DATE DUE

DEMCO 38-296

1975
The Supreme Court Review

1975

The

"Judges as persons, or courts as institutions, are entitled to
no greater immunity from criticism than other persons
or institutions . . . [J]udges must be kept mindful of their limitations and
of their ultimate public responsibility by a vigorous
stream of criticism expressed with candor however blunt."
—*Felix Frankfurter*

". . . while it is proper that people should find fault when
their judges fail, it is only reasonable that they should recognize the
difficulties. . . . Let them be severely brought to book,
when they go wrong, but by those who will take the trouble
to understand them."
—*Learned Hand*

THE LAW SCHOOL

THE UNIVERSITY OF CHICAGO

Supreme Court Review

EDITED BY

PHILIP B. KURLAND

 THE UNIVERSITY OF CHICAGO PRESS

CHICAGO AND LONDON

TO

E. P. K.

In Memoriam

She has a real thread of courage running
through her, which is better than genius,
and better than virtue; indeed I put it first
of all qualities.

O no more—darkness has vanquished
Light.

—Virginia Stephen

INTERNATIONAL STANDARD BOOK NUMBER: 0-226-46426-1

LIBRARY OF CONGRESS CATALOG CARD NUMBER: 60-14353

THE UNIVERSITY OF CHICAGO PRESS, CHICAGO 60637

THE UNIVERSITY OF CHICAGO PRESS, LTD., LONDON

PRINTED IN THE UNITED STATES OF AMERICA

CONTENTS

RUTH BADER GINSBURG

GENDER IN THE SUPREME COURT:

THE 1973 AND 1974 TERMS

Supreme Court discourse on gender[1] and the Constitution, as the record stood at the start of 1975, bemused lower courts and law review contributors. As the Court of Appeals for the District of Columbia described the state of adjudication, precedent was "still evolving," "rapidly changing, and variously interpreted."[2] A concerned and perceptive Court watcher in this area concluded: "[T]he Court is not certain what constitutes sex discrimination, how virulent this form of discrimination is or how it should be analyzed in terms of due process and equal protection."[3]

These appraisals derived from the vacillation that followed the Court's break from a consistent affirmation of governmental authority to classify by gender unbroken until 1971. There was quick movement in a new direction in 1971–73. 1974 saw retrenchment or at least lineholding. 1975 brought the Court back to the 1971–73 track. Momentum in the new direction built up, but the

Ruth Bader Ginsburg is Professor of Law, Columbia University, and General Counsel, American Civil Liberties Union. She was counsel in many of the cases discussed herein.

[1] For impressionable minds, the word "sex" may conjure up improper images of issues like those that the Supreme Court has left to "contemporary community standards." See Paris Adult Theatre I v. Slaton, 413 U.S. 49 (1973). The denotation and connotations of the word "gender" make it more appropriate than "sex" for use in the context of this set of problems. Both terms are used herein always with the meaning of the latter.

[2] Waldie v. Schlesinger, 509 F.2d 508, 510 (D.C. Cir. 1974); see also Dahl v. State Tax Commission, 96 Idaho 174 (1974).

[3] Johnston, *Sex Discrimination and the Supreme Court—1971–1974*, 49 N.Y.U.L. Rev. 617, 689 (1974).

Justices who wrote the opinions shied from doctrinal development. This article analyzes developments of the 1973 and 1974 Terms.

I. The Backdrop: From "Anything Goes" to Reed and Frontiero

For nearly a century after the Fourteenth Amendment became part of our fundamental law, the judiciary routinely upheld legislative classifications by gender.[4] Utmost deference to political judgments seemed the course Constitution-makers intended. Neither the founding fathers[5] nor the framers of the post–Civil War amendments[6] questioned the traditional assumptions: women's place in a world controlled by men is divinely ordained;[7] the law's differential treatment of the sexes operates benignly in women's favor.[8]

By the late 1960s a revived and burgeoning feminist movement spotlighted the altered life patterns of women, which were also revealed in U.S. Current Population Reports. The virtual disappearance of food and goods cultivated or produced at home and "repeal of the motherhood draft"[9] contributed to a phenomenal growth in women's participation in the paid labor force.[10] Enforce-

---

[4] See Ginsburg, Constitutional Aspects of Sex-Based Discrimination 2–35 (1974). Three Supreme Court decisions set the pattern that persisted until 1971: Muller v. Oregon, 208 U.S. 412 (1908); Goesaert v. Cleary, 335 U.S. 464 (1948); Hoyt v. Florida, 368 U.S. 57 (1961).

[5] Thomas Jefferson once commented: "Were our state a pure democracy there would still be excluded from our deliberations women, who, to prevent deprivation of morals and ambiguity of issues, should not mix promiscuously in gatherings of men." Quoted in Gruberg, Women in American Politics 4 (1968). See also Forrester, The Feminists— Why Have They Not Yet Succeeded? 61 A.B.A.J. 333 (1975), reporting on the exchange of views between Abigail and John Adams.

[6] See Flexner, Century of Struggle 142–55 (1959).

[7] See Myrdal, An American Dilemma 1073 (2d ed. 1962); Bradwell v. Illinois, 16 Wall. 130, 141 (1873) (concurring opinion).

[8] 1 Blackstone's Commentaries *445 (3d ed. 1768).

[9] The phrase is taken from Professor Alfred Conard. See 16 Law Quadrangle Notes 11 (Fall 1971).

[10] See Taylor v. Louisiana, 419 U.S. 522, 535 n.17 (1975). In 1920, 23 percent of women over the age of fourteen were in the labor force. In 1940, the percentage had reached 25. By 1950, the percentage of women over sixteen in the labor force was 34; it was 38 percent in 1960, 43 percent in 1970, and 45 percent by 1973. See Economic Report of the President Table 21, at p. 91 (January 1973); U.S. Dep't of Labor, Bureau of Labor Statistics, Special Labor Force Report 163, at A-6 (1974), Reports of the Advisory Council on Social Security 176–81 (March 1975) asserts: (1) Married couples with the husband as the only working member no longer constitute the majority of families in the United States. (2) In all industrialized societies, the greater the percentage of working women, the smaller the birth rate.

ment of the Equal Pay Act of 1963[11] and Title VII of the Civil
Rights Act of 1964[12] began to focus national attention on the adversely discriminatory treatment encountered by women outside
the home.

The first Title VII gender discrimination case to reach the
Supreme Court, *Phillips v. Martin Marietta Corp.*,[13] was decided
in complainant's favor early in 1971. The Court held that an employer willing to hire fathers, but not mothers, of preschool children, engaged in sex discrimination within the compass of Title
VII.[14] Later that year, in *Reed v. Reed*,[15] all seven members of
the Court invalidated, as violative of the Equal Protection Clause,
an Idaho statute requiring, as between persons "equally entitled"
to administer a decedent's estate, that "males . . . be preferred to
females." The laconic *Reed* opinion acknowledged no break with
precedent, but as Professor Gunther commented:[16]

> It is difficult to understand [the *Reed*] result without an as-
> sumption that some special sensitivity to sex as a classifying
> factor entered into the analysis. . . . Only by importing some
> special suspicion of sex-related means . . . can the result be
> made entirely persuasive.

A few months later, in *Stanley v. Illinois*,[17] the Court divided
4–1–2 on the question whether a state could deny to an unwed
father, who had in fact lived with his children, a presumed right
to custody after the death of the mother. Although ruling for the
father, the Court avoided the equal protection argument tendered
by Stanley's counsel. It held that due process required a hearing
for Stanley of the kind that would be accorded a mother or a wed
father.[18]

---

[11] 29 U.S.C. § 206(d).   [12] 42 U.S.C. § 2000(e).   [13] 400 U.S. 542 (1971).

[14] In dictum, the Court said that a defense might "arguably" be established under the
statute's bona fide occupational qualification exception if the employer were to prove
that "conflicting family obligations [are] demonstrably more relevant to job performance
for a woman than for a man." Id. at 544. The 1972 E.E.O.C. guidelines interpret the
"bona fide occupational qualification exception" very narrowly. 29 C.F.R. § 1604.2.

[15] 404 U.S. 71 (1971).

[16] Gunther, *In Search of Evolving Doctrine on a Changing Court: A Model for a Newer
Equal Protection*, 86 HARV. L. REV. 1, 34 (1972).

[17] 405 U.S. 645 (1972).

[18] On the utilization of the impermissible presumption rule as an alternative to equal
protection, see authorities cited in note 48 *infra*.

In 1973, the Supreme Court rendered what was greeted as a landmark decision. In *Frontiero v. Richardson*,[19] the Court held that married male and female members of the uniformed services must be granted the same fringe benefits. It held invalid federal[20] statutes indulging the presumption that a serviceman's wife, but not a servicewoman's husband, is "dependent." In *Frontiero* four of eight Justices in the majority joined in a plurality opinion declaring sex, like race and national origin, an "inherently suspect" criterion for legislative line drawing. A widely read publication asserted: "The Court came within one vote of rendering state ratification of the Equal Rights Amendment superfluous."[21]

II. The Hard Cases of 1974: Kahn, Ballard and Aiello

Reed and *Frontiero*, contrary to fact, gave the appearance of well-planned first steps in a sustained litigation campaign.[22] Both presented situations in which gross sex lines, drawn for purposes of administrative convenience, favored men and operated to the manifest disadvantage of similarly situated women. Sally Reed had been denied appointment as an administrator for no reason other than her sex. In essence, Sharron Frontiero had been denied equal pay. In the 1973 Term, harder cases reached the Court. *Kahn v. Shevin*[23] involved a state real property tax exemption for the blind, the totally disabled, and widows (but not widowers). *Cleveland Board of Education v. LaFleur*[24] and *Geduldig v. Aiello*[25] tendered the question whether disadvantageous treatment of pregnancy is invalid gender discrimination. And the first in the 1974 Term was a tangled, idiosyncratic case, *Schlesinger v. Ballard*.[26]

A. WITH THE BLIND AND THE LAME: KAHN V. SHEVIN

Mel Kahn was a Florida widower who sought a real property tax exemption, worth $15 annually, granted by Florida law to

---

[19] 411 U.S. 677 (1973).

[20] *Frontiero* rested on the Fifth rather than the Fourteenth Amendment because a federal statute was at issue. The Court has declared implicit in the Fifth Amendment a prohibition against discrimination "precisely the same" in tenor as the express guarantee in the Fourteenth Amendment. Weinberger v. Wiesenfeld, 420 U.S. 636, 638 n.2 (1975); see Johnson v. Robison, 415 U.S. 361, 364–65 n.4 (1974).

[21] 42 U.S.L. Week 3057 (17 July 1973).

[22] Cf. Greenberg, *Litigation for Social Change: Methods, Limits and Role in Democracy,* 29 Record 320 (1974).

[23] 416 U.S. 351 (1974).

[24] 414 U.S. 632 (1974).

[25] 417 U.S. 484 (1974).

[26] 419 U.S. 498 (1975).

"every widow or person who is blind or totally and permanently disabled."[27] Widower Kahn argued, as had Sharron and Joseph Frontiero, that gender classification as a proxy for some other individual or social characteristic, for example, physical or economic incapacity or need, violated the Equal Protection Clause. Acknowledging the proposition that "wives are typically dependent" may correctly describe the generality of cases, widower Kahn questioned the reasonableness of treating men and women who do not match the gross generalization as if they did, and of using a gender pigeonhole in lieu of a functional description.

Two factors doomed widower Kahn's case in the eyes of the Court's majority. One was a solid body of decisions holding that states have "large leeway" in framing their tax systems. The other was the sex of the complainant. In contrast to *Reed* and *Frontiero*, *Kahn* seemed to the Court a case in which some women were helped, and no women were harmed by the classification. Real property–owning widows[28] were accorded a small favor, which Mr. Justice Douglas, author of the *Kahn* opinion, rationalized by reference to the economic dependency of most wives, and the inhospitable climate women encounter in the job market.[29] Returning to the old thesis of benign preferences, Mr. Justice Douglas referred to the Court's 1908 opinion in *Muller v. Oregon*,[30] permitting protective labor legislation for women only, because "the special physical structure of women has a bearing on the 'conditions under which she should be permitted to toil.' "[31]

The widow's exemption at issue in *Kahn* came into Florida law in 1885, decades before women achieved the franchise and at a time

---

[27] FLA. CONST., Art. 7, § 3(b); FLA. STAT. § 196.202 (1971). Property was exempted to the value of $500. At the applicable rate, the exemption reduced the tax bill by approximately $15.

[28] Single and divorced women, regardless of age, were accorded no exemption. FLA. CONST., Art. 7, § 3(b).

[29] Cf. DOUGLAS, GO EAST YOUNG MAN 17–30 (1974). The statistics set out in the *Kahn* opinion, 416 U.S. at 353–54 nn.4–6, indicate the earnings gap between men and women. They do not relate to the economic needs of widows as compared with widowers. They may bear more realistically on the plight of single women than of widows.

[30] 208 U.S. 412 (1908).

[31] 416 U.S. at 356 n.10. Mr. Justice Douglas observed in the same footnote: "Gender has never been rejected as an impermissible classification in all instances. Congress has not so far drafted women into the Armed Services. 50 App. U.S.C. § 454." But the Supreme Court has not yet passed on the constitutionality of limiting the draft to men. And at least one District Court has held such classification invalid. See United States v. Reiser, 394 F. Supp. 1060 (D. Mont. 1975).

when married women were treated as disabled in many legal contexts.[32] Florida maintained that the tax break was remedial, hence permissible under the Equal Protection Clause.[33] *Kahn* urged skeptical appraisal of the state's justification:[34]

> The exemption surely does not address "the plight of women in the economic area" through means calculated to aid them "to sustain themselves in today's job market." For such means address the problem at its source; principal examples are laws prohibiting gender discrimination in education, employment, financing, housing and public accommodations.

Eight of the Justices agreed that the Equal Protection Clause accommodated such compensatory legislation. Two of them, Justices Brennan and Marshall, would have accepted the widow's preference if it incorporated a means test.[35] The six composing the majority found the tax exemption acceptable as it was written. The opinion did not address Kahn's contention that a gender-specific tax exemption reinforced rather than remedied double standards that confined women's opportunities.[36] Nor did the majority spokesman in *Kahn* attempt to reconcile that opinion with his statement the day before as sole Justice to reach the merits in *DeFunis v. Odegaard*,[37] the University of Washington law school admission

---

[32] See Johnston, *Sex and Property: The Common Law Tradition, the Law School Curriculum, and Developments toward Equality*, 47 N.Y.U. L. Rev. 1033, 1057–70, 1082–83 (1972).

[33] Cf. *In re* Humphrey's Estate, 299 So.2d 595 (Fla. 1974), in which the Florida Supreme Court declined to consider a constitutional challenge to legislation providing dower for widows, but no similar forced shares for widowers. The remedial classification argument derived from a footnote to the plurality opinion in *Frontiero*, where Mr. Justice Brennan noted that the statutes in issue were "not in any sense designed to rectify the effects of past discrimination against women." 411 U.S. at 689 n.22.

[34] Reply Brief for Appellant at 3, 4, Kahn v. Shevin.

[35] The position of Justices Brennan and Marshall raised an interesting question about the appropriate remedy. Kahn's complaint argued that the classification was underinclusive. The two Justices found the classification overinclusive. Kahn sought extension of the benefit to widowers; he was not interested in removing the benefits from widows. Cf. Colburn v. Colburn, 316 A.2d 283, 287–88 (Md. Ct. Spec. App., 1974), where the court held that a husband not seeking alimony for himself could not challenge a statute authorizing alimony for women only. See generally, *Extension versus Invalidation of Statutes That Unconstitutionally Differentiate between Men and Women*, in GINSBURG, *supra* note 4, at 94–99. Since a state law was in issue in *Kahn*, the choice of eliminating or extending the category would have been left to the Florida courts for resolution. See Stanton v. Stanton, 421 U.S. 7, 15 (1975).

[36] See Brief for Appellant at 16–25; Reply Brief for Appellant at 1–6, Kahn v. Shevin.

[37] 416 U.S. 312 (1974).

case. There he had announced: "There is no constitutional right for any race to be preferred."[38]

B. AN IDIOSYNCRATIC CASE: SCHLESINGER V. BALLARD

On 15 January 1975, the Court again rejected a male's complaint of unconstitutional gender discrimination, and cited *Kahn* in support of the result. In a 5-to-4 decision in *Schlesinger v. Ballard*,[39] the Court held that it was not a denial of equal protection of the laws to hold a male naval officer to a strict "up or out" system while guaranteeing female officers thirteen years before mandatory discharge for lack of promotion. *Ballard* presented a tangled problem. The Court was asked to intercede at the point where the system operated to the disadvantage of a particular male officer. The contending parties did not challenge the anterior discrimination against women officers by way of statute and regulations that barred females from assignments most likely to generate promotions. Moreover, the litigation was motivated by a retirement benefit consideration peculiar to Lieutenant Ballard's situation. Tacking his seven years' service as an enlisted member to his nine years' service as an officer, he had a total of sixteen years' service at the time his discharge was ordered. With a guaranteed officer tenure of thirteen years, he could have attained the twenty years required for retirement benefits.

Ballard illustrates the problem courts encounter when asked to review in isolation one small facet of a large and complex scheme. Sex-based differentials are still pervasive in the congeries of rules governing military service entrance, promotion, discharge, and retirement.[40] Many of these differentials favor men, and even the one challenged by Lieutenant Ballard had been viewed by a female officer as detrimental to her, because it deferred her eligibility for severance pay.[41]

C. A PREGNANT PROBLEM: GEDULDIG V. AIELLO

Although *Kahn* indicated a Court without sharp perception of the root causes and fundamental unfairness of gender lines in the

---

[38] 416 U.S. at 336 (dissenting).

[39] 419 U.S. 498 (1975).

[40] See Note, 82 YALE L.J. 1533 (1973).

[41] See Two v. United States, 471 F.2d 287 (9th Cir. 1972).

law,[42] the decision was not generally seen as a retreat from *Reed* and *Frontiero*.[43] The Court took note of "firmly entrenched practices" operating to the economic disadvantage of women and accepted the state's assertion of a remedial purpose. Dr. Pangloss might have surveyed the development from *Reed* through *Kahn* with satisfaction: woman had "the best of both worlds," the opportunity to "attack laws which unreasonably discriminate against women while saving some . . . which favor them."[44] But *Geduldig v. Aiello*,[45] decided some weeks after *Kahn*, was universally recognized as a setback for feminist advocates.

Aiello concerned a formidable obstacle to equal opportunity for women: employment regulation applicable to childbirth. Questions novel to the Court were raised. Is disadvantageous treatment of pregnancy sex discrimination? Must disability due to pregnancy be blanketed with other disabilities in laws regulating employment-related benefits? Is the answer that pregnancy can't happen to a man, therefore pregnancy classifications can't discriminate on the basis of sex? Or because they affect women exclusively do pregnancy classifications merit particularly careful inspection?

Earlier in the 1973 Term, in *Cleveland Board of Education v. LaFleur*,[46] the Court had ruled, on a due process–conclusive presumption ground, that pregnant public school teachers could not be forced out of work after only four or five months of pregnancy. Reminiscent of its approach in *Stanley v. Illinois*,[47] the Court in *LaFleur* reasoned that an inflexible rule sending every pregnant teacher home months in advance of the expected delivery date established a conclusive presumption of unfitness, impermissibly burdening exercise of the fundamental right to bear a child.

Conclusive presumption analysis, though popular for a spell in recent Supreme Court Terms, has not fared well under analyses.[48]

---

[42] See Johnston, note 3 *supra*, at 661–73.

[43] See Note, 88 HARV. L. REV. 129 (1974).

[44] The remarks quoted are attributed to Mr. Justice Stewart in the course of an informal talk to Harvard students. 56 HARV. L. REC. 15 (23 March 1973).

[45] 417 U.S. 484 (1974).   [46] 414 U.S. 632 (1974).

[47] 405 U.S. 645 (1972); see text *supra*, at notes 17–18.

[48] See Bezanson, *Some Thoughts on the Emerging Irrebuttable Presumption Doctrine*, 7 IND. L. REV. 644 (1974); Note, 87 HARV. L. REV. 1534 (1974); Note, 72 MICH. L. REV. 800 (1974); Note, 27 STAN. L. REV. 499 (1974). But see Tribe, *Structural Due Process*, 10 HARV. CIV. RTS.–CIV. LIB. L. REV. 269 (1975); Tribe, *From Environmental Foundations to Constitutional Structures*, 84 YALE L.J. 545, 553–56 (1975); Note, 62 GEO. L.J. 1173 (1974).

As one student writer pointed out, conclusive or irrebuttable presumptions are not "evidentiary rules involved in the process of fact-finding," they "are nothing more than statutory classifications."[49] Professor Gunther refers to a colleague's descriptive name for the technique as the "New Old Equally Protective Substantively Procedural Due Process."[50] At the end of the 1974 Term, in *Weinberger v. Salfi*,[51] the Court appeared to join the critics of the presumption notion. *Geduldig v. Aiello*[52] may clarify why the Court avoided the Equal Protection Clause, in *LaFleur*, although that was the ground relied upon in the lower courts and emphasized in the arguments to the Court. In *LaFleur* the Court had accorded a measure of protection to a woman's right to work while pregnant, but not disabled. In *Aiello* it rejected a wage-earning woman's claim to income maintenance when pregnancy in fact disabled her. Six of the Justices held it did not violate the Equal Protection Clause to single out disability due to normal pregnancy for exclusion from California's income protection program for disabled workers.[53]

Acknowledging that pregnancy was related to sex, the Court did not perceive in the *Aiello* classification gender discrimination of the kind involved in *Reed* or *Frontiero*. It noted that the pregnancy exclusion was not based on "gender as such" for "[t]he program divides potential recipients into two groups—pregnant women and nonpregnant persons."[54] Further, "[t]here is no risk from which men are protected and women are not. Likewise, there is no risk from which women are protected and men are not."[55]

Plainly, no "benign," "compensatory," or woman-protective

---

[49] Note, 87 HARV. L. REV. at 1556.

[50] GUNTHER, CONSTITUTIONAL LAW 893 n.8 (1975).

[51] 95 S. Ct. 2457 (1975). Mr. Justice Rehnquist, writing for a six-member majority, declined an invitation to apply conclusive presumption analysis and cautioned against turning the doctrine "into a virtual engine of destruction for countless legislative judgments."

[52] 417 U.S. 484 (1974).

[53] A state court had interpreted the statute to exclude only normal deliveries and recuperation and not disability due to abnormal conditions or medical complications connected with a pregnancy. 417 U.S. at 490.

[54] *Id.* at 497 n.20. Cf. Phillips v. Martin Marietta Corp., 400 U.S. 542 (1971), where the Court rejected the "sex plus" analysis relied upon by the court below. In *Phillips*, the "plus" was motherhood or pre-school children, a condition for which there is a male counterpart.

[55] 417 U.S. at 496–97.

purpose could rationalize the pregnancy exclusion challenged in
Aiello. Discussed at length in Appellees' brief[56] were the stereo-
typical attitudes and generalizations about sex roles in society underlying disadvantageous job-related treatment of pregnant women.
This presentation invited close inspection of the State's claim that
the pregnancy exclusion was the product of an entirely sex-neutral
decision on risk selection in the California insurance program.
Commentary on *Aiello*[57] suggests that the analogy of pregnancy
to other temporary disabilities pressed in the briefs supporting appellees[58] may have foundered for a reason not fully acknowledged
in the Supreme Court's opinion: assessment of childbirth not as
a short-term medical episode, but as an integral part of a long-term
process, a process commencing with pregnancy and ending years
later when child-rearing work is done. Viewed in that frame,
childbirth has no place in a worker's disability benefit program.

Whether disadvantageous treatment of pregnancy in employment contexts is invalid sex discrimination remains a live issue under Title VII.[59] The E.E.O.C. Guidelines, issued two years before
the Supreme Court's *Aiello* decision, provide: "Disabilities caused
or contributed to by pregnancy, miscarriage, abortion, childbirth,
and recovery therefrom are, for all job-related purposes, temporary disabilities and should be treated as such under any health or
temporary disability insurance or sick leave plan available in connection with employment."[60] In other words, the Commission has
interpreted Title VII to require employers to accord women disabled by pregnancy the same protection, no more no less, that

---

[56] Brief for Appellees at 28–46, Geduldig v. Aiello.

[57] Johnston, note 3 *supra*, at 646–47, 678–80; Bartlett, *Pregnancy under the Constitution:
The Uniqueness Trap*, 62 CALIF. L. REV. 1532, 1535, 1563–66 (1974); Note, 75 COLUM.
L. REV. 441 (1975); see also Ginsburg, *Gender and the Constitution*, 44 U. CIN. L. REV. 1,
34–40 (1975).

[58] The analogy was drawn in terms of the two factors that pregnancy shares with
other physical conditions causing temporary disability: (1) loss of income due to temporary inability to work; (2) medical expenses.

[59] The resolution of the issue under Title VII will bear significantly on the vitality of
the *Aiello* exclusion rule after promulgation of the Equal Rights Amendment. See Peratis
& Rindskopf, *Pregnancy Discrimination as a Sex Discrimination Issue*, 2 WOMEN'S RTS. L.
REP. No. 4 (1975); Note, 75 COLUM. L. REV. 441 (1975); cf. Brown, Emerson, Falk &
Freedman, *The Equal Rights Amendment: A Constitutional Basis for Equal Rights for
Women*, 80 YALE L.J. 871, 929 (1971); Note, 72 MICH. L. REV. 800, 813 n. 90 (1974).

[60] 29 C.F.R. § 1604.10; 37 FED. REG. 6837 (1972). For an early statement on the
subject, see Citizens' Advisory Council on the Status of Women, Job Related Maternity
Benefits (CACSW Item No. 15-N, Nov. 1970).

would be accorded any employee temporarily away from work for other nonoccupational disabilities, for example, a broken leg, prostate operation, cosmetic surgery. Noting the deference due Commission guidelines,[61] the Courts of Appeals for the Second, Third, Fourth, Sixth, Eighth, and Ninth Circuits have reasoned that Title VII requires rigorous review of employment practices which place women at a disadvantage in the labor market, not the restrained equal protection review applied in *Aiello*.[62] Cautioning against unguarded reading of "footnotes or other 'marginalia' in Supreme Court opinions," the Second Circuit considered it "inconceivable" that the Supreme Court intended to foreclose the Title VII issue "without even a mention of [the statute] or the guidelines."[63] All six courts of appeals posited the distinction: *Aiello* for equal protection purposes; a more stringent, effect-oriented analysis for Title VII.[64]

III. Gender Discrimination's Place on the Equal Protection Spectrum: Rational Relationship, Compelling State Interest, or Something in Between

The two-definition approach developed in the Title VII pregnancy classification cases, distinguishing a strict statutory antidiscrimination command from a less rigorous constitutional requirement, bears a resemblance to the two-tier Equal Protection Clause analysis developed in Warren Court adjudications and still formally retained by the Burger Court. In the generality of cases, rational relationship is the controlling rubric. For classifications regarded as "suspect" and for rights ranked as "fundamental," the "strict scrutiny" standard applies, a standard requiring the proponent of the classification to demonstrate that a "compelling state interest" justifies it. The "rational relationship" label, at least until

[61] See Griggs v. Duke Power Co., 401 U.S. 424, 433–34 (1971).

[62] Communication Workers v. American Telephone & Telegraph Co., 513 F.2d 1024 (2d Cir. 1975); Liberty Mutual Ins. Co. v. Wetzel, 511 F.2d 199 (3d Cir. 1975), cert. granted, 421 U.S. 987 1975); Gilbert v. General Electric Co., 519 F.2d 661 (4th Cir. 1975); Satty v. Nashville Gas Co., 522 F.2d 850 (6th Cir. 1975); Holthaus v. Compton & Sons, Inc., 514 F.2d 651 (8th Cir. 1975); Hutchison v. Lake Oswego School District, 519 F.2d 961 (9th Cir. 1975). Accord, Union Free School District No. 6 v. Human Rights Appeal Board, 35 N.Y.2d 371 (1974).

[63] 513 F.2d at 1028.

[64] Adverse effect on a protected group has sufficed to render an employment practice suspect under Title VII and, thus, to cast a burden of justification on the employer. See Cooper, *Equal Employment Law Today*, 5 Colum. Hum. Rts. L. Rev. 263 (1973).

1971, meant a virtually automatic pass for challenged legislation. The "strict scrutiny" stamp signaled a failing grade.[65]

The "fundamental rights" concept had limited utility in gender discrimination cases, even under forecasts of a more elastic definition of "fundamental" than the Court now embraces.[66] Sally Reed, for example, asserted no right, fundamental or otherwise, to administer a relative's estate. Sharron Frontiero claimed no right to a housing allowance. But both objected to the use of sex as a classifying factor. And both urged designation of sex as a "suspect" criterion commanding upper tier equal protection review.

Consistent with the core purpose of the Fourteenth Amendment,[67] race became and remains the prime "suspect" criterion. Two other criteria distinguishing between persons on the basis of who they are rather than what they have done or are capable of doing, however, have been stamped as "suspect": national origin and alienage.[68] These expansions encouraged gender equality advocates, along with advocates for other constituencies, notably the poor[69] and children born out of wedlock,[70] to argue for a place on the upper tier list.

In *Frontiero*,[71] Mr. Justice Powell, joined by Chief Justice Burger and Mr. Justice Blackmun, said it was "unnecessary for the Court . . . to characterize sex as a suspect classification, with all of the far-reaching implications of such a holding."[72] *Reed* was enough to support the result, therefore the broader approach of the *Frontiero* plurality (Justices Brennan, Douglas, Marshall, and White) was unwarranted. Moreover, "suspect" categorization for sex was premature. The Court should not assume "a decisional responsi-

---

[65] See generally Gunther, note 16 *supra*; *Developments in the Law—Equal Protection*, 82 HARV. L. REV. 1065 (1969); GINSBURG, note 4 *supra*, at 99–107.

[66] In San Antonio Independent School District v. Rodriguez, 411 U.S. 1, 33, 34 (1973), the Court defined fundamental rights as those "explicitly or implicitly guaranteed by the Constitution," including travel interstate, voting, and reproduction. Education was declared to be "important" but not "fundamental."

[67] See Bickel, *The Original Understanding and the Segregation Decisions*, 69 HARV. L. REV. 1 (1955).

[68] See *In re* Griffiths, 413 U.S. 717 (1973); Graham v. Richardson, 403 U.S. 365 (1971).

[69] See *Rodriguez*, note 66 *supra*, at 25–28; Reid, *Equal Protection or Equal Denial, Is It Time for Racial Minorities, the Poor, Women and Other Oppressed People to Regroup*, 3 HOFSTRA L. REV. 1 (1975).

[70] See Jimenez v. Weinberger, 417 U.S. 628 (1974); Note, 49 N.Y.U. L. REV. 479 (1974); GINSBURG, note 4 *supra*, at 103.

[71] See text *supra*, at notes 19–21.   [72] 411 U.S. at 691–92.

bility at the very time when state legislatures, functioning within the traditional democratic process, are debating the proposed [Equal Rights] Amendment."[73]

Mr. Justice Stewart announced only his agreement that the legislation at issue in *Frontiero* worked "an invidious discrimination in violation of the Constitution."[74] His opinions for the Court in *LaFleur* and *Aiello* and his alignment with the majority in *Kahn* indicated that he would not likely be the fifth vote putting gender within the suspect category. The other member of the Court, Mr. Justice Rehnquist, dissented in *Frontiero* and *LaFleur*. He was not on the Court when the unanimous *Reed* decision issued.

By the 1974 Term, it appeared reasonably clear that sex would not be a "suspect classification" for a majority of the Court. Moreover, the *Aiello* decision dampened enthusiasm for keeping the argument in the front line. Ground lost in *Aiello* might be regained in cases covered by Title VII[75] through distinguishing the meaning of the statute, a measure centrally focused on sex as well as race discrimination,[76] from the relatively weaker thrust of the Fourteenth Amendment, where race but not sex was the central concern.[77] Further, the two-tier equal protection model had critics on the Court[78] as well as in the law reviews.[79] *Reed* and *Frontiero* were prime examples of decisions that did not fit the model. And cases on the 1974–75 docket might be argued successfully on the basis of those judgments.

IV. THE COURT BACK ON TRACK: TAYLOR, WIESENFELD, STANTON

In *Taylor v. Louisiana*,[80] decided the week after the *Ballard* decision,[81] the Court overruled *Hoyt v. Florida*,[82] a 1961 prece-

---

[73] *Id.* at 692.   [74] *Id.* at 691.

[75] See notes 59–64, *supra*, and accompanying text.

[76] See, *e.g.*, Rosenfeld v. Southern Pac. Co., 444 F.2d 1219 (9th Cir. 1971); Sprogis v. United Air Lines, Inc., 444 F.2d 1194 (7th Cir. 1971).

[77] See authorities cited in notes 6, 65, and 67 *supra*.

[78] See, *e.g.*, Vlandis v. Kline, 412 U.S. 441, 458–59 (1973) (White, J., concurring); Marshall v. United States, 414 U.S. 417, 432–33 (1974) (Marshall, J., dissenting). Discomfort with the dichotomy extends to the upper tier as well as the lower. See Dunn v. Blumstein, 405 U.S. 330, 363–64 (1972) (Burger, C.J., dissenting).

[79] See Gunther, *supra* note 16; Note, 58 VA. L. REV. 1489 (1972).

[80] 419 U.S. 522 (1975).

[81] 419 U.S. 498 (1975), discussed in text *supra*, at notes 39–41.

[82] 368 U.S. 57 (1961).

dent that had routinely rejected a woman's complaint of unconstitutional gender discrimination.[83] *Hoyt* had sustained a Florida statute limiting jury service by women to those who registered with the court their desire to be placed on the jury list. *Taylor* rejected, 8 to 1, a virtually identical Louisiana arrangement. Two months later, in *Weinberger v. Wiesenfeld*,[84] a unanimous Court declared unconstitutional the Social Security Act's provision of a mother's benefit for the caretaker of a deceased wage earner's child, but no corresponding father's benefit. In effect, the judgment in *Wiesenfeld* substitutes functional description (sole surviving parent) for the gender classification (widowed mother) employed in the statute. Fair weather signals continued in *Stanton v. Stanton*,[85] decided 15 April 1975, when the Court rejected, 8 to 1, Utah's age of majority differential, 18 for girls, 21 for boys, applicable to a parent's child support obligation.

A. HOYT V. FLORIDA IS OVERRULED

Taylor was argued in tandem with *Edwards v. Healy*,[86] a class action challenge to Louisiana's jury selection system, decided in plaintiff's favor by a three-judge federal district court. A new Louisiana Constitution, eliminating the "volunteers only" provision for female jury service, became effective 1 January 1975. Pursuant to that Constitution, the Louisiana Supreme Court established a rule governing jury service exemption, which includes no gender-based differential. Pointing to these developments, the Louisiana attorney general suggested that *Healy* had become, or was fast becoming, moot, for the named plaintiffs in *Healy* were civil litigants still awaiting trial.[87] Taylor, however, had been tried and convicted in 1972. Hence mootness was not an issue in his case.

Three threshold determinations were made in *Taylor*. (1) Appellant, a man, had standing to challenge the exclusion of women from his jury.[88] (2) The Sixth Amendment required a

---

[83] See note 4 *supra* and accompanying text.

[84] 420 U.S. 636 (1975).   [85] 421 U.S. 7 (1975).

[86] No. 73-759, decision below, Healy v. Edwards, 363 F. Supp. 1110 (E.D. La. 1973).

[87] The judgment in *Healy* was vacated and the case remanded to the three-judge court "to consider whether in light of recent changes in the state constitutional, statutory and other rules applicable to [the] case the cause has become moot." 421 U.S. 772 (1975).

[88] Cf. Peters v. Kiff, 407 U.S. 493 (1972).

petit jury selected from a representative cross-section of the community.[89] (3) "[W]omen are sufficiently numerous and distinct from men that if they are systematically eliminated from jury panels, the Sixth Amendment's fair cross-section requirement cannot be satisfied."[90] The Court then turned to a reconsideration of *Hoyt v. Florida*, the prime justification tendered by Louisiana for retaining the system into the 1970s.

The complainant in *Hoyt* was a woman charged with killing her husband by assaulting him with a baseball bat, thus terminating an altercation in which she claimed he had insulted and humiliated her to the breaking point. Convicted of second degree murder by an all-male jury, Hoyt had asserted that female peers might better comprehend her state of mind and her defense of temporary insanity. (Ironically, complainant Taylor was initially charged with rape.) The Supreme Court held that Hoyt was not denied due process or equal protection, for the blanket exclusion of women who did not volunteer was rationally based: "[W]oman is still regarded as the center of home and family life."[91] "Weightier reasons" were demanded in *Taylor* because defendant's Sixth Amendment right was implicated, a right not established until seven years after *Hoyt*.[92]

At oral argument in *Healy* and *Taylor*, the Court expressed concern regarding the "cavalier" treatment of the *Hoyt* precedent by the *Healy* three-judge court. The district court had written: "When today's vibrant principle is obviously in conflict with yesterday's sterile precedent, trial courts need not follow the outgrown dogma. Hence we consider that *Hoyt* is no longer binding."[93] "Yesterday" was only a dozen years earlier, and the "sterile precedent" was a unanimous decision.[94] Since *Taylor* was predicated on the Sixth Amendment, head-on collision with the 1961

---

[89] Cf. Duncan v. Louisiana, 391 U.S. 145 (1968), holding the Sixth Amendment applicable to the States through the Fourteenth Amendment.

[90] 419 U,S. at 531. *Healy* and *Taylor* derived from the same Louisiana parish. On the stipulation in *Healy*, the three-judge court found that women were represented on parish jury panels to the extent of 5 percent or less.

[91] 368 U.S. at 62. See the earlier treatment of the problem in Fay v. New York, 332 U.S. 261, 290 (1947).

[92] See note 89, *supra*.   [93] 363 F. Supp. at 1117.

[94] Cf. National Organization for Women v. Goodman, 374 F. Supp. 247 (S.D. N.Y. 1974), holding that the lower federal courts were bound by *Hoyt* until it was overruled by the Supreme Court.

precedent was averted. Mr. Justice White's opinion for the Court in *Taylor*, however, finds not even "lightweight" reasons left for *Hoyt*. Statistics on women's participation in the labor force compiled by the Department of Labor in 1974, Mr. Justice White concluded, "certainly put to rest the suggestion that all women should be exempt from jury service based solely on their sex and the presumed role . . . in the home."[95]

B. NEUTRALITY IN ROLE DESCRIPTION: WEINBERGER V. WIESENFELD

In 1939, Congress extended social security benefits to a widowed parent who has in her care a minor child of the insured wage earner. In the Wiesenfeld family, the insured wage earner was a woman, consequently the widowed parent, who had a child left in his sole care when mother died in childbirth, was the father.[96] The statute in question had left no room for functional interpretation. It is captioned "mother's insurance benefits."[97]

Appellee Stephen Wiesenfeld claimed that the exclusion of male beneficiaries entailed three forms of illegal discrimination. Stephen Wiesenfeld, the widowed father, was denied social insurance that would have been paid to a similarly situated widowed mother. Jason Paul Wiesenfeld, newborn child of a fully insured individual, was denied the opportunity for the personal care of his sole surviving parent. And Paula Wiesenfeld, the deceased wage earner, did not secure the family protection that would be afforded the family of a male wage earner.

Wiesenfeld came to the Court bracketed by *Frontiero* and *Kahn*, the former declaring married male and female members of the uniformed services entitled to the same family benefits, the latter upholding exclusion of widowers from a real property tax exemp-

---

[95] 419 U.S. at 535 n. 17. The rule in *Taylor* was held not to be retroactively applicable, even to cases already on the Supreme Court docket raising the same issues. Daniel v. Louisiana, 420 U.S. 31 (1975). Two of the docketed cases involved female defendants. Stubblefield v. Tennessee, *app. dism.*, 420 U.S. 903 (1975); Normand v. Louisiana, *cert. den.*, 420 U.S. 908 (1975).

A comprehensive article on women and jury service appeared on the eve of argument in *Healy* and *Taylor*, in 9 HARV. CIV. RTS.–CIV. LIB. L. REV. 561 (1974).

[96] During the marriage, the wife's earnings exceeded those of the husband. Brief for Appellant at 4, Weinberger v. Wiesenfeld, attributed the difference to the fact that the husband was "in pursuit of an education." Inspection of the record on this point would have revealed to the solicitor general that the husband had completed his education eighteen months prior to the marriage. See Brief for Appellee, at 4.

[97] 42 U.S.C. § 402(g); cf. 1 U.S.C. § 1.

tion accorded widows. Relying on *Kahn*, the Solicitor General described the mother's benefit at issue in *Wiesenfeld* as a provision designed "to rectify the inferior economic status of women."[98] Appellee Wiesenfeld cautioned against continued acceptance of government-tendered "benign" or "compensatory" rationalizations for laws based on two assumptions: (1) that man's place is at work, woman's at home; (2) that women who do work are secondary breadwinners whose employment is implicitly less valuable to, and supportive of the family than the employment of the family's man.[99]

In an exhaustive review of legislative history, Mr. Justice Brennan, writing for the majority, concluded that alleviating gender-based job market discrimination was not what Congress had in mind when it stipulated a mother's benefit, in lieu of a parent's benefit. It was, he said, rather the twin couplings familiar to legislators in the 1930s: men and breadwinning; women and children.[100] Mr. Justice Brennan noted the Court's recognition in *Taylor* that current statistics belie the "presumed role in the home" of contemporary women.[101]

For seven of the Justices, the principal flaw in the scheme was that it denigrated the efforts of the wage-earning woman by providing her family less protection than it provided the family of a wage-earning man.[102] Mr. Justice Rehnquist's attention focused on the child. He found no rational purpose served by a distinction between mothers and fathers when the issue is "whether a child of a deceased contributing worker should have the opportunity to receive the full-time attention of the only parent remaining to it."[103]

While Mr. Justice Rehnquist labeled the exclusion of widowed fathers "irrational," none of the other Justices particularized the standard of review applied. "Suspect classification" was not argued

---

[98] Brief for Appellant, at 14, Weinberger v. Wiesenfeld.

[99] Brief for Appellee, at 16–26, Weinberger v. Wiesenfeld.

[100] 420 U.S. at 648–53; see Griffiths, *Sex Discrimination in Income Security Programs*, 49 NOTRE DAME L. 534 (1974); Note, 49 IND. L.J. 181 (1973).

[101] 420 U.S. at 643 n.11.

[102] Mr. Justice Powell's concurring opinion, in which Chief Justice Burger joined, relied heavily on the different treatment of male and female wage earners. Noting that the benefits under the statute are "not conditioned on the surviving parent's decision to remain at home," he did not attach to the statute's child care purpose the significance accorded that factor by the majority. 420 U.S. at 654.

[103] *Id.* at 655.

by Wiesenfeld,[104] nor was it mentioned by the Court. Despite the absence of doctrinal clarification, *Wiesenfeld* augurs movement beyond *Frontiero* in significant respects. For one thing, it represents the Court's first affirmative response to a gender discrimination claim in which the defender of the differential emphasized the factor of cost. Several months before the Court heard argument in *Frontiero*, the Department of Defense had informed Congress that equalization of fringe benefits for married military personnel, regardless of sex, would result in no increased budget requirements.[105] By contrast, the Solicitor General told the Court in *Wiesenfeld* that "the [annual] cost of [extending benefits to widowed fathers] would be $20 million (and over $300 million if other closely analogous provisions were extended)."[106] Further, Mr. Justice Brennan's opinion dealt sharply with the proposition that in reviewing gender classifications in the social security program, extreme deference should be the judicial perspective.

C. JUDICIAL NOTICE OF THE PRESENCE OF WOMEN IN ALL WALKS
   OF LIFE: STANTON V. STANTON

Utah's legislature and Supreme Court found a reasonable basis for requiring a parent to support a boy until he reaches age 21, but a girl only until age 18; because the boy needs more education and training to equip him for his role as family provider. Invalidating that gender line in *Stanton*, the Court again found it "unnecessary . . . to decide whether a classification based on sex is inherently suspect,"[107] for the male/female age differential failed "under any test—compelling state interest, or rational basis, or

---

[104] See text *supra*, at notes 75–79. The decision below found that the classification was a rational attempt to protect women but that sex ranked as a "suspect" classification and, therefore, the statutory classification failed because it "discriminates against some of the group which it is designed to protect." 367 F. Supp. 981, 990–91 (D. N.J. 1973).

[105] S. REP. No. 92-1218, 92d Cong., 2d Sess. 2 (1972).

[106] Brief for Appellant at 22, Weinberger v. Wiesenfeld.

Subject matter jurisdiction in *Wiesenfeld* was invoked under 28 U.S.C. § 1331 (general federal question jurisdiction). See 420 U.S. at 641–42 nn. 9, 10. In Weinberger v. Salfi, 95 S. Ct. 2457 (1975), decided some three months after *Wiesenfeld*, the Court ruled, sua sponte, that social security benefit claims, even when the sole question is the constitutionality of a statutory provision excluding claimant from benefits, must be presented in accordance with 42 U.S.C. § 405(g) (judicial review of final administrative determination), and may not be adjudicated under 28 U.S.C. § 1331. In a footnote in *Salfi*, 95 S. Ct. at 2468 n. 10, Mr. Justice Rehnquist, writing for the Court, reached back and recast the *Wiesenfeld* jurisdictional base to fit the 42 U.S.C. § 405(g) frame.

[107] Stanton v. Stanton, 421 U.S. 7, 13 (1975).

something in between."[108] Mr. Justice Blackmun, writing for eight members of the Court, referred to newer notions of women's place. He considered the changing roles played by women appropriate fare for judicial notice:[109]

> A child, male or female, is still a child. No longer is the female destined solely for the home and the rearing of the family, and only the male for the marketplace and the world of ideas. [Citation to *Taylor*.] Women's activities and responsibilities are increasing and expanding. . . . The presence of women in business, in the professions, in government and, indeed, in all walks of life where education is a desirable, if not always a necessary antecedent, is apparent and a proper subject of judicial notice. If a specific age of minority is required for the boy in order to assure him parental support while he attains his education and training, so, too, it is for the girl. To distinguish between the two on educational grounds is to be self-serving: if the female is not to be supported as long as the male, she hardly can be expected to attend school as long as he does, and bringing her education to an end earlier coincides with the role-typing society has long imposed.

V. Looking Back on the Last Two Terms

Taylor, *Wiesenfeld*, and *Stanton* suggest the Court's readiness to reassess classifications based on the assumption that social roles are ordained by sex, that woman's first job is wife and mother, man's, doctor, lawyer, or Indian chief. All three cases dealt with laws based on sharp sex-role delineation, the traditional notion that the adult world is (and should be) divided into two classes: (1) independent men, whose primary responsibilities are income production and participation in civic affairs outside the home; (2) dependent women, whose primary responsibility is care of household and children. Without attempting reformulation of the standard of review applicable to gender classifications, the

---

[108] *Id.* at 17. The question whether the age of majority should be 21 for all or 18 for all is "plainly . . . an issue of state law to be resolved by the Utah courts on remand." *Ibid.*

[109] *Id.* at 14–15. Cf. Women's Liberation Union of Rhode Island v. Israel, 512 F.2d 106, 109 (1st Cir. 1975): "Appellants place their major reliance . . . on cases in which the Court did indeed content itself with stereotypes. . . . But the authority of those precedents . . . has waned with the metamorphosis of the attitudes which fed them. What then was gallantry now appears Victorian condescension or even misogyny, and this cultural evolution is now reflected in the Constitution."

Court had in fact traveled almost full circle from its 1948 position in *Goesaert v. Cleary*,[110] where it reasoned:

> Michigan could, beyond question, forbid all women from working behind a bar. This is so despite the vast changes in the social and legal position of women. The fact that women may now have achieved the virtues that men have long claimed as their prerogatives and now indulge in vices that men have long practiced, does not preclude the States from drawing a sharp line between the sexes . . . . The Constitution does not require legislatures to reflect sociological insight, or shifting social standards . . . .

"Shifting social standards" and "vast changes" in women's activities and responsibilities became, in 1975, fare for judicial notice.

"[O]ld notions"[111] also figured in the 1885 legislation at issue in *Kahn*, the Florida widower's case. Up to 1968, Florida law required husband's consent to a married woman's transfer of her own interest in real property.[112] Appellant Kahn noted that a paternalistic legislator might well deem the married woman worthy of special solicitude on the death of the person the law regarded more as her guardian than her peer. He argued that although exclusion of widowers from the exemption discriminates most obviously against men, more subtly but as surely, it discounts the contribution made to the marital unit and the family economy by the female partner.

The afternoon following conclusion of oral argument in *Kahn*, the Court heard *DeFunis v. Odegaard*,[113] in which a white applicant to the University of Washington Law School claimed he had been denied the right to have his application considered in a racially neutral manner. The juxtaposition of *Kahn* and *DeFunis* may have been a factor in the assessment of some of the Justices in *Kahn*. It was not a clear day for perception of Sarah Grimke's 1837 plea: "I ask no favors for my sex. I surrender not our claim to equality. All I ask of our brethren, is that they will take their feet off from our necks."[114] Not only the *Kahn* majority opinion, au-

---

[110] 335 U.S. 464, 465 (1948).   [111] 421 U.S. at 14.

[112] See FLA. CONST., Art. 10. § 5; FLA. STAT. § 708.08 (1970).

[113] 416 U.S. 312 (1974).

[114] GRIMKE, LETTERS ON THE EQUALITY OF THE SEXES AND THE CONDITION OF WOMEN 10 (1838); cf. Matthews, *Women Must Have Equal Rights with Men: A Reply*, 12 A.B.A.J. 117, 120 (1926).

thored by Mr. Justice Douglas, but also the dissenting opinion of Mr. Justice Brennan, in which Mr. Justice Marshall joined, left room for "compensatory" gender classifications, among them, benefits for widows, but not widowers. Mr. Justice Brennan's dissenting opinion in *Kahn* perhaps was framed with one eye on *DeFunis*.[115] Mr. Justice Douglas, on the other hand, although he continued, after *Kahn*, to join minority opinions categorizing sex as a "suspect" criterion,[116] appears to discern degrees of suspectness. On 24 April 1974, he spoke for the majority in *Kahn*. On 23 April, in *DeFunis*, he declared: "So far as race is concerned, any state-sponsored preference to one race over another" is invidious.[117]

In the 1974 Term cases, *Taylor*, *Wiesenfeld*, and *Stanton*, it was made clear to the Court that women were harmed by the classifications. Though Taylor was a man (convicted of an aggravated kidnapping involving two female victims), his case was argued together with *Edwards v. Healy*,[118] in which female complainants charged that Louisiana's "benign dispensation" served to keep women in their place. Appellees in *Healy* asserted that a system treating "male participation in the administration of justice [as] essential, female participation [as] expendable, stigmatizes all women, even those who do not wish to serve."[119] *Stanton* was brought to secure support for a daughter. The brief and oral argument for appellee in *Wiesenfeld* concentrated on the discrimination against Paula Wiesenfeld, the deceased wage earner, whose contributions to social security did not secure for her family the benefits that were available to the family of a male wage earner.

Looking back over the two Terms, *Kahn* might be appraised as the wrong case brought to the Court at the wrong time, but a case with scant growth potential, a "state tax case" that may not carry over into other areas.[120] *Aiello*, in which the Court deferred

---

[115] On differences between the forces generating race and sex discrimination and the failure to distinguish problems of women and ghettoized minorities, see Ginsburg, note 57 *supra*, at 28–29; cf. Bartlett, note 57 *supra*, at 1548–51.

[116] Geduldig v. Aiello, 417 U.S. at 503 (dissent); Schlesinger v. Ballard, 419 U.S. 498, 511 (1975) (dissent).

[117] 416 U.S. at 343–44 (dissent).   [118] See notes 86 and 87 *supra*.

[119] Brief for Appellees at 9, Edwards v. Healy.

[120] If the classification had been found vulnerable to the widower's claim, others falling in line might have included single women, deaf persons, partially disabled persons. Cf. Bittker & Kaufman, *Taxes and Civil Rights: "Constitutionalizing" the Internal Revenue Code*, 82 YALE L. J. 51 (1972).

to a legislative judgment excluding from California's workers disability program institutionalized drug addicts, alcoholics, and sexual psychopaths, and women with normal pregnancies, remains the most troublesome recent decision. It presented an issue of critical importance to achievement of genuine equal opportunity for women, an issue perhaps brought to the Court too soon, but an issue destined to return for another airing at another Term.[121]

VI. In Conclusion: The Continued Need for the Equal Rights Amendment

The Court's performance in sex discrimination cases since 1971, compared to the record of the preceding century, may be legitimately characterized as a dramatic shift,[122] "a smashing success for proponents of equal treatment."[123] The majority of the Justices, however, have avoided articulating any standard of review for gender-based classifications distinct from the command of rational relationship. *Kahn* and *Aiello* indicate that the Court does not yet fully perceive, or is unwilling to confront, particular gender discrimination cases presented to it as part of a pervasive design of sex-role allocation shored up by laws that impede social change. Rather, the tendency has been to deal with each case in its own frame, and to write an opinion for that case and that day alone.[124]

The Court's reluctance to develop new doctrine is understandable. Under the Fifth and Fourteenth Amendments, a considerable stretch of historical meaning is necessary to cover gender discrimination at all.[125] Mr. Justice Powell's concurring opinion in *Frontiero*[126] cautions the Court to act with particular circumspection

---

[121] The Court has agreed to review Liberty Mutual Ins. Co. v. Wetzel, 511 F.2d 199 (3d Cir. 1975), holding that exclusion of disabilities due to pregnancy from employee disability coverage violates Title VII. 421 U.S. 987 (1975).

[122] See New York Times, 18 May 1975, § 4, p. 11, col. 1.

[123] See Johnston, note 3 *supra*, at 688.

[124] In *Reed*, administrative efficiency was not an adequate justification; in *Stanley* and *LaFleur*, there was an impermissible presumption trenching upon fundamental rights; in *Kahn*, there was leeway for state tax classification; in *Aiello*, deference to social legislation classification; and in *Taylor*, there was a criminal defendant's fundamental right to a jury drawn from a cross section of the community.

[125] See text *supra*, at notes 4–8, 67–72.

[126] See text *supra*, at note 73.

in the dim zone between dynamic interpretation and constitutional amendment.

Computer key-word runs on federal and state statutes have revealed hundreds of laws in each jurisdiction containing sex-based references.[127] Few of these laws have been revised. Legislators' behavior to date suggests that Mr. Justice Powell's counsel of restraint in *Frontiero* is paralleled by the position of the most political branch which seems to be that if the Equal Rights Amendment is adopted, the task of revising and adding particular legislation will be undertaken in earnest, but absent ratification, legislative revision may continue to be regarded as "premature."

The substantive section of the Equal Rights Amendment reads: "Equality of rights under the law shall not be denied or abridged by the United States or by any State on account of sex." Like other basic constitutional guarantees, the Amendment is drafted as general principle, the appropriate form for a text designed to govern through the ages. The Amendment would eliminate the historical impediment to judicial recognition of the legal equality of men and women: the absence of any intention by eighteenth- and nineteenth-century Constitution-makers to deal with gender-based discrimination. It would add to the text of the Constitution a principle under which a more complete and coherent opinion pattern may be developed.[128] It would end legislative inertia that keeps

---

[127] A Department of Justice computer printout, now under study by the United States Commission on Civil Rights, turned up over 800 sections of the United States Code that contain gender-based references. See Brief for Appellees, at 20 n.17, Frontiero v. Richardson. State reports include WISCONSIN LEGISLATIVE COUNCIL, REPORT ON EQUAL RIGHTS TO THE 1973 LEGISLATURE (1973); REPORT BY THE OHIO TASK FORCE FOR THE IMPLEMENTATION OF THE EQUAL RIGHTS AMENDMENT (1975); CALIFORNIA COMM'N ON THE STATUS OF WOMEN, ERA CONFORMANCE; AN ANALYSIS OF THE CALIFORNIA STATE CODES (1975).

[128] Walker v. Hall, 399 F. Supp. 1304 (W.D. Okla. 1975), illustrates the confusion still evident in the lower courts. The court there, in reliance on *Reed* and *Kahn*, distinguishing *Stanton*, upheld an Oklahoma statute permitting 18-year-old females to purchase 3.2 beer, while males had to be 21 years old to do so.

Taylor did not supply a principle broad enough to cover the range of women's jury service exemptions still prevalent in state and federal courts. The Court denied certiorari in Marshall v. Holmes, 365 F. Supp. 613 (N.D. Fla. 1973), aff'd, 495 F.2d 1371 (5th Cir. 1974), concerned with an exemption of "expectant" mothers and mothers with children under the age of 18. See also Foster v. Sparks, 506 F.2d 805, 827 (5th Cir. 1975).

Motherhood remains an area in which the stereotype holds sway. The Court denied review also in Arends v. Arends, 517 P.2d 1019 (Utah, 1974), 419 U.S. 881 (1975). And *Aiello* has put off the Fourteenth Amendment track the unique physical characteristic conundrum.

discriminatory laws on the books despite the counsel of amendment opponents that removal or revision of these laws is "the
way."[129] And it would serve as a forthright statement of the
nation's moral and legal commitment to a system in which women
and men stand as full and equal individuals under the law.

---

[129] Freund, *The Equal Rights Amendment Is Not the Way*, 6 HARV. CIV. RTS.–CIV.
LIB. L. REV. 234 (1971).

J. HARVIE WILKINSON III

GOSS v. LOPEZ: THE SUPREME COURT AS SCHOOL SUPERINTENDENT

No Term of the United States Supreme Court now seems complete without a school case. The Court has now afforded judicial review to most significant aspects of educational policy: school desegregation,[1] school finance,[2] school curriculum,[3] school personnel practices,[4] and, now, school discipline.[5] Though some constitutional challenges to educational authority have been rejected,[6] the trend has been unmistakably toward greater judicial intervention, in higher[7] and secondary[8] education alike. Indeed, if the last

---

J. Harvie Wilkinson III is Associate Professor of Law, University of Virginia.

AUTHOR'S NOTE: I am much indebted to my student assistant, Jack Costello, Jr., for diligent research and stimulating disagreement. Conversations with colleagues Peter W. Low and Warren F. Schwartz greatly helped my thinking. They are not, of course, responsible for points of view or errors found herein.

[1] *E.g.*, Swann v. Charlotte-Mecklenburg Bd. of Education, 402 U.S. 1 (1971); Wright v. City Council of Emporia, 407 U.S. 451 (1972); Keyes v. School District No. 1, 413 U.S. 189 (1973); Milliken v. Bradley, 418 U.S. 717 (1974).

[2] San Antonio Independent School Dist. v. Rodriguez, 411 U.S. 1 (1973).

[3] Epperson v. Arkansas, 393 U.S. 97 (1968).

[4] Cleveland Bd. of Education v. LaFleur, 414 U.S. 632 (1974).

[5] Goss v. Lopez, 419 U.S. 565 (1975); Wood v. Strickland, 420 U.S. 308 (1975).

[6] See Milliken v. Bradley, 418 U.S. 717 (1974); San Antonio Independent School Dist. v. Rodriguez, 411 U.S. 1 (1973).

[7] Healy v. James, 408 U.S. 169 (1972); Perry v. Sindermann, 408 U.S. 593 (1972); Papish v. Board of Curators, 410 U.S. 667 (1973); Vlandis v. Kline, 412 U.S. 441 (1973).

[8] In addition to the cases cited *supra*, in notes 1–5, see Tinker v. Des Moines School Dist., 393 U.S. 503 (1969).

decade saw the assertion of Supreme Court preeminence over state election law[9] and state systems of criminal justice,[10] the present one is witnessing the Court's gradual assumption of hegemony over state education. To more traditional matters such as school desegregation and state aid for parochial schools, the Court has now added a generalized concern with the fairness of educational policy. Surely the time has come to examine the implications of so far-reaching a development.

Along with the growth of the Court's interest in state education has been the revival of the doctrines of procedural due process. The recent line of procedural due process decisions began in 1969 with *Sniadach v. Family Finance Corporation*[11] and has continued largely uninterrupted despite dramatic shifts in the Court's personnel. Procedural safeguards of varying elaborateness now protect the right to one's wages[12] and commercial bank account,[13] welfare payment,[14] household possessions,[15] driver's license,[16] parole[17] and good time credits,[18] employment,[19] custody of children,[20] and good name.[21]

It was inevitable that two such flourishing lines of decision would converge, and that the Court would apply its ever more versatile tool of procedural due process to that ever more prevalent

---

[9] *E.g.*, Baker v. Carr, 369 U.S. 186 (1962); Harper v. Virginia Bd. of Elections, 383 U.S. 663 (1966); Williams v. Rhodes, 393 U.S. 23 (1968).

[10] *E.g.*, Mapp v. Ohio, 367 U.S. 643 (1961); Gideon v. Wainwright, 372 U.S. 335 (1963); Duncan v. Louisiana, 391 U.S. 145 (1968).

[11] 395 U.S. 337 (1969).   [12] *Ibid.*

[13] North Georgia Finishing, Inc. v. Di-Chem, Inc., 419 U.S. 601 (1975).

[14] Goldberg v. Kelly, 397 U.S. 254 (1970).

[15] Fuentes v. Shevin, 407 U.S. 67 (1972). But *cf.* Mitchell v. W. T. Grant Co., 416 U.S. 600 (1974).

[16] Bell v. Burson, 402 U.S. 535 (1971).

[17] Morrissey v. Brewer, 408 U.S. 471 (1972).

[18] Wolff v. McDonnell, 418 U.S. 539 (1974).

[19] Perry v. Sindermann, 408 U.S. 593 (1972). In Arnett v. Kennedy, 416 U.S. 134 (1974), Mr. Justice Rehnquist, in announcing the judgment of the Court, gave Congress wide latitude in setting predismissal procedures for non-probationary federal civil service employees. It is clear, however, from the concurring and dissenting opinions that a majority of Justices felt that due process required at least some minimal procedural protection before the employees could be discharged.

[20] Stanley v. Illinois, 405 U.S. 645 (1972).

[21] Wisconsin v. Constantineau, 400 U.S. 433 (1971).

judicial subject, the public schools. In *Goss v. Lopez*,[22] the Court held by a vote of 5 to 4 that in suspensions of ten days or less the Due Process Clause requires that the "student be given oral or written notice of the charges against him . . . an explanation of the evidence the authorities have and an opportunity to present his side of the story." And in a related 5 to 4 decision, *Wood v. Strickland*,[23] the Court declared that while a public school official enjoyed a qualified good faith immunity from liability for damages under 42 U.S.C. § 1983, he was not immune "if he knew or reasonably should have known that the action he took within his sphere of official responsibility would violate the constitutional rights of the student affected."

Goss v. Lopez, the decision on which this article focuses, is by any index a "modern" constitutional decision. It implicitly rejected the view that attendance at public school is a privilege to be withdrawn by school authorities at will.[24] It rejected the notion that school authorities stand *in loco parentis* to the student and therefore have full parental discretion in matters of discipline.[25] It rejected, too, any claim that presumed benevolence on the part of school authorities will suffice to protect the child's welfare.[26] In short, *Goss* evinced that skepticism toward the actions of local officialdom which is a hallmark of the modern Court. As in the area of criminal procedure, procedural safeguards are constitutionally required to check the officials' potential negligence, ignorance, or ill will.

Goss is thus certain to be hailed as an advance in human dignity

---

[22] 419 U.S. 565, 581 (1975).

[23] 420 U.S. 308, 322 (1975). Mr. Justice White wrote the opinion for the Court in both cases and was joined by Justices Douglas, Brennan, Stewart, and Marshall. Mr. Justice Powell, joined by the Chief Justice and Justices Blackmun and Rehnquist, dissented in *Goss* and dissented in part in *Wood v. Strickland*.

[24] The rejection of the rights-privileges distinction is, of course, not novel. See, *e.g.*, Graham v. Richardson, 403 U.S. 365, 374 (1971); Board of Regents v. Roth, 408 U.S. 564, 571 (1972).

[25] Professor Buss has noted that "when a parent sends a child to school, because the law so directs, he delegates no power. And to suggest that the parent delegates unrestricted power, especially when he objects to the discipline imposed, is patently absurd." Buss, *Procedural Due Process for School Discipline*, 119 U. PA. L. REV. 545, 560 (1971).

[26] 419 U.S. at 580, 581. A similar rationale for the juvenile court system was rejected in *In Re Gault*, 387 U.S. 1 (1967). See Paulsen, *The Constitutional Domestication of the Juvenile Court*, 1967 SUPREME COURT REVIEW 233.

and as a blow for fair treatment of the nation's schoolchildren. It is likely to be regarded as one of those narrow and modest victories for personal freedoms which occasionally emerge when Justices White and Stewart combine with the Court's liberal wing against the four appointees of President Nixon.[27] It is to such plaudits that I wish to register dissent. However welcome a development in individual rights the decision may appear, it symbolizes two of the more disquieting trends of modern constitutional decision-making. *Goss* affords a suitable vehicle to explore the recent topsy-turvy expansion of procedural due process and the concurrent inflation in the Supreme Court's supervision of our public schools.

I

I would begin by placing the *Goss* decision in perspective, for by itself, it is hardly a momentous case. Even those deeply disenchanted with the course of modern constitutionalism would have a difficult time regarding *Goss* as a dire moment for the Republic. Mr. Justice White's majority opinion is characteristically a measured one and comes wrapped in the usual cautionary platitudes: "By and large, public education in our Nation is committed to the control of state and local authorities,"[28] "Judicial interposition in the operation of the public school system . . . raises problems requiring care and restraint,"[29] and, of course, "Some modicum of discipline and order is essential if the educational function is to be performed."[30] Moreover, *Goss* flows smoothly and easily from the Court's recent precedents. Indeed, if one is to be loyal to precedent, there may be no fair way to reject the Court's result. Finally, *Goss* may be seen not only as a modest and logical extension of the Court's past decisions. There is a case to be made in *Goss*, as there always is, for due process in terms of fair and humane individual treatment.

Goss is not, of course, the first Supreme Court decision to vindicate student rights. In 1943, in *West Virginia State Board of Education v. Barnette*, the Court held that public school children, in this case Jehovah's Witnesses, could not be required to salute the

---

[27] *E.g.*, Wright v. City Council of Emporia, 407 U.S. 451 (1972); Furman v. Georgia, 408 U.S. 238 (1972).

[28] 419 U.S. at 578, *quoting* Epperson v. Arkansas, 393 U.S. 97, 104 (1968).

[29] 419 U.S. at 578.   [30] *Id.* at 580.

American flag in violation of their religious beliefs.[31] Over a decade later came *Brown v. Board of Education*[32] with its promise that a student's place in public education cannot be determined by race. The most significant student rights case of recent years, *Tinker v. Des Moines School District*,[33] upheld under the First Amendment the right of high school students to wear black armbands to protest the Vietnam war and, more generally, of high school students to engage in protest that does not materially disrupt normal school activity. *Goss* not only bears an obvious kinship with each of these decisions. *Goss* may represent the necessary culmination of all the Court's major student rights cases. It can be argued that without *Goss*, those decisions would remain vulnerable to the discretion of local school officials.

A student's rights to nondisruptive protest or free religious exercise, for example, may not be worth a farthing, if a school principal remains free to order summary suspensions.[34] First Amendment rights are theoretically vulnerable to school disciplinarians in at least three basic ways. First, the disciplinarian may act on an incorrect constitutional standard and find that something less than disruptive expression justifies suspension. Second, he may suspend the student on the basis of insufficient evidence as to whether, for example, a protest actually did take place or interfere with normal school operations. Third, the disciplinarian might fabricate or seize upon some later, alleged disciplinary violation to retaliate against the student's prior exercise of First Amendment rights.

Goss has little to say about the substantive standards under which disciplinarians operate. The requirement from the discipli-

---

[31] 319 U.S. 624. *Barnette* rested on more general First Amendment grounds than the religious freedom clause, see Kurland, *The Supreme Court, Compulsory Education, and the First Amendment's Religion Clauses*, 75 W. VA. L. REV. 213, 224 (1973). Later cases did uphold student rights on establishment grounds. *E.g.*, Engel v. Vitale, 370 U.S. 421 (1962); School District v. Schempp, 374 U.S. 203 (1963).

Nor is *Barnette* necessarily the Court's first "student rights" case. The Court in *Tinker*, for example, cited Meyer v. Nebraska, 262 U.S. 390 (1923) as an instance of an unconstitutional interference with a student's liberty, presumably to learn a foreign language. 393 U.S. at 506 (1969). And see Pierce v. Society of Sisters, 268 U.S. 510 (1925).

[32] 347 U.S. 483 (1954).   [33] 393 U.S. 503 (1969).

[34] "Without procedural safeguards the substantive protections would be virtually useless. There would be no point in an elaborate doctrine that students may be disciplined for disruptive action but not for mere expression if some administrator were permitted to make an ex parte and unreviewable determination that particular behavior was 'disruptive action' and that a particular student had participated in it." Wright, *The Constitution on the Campus*, 22 VAND. L. REV. 1027, 1059 (1969).

narian of some statement of charges and explanation of evidence against the student may, however, assist in curbing groundless or vindictive reaction to a student's exercise of First Amendment freedoms. Nevertheless, the bare procedural safeguards afforded in *Goss* hardly seem sufficient to protect fully the student's First Amendment interests against deprivation by pretext. Mr. Justice Douglas has suggested, in a related context, for instance, that "[w]hen a violation of First Amendment rights is alleged, the reasons for dismissal or for nonrenewal of an employment contract must be examined to see if the reasons given are only a cloak for activity or attitudes protected by the Constitution."[35] Yet, under *Goss*, where the student lacks the constitutional right to cross-examine or even to present witnesses of his own, examination of the disciplinarian's evidence or the true basis for his action may be anything but searching. It is difficult to believe, in fact, that several members of the *Goss* majority will ultimately rest content with its minimal requirements.[36]

In one respect, *Wood* resumed where *Goss* left off. In subjecting official action in violation of students' "basic, unquestioned constitutional rights"[37] to § 1983 liability, *Wood*, unlike *Goss*, affords protection against official ignorance of substantive First Amendment standards. By holding open the possibility of a damage action, *Wood* created protections against suspensions so groundless or so transparently a pretext as to evince official bad faith. Though, in this regard, the decisions are complementary, *Goss* in another sense only buffers school officials from the reach of *Wood*. For disciplinarians who follow the procedures in *Goss* would seem to present at least a *prima facie* case of actions in good faith for purposes of a subsequent § 1983 suit.

Thus, on its face, *Goss* is a logical successor to *Tinker* and *Barnette* in providing some procedural protection for the First Amendment rights extended in those cases. Yet *Goss* ultimately represents more of a sequel to *Brown v. Board of Education* than to the free speech cases. If in *Brown* the racial question was very much on the surface, in *Goss* it lay not very far below. In the years since *Brown*, the problem of race has moved from the perpetuation of

---

[35] Board of Regents v. Roth, 408 U.S. 564, 582 (1972) (dissenting opinion).

[36] In *Goss*, the Court left the door ajar for requiring more elaborate procedures in short suspensions involving "unusual situations." 419 U.S. at 584.

[37] 420 U.S. at 322.

segregation to one involving the implementation of integration. The difficulties confronting today's black students in mixed schools have been termed "second generation" problems and involve, in addition to school discipline, such matters as "discriminatory tracking and testing patterns."[38] School discipline remains perhaps the foremost source of aggravation. Many in the black community view the suspension of minority students as the rearguard attempt of school officials to perpetuate dual school systems, a problem calling for the exercise of judicial remedial powers just as surely as the breakup of de jure segregation mandated by *Brown*.[39]

Disciplinary problems, according to one study, are more common in integrated than in one-race schools,[40] and it is claimed that "in most localities a Black is at least two or three times more likely than a White to be suspended from public school."[41] For blacks the consequences of suspension may be especially severe: "Disadvantaged Black children, who are uniquely dependent upon public education to achieve full equality, frequently enter school at an academic disadvantage relative to their White classmates, and can be expected to fall further and further behind if their schooling is interrupted by unjustified suspensions."[42]

Such consequences are particularly hard to endure if the punishment itself is thought to be a product of racial discrimination. Many black students undoubtedly see the school "as a white world hostile to blacks, full of subtle and not-so-subtle racial slights and innuendos that cut deep and have caused the hostilities to escalate on both sides."[43] Whites are believed to "see black and think trouble." School regulations and their enforcement appear aimed at blacks, and dress codes may impinge primarily on black fashions

---

[38] NAACP Legal Defense Fund, Division of Legal Information and Community Service, Report on Black Student "Pushouts"—A National Phenomenon, 1–2 (1972). See also Task Force on Children out of School, The Way We Go to School: The Exclusion of Children in Boston (1971).

[39] Brief Amicus Curiae NAACP and the Southern Christian Leadership Conference in *Goss*, at 8; Southern Regional Council and Robert F. Kennedy Memorial, The Student Pushout: Victim of Continued Resistance to Desegregation (1973).

[40] Havighurst, Smith, & Wilder, *A Profile of the Large-City High School*, National Association of Secondary School Principals Bulletin 76 (January 1971).

[41] NAACP Amicus Brief note 39 *supra*, at 3–4.

[42] *Id*. at 4.

[43] U.S. Senate Committee on the Judiciary, Subcommittee to Investigate Juvenile Delinquency, *Our Nation's Schools—A Report Card: "A" in School Violence and Vandalism*, 94th Cong., 1st Sess. 29 (Comm. Print 1975).

and styles.[44] White students and parents respond in turn that blacks are more prone to physical aggression and claim that "the influx of blacks had lowered the quality of teaching by causing teachers to spend increasing amounts of time disciplining black students."[45]

In such a climate of mistrust, the Court in *Goss* set about to vindicate the promise of *Brown*. The silent expectation of *Goss* is that a hearing, however abbreviated, may help relieve racial tensions by enhancing the appearance of evenhanded discipline, by reducing the number of arbitrary or mistaken suspensions of minority students, and perhaps by encouraging communication between school officials and suspected student troublemakers and malcontents. *Goss* echoes much of the old Warren Court's faith that greater procedural formality, whether a search warrant, counsel, or arrest warnings, would spare poor and minority citizens from discriminatory law enforcement. Beneath the Court's split in *Goss* lies some of the tension between race and order that so badly divides the country. Differences in the Justices' own perceptions obviously run deep. To some, minority students and criminal suspects are disadvantaged and misunderstood citizens badly in need of some protection against the harassments of low-level state officials. The other view is that law violators and offenders, minority or not, merit a firm and sometimes swift response, minimally encumbered by constitutional obstacles. *Goss* represents a limited and uneasy victory for the former viewpoint, but makes it likewise unmistakable that proposed solutions for second-generation racial problems cannot command the unanimity of the 1954 decision and its immediate successors.

II

Goss is thus, by one view, a consummation of the Court's decisions in the field of substantive student rights. No less is it the product of the Court's recent expansion of procedural due process. With reference to that expansion, *Goss* is almost an anticlimax.

---

[44] See CHILDREN'S DEFENSE FUND OF THE WASHINGTON RESEARCH PROJECT, CHILDREN OUT OF SCHOOL IN AMERICA (1974). This extensive report notes that one school district "amended its conduct code, for example, to include possession of a metal pick as a weapons offense. Metal picks are used by black children to comb Afro hair styles." *Id.* at 132.

[45] Note 43 *supra*, at 29.

Having bestowed at least some due process protection upon
nearly everything else, the Court, in *Goss*, could not comfortably
find education excluded. It would have been awkward, for example, for the Court to surround the right of retention of such
mundane items as a driver's license,[46] gas stove, and stereo set[47]
with procedural safeguards but to deny them to education. Nor
would it have been easy to justify the view that the prison inmate
deserves protection against his supervisors[48] but that the schoolchild
does not. And, it is hardly obvious why a temporary deprivation
of education should rank, in due process terms, below the interim
freezing of wages in a prejudgment garnishment action.[49] Any
contention that deprivation of education is somehow the lesser interest because it may not drive one to the edge of survival would
mock the Court's evangelical rhetoric on the importance of education to the American way of life.[50]

Other recent developments in the law of procedural due process
foreshadowed the result in *Goss*. Much of the State's case in *Goss*
obviously rested upon the idea that educational discipline is principally the domain of the educator, next the legislator, and almost
never the judge. Or, as Mr. Justice Powell put it, school officials,
not the federal courts, should have "the authority to determine the
rules applicable to routine classroom discipline of children and
teenagers in the public schools."[51] Whatever vitality this theory
may still have possessed after the recent spate of school decisions
necessarily diminished after the 1974 prison discipline cases, chiefly
Wolff v. McDonnell,[52] which applied minimum due process safeguards to the deprivation of inmates' good time credits by prison
officials. If, as Mr. Justice White declared in *Wolff*, "[t]here is
no iron curtain drawn between the Constitution and the prisons of

---

[46] Bell v. Burson, 402 U.S. 535 (1971).

[47] Fuentes v. Shevin, 407 U.S. 67 (1972).

[48] Wolff v. McDonnell, 418 U.S. 539 (1974).

[49] Sniadach v. Family Finance Corp., 395 U.S. 337 (1969).

[50] *E.g.*, Brown v. Board of Education, 347 U.S. 483, 493 (1954).

[51] 419 U.S. at 585. Even after *Goss*, of course, state legislatures and school authorities
retain broad authority in formulating substantive rules of conduct.

[52] 418 U.S. 539 (1974). See also Procunier v. Martinez, 416 U.S. 396 (1974), where
the Court upheld prisoners' challenges against mail censorship, and Pell v. Procunier,
417 U.S. 817 (1974), and Saxbe v. Washington Post Co., 417 U.S. 843 (1974), where
challenges to prison bans on media interviews with inmates were rejected.

this country,"[53] there may be no curtain of any sort between the Constitution and the schools where the environment is less grim than in prisons,[54] the need for discipline less a life-or-death matter, and where creativity, even some deviance, is ideally to be encouraged. The irony of all this, however, is that the Burger Court, popularly portrayed as a conservative one, is eroding through procedural due process the notion that prison officials and school principals are free to order and maintain their own baronies, immune and removed from constitutional scrutiny.[55]

The lower federal courts had, of course, carried procedural due process to public education long before *Goss*. In *Dixon v. Alabama State Board of Education*,[56] the Fifth Circuit held that "due process requires notice and some opportunity for hearing before students at a tax-supported college are expelled for misconduct." *Dixon* was somewhat removed from the circumstances of *Goss*. It was concerned with higher education, not secondary and elementary schools, and, more importantly, it involved the expulsion of students, not short-term suspensions of ten days or less. While *Dixon* gained quick acceptance as to expulsions, the lower courts splintered hopelessly over just how long a suspension from school was necessary to invoke some due process protection.[57] A holding that procedural due process is required for suspensions of ten but not of seven days contributes little to solution of the problem.[58]

In *Board of Regents v. Roth*,[59] the Court had gone far toward making such line drawing unnecessary. There the Court declared that "to determine whether due process requirements apply in the first place, we must look not to the 'weight' but to the *nature* of

[53] 418 U.S. at 555–56.

[54] In some quarters, this statement would be disputed. See Haney & Zimbardo, *It's Tough to Tell a High School from a Prison*, PSYCHOLOGY TODAY 26 (June 1975); SILBERMAN, CRISIS IN THE CLASSROOM 142, 146 (1970); KOZOL, DEATH AT AN EARLY AGE 178 (1967).

[55] But as to the barony of military officers, see *e.g.*, Parker v. Levy, 417 U.S. 733, 752 (1974), where the Court rejected vagueness and overbreadth challenges to Capt. Levy's court-martial conviction partly on the basis of the "very significant differences . . . between the military community and the civilian community."

[56] 294 F.2d 150, 151 (5th Cir. 1961).

[57] See the cases cited by the Court in *Goss*, 419 U.S. at 576 n. 8.

[58] *Compare* Black Students of North Fort Meyers Jr.-Sr. High School v. Williams, 470 F.2d 957 (5th Cir. 1972), *with* Linwood v. Bd. of Education, 463 F.2d 763 (7th Cir. 1972).

[59] 408 U.S. 564 (1972).

the interest at stake."[60] Thus, whether the suspension was for one, five, or ten days was rendered irrelevant in determining whether some form of due process requirement applies. As to the nature of the interests requiring due process protection, *Roth* defined property as a "legitimate claim of entitlement to" a benefit conferred by state statute or policy or by contract or even some less formal understanding with a public agency.[61] In *Goss*, the student's property interest constituted an "entitlement" to public education established both by Ohio statutes providing free public education to all residents between six and twenty-one, and by Ohio's compulsory school attendance law.[62] Liberty interests, protected in *Roth* against public actions "that might seriously damage [one's] standing and associations in his community,"[63] were also implicated in *Goss*, since suspensions, however short, "could seriously damage the students' standing with their fellow pupils and their teachers as well as interfere with later opportunities for higher education and employment."[64]

If the application of some form of due process to student suspensions was heavily foreshadowed by *Roth*, *Goss* nonetheless added two notable elements to that decision. From old concurring opinions of Justices Frankfurter and Harlan, the Court had collected and banded loosely two alternate notions of when due process was to be required. One was that due process requirements had to be met where an individual may suffer "grievous loss."[65] The second was that the Due Process Clause applied wherever the deprivation was not de minimis.[66] *Goss* now announces that the second, de minimis, standard is the correct one, and thus potentially sweeps all property deprivations but the most trivial and harmless within the already spacious language of the Fourteenth Amendment.

The vagueness of the de minimis standard will, over time, sow

---

[60] 408 U.S. at 570–71. See also Fuentes v. Shevin, 407 U.S. 67, 90 n.21 (1972).

[61] 408 U.S. at 577.   [62] 419 U.S. at 573.

[63] 408 U.S. at 573. See also Wisconsin v. Constantineau, 400 U.S. 433, 437 (1971).

[64] 419 U.S. at 575.

[65] Joint Anti-Fascist Refugee Committee v. McGrath, 341 U.S. 123, 168 (1951) (Frankfurter, J., concurring), quoted in *Goldberg*, 397 U.S. at 262–63, and *Morrissey*, 408 U.S. at 481 (1972).

[66] Sniadach v. Family Finance Corp., 395 U.S. 337, 342 (1969) (Harlan, J., concurring); Boddie v. Connecticut, 401 U.S. 371, 379 (1971); Board of Regents v. Roth, 408 U.S. at 570 n.8.

its own inconsistencies and confusions. Meanwhile, the list of marginal adversity potentially protected by due process demands must rapidly expand. For if, under *Goss,* even a one-day suspension from school is not de minimis, then one must ask whether an equally brief suspension of welfare benefits or a driver's license is any more so.[67] Slight reductions of welfare payments, transfers from larger to smaller public housing units, minor changes in treatment programs for mental health patients, can all be seen by a sympathetic judiciary to have more than de minimis impact. If district judges then must fashion varying levels of procedural protections prior to every short-term cutoff or minor reduction of innumerable public benefits, then yet another wholesale displacement of political power by judicial command lies at hand.

Goss also rejected as a theory of procedural due process Mr. Justice Rehnquist's opinion in *Arnett v. Kennedy,*[68] which, if expanded, would have sharply limited the reach of *Roth.* The Rehnquist view was "that where the grant of a substantive right is inextricably intertwined with the limitations on the procedures which are to be employed in determining that right, a litigant . . . must take the bitter with the sweet."[69] This thesis thus strikes at the very heart of the division of powers between legislatures and courts. It envisions congressional paramountcy in the planning of public programs and the provision of procedures for their enforcement as well as a severe constriction of the role of courts as protectors of personal liberties. Ultimately it might allow the State to escape the imposition of the Due Process Clause by conditioning almost any public benefit with summary procedures for its termination.

Mr. Justice Powell, who rejected the Rehnquist rationale in *Arnett,*[70] inexplicably embraced it in his *Goss* dissent, noting that the "Ohio statute that creates the right to a 'free' education also explicitly authorizes a principal to suspend a student for as much as 10 days," and that "the very legislation which 'defines' the 'dimen-

---

[67] As Professor O'Neil has noted, *Goldberg v. Kelly* did not deal explicitly "with the recurrent problem of temporary suspension rather than final termination of payments," although the Court may have meant "to assimilate suspension and termination without quite saying so." *Of Justice Delayed and Justice Denied: The Welfare Prior Hearing Cases,* 1970 SUPREME COURT REVIEW 177. *Goss* surely makes such an assumption more plausible.

[68] 416 U.S. 134 (1974). Mr. Justice Rehnquist's opinion, which announced the judgment of the Court in *Arnett,* was joined by Chief Justice Burger and Mr. Justice Stewart.

[69] *Id.* at 153–54.   [70] *Id.* at 164 (Powell, J., concurring).

sion' of the student's entitlement, while providing a right to education generally, does not establish this right free of discipline imposed in accord with Ohio law."[71] Mr. Justice Stewart, on the other
hand, who had joined the Rehnquist opinion in *Arnett,* then rejected it in *Goss.* The majority in *Goss,* of course, declined the
Rehnquist view, and, with it, one of the last chances to contain the
Roth opinion. For there may be few public programs or facilities to which one cannot assert claims of property entitlement, and
the denial of any public benefit is not without some reputational
scar or blemish.

Determining that the Due Process Clause applies is, of course,
only half the battle. The consequent inquiry is what process is due.
If this second inquiry is, as the Court has so often repeated, an
"intensely practical" matter,[72] requiring great flexibility,[73] the question arises why those administrators who are on the scene are
not permitted greater leeway. In this, as in other contexts, the
Court has claimed a versatile expertise of extraordinary precision.
It has constitutionalized these "practical" and "flexible" judgments
and meticulously set forth exactly what set of procedures must
govern each given situation. Sometimes the mandated procedures
are quite sparse,[74] and, on occasion, the Court simply states that
due process applies and refrains from particularizing its content.[75]
But in a growing number of instances, the Court has assumed for
itself the capacity to understand exactly what minutiae of procedure parole boards, prison officials, welfare boards, and school
administrators require to best accommodate individual interests to
administrative ones.[76] Not only is the wisdom of its procedural
codes suspect,[77] but serious doubts exist over the ability of the

---

[71] 419 U.S. at 586. The inconsistency may be due to the heavy weight Justice Powell
places on the autonomy of public schools, see text *infra,* at notes 118 *et seq.* Even so,
the doctrinal shift was not necessary to his dissent in *Goss.*

[72] *E.g.,* 419 U.S. at 478.

[73] Cafeteria Workers Local 973 v. McElroy, 367 U.S. 886, 895 (1961); *Morrissey,*
408 U.S. at 490.

[74] *E.g.,* Wolff v. McDonnell, 418 U.S. 539 (1974).

[75] *E.g.,* Sniadach v. Family Finance Corp., 395 U.S. 337 (1969); Bell v. Burson, 402
U.S. 535 (1971); Stanley v. Illinois, 405 U.S. 645 (1972).

[76] See *Morrissey, Wolff, Goldberg,* and *Goss, supra.*

[77] One careful student of the social welfare system has concluded: "The information
which is available on the AFDC program should substantially decrease our confidence
that the procedural rights afforded recipients in *Goldberg* v. *Kelly* provide substantial

Court to achieve genuine compliance.[78]

Though some of the procedures recently challenged before the Court provided the complaining individual a post-deprivation hearing,[79] and others granted an informal pre-termination hearing followed by a fuller and more elaborate post-deprivation one,[80] the Court has generally emphasized that the pre-termination stage is critical.[81] Such emphasis is due to the danger of mistake in summary pre-termination proceedings, the hardship suffered by individuals waiting for erroneous decisions to be rectified, the lack of knowledge or incentive on the part of those already deprived to seek relief, and the likelihood that post-termination hearings may become after-the-fact rationalizations of bureaucratic decisions already made.[82] All these factors undoubtedly helped persuade the Court in *Goss* of the need for some hearing prior to even a short suspension. If hardship may not loom as large with school-children as with wage earners and welfare recipients, there is arguably the added factor that missing time in education, unlike back wages and welfare payments, cannot easily be restored, and the collateral and psychological consequences on the suspended schoolchild may not be easily reversed.[83]

It is not my purpose here to survey all possible elements of a due process hearing. This Judge Friendly has done recently with characteristic thoroughness and pungency.[84] The important thing

---

assurance of fairness and accuracy." Mashaw, *The Management Side of Due Process: Some Theoretical and Litigation Notes on the Assurance of Accuracy, Fairness, and Timeliness in the Adjudication of Social Welfare Claims,* 59 Corn. L. Rev. 772, 811 (1974).

[78] Professor Mashaw noted that "the only systematic study that seems to have been made of the compliance of agency practice with post-*Goldberg* fair hearing regulations found that the New York City public welfare agencies failed to provide a procedurally regular hearing in a significant number of cases." *Id.* at 813.

[79] *E.g., Sniadach, Fuentes,* and *Mitchell, supra.*

[80] *E.g., Goldberg* and *Arnett, supra.* In *Bell v. Burson, supra,* the post-suspension hearing was a full trial on the merits, whereas the pre-suspension hearing excluded altogether the critical consideration of the motorists' fault.

[81] *E.g., Sniadach,* 395 U.S. at 338–39; *Goldberg,* 397 U.S. at 260–61; *Constantineau,* 400 U.S. at 437; *Boddie,* 401 U.S. at 379; *Burson,* 402 U.S. at 542; *Fuentes,* 407 U.S. at 81–82.

[82] The Court has, in general, been discouragingly conclusory about the rationale for *pre-termination* hearings. A good analysis of the need for such hearings, at least in the welfare area, is O'Neil, note 67 *supra,* at 168–75.

[83] In *Sniadach* and *Goldberg,* moreover, there was available to the wage earner and welfare recipient a later trial on the merits of the case, something not always granted suspended students.

[84] Friendly, "*Some Kind of Hearing,*" 123 U. Pa. L. Rev. 1267 (1975).

to recognize is that three quite different constitutional models of pre-termination hearings have emerged under recent Supreme Court decisions. The models diverge sharply in their procedural formalities:

1. *Full dress due process.* This most elaborate system of due process governs trials of adult criminal defendants in the United States. The familiar protections of the Bill of Rights apply: the right to a speedy and public trial by an impartial jury (or judge); the right to notice of the charges, to be present at trial, to confront and cross-examine adverse witnesses and to compulsory process of favorable ones, the right to retained or appointed counsel, to have excluded wrongly seized evidence and illegally obtained confessions, protection against being put twice in jeopardy, and a standard of proof of beyond a reasonable doubt. The litany continues through a host of protections, some constitutional, others almost universally provided by statute: the right to a transcript, to appeals and post-conviction relief, to protection against unreliable, intimate, prejudicial, and irrelevant evidence. For those not on bail whose liberty has been taken, the trial comes too late to be classed pre-deprivation relief,[85] and the appeal and post-conviction proceedings find all but a few defendants already in custody.

2. *Medium due process. Goldberg v. Kelly* and *Morrissey v. Brewer* are the best examples of this middle level of due process which borrows freely from the criminal model. Some of the more formal manifestations of the criminal trial, such as the jury, complex rules of evidence, and stricter standards of proof,[86] are absent at this level, reflecting, as in *Goldberg* and *Morrissey*, the less formal setting of an administrative determination, or, as in *Morrissey*, the fact that an earlier conviction has been obtained. At this middle level, the right to cross-examine is accorded, but the Court's attitude toward counsel is more ambivalent. *Goldberg* notes oddly that counsel need not be provided at the pre-termination stage, but that "the [welfare] recipient must be allowed to

---

[85] So too does the magistrate's initial determination of probable cause often follow the deprivation of liberty through arrest. See Gerstein v. Pugh, 420 U.S. 103, 120–21 (1975).

[86] *Morrissey* explicitly identified the standard of proof in parole revocation hearings as one of "probable cause." 408 U.S. at 485.

retain an attorney if he so desires."[87] *Morrissey's* blueprint for parole revocation proceedings was shortly supplemented by *Gagnon v. Scarpelli*[88] in which the Court held that due process required the appointment of counsel only where there was a colorable factual dispute or that the evidence on behalf of the parolee was difficult for a layman to develop.[89] Significantly, the pre-termination hearing required by *Goldberg* does provide the welfare recipient with notice of the proposed termination of benefits, an opportunity to present his evidence orally and to confront and cross-examine any adverse witnesses and, finally, the right to a statement of reasons based on the hearing from an impartial decision maker.[90] *Morrissey's* requirements were substantially similar.[91]

3. *Skeletal due process.* The chief difference between medium and skeletal due process is that in the latter the rights to counsel and cross-examination are almost wholly absent. Skeletal due process contemplates only the barest rudiments: advance notice of the charges, a statement of the evidence backing them, some chance to present one's own side of the story, and perhaps a brief statement of reasons for adverse action. In *Arnett*, a majority of Justices accepted a roughly similar set of safeguards as constitutionally sufficient for a pre-dismissal hearing for federal civil service employees, and in *Wolff* skeletal due process was all that was required before taking prison disciplinary action. Both decisions left the Court's liberal wing disgruntled. Skeletal due process, complained Mr. Justice Marshall in *Wolff*, meant "little more than empty promises."[92]

Goss v. Lopez, of course, represents skeletal due process even more than *Wolff*. The Court conferred upon the student faced with a short suspension only a constitutional right to oral or written notice of the charges, an explanation of the evidence held by au-

---

[87] 397 U.S. at 270. How most indigent recipients are to retain attorneys is a puzzling question.

[88] 411 U.S. 778 (1973).

[89] See *id.* at 790–91 for the full explanation of when counsel may be necessary in parole revocation proceedings.

[90] 397 U.S. at 266–71. An impartial decision-maker here means no more than someone other than the one who made the decision under review.

[91] In *Morrissey*, unlike *Goldberg*, the right to cross-examine is qualified and subject to suspension "if the hearing officer determines that an informant would be subjected to risk of harm if his identity were disclosed." 408 U.S. at 487.

[92] 418 U.S. at 581.

thorities,[93] and an opportunity to tell his side of the story to the disciplinarian. Though *Wolff* stipulated that prior notice be written, *Goss* did not. And unlike *Wolff*, the Court in *Goss* refused to require the disciplinarian to set forth written reasons for his action. The Court in *Goss* also explicitly declined to require any constitutional right to counsel, cross-examination, or even the chance for the student "to call his own witnesses to verify his version of the incident."[94] Once again the protection afforded was even skimpier than in *Wolff*, which at least permitted "the inmate facing disciplinary proceedings . . . to call witnesses and present documentary evidence in his defense when permitting him to do so will not be unduly hazardous to institutional safety or correctional goals."[95] So narrow, in fact, was the holding in *Goss* that the debate on the Court was not, as in *Wolff*, whether to require skeletal or medium due process but whether to require skeletal due process or none at all. And the Court's three most liberal members, so dissatisfied with skeletal due process in *Arnett* and *Wolff*, joined the majority in *Goss* without so much as the bare murmur of a separate opinion.[96]

Upon close inspection, *Goss* comes to seem even more deferential to school authorities. There need be no delay between notice and the holding of the hearing and in "the great majority of cases the disciplinarian may informally discuss the alleged conduct with the student minutes after it has occurred."[97] Presumably, one hearing will suffice. There is no mention in the Court's opinion of any record to be kept of the hearing, of fuller post-suspension proceedings, or, indeed, of any further administrative review of the

---

[93] One important unanswered question is how far the disciplinarian must go in revealing the sources of adverse evidence against the student. The tenor of the Court's opinion would appear to leave school administrators substantial discretion in such matters, especially where divulgence of the names of "student-informants" would subject them to risks of reprisal.

[94] 419 U.S. at 583.   [95] 418 U.S. at 566.

[96] It is tempting to speculate on the "politics" of this development. The Court majority may have been impressed with the need for a solid front in a close and controversial decision. Perhaps the Court's more liberal members joined the opinion in order to win the principle of due process application, waiting to add substance another day. Perhaps, also, *Goss* represented the most that Justices such as Stewart and White would accept. At any rate, the Court's opinion leaves clues of compromise among members of the majority, such as the Sphinx-like statement: "Nor do we put aside the possibility that in unusual situations, although involving only a short suspension, something more than rudimentary procedures will be required." 419 U.S. at 584.

[97] *Id.* at 582.

disciplinarian's initial decision. In addition, the Court loosely exempted from the general requirement of a prior hearing "[s]tudents whose presence poses a continuing danger to persons or property or an ongoing threat of disrupting the academic process."[98] In such cases, the student "may be immediately removed from school" and the necessary notice and hearing should "follow as soon as practicable."[99] Because the school principal is the most likely and practical hearing officer, the Court refrained even from speculating on his impartiality, something it surely could not have assumed.[100] Finally, the Court omitted mention of rights of parents or other persons either to notice or to be present.[101]

It was not inevitable that the procedures required by *Goss* be so threadbare. The extent to which procedural due process must be afforded always depends upon a simple balancing process, "a determination of the precise nature of the government function involved as well as of the private interest that has been affected by governmental action."[102] In such an equation, one might argue, the schoolchild's interests are not insignificant. The consequences of mistaken suspensions are, in the eyes of some educators, severe: time lost from school with poor grades or zeros often awarded for missed tests, the acquisition of a troublemaker's reputation both with teachers and fellow classmates, a lowering of the student's self-esteem and self-confidence, a sense of non-belonging and exclusion from the community, and a feeling of cynicism and frustra-

---

[98] *Ibid.*   [99] *Id.* at 582–83.

[100] As two observers assessed it: "Given a choice between supporting the teachers or the students, most school officials have no difficulty recognizing their natural allies. Among the school administrators we interviewed, one told us candidly he would never support a student in a dispute with a teacher, but would only try to convey an impression of fairness 'to prevent parents from getting involved.' " Haney & Zimbardo, note 54 *supra*, at 29–30.
Apart from any such institutional bias, the principal or his assistant may be heavily involved with the parties or situation under review. In cases where an exceptional bias might be provable, the disciplinarian would do well to disqualify himself.

[101] There are threshold difficulties with bringing a parent into brief suspension hearings. A requirement of prior notice to a parent and a right to be present might have defeated the Court's expectation that most hearings would quickly follow the alleged disciplinary violation. Parents may also be quite unaware of the facts or circumstances underlying an incident and in some instances even have interests and viewpoints opposed to the student. Called quickly to the scene with little prior knowledge, their presence would often be diversionary and delaying. In any event, most parents will learn soon enough of the suspension and be able to request a conference with school officials at that time.

[102] Cafeteria Workers Local 973 v. McElroy, 367 U.S. 886, 895 (1961), quoted in *Goldberg*, 397 U.S. at 263.

tion toward authorities for an arbitrary and unjust decision.[103] The most enduring consequence of a mistaken suspension may be a notation of the disciplinary action in the student's file or record. Even where actual access of employers and other educational institutions to the file is limited, teachers often use such files in preparing recommendations and students themselves are often requested by employers and prospective colleges to reveal and explain any prior misconduct.[104]

A principal purpose of procedural due process is to prevent mistaken judgments, and the risk of error in short suspensions is not slight. Unlike the actions of creditors to repossess commercial goods, which the Court has characterized as "ordinarily uncomplicated matters that lend themselves to documentary proof,"[105] student suspensions present the classic case of inquiry into fault. Dispute may abound on who actually committed the offense, and under what circumstances. The accuracy of factual determinations may be undermined by "[m]istakes of identity, distortions caused by the failure of information sources, faulty perceptions or cloudy memories, as well as fabrications born of personal antagonisms,"[106] in other words the very factors that gave rise to the elaborate constitutional safeguards of the criminal trial. But unlike the criminal trial, the decision to discipline a student is not reached in the more detached atmosphere of a courtroom but rather exclusively by a layman in or near the harried climate of the public schools, with "bells ringing, buzzers sounding, public address systems making all those announcements, thousands of noisy adolescents pushing and shoving their way through crowded halls and stairways, locker doors banging . . . and so on."[107]

> In this charged atmosphere, arbitrariness inevitably takes
> root and flourishes. The motivations for arbitrary, even mali-

---

[103] Lines, *The Case against Short Suspensions*, 12 INEQUALITY IN EDUCATION 39, 41–42 (1972); CHILDREN'S DEFENSE FUND, note 44 *supra*, at 135–39; and Brief Amici Curiae for the Children's Defense Fund and the American Friends Service Committee, at 14–15.

[104] 419 U.S. at 575, n.7.

[105] *Mitchell*, 416 U.S. at 609. Other factors, not present in the school discipline context, reduced the risk of mistake in the *ex parte* proceeding in *Grant:* the requirement that the seller post a bond to guarantee the buyer against damage or expense; the presence of a judge, as opposed to a school principal, as the decision-maker; and the creditor's own interest in not interrupting the transaction.

[106] *Arnett*, 416 U.S. at 214 (Marshall, J., dissenting).

[107] BAILEY, DISRUPTION IN URBAN PUBLIC SECONDARY SCHOOLS 28 (1970).

cious, accusations of misconduct are legion. Outside quarrels may carry over into the school. A student may make a false accusation against a rival; a member of one racial or ethnic group may make a false accusation against a member of another. And, more important, an administrator or teacher, harried and wishing to be rid of certain students, may color ambiguous facts, or simply lie, out of frustration.[108]

In such cases and "[i]n almost every setting where important decisions turn on questions of fact, due process requires an opportunity to confront and cross-examine adverse witnesses."[109] Why, then, did the Court in *Goss* opt for a mere wisp of due process? The major reason was, as the Court noted, the sheer volume of brief disciplinary suspensions and that to "impose in each such case even truncated trial-type procedures might well overwhelm administrative facilities in many places and, by diverting resources, cost more than it would save in educational effectiveness."[110]

There are more specific reasons not mentioned by the Court that militate against further formalizing the process of short suspensions. Take, for example, the right to cross-examine adverse witnesses. If, as *Goss* contemplates, the hearing will occur in most cases almost immediately after the alleged violation, there is hardly the kind of prior notice to make cross-examination effective. Cross-examination of one student by another would quickly dissolve into mutual shoutings of recriminations, especially where the antagonists lacked time to cool off. In fact one wonders how artful cross-examiners most students will make under any circumstances. Especially with younger schoolchildren, there will be pressure to bring into the proceedings some adult, perhaps a parent or even counsel, to conduct the examination. The resulting formalization of brief suspension proceedings could be staggering.[111] Where a teacher rather than another student is the principal accuser, affording the student the right to confrontation may only increase the level of acrimony and undermine the teacher's authority which

---

[108] Children's Defense Fund Amicus Brief, at 59.

[109] *Goldberg*, 397 U.S. at 269.   [110] 419 U.S. at 583.

[111] "In a school proceeding the attorney for the student will be the only professionally trained advocate in the proceeding. . . . Would not a natural consequence seem to be that, after an initial period of layman trying to deal with lawyers, lawyers would also be introduced for the "prosecuting" school authorities and, indeed, for the deciders? Such seems to be the tendency in college disciplinary proceedings that become very formalized." GOLDSTEIN, LAW AND PUBLIC EDUCATION, CASES AND MATERIALS 511 (1974).

would be difficult to reassert once the brief suspension had passed. If hearings are to be held promptly and prior to suspension, it will often be disruptive for a principal to remove teachers and students from the classroom to undergo cross-examination. Finally, in those cases where the adverse witness is not immediately known, summoning him for cross-examination may subject him, in today's school environment, to the risk of serious reprisals.[112]

The foregoing does not, of course, mean that a student is bereft of all opportunity to counter adverse evidence through lesser means. Under *Goss* the authorities still must inform the student of the evidence they possess and grant him the opportunity to present his version of the incident. But objections similar to those raised against cross-examination can readily be leveled at most other suggestions for more formalized procedures in brief disciplinary suspensions. For now, at least, the Court has wisely left further elaboration to the discretion of school authorities, noting there may be instances where the disciplinarian himself would "summon the accuser, permit cross-examination and allow the student to present his own witnesses. In more difficult cases, he may permit counsel."[113]

If *Goss*, then, is so modest a step, why so closely and vigorously divided the Supreme Court? The decision provoked Mr. Justice Powell to his first verbal dissent from the bench. To understand this, one must look to the broader contours of the Justice's philosophy. Mr. Justice Powell's posture in *Goss* and in *Wood v. Strickland* reflects what is becoming a most prominent theme of his tenure: the determination to contain constitutional interference with the operations of the public schools.[114] This cause has certainly enlisted his most strenuous efforts, and possibly his most distinguished ones, including the Court's opinion in *San Antonio Independent School District v. Rodriguez*[115] rejecting a constitutional

---

[112] A thoughtful discussion of the pros and cons of the more formal procedural safeguards in disciplinary hearings can be found in Buss, note 25 *supra*, at 589–641. Professor Buss was concerned with longer student suspensions and expulsions than those involved in *Goss*.

[113] 419 U.S. at 584.

[114] The Justice has not, however, advocated complete immunity for educators from constitutional scrutiny. See his opinion for the Court in Healy v. James, 408 U.S. 169 (1972), and his concurrence in Cleveland Bd. of Education v. LaFleur, 414 U.S. 632, 651 (1974).

[115] 411 U.S. 1 (1973).

challenge to the Texas system of public school finance and the thirty-six-page opinion in *Keyes v. School District No. 1* urging reduced judicial resort to the compulsory transportation of school-children to desegregate the public schools.[116]

Much of the rhetoric in these opinions seems almost interchange-able. *Rodriguez* involved "the most persistent and difficult ques-tions of educational policy, another area in which this Court's lack of specialized knowledge and experience counsels against pre-mature interference with the informed judgments made at the state and local levels."[117] In *Keyes,* the Justice concluded that "[c]om-munities deserve the freedom and the incentive to turn their atten-tion and energies to [the] . . . goal of quality education, free from protracted and debilitating battles over court-ordered student trans-portation."[118] His *Goss* dissent warns that "the discretion and judgment of federal courts across the land often will be substituted for that of the 50 state legislatures, the 14,000 school boards and the 2,000,000 teachers who heretofore have been responsible for the administration of the American public school system."[119] The thrust of such comments may result from Mr. Justice Powell's own extensive experience in the administration of the public schools. Prior to coming on the Court, he had served both as chair-man of the Richmond School Board and as a member of the Vir-ginia State Board of Education.[120]

One may fairly ask whether the Powell dissent really suited the occasion. School finance and the forced transportation of school-children are momentous questions that call for grand efforts. But can the same be said of the few paltry protections tendered by *Goss?* The Court by its own appraisal had done no more than imposed procedures on school disciplinarians "which are, if any-thing, less than a fair-minded school principal would impose upon himself in order to avoid unfair suspensions."[121] Does the Powell dissent, while less shrill than that of Justice Black in *Tinker,* still overplay the significance of the decision? Consider the following passages:[122]

---

[116] 413 U.S. 189, 238 (1973) (concurring in part and dissenting in part).

[117] 411 U.S. at 42.   [118] 413 U.S. at 253.   [119] 419 U.S. at 599.

[120] For an appraisal of that service, see Howard, *Mr. Justice Powell and the Emerging Nixon Majority*, 70 MICH. L. REV. 445, 458–59 (1972).

[121] 419 U.S. at 583.   [122] *Id.* at 597–600.

Teachers and other school authorities are required to make
many decisions that may have serious consequences for the
pupil. They must decide, for example, how to grade the student's work, whether a student passes or fails a course, whether
he is to be promoted, whether he is required to take certain
subjects, whether he may be excluded from interscholastic
athletics or other extracurricular activities, whether he may be
removed from one school and sent to another, whether he may
be bused long distances when available schools are nearby, and
whether he should be placed in a "general," "vocational" or
"college-preparatory" track.

In these and many similar situations claims of impairment of
one's educational entitlement identical in principle to those
before the Court today can be asserted with equal or greater
justification.

.   .   .   .

If, as seems apparent, the Court will now require due process
procedures whenever such routine school decisions are challenged, the impact upon public education will be serious indeed.

.   .   .   .

As it is difficult to think of any less consequential infringement
than suspension of a junior high school student for a single
day, it is equally difficult to perceive any principled limit to
the new reach of procedural due process.

The above matters cannot, however, be so quickly assimilated.
Grades, promotions, tracking, and curriculum decisions represent
academic as opposed to disciplinary judgments though the two are
not always unrelated. Perhaps, as Professor Wright urges, the
courts will recognize that "the persons on campus are the experts
in deciding the academic value of a particular piece of work."[123]
Moreover, proceedings over misconduct bear closer analogy than
academic judgments to the criminal and juvenile process, a traditional subject of judicial competence. At bottom of matters of
misconduct are questions of fact: Did student X commit offense Z?
Indeed, most of the recent extensions of procedural due process
have involved very similar inquiries into historical fact: whether,
for example, unpaid debt exists or someone violated the conditions

---

[123] Wright, note 34 *supra*, at 1070. Extensions of procedural due process will, however,
inevitably be explained not as substitutes for academic judgments but simply as ways to
make those judgments fair.

of parole. Academic judgments are more often subjective and involve a cumulative assessment of a student's intellectual and emotional capacities. There is, to be sure, the danger of mistake and arbitrariness in such judgments, and rudimentary procedures, such as notice of adverse action on a promotion, some explanation of the evidence on which the decision is based, and a conference at which the student or his parents could present their views could conceivably be required. But beyond this, hard questions arise on the standard of proof required for academic decisions, the role of cross-examination in testing academic judgment, whether counsel or someone with more educational expertise is an appropriate representative of the student, and what authority, if any, should review an initial decision on, for example, a denial of promotion. Such questions may not be unresolvable,[124] but they present rougher terrain for the Court than the straight disciplinary proceeding.

A more critical constitutional question is whether a student's desire for a passing grade, a promotion, participation in interscholastic athletics or placement in a college-preparatory track establishes a property or liberty interest sufficient to confer due process protection. Once again, *Roth* cautions that the sheer weight or importance to the student of some of these decisions such as tracking or promotion will not alone entitle them to constitutional recognition.[125] Professor Roth undoubtedly felt the keenest interest in being rehired by Wisconsin State, but the Court did not on that account confer constitutional status on his claim.

In *Goss*, the students enjoyed a statutory entitlement to attend school which their suspensions took away. This property interest was clearly established both by Ohio's compulsory attendance and free public education laws. In most jurisdictions there will be no such clear statutory entitlement to receive a certain grade or promotion, to participate in interscholastic athletics, or to be placed in a college-preparatory track. The Court, however, does not require that the property interest always be embodied in state statute. In *Sindermann*, the claimant relied not upon state statutes but rather on written rules and guidelines promulgated in the official college Faculty Guide as well as by the Coordinating Board of the Texas College and University System.[126] The irony here is

---

[124] See the provocative effort in Kirp, *Schools as Sorters: The Constitutional and Policy Implications of Student Classification*, 121 U. PA. L. REV. 705, especially 775–93 (1973).

[125] 408 U.S. at 570–71.   [126] 408 U.S. at 600.

that the more explicit, open, and fair-minded in their rules that
school officials try to be, the more likely they are to create property interests protected by due process. Those school districts that
try to spell out standards for grades and promotions, for assignment to particular tracks or schools, have simultaneously engendered a legitimate reliance and hence a property interest on the
part of students within their jurisdiction.[127]

Even where there are no written rules promulgated by school
officials, there may yet be a property interest for purposes of due
process. The question then becomes whether one's desire to be
promoted, to be placed in a better track, or to participate in interscholastic athletics becomes merely "a unilateral expectation," or
"an abstract need or desire"—in which case a property interest does
not exist—or rather "a legitimate claim of entitlement" or legitimate reliance fostered by some institutional practice or understanding, in which case a property interest is present.[128] If oral
promises or representations have been made to a student, the Court
will be more likely to find some property interest created. But
absent this factor, the inquiry becomes exceedingly murky and
subtle. *Sindermann* may be viewed as establishing some property
interest in the individual to be treated according to an institution's
usual and customary practices.[129] The Court might thus be more
willing to find a property entitlement in a promotion, for example,
than in interscholastic athletics on the ground of an implicit understanding that upon entering school one will, absent some good
cause, progress yearly from one grade to the next. Persons excluded
from the more universally conferred step of promotion may stand
on a different footing for purposes of a hearing than those rejected
under the more selective standards of the high-school football
program. Below the level of written entitlement, however, the
lines become quite difficult to draw persuasively. Not surprisingly,
lower court cases struggling with property entitlements fall all over
the lot.[130]

---

[127] A similar irony underlies the whole constitutional concept of property "entitlements." The more beneficent the State attempts to be with its citizens, the greater the
constitutional constraints to which it is subjected.

[128] *Roth*, 408 U.S. at 577–78; *Sindermann*, 408 U.S. at 599–603.

[129] 408 U.S. at 602, speaking of "an unwritten 'common law' in a particular university
that certain employees shall have the equivalent of tenure."

[130] *Compare* Johnson v. Fraley, 470 F.2d 179, 183 (4th Cir. 1972) (Boreman, J.,
concurring); Hostrop v. Board of Junior College Dist. No. 515, 471 F.2d 488 (7th Cir.

It is apparent, at any rate, that one's property interests in grades, promotions, and college-preparatory tracks are much less clear than the property entitlements present in *Goss*. Yet another important distinction separates *Goss*, and indeed almost all the Court's recent procedural due process cases, from such matters as promotions or tracking. Recent Court decisions interpreting the property component of the Due Process Clause have had some implicit notion of physical severance, with its requirement that the individual face the actual physical separation, if only for a time, from the property interest. Many of those cases involved personal property that had, at the time of Court review, actually been removed from the claimant's use or enjoyment. In *Fuentes*,[131] the gas stove and stereo had been transported from the claimant's possession and use; the wages in *Sniadach* were at least temporarily withheld from the worker; the preacher in *Bell* had lost, at least for a time, the use of his license; the welfare recipient in *Goldberg* faced the termination of benefits; and in *Stanley* the father had lost custody of his child. There was in all these cases the core notion of actual or impending physical severance, however temporary. This concept has applied as well to those cases dealing with the individual's property interest in remaining within a particular environment. Thus, in *Roth*, *Sindermann*, and *Arnett*, the claimants faced loss of a job or, rather, physical separation from the working environment. And in *Goss*, of course, the students were actually forced to leave the physical premises of the school system. Students denied promotions or a college preparatory track do, however, remain within the school system. Their status while within that environment may not be the preferred one, but an education is still being afforded and there is missing the element of physical excommunication so central to the concept of property interests in recent procedural due process decisions.

1972); and Roane v. Callisburg Independent School Dist., 511 F.2d 633 (5th Cir. 1975), which found property entitlements, *with* Calvin v. Rupp, 471 F.2d 1346 (8th Cir. 1973); Patrone v. Howland Local School Bd. of Education, 472 F.2d 159 (6th Cir. 1972); and Cusumano v. Rutchford, 507 F.2d 980 (8th Cir. 1974), which did not. All of the above cases involved dismissals of educational personnel. See also in connection with an alleged entitlement to remain in the armed forces, Sims v. Fox, 505 F.2d 857 (5th Cir 1974) (*en banc*), holding, by vote of 10 to 6, that no property interest was violated in the failure to grant a pre-discharge hearing.

[131] See notes 11–20 *supra* for the full citations of cases discussed in this paragraph. *Wolff v. McDonnell*, 418 U.S. 539 (1974), which does not involve the notion of physical severance, was decided under the liberty, not the property, component of due process.

This requirement of physical severance will doubtless be decried as stilted, formalistic, and as immunizing deeply harmful public decisions from constitutional reach. It should not, however, be so easily dismissed. It has textual support in the use of the word "deprive"—take away—in the Due Process Clauses of the Fifth and Fourteenth Amendments. That word seems to demand something more than any state action which somehow adversely affects an individual and it cannot be circumvented simply by pleading that all unfavorable state-created impacts somehow amount to "deprivations." More importantly, the requirement of physical severance serves the substantial interest of saving courts from review of all those infinite changes in property status that can occur short of outright suspension or loss. For example, a person may be denied raises, promotions, a larger office, or greater responsibility in public employment. But it is doubtful the courts would sweep within due process all those myriad matters with the concurrent responsibility of setting the constitutional requirements of procedural fairness in each of them. Similar consequences would attend the puncture of the physical severance requirement in the educational context.[132]

There remains the issue of whether school tracking or promotional decisions deny a liberty interest and thus fall within that ambit of procedural due process. To such classic elements of liberty as getting or remaining out of jail, the Court has recently added one's stake in his or her personal reputation. Not being promoted or being assigned to an inferior track or special education class does undoubtedly carry a reputational stigma of sorts. Professor Kirp, upon reviewing *Wisconsin v. Constantineau*[133] and *Roth*, concluded that "if the label 'alcoholic,' or dismissal clouded by allegations of dishonesty, stigmatize, the argument for treating similarly the adverse school classifications which have equally devastating social and economic effects assumes considerable force."[134] But there remains a difference between one's interest in his repu-

---

[132] Professor Kirp would have courts overlook this factor and concentrate on special education and tracking decisions on the grounds that those decisions are relatively infrequent, visible, stigmatizing, prone to mistake, and leave consequences of a deep and often irreversible nature. The very statement of such factors, however, reveals their amorphous nature and the difficulty courts would have in deciding which school decisions and classifications were reviewable and which were not. Kirp, note 124 *supra*, at 713–14.

[133] 400 U.S. 433 (1971).

[134] Kirp, note 124 *supra*, at 778.

tation for honesty and moral rectitude and one's interest in his educational ranking. The former speaks to one's very worth or essence as a person, the latter more to one's prospects of worldly success. If the prospects for such success are to form the basis of a new liberty interest,[135] then almost nothing the school does in the way of grading, tracking, curriculum, or promotions[136] would escape the new procedural due process. But *Constantineau* and *Roth* assess liberty interests in terms of government actions that tar "a person's good name, reputation, honor, or integrity"[137] or that "might seriously damage his standing and association in his community" such as non-renewal of an employment contract on charges of "dishonesty, or immorality."[138] Suspension for misbehavior at school readily fits within this category. Lack of attainment within the classroom does not.

The foregoing discussion provides no ironclad assurance that *Goss* will not extend to the academic matters Mr. Justice Powell's dissent describes.[139] The entanglement of the Court with the classroom would then be well-nigh complete. *Goss* may indeed portend these consequences, but the Court still has open to it principled means of withdrawal.

III

Goss v. Lopez is a case closely rooted in the Court's recent precedent. In the student rights and procedural due process area, *Goss* by itself is rather a modest holding whose implications can

---

[135] The connection of such an interest with any common understanding of the word "liberty" would be a remote one.

[136] Or, indeed, interscholastic athletics which surely carries make or break career potential for many.

[137] *Constantineau*, 400 U.S. at 437.

[138] *Roth*, 408 U.S. at 573. *Goss* relies heavily upon the quoted passages from *Roth* and *Constantineau* in finding a "liberty" interest implicated in short disciplinary suspensions. 419 U.S. at 574. Nothing in the Court's subsequent statement that short disciplinary suspensions could "interfere with later opportunities for higher education and employment" indicates the Court meant to construct a new liberty interest whenever future employment opportunities might be affected. 419 U.S. at 575.

[139] It is worth noting finally, in connection with possible extensions of *Goss*, that the opinion affords little support to claims for a hearing upon denial of an application for some benefit, as opposed to deprivation of a benefit already possessed. The Court in *Morrissey* has recognized the importance of this distinction, 408 U.S. at 482 n.8, as have commentators, Gellhorn & Hornby, *Constitutional Limitations on Admissions Procedures and Standards—Beyond Affirmative Action*, 60 VA. L. REV. 975, 989 (1974); Friendly, note 84 *supra*, at 1296.

be limited. And the case is not without support in policy. Nonetheless, the decision is disturbing for its contributions to two trends. The first is the growth of the new procedural due process[140] and the second the Court's deepening involvement with our public schools.

One should be forgiven for wondering, after the Court's meanderings for the first three-quarters of this century, if any part of § 1 of the Fourteenth Amendment is really very different from any other part. After exhausting one clause of that Amendment, the Court shifts to another, thus eluding for a time fallout from its previous misadventure.[141] Economic substantive due process has yielded as a tool of intervention to equal protection[142] which in turn shows signs of giving way to such doctrines as the distaste for "conclusive presumptions,"[143] a concept designed, unsuccessfully, to divert attention from the Court's problems and transgressions under the Equal Protection Clause. But the overlap of all Fourteenth Amendment doctrine provides the Court precious little room for escape.

Boddie v. Connecticut,[144] where the Court voided as applied to indigents filing fees for divorce, at once involved the equal protection concern over discrimination against indigents with regard to court access, a substantive due process right of divorce, and the procedural due process theme of the right of prospective divorcees to a hearing. *Stanley v. Illinois*,[145] where the Court granted unwed fathers a right to a hearing before their children were removed from their custody, is a potpourri of equal protection overtones of sex discrimination, the substantive due process right to rear a child, a conclusive presumption that unwed fathers are unfit as parents, and a father's procedural due process claim to a hearing. Such obvi-

---

[140] I use the word "new" because the Due Process Clause "had produced only a few Supreme Court constitutional decisions with respect to executive or administrative action until *Goldberg* v. *Kelly* in 1970 . . . indeed, we have witnessed a greater expansion of procedural due process in the last five years than in the entire period since ratification of the Constitution." Friendly, note 84 *supra*, at 1267–68, 1273.

[141] See Kurland, *The Privileges or Immunities Clause: "Its Hour Come Round at Last?"* 1972 WASH. U. L. Q. 405.

[142] See McCloskey, *Economic Due Process and the Supreme Court: An Exhumation and Reburial*, 1962 SUPREME COURT REVIEW 34.

[143] Vlandis v. Kline, 412 U.S. 441 (1973); United States Dept. of Agriculture v. Murry, 413 U.S. 508 (1973); Cleveland Bd. of Education v. LaFleur, 414 U.S. 632 (1974).

[144] 401 U.S. 371 (1971).   [145] 405 U.S. 645 (1972).

ous intermeshing might have led the Court to some consistent body of Fourteenth Amendment principles. By and large it has not, however, and at the very core of the inconsistency lies the doctrine of the new procedural due process.

Procedural due process, the Court must believe, affords an intrinsically more limited and justifiable method of intervention than either substantive due process or equal protection. At least the Court's ventures into procedural due process make clear a double standard. While *Rodriguez* found education not to be a fundamental right under the Equal Protection Clause, *Goss* proclaimed a student's interest in education deserving of protection under due process.[146] A similar development occurred with welfare, which the Court in *Dandridge v. Williams*[147] proclaimed not to be a fundamental equal protection right but surrounded, in *Goldberg*, with procedural safeguards in the name of due process. Individual Justices, most notably Harlan and Stewart, who were often outspoken opponents of the Court's equal protection activism, frequently found in procedural due process a more congenial basis for intervention.[148] One important analytical difference between the doctrines has recently been made clear. Strict scrutiny under equal protection may require a right to be "explicitly or implicitly guaranteed by the Constitution,"[149] while property rights under due process are created, not by the Constitution, but "by existing rules or understandings that stem from an independent source such as state law."[150]

There is yet more dramatic evidence that the Court regards the doctrines of procedural due process and equal protection very

---

[146] One can argue over whether a student's interest in education was more seriously affected in *Rodriguez* or *Goss*. The Court's constitutional analysis in the two cases, however, did not proceed on that basis.

[147] 397 U.S. 471 (1970).

[148] *Compare* Justice Harlan's disillusionment over modern equal protection, in Shapiro v. Thompson, 394 U.S. 618, 655 (1969), *with* his concurrence in *Sniadach*, 395 U.S. at 342, his opinion for the Court in *Boddie*, and the opinions in *Goldberg* and *Burson*, which he joined. *Compare* Justice Stewart's Court opinion in *Dandridge*, and his concurrence in *Rodriguez*, 411 U.S. at 59, *with* his opinions for the Court in *Fuentes*, *Roth*, and *Sindermann*. While *Roth* itself found no protected interest under due process, it did establish the framework for the discovery of many later interests such as in *Goss* which Stewart joined.

[149] 411 U.S. at 33–34.

[150] *Roth*, 408 U.S. at 577; *Goss*, 419 U.S. at 572–73.

differently. The principle that supposedly emerged above all others
in reaction to the *Lochner* era was that laws "regulatory of business and industrial conditions"[151] and "state regulation[s] in the
social and economic field"[152] were now largely beyond the province
of the Court. This article of faith has proved largely meaningless,
however, in the realm of procedural due process. One is struck
that so many of the state statutes found wanting under the new
procedural due process are laws regulating business and commercial transactions such as wage garnishment in *Sniadach* and creditors' writs of replevin in *Fuentes* or laws in the area of social welfare such as automobile accident liability in *Burson* and public
benefit programs in *Goldberg*.

It is true, to be sure, that modern equal protection has also been
invoked to invalidate some social and economic legislation such as
public welfare laws, and wrongful death and workmen's compensation programs.[153] But with equal protection the Court has been
careful to emphasize the presence of some personal, noneconomic
liberty such as the right to travel or the avoidance of stigmatizing
classifications without which the individual economic interest would
be constitutionally insufficient.[154] In many of the new procedural
due process cases, however, the ultimate substantive rights at stake
are often solely economic and proprietary.[155] Thus these cases may
indeed be foreshadowing an erosion of the distinction between
personal and economic liberty which has characterized so much of
the Court's modern jurisprudence in the equal protection and substantive due process area.[156] The distinction between personal and
economic liberty has, of course, never been pellucid.[157] Marital
privacy is not the same in the ghetto as in the suburban villa and
the right to travel can hardly seem so real without the means to pay

---

[151] Williamson v. Lee Optical, Inc., 348 U.S. 483, 488 (1955).

[152] *Dandridge*, 397 U.S. at 484.

[153] *E.g.*, Shapiro v. Thompson, 394 U.S. 618 (1969); Levy v. Louisiana, 391 U.S. 68
(1968); Weber v. Aetna Casualty & Surety Co., 406 U.S. 164 (1972).

[154] For examples of such insufficiency, see *Dandridge;* James v. Valtierra, 402 U.S. 137
(1971); Lindsey v. Normet, 405 U.S. 56 (1972). But *cf.* United States Dept. of Agriculture v. Moreno, 413 U.S. 528 (1973).

[155] See, *e.g.*, *Sniadach, Goldberg, Burson, Fuentes*, cited fully *supra*, at notes 11–15.

[156] As to the latter, see Griswold v. Connecticut, 381 U.S. 479 (1965), and Roe v.
Wade, 410 U.S. 113 (1973).

[157] *Cf.* Lynch v. Household Finance Corp., 405 U.S. 538 (1972).

the fare. The enjoyment of personal liberty, it hardly seems novel to observe,[158] is heavily dependent on an economic base.

The modern Court thus feels it may intervene more freely and with different criteria under procedural due process than under either substantive due process or equal protection. The existence of this double standard, however, proves easier to discover than its basis. The most noticeable difference between equal protection and due process is that the Due Process Clause makes explicit reference to liberty and property, thus giving it a focus that equal protection lacks. Yet what other than this perennial invitation of due process to define "liberty" and "property" has brought on so much of the Court's twentieth-century woe? *Lochner* and its progeny defined "liberty" in the Due Process Clause to include the "liberty of contract," and the Justices were roundly and ultimately fatally criticized for promoting a personal economic philosophy, for favoring the interests of business and property to the detriment of the political gains of the working classes, and for creating, to serve such low purposes, a non-textual Fourteenth Amendment right. The modern substantive due process cases, with their rights of marital and maternal privacy, are not, the commentators have been quick to observe, noticeably less subjective.[159]

To go only so far, however, leaves analysis hanging. The dissenters in *Griswold* and *Roe* were quick to throw *Lochner* at the majority,[160] but citation of that case is eerily absent in dissents from the modern procedural due process. Such need not be the case. The concept of "property" which ultimately surfaces in *Goss v. Lopez* is no less subjectively divined than the concept of "liberty" was by Justice Peckham in 1905. The "property" of *Goldberg*, *Roth*, and *Sindermann*, and now *Goss*, is at bottom an academically hatched concept, which the Court, to serve its inclinations, found it convenient to swallow whole. Professor Charles Reich in two imaginative articles written in the middle 1960s[161]—before America

---

[158] See, *e.g.*, HAND, THE BILL OF RIGHTS esp. 50–52 (1958).

[159] Ely, *The Wages of Crying Wolf: A Comment on Roe v. Wade*, 87 YALE L.J. 920, 937–43 (1973); Epstein, *Substantive Due Process by Any Other Name: The Abortion Cases*, 1973 SUPREME COURT REVIEW 159.

[160] See especially Justice Black's dissent in *Griswold*, 381 U.S. at 507, and Mr. Justice Rehnquist's dissent in *Roe*, 410 U.S. at 171.

[161] Reich, *The New Property*, 73 YALE L.J. 733 (1964); Reich, *Individual Rights and Social Welfare: The Emerging Legal Issues*, 74 YALE L. J. 1245 (1965), cited in *Goldberg*, 397 U.S. at 262 n.8.

was "greened"—argued that modern society is characterized by the omnipresence of different forms of governmental largesse upon which individuals are becoming ever more dependent. This largesse was not merely something the individual was merely privileged to receive but rather something to which he was entitled. The new concept of entitlement adopted by the Court in *Goldberg* and *Roth* was thus closely forged to the demise of the distinction between rights and privileges, a development that likewise met with academic applause.[162] Under "entitlement," what had previously been thought privileges suddenly took on many attributes of rights. Public welfare, housing, education, electrical service,[163] employment, professional licenses, and so on are now more and more matters of "entitlement," whose deprivation calls into play some form of due process.

It is difficult, really, to overstate the impact of the indiscriminate constitutionalization of Professor Reich on our personal and national consciousness.[164] Granted that government is involved more intimately and pervasively in our personal lives than ever before and granted that we want that involvement to be fair. Still, the price we as a society pay for such concepts as entitlement may be dear. "Entitlement" may rework our self perceptions to the point where we seem less often persons with paramount obligations to others but rather beings to whom government for one reason or another remains perpetually in debt. The implications of this outlook for personal productivity and generosity are not hopeful, for the point of emphasis under "entitlement" must always be on what rights we as individuals have been wrongly denied. Justice Black perhaps foresaw this, for with a kind of old-fashioned testiness he insisted in *Goldberg* that welfare remained a charity and gratuity, not classifiable as a property right and hence undeserving of due process protection.[165] To his credit, Justice Black recognized in

---

[162] See Van Alstyne. *The Demise of the Right-Privilege Distinction in Constitutional Law*, 81 HARV. L. REV. 1439 (1968).

[163] See Jackson v. Metropolitan Edison Co., 419 U.S. 345 (1974), where such an alleged entitlement went unresolved by the Court because of a lack of state action.

[164] I say "indiscriminate" because some of the matters Professor Reich terms entitlement may constitute severe enough personal losses to merit some protection from the Due Process Clause. Comparing and evaluating the severity of a loss free from the overtones of the entitlement concept is a difficult, but surely not impossible task. See Friendly, note 84 *supra*, at 1295–1305.

[165] 397 U.S. at 272, 275.

his last years on the Court that the new procedural due process was no less a political judgment than many that had gone before and that the federal judiciary had "transgress[ed] into the area constitutionally assigned to the Congress and the people."[166]

As much of the motivation of the Court's long *Lochner* era was to protect the prerogatives of employers against the social gains of the working classes, so the central ideological thrust of the new procedural due process has been simply to help the poor.[167] *Sniadach* speaks movingly and at length of the "tremendous hardship [imposed by prejudgment garnishment] on wage earners with families to support";[168] *Goldberg* talks of welfare as a means to "help bring within the reach of the poor the same opportunities that are available to others to participate meaningfully in the life of the community";[169] *Boddie* sought to give indigents an equal right to dissolve their marriages;[170] *Fuentes* argues that "a stove or a bed may be equally essential to provide a minimally decent environment for human beings in their day-to-day lives."[171] Though the interests of the poor are less openly at issue in *Goss*, the fact remains that minority and disadvantaged children are the more frequent victims of suspension.[172] In *Dandridge*, however, the fact that "the most basic economic needs of impoverished human beings" were involved[173] was not alone enough to cause the Court to overcome its customary reluctance to invalidate social and economic legislation. In *Goldberg*, however, the poverty factor appears critical.

This difference between *Dandridge* and *Goldberg* may suggest yet another reason for the lesser inhibitions the Court experiences in dealing with the new procedural due process. That doctrine, it is argued, does not interfere with a state's substantive lawmaking capacity. *Goldberg* impairs not at all a state's right to set standards

---

[166] *Id*. at 274. See also his dissents in *Sniadach*, 395 U.S. at 344; and *Boddie*, 401 U.S. at 389. Justice Black, in fact, took strong exception to much of Professor Reich's thinking. See MEADOR, MR. JUSTICE BLACK AND HIS BOOKS 12 (1974).

[167] One standard justification of the difference is, of course, that the poor are politically powerless, an assumption I think Professor Winter, among others, effectively put down. Winter, *Poverty, Economic Equality, and the Equal Protection Clause*, 1972 SUPREME COURT REVIEW 41, 98.

[168] 395 U.S. at 340.   [169] 397 U.S. at 265.   [170] 401 U.S. 371.

[171] 407 U.S. at 89. But *cf*. North Georgia Finishing, Inc. v. Di-Chem, Inc., 419 U.S. 601, 608 (1975).

[172] See section I *supra*.   [173] 397 U.S. at 485.

of eligibility for public welfare recipients and *Goss* and *Wolff* still let schools and prisons write their own codes of conduct. The whole concept of entitlement, in fact, only takes its cue from state or federal substantive law. Thus explained, procedural due process seems benign enough compared to equal protection or substantive due process which may find state substantive judgments wanting. The only state interests opposed to a hearing are often said to be the rather prosaic ones of bureaucratic efficiency and conservation of public funds which the Court belittles as "rather ordinary costs" which cannot "outweigh the constitutional right."[174] We are told in one overheated and widely quoted moment, "the Constitution recognizes higher values than speed and efficiency," it is meant "to protect the fragile values of a vulnerable citizenry from the overbearing concern for efficiency and efficacy" of every kind of government official, and thus, by implication, the State's efforts and experiments at more effective public programs are to be correspondingly downgraded in the constitutional scale.[175] The State is often counseled by the Court to preserve its interests "by skillful use of personnel and facilities,"[176] something surely easier for the Justices to suggest than for a state to put into practice.

Posed thus pejoratively as a conflict between human needs and mere administrative ones, the expansion of procedural due process can hardly be denied. But this framing of the issues quite overlooks the real nature of the interests at stake as well as the extraordinary substantive overlay of procedural due process. The new procedural due process may in fact be reworking bureaucratic behavior to substantial public detriment, a possibility the Court only begrudgingly recognizes and consistently downplays.

The following example will somewhat oversimply illustrate. Suppose a school district has imposed upon it constitutional requirements for disciplinary hearings more elaborate than those it has heretofore held. Assume further that the school district wishes genuinely to comply, something that, given the low visibility of the suspension process and likely resentment of school officials to its constitutionalization, will not always be the case. Compliance might occur in a mixture of ways, each of which has significant public ramifications. Funds could be diverted from some unrelated

---

[174] *Fuentes,* 407 U.S. at 90, n.22.

[175] *Stanley,* 405 U.S. at 656.   [176] *Goldberg,* 397 U.S. at 266.

public program to staff the suspension hearing, in which case that program is correspondingly deprived.[177] Or, the energies of educators might be diverted from more purely educational pursuits to hold the hearing. If such a diversion of resources is unappealing, however, the school district may simply hold fewer hearings in order that those which are held may meet constitutional standards. Fewer and more elaborate hearings may result in quite different consequences. They may result in a more accurate and less arbitrary use of the suspension power and more discernment in the selection of cases in which event a real improvement in school discipline will be realized. The other possible consequence of more elaborate hearings, however, is that violators may simply remain in school because the costs of removing them are perceived by officials to be too great. Potential violators will then soon perceive the diminished capacity of official response and become more likely to break school rules themselves.

Thus procedural due process at least potentially involves a substantial diversion of resources from other public needs, the inhibition of desired official action, and some possible loss in legal deterrence. Whether these should be the prevailing values in a particular decision is disputable, but they surely represent more serious public concerns than what the Court termed in *Goss* the desire of administrators for "the untrammeled power to act unilaterally."[178] These public concerns grow as the level of due process required by the Court becomes more formal and as the volume of incidents increases to which the new requirements apply. Such concerns are also prominent in most of the Court's recent procedural due process cases. Where and how, for example, will states fund the welfare termination and parole revocation hearings *Goldberg* and *Morrissey* require? More pertinently, what magnitude of effort is required to do so? Will the heightened costs of termination and revocation make the workings of the welfare and parole systems more rational or will they simply result in more ineligible recipients remaining on the rolls and more parole violators remaining at liberty? Such questions have a somewhat impenetrable aura,

---

[177] Increased taxes could also be levied, possibly resulting in a lesser public tolerance or capacity to support a tax increase for other purposes.

[178] 419 U.S. at 580.

and I doubt the Court or anyone else will arrive at final answers.[179] Yet the Court's treatment of such questions can hardly afford to remain so cavalier. Unfortunately, such decisions as *Morrissey*, *Goldberg*, and *Goss* only crudely assess the magnitude of resource commitment demanded of the states[180] and none of the opinions even addresses or admits any likelihood that more elaborate hearings will cause violations of disciplinary rules and eligibility standards simply to go unattended.[181]

The failure to undertake such analysis points to one last irony. For all its compassion, the new procedural due process may harbor ill side-effects for the country's dispossessed. One may foresee in all of these cases that greater difficulty in terminating any benefit will lead to greater resistance in granting it. It is still a live question, for example, whether the result of *Goldberg* will be that "many will never get on the rolls, or at least that they will remain destitute during the lengthy proceedings followed to determine initial eligibility."[182] A similar question arises as to grants of parole, although *Morrissey* states with some reason that the high costs of imprisonment will afford authorities ample economic incentive to continue paroling inmates, whatever the costs of revocation.[183]

---

[179] A growing body of economic literature, whose impact on constitutional litigation is as yet slight, would approach such questions from the standpoint of "efficiency" as opposed to "a purely visceral sense of fairness." *E.g.*, Posner, *An Economic Approach to Legal Procedure and Judicial Administration*, 2 J. Leg. Studies 399, 401 (1973); Schwartz & Tullock, *The Costs of a Legal System*, 4 J. Leg. Studies 75 (1975). A pioneering effort in the application of the economic approach to the area of creditor remedies is Scott, *Constitutional Regulation of Provisional Creditor Remedies: The Cost of Procedural Due Process*, 61 Va. L. Rev. 807 (1975).

[180] *Goss*, for instance, notes vaguely that brief disciplinary suspensions are "almost countless," 419 U.S. at 583, but it is only the dissent that begins to try to count them, 419 U.S. at 592 n.10. *Morrissey* mentions "[t]hirty States provide in their statutes that a parolee shall receive some type of hearing," without telling us what type, surely a more critical question. 408 U.S. at 488 n.15. Neither *Goldberg* nor *Morrissey* bothers to estimate the number of welfare terminations or parole revocations annually attempted, much less the percentage of cases in which a recipient or parolee would be likely to challenge the state's proposed action.

What is nearly always ignored is that the cost in resources of a constitutional rule is not measured alone in what it demands of the state to achieve compliance. A second cost comes when, once having complied, and believing a simpler proceeding will work better, the state is not free to change.

[181] This seems less a problem in *Goss*, where skeletal due process prevails, than in *Goldberg* and *Morrissey*.

[182] 397 U.S. at 279 (Black, J., dissenting).

[183] 408 U.S. at 483 n.10.

After *Fuentes*, "the availability of credit may well be diminished or, in any event, the expense of securing it increased."[184] If disciplinary hearings for longer suspensions or expulsions were to become too elaborate or formalized, college and school administrators might be reluctant to risk admission or readmission of those whom they suspect, perhaps irrationally, to be potential troublemakers. The most serious blow of procedural due process to the interests of the disadvantaged may be, as hinted earlier, that "new layers of procedural protection may become an intolerable drain on the very funds earmarked for food, clothing, and other living essentials,"[185] or, in the case of more formalized school disciplinary hearings, a drain on funds and energies devoted to purposes of instruction.

I do not mean by all of this to denigrate the generosity of impulse whence these decisions sprang. But they seem so manifestly flawed by political preference and so inappropriately self-assured as to be regarded, not too many years hence, as period pieces, more than a little blinkered and naive. Modern procedural due process has come to involve troublesome concepts of contract, property, procedure, criminal deterrence, and the related fields of sociology, psychology, and economics in which certainly a beginning constitutionalist, but perhaps even venerable Justices, are inexpert. I have argued at length in the context of the Equal Protection Clause that ordering the commitment of specific kinds of resources to the disadvantaged is basically not, with its highly complex and fiercely political overtones, a judicial judgment to make.[186] Because procedural due process commits those resources in the form of a hearing does not necessarily make it more acceptable or right.

IV

I come then to the brunt of my final disagreement with the Court's 1975 school discipline cases. I do not mean to imply here that education is not important to a child's development. Clearly it is essential to any process of self-realization and to taking "best advantage of our personal potential."[187] Nor do I nurture any spe-

---

[184] 407 U.S. at 103 (White, J., dissenting).

[185] Wheeler v. Montgomery, 397 U.S. 280, 284 (1970) (Burger, C.J., dissenting).

[186] Wilkinson, *The Supreme Court, the Equal Protection Clause, and the Three Faces of Constitutional Equality*, 61 VA. L. REV. 945, 998–1017 (1975); Winter, note 167 *supra*.

[187] Wilkinson, *supra* note 186, at 986.

cial faith in the goodness of school officials who are often, no less than the rest of us, unimaginative, autocratic, and distrustful of change.[188] But conceding such truisms does not redeem what the Court has done in *Goss* or in *Wood*. Once more, in those decisions, the modern Court has demonstrated a faith that judicial competence knows few horizons, that the deep-felt needs of the American people can be largely irrelevant to so heady an exercise as constitutional writing, and that constitutional resolution of public controversy need rest on little more than uninformed good will. Those who distrust the Court's assumptions—and there are many —are left to fear that the damage done in that most important setting of our public schools may not be easily repaired or reversed.

One preliminary point on the workings of the adversary process, as exemplified by *Goss*, is in order. The caliber of written advocacy before the Court in that case might charitably be described as a mismatch. Both in quantity and in quality of presentation the State's position was badly outclassed. Several persuasive and artfully couched briefs were filed on behalf of Appellees, urging the Court to accord due process protection to students facing short suspensions,[189] while Appellants had to be corrected by the Court on the elementary point that rights need not be mentioned in the Constitution in order to qualify for due process protection.[190] Add to this the fact that the overwhelming body of legal literature on the subject favored greater protection for students facing suspension or expulsion,[191] and the Court faced an insistent clamor for a "libertarian" result. While I have no figures to document, for

---

[188] See Ladd, *Allegedly Disruptive Student Behavior and the Legal Authority of School Officials*, 19 J. Pub. Law 209 (1970).

[189] Especially persuasive is the amicus brief filed by Marian Wright Edelman and Richard D. Parker on behalf of the Children's Defense Fund of the Washington Research Project Inc. and the American Friends Service Committee. Note also the amicus briefs of the American Civil Liberties Union, the NAACP, and the National Committee for Citizens in Education.

[190] 419 U.S. at 572–73.

[191] *E.g.*, Children's Defense Fund, note 44 *supra*; Comment, *Procedural Due Process in Secondary Schools*, 54 Marq. L. Rev. 558 (1971); Flvgare, *Short-Term Student Suspensions and the Requirements of Due Process*, 3 J. Law & Ed. 529 (1974); Hudgins, *The Discipline of Secondary School Students and Procedural Due Process: A Standard*, 7 Wake F. L. Rev. 32 (1970); Ladd, *Civil Liberties for Students—At What Age?* 3 J. Law & Ed. 251 (1974); Lines, note 103 *supra*; McClung, *The Problem of the Due Process Exclusion: Do Schools Have a Continuing Responsibility to Educate Children with Behavior Problems?* 3 J. Law & Ed. 491 (1974); and Note, *Student Discipline in the Public Schools*, 2 J. Law & Ed. 491 (1973).

example, the number of amicus briefs filed with the Court on respective sides of a controversy, nor have I undertaken any systematic study of the quality of advocacy, my impression is that, in cases where civil liberties are made the issue, the libertarian viewpoint, as in *Goss v. Lopez,* fares much the better.[192] This is unfortunate not only in that it may distort the controversy before the Court, but because it comparatively disables those Justices seeking to place the State's point of view in its most favorable light.[193]

It is unfortunate, also, because the blandishments of the commentators and the Court's *amici* may have precious little relevance beyond the citadel. For example, it is disheartening how frequently scholarly proponents of greater student rights soft-pedal or even forgo discussion of the true dimensions of the disciplinary problem overtaking our nation's schools.[194] Those problems have passed well beyond the comical and traditional brand of mischief in *Wood v. Strickland,* where two tenth-grade girls in Mena, Arkansas, harmlessly spiked the punch at a parent-student gathering with "Right Time" malt liquor. Instead, "crime and violence, in varying degrees, have become the norm in schools throughout the country," reported the *New York Times* in a recent survey.[195] "Many officials have become so anesthetized to the scope of the problem that they now consider a certain number of serious incidents inevitable." The *Washington Post* noted that "it is estimated by the National Educational Association that at least 70,000 teachers are

[192] This is not the case in litigation involving federal laws and regulations, however, when the Solicitor General's office argues the Government position or in rare cases of great public moment such as De Funis v. Odegaard, 416 U.S. 312 (1974), where the Court was treated to high quality advocacy on all sides of the controversy.

[193] It is questionable, for example, whether Mr. Justice Powell, the author of Healy v. James, 408 U.S. 169 (1972), really wished in his *Goss* dissent to cite as an authority on school discipline the work mentioned in appellant's Reply Brief, DOBSON, DARE TO DISCIPLINE (1972). The author advocates, among other things, that "Students for a Democratic Society and all similar revolutionary organizations should be banned from American campuses," that "faculty members encouraging revolution should be dismissed," and that "in the event of a campus riot, national guard troops or security police should surround the students offering to let everyone leave within a few minutes time. Notification should be given to the rioters that *every* student remaining will be arrested, expelled, and prosecuted to the fullest extent of the law. If eight hundred students or more were sent home to dad, rioting might become less fashionable at good old Ivy U." *Id.* at 115–16.

[194] Again the amicus brief filed by the Children's Defense Fund, at 22–23, may be something of an exception.

[195] Nemy, *Violence in Schools Now Seen as Norm across the Nation,* N.Y. Times, 14 June 1975, p. 1.

being assaulted every year by students and that 155,000 have had personal property stolen or vandalized. In the school year 1972–73, 100 students were murdered throughout the nation and countless numbers were assaulted, beaten, stabbed, robbed or shot."[196] Of primary concern in many school districts is the proliferation of weapons carried by students. "These kids bring in everything," said Mary Ellen Riordon, president of the Detroit Federation of Teachers, "guns, knives, baseball bats, karate sticks, Afro picks, razor blades, brass knuckles, you name it."[197]

A subcommittee of the Senate Judiciary Committee, chaired by Senator Birch Bayh, conducted the most extensive study on the subject of student violence for the school years 1970–71, 1971–72, and 1972–73. It concluded:[198]

> It is alarmingly apparent that student misbehavior and conflict within our school system is no longer limited to a fist fight between individual students or an occasional general disruption resulting from a specific incident. Instead our schools are experiencing serious crimes of a felonious nature including brutal assaults on teachers and students, as well as rapes, extortions, burglaries, thefts and an unprecedented wave of wanton destruction and vandalism. Moreover our preliminary study of the situation has produced compelling evidence that this level of violence and vandalism is reaching crisis proportions which seriously threaten the ability of our educational system to carry out its primary function.

The costs of vandalism, thefts, and arson were conservatively estimated at the end of the 1973 school year at an average of $63,031 per school district and a national figure of $500 million, which equaled the total amount expended on textbooks throughout the country in 1972.[199] Not surprisingly, a 1974 Gallup Poll found that "most adults and high school students surveyed cited the lack

---

[196] *Violence Proliferates in Area Schools*, Washington Post, 18 May 1975, p. 1. See also *Violence Soars in U.S. Schools*, Washington Post, 10 April 1975, p. 1.

[197] New York Times, note 195 *supra*, at 57.

[198] Note 43 *supra*, at 3. The subcommittee's members were, in addition to Chairman Bayh, Senators Hart, Burdick, Kennedy, Tunney, Hruska, Fong, and Mathias. The extent of the subcommittee's hearings and questionnaires is described in pp. 1–2 of the Report.
The Report found the outbreak of violence to be a phenomenon of recent vintage and of nationwide scope. On page 12 of its Report, the subcommittee does mention briefly and indeed favorably the Court's decision in *Goss*.

[199] *Id*. at 6.

of discipline as the chief problem confronting schools today."[200]
In the same vein, the Senate subcommittee prominently quoted
Dr. Frank Brown, chairman of the National Commission for Reform of Secondary Education, that the chief concern of secondary
schools today "is the climate of fear where the majority of students
are afraid for their safety."[201]

My point is not that Dr. Gallup's findings should bind the
Supreme Court and certainly not that public reaction to disruptive
behavior always deserves free rein. But I do question the sensitivity of any decision to begin constitutionalizing the disciplinary
process at its lowest rungs at precisely that time when the public
is deeply anxious over a lack of discipline in the schools and when
the maximum flexibility may be required by school officials in different parts of the country to reduce the level of violence in secondary education. Though fortunately the Court required only
skeletal due process in the case of most short suspensions, we do not
yet know what it will require in short suspensions raising "unusual" situations,[202] in longer suspensions or expulsions, or in the
academic matters mentioned in Mr. Justice Powell's dissent. There
remain ways, which I have tried to suggest, in which the consequences of *Goss* may yet fairly be limited.[203] If the Court disre-
gards them, it will have embarked on a constitutionalization of
school discipline and administration which will surely rival in public dissatisfaction its championship of the criminally accused at
a time of rising crime.

I would not, of course, exclude the possibility that *Goss* and
Wood may help rather than hinder a solution to the problem of
student lawlessness. " 'Normal' children may develop hostile and
aggressive behavior patterns if school authorities respond to them
too severely or inadequately."[204] A student understandably reacts
adversely "to what he consider[s] the pointless exercise of authority within the school, treating him as a subject rather than a
person."[205] To the extent that the erroneous or vindictive exercise

---

[200] *Id.* at 3–4.

[201] *Id.* at 3.

[202] 419 U.S. at 584.

[203] See section II *supra.*

[204] Task Force on Children Out of School, note 38 *supra,* at 44 (1971), quoted in
McClung, *The Problem of the Due Process Exclusion: Do Schools Have a Continuing Responsibility to Educate Children with Behavior Problems?* 3 J. Law & Educ. 491, 516 (1974).

[205] McClung, note 204 *supra,* at 516.

of school authority has contributed to student frustration and bit-
terness, *Goss* may help by making the appearance and the substance
of justice a little more fair. *Goss* may also provide that principal,
beleaguered by teachers and teacher unions, an excuse to be fair, to
remind teachers that while he trusts and supports them, he is constitutionally obligated at least to listen to the student's side.

Likewise it should not be the purpose of education to vest school
authorities with an iron fist, even if such a step would bring serious disciplinary infractions to an end. The Soviet prison camps
where Ivan Denisovich labored no doubt eliminated open disruption, but at the price of dulling and decomposing all that was
worthy in the spirit of man. A not dissimilar atmosphere pervades,
in the view of Charles Silberman's polemic, American public
schools:[206]

> The public schools—those "killers of the dream," to appropri-
> ate a phrase of Lillian Smith's—are the kind of institution one
> cannot really dislike until one gets to know them well. Be-
> cause adults take the schools so much for granted, they fail to
> appreciate what grim, joyless places most American schools
> are, how oppressive and petty are the rules by which they are
> governed, how intellectually sterile and esthetically barren the
> atmosphere, what an appalling lack of civility obtains on the
> part of teachers and principals, what contempt they uncon-
> sciously display for children as children.

Thus apparently we can believe that *Goss* and *Wood* may be
helpful in resolving problems of school discipline and that of
course those decisions are in the best interests of students within
the custody of potentially arbitrary or mistaken officials. This is
the case the Court ultimately asks us to accept. Identification of the
core assumptions on which the Court's case rests indicates the seriousness of the challenges that may be raised against those assumptions, challenges which the Court has barely come to acknowledge,
much less to meet.

The value of *Goss* and *Wood* depends chiefly upon whether
the Court has correctly estimated the impact of procedural safeguards and particularly § 1983 actions on the psychology of school
officials. The Court assumes, in the accepted fashion, that the
presence of procedure and the potential of a § 1983 suit will help

---

[206] SILBERMAN, note 53 *supra*, at 10.

prevent hasty or vindictive official action. But that will most as-
suredly not be the only or maybe even the primary effect of those
decisions. The further entry into school discipline of so formidable a force as the courts and the judicial process may simply discourage some school officials from taking firm disciplinary action.
For many persons there exist few things quite so viscerally un-
settling as the prospect of a lawsuit. Those school administrators
who are already by temperament overcautious and indecisive will
become all the more so with the increasing likelihood of legal
action. To be sure, the Court in *Wood* hopes, in its nebulous way,
that "public school officials understand that action taken in the
good-faith fulfillment of their responsibilities and within the bounds
of reason under all the circumstances will not be punished and
that they need not exercise their discretion with undue timidity."[207]
But such a statement simply belies the fact that a lawsuit, even
if unsuccessful, may involve time, inconvenience, constant pub-
licity, depositions and cross-examination by hostile counsel, expense,
and so on. Most Americans, including the decent and fair-minded,
do not greatly relish such disruptions of their personal lives, and
the human response in all too many instances will be to avoid the
fuss and threat of court action by avoiding disciplinary action as
well.[208] It was Learned Hand who remarked: "I must say that, as
a litigant, I should dread a lawsuit beyond almost anything else
short of sickness and of death."[209]

It can be argued that school officials may avoid most such hardship by being fair-minded in their rulings and complying with the
Court's rather innocuous requests.[210] Such reassurance, however, is
of limited value. To begin with, the Court's requirements are less
than clear. *Goss* leaves hanging, among other things, what procedure will be required even in short suspensions involving, in the

---

[207] 420 U.S. at 321.

[208] This is not to say there will not be some school principals willing to ignore or even
resist whatever student rights are established. Note the behavior of principal Louis A.
Schuker and others discussed in Glasser & Levine, *Bringing Student Rights to New York
City's School System*, 1 J. LAW & EDUC. 213, 226–27 (1972). The authors contend the
refrain of some principals was " 'I don't care what the law is; I'm the one who runs this
school.' " *Id.* at 228.

[209] Quoted in FRANK, COURTS ON TRIAL 40 (1949).

[210] This argument may not be wholly without merit. I have noted earlier, for example,
that school officials following *Goss* may present a prima facie case of good faith under
Wood.

mystic language of the Court, "unusual situations."[211] *Wood*, as
Mr. Justice Powell's dissent reminds, selects the highly fluid and
unpredictable area of students' constitutional rights to speak of
"ignorance or disregard of settled, indisputable law" as a standard
of § 1983 liability.[212] Even if the Court's standards had been clearer,
there is no assurance that school officials in all the different districts of the country would either be or feel sufficiently certain of
the standard of liability to take firm action.[213] It is ironic that the
Court has coined the phrases "chilling effect" and "void for vagueness" primarily to redress inhibitions worked on citizens by government regulation in the area of free expression. In so doing, the
Court has somehow overlooked those chilling effects created from
vague pronouncements of its own and the fact that public officials, especially those faced with prospects of damage actions under § 1983, will now likely give to all Supreme Court decisions in
the student rights area a very wide berth.

Given the climate of today's schools, it would seem an inappropriate moment for the Court to risk creating such inhibitions on
the part of disciplinarians and to arm alleged offenders with enhanced prospects for judicial recourse. Given the level of disruption in the public schools, the Court would not seemingly wish
to risk turning the tables in this way. But it is necessary, the Court
reasons in *Goss*, because disciplinarians are fallible in their judgments, because the disciplinary process is not "a totally accurate,
unerring process, never mistaken and never unfair. . . . The risk
of error is not at all trivial, and it should be guarded against if
that may be done without prohibitive cost or interference with
the educational process."[214]

It is quite true that disciplinarians make mistakes.[215] That in
itself is hardly earthshaking; human activity is, by its nature, prone

---

[211] 419 U.S. at 584.

[212] The Court's full quotation is "The official must himself be acting sincerely and
with a belief that he is doing right, but an act violating a student's constitutional rights
can be no more justified by ignorance or disregard of settled, indisputable law on the
part of one entrusted with supervision of students' daily lives than by the presence of
actual malice." 420 U.S. at 321.

[213] Mr. Justice Powell's opinion in *Wood* notes that even if counsel's advice were to
constitute a defense to a § 1983 action, few school boards and officials enjoy ready access
to counsel or had thought it necessary to consult counsel on countless school management
decisions. 420 U.S. at 331.

[214] 419 U.S. at 579–80.   [215] See section II *supra*.

to error. But the fact that some process is operated under the direction of mortals and thus fallible is hardly a discriminating method of deciding when to inhibit it by constitutional norms. All aspects of popular government and its administration would soon be blanketed. The question cannot be solely whether mistakes might be made, but whether means, less drastic than the promised constitutional standards with all their trappings and effects, generally exist to correct and prevent them.

In this regard, the process of short disciplinary suspensions was hardly shown to be so error-ridden or irrational as the Court makes it appear. It did, generally on its own, more than the Court and Constitution would now require of it. A blameless student need not and presumably will not stand mute if he is wrongly suspended. Almost certainly, before departing, the student, or perhaps a friend, would communicate his "side" in some way to a teacher or principal. If his explanation seems at all plausible, one would expect most teachers or principals to listen.[216]

The typical principal is not always the autocrat he is pictured to be. He acts in a setting of accountability more real and sensitive than is generally admitted. If his disciplinary action is not warranted, and often even if it is, he faces the unwelcome prospect of an irate parent in his office or over the telephone. If his explanation fails to appease, the parent may approach some member of the school board or perhaps some other elected local official. The school board, as Mr. Justice Powell's dissent makes plain, is "usually elected by the people and sensitive to constituent relations, [and] may be expected to identify a principal whose record of suspensions merits inquiry."[217] The rejection of such informal correctives by the Court is, in the end, nothing less than a rejection of the workings of the democratic process. And introducing the Constitution to do what the disciplinary process so often accomplishes on its own makes all the good sense of traveling from New York to Washington by way of San Francisco.

There is a further assumption that necessarily underlies the *Goss* opinion, though the Court does not explicitly refer to it. This as-

---

[216] I say "most" will listen, because there are always undoubtedly some who will not. A critical value choice is whether those who will not are sufficiently numerous, injurious, and unaccountable to justify what I have attempted to identify as the serious risks and costs of constitutionalizing the short suspension process.

[217] 419 U.S. at 596.

sumption involves a basic faith in the educative and rehabilitative effects of fair procedural treatment and, conversely, in the disintegration of order and respect engendered by arbitrariness. The point is most often raised with respect to prisons. Refusal to accord an inmate the right to confrontation before deprivation of good time credit reflects, so Mr. Justice Douglas has told us, "a view of prison administration which is outmoded and indeed anti-rehabilitation, for it supports the prevailing pattern of hostility between inmate and personnel which generates an 'inmates' code' of non-cooperation, thereby preventing the rapport necessary for a successful rehabilitative program."[218] Justice Jackson made the similar point as to schools over thirty years ago: "That they [school officials] are educating the young for citizenship is reason for scrupulous protection of Constitutional freedoms of the individual, if we are not to strangle the free mind at its source and teach youth to discount important principles of our government as mere platitudes."[219]

And this basic lesson was strenuously, if less elegantly, urged on the Court in *Goss:*[220]

> our schools may be turning out millions of students who are not forming a strong and reasoned allegiance to a democratic political system, because they receive no meaningful experience with such a democratically-oriented system in their daily lives in school. For them we should remember, public school is the governmental institution which represents the adult society in its most direct and controlling aspect. If we do not teach the viability of democratic modes of conflict-resolution, and win respect for these as just and effective processes, we will lose more and more potential democrats.

It may be true that procedural regularity in disciplinary proceedings promotes a sense of institutional rapport and open communication, a perception of fair treatment, and provides the offender and his fellow students a showcase of democracy at work. But nothing the Court has as yet adduced ought to convince us

---

[218] *Wolff*, 418 U.S. at 596–97. *Morrissey* notes similarly that "fair treatment in parole revocations will enhance the chance of rehabilitation by avoiding reactions to arbitrariness." 408 U.S. at 484.

[219] West Virginia Bd. of Education v. Barnette, 319 U.S. 624, 637 (1943).

[220] CENTER FOR RESEARCH AND EDUCATION IN AMERICAN LIBERTIES, CIVIC EDUCATION IN A CRISIS AGE 1–2 (1970) (quoted in ACLU Amicus Brief at 12–13).

of it. Respect for democratic institutions will equally dissipate if they are thought too ineffectual to provide their students an environment of order in which the educational process may go forward. Is it not possible, for example, that the more elaborate disciplinary hearings simply communicate to today's students society's willingness to temporize with even the most hard-core offenders, the relative inability of society to act effectively to redress injury to its members, or even the uncertainty on the part of society of its justification and mandate for acting at all? In the case of *Goss*, where only rudimentary procedures are required, the proceeding may appear, at least in some instances, not an exercise in democracy, but more a charade which authorities play as quickly as possible in order to reach the predetermined result. If, as the Court says, the fair-minded school principal would quickly impose such rudimentary requirements on himself,[221] the unfair principal will hardly be led by the slight protections of *Goss* to a more elevated frame of mind. He may comply with the Court's requirements, to be sure, but the alleged offender may only receive the shell of compliance with cynicism and contempt.

Student perception of disciplinary proceedings is a deeply complicated matter, the psychology of which the Court shies from considering in other than the spirit of democratic idealism noted above. A second point of psychology, perhaps equally at work on the Court in *Goss*, is the importance of suspensions on the outlook of schoolchildren. The courts have reacted to this quite differently. One district judge has extravagantly compared the suspended student to "the public penitent of medieval Christendom and colonial Massachusetts, the outlaw of the American West, and the ostracized citizen of classical Athens."[222] Mr. Justice Brennan has observed with less hyperbole that " 'the excluded pupil loses caste with his fellows, and is liable to be regarded with aversion, and subjected to reproach and insult.' "[223]

It is a long way from such statements to Mr. Justice Powell's criticism of the Court in *Goss*:[224]

---

[221] 419 U.S. at 583.

[222] Sullivan v. Houston Indep. School Dist., 333 F. Supp. 1149, 1172 (S. D. Tex. 1973), *rev'd on other grounds*, 475 F.2d 1071 (5th Cir. 1973).

[223] School Dist. v. Schempp, 374 U.S. 203, 292 (1963), quoting from Weiss v. District Bd. of School Dist. No. 8, 76 Wis. 177, 200 (1890).

[224] 419 U.S. at 598 n.19.

In my view we tend to lose our sense of perspective and proportion in a case of this kind. For average, normal children—
the vast majority—suspension for a few days is simply *not* a
detriment; it is a commonplace occurrence, with some 10% of
all students being suspended; it leaves no scars; affects no repu-
tations; indeed, it often may be viewed by the young as a badge
of some distinction and a welcome holiday.

I have no competence to choose between such competing theories of child psychology—nor does the Court. For some children,
it undoubtedly is disturbing psychologically to be compelled to
leave school, even for so short a time. But that does not alone indicate a problem of constitutional magnitude. Concern for the psychological consequences of short suspensions, to the extent it influenced the result in *Goss*, may be a prime example of judicial
overprotectiveness. Schools, and indeed later life, abound in psychological reverses, as severe as the short suspension, and from
which courts cannot guard. We may all undergo unfair and unwarranted exclusions, beginning with those from playground groups
and athletic teams, and continuing, perhaps, through social organizations, professional societies, and friendship circles of which adults
would like to be part. Not only school discipline but academic
disappointment, career failure, family breakdown, all carry the
potential for acute psychological distress. While due process retains
an important role in redressing particular kinds of publicly and
governmentally inflicted injury, it is little more than an illusion to
imply that psychological discomfort bears any direct relationship
to constitutional redress. Any discussion of psychological consequence readily expands to the whole range of consequences presumed to attend short disciplinary suspensions: whether psychological, social, reputational, educational, or economic. Life deals
so many situations of comparable and much greater adversity that
it seems fastidious and ultimately just plain silly for the Court
to have singled out even a one-day suspension from school for an
exercise in constitutional compassion.

Goss v. Lopez may in the end be too inoffensive an occasion to
make doleful predictions or to talk of Armageddon. But we must
face frankly the possibility that one chief effect of the Court's recent educational cases has been to erode the public's faith and support of the public schools. As the Court loads upon the public
school system disciplinary hearings, compulsory student transpor-

tation programs and other constitutional baggage, it only enlarges the gap between public and private education and enhances the attractiveness of the latter. Many parents, whose support is essential for a strong public school system, are concerned over nothing so much as a loss of neighborhood schooling and a basic breakdown of order. They will not forever support with their tax dollars, their civic efforts, or their child's attendance, a deteriorating public school situation which the Court each year removes farther and farther from their capacity to influence. Capable persons who once sought a career in the public school system may become increasingly dissuaded. In expanding student rights, quite possibly at the expense of student discipline, the Court in *Goss* and *Wood* has struck for American public education a sour and untimely note.

This brings me to a broader point, and one on which I will conclude. The well-being of any society depends ultimately on a fragile equilibrium between duties and rights. A citizen's appreciation of his basic rights must not go unaccompanied by some recognition of his obligations. This balance seems to me increasingly endangered in this country, where the question "What rights do I have?" too often has supplanted rather than joined with the question "What responsibilities do I owe?" American society experimented extensively with greater rights in the late 1960s, and the results we have been reaping from that experiment have not all been happy ones. Midge Decter's poignant epitaph to some of the high hopes for the generation that came to maturity at the end of the last decade is relevant here:[225]

> It might sound a paradoxical thing to say—for surely never has a generation of children occupied more sheer hours of parental time—but the truth is that we neglected you. We allowed you a charade of trivial freedoms in order to avoid making those impositions on you that are in the end both the training ground and proving ground for true independence. We pronounced you strong when you were still weak in order to avoid the struggles with you that would have fed your true strength. We proclaimed you sound when you were foolish in order to avoid taking part in the long, slow, slogging effort that is the only route to genuine maturity of mind and feeling. Thus, it was no small anomaly of your growing up that while you were the most indulged generation, you were also in many ways the most abandoned to your own meager devices by those into whose safekeeping you had been given.

---

[225] *What Has Gone Wrong with the Children?* Washington Post, 13 July 1975, at C2.

The Supreme Court, since the early 1960s, has helped inspire and lead this national passion for individual rights. It has acted, sincerely, from fear of a loss of personal freedoms. That was and is a real fear, but not the only real fear. The danger to America increasingly approaches from quite an opposite direction. For this reason the larger, faintly nostalgic message of the *Goss* dissent does not lack for modern meaning:[226]

> Education in any meaningful sense includes the inculcation of an understanding in each pupil of the necessity of rules and obedience thereto. . . . One who does not comprehend the meaning and necessity of discipline is handicapped not merely in his education but throughout his subsequent life. . . .
>
> The lesson of discipline is not merely a matter of the student's self-interest in the shaping of his own character and personality; it provides an early understanding of the relevance to the social compact of respect for the rights of others. The classroom is the laboratory in which this lesson of life is best learned.

---

[226] 419 U.S. at 593.

CHARLES A. LOFGREN

MISSOURI v. HOLLAND IN

HISTORICAL PERSPECTIVE

In April 1920 the Supreme Court rejected state claims based on the Tenth Amendment and upheld federal legislation which implemented a treaty to protect migratory birds. *Missouri v. Holland*[1] has since become, in the words of Professor Henkin, "perhaps the most famous and most discussed case in the constitutional law of foreign affairs."[2] Foreshadowed by debate prior to the decision, the dispute over *Holland* grew especially heated in the 1950s and has never entirely subsided. Some critics have read the Holmes opinion as creating a license for unlimited federal authority through the treaty power; more favorable commentators have argued that the decision did no more than ratify existing law.[3] By examining

---

Charles A. Lofgren is Roy P. Crocker Associate Professor of American History, Claremont Men's College.

[1] 252 U.S. 416 (1920).

[2] HENKIN, FOREIGN AFFAIRS AND THE CONSTITUTION 144 (1972) [hereafter HENKIN].

[3] For the early controversy, see Boyd, *The Expanding Treaty Power*, in A.A.L.S., SELECTED ESSAYS ON CONSTITUTIONAL LAW 410, 422–28 (1938); Note, 33 HARV. L. REV. 281 (1919); Note, 8 CALIF. L. REV. 177 (1920); Note, 20 COLUM. L. REV. 692 (1920); Note, 29 YALE L. J. 445 (1920) (all supporting the position taken by the Court in *Holland*); Thompson, *State Sovereignty and the Treaty-Making Power*, 11 CALIF. L. REV. 242, 247–51 (1923); Black, Missouri v. Holland—*A Judicial Milepost on the Road to Absolutism*, 25 ILL. L. REV. 911 (1931); Note, 6 CORN. L.Q. 91 (1920); Note, 68 U. PA. L. REV. 160 (1920) (all adversely critical). Professor Corwin noted *Holland*'s significance without overt approval, in *Constitutional Law in 1919–1920, II*, 15 AM. POL. SCI. REV. 52, 52–54 (1920), but had earlier supplied his imprimatur to similar arguments in NATIONAL SUPREMACY: TREATY POWER V. STATE POWER (1913). Professor T. R. Powell likewise withheld open expression of judgment but seemed to think that the

Holland in historical context and by assessing its impact on subsequent constitutional law, this article seeks to shed some additional light on its meaning and on its capacity for raising controversy.

I. The Development of Federal Migratory Bird Legislation

The active effort in Congress to gain federal protection for migratory birds dates to a bill introduced in 1904. Each succeeding Congress saw one or more similar bills introduced, until, on 3 March 1913, a measure passed both houses as an amendment to the Department of Agriculture Appropriation Act and received President Taft's signature.[4] State and national conservation organizations, progressive sportsmen's associations, state game officials, and members of the federal Department of Agriculture had backed the legislation. These groups feared for the birds' survival in the face of large-scale shooting not only of game birds but of such insectivorous birds as the robin, particularly during the spring breeding season. State protective legislation existed, but "strong temptation pressing upon every State to secure its full share of edible game birds during the spring and fall migrations . . . rendered harmonious and effective State supervision impossible."[5] Moreover, testimony established that the endangered birds destroyed insects which otherwise would damage millions of dollars of crops each year.[6]

Professing agreement with its objectives, opponents of federal legislation mainly disputed its constitutionality. Migratory bird protection not only exceeded the federal government's delegated powers, they contended; it also clearly fell within the police power reserved to the states.[7]

---

decision opened the way to constitutional amendment via treaties. See Powell, *Constitutional Law in 1919–1920,* 19 Mich. L. Rev. 1, 11–13 (1920).

For the debate of the 1950s, see notes 219–31 *infra* and accompanying text.

The present legal status of the *Holland* case is set out in Henkin 137–48, 383–96.

[4] See Palmer, *Memorandum concerning the Movement in Favor of Federal Protection,* in Protection of Migratory and Insectivorous Game Birds of the United States, H.R. Rep. No. 680, 62d Cong., 2d Sess. 4–5 (1912); 49 Cong. Rec. 4799 (1914); 37 Stat. 828, 847.

[5] S. Rep. No. 675, 62d Cong., 2d Sess., 1 (1912).

[6] See *id.,* *passim;* H.R. Rep. No. 680, note 4 *supra,* *passim;* H.R. Rep. No. 1424, 62d Cong., 3d Sess. *passim* (1913); Pearson, *The Federal Government to Protect Migratory Birds,* 24 Craftsman 395 (1913); Gladden, *Federal Protection for Migratory Birds,* 62 Outing 345 (1913); *Weeks-McLean Law,* 15 Bird Lore 137 (1913).

[7] See 48 Cong. Rec. 8547–49 (Rep. Mondell, 1 July 1912); 49 *id.* at 2725–27, 4330, 4337–39 (Reps. Mondell, Bartlett, Cox, 7, 28 Feb. 1913). *Cf. id.* at 1493 (Sen. Reed, 14 Jan. 1913). See also citations in note 16 *infra* for similar constitutional attacks on appropriations for bird protection after the legislation passed.

The opposition's certainty in these regards was not matched by the advocates of protection. Senator George McLean, the sponsor of the bill which passed in 1913, was so unsure at first whether the legislation could stand on its own that he introduced a constitutional amendment to validate it. Later reversing himself on the need for an amendment, he still could not cite a specific constitutional clause to which the proposed legislation could be tied. Instead, he theorized that the national government held "implied attributes of sovereignty" with respect to those objects which the states acting alone could not achieve.[8] But this was a weak support in view of the Supreme Court's decision in *Kansas v. Colorado*, where Justice Brewer, writing for the Court, had explained:[9]

> The powers affecting the internal affairs of the states not granted to the United States by the Constitution, nor prohibited by it to the States, are reserved to the States respectively, and *all powers of a national character which are not delegated to the National Government by the Constitution are reserved to the people of the United States.*

McLean's exposition was otherwise dubious. It rested partly on a strained interpretation of several cases which had held that the states, acting in their sovereign capacities, were trustees for their citizens of animals *ferae naturae* within their boundaries. In these, the Court had in effect reserved decision on the extent of state power in the face of positive federal action.[10] To make his point, McLean equated such reservations with specific holdings favorable to federal power.[11] He also relied on an article by Senator George Sutherland in which the future Justice strove to show that dual federalism in domestic affairs and plenary national power in foreign affairs could constitutionally coexist.[12] By selective quotation, McLean portrayed Sutherland as arguing for plenary national

---

[8] See 47 CONG. REC. 2564 (28 June 1911); 49 *id.* at 1489–94 (14 Jan. 1913). *Cf. id.* at 4331–32 (Rep. Lamb, 28 Feb. 1913).

[9] Kansas v. Colorado, 206 U.S. 46, 90 (1907). (Emphasis added.)

[10] See Manchester v. Massachusetts, 139 U.S. 240, 264–66 (1891); Geer v. Connecticut, 161 U.S. 519, 528 (1896); The Abby Dodge, 223 U.S. 166, 173–75 (1912) (all mentioned by Sen. McLean, 49 CONG. REC. 1490).

[11] See 49 CONG. REC. 1490 (14 Jan. 1913). Indeed, the opposition read the case law quite differently. See *id.* at 4337 (Rep. Sisson, 28 Feb. 1913).

[12] See INTERNAL AND EXTERNAL POWERS OF THE NATIONAL GOVERNMENT, S. DOC. No. 417, 61st Cong., 2d Sess. *passim* (1910), also printed in 191 NORTH AM. REV. 373 (1910).

power in both arenas, whenever the states were severally incompetent.[13] All told, the frankness of another supporter of protective legislation was much in order: "I do not know whether [the bill] is constitutional," he allowed, "but I do know that it is eternally right and in the end right will prevail."[14]

Passage of the Migratory Bird Act on 3 March 1913 failed to end the constitutional dispute. Even as some enforcement and evidently much voluntary compliance had a salutary effect on the bird population,[15] constitutional doubts figured in attacks on appropriations for continued enforcement.[16] Significantly, the Department of Agriculture, which held responsibility for enforcement, showed little eagerness for a court test of the legislation.[17] And when prosecutions did occur, two federal courts handed down decisions ad-

---

[13] See 49 CONG. REC. 1491.

[14] Id. at 4332 (Rep. Weeks, 28 Feb. 1913). The favorable House and Senate Reports on the bird protection bill further illustrate the uncertain grounds on which the legislation rested in the eyes of its proponents. While the House Report pictured the "interstate bird" as being in interstate commerce, it also included an admission from a supporter of bird protection that doubts about the bill's constitutionality plagued some who were "strongly in favor of [its] purpose." H.R. REP. No. 680, note 4 supra, at 2, 4–5. The Senate Report found support in the allegedly (but dubiously) analogous "power of the Federal Government to regulate by treaty the taking of migratory seals and fish," which of course overlooked the fact that no bird treaty yet existed. S. REP. No. 675, note 5 supra, at 2.

[15] See the ANNUAL REPORTS OF THE DEPARTMENT OF AGRICULTURE: For 1915, at 246 (1916); for 1916, at 251–52 (1917); for 1917, at 265 (1918); for 1918, at 273–74 (1919).

[16] See 51 CONG. REC. 8349–58, 8423–54 (Senate, 9, 12 May 1914); 53 id. at 6763–70, 6804–06 (House, 24, 25 April 1916); id. at 10682–98 (Senate, 10 July 1916); 54 id. at 968–70 (House, 6 Jan. 1917). Not all opponents of the law, however, opposed appropriations to enforce it. One argued: "If this law had been rigidly enforced, there would have been not three judicial decisions against its constitutionality, but a score. . . . Of course, the Supreme Court will overturn this law when the court reaches it; and the surest way to have the law pronounced unconstitutional, the most certain and effective way to arouse public sentiment against the effort to extend Federal police power throughout the country, is to enforce the law. Therefore I am in favor of the appropriation." 53 id. at 6804–05 (Rep. Mondell, 25 April 1916). For a background, from a Progressive perspective, on the drive against bird protection after the 1913 law was enacted, see Phillips, The Missouri Campaign: How the Middle West Has Organized to Defeat the Federal Migratory Bird Law, 69 OUTING 77 (1916).

[17] "The prosecution of cases arising under the law is under the jurisdiction of the Department of Justice. So far no case has been presented to this department [i.e., Agriculture] which our solicitor has deemed it advisable to present to the Department of Justice." Letter from Secretary of Agriculture David F. Houston to Senator Robinson, 24 April 1914. 51 CONG. REC. 8350–51 (1914). "As to the matter of testing the law, I personally have no desire to press the matter. The only question is whether it can be kept out of the courts. There is pressure on the Department of Justice to have the law tested." Letter from Houston to Senator McLean, 23 April 1914. Id. at 8355. See generally id. at 8350–55, 8450–53 (Senate debates of 9, 12 May 1914, discussing the government's reticence over a court test of the 1913 law).

verse to the Act,[18] with these in turn giving new ammunition to its congressional opponents.[19]

Faced by these doubts and attacks, the birds' defenders called for a bird protection treaty with other North American nations. Indeed, the day the Senate passed the 1913 protection bill, Senator McLean had guardedly questioned whether "Congress can in the absence of a treaty exercise control over migratory birds or fishes."[20] Senator Elihu Root proceeded to introduce a resolution recommending negotiation of a treaty.[21] He remarked that "it may be that under the treaty-making power a situation can be created in which the Government of the United States will have constitutional authority to deal with this subject."[22] Nothing came of Root's resolution, but in the next session one by McLean passed the Senate.[23]

In the treaty-related discussions during the appropriation debates, and in the debates on implementing the treaty, which was quickly concluded with Great Britain (acting on behalf of Canada) and approved in 1916,[24] two general constitutional positions emerged. One held that bird protection, being a legitimate object of international concern, was a proper subject for a treaty, and that legislation implementing such a treaty was therefore constitutional because the treaty had status as supreme law and because the legis-

---

[18] United States v. Shauver, 214 F. 154 (E.D. Ark. 1914); United States v. McCullagh, 221 F. 288 (D. Kans. 1915).

[19] See 53 CONG. REC. 6763–69 (House, 24 April 1916); id. at 10682–93 (Sen. Reed, 10 July 1916); 54 id. at 968 (Rep. Doolittle, 6 Jan. 1917); 55 id. at 5547–48 (Sen. Reed, 30 July 1917); 56 id. at 7363, 7365 (Reps. Huddleston, Graham, 4 June 1918).

[20] 49 id. at 1490 (14 Jan. 1913).   [21] Id. at 1494.

[22] Quoted by Sen. Robinson in 51 id. at 8349 (9 May 1914). This remark was omitted from the permanent edition of volume 49 of the Congressional Record, but from the context of Robinson's use of it, there seems no reason to doubt its accuracy.

Proponents of protection did not see a treaty merely as a means to remedy possible constitutional defects in the 1913 legislation. They also believed that international effort was needed for its real protective benefits. Finley, Uncle Sam, Guardian of the Game, 107 OUTLOOK 481, 487 (1914).

[23] 50 CONG. REC. 2339–40 (7 July 1913). Forty years later, John W. Davis, who had been solicitor general from 1913 to 1918 under President Wilson, took credit for having suggested, in a conversation with Secretary of State Robert Lansing, the idea of concluding a treaty in order to establish a constitutionally viable basis for bird protection. See Report of the Committee on International Law, N.Y. State Bar Assoc., 30 Jan. 1953, at 60, quoted in Hearings on S.J. Res. 1 before a Subcommittee of the Senate Committee on the Judiciary, 84th Cong., 1st Sess. 139 (1955). Clearly, however, the idea antedated not only Lansing's tenure as secretary of state, but also Wilson's presidency. See notes 20–22 supra and accompanying text.

[24] Convention with Great Britain for the Protection of Migratory Birds, 39 STAT. 1702 (1916).

lation violated no constitutional prohibition.[25] Opponents denied
that a treaty could validate otherwise unconstitutional legislation,
particularly when the legislation trenched on state police powers
protected by the Tenth Amendment.[26] But after approval and ratification of the 1916 treaty, the opponents were less certain of their
grounds than they had been in attacking legislation unaided by
a treaty.[27] This is not surprising, for the advocates of protection
on balance now constructed the better argument, having the relevant case law and treatises more clearly on their side.[28]

Legislation implementing the Migratory Bird Treaty of 1916
passed the Senate by voice vote on 30 July 1917 and cleared the
House almost a year later, on 6 June 1918, on a 236 to 49 roll
call.[29] After minor differences in the two versions were resolved,
President Wilson signed the measure into law on 3 July 1918. The
act forbade the hunting, killing, or subsequent sale and shipment
of the bird species covered by the treaty, except as allowed by
regulations to be established by the Secretary of Agriculture.[30]
These regulations were quickly issued on 31 July.[31]

---

[25] See 51 Cong. Rec. 8352–53, 8447–49, 8452–54 (Sen. McLean, 9, 12 May 1914);
53 id. at 10698–99 (Sen. McLean, 10 July 1916); 56 id. at 7361–62, 7367–71, 7377
(Reps. Stedman, Temple, Miller, Small, 4 June 1918); H.R. Rep. No. 243, 65th Cong.,
2d Sess. 1–2 (1918). Cf. 54 Cong. Rec. 970 (Reps. Platt, Raker, 6 Jan. 1917); 55 id. at
4400 (Sens. Lodge, Hitchcock, McLean, 28 June 1917).

[26] See 51 id. at 8351–54, 8447–49, 8452–54 (Sens. Robinson, Borah, Reed, Gore,
9, 12 May 1914); 53 id. at 10698 (Sen. Reed, 10 July 1916); 54 id. at 969 (Rep. Sisson,
6 Jan. 1917); 56 id. at 7363–66, 7450–51 (Reps. Tillman, Huddleston, Graham, Mondell,
4, 6 June 1918).

[27] See, e.g., 55 id. at 4815 (Sen. Reed, 30 July 1917, admitting that Congress might
have some power to legislate "touching the matters named in the treaty"); 54 Cong.
Rec. App. 308 (1917). Similarly revealing the opponents' uncertainty was the amendment
to the Migratory Bird Treaty Bill unsuccessfully proposed by Rep. Bland: "[T]his act
shall not become effective until the provisions of the treaty between the United States
and Great Britain covering the question of migratory birds shall have been ratified or
approved by the legislatures of all the States of the Union." 56 id. at 7460 (6 June 1918).

[28] Compare, e.g., 56 id. at 7361–62, 7367–71 (Reps. Stedman, Temple, Miller, 4 June
1918, favoring the bill) with id. at 7365–66, 7450–52 (Reps. Graham, Mondell, Huddleston, 4, 6 June 1918, opposing the bill). See also note 27 supra. Representative Miller
in his comments defending the bill somewhat anticipated the organic view of constitutional development that Holmes was to advance in his opinion in Holland. Compare 56
Cong. Rec. 7371 with Holland at 433; see also note 134 infra and accompanying text.

[29] See 55 Cong. Rec. 5548 (30 July 1917); 56 id. at 7461–62, 8430, 8462 (6, 28, 29
June 1918).

[30] 40 Stat. 755 (1918).

[31] Report of the Solicitor, October 3, 1919, in Annual Reports of the Department
of Agriculture for 1919 490 (1920).

II. The Migratory Bird Act of 1913 in the Courts

By the time the 1918 law took effect, prosecution under the earlier legislation had virtually halted because of doubts concerning its constitutionality.[32] Although in April 1914 the 1913 act was upheld against a constitutional challenge in one trial court,[33] the next month in another district Judge Trieber ruled against the legislation on a demurrer to an indictment in *United States v. Shauver*,[34] and other adverse rulings followed.[35] Trieber's opinion attracted attention in the continuing constitutional debates in Congress and typified the other opinions.

Approaching the constitutional issue with caution, Trieber stated that a holding of unconstitutionality could come "[o]nly if the question is practically free from real doubt."[36] He also recognized "that the United States . . . possess[ed] what is analogous to the police power, which every sovereign nation possesses, as to its own property."[37] This concession took on importance because the Government initially conceded that the law found no support in the Commerce Clause[38] and instead rested its case on the grant in Art. IV, § 3, that "[t]he Congress shall have power to . . . make all needful rules and regulations respecting the territory or other property belonging to the United States."[39] Trieber refused, however, to accept the claim that even though the Constitution made no affirmative grant, the national government possessed "implied attributes of sovereignty" which allowed it to act "where the state is clearly incompetent to save itself."[40] He bolstered his assertion of vintage

---

[32] In its five years of operation by 30 June 1918, game wardens of the Department of Agriculture had reported 1,132 violations of the 1913 act, but prosecution in all but 29 of these had been withheld pending the Supreme Court's disposition of United States v. Shauver, 214 F.2d 154 (E.D. Ark. 1914), which is described in the text *infra*, at notes 52–53. See Annual Reports of the Department of Agriculture for 1918 274 (1919). The growth of this backlog can be traced in the Annual Reports for 1915–1917. See also note 17 *supra*.

[33] United States v. Shaw (D.S.D., 18 April 1914), unreported but mentioned in *The Federal Migratory-Bird Law in the Courts*, 16 Bird Lore 322 (1914), and alluded to in State v. McCullagh, 96 Kansas 786, 790 (1915).

[34] 214 Fed. 154 (E.D. Ark. 1914).

[35] United States v. McCullagh, 221 F. 288 (D. Kan. 1915); State v. Sawyer, 113 Maine 458 (1915); State v. McCullagh, 96 Kansas 786 (1915). The state court rulings came when defendants raised the federal act as a bar to state prosecution for violation of state game regulations.

[36] 214 Fed. at 156.   [38] *Id.* at 160.   [40] *Id.* at 156–57.

[37] *Ibid.*   [39] *Id.* at 156.

dual federalism with a long excerpt from Justice Brewer's opinion in *Kansas v. Colorado*,[41] which, among other things, remarked that "this is a government of enumerated powers," and that "[t]his natural construction of the original body of the Constitution is made absolutely certain by the tenth amendment."[42]

Trieber's reaffirmation of the Tenth Amendment made constitutionally irrelevant a mere showing that the states severally could not protect the birds.[43] *Shauver* thus turned on whether migratory birds were property of the United States or of the individual states. The long-standing American rule, which had evolved from English law and had been elaborated in the leading case of *Geer v. Connecticut*,[44] was that animals *ferae naturae* were the common property of the people of the individual states, with the states acting as trustees over that property for their citizens. Even after people reduced game to their own possession (as by killing a bird), the resulting personal ownership was qualified by a continuing state interest in its subsequent shipment or disposal.[45] Trieber therefore concluded that Art. IV, § 3, provided no support for the legislation.[46]

Nevertheless, after Trieber observed that government counsel had not argued "that the power to enact such legislation exists under the commerce clause,"[47] the Government advanced a Commerce Clause claim in its motion for rehearing. If it was true, as

---

[41] 206 U.S. 46 (1907).   [42] Quoted in 214 Fed. at 157.

[43] Trieber repeated this point, explaining that the expediency of the legislation did not remove the constitutional problems besetting it, because "[i]t is the people alone who can amend the Constitution to grant Congress the power to enact such legislation as they deem necessary." *Id.* at 160. The courts thus had to take the Constitution as they found it. *Ibid.* He distinguished the examples of federal regulation of such objects as interstate lotteries, food and drugs, mailable packages, and prostitution. In those and similar instances, federal involvement had been "upheld under some provision of the Constitution, either that of the Post Office Department, the commerce clause, the taxing power, or some other grant." *Id.* at 159.

[44] 161 U.S. 519 (1896).

[45] See *id.* at 522–34. Justice White's analysis in *Geer* is summarized in *Shauver*, 214 Fed. 157–59, with attention there also to the subsequent conforming cases of New York *ex rel.* Silz v. Hesterberg, 211 U.S. 311 (1908), and The Abby Dodge, 223 U.S. 166 (1912).

[46] 214 Fed. at 156–59.

[47] *Id.* at 156. Indeed, according to Judge Trieber's later opinion on the Government's motion for rehearing, rather than simply not advancing a Commerce Clause claim, government counsel had "conceded that the act cannot be sustained under the commerce clause." *Id.* at 160.

Trieber had averred in his original opinion, that a bird while in one state was owned by that state's citizens in their collective capacity, and after passing to another state was likewise owned by the latter's citizens, then the bird was an article in commerce.[48] But this argument similarly failed to impress Trieber. Again quoting from *Geer*, in which a state game regulation had been unsuccessfully attacked as trenching on the federal commerce power, Trieber denied the motion for rehearing.[49]

In the absence of the Government's case file for *Shauver*, which cannot be located,[50] it is difficult to determine accurately how important Trieber's ruling was for the Justice and Agriculture Departments. Yet they must have attached some importance to the defeat: Assistant Attorney General E. Marvin Underwood came from Washington to argue the motion for rehearing.[51] When that failed, the Government appealed on writ of error to the Supreme Court, which heard arguments on 18 October 1915 and assigned the case for reargument during the October 1916 Term.[52]

It seems probable, however, that the Migratory Bird Treaty with Britain, along with the legislation expected to implement it, now entered the Government's calculations, for government counsel first moved to postpone reargument, and eventually to dismiss, which the Court did in January 1919.[53] By this time, the Justice and Agriculture Departments probably concluded they would be

---

[48] See Brief for the United States on Motion for Rehearing, quoted at 214 Fed. 160–61. Besides advancing this new argument in its motion for rehearing, the Government reiterated its two claims that the law should be accorded a strong presumption of constitutionality and that the birds in question were property of the United States. Judge Trieber agreed with the first of these, just as he had in his first opinion, and he almost summarily found no reason to change his conclusion respecting the second. *Id.* at 160.

[49] *Id.* at 161.

[50] Letter from Assistant Attorney General Henry E. Peterson, by John L. Murphy, Chief, Government Regulations Section, Department of Justice, to the Author, 23 May 1974, in author's possession. The Department's case file for *Holland* is also missing. *Ibid.*

[51] 214 Fed. at 160.

[52] ANNUAL REPORT OF THE ATTORNEY GENERAL OF THE UNITED STATES FOR 1916 42 (1916).

[53] United States v. Shauver, 248 U.S. 594 (1919). The Supreme Court's file for *Shauver* (Supreme Court Appellate Case 24323, National Archives, Washington, D.C.) fails to disclose the government's reasons for requesting postponement of reargument. Letter from Mr. M. M. Johnson, Legislative, Judicial, and Fiscal Branch, Civil Archives Division, National Archives and Records Service, to the Author, 11 September 1974, in author's possession.

on firmer ground in arguing for the 1918 act. They may also have wished to avoid an outright defeat in the Supreme Court on the 1913 legislation. Such a defeat would not make the new law any easier to defend.

Support for this construction of the Government's strategy and reasoning may be derived from a review of its brief before the Supreme Court in *Shauver*;[54] this elaborated the Government's two key arguments in District Court, but still lacked persuasiveness. A review of the brief also explains further why the 1913 law failed in the lower courts, and it offers added insight into why the Government in *Holland* placed major emphasis on the sweep of the treaty power and why Justice Holmes in his opinion took the same route.

The first of the Government's arguments in *Shauver* again rested on Art. IV, § 3, giving federal authorities power to regulate United States property. Admitting control over animals *ferae naturae* rested with the sovereign in his capacity as trustee for the animals' collective owners, the Government nevertheless denied that the states severally stood as sovereigns *qua* trustees in relation to game not permanently within any one state. A state, it argued, could not effectively preserve property which resided within its borders for only a portion of the year.[55] Nor could the states act jointly to preserve game through interstate compacts without approval of Congress. Here the Government's brief had a curious twist, in light of the fact that the 1913 legislation lacked a treaty base:[56]

> By ratifying the Constitution, the people expressly delegated to the Federal Government the exclusive right to protect wild life by treaties with foreign nations, and at the same time withdrew from the States the right, without the consent of Congress, to make among themselves agreements for such purpose, thus vesting in Congress the ultimate control and protection of same. By thus stripping the States of all power to protect migratory wild life for the greater part of the time, and expressly granting such power to the Federal Government, the people, by necessary implication from these express grants and the nature of the property, changed their trustee and vested

---

[54] Not otherwise conveniently available, the Brief for the United States in *Shauver* [hereinafter cited as Shauver Brief] appears as Appendix A in Brief for Appellee, Missouri v. Holland, 252 U.S. 416 (1920), and also in 55 CONG. REC. 4816–18 (1917). Citations hereinafter for the Shauver Brief are to the *Holland* Brief's appendix.

[55] See Shauver Brief at 48–52.   [56] *Id.* at 52–53.

the title to all migratory animals *ferae naturae* in the Federal Government in trust for themselves, the people of the United States and the common owners of such animals.

The Government also stressed that ownership of game found its basis in common law, and that no such law respecting migratory animals had ever been declared in the United States, so far as it concerned the federal government's interest.[57] Existing cases either had involved animals resident solely in one state or, to the extent migratory animals were involved, had not raised the issue of their migratory character. In the absence of federal law, the Court had not reached the question of federal control in the face of the states' police powers.[58] The Court was now being asked in a case of first impression to declare in favor of federal ownership.

In short, the 1913 legislation did not seek to establish an independent federal police power, which had been disallowed in *Kansas v. Colorado*, or to trench on the states in the exercise of their police power over game, which had been recognized in *Geer*.[59] It "merely provide[d] 'needful rules and regulations' respecting *property* of the United States within the territory of the several States, a power daily exercised by the Federal Government."[60]

The Government's second line of argument stressed that denial of its position concerning federal ownership of migratory game —that is, affirmation of state ownership—led to the conclusion that such game was in interstate commerce, for when the game crossed state lines, ownership in property was then transferred.[61] Commerce, the Government admitted, was not susceptible to precise definition, but "the mere 'transit' of persons or property, independently of purchase, sale, or exchange, was such intercourse as falls within the meaning of the word 'commerce.'"[62]

Certain problems are apparent in the Government's position in its *Shauver* brief. True, existing cases had not reached the question of federal powers over migratory game, but overall they hardly supported the Government's position. In *Geer v. Connecticut*, for example, Justice White had detailed at length how the sovereign had come to be regarded as trustee for animals *ferae naturae*

---

[57] *Id.* at 48.

[58] *Id.* at 54–56, citing and quoting especially *The Abby Dodge, Geer*, and *Manchester*.

[59] Shauver Brief at 57.   [61] *Id.* at 59–62.

[60] *Ibid.*   [62] *Id.* at 61.

and how, in America, this sovereign authority had vested first in the colonies and then in the states.[63] It "remains in them [the states] at the present day," he concluded, "in so far as its exercise may not [be] incompatible with, or restrained by, the rights conveyed to the Federal government by the Constitution."[64] On its face, perhaps, that formulation left an opening for federal regulation, but in reality it merely returned the question to whether the Constitution affirmatively granted the federal government either express or implied power over game.

On this score, the Government's federal trusteeship theory was dubious, for it essentially repeated the constitutionally irrelevant claim that since the states severally could not protect game and hence could not act effectively as trustees, there must exist a federal power to do so. Resting on no evidence beyond simple assertion, the theory ignored Justice Brewer's remark in *Kansas v. Colorado* that where powers of a national nature had not been positively assigned to the federal government, they remained with the people.[65] Despite Justice White's passing reservation in *Geer* of the question of federal power, the Government theory also ran against White's actual emphasis in *Geer* on the states as trustees for animals *ferae naturae*.[66] And in the same year White had reiterated this emphasis when, speaking for the Court in *Ward v. Race Horse*,[67] he maintained "the complete power to regulate the killing of game within its borders" was "a necessary incident of . . . [state] authority." In *Patsone v. Pennsylvania*,[68] Justice Holmes had read *Geer* as establishing "the protection of wild life" as a "lawful [state] object" in the face of a claim that certain state regulations worked a deprivation of Fourteenth Amendment rights. Wild game, he

---

[63] 161 U.S. at 522–29. As already mentioned, *Geer* was the leading case; it summarized previous developments and was followed in subsequent cases. See *e.g.*, McCready v. Virginia, 94 U.S. 391 (1877); notes 45 *supra* and 67–70 *infra*.

[64] 161 U.S. at 528.

[65] 206 U.S. at 90. Although Hammer v. Dagenhart, 247 U.S. 251 (1918), had not yet been decided, it is similarly instructive to consider the Government's argument in *Shauver* in light of the Court's opinion in *Dagenhart*. See note 111 *infra* and accompanying text; note 139 *infra*.

[66] 161 U.S. at 527–29.

[67] 163 U.S. 504, 510 (1896). Later in the same opinion White reiterated: "The power of all the States to regulate the killing of game within their borders will not be gainsaid." *Id.* at 514.

[68] 232 U.S. 138, 143 (1914).

said, was something "which the State may preserve for its own citizens if it pleases."[69] As if to ratify this line of interpretation, White, now the Chief Justice, observed later in the same Term in which *Shauver* was argued that "[i]t is not to be doubted that the power to preserve fish and game within its borders is inherent in the sovereignty of the state."[70]

Arguably, too, the Government's Commerce Clause argument fell before *Geer*. There, as a bar to state prosecution, the defendant had claimed that the birds he had killed and sold out of state had entered interstate commerce. Not so, Justice White had held, finding that "the errors which this argument involves are manifest."[71] For one thing, personal ownership of such game remained qualified by the state's authority, under its trusteeship and police powers, to fix conditions on the killing and sale of game to such an extent that "it may well be doubted whether commerce is created" by those acts.[72] For another, even if it were conceded that the acts in question created commerce, "it [did] not follow that such internal commerce became necessarily the subject matter of interstate commerce, and therefore under the control of the Constitution of the United States. The distinction between internal and external commerce and interstate commerce is marked, and has always been recognized by this court."[73]

Of course, one could question whether White's remarks about commerce in *Geer* were relevant to the migratory bird legislation of 1913. The game involved in *Geer* had already been killed and

---

[69] *Id.* at 145–46. Like Justice White's argument in *Ward*, Holmes's narrow argument in *Patsone* was that if a treaty were to confer rights in derogation of a state's customary and well-established powers of police, it would have to do so explicitly and could not do so by implication.

[70] New York *ex rel.* Kennedy v. Becker, 241 U.S. 556, 562 (1916) (citing *Geer* and *Race Horse*). Though delivered by Chief Justice White, this opinion had been written by Justice Charles Evans Hughes prior to his resignation. *Id.* at 559. The remainder of the statement quoted in the text was: "subject, of course, to any valid exercise of authority under the provisions of the Federal Constitution." *Id.* at 562. So here again the question of state power in the presence of valid federal regulation was reserved, but, like the Government brief in *Shauver*, see text at note 64 *supra*, at most this too only returned the issue to what constituted valid federal regulation. More specifically, in context, the Court doubtless meant to reserve the question with reference to the exercise of the federal government's treaty power, for the case involved (and the Court disallowed) an Indian claim that a federal treaty conveying hunting and fishing rights acted as a bar to state prosecution for violations of state game laws. Hence, although the Court had already heard arguments in *Shauver*, it probably was not referring to an exercise of federal authority lacking a treaty base, as in *Shauver*.

[71] 161 U.S. at 530.   [72] *Ibid.*   [73] *Id.* at 530–31.

reduced to personal possession within a particular state. The 1913 law, although regulating the killing of game within individual states, aimed to preserve live birds in their flights across state lines. Yet the Government could not cite a single case in which the item being regulated as interstate commerce had crossed state lines of its own volition and not as a result of its owner's will or act.[74] In seeking to establish "transit" as a sufficient condition to define "commerce," it could only "submit" that self-volition in movement was constitutionally irrelevant.[75]

The remaining constitutional support the Government offered in *Shauver* was the Treaty Clause. The clear implication of the Government's brief was that the existence of the treaty power created an authority to regulate migratory birds independent of the actual conclusion of a treaty on the subject.[76] Yet, however prescient reference to the treaty power was with respect to the 1918 legislation, it provided no base for the 1913 legislation or for any action in the absence of a treaty. The necessity to resort to such sophistry simply underscores the constitutional infirmities which beset the Government's case within the doctrinal climate of the decade.

This critique of the Government's brief is not intended to suggest that no way existed by 1920 to uphold a bird protection law that lacked treaty support.[77] Under the guise of approving commercial regulation and taxation, the Court had already legitimated what in fact constituted federal police power in other areas.[78] The

---

[74] See Shauver Brief at 61–62.

[75] "Undoubtedly, under *Kelley* v. *Rhoads*, 188 U.S. 1, the Federal Government could prevent the owner from driving diseased cattle from the quarantined State into the other. It is submitted that the fact that the same cattle cross the quarantine line of their own volition instead of that of their owner does not so change their status as participants in interstate intercourse as to destroy the power of Congress to prevent their crossing the State line." *Id.* at 62. Later, to be sure, the Court held that freely ranging cattle which crossed state lines were in interstate commerce, but this conclusion rested on the argument that movement of the cattle was "made possible by the failure of their owners to restrict their ranging, and [was] due, therefore, to the will of their owners." Thornton v. United States, 271 U.S. 414, 425 (1926).

[76] Shauver Brief at 52–53.

[77] In 1916, for instance, Professor Corwin entered a vigorous defense of the 1913 act on grounds similar to those advanced by the Government in *Shauver*. Corwin, *Game Protection and the Constitution*, 14 MICH. L. REV. 613 (1916).

[78] See, *e.g.*, Champion v. Ames, 188 U.S. 321 (1903) (lotteries); McCray v. United States, 195 U.S. 27 (1904) (colored oleomargarine); Hipolite Egg Co. v. United States, 220 U.S. 45 (1911) (pure food and drugs); Hoke v. United States, 227 U.S. 308 (1913) (prostitution).

point instead is that, compared with the ease offered by the treaty route, the task clearly would have been a more difficult one, particularly in view of the willingness in 1918 of a five-man majority to strike down federal child labor legislation which rested on the Commerce Clause.[79]

III. THE MIGRATORY BIRD TREATY ACT OF 1918: JUDICIAL PRELIMINARIES

The Migratory Bird Treaty Act of 1918, unlike its predecessor, immediately received favorable treatment in the federal district courts. In fact, the first decision, in *United States v. Thompson*,[80] came from Judge Trieber. The Government, evidently attaching considerable importance to the case, was represented in *Thompson* not only by the resident United States attorney but also by an assistant attorney general and by the solicitor of the Department of Agriculture.[81] Trieber reached his finding of constitutionality without noticeably more difficulty than had attended his opposite conclusion in *Shauver*. He at first stressed the wording of the Supremacy Clause: "when referring to treaties, the only limitation is 'which shall be made under the authority of the United States,' omitting the words 'in pursuance of the Constitution.' "[82] Later, though, he recognized other limitations on treaty-making.[83] While a court might therefore hold a treaty void, it should do so only " 'in a very clear case indeed,' "[84] and the treaty with Britain was not such a case, even though it involved a subject otherwise governed by state regulation.[85] The major contrast

---

[79] Hammer v. Dagenhart, 247 U.S. 251 (1918); Henkin, *The Treaty Makers and the Law Makers: The Law of the Land and Foreign Relations*, 107 U. PA. L. REV. 903, 915 n.24 (1959). Justice Day's opinion for the Court in *Dagenhart* abounds with passages which could as easily have applied to bird regulation devoid of a treaty base. Consider, for example: "[T]he act in a twofold sense is repugnant to the Constitution. It not only transcends the authority delegated to Congress over commerce but also exerts a power as to a purely local matter to which the federal authority does not extend." 247 U.S. at 276. That the situation regarding federal regulation was becoming clouded is further indicated by United States v. Doremus, 249 U.S. 86 (1919), in which the Court, per Justice Day, upheld federal narcotics legislation by only a 5-to-4 vote.

[80] 258 Fed. 257 (E.D. Ark. 1919).

[81] *Ibid.*   [82] *Id.* at 258, and see 258–61.

[83] *Id.* at 262, relying especially on Geofroy v. Riggs, 133 U.S. 258, 266–67 (1890).

[84] 258 Fed. at 268, quoting Chase, J., in Ware v. Hylton, 3 Dall. 199, 237 (1796) (separate opinion).

[85] *Compare* 258 Fed. at 268 *with id.* at 258–59.

with *Shauver* was that the Tenth Amendment now did not apply. The Constitution specifically granted the treaty power to the federal government and forbade its exercise to the states.[86]

Although supported by opinions differing in emphasis and detail (and shorter as well), subsequent district court decisions were essentially similar.[87] That these later cases were prosecuted by local United States attorneys without assistance on argument from Washington may indicate that the Government itself was confident of their outcome. Relatedly, the Bureau Chief in Agriculture charged with implementing the act claimed that the lower court victories "[had] removed to a large extent the doubt existing in some quarters concerning the validity of the act, and . . . [were] a decided deterrent to those inclined to violate the law."[88] Certainly the statistics on prosecutions and convictions, when compared with the virtual hiatus in enforcement under the 1913 act after the *Shauver* case had come before the Supreme Court, reveal a more active and confident enforcement policy.[89]

The case which eventually confronted the Supreme Court arose in Missouri when two local citizens were indicted for violating the new federal game regulations. This led the state to sue to enjoin further enforcement of the act by the federal game warden, Ray P. Holland. After argument on defendants' demurrers to their indictments and on the Government's motion to dismiss Missouri's bill in equity for an injunction against Holland, Judge Van Valkenburgh overruled the demurrers and dismissed the bill, but not

---

[86] *Id.* at 262–67.

[87] United States v. Samples, 258 Fed. 479 (W.D. Mo. 1919); United States v. Selkirk, 258 Fed. 775 (S.D. Tex. 1919); United States v. Rockefeller, 260 Fed. 346 (D. Mont. 1919).

[88] ANNUAL REPORTS OF THE DEPARTMENT OF AGRICULTURE FOR 1919 at 295 (1920).

[89] In the first year of the new law's operation, the Government obtained 110 convictions, and 393 in its second year. For these and similarly revealing figures on enforcement of the 1918 law, see the ANNUAL REPORTS OF THE DEPARTMENT OF AGRICULTURE: For 1918, at 274 (1919); for 1919, at 490–91 (1920); for 1920, at 599–600 (1921). There are minor discrepancies between the Department of Agriculture's statistics and those found in the *Reports of the Attorney General* for these years. I have used Agriculture's figures because they are more detailed. For figures on the 1913 law, see note 32 *supra*. Interestingly, about the time prosecutions under the 1918 law were beginning and the law was being upheld in the lower courts, the Supreme Court in May 1919 sidestepped a final opportunity to rule on the earlier 1913 act. When a South Dakota defendant raised the 1913 law as a bar to state prosecution for violation of state game laws, the State argued, *inter alia*, that the federal law was unconstitutional. The Court, per Justice Brandeis, upheld the defendant's state conviction by finding no conflict between the state and federal acts. Carey v. South Dakota, 250 U.S. 118 (1919).

without remarking that the 1918 Act would have been unconstitutional without its treaty base.[90] Missouri then appealed to the Supreme Court and was joined in its attack on the 1918 law by the State of Kansas as amicus curiae. The Association for the Protection of the Adirondacks filed an amicus brief supporting the legislation.[91]

The Missouri and Kansas briefs anticipated a major criticism of the eventual decision. If an enactment which is otherwise unconstitutional becomes constitutional when passed pursuant to a treaty, the states argued, then for all practical purposes the Constitution can be amended without resort to the formal amendment process.[92] Accordingly, to uphold the Migratory Bird Treaty Act would set the stage for the President and Senate, acting with the assistance of some obliging foreign power (at one point Missouri mentioned Turkey),[93] to invade all internal state affairs, regulate child labor, cede state territory, alter modes of elections, and even force the introduction of opium.[94] Missouri warned that "[w]hen the power of the states over their purely internal affairs is destroyed, the system of government devised by the Constitution is destroyed."[95]

Maintaining that treaties must be subordinate to the Constitution,[96] both states rejected the notion that the Supremacy Clause freed treaties from the need to conform to the Constitution. The clause admittedly spoke not of treaties made pursuant to the Constitution, but of "[t]reaties made, or which shall be made, under the Authority of the United States." The two states explained, however, that this phrasing derived only from the necessity in 1787 to validate preexisting treaties.[97] Included in the resulting limitations on treaties were the reservations incorporated in the Tenth

---

[90] 258 Fed. 479 (W.D. Mo. 1919). Although conceding that the Migratory Bird Treaty Act of 1918 would have been unconstitutional in the absence of the 1916 treaty, id. at 481, and recognizing that treaties inconsistent with the Constitution were invalid, id. at 482–83, the judge found that the treaty violated no constitutional provisions and involved a matter of mutual interest between nations. 258 Fed. at 483–85.

[91] 252 U.S. at 430.

[92] Brief for Appellant, esp. at 41–42, 63–73; Brief for Kansas at 29–37; cf. id. at 25–29, 37–71.

[93] Brief for Appellant at 63.

[94] Brief for Appellant at 63, 73; Brief for Kansas at 28–29.

[95] Brief for Appellant at 64.

[96] Id. at 43–59, 78–86; Brief for Kansas at 37–77.

[97] Brief for Appellant at 83–84; Brief for Kansas at 31–32.

Amendment.[98] One of the powers thereby reserved to the states, in both their trusteeship and police capacities, was the regulation of game.[99]

Like the opinions in the favorable decisions below, the Government in its brief on behalf of Holland found the Tenth Amendment "wholly irrelevant" where treaties were involved.[100] The power to make treaties had been expressly granted to federal authorities by the Constitution and hence was not reserved.[101] It agreed that treaties were subject to prohibitions found in the Constitution, but failed to enumerate those prohibitions and merely contended that no prohibition barred a treaty dealing with a subject of mutual interest and proper negotiation between nations.[102] Although conceding dual federalism characterized domestic federal-state relationships, the brief explained that "when we come to deal with national questions affecting the interests not only of our own country but of other countries as well, we confront a different situation."[103] This position, the Government noted,[104] was consistent with the Court's earlier ruling in *Geer*, which legitimated state regulation only "in so far as its exercise may not be incompatible with, or restrained by, the rights conveyed to the Federal Government by the Constitution."[105]

The issue thus became whether bird protection was a proper subject of international negotiation. It would "not admit of doubt," argued the Government, that protection was "a matter of very great importance to both countries."[106] In fact, because the birds crossed international borders, such protection was only possible through a treaty.[107] To illustrate the importance of the birds, the brief included data on their economic value in preserving crops and forests from insects.[108]

---

[98] Brief for Appellant at 56–59; Brief for Kansas at 13, 40–45.

[99] Brief for Appellant at 30–44, 64–73; Brief for Kansas at 9–13, 57–59.

[100] Brief for Appellee at 18.   [103] *Id*. at 13–14.

[101] *Id*. at 8–14, 24–27.   [104] *Id*. at 30–31.

[102] *Id*. at 33–34, 36–41.

[105] 161 U.S. at 528, quoted *id*. at 31. Whether the Court in *Geer* specifically meant the exercise by the federal government of its treaty power is problematic, but in at least one more recent case, when it entered a similar reservation, the Court probably did specifically have in mind possible exercise of the treaty power. New York *ex rel*. Kennedy v. Becker, 241 U.S. 556, 562 (1916). See notes 69 and 70 *supra* and accompanying text.

[106] Brief for Appellee at 42.

[107] *Id*. at 42–43.   [108] *Id*. at 63–79 (Appendix B).

The Government also contended that the legislation of 1918 was valid even in the absence of a treaty.[109] However, it elaborated this point merely by including its earlier *Shauver* brief as an appendix,[110] which may suggest the Government suspected—and not without cause—that such an argument would likely have but marginal, if any, effect on the Court.[111] The Association for the Protection of the Adirondacks nevertheless gave the point greater emphasis, plus a new dimension. Perhaps recognizing that federal title to migratory birds was difficult, if not impossible, to establish, the Association massed a plethora of facts to demonstrate how birds were necessary to the preservation of national forests.[112] Federal bird regulation was therefore a necessary and proper means of regulating objects—that is, the forests—which were themselves undeniably federal property within the meaning of Art. IV, § 3.[113] Of course, this argument reinforced as well the Government's contention that the birds constituted a substantial national interest.

IV. JUSTICE HOLMES'S OPINION FOR THE COURT: AN EXPLICATION

The effort to put the federal government in the business of protecting migratory birds now squarely faced its final constitutional test. In outline, the Court's opinion, written by Justice Holmes, is simple enough. Quickly conceding Missouri's standing to sue,[114] Holmes narrowed the issue to "whether the treaty and statute are void as an interference with the rights reserved to the States."[115] He next explored possible tests for determining the constitutional validity of treaties and pursuant statutes, concluding that they must involve matters of national interest and must not contravene specific constitutional prohibitions.[116] Finally, he applied these tests to the challenged treaty and statute and held them con-

---

[109] *Id.* at 7–8.   [110] *Id.* at 47–62 (Appendix A).

[111] It should be recalled in this connection that the lower court in *Holland* had remarked that the 1918 law would have been unconstitutional without its treaty base. Perhaps also contributing to the Government's deemphasis of the non-treaty arguments was the Court's recent surprising and highly unexpected invalidation of the 1916 Child Labor Law in Hammer v. Dagenhart. On the surprised reactions to *Dagenhart*, see WOOD, CONSTITUTIONAL POLITICS IN THE PROGRESSIVE ERA: CHILD LABOR AND THE LAW 169–70 (1968).

[112] *See* Brief for Association for the Protection of the Adirondacks *passim*.

[113] *Id.* at 11–28.   [115] *Id.* at 432.

[114] 252 U.S. at 431.   [116] *Id.* at 432–35.

stitutional.[117] Only Justices Van Devanter and Pitney dissented, and without opinion.[118] But to argue that the majority opinion is a model of clarity would be to fly in the face of a half-century of dispute over its meaning. A close reading reveals the complexities of Holmes's handiwork.

Holmes focused his analysis on the treaty and not on the statute implementing it, for "[i]f the treaty is valid there can be no dispute about the validity of the statute under Article I, § 8, as a necessary and proper means to execute the powers of the Government."[119] Such a focus gave a nearly irrebuttable presumption of constitutionality to the challenged legislation. To be sure, the Tenth Amendment reserved to the states or the people those powers not delegated to the United States, but the Constitution expressly delegated the power to make treaties and declared that "treaties made under the authority of the United States, along with the Constitution and laws of the United States, made in pursuance thereof," were the supreme law of the land.[120] With such a foundation, the decision no longer turned on whether the substantive power to be exercised by a treaty and pursuant statute had itself been delegated. "The language of the Constitution as to the supremacy of treaties being general," Holmes declared, "the question before us is narrowed to an inquiry into the ground upon which the present supposed exception is placed."[121]

He thereupon explored the possible limits to a valid treaty. "One such limit," he wrote, "is that what an act of Congress could not do unaided, in derogation of the powers reserved to the States, a treaty cannot do."[122] But whether or not the district courts had been correct in striking down the 1913 bird protection law as an invasion of the reserved powers of the states,[123] this limit ran afoul of the text of the Constitution by which "[a]cts of Congress are the supreme law of the land only when made in pursuance of the Constitution, while treaties are declared to be so when made under the authority of the United States."[124] That textual distinction led Holmes into the comment probably most responsible for the later criticism of *Missouri v. Holland:* "It is open to question

---

[117] *Id.* at 434–35.   [119] *Id.* at 432.   [121] *Ibid.*

[118] *Id.* at 435.   [120] *Ibid.*   [122] *Ibid.*

[123] See *id.* at 432–33. Holmes cited *Shauver* and *McCullagh.*

[124] 252 U.S. at 433.

whether the authority of the United States means more than the formal acts prescribed to make the convention."[125] By itself, this statement suggested that any treaty, when duly made, approved, and ratified, held status as supreme law, other constitutional provisions notwithstanding.

Holmes, however, had only raised a question. Although the question contained far-reaching implications, he promptly limited their reach by recognizing that limitations to the treaty power did exist.[126] Yet a distinction remained between treaties and legislation unaided by treaties, for the limitations to treaties "must be ascertained in a different way."[127] This, of course, was but a restatement of the view that while the federal government held no general power of legislation, it did hold a general treaty power. So Holmes to this point had rejected the argument that the alleged unconstitutionality of the Migratory Bird Act of 1913 doomed the 1918 act. He still faced the task of specifying the limits to the treaty power.

Perhaps taking his cue from the Government's argument, Holmes did not initially specify the outer limits of valid treaties, but instead offered, at least by implication, a threshold test which can be labeled the "national interest test." A constitutionally valid treaty, he implied, must deal with a national concern. His precise wording was this:[128]

> It is obvious that there may be matters of the sharpest exigency for the national well being that an act of Congress could not deal with but that a treaty followed by such an act could, and it is not lightly to be assumed that, in matters requiring national action, "a power which must belong to and somewhere reside in every civilized government" is not to be found.

But this formulation left open whether, in order to be appropriate objects for the treaty power, such matters of "sharpest exigency for the national well being"—that is, matters of national concern— need be susceptible only to actual international action for their solution. The passage can be read thus, or it can be read as defending the exercise of the treaty power for the primary purpose of

---

[125] *Ibid.*

[126] "We do not mean to imply that there are no qualifications to the treaty-making power." *Ibid.*

[127] *Ibid.*   [128] *Ibid.*

dealing with matters of national concern susceptible to domestic solution but which are constitutionally beyond the unaided legislative power of Congress.[129]

His next sentence hinted that Holmes had in mind the second of these alternatives. Referring to *Andrews v. Andrews*,[130] which he had just cited and quoted, he wrote: "What was said in that case with regard to the powers of the States applies with equal force to the powers of the nation in cases where the States individually are incompetent to act."[131] In other words, because "a power which must belong to and somewhere reside in every civilized government" *had* to exist somewhere in American government, a treaty followed by a statute could serve to clothe the national government with needed plenary power that the Constitution otherwise failed to grant. That he thought a requirement for actual international action was not a requisite to valid exercise of the treaty power follows also from Holmes's later affirmation that even if state action would suffice, this would not withdraw the subject of bird protection from the treaty power.[132]

If such was Holmes's intended meaning, it was arguably dictum. He not only concluded that in reality state action was insufficient; he seems to have accepted the Government's argument that national action by itself was similarly insufficient and thus a truly international effort was in fact required.[133] Accordingly, he had no need to decide whether a matter not requiring international action, and not within the federal government's delegated powers, might still be confided in it by a treaty with some willing foreign power.

---

[129] For the view that the second alternative was Holmes's intended meaning, see, *e.g.*, Nicholson, *The Federal Spending Power*, 9 TEMPLE L.Q. 3, 5 n.10 (1934).

[130] 188 U.S. 14 (1903). At issue there was whether a fraudulently obtained South Dakota divorce, which had not been challenged in South Dakota, must be recognized in Massachusetts pursuant to the Full Faith and Credit Clause of Art. IV, § 1. The Court, per Justice White, held that to require recognition would emasculate Massachusetts's control over an important area of internal police and thereby effectively destroy a power which must exist "in every civilized government." *Id.* at 32–33.

[131] 252 U.S. at 433.

[132] *Id.* at 435. Because Holmes denied that state incompetency was necessary in order to commit a subject to the treaty power, I believe that Professor Powell was mistaken in writing, in his critique of *Holland*, that "[t]he fact that the states are individually incompetent to deal with the subject matter seems to be regarded as important [in establishing the existence of a national interest for treaty purposes]." Powell, note 3 *supra*, at 12.

[133] 252 U.S. at 435.

In any event, to lay the basis for his eventual conclusion that the Migratory Bird Treaty concerned a matter of national interest, Holmes had to establish that the category "national interest" was not a fixed, unchanging one. (One can imagine him anticipating the objection that the founding fathers would hardly have thought bird protection a significant enough problem to warrant a treaty.)[134] He argued:[135]

> [W]hen we are dealing with words that also are a constituent act, like the Constitution of the United States, we must realize that they have called into life a being the development of which could not have been foreseen completely by the most gifted of its begetters. It was enough for them to realize or to hope that they had created an organism; it has taken a century and has cost their successors much sweat and blood to prove that they created a nation. The case before us must be considered in the light of our whole experience and not merely in that of what was said a hundred years ago.

Besides conjuring up young Captain Holmes, thrice wounded in the Civil War, this language unambiguously displayed the Constitution as a flexible, dynamic instrument. It led, however, to a superficially more cryptic comment about the Tenth Amendment. "The only question," wrote Holmes, "is whether it [the treaty] is forbidden by some invisible radiation from the general terms of the Tenth Amendment."[136] Finally there came the sentence relating Holmes's comment about an organic constitution to Missouri's Tenth Amendment claim: "We must consider what this country has become in deciding what that Amendment has reserved."[137]

These last comments—about "invisible radiation" and the need to consider what the country has become—were phrased and positioned so that taking them out of context is easy.[138] This has

---

[134] During debate on the Migratory Bird Treaty Bill, one of its congressional supporters had anticipated such an argument and had proceeded to counter it with an argument similar in many respects to the one developed by Holmes at this point in *Holland*. 56 CONG. REC. 7371 (Rep. Miller, 4 June 1918).

[135] 252 U.S. at 433.   [136] *Id.* at 433–34.   [137] *Id.* at 434.

[138] Although Holmes had sufficient warrant to refer to the Tenth Amendment's "invisible radiation," the phrase greatly disturbed those who saw the Amendment as a most concrete and highly visible bulwark of the federal system, and this probably contributed to their focusing narrowly on the phrase as derogatory of the Amendment itself. See, *e.g.*, Appellant's Petition for Rehearing at 9. Moreover, Holmes's remark that "[w]e must consider what this country has become in deciding what that amendment has reserved" was separated by most of a fairly long paragraph from the main body of his related comments about matters involving an expansible national interest, with which *treaties* could deal. 252 U.S. at 433–34.

further contributed to the controversy surrounding the opinion, because, out of context, the remarks surely conflict with the restrictive gloss Justice Brewer had put on the Tenth Amendment in *Kansas v. Colorado,* a gloss comparable to that put on it by the opponents of the earlier bird protection act of 1913, by Missouri in the instant case, and so recently by the Court in *Hammer v. Dagenhart.* Whether Holmes, a dissenter in *Dagenhart*[139] and a master of the English language, deliberately phrased and positioned the remarks to achieve this appearance of conflict makes for intriguing speculation. Yet they must not be read as part of a general gloss on the Amendment. Indeed, had the 1920 Court so understood them, one suspects Holmes's opinion would have failed to command the 7 to 2 majority it did. They instead must be read more narrowly as part of an explication of the role of the Amendment in treaty adjudication.

For Holmes was still exploring the limits to valid treaties. Particularly, he was ruling on Missouri's Tenth Amendment claim. With this in mind, a sorting out of Holmes's thoughts reveals the following line of reasoning: Matters of national interest, and certainly those requiring international action for their solution, fall within the treaty power, a power which is expressly granted to the federal government, expressly denied to the states, and thus clearly excepted from the Tenth Amendment's restrictions. Because the category of national interest has grown with the nation, the permissible scope of treaties has likewise grown. This being the case, the growth of the nation has correspondingly and (to adapt Holmes's usage) visibly narrowed the reach of the Tenth Amendment, so far as treaties were involved. To be sure, a reversal of roles occurred in Holmes's argument. Contemporaries more commonly regarded the Tenth Amendment as the restricting, rather than the restricted, constitutional element. Nonetheless, since the Amendment did not visibly restrict treaties, all that remained was to inquire whether it had "some invisible radiation" which did so. Holmes gave no direct answer;[140] to ask the question was to answer it in the negative.

---

[139] 247 U.S. at 277. In conjunction with his remarks about the Tenth Amendment in *Holland,* consider, for example, this remark from Holmes's *Dagenhart* dissent: "I should have thought that the most conspicuous decisions of this Court had made it clear that the power to regulate commerce *and other constitutional powers* could not be cut down or qualified by the fact that it might interfere with the carrying out of the domestic policy of any State." 247 U.S. at 278. (Emphasis added.)

[140] 252 U.S. at 434.

Holmes, however, did not stop at that point. Instead, in the midst of his remarks on the organic nature of the Constitution and on the inapplicability of the Tenth Amendment, he observed that the Bird Treaty "d[id] not contravene any prohibitory words to be found in the Constitution."[141] He thereby implied another and more general test for assessing the constitutional validity of treaties. This, which can be labeled the "no-conflict test," was perhaps required to square Holmes's organic conception of the Constitution with the more general American notion of constitutionalism in the sense of limited government. For if national interest were an expansible concept, then, by itself, the national interest test gave the treaty power a potentially unlimited reach. But the no-conflict test set outer limits beyond which not even the growth of national interest could carry the treaty power. In that sense, the no-conflict test was superior to the national interest test.

At the same time, the no-conflict test bolstered the national interest test within those limits, and this was its immediate role within the *Holland* opinion. Even if the states were competent to preserve migratory birds, said Holmes, "the question is [still] whether the United States is forbidden to act."[142] National interest in birds would not cease to afford constitutional support to the Migratory Bird Treaty even in the face of a showing that the states severally could protect the creatures. National interest became irrelevant only if there was a specific provision barring federal action. Thus emerges the fundamental importance of Holmes's review of the Tenth Amendment's relation to treaty adjudication. It aimed at determining whether the Amendment contained restrictions which would set limits on treaties under the no-conflict test.

V. Justice Holmes's Opinion: An Evaluation

Justice Holmes eschewed defending the Migratory Bird Treaty Act of 1918 as a proper regulation of interstate commerce or federal property. This is understandable. While such non-treaty arguments remained available despite their rejection by lower courts in *Shauver* and related cases and while they may have been persuasive to Holmes himself, it is doubtful that they could have carried a majority of the Supreme Court in 1920. Proponents of the 1913 bird protection law had themselves been uncertain of its

---

[141] *Id.* at 433.   [142] *Id.* at 435.

constitutionality, but saw a treaty as offering a firm foundation. Moreover, the differing responses of the lower courts to the two bird protection laws is instructive. The treaty did make a difference in judicial outcome. In *Holland* itself, the district court had agreed that the 1918 law would have been unconstitutional were it not enacted pursuant to a treaty. Finally, in its brief before the Supreme Court in *Holland*, the Government relegated its non-treaty arguments to an appendix, indicating what several well-placed and interested contemporaries thought would impress the Court.

In operative terms, Holmes approached the testing of treaties far differently than most of his judicial contemporaries would have approached the testing of ordinary legislation. The minimal requirement for any federal action was an express or implied constitutional authorization, and there were also relevant prohibitions to be accommodated. With legislation, both these considerations imposed real limitations. However, because the Constitution gave blanket authorization to the President to make treaties with the advice and consent of the Senate, the only substantial restriction on treaties for Holmes was that they not violate constitutional prohibitions. To be sure, they had to involve matters of national interest, but "national interest" was hardly a narrow category, particularly with Holmes's organic view of the Constitution.

Although Holmes did not review it in his opinion, there was solid judicial precedent for testing treaties by the no-conflict and national interest requirements, even in 1920.[143] The best-known

---

[143] See, *e.g.*, New Orleans v. United States, 10 Peters 662, 736 (1836); Doe v. Braden, 16 How. 635, 657 (1853); The Cherokee Tobacco, 11 Wall. 616, 620–21 (1870); Holden v. Joy, 17 Wall. 211, 242 (1872); Geofroy v. Riggs, 133 U.S. 258, 266–67 (1890); Downes v. Bidwell, 182 U.S. 244, 294 (1901) (White, Shiras, and McKenna, JJ., concurring); *id*. at 370 (Fuller, C.J., Harlan, Brewer, and Peckham, JJ., dissenting). For non-judicial comment affirming this point during the two decades preceding, and also roughly contemporaneous with, the *Holland* case, see 1 BUTLER, THE TREATY-MAKING POWER OF THE UNITED STATES 349–64 (1902); 1 WILLOUGHBY, THE CONSTITUTIONAL LAW OF THE UNITED STATES 493–504 (1910); CORWIN, NATIONAL SUPREMACY: TREATY POWER VS. STATE POWER (1913); TUCKER, LIMITATIONS ON THE TREATY-MAKING POWER 332–40 (1915); SUTHERLAND, CONSTITUTIONAL POWER AND WORLD AFFAIRS 141–62 (1919); Wright, *The Constitutionality of Treaties*, 13 AM. J. INT'L L. 242, 252–60 (1919); Boyd, note 3 *supra*, at 414–21. Of these commentators, it is especially noteworthy that even Butler, who sought to document the sweeping scope of the treaty power, recognized limitations to it largely comparable to those stated by Justice Field in Geofroy v. Riggs, *supra*, as quoted in text *infra*, at note 144. He nevertheless found discussion of such limitations "necessarily academic" and "practically of little value." 1 BUTLER, *supra*, at 363. For background to the specific issue presented in *Holland*, the best account is CORWIN, *supra*. For recent commentary on the constitutional status of treaties, see HENKIN 137–56, 383–404 nn.33–92.

formulation came from Justice Field, speaking for the Court in *Geofroy v. Riggs*:[144]

> The treaty power, as expressed in the Constitution, is in terms unlimited except by those restraints which are found in that instrument against the action of the government or of its departments, and those arising from the nature of the government itself and of that of the States. It would not be contended that it extends so far as to authorize what the Constitution forbids, or a change in the character of the government or in that of one of the States, or a cession of any portion of the territory of the latter, without its consent. . . . But with these exceptions, it is not perceived that there is any limit to the questions which can be adjusted touching any matter which is properly the subject of negotiation with a foreign country.

As Professor Henkin has observed, this statement and those like it "assert[ed] the fullness of [the treaty] power rather than restrictions upon it."[145] With the exception of the restriction, probably outmoded by 1920,[146] on ceding state territory, Field specified no well-defined limitations other than the requirement that a treaty not "authorize what the Constitution forbids." And as regards the supremacy of treaties over state constitutions and laws, this had received judicial recognition as early as 1796 in *Ware v. Hylton*,[147] as well as in subsequent cases.[148] (In this instance, Holmes did review the precedents.)[149] In short, Holmes's opinion hardly turned on novel judicial doctrine. Indeed, his approach had been anticipated by the lower court decisions favorable to the 1918 law,[150] and even by that guardian of the Tenth Amendment, Justice Brewer, some eleven years earlier.[151]

---

[144] 133 U.S. 258, 267 (1890) (dictum).

[145] HENKIN 141.

[146] CORWIN, note 143 *supra*, at 133–34, 190–91.

[147] 3 Dallas 199 (1796).

[148] See cases cited 252 U.S. at 434–35. In 1913, Professor Corwin was able to find only one federal case after the early 1880s in which a state's so-called reserved powers were recognized, and then only in dictum, as a limitation on the federal treaty power. That case was Cantini v. Tillman, 54 Fed. 969, 976 (C.C.D. S.C. 1893). See CORWIN, note 143 *supra*, at 195.

[149] 252 U.S. at 434–35.

[150] See cases cited in notes 80 and 87 *supra*.

[151] Keller v. United States, 213 U.S. 138, 147 (1909). Here the Court, per Justice Brewer, held unconstitutional, as beyond the delegated powers of the federal govern-

To go beyond an examination of judicial precedent and ask whether *Holland* accorded with the understandings of those who framed and ratified the Constitution might seem to impose an unfair standard. On quick reading, Holmes appeared to rule out recourse to the original understanding when he advanced his organic view of the Constitution. In fact, however, he only said that *Holland* should "be considered . . . *not merely* in [light] of what was said a hundred years ago."[152] In context, he was further arguing not that constitutional tests changed over time, but that the concept of national interest, which was central to one of his constitutional tests, was expansible; and this, he implied at least, was realized by those who called the nation into life.[153] So an examination of the original understanding of treaties is in order.

Consistent with the "plain words" of the document, the consensus in 1787–88 of Federalists and Antifederalists alike was that the Constitution made treaties supreme over state constitutions and laws.[154] In fact, one of the complaints which led to the Federal Convention of 1787 was the inability of the Confederation govern-

---

ment, a statutory provision that prohibited the willful and knowing harboring of a female alien within three years of her arrival in the United States for purposes of prostitution. In reviewing possible grounds for upholding the provision, Justice Brewer commented: "By § 2 of Article II of the Constitution, power is given to the President, by and with the advice and consent of the Senate, to make treaties, but there is no suggestion in the record or in the briefs of a treaty with the King of Hungary [of whom the harbored alien was a subject] under which this legislation can be supported." 213 U.S. at 147. Brewer, it should be noted, had written the opinion of the Court in Kansas v. Colorado, 206 U.S. 46 (1907), on which opponents of both the 1913 and the 1918 bird protection laws placed so much reliance. Hence the implication of his remark in *Keller* seems particularly significant in illustrating the unexceptional nature of the doctrine Holmes advanced in *Holland*.

152 252 U.S. at 433. (Emphasis added.)   153 *Ibid.*

154 THE FEDERALIST, No. 64, at 436–37 (Cooke ed., 1961) (John Jay); [James Iredell], *Answers to Mr. Mason's Objections to the New Constitution* . . . , in PAMPHLETS ON THE CONSTITUTION OF THE UNITED STATES . . . 1787–1788, at 355–56 (Ford ed., 1888) [hereinafter cited as FORD, PAMPHLETS], [David Ramsey], *An Address to the Freemen of South Carolina* . . . , *id.* at 376; *Letters of Luther Martin, IV*, in ESSAYS ON THE CONSTITUTION OF THE UNITED STATES . . . 1787–1788, at 361 (Ford ed., 1892); [Samuel Bryan(?)], *Letters of Centinel*, in PENNSYLVANIA AND THE FEDERAL CONSTITUTION, 1787–1788, at 580, 582, 610–11 (McMaster & Stone eds., 1888); *Petition of Group Chaired by Blair M'Clenachan to Pennsylvania General Assembly, id.* at 564; *Reasons of Dissent of the Minority, id.* at 476; 2 ELLIOT, DEBATES IN THE SEVERAL STATE CONVENTIONS ON THE ADOPTION OF THE FEDERAL CONSTITUTION . . . IN 1787 . . . , at 506–07 (2d ed. 1888) (James Wilson, Pennsylvania) [hereinafter cited as ELLIOT]; 3 *id.* at 500–14 (various speakers, Virginia). See generally 1 BUTLER, note 143 *supra*, at 341–92; Corwin, note 143 *supra*, at 66–74; CRANDALL, TREATIES: THEIR MAKING AND ENFORCEMENT 53–63 (2d ed. 1916); COWLES, TREATIES AND CONSTITUTIONAL LAW: PROPERTY INTERFERENCES AND DUE PROCESS OF LAW 18–49 (1941).

ment to obtain state compliance with treaty provisions.[155] And *Ware v. Hylton,* besides providing strictly judicial precedent, further evidences the understanding of those close in time to the period of framing and ratification.[156]

The more difficult task is to determine whether Holmes's view of the relation of treaties to the federal Constitution is historically correct. Here, in questioning whether treaties need meet any test other than being properly made, approved, and ratified, Holmes at least superficially ignored the conventional explanation for the wording of the Supremacy Clause. That explanation stresses that the clause was dictated not by a desire on the founders' part to place treaties above the Constitution but by the need to ensure continued validity for treaties made prior to the adoption of the Constitution.[157] Professor Henkin opines that "[p]erhaps Holmes did not know of that suggestion; perhaps he did not accept it."[158] The first possibility is doubtful. Missouri and Kansas advanced the explanation in their briefs before the Court. It is more likely that Holmes either did not accept the explanation or, accepting it, still concluded that treaties were to be held to tests different in practice from those applied to ordinary laws. Which of these alternatives is correct cannot be determined conclusively. The second, is consistent with the history that Holmes probably knew well,[159]

---

[155] *E.g.,* Farrand, *The Federal Constitution and the Defects of the Confederation,* 2 Am. Pol. Sci. Rev. 532, 535–36 (1908); see also Marks, Independence on Trial: Foreign Affairs and the Making of the Constitution 3–15, 151–52 (1973).

[156] "[T]he contemporaries of the constitution have claims to our deference . . . because they had the best opportunities of informing themselves of the understanding of the framers of the constitution, and of the sense put upon it by the people, when it was adopted by them. . . ." Ogden v. Saunders, 12 Wheat. 212, 290 (1827) (Johnson, J., separate opinion). The same consideration is pertinent to the following discussion of the ratification debates of 1787–88, the Judiciary Act of 1789, and the Jay Treaty debate.

[157] See, *e.g.,* Reid v. Covert, 354 U.S. 1, 16–17 (1957) (Black, J., plurality opinion); Rawle, A View of the Constitution of the United States of America 66–67 (2d ed. 1829); Corwin, The President: Office and Powers, 1787–1957, at 421 n.17 (1957); Schwartz, A Commentary on the Constitution of the United States: The Powers of Government 135–36 (1963); citations in note 97 *supra. Cf.* 1 Butler, note 143 *supra,* at 321; Corwin, note 143 *supra,* at 64; Crandall, note 154 *supra,* at 50.

[158] Henkin, 138.

[159] Consider for example, what Holmes must have reviewed in editing Kent's *Commentaries,* which include this footnote: "The treaty-making power is necessarily and obviously subordinate to the fundamental laws and constitution of the state, and it cannot change the form of the government, or annihilate its constitutional powers." Kent, Commentaries on American Law *287 n.(a) (Holmes ed. 1873) (quoting Joseph Story). See generally Howe, Justice Oliver Wendell Holmes: The Proving

and with the fact that he ultimately did offer constitutional tests
for treaties, whereas rejection of the conventional explanation could
tend to endow treaties with an extra-constitutional status.

The direct evidence from 1787 in support of the conventional
explanation for the wording regarding treaties in the Supremacy
Clause, and thus in support of the subordination of treaties to the
Constitution, is slim. The phrase "authority of the United States"
appeared early in the Philadelphia Convention, on 31 May 1787.[160]
Finally, on 23 August, the Convention approved the Supremacy
Clause with wording that "all Treaties made under the authority
of the U.S. shall be the supreme law."[161] On 25 August, the clause
"was reconsidered and after the words 'all treaties made,' were inserted . . . the words 'or which shall be made [.]' This insertion
was meant to obviate all doubt concerning the force of treaties
preexisting, by making the words 'all treaties made' to refer to them,
as the words inserted would refer to future treaties."[162] This passage from Madison's notes hints—but only hints—that "the authority of the United States" was designed to encompass both past and
future treaties. It also reveals that the phrase itself did not have
a precise enough intension to satisfy the delegates. Aside from this,
there is no direct evidence one way or another in the extant records
of the Convention to illuminate the status of treaties vis-à-vis the
Constitution. What seems likely is that, had the delegates firmly
sensed the wording of the Supremacy Clause freed treaties from
all constitutional controls save the requirements regarding their

<hr>

YEARS, 1870–1822, at 12–23 (1963). Holmes was familiar, too, with the Judiciary
Act of 1789, which in § 25, contained implications for the status of treaties under the
Constitution.

[160] See 1 FARRAND, THE RECORDS OF THE FEDERAL CONVENTION OF 1787, at 47 (rev.
ed. 1937) (amendment by Benjamin Franklin, 31 May 1787, to the "Virginia Plan")
[hereinafter cited as FARRAND]. The phrase also appeared in the provision of the initial
draft of the "New Jersey Plan" which evolved into the Supremacy Clause of the finished
Constitution. See id. at 245 (15 June 1787). The history of the phrase is conveniently
summarized in Myers, Treaty and Law under the Constitution, 26 DEPT. STATE BULL.
371, 373–76 (1952).

[161] 2 FARRAND, 389.

[162] Id. at 417. Professor Henkin correctly observes that the element of the Supremacy
Clause which is crucial to its encompassing preexisting treaties is the phrase "made, or
which shall be made." HENKIN, 138, 385 n.38. If, however, he means to suggest that
retention of "the Authority of the United States" was therefore designed to accomplish
other purposes (his text is not entirely clear about his position), I would disagree.
Clarity, rather than a studied avoidance of all redundancy, emerges as the object in
reformulating the clause on 25 August. See 2 FARRAND, 417; McLaughlin, The Scope of
the Treaty Power in the United States, I, 42 MINN. L. REV. 709, 730–31 (1958).

making and approval, then someone would have commented how the clause transgressed American notions of limited government.

Somewhat better evidence comes from the state ratification contests in 1787–88. Here, admittedly, the main concern was the impact treaties would have on state constitutions and laws. As already noted, Federalists and Antifederalists agreed that, consistent with the plain wording of the document, the clause did in fact establish the supremacy of treaties over state constitutions and laws.[163] Even the Antifederalist Federal Farmer, who observed that "[i]t is not said that these treaties shall be made in pursuance of the constitution—nor are there any constitutional bounds set to those who shall make them,"[164] most feared their impact on state law. In context, in fact, the "constitutional bounds" he was concerned with are the bounds necessary to preserve state constitutions and bills of rights. Still, the Federal Farmer's comment gives an inkling that he saw treaties as paramount to the United States Constitution.[165] The same suggestion emerges from an amendment proposed in Pennsylvania that "neither shall any treaties be valid which are in contradiction to the Constitution of the United States."[166] But the hint is again weak. The amendment may have reflected anxiety that treaties would have an extra-constitutional status, or it may simply have reflected the common Antifederalist desire to clarify the Constitution.

Running counter to such fears, and presumably better indicators of the Constitution's design, are several statements by Federalists in the Virginia ratifying convention, where the most extensive debate on treaties occurred. Responding to charges from Patrick Henry, the Federalists pointed primarily to the political check on treaties which the two-thirds rule in the Senate provided.[167] Three

---

[163] See citations in note 154 *supra*. For an example, apropos *Holland*, of what I believe to be an incorrect reading of the Antifederalists' concerns respecting treaties and the Supremacy Clause (that is, that they were fearful the Supremacy Clause made treaties supreme over the *federal* Constitution), see Deutsch, *Treaty-Making Clause: A Decision for the People of America*, 37 A.B.A.J. 659, 662 (1951).

[164] *Letters from the Federal Farmer to the Republican* in FORD PAMPHLETS, at 312. The "Federal Farmer," formerly thought to have been Richard Henry Lee, now appears unidentifiable. See Wood, *The Authorship of the* Letters from the Federal Farmer, 31 WM. & MARY Q. 299 (3d ser. 1974).

[165] See FORD PAMPHLETS, at 312–13. *Cf.* 4 ELLIOT, 215 (William Lancaster, North Carolina).

[166] PENNSYLVANIA AND THE FEDERAL CONSTITUTION, note 154 *supra*, at 463.

[167] 3 ELLIOT, 499–516. The issue also received less focused attention throughout the Virginia convention.

Federalists went further, however. James Madison denied the treaty power carried the authority to dismember the nation.[168] He also argued that "exercise of the power must be consistent with the object of the delegation," which, in the case of treaties, was "the regulation of intercourse with foreign nations, and is external."[169] Citing the provision of Article IV that "nothing in this Constitution shall be so construed as to prejudice any claims of the United States, or of any particular state," Governor Edmund Randolph concurred that the power carried no potential of dismemberment.[170] Moreover, the President and Senate, being subordinate to the Constitution whose creatures they were, could not by treaty alter the functions of the various departments of government.[171] The most restrictive reading came from George Nicholas, who interpreted the requirement that treaties be under "authority of the United States" as meaning "no treaty . . . shall be repugnant to the spirit of the Constitution, or inconsistent with the delegated powers."[172]

Those Virginia Federalists who discussed the issue thus perceived constitutional limits to treaties beyond the minimal requirement that they be properly made. That they failed to enumerate these limits in detail is not surprising. The problem which set the context for the Virginia debate was the narrow one of the threatened closing of the Mississippi River,[173] which explains the special concern about dismemberment of the nation. Furthermore, in the absence of a well-developed notion that the courts would exercise the power of constitutional review,[174] the question of well-defined limitations, such as might be applied by courts, was unlikely to arise. And, as Madison indicated, future developments would influ-

---

[168] *Id.* at 500, 514.   [170] *Id.* at 504.   [172] *Id.* at 507.

[169] *Id.* at 514.   [171] *Ibid.*

[173] See *e.g.*, *id.* at 500–02; MARKS, note 155 *supra*, at 197–98; Warren, *The Mississippi River and the Treaty Clause of the Constitution*, 2 GEO. WASH. L. REV. 271, 296–98 (1934); see also Bestor, *Separation of Powers in the Domain of Foreign Affairs: The Intent of the Constitution Historically Examined*, 5 SETON HALL L. REV. 527, 613–60 (1974).

[174] Although debate continues over the original understanding of judicial review, Professor Levy has aptly summed up the situation: "The precedents [as of 1787–88] tend not to show that the courts could pass on the constitutionality of the general powers of the legislatures." Levy, *Judicial Review, History, and Democracy: An Introduction*, in JUDICIAL REVIEW AND THE SUPREME COURT 1, 11 (1967). Hence, whatever germs of judicial review were present in the Constitution and in American constitutional thought at this time, I think it safe to conclude that the concept was not sufficiently developed so as to force contemporaries to face comprehensively the question of how courts would test treaties.

ence what objects might come within the scope of the treaty power.[175] In short, the occasion did not demand close attention to specific limitations. What does emerge, however, is (1) the view that treaties would be restricted to foreign objects (but with recognition that this was an expansive category), and (2) the implication, arising in various ways, that treaties could not infringe constitutional guarantees and prohibitions.

Consistent with these comments from the Virginia convention, the Judiciary Act of 1789 also hints that Americans originally concluded that treaties would be subject to constitutional tests. In its crucial § 25, the act provided for appeals to the Supreme Court by writ of error when the highest court of a state had questioned the validity of a treaty.[176] This, unfortunately, indicates nothing about what specific tests the framers of the act thought might be applied to treaties.

The fullest indication of early American conclusions about the constitutional status of treaties comes from a largely neglected aspect of the Jay Treaty debate in the House of Representatives in March and April of 1796.[177] The immediate issue in the debate was whether the House might, consistent with the Constitution's treaty provisions, pass independent judgment on the merits of a treaty in the course of appropriating funds needed to implement it, and thus whether the House could call on the President to provide papers relating to the negotiation of the treaty. (This is the aspect of the debate which has attracted the main attention of constitutional scholars.)[178] Nonetheless, the constitutional status of treaties also received comment, for the Federalists conceded that the House could pass independent judgment on treaties, but in only two instances: (1) where the treaty was, on its face, patently contrary to the nation's interests (in which case impeachment of the Presi-

---

[175] 3 Elliot, 514–15.

[176] 1 Stat. 73, 85–87, § 25 (1789).

[177] The only study I have found which gives extended attention to the debate's implications for the early understanding regarding constitutional limitations on treaties, as opposed to its implications for the House's role in the treaty process, is Byrd, Treaties and Executive Agreements in the United States 35–59 (1960). My conclusions from the debate largely parallel Byrd's. The subject is also briefly discussed in McLaughlin, A Constitutional History of the United States 260–61 (1935).

[178] See, e.g., Corwin, note 157 supra, at 182; Henkin, 161–62; Schlesinger, The Imperial Presidency 16–17 (1973); Berger, Executive Privilege A Constitutional Myth 171–79 (1974).

dent was a proper recourse), and (2) where it was contrary to the Constitution.[179]

Of interest here is the latter concession, although like the Judiciary Act of 1789 it does not by itself reveal what tests the Federalists were willing to apply to treaties. Abstractly, they had a range of options. They may only have been conceding that a treaty must be properly made and approved. At the other extreme, they may have been admitting the Republican contention that at least without implementing legislation, a treaty could not infringe on the legislative power shared by the House of Representatives.[180]

While most Federalists did not carefully elaborate what they conceived would constitute an unconstitutional treaty, they clearly rejected the Republican position, but stopped short of simply requiring proper form. The common assumption was given voice by Theophilus Bradbury of Massachusetts, who, after remarking that "no laws inconsistent with that [the Constitution] can be passed, either by the Treaty or Legislative power," said that "the only *other* checks" on the treaty power of the President were the requirement for Senate approval and the possibility of impeachment.[181] So the requirement that a treaty be properly made and approved was in addition to the requirement that it be consistent with the Constitution.

Two other Federalists were more specific. Republican James Madison had charged that the Federalist position would allow treaties to contravene specific prohibitions placed on Congress in the body of the Constitution and in the Bill of Rights.[182] James Hillhouse of Connecticut denied the accusation, commenting that "it is a sound rule of construction, that what is forbidden to be done by all branches of the government conjointly, cannot be done by one or more of them separately."[183] Daniel Buck of Vermont added detail:[184]

---

[179] For Federalist statements developing various aspects of this position, see 5 ANNALS, cols. 426–27, 430–35, 438–39, 462, 530–32, 551, 593–94, 609–10, 621, 660–62, 671, 684–703, 712, 715–16, 989, 1016, 1160, 1204 (1849) (7 March–27 April 1796). (There are two editions of the *Annals;* all citations herein are to the edition which carries the running head "History of Congress" on *each* page.)

[180] See, *e.g., id.,* cols. 493–94 (Madison, 10 March 1796), 738–43 (Gallatin, 24 March 1796).

[181] *Id.,* col. 551 (14 March 1796) (Emphasis added.)

[182] *Id.,* col. 491 (10 March 1796).

[183] *Id.,* col. 671 (22 March 1796).　　　　　[184] *Id.,* cols. 715–16 (24 March 1796).

Is it not agreed by all, that if a Treaty violates the Constitution, it is void in itself? Does not the Constitution particularly point out how the Legislature shall be formed; what shall be the qualifications of its members, and how they shall be elected? Does it not point out, with the same precision, how each other department of Government shall be constituted and organized; and does it not mark out the powers and limits of each? Does it not guaranty to each State its republican form of Government; and is not the right of altering or creating anew the Constitution reserved to the People? Look to the Constitution, and it will be found that the PRESIDENT, Senate, and this House, cannot, with all their combined powers, interfere with the personal security, personal liberty, or private property of the people, unless in raising taxes, and the mode in which this is to be done is directed by the Constitution.

Significantly, Republican William Giles of Virginia had already admitted the Federalists were not contending for an unlimited treaty power, but were qualifying it to the extent that "it is not to be supreme over the head of the Constitution."[185]

Besides agreeing that treaties must not contravene specific prohibitions of the Constitution, Federalists accepted another limit. James Hillhouse put it that a treaty must relate "to objects within the province of the Treaty-making power, a power which is not unlimited. The objects upon which it can operate are understood and well defined." "A treaty," he said, "is a compact entered into by two independent nations, for mutual advantage."[186] The same position was advanced by Theodore Sedgwick of Massachusetts. Of all those Federalists who spoke in the debate, Sedgwick was probably the most extreme advocate of a broad treaty power. For instance, while not actually contradicting his fellows on the point, he did not clearly admit that treaties could not contravene the Constitution.[187] But even he proposed a limited subject matter for treaties when he stated:[188]

---

[185] *Id.*, col. 506 (10 March 1796). He added: "[B]ut in every other respect they contend that it shall be unlimited, supreme, undefined." In context, this referred to the Federalist claim that treaties might properly involve the usual objects of international negotiation and that the House had no authority to pass further judgment on their merits after Senate approval had been given. *Id.*, cols. 505–07.

[186] *Id.*, cols. 660, 662 (22 March 1796).

[187] *Id.*, cols. 514–30 (11 March 1796).

[188] *Id.*, col. 516.

The power of treating between independent nations might be classed under the following heads: 1. To compose and adjust differences whether to terminate or to prevent war. 2. To form contracts for mutual security or defence; or to make Treaties, offensive or defensive. 3. To regulate an intercourse for mutual benefit, or to form Treaties of Commerce.

What emerges, then, from the Jay Treaty debate is a consensus. However they differed about the propriety of the House's calling on the President for papers and about the need to engage the House when treaties dealt with subjects ordinarily falling within the legislative realm, Federalists and Republicans saw treaties as subordinate, at minimum, to the Constitution. They agreed that treaties could not contravene its prohibitions and guarantees and could properly encompass only those objects of mutual interest between nations.[189]

Consistent with this consensus, and apropos *Missouri v. Holland*, the Jay Treaty debate also provides the earliest explicit instance I have found of what has become the common explanation of the wording of the Supremacy Clause. Several Federalists explained that the phrase "authority of the United States" was simply a convenient means of encompassing preexisting treaties made by the Continental and Confederation Congresses as well as those made under the Constitution by the President with the approval of the Senate.[190]

The difficulty with Holmes's opinion therefore consists not in its reliance on the treaty power, nor, in the main, in the judicial and historical warrants underlying the tests he proposed for treaties.

---

[189] Accordingly, it is not surprising to find that a 1796 statute regulating the conveyance of Indian lands used the wording "treaty, or convention, entered into *pursuant* to the constitution." 1 STAT. 469, 472. (Emphasis added.) On the other hand, the Louisiana Purchase Treaty gave France and Spain commercial advantages in ports of Louisiana which they did not enjoy in other ports of the United States, and the treaty correspondingly made these Louisiana ports more attractive than others to French and Spanish shipping. The advantages continued for a period after Louisiana obtained statehood, in apparent violation of the clause of Art. 1, § 9, that "[n]o Preference shall be given by any Regulation of Commerce or Revenue to the Ports of one State over that of another." Farrand, *The Commercial Privileges of the Treaty of 1803*, 7 AM. HIST. REV. 494 (1902).

[190] 5 ANNALS, cols, 548 n.† (Bradbury, 14 March 1796), 669 (Hillhouse, 22 March 1796), 721 (Goodrich, 24 March 1796). *Cf. id.*, col. 558 (Page, 15 March 1796). One Republican made explicit the more restrictive reading that was implicit in many other Republican comments: that the "authority of the United States," under which treaties were to be made, comprised not only the Constitution, but also all existing laws. Hence a treaty contrary to existing law would be invalid. *Id.*, col. 578 (Brant, 15 March 1796). *Cf. id.*, cols. 592–93 (Findley, 16 March 1796).

Instead, the problem is this: Holmes raised the question whether there were any limits to treaties so as to hint that there were none, and he then buried his actual answer—that is, his proposed limitations—in passages which lacked precision and were far more striking for their general constitutional ideas and aphorisms. As a result, he practically encouraged misinterpretation of the Court's decision. Thus, at one extreme, citing and quoting *Missouri v. Holland*, a California judge commented in 1937 that "[u]nder the present state of the law it may be conceded that it is uncertain whether there is any limitation at all on the treaty-making power of the federal government."[191] At the other, a congressman alleged in 1974 that the decision supported the proposition "that one . . . limit [to the treaty-making power] is that what an act of Congress could not do unaided, in derogation of the power of the Constitution, a treaty cannot do."[192]

Now state judges and federal congressmen, while bound to uphold the Constitution, are not always the most astute commentators on it. Yet the intense controversy which raged over *Missouri v. Holland* in the 1950s, during the Bricker Amendment debate, reveals a similar picture. Not only congressmen, who might be accused of political perversity in the episode, but also legal scholars were able to read quite different meanings into the *Migratory Bird* opinion. And some thirty years earlier, even so highly regarded a constitutionalist as Thomas Reed Powell could say of the opinion, in evident disregard of certain of Holmes's comments, that "[i]ts hint that there may be no other test to be applied than whether the treaty has been duly concluded indicates that the court might hold that specific constitutional limitations in favor of individual liberty and property are not applicable to deprivations wrought by treaties."[193] In fine, the opinion fits the pattern suggested by

---

[191] Tokaji v. State Bd. of Equalization, 20 Cal. App.2d 612, 617 (1937). See United States v. Reid, 73 F.2d 153, 155 (9th Cir. 1934). Quite inexplicably, the quoted statement from *Tokaji* was followed by a quotation from *Holland* which included Holmes's comment, "We do not mean to imply that there are no qualifications to the treaty-making power; but they must be ascertained in a different way." 20 Cal. App.2d at 617.

[192] 120 CONG. REC. at S.465 (daily ed. 1974) (Sen. William L. Scott, 28 Jan. 1974, discussing the proposed American adherence to the Genocide Convention).

[193] Powell, *supra* note 3, at 13. Admittedly Professor Powell's next sentence read: "It would be going a step further to extend the same immunity to legislation enforcing treaties." *Id.* But I fail to see that this addition substantially rectified his interpretation of the limits Holmes placed on treaties. If anything, it compounded the error by ignoring Holmes's evident willingness to judge treaties and legislation implementing them by the same standards. See text *supra*, at note 119.

Justice Frankfurter, surely an admirer of Holmes, when he wrote that Holmes "spoke for the Court, in most instances tersely and often cryptically."[194] Similarly, Justice Brandeis, Holmes's colleague on the bench, might have had *Holland* in mind in remarking that Holmes did not "sufficiently consider the need of others to understand."[195]

VI. HOLLAND'S IMPACT AND LATTER-DAY SIGNIFICANCE

Did *Missouri v. Holland* have an impact on the law of the Constitution? At one level, obviously yes. In the 1930s and early 1940s, to be sure, courts evidenced a willingness to uphold conservation activities under the Commerce Clause, independent of a treaty base.[196] But in the doctrinal climate of the 1920s and early 1930s, the decision in *Holland* did facilitate federal conservation policy and thus influenced not only law but also America's natural environment. It established the validity of the 1918 Migratory Bird Treaty Act,[197] thereby "first plac[ing] this new policy [of bird protection] on a firm foundation."[198] It also contributed a constitutional base for such further conservation efforts as federal

---

[194] Federal Maritime Board v. Isbrandtsen Co., 356 U.S. 481, 523 (1958) (dissenting).

[195] Quoted in BICKEL, THE UNPUBLISHED OPINIONS OF MR. JUSTICE BRANDEIS 226–27 (1957). Regarding Holmes's cryptic style, see Rogat, *Mr. Justice Holmes: A Dissenting Opinion*, 15 STAN. L. REV. 3, 9–10 & nn.26–33 (1962).

[196] Bogle v. White, 61 F.2d 930, 931 (5th Cir. 1932); Cerritos Gun Club v. Hall, 96 F.2d 620, 623–28 (9th Cir. 1938); Bailey v. Holland, 126 F.2d 317, 321 (4th Cir. 1942). Interestingly, the Court of Appeals in the *Cerritos Gun Club* case took issue with Holmes's contention in *Holland* that title to migratory birds was a dubious concept. Said the Court: "Naturalists and the public at large have learned much about the habits and actual and possible domestication of these migratory fowl since Mr. Justice Holmes wrote [his] opinion." 96 F.2d at 624. As items of property, the birds were thus articles in commerce. *Id.* at 623–27. But *cf.* Toomer v. Witsell, 334 U.S. 385, 401 (1948); Takahashi v. Fish and Game Commission, 334 U.S. 410, 421 (1948) (both using *Holland* to support contention that fish are not in the possession of anyone in the ordinary property sense); Russo v. Reed, 93 F. Supp. 554, 560 (D. Me. 1950); Koop v. United States, 296 F.2d 53, 59 (8th Cir. 1961) (both using *Holland* to support contention that state ownership of wildlife is doubtful).

[197] For cases citing *Holland* in this connection, see Shouse v. Moore, 11 F. Supp. 784, 785 (E.D. Ky. 1935); Cerritos Gun Club v. Hall, 21 F. Supp. 163, 165 (S.D. Cal. 1936), *aff'd* 96 F.2d 620 (9th Cir. 1938); Cochrane v. United States, 92 F.2d 623, 626–27 (7th Cir. 1937); United States v. Reese, 27 F. Supp. 833, 836 (W.D. Tenn. 1939); Lansden v. Hart, 180 F.2d 679, 683 (7th Cir. 1950); Bishop v. United States, 126 F. Supp. 449, 450–51 (Ct. Cl. 1954); Converse v. United States, 227 F.2d 749, 750 (6th Cir. 1955).

[198] United States v. Otley, 34 F. Supp. 182, 191 (D. Ore. 1940).

wildlife preserves, reforestation projects, and associated state land donations.[199]

At another level, the case's impact is more difficult to assess. Precisely because it accorded with judicial precedent as to the supremacy of treaties over state law, and because it recognized, however cryptically, the commonly accepted limits to treaties, it hardly staked out new ground. It nevertheless fulfilled the prophecy of one commentator ten years earlier "that the *obiter* doctrine that the reserved rights of the States may never be infringed upon by the treaty-making power will sooner or later be frankly repudiated by the Supreme Court."[200] Accordingly, it served as convenient precedent in later cases which drew into issue the supremacy of treaties or executive agreements over state law.[201] Meanwhile, it also bolstered dicta that treaties could not authorize what the Constitution forbade and must involve matters of national interest.[202] Finally, in 1957, Justice Black explained that "nothing in *Missouri v. Holland* . . . is contrary to the position taken here [that treaties must not contravene constitutional guarantees]. There the Court carefully noted that the treaty involved was not inconsistent with any specific provision of the Constitution."[203]

More specifically, Holmes's passage about an organic constitution that takes shape from, and grows with, the nation's history and needs[204] has proved eminently quotable and serviceable. In the

---

[199] United States v. 2,271.29 Acres, 31 F.2d 617, 621 (W.D. Wis. 1928); United States v. 546.03 Acres, 22 F. Supp. 775, 777 (W.D. Pa. 1938); *In re* United States, 28 F. Supp. 758, 763–64 (W.D. N.Y. 1939); Swan Lake Hunting Club v. United States, 381 F.2d 238, 242 (5th Cir. 1967).

[200] 1 WILLOUGHBY, note 143 *supra*, at 503. Whether Willoughby himself thought *Holland* fulfilled his prediction is unclear, for he included the same statement at page 569 in his 1929 edition.

[201] Asakura v. Seattle, 265 U.S. 332, 341 (1924); Santovincenzo v. Egan, 284 U.S. 30, 40 (1931); United States v. Belmont, 301 U.S. 324, 331–32 (1937); Amaya v. Stanolind Oil and Gas Co., 158 F.2d 554, 556 (5th Cir. 1947); Power Authority of New York v. F.P.C., 247 F.2d 538, 545 (D.C. Cir. 1957) (Bastion, J., dissenting). *Cf.* United States v. California, 332 U.S. 19, 45 (1947) (Frankfurter, J., dissenting); Sohappy v. Smith, 302 F. Supp. 899, 912 (D. Ore. 1969).

[202] Asakura v. Seattle, 265 U.S. 332, 341 (1924); Amaya v. Stanolind Oil and Gas Co., 158 F.2d 554, 556 (5th Cir. 1947); Power Authority v. Federal Power Commission, 247 F.2d 538, 542 (D.C. Cir. 1957); Pierre v. Eastern Air Lines, 152 F. Supp. 486, 488 (D.N.J. 1957).

[203] Reid v. Covert, 354 U.S. 1, 18 (1957) (plurality opinion).

[204] 252 U.S. at 433.

Mortgage Moratorium Case,[205] this comment, along with Chief Justice Marshall's in *McCulloch v. Maryland* about "a constitution intended to endure for ages to come,"[206] aided Chief Justice Hughes in demonstrating that "[i]t is no answer to say that this public need [for mortgage payment relief] was not apprehended a century ago, or to insist that what the provision of the Constitution [concerning the obligation of contracts] meant to the vision of that day it must mean to the vision of our time."[207] The same passage from Holmes's opinion has been enlisted to support broadened individual protection in the areas of denaturalization,[208] racial discrimination,[209] and malapportionment of voting districts.[210] But *Holland* also carries the contrary potential as illustrated by Justice Frankfurter's use of it in *Dennis,* to the end that the federal government possessed authority, commensurate with national needs, to protect national security.[211] And again emerging on the side of governmental authority over the individual, the case has received mention in lower

---

[205] Home Building and Loan Assoc. v. Blaisdell, 290 U.S. 398 (1934).

[206] McCulloch v. Maryland, 4 Wheat. 316, 407 (1819), quoted more extensively in 290 U.S. at 443.

[207] 290 U.S. at 443. For quotations, in turn, of Hughes's quoting Holmes, see, *e.g.,* Campbell v. Alleghany Corp., 75 F.2d 947, 955 (4th Cir. 1935) (upholding Federal Bankruptcy Act of 1934); Gomillion v. Lightfoot, 270 F.2d 594, 604 (5th Cir. 1959) (Brown, J., dissenting, and contending that a gerrymander had occurred, contrary to the spirit of the Constitution). *Rev'd* 364 U.S. 339 (1960) (held to be violation of Fifteenth Amendment). Intriguingly, four years before the *Mortgage Moratorium* case, a federal district judge used the same passage from *Holland* that Hughes quoted, but for the opposite purpose of restricting governmental power. Simply because the Constitution specified an amendment process, the judge argued, its terms could not always be followed literally, for the spirit of the document had to be considered. See United States v. Sprague, 44 F.2d 967, 981 (D.N.J. 1930) (holding the Prohibition Amendment unconstitutional), *rev'd* in 282 U.S. 716 (1931).

[208] Baumgartner v. United States, 322 U.S. 665, 673 (1944).

[209] Bell v. Maryland, 378 U.S. 226, 316–16 (1964) (Goldberg, J., concurring).

[210] Fortson v. Morris, 385 U.S. 231, 247–48 (1966) (Fortas, J., dissenting).

[211] Dennis v. United States, 341 U.S. 494, 519–20 (1951) (Frankfurter, J., concurring). For other uses of *Holland* to support the proposition that where national action is required, the necessary power will likely be found to exist, see United States v. American Bond & Mortgage Co., 31 F.2d 448, 454 (N.D. Ill. 1929); *In re* United States, 28 F. Supp. 758, 763–64 (W.D. N.Y. 1939). *Cf.* Kentucky Whip and Collar Co. v. Illinois Central Railroad Co., 12 F. Supp. 37, 42 (W.D. Ky. 1935). Apropos the 1974 impeachment debate, a federal Court of Appeals judge, speaking off the bench, found *Holland* to support the notion that a President has considerable latitude in the exercise of his duties; hence for him to be impeached and convicted for exercising such discretion might provide grounds for Supreme Court review of his conviction. Gibbons, *The Interdependence of Legitimacy: An Introduction to the Meaning of Separation of Powers,* 5 SETON HALL L. REV. 435, 485–86 n.218 (1974).

court dicta that even absent other constitutional grounds, federal narcotic drug legislation could be upheld as a necessary and proper means of implementing various drug treaties to which the United States is a party.[212]

Still, Professors Chafee, Sutherland, and Henkin have argued persuasively that the Court's post-1937 acquiescence in federal programs based on the taxation and commerce powers and on the Fourteenth Amendment has deprived *Missouri v. Holland* of much of its earlier significance. Legislation which in the 1920s and early 1930s might only have passed judicial scrutiny were it pursuant to a treaty now could easily stand alone.[213] The obvious example involves regulation of child labor.[214] After the Court twice struck down child labor laws, in 1918 and 1922,[215] some proponents of regulation toyed with the treaty route, seeing no other alternative save the uncertain course of constitutional amendment.[216] (An amendment was sent to the states but received only twenty-eight ratifications.)[217] Then, in 1941, the Court upheld the New Deal's Fair Labor Standards Act, which included child labor provisions, on grounds that Congress had absolute control over commerce.[218] But, somewhat paradoxically, the *Migratory Bird Case* may itself

---

[212] United States v. Eramdjian, 155 F. Supp. 914, 920 (S.D. Cal. 1957); United States v. Contrades, 196 F. Supp. 803, 812 (D. Hawaii 1961); United States v. Rodriguez-Camacho, 488 F.2d 1220, 1222 (9th Cir. 1972); United States v. LaFroscia, 354 F. Supp. 1338, 1341 (S.D. N.Y. 1973); United States v. Maiden, 355 F. Supp. 743, 749 n.5 (D. Conn. 1973). The suggestion appeared earlier, but without reference to *Holland*, in Stutz v. Bureau of Narcotics, 56 F. Supp. 810 (N.D. Cal. 1944).

[213] Chafee, *Federal and State Powers under the U.N. Covenant on Human Rights*, 1951 Wis. L. Rev. 389, 400–24; Sutherland *Restricting the Treaty Power*, in A.A.L.S. Selected Essays on Constitutional Law, 1938–1962, at 160, 180 (1963); Henkin, note 79 *supra*, at 913–22; Henkin, 147.

[214] Wood, note 111 *supra, passim*. The drive to enact child labor legislation and to obtain its validation by the Supreme Court contains striking similarities to the movement for protection of migratory birds. The striking dissimilarity, of course, is the ultimate fate of the two efforts in the pre-1937 Court: the birds fared far better than the children, for reasons quite understandable within the doctrinal climate of the day.

[215] Hammer v. Dagenhart, 247 U.S. 251 (1918); Bailey v. Drexel Furniture Co., 259 U.S. 20 (1922).

[216] *See* Boyd, note 3 *supra*, at 429–31; Jackson, *The Tenth Amendment versus the Treaty-Making Power*, 14 Va. L. Rev. 331, 332 (1928) (attacking the validity of a child labor treaty); Note, 22 Mich. L. Rev. 457 (1924) (defending the validity of a child labor treaty).

[217] Congressional Quarterly, Guide to the Congress of the United States 287 (1971).

[218] United States v. Darby, 312 U.S. 100 (1941).

have aided the judicial transformation which diminished its own importance, for Holmes's opinion arguably bolstered governmental activism.

Holland's faded significance did not prevent it from figuring in an attempted constitutional change which, had it succeeded, would have had consequences far beyond anything Holmes and his brethren in 1920 could have imagined they were setting afoot.[219] In 1952, Senator John Bricker introduced an Amendment to the Constitution to limit the treaty power.[220] As reported out of committee in June 1953, the Amendment provided, among other things, that "[a] treaty shall become effective as internal law only through legislation which would be valid in the absence of a treaty."[221]

Although omitted from the version that came within one vote of Senate passage in February 1954,[222] this so-called "which" clause is a clue to part of the reasoning underlying the proposed Amendment. Bricker and others wished to eliminate what they saw as the Court-sanctioned route of amending the Constitution through treaty-making.[223] Highlighting the danger which the Amendment's backers thought needed remedying, Bricker characteristically told

---

[219] See, *e.g.*, Sutherland, note 213 *supra*, at 173–80.

[220] 98 CONG. REC. 899, 907–08 (1952). For background to the Amendment and the political dimensions of the fight over it, see Sutherland, note 213 *supra*, at 160–73; Schubert, *Politics and the Constitution: The Bricker Amendment during 1953*, 16 J. POL. 257 (1954); EISENHOWER, THE WHITE HOUSE YEARS: MANDATE FOR CHANGE, 1953–1956, at 340–48 (Signet ed. 1965); PARMET, EISENHOWER AND THE AMERICAN CRUSADES 305–12 (1972).

[221] S. REP. No. 412, 83d Cong., 1st Sess. 1 (1953). Between 1952 and 1957, the Amendment appeared in several versions. These are reprinted and compared in *Hearings on S.J. Res. 3 before a Subcommittee of the Senate Committee on the Judiciary*, 85th Cong., 1st Sess., foldout facing 373 (1958).

[222] 100 CONG. REC. 2358, 2374–75 (1954).

[223] "This decision [*Holland*] in effect, and really for the first time, opened the way for amending the Constitution of the United States by and through a treaty, because it proclaims that an otherwise unconstitutional law may become constitutional when, as, and if the President negotiates a treaty on the subject and obtains approval of the Senate." Holman, *Treaty Law Making: A Blank Check for Writing a New Constitution*, 36 A.B.A.J. 707, 709 (1950). Holman, a former president of the American Bar Association, was one of the chief instigators of the Bricker Amendment and had been advocating such action for several years. See PARMET, note 220 *supra*, at 306–07. Three years later, another supporter explained: "The 'which clause' . . . would restrict implementing legislation to legislation valid in the absence of a treaty and is imperative because the case of *Missouri* v. *Holland* . . . made it perfectly clear that the Federal Government may, so long as that decision stands, invade and destroy all reserved powers of the states, arrogate to itself fields of legislative competence within the area of reserved powers where none existed without treaty, and regulate the purely internal concerns of the states, and the affairs of the citizens through the use of the treaty making power." Hatch, *The Treaty-Making Power: "An Extraordinary Power Liable to Abuse,"* 39 A.B.A.J. 808, 809 (1953).

the Senate in January 1954 that Holmes had "suggested that 'under the authority of the United States' might mean 'nothing more than the formal acts required to make the convention.' " He further charged *Holland* had "repudiated" the early dictum "that the treaty power does not extend 'so far as to authorize that the Constitution forbids.' "[224] "One of the premises of that case [*Holland*]," he declared a week later, "is that Congress has unlimited power to legislate in implementation of a treaty."[225] Other supporters of the Amendment elaborated the need to correct the doctrines they alleged Holmes had advanced in legitimating a treaty made, as one article charged, "for the express purpose of conferring on [the federal government] legislative competence in domestic fields where it had none before."[226] For good reason an early student of the Bricker amendment debate labeled *Holland* "the *bête noire* of the [Amendment's] proponents."[227] Opponents correspondingly stressed that *Holland* did not place treaties and consequent legislation above the Constitution.[228]

---

[224] 100 CONG. REC. 942–43 (28 Jan. 1954). For virtually identical comments from Bricker, see Bricker & Webb, *Treaty Law vs. Domestic Constitutional Law*, 29 NOTRE DAME L. 529, 534–35 (1954).

[225] 100 CONG. REC. 1333 (4 Feb. 1954). This remark would of course have been accurate had Bricker said "in implementation of a *valid* treaty."

[226] Hatch, Finch & Ober, *The Treaty Power and the Constitution: The Case for Amendment*, 40 A.B.A.J. 207, 254 (1954). See Deutsch, *The Need for a Treaty Amendment: A Restatement and a Reply*, 38 A.B.A.J. 735 (1952); Finch, *The Need to Restrain the Treaty-Making Power of the United States within Constitutional Limits*, 48 AM. J. INT'L L. 57, 66–67 (1954); *Hearings on S.J. Res. 130 before a Subcommittee of the Senate Committee on the Judiciary*, 82d Cong., 2d Sess. 36–37 (1952) (statement of Alfred J. Schweppe, Chairman, Committee on Peace and Law through the United Nations of the American Bar Association) [hereinafter cited as *1952 Bricker Hearings*]; *Hearings on S.J. Res. 1 & 43 before a Subcommittee of the Senate Committee on the Judiciary*, 83d Cong., 1st Sess. 817 (1953) (testimony of Clarence Manion, former Dean of College of Law, University of Notre Dame) [hereinafter cited as *1953 Bricker Hearings*]; *Hearings on S.J. Res. 1 before a Subcommittee of the Senate Committee on the Judiciary*, 84th Cong., 1st Sess. 36–37 (1955) (comments of Sen. Dirksen) [hereinafter cited as *1955 Bricker Hearings*]; S. REP. No. 412, 83d Cong., 1st Sess. *supra* note 224, at 4, 6–7, 14, 16; 100 CONG. REC. 853–54, 1061–62, 1309–10, 1786–87, 2121, 2351 (comments of Sens. Butler of Md., Dirksen, Ferguson, Jenner, and Daniel, 27 Jan., 1, 4, 16, 23, 26 Feb. 1954). By 1955, however, at least some proponents of the Amendment were examining *Holland* more carefully. The majority committee report of that year stated: "Insofar as that decision relates to the first [that is, central] section of this amendment . . . the concern is not with the conclusion reached but rather with the expressions used in the course of the opinion." S. REP. No. 1716, 84th Cong., 2d Sess. 3 (1956).

[227] Schubert, note 220 *supra*, at 286 n.121.

[228] *E.g.*, Chafee, *Stop Being Terrified of Treaties: Stop Being Scared of the Constitution*, 38 A.B.A.J. 731, 732 (1952); Chafee, *Amending the Constitution to Cripple Treaties*, 12 LA. L. REV. 345, 354–56 (1952); Whitton & Fowler, *Bricker Amendment—Fallacies and Dangers*, 48 AM. J. INT'L L. 23, 30–40 (1954); Mathews, *The Constitutional Power*

The Bricker Amendment did not pass Congress, let alone enter the Constitution. At most, then, *Missouri v. Holland* served only to trigger and help fuel a national debate, although even in this regard its role needs qualifying. While the debate in legal periodicals and in the Senate contained frequent references to the case,[229] *Holland*'s importance pales amidst the complexities of historical causation. Reaction to several World War II agreements, alleged threats posed by the United Nations Human Rights and Genocide Conventions, and the frustrating "police action" in Korea all encouraged the movement for some kind of limitation on treaties and executive agreements.[230] In the absence of Holmes's holding that the Tenth Amendment was no bar to exercise of the treaty power and his easily misinterpreted remarks about other limitations on treaties, the legal and senatorial proponents of an Amendment might have lacked some of their ammunition. Also, the Amendment might have taken a different initial shape, perhaps without the "which" clause.[231] But such possibilities concerning an unsuccessful Amend-

---

of the President to Conclude International Agreements, 64 YALE L.J. 345, 377 (1955); Corwin, *Memorandum on Senate Joint Resolution 1 as Reported by the Judiciary Committee, January 11, 1954*, printed in 100 CONG. REC. 859 (1954); *1952 Bricker Hearings* 78–80 (testimony of Theodore Pearson of Bar Association of the City of New York); *id.* at 413 (memorandum submitted by Solicitor General Philip B. Perlman); *1953 Bricker Hearings* 905–06, 908, 910–12, 924–25 (statement of Attorney General Herbert Brownell); *1955 Bricker Hearings* 272–73 (statement of Bethuel M. Webster, former president of the Bar Association of the City of New York); S. REP. No. 412, note 221 *supra*, at 47 (minority views); S. REP. No. 1716, note 226 *supra*, at 26–27 (individual views of Sen. Kefauver); 100 CONG. REC. 658–59, 665, 1069–70, 2058–59 (Sen. Wiley, 22 Jan., 1, 19 Feb. 1954). See McLaughlin, *The Scope of the Treaty Power in the United States, II*, 43 MINN. L. REV. 651, 704–08 (1959).

[229] See, *e.g.*, citations in notes 223–28 *supra*. In his memoirs, President Eisenhower also recognized the role of *Holland* in the Bricker Amendment controversy. See EISENHOWER, note 220 *supra*, at 340–41.

[230] See, *e.g.*, Deutsch, note 163 *supra*, at 660–62; 98 CONG. REC. 907–14 (1952) (comments of Sen. Bricker and others on introduction of Bricker Amendment, 7 Feb. 1952); 100 *id.* at 934–37 (speech of Sen. McCarren, 28 Jan. 1954); Lofgren, *Mr. Truman's War: A Debate and Its Aftermath*, 31 REV. POL. 223, 236 (1969); PARMET, note 220 *supra*, at 308–09; THEOHARIS, THE YALTA MYTHS: AN ISSUE IN U.S. POLITICS, 1945–1955 105–06 & n.1, 131–33, 180–85 (1970).

[231] For example, Alfred J. Schweppe, chairman of the American Bar Association's Committee on Peace and Law through the United Nations, testified in 1953 that the "which" clause "[was] intended specifically to limit the doctrine of *Missouri v. Holland*." *1953 Bricker Amendment Hearings* 56. Similarly, the Majority Report on the Amendment in June 1953 indicated that *Holland* made necessary the "which" clause. S. REP. No. 412, note 221 *supra*, at 16. But the Report also indicated that the clause was "intended to correct the broad language in *U.S. v. Curtiss-Wright Export Corporation* [299 U.S. 304 (1936)]." *Id.* If the Amendment had passed Congress and then the states by narrow margins, it would be easier to assign a crucial influence to *Holland*.

ment hardly suggest that *Holland* substantially influenced the actual course of events.

VII. CONCLUSION

This much is unexceptionable: The Supreme Court's doctrinal commitments, *circa* 1910–20, doubtless dictated that if the Court were to uphold federal migratory bird legislation, it would have to do so on grounds other than the federal government's authority over interstate commerce or federal property. Advocates of bird protection suspected this, perhaps as early as 1911. A treaty with Great Britain was subsequently concluded in 1916 and provided a base for new legislation in 1918 to replace the constitutionally questionable Migratory Bird Act of 1913. The strategy of the bird lovers, as well as that of the government in declining to push a test of the 1913 act, bore fruit in 1920. Justice Holmes, speaking for the Court, upheld the 1918 law as a necessary and proper means of implementing the Migratory Bird Treaty. The treaty itself, he argued, was a proper exercise of the treaty power, involving a subject of national concern and contravening no constitutional prohibitions.

Less certain are the reasons for the controversy surrounding *Missouri v. Holland*. Three considerations, however, seem important to its origins. First, the decision validated federal legislation which would arguably have failed had the Court ruled on it in its original form, devoid of a treaty base. This gave superficial plausibility to contention that for practical purposes the Court had held a treaty could amend the Constitution. Second, the result in *Holland* was put into bolder relief by virtue of the narrow play the "old" Court normally allowed to federal activity. Third, Holmes's opinion, while resting on grounds which were well established and historically warranted, failed to explicate those grounds fully and carefully and failed as well to clarify sufficiently the limits to the treaty power.

If these considerations were in fact crucial, then because of his cryptic remarks Holmes must bear some responsibility for the ensuing debate. Yet it should be remembered that he spoke with the approval of the Court. In a broader sense, the Court, but not so much Holmes, bears responsibility for helping to create the doctrinal climate which both forced reliance on the treaty power and put into sharp relief the result accomplished through that reliance.

What remains unexplained is why the controversy should have persisted into the 1950s, by which time the Court's commitments had markedly changed. Viewed objectively, the case now lacked importance as a potential source of domestic federal authority; the post-1937 Court had discerned new bases for expanded federal activity. In the new climate of concern over foreign involvement and enlarged federal authority, politics of course figured prominently in the renewed debate, with Holmes's passages making good targets. In part, too, the proponents of the Bricker Amendment may simply have overlooked how the Court's post-1937 flexibility rendered *Holland* largely redundant.[232] But something deeper may have been at work. The "Golden Age" of the judiciary for *Holland*'s critics in the 1950s was undoubtedly the period from the 1890s to 1937. Yet it was during this period that the Court had decided *Holland*. So, to speculate, reversal of the decision through constitutional amendment promised not only protection from "internationalist" schemes in the post–World War II era; it also promised to close off an avenue of encroachment on state authority and individual liberty which even a future right-headed Court might otherwise again follow.

A similar congeries of fears, frustrations, and yearnings could conceivably revive national interest in the case.[233] More likely, *Missouri v. Holland* will remain interred in the casebooks and history texts—and properly so. What is unlikely is that it will find crucial new applications in the development of the American Constitution.

---

[232] HENKIN, 147.

[233] *Cf.* former Senator Bricker's plea in 1974: "[T]his matter [that is, the danger of treaties and executive agreements overriding the Constitution] is just as important now as it was twenty years ago. It is time for the public interest to be aroused—if the Constitution and the rights it guarantees are to be preserved." Bricker, *Bricker Amendment Still Apt Today*, Los Angeles Times, 10 Feb. 1974, § VI, p. 4, col. 5.

PETER G. FISH

WILLIAM HOWARD TAFT AND CHARLES EVANS HUGHES: CONSERVATIVE POLITICIANS AS CHIEF JUDICIAL REFORMERS

In the twentieth century the Chief Justice of the United States has played a leading part in judicial reform. A variety of conditions have been responsible for the development of this role, and foremost among them has been the creation of explicit institutional structures designed to facilitate reform.

The Chief Justice is "first among equals" on the Supreme Court over which he presides. Whether or not he is, in fact, more influential than his eight colleagues depends largely on his own skills and competencies.[1] But since 1922, the Chief Justice has sat as Chairman of the Judicial Conference of the United States. This institution composed of judges from the "inferior" federal courts, exercises broad responsibility for administration of business in the federal courts. Within its purview lie traditional subjects of judicial reform as well as more mundane housekeeping aspects of the court system. Thus the Chief Justice cannot avoid exposure to and direct involvement in judicial reform at the federal level and, to the extent issues of judicial federalism arise, at the state level as well. As conference

---

Peter G. Fish is Associate Professor of Political Science, Duke University.

[1] See Murphy, Elements of Judicial Strategy, c. 3 and authorities cited in n.1 of c. 3 (1964).

chairman in a periodic gathering of "unequals," the Chief Justice
is undisputed leader.[2]

During the decades of the twenties and thirties, the Chief Justice
of the United States came to fill a role which would gain permanence, that of chief judicial reformer. It was a role, however neutral in appearance, which permitted the presiding officer of the
nation's highest court to foster seemingly prosaic reforms of court
organization, jurisdiction, administration, and procedure. Yet such
alterations could pose far-reaching consequences for value alloca-
tions and power distribution among and between elements of the
larger political system.

At the annual Judicial Conference of the United States, the
American Law Institute, the American Bar Association meetings,
and circuit judicial conferences, William Howard Taft and Charles
Evans Hughes sounded reform themes strikingly similar in their
symptomatic analysis of judicial problems, yet very different in
their political theories and reform strategies. That they exhibited
similarities is hardly unexpected given the common threads coursing
through their backgrounds: Republicanism, previous judicial experience, presidency of the American Bar Association, prior elective office as President in the case of Taft and as Governor of New
York in that of Hughes, important appointive positions, Taft as
Secretary of War and Governor-General of the Philippines, and
Hughes as Secretary of State. As advocates of change in the judicial system, Taft and Hughes fell squarely into the mainstream of
the conservative reform tradition so dominant in the world of the
bench and bar. Both labored assiduously to ward off specific threats
to an independent federal judiciary and to preserve a social and
political equilibrium which seemed ever precarious.

I. Taft and Progressivism

To William Howard Taft, even the last days of the Ed-
wardian era were fraught with dangers. All about him churned
a "lack of respect for law and the weakened supremacy of the
law." Physical force and lawless violence appeared increasingly
"a calculated element in the winning of political and social issues."[3]

---

[2] See Fish, The Politics of Federal Judicial Administration cc. 1 & 2 (1973).

[3] Taft, *The Attacks on the Courts and Legal Procedure*, before the Economic Club of
Worcester, Mass., 13 May 1914, Series 9C. Taft Papers (Library of Congress).

Aider and abetter, if not prime cause, of this deplorable condition lay with progressivism of the social reform variety as distinguished from "efficiency progressivism" supported by leading members of the legal community.[4] It was the former that composed, in the words of the organizing committee of the American Law Institute "that radical section of the community which would overthrow existing social, economic and political institutions."[5]

Theodore Roosevelt, Robert M. La Follette, and George W. Norris numbered among the conservative reformers' chief antagonists. Such social progressives looked to government to ameliorate defects in the fabric of society.[6] But often they looked in vain as courts, particularly federal courts, struck down or otherwise emasculated legislative efforts to meet new industrial conditions. To progressives the "activist" superlegislative role of judges in construing constitutions and statutes in a manner according extensive protection to corporate property ranked as their fundamental objection to the judiciary.[7]

There existed two judicial systems, said Senator Norris, "one for the poor and the other for the well-to-do."[8] The poor were disadvantaged in the judicial process, not because the process was slow, costly, or inefficient, as conservative reformers argued. They lost out because federal judges had usurped the sovereignty of the people by means of judicial review and because the judges themselves were "not responsive to the pulsations of humanity."[9] The 1912 Progressive Party Platform minced no words in delineating a remedy. It demanded "such restriction of the power of the courts as shall leave to the people the ultimate authority to determine fundamental questions of social welfare and public policy."[10] The social progressive's answer to judicial supremacy was popular democracy. With it, fundamental changes could be expected

---

[4] WIEBE, THE SEARCH FOR ORDER: 1877–1920, at 176 (1967).

[5] *Report of the Committee on the Establishment of a Permanent Organization for the Improvement of the Law Proposing the Establishment of an American Law Institute*, 1 A.L.I., PROCEEDINGS 1 (1923).

[6] MOWRY, THEODORE ROOSEVELT AND THE PROGRESSIVE MOVEMENT 10–11 (1946).

[7] *Id.* at 214–15.

[8] New York Times, § VI, p. 5, col. 1, 23 April 1922.

[9] *Id.* at col. 3.

[10] *The Progressive Party Platform of 1912*, in HOFSTADTER, ed., THE PROGRESSIVE MOVEMENT: 1900–1915, at 129–30 (1965).

in the substance of judicial decisions, the selection and tenure of judges, restriction of their powers over juries, contempt and injunction powers, and the jurisdiction of their courts. The major premise, as Theodore Roosevelt put it in 1912, was that "the judge is just as much the servant of the people as any other official."[11] Democratic responsibility became the keystone of the Progressive arch.

But for Taft a popularly responsive judiciary was complete anathema. As President of the American Bar Association he decried the agitation with reference to the courts, the general attacks upon them, the grotesque remedies proposed of recall of judges and recall of judicial decisions.[12] Such progressive-sponsored proposals were "radically erroneous and destructive . . . a form of muckraking of the courts."[13] He objected to them precisely because they threatened to break down the independence or insularity of federal judges from the political process. For Taft found few of the virtues of the federal judiciary duplicated in the states. Elective judges and a tradition of lay judges in limited jurisdiction courts contrasted unfavorably with United States judges who received executive appointments and held tenure during good behavior. These two factors, he thought, assured not only independence from political influence but higher quality magistrates as well.[14]

"Why is it," Taft queried, "that every law-breaker prefers to be tried in a state court? Why is it that the federal courts are the terrors of evil-doers?"[15] The obvious answer was that in addition to presumed competence arising from their manner of appointment, federal judges enjoyed formidable powers over trials conducted in their courts, especially over juries. How different the situation in state courts "where opportunity is too frequently given to the jury to ignore the charge of the Court, to yield to the histrionic eloquence of counsel, and to give a verdict according to their emotions instead of . . . reason and their oaths."[16]

As Taft saw it, however, the real dangers of progressivism related to modification of then controlling case law, to the substance

[11] PRINGLE, THEODORE ROOSEVELT: A BIOGRAPHY 558 (1931).

[12] Taft, *Attacks on the Courts and Legal Procedure*, 5 KY. L.J. 1, 4 (1916).

[13] *Ibid.*

[14] Taft, *The Selection and Tenure of Judges*, address delivered at the American Bar Association Meeting, Montreal, 1–3 Sept. 1913, p. 10, Series 9C, Taft Papers.

[15] *Id.* at 11.   [16] *Ibid.*

of the judicial product. The more he thought about it, the more certain he became "that the real issue is the right of property and [of] socialism."[17] "[T]he whole Progressive Party program, including those portions affecting the judiciary, Taft argued, "intends the taking from the successful and the conferring on the unsuccessful that which the successful have earned."[18] Such welfarist policies would inevitably produce dire consequences for the individual and for society as a whole. As Taft saw it: "The great and tremendous advantage of the right of property is that it furnishes a motive to a man to exercise industry and self-restraint, and the more he saves and uses to reproduce itself the more he improves the general prosperity of the community."[19] Thus Taft devoutly believed that "the institution of property is civilization."[20]

Yet that fundamental institution appeared under siege. Responsive state legislatures had enacted legislation hostile to resident and nonresident corporations alike. Such laws called for discriminatory taxation, rate regulation, "sometimes . . . direct deprivation of vested rights," and "restrictions upon interstate commerce."[21] Injured by state laws, corporations sought out federal forums and protections there accorded them under the Fourteenth Amendment's Due Process Clause and Article I's Commerce Clause.[22] It was the mere existence of this jurisdiction which Taft believed to be the root cause of "the popular impression . . . that the Federal courts are the friends of corporations and protectors of their abuses."[23] After all, the federal courts had no choice. Their unpopular decisions arose directly from their jurisdiction. Furthermore, the people of the South and West, where winds of progressivism blew strongest, had materially benefited from investments of foreign, usually eastern, capital. The original investments were made on reasonable terms solely because of "the presence of . . . federal courts, where

---

[17] Taft to Gus Karger, 27 May 1913, Series 8, Taft Papers.

[18] Taft, *Address*, at the Banquet of the Union League Club of New York, the Union League of Philadelphia, the Republican Club of Boston, and the Republican Club of New York, 4 Jan. 1913, Series 9C, Taft Papers.

[19] *Ibid.*

[20] Taft, *Address*, before the New England Society of Detroit, 19 Dec. 1914, p. 15, Series 9C, Taft Papers.

[21] Taft, *Recent Criticism of the Federal Judiciary*, 18 A.B.A. ANN. REPTS. 247 (1895).

[22] Taft, note 14 *supra*, at 12–13; *Hearings on H.R. 661 on Additional Judges for the Eighth Circuit before the House Committee on the Judiciary*, 68th Cong., 1st Sess. 2 (1924).

[23] Taft, note 21 *supra*, at 249.

the owners of foreign capital think themselves secure in the maintenance of their just rights when they are obliged to resort to litigation."[24] Slings and arrows of unpopularity proved unavoidable
for the federal courts because as Taft put it with his usual clair-
voyance: "Men borrow with avidity, but pay with reluctance, and
do not look on the tribunal that forces them to pay with any degree
of love or approval."[25]

There would be a rising tide of attacks on the federal judiciary
as long as the states remained "laboratories of experimentation" and
fundamental rights constituted the chief subject of experimentation.
Even if states adopted direct democracy, or "nostrums," as Taft
termed them, their citizens' basic rights remained unimpaired "because the Federal Constitution and the Federal Courts offer a bulwark of protection upon which they can still rely."[26] He queried
a gathering of New York lawyers: "If it were not for the bulwark
of the Fourteenth Amendment . . . what might happen in such states
as Arizona, California, Oregon and other states which seem fad-
ridden?"[27]

Subversion of an independent federal judiciary marked a key
step on the progressive's path to social democracy. That path was
well marked. Its beginnings would require transformation of "a
Republican representative system of government to one of direct
and pure democracy."[28] Thereafter, law would become dependent "on the momentary passions of a people," expressed via initiative, referenda, and recall of judicial officials and decisions.[29] Taft,
for one, refused "to acquiesce in the substitution for the deliberate judgment of trained lawyers in the interpretation of . . . constitution and statutes, the fitful and uncertain vote of a probable
minority of an electorate that cannot in the nature of things understand . . . frequently complicated issues."[30] Judicial recall could
be defined neither as due process nor as binding legal precedent.

---

[24] Taft, note 14 *supra*, at 12.   [25] *Ibid.*

[26] Taft, *Address*, before the Electrical Manufacturers' Club, at Hot Springs, Virginia,
6 Nov. 1913, p. 14, Series 9C, Taft Papers.

[27] Taft, *Address*, before the New York State Bar Association at Buffalo, 22 Jan. 1915,
pp. 3–4, Series 9C, Taft Papers.

[28] Taft, note 3 *supra*, at 3.

[29] 2 PRINGLE, THE LIFE AND TIMES OF WILLIAM HOWARD TAFT: A BIOGRAPHY 766
(1939).

[30] Taft, *The Courts and the Progressive Party*, 186 SAT. EVE. POST 47 (28 March 1914).

It was "legalized terrorism," Taft as President argued when he vetoed the Arizona enabling act in 1911.[31] How, he asked, could a recall election take property from an individual who, but for the election, would have owned the property by virtue of a favorable judicial decision? "An election," he argued, "is not a judicial hearing. The parties in an electoral controversy do not have their day in court, and a day in court has been vouchsafed to parties litigant since the dawn of civilization."[32] Even if the sun had set on civilization, how could a recall decision be regarded as binding legal precedent? "It could not be," he maintained, "because there is no method of determining what the ground of the decision is. It is to be an exception grafted on the Constitution, an excrescence on a symmetrical body."[33] In short, democratization of the judicial process threatened to open the doors wide to majoritarian suppression of individual rights, especially property rights. As Taft told the Augusta Georgia Bar Association, the Progressives advocated an appeal "from that very independent judiciary that [is] to save us from a possibly tyrannous majority, to the tyrannous majority itself."[34]

Confronted by attacks and remedies advanced by those whom he considered "ultra reformers" and " 'hair trigger' gentlemen,"[35] Taft told the House Judiciary Committee in 1914 of his eagerness "to vindicate the [federal] courts by remedying the real objections to their administration of justice."[36] But he emphatically denied "that there is in the decisions of the courts, or the character of the judges, or the result of litigation that which justifies . . . radical innovation."[37] As he saw it, "the real difficulty with the courts is not in the courts themselves, and is not in the lawyers." The "real difficulty," Taft thought, "is a lack of dispatch of business and

---

[31] Quoted in MOWRY, note 6 *supra*, at 171. The proposed Arizona constitution provided for judicial recall.

[32] Taft, note 30 *supra*, at 10.   [33] *Ibid.*

[34] Taft, *Address*, before the Augusta, Ga., Bar Association, 14 March 1913, p. 6, Series 9C, Taft Papers.

[35] TAFT, POPULAR GOVERNMENT, ITS ESSENCE, ITS PERMANENCE AND ITS PERILS 182 (1913).

[36] *Hearings on Reforms in Judicial Procedure—American Bar Association Bills, before the House Committee on the Judiciary*, 63d Cong., 2d Sess. 17 (1914).

[37] Taft, *Address*, to the General Court of the Legislature of Massachusetts, at Boston, Mass., 18 March 1912, S. Doc. No. 451, 62d Cong., 2d Sess. 6–7 (1912).

the cost of litigation."[38] Tinkering with structures, administrative systems, and procedures could go far in resolving such mechanical problems. Clearly, reform to Taft meant "efficiency-as-economy" not "efficiency-as-social service."[39]

II. Hughes and F.D.R.

Chief Justice Charles Evans Hughes, like his predecessor, fit into the classic conservative reformer mold. Whatever his social reform and economic regulation achievements as Governor of New York,[40] his view of judicial reform was indistinguishable from that of Taft. As with Taft, valid judicial reform related to structure and procedure rather than to substance. In his 1932 address to the Fourth Circuit Judicial Conference at Asheville, North Carolina, he declared:[41]

> Criticism of courts should never be confused with criticism of the judicial function. It is the imperfection of the discharge of that function that is the target. It is the adaptation, the operation, of the machinery, not its purpose, that is called in question.

"Now, our business," he told the conference participants, "is to diminish friction in the machinery of the administration of justice, to improve that administration by preventing unnecessary delays, by dispensing with useless formalities, by cutting through a web of meaningless technicalities, by insuring speedy, expert, impartial, application of our laws, thus enabling our courts as completely as possible to achieve their aims."[42] Mobilizing bench and bar to oil and occasionally overhaul judicial machinery would prevent charges "well-laid by the public, of maladministration of justice in the United States."[43] Unlike Taft, however, Hughes demonstrated greater willingness to place blame for valid criticism of the courts on the behavior of crafty lawyers who "constantly foul our

---

[38] Taft, *Address*, before Connecticut State Bar Association, New London, Conn., 2 Feb. 1914, p. 9, Series 9C, Taft Papers.

[39] Wiebe, note 4 *supra*, at 176.

[40] See Wesser, Charles Evans Hughes, Politics and Reform in New York: 1905–1910 c. 13 (1967).

[41] Hughes, *Chief Justice Hughes Addresses Judicial Conference of Fourth Circuit*, 18 A.B.A.J. 445, 446 (1932).

[42] *Id.* at 447.   [43] New York Times, 28 April 1925, p. 4.

reputation by their utterances and their acts."⁴⁴ In the wake of several impeachment proceedings, he assailed judges "who by pettiness, petulance, arbitrary conduct or procrastination in rendering decisions . . . brought [their offices] into disrepute."⁴⁵ The process and personnel constituted sources of remediable judicial defects. The substantive law, the judicial function, remained sound. And given the prevailing influence of the Blackstonian view of judges as finders and expounders, not makers of law, little could be done about preordained substance. In fact nothing should be done. As president of the Association of the Bar of the City of New York, he told the assembled lawyers and judges that "there are fundamental difficulties arising from social conditions which lie beyond the reach of corrective means within our power."⁴⁶

President Franklin D. Roosevelt's Court-Packing Plan, announced on 5 February 1937, electrified the nation and galvanized Hughes into action. He had assumed the mantle of chief judicial reformer bequeathed by Taft by implementing reforms either instituted or advocated by his energetic predecessor: the Judicial Conference of the United States, the Judiciary Act of 1925, and the development and ultimate enactment in 1938 of the Federal Rules of Civil Procedure. The Court-Packing Plan, however, resembled in its ultimate source and configuration the kind of threat always feared by Taft. Its immediate source, however, was a coordinate branch of government, not remote states and their congressional representatives. It was a political attack from without the judiciary aimed squarely at the judicial function and the existing state of the substantive law. For his part, the President cloaked his proposal in the rhetoric of conservative judicial reform. He cited complaints "of the complexities, the delays, and the expenses of litigation in United States Courts. . . . Only by speeding up the processes of the law and thereby reducing their cost, can we eradicate the growing impression that the courts are chiefly a haven for the well-to-do."⁴⁷ Reorganization would promote efficiency and economy in the judicial branch. But Roosevelt's motives were transparent. He objected

---

⁴⁴ *Ibid.*

⁴⁵ *Address of the Chief Justice, Honorable Charles Evans Hughes,* 15 A.L.I., PROCEEDINGS 34 (1938).

⁴⁶ New York Times, 9 May 1928, p. 11.

⁴⁷ 6 ROSENMAN, ed., THE PUBLIC PAPERS AND ADDRESSES OF FRANKLIN D. ROOSEVELT 52 (1937).

to the Court's treatment of New Deal legislation designed to miti-
gate economic adversity by expansive national action. The country, he argued in a "fireside chat," could not yield its "constitutional
destiny to the personal judgment of a few men who, being fearful
of the future, would deny us the necessary means of dealing with
the present."[48] Interior Secretary Harold Ickes, a former Bull Moose
Progressive, exclaimed: "What a blow this will be to the prestige
of Chief Justice Hughes. . . . Of course, the proposal . . . is a distinct slap in his face, and in those of Van Devanter, McReynolds,
Roberts, and Sutherland, who have constituted the old guard
majority."[49] Hughes responded first with a short-run political strategy involving public refutation of the President's allegation of
delayed justice in the Supreme Court and subsequently in the inferior federal courts;[50] second, with a shift in judicial strategy,
which by altering the substantive work of the Court, reputedly
saved that institution from political attack;[51] and third, with a reform plan designed to insulate United States courts, and particularly the Supreme Court, from similar future onslaughts.

To the Chief Justice, the New Deal generally and the Court
Plan specifically merely symbolized an accelerating worldwide
trend toward national executive-centered government accompanied
by threats not only to courts and legislatures but also to federalism and ultimately to the rule of law.[52] With the strident sounds of
totalitarianism ringing out from Germany, Italy, the Soviet Union,
and Spain, he warned the 1938 Conference of Senior Circuit
Judges:[53]

> We are living in a time when all legal processes, all processes
> of reason, here and abroad throughout the world, are more or
> less subject to attack. We are living at a time when the dis-

---

[48] S. Rep. No. 711, 75th Cong, 1st Sess. 44 (1937).

[49] 2 Ickes, The Secret Diary of Harold L. Ickes: The Inside Struggle: 1936–39,
at 66 (1954).

[50] See communications between Hughes and members of the Senate Judiciary Committee on the state of the Supreme Court's docket, in 2 Pusey, Charles Evans Hughes
754–57 (1951). On the state of district court business, see New York Times, 29 Sept.
1937, p. 17, col. 3. For Attorney General Cummings's rebuttal of Hughes, see id., 30
Sept. 1937, p. 2, col. 2.

[51] See Mason, The Supreme Court from Taft to Warren 106 et seq. (1968).

[52] New York Times, 30 Sept. 1931, p. 26.

[53] Extract from the Proceedings of the Judicial Conference 174–92 (Sept. 1938);
Administration in the Federal Courts—Administrative Office Bill 12–13 (1938) (mimeo).

position . . . to control by executive force, makes a strong appeal to a multitude of people. . . .

Now the maintenance of this form of government [of limited powers] rests peculiarly with the Judiciary. . . . It is of vital importance that every step should be taken to keep the work of the courts so far as practically possible in the good opinion of the country. It is of the greatest importance that everything should be done to conserve the confidence of the people in the administration of justice.

So motivated, Hughes moved to take a leadership role in judicial reform. And when he last addressed the American Law Institute in the spring of 1941, he proclaimed success. The Chief Justice then observed that though "[T]he lamps of justice are dimmed or have wholly gone out in many parts of the earth . . . these lights are still shining brightly here."[54]

Like Taft, Hughes too believed "[o]ur government is based upon the principles of individualism and not upon those of socialism."[55] Property rights were of high importance; they were not absolute. Government might be required to intervene "with necessary restrictions and regulations not to curtail the liberty of the people, but to protect it."[56] Thus, Hughes recognized, in the words of Samuel Hendel, "the necessity for an extension of governmental activities to cope with the problems of modern life."[57] But the national government was not necessarily the sole source of such extension.

The key to protection of individual rights, including those relating to property, lay with development and maintenance of limited government. Balance not dominance constituted the hallmark of such government. During the 1924 presidential campaign Hughes had hammered at candidate Robert La Follette's judicial platform. That platform, he thought, would "destroy our system of government by its assault upon the jurisdiction of the Supreme Court in the interpretation of the Constitution."[58] It would un-

---

[54] *Address of the Honorable Charles Evans Hughes, Chief Justice of the Supreme Court of the United States*, 18 A.L.I., PROCEEDINGS 29 (1941).

[55] HUGHES, ADDRESSES AND PAPERS OF CHARLES EVANS HUGHES, GOVERNOR OF NEW YORK: 1906–1908, at 45 (1908).

[56] *Ibid.*

[57] HENDEL, CHARLES EVANS HUGHES AND THE SUPREME COURT 6 (1951).

[58] New York Times, 29 Oct. 1924, p. 8, col. 3. La Follette proposed a constitutional amendment that would permit Congress to overrule decisions of the Supreme Court.

balance the existing political structure, weaken national judicial power, and threaten "our stability without which the security and expansion of American enterprise are impossible."[59] Above all, the La Follette proposal endangered a viable federalism. Hughes argued that:[60]

> . . . the very existence of State governments depends upon the maintenance of the provisions of the Constitution. If Congress by passing a measure twice could make it effective despite the decision of the Supreme Court, then a majority in Congress could pass any act it pleased and override the authority of the States. Congress could destroy the States.

For Hughes, the path to ordered individual freedom lay through dual federalism judicially safeguarded. As early as 1908, he warned against "an unnecessary exercise of Federal power, burdening the central authority with an attempted control which would result in the impairment of proper local autonomy, and extending it so widely as to defeat its purpose."[61] Nearly twenty years later, he admonished the American Bar Association: "There may be an imperialism at home as well as abroad," and urged his listeners to rally to the defense of "our dual system of government" because it promoted freedom.[62] Concern for the political position of the Supreme Court and for the theory of dual federalism would be revealed not only in the jurisprudence of the Hughes Court but also in the essentials of the Chief Justice's major judicial reform, the Administrative Office Act of 1939.[63]

III. Reform Strategies: Taft

As judicial reformers, Taft and Hughes followed quite different paths although their goal of an independent, even a less popularly responsive and more insulated, federal judiciary remained identical. Nationalism ranked as the capstone of Taft's reform philosophy. How to enhance the power, legitimacy, and status of the national government's legal institutions? How to strengthen the kind of federal trial and appellate magistrates who were standing

---

[59] New York Times, 2 Nov. 1924, p. 17, col. 5.

[60] *Ibid.*   [61] Hughes, note 55 *supra*, at 51.

[62] Hughes, *Liberty and Law*, 11 A.B.A.J. 563, 565 (1925).

[63] 53 Stat. 1223 (1939).

firm against attempts by social reformers, labor organizers, and direct democracy advocates to subvert the then constitutionally protected right of property?

He entertained no illusions as to the source of threats to federal institutions and to private property. It was the states. They could be trusted neither to protect individual rights nor even to guarantee basic order. When violence erupted in the Colorado minefields in 1914, Taft thought it "noteworthy that Colorado is the only State in the Union that has adopted the recall of judicial decisions."[64]

Strong federal law and institutions were Taft's answer to ever unpredictable and sometimes dangerous exercises of state power. As Chief Justice, he and his colleagues would set records for wielding their power of judicial review to nullify state economic and social reform legislation. Taft, Willis Van Devanter, Pierce Butler, George Sutherland, and Edward T. Sanford constituted a majority bloc decidedly antagonistic to exercises of state authority. In fact in the 1929 Term of Court, Taft, Van Devanter, and Butler were the only members who never dissented in a direction favorable to state authority.[65] Taft's broad construction of national commerce power preempted state regulation, yet validated national legislation regulating social and economic forces.[66] In the realm of judicial reform Taft similarly sought to augment the power and status of the United States courts and thereby enhance their independence. Specifically he pressed for enactment of proposals which had long been germinating: (1) centralization of federal judicial administration; (2) nationalization of procedural rules; and (3) enhancement of the status and power enjoyed by federal appellate courts.

Establishment of the Conference of Senior Circuit Judges in 1922 capped Taft's campaign to bring at least some centralizing influence to administration of the United States courts. For a decade he had called for institutional machinery "to keep close and current watch upon the business awaiting dispatch in all the districts and circuits of the United States, and likely to arise during the ensuing year [and to estimate] the number of judges needed in

---

[64] Taft to George W. Wickersham, 29 April 1914, Series 8, Taft Papers.

[65] See SPRAGUE, VOTING PATTERNS OF THE UNITED STATES SUPREME COURT: CASES IN FEDERALISM, 1889–1959, at 89–97 (1968).

[66] See Kutler, *Chief Justice Taft, National Regulation, and the Commerce Power*, 51 J. AM. HIST. 651–58 (1965).

the various districts to dispose of such business."[67] Reflecting his hierarchical theory of administration which became apparent in *Myers v. United States*,[68] he argued for introducing "into the administration of justice the ordinary business principles in successful executive work, of a head charged with the responsibility of the use of the judicial force at places and under conditions where the judicial force is needed."[69]

The Act of 1922 provided Taft and his successors with an information and communication system, at first quite rudimentary, a policy-making institution with ready access to Congress and the media, and a vehicle for centralized supervision of the geographically remote district courts.[70] The act failed, however, to provide him with a "flying squadron" of national judges-at-large who might be freely assigned to congested courts. Such a departure from historic principles of localism fell before heated congressional opposition. Nevertheless, the Conference, together with the expanded power of the intercircuit assignment of resident judges,[71] offered Taft some hope of meeting those criticisms of the courts which he regarded as valid: delayed justice, immobile and dilatory judges, high court fees,[72] abuses in the appointment of receivers, and misconduct in the court clerk's office.[73] The Judicial Conference would act as a centralized catalyst to promote speedy, economical, efficient, and honest federal justice.

Nationalization of federal civil procedure ranked high among Taft's goals. As President he had declared: "One great crying need in the United States is cheapening the cost of litigation by simplifying judicial procedure and expediting final judgment."[74] Delays and confusion in the administration of federal justice arose from the Conformity Act of 1872.[75] Requiring adherence by federal courts to state procedures in all civil cases at common law, that act spawned a great diversity of procedures in federal tribunals. These

---

[67] Taft, *Address of President*, 39 A.B.A. REPT. 384 (1914).

[68] 272 U.S. 52 (1926).   [69] Taft, note 3 *supra*, at 16.

[70] Taft, *Informal Address*, 46 A.B.A. REPT. 561, 564 (1921).

[71] 42 STAT. 837, 839 (1922). Section 3 extended the intercircuit assignment power formerly confined to the Second Circuit. 38 STAT. 203 (1913).

[72] Taft, *The Delays of the Law*, 18 YALE L.J. 28, 35 (1908).

[73] TAFT, note 35 *supra*, at 212–13.

[74] MASON, WILLIAM HOWARD TAFT: CHIEF JUSTICE 114 (1965).

[75] 17 STAT. 197 (1872).

variations reflected, of course, different state procedures on which, by the act, federal procedure was patterned. Thus, common law pleadings, rooted in the old forms of action, characterized federal procedure in some United States district courts while modern code pleading typified that in adjacent districts.

Under the leadership of Taft, Roscoe Pound, and its congressional lobbyist, Thomas W. Shelton, the American Bar Association launched, in 1912, what became a long-term battle for a uniform system of judicial procedure. Ten years later, the proposed reform was expanded to include not merely modernization of procedures at law but also the merger of law and equity procedures in one form of civil action.[76] Billed by conservative reformers as a cost-reduction step of particular benefit to poor litigants, federal procedural reform enjoyed strong support from the business community. The Credit Men's Association, Chamber of Commerce of the United States, Southern Commercial Congress, and National Civic Federation all endorsed it.[77] Under the existing system, interstate business involved in federal court litigation required the assistance of numerous different expert federal practitioners familiar with state procedures used in the various district courts.[78] Corporation lawyers with multistate federal practices would derive substantial advantages from a single, simplified procedural code.[79] Taft eschewed articulation of the subtle direct benefit of procedural reform to corporate property interests seeking access to and a haven in federal courts.[80] Shelton, however, minced no words in telling the House Judiciary Committee that "it must appeal to you that the courts were created for the benefit of commerce and society, and that if there were no businesses we would need no courts. Therefore . . . you ought to do that thing which will meet most largely with the approval of the business men of the country."[81]

Congress hesitated chiefly because of opposition from Progres-

---

[76] *Hearings on S. 2060 and S. 2061 on Procedure in Federal Courts before the Senate Committee on the Judiciary*, 68th Cong., 1st Sess. 75–77 (1924).

[77] *Hearings*, note 36 *supra*, at 19.

[78] *Hearings on H.R. 2377 and H.R. 90 on Procedure in Federal Courts before House Committee on the Judiciary*, 67th Cong., 2d Sess., 11 (1922).

[79] *Id.* at 25.

[80] Taft, *Delays and Defects in the Enforcement of Law in This Country*, 187 No. Am. Rev. 851, 853 (1908).

[81] *Hearings*, note 36 *supra*, at 19–20.

sives and southern and western Democrats led by Senator Thomas J. Walsh of Montana.[82] They objected that local attorneys would be disadvantaged by the virtual necessity of learning two sets of procedures and that, as the Supreme Court would formulate the new rules, rule-making power, once lodged in accessible and responsive state legislatures, would now be delegated to that remote national court.[83]

As Walsh and his allies saw it, the Supreme Court had already manifested acute conservatism in its existing procedural rule-making role. Not only was it overburdened by its normal caseload but:[84]

> its work is of such a character that the justices have no opportunity, or at least little opportunity, from their own experience and observation, to know whether the system as a whole or in any detail works satisfactorily or not. They are not thrown into such intimate contact with the members of the bar or the judges of the trial courts as would serve to enlighten them touching defects. While not exactly recluses, something of the sanctity and the solitude of the priesthood attends them.

How, asked reform opponents, "would those who have any complaint to make against the rules as a whole or against any specific provision of the rules . . . make themselves heard?"[85] If state legislatures readily accessible to local lawyers and bar organizations were to be superseded, the rule-making power should be transferred not to the Supreme Court but to Congress.[86] At least in the latter forum all interests, especially local ones, would be guaranteed access. Procedural reform failed during Taft's lifetime, largely because of Walsh's opposition, but it would be revived and brought to fruition under his successor in company with President Roosevelt's Attorney General, Homer S. Cummings.

More successful was Taft's quest to elevate the status of federal appellate courts by reducing the Supreme Court's obligatory jurisdiction, expanding its discretionary review powers, and thereby rendering courts of appeals the courts of last resort in many cases. Again, Taft offered his proposal as an efficiency measure designed

---

[82] S. Rep. No. 892, pt. 2, 64th Cong., 2d Sess. (1917).

[83] *Id.* at 1–3. See Walsh, *Reform of Federal Procedures*, S. Doc. No. 105, 69th Cong., 1st Sess. 1–3 (1926).

[84] Note 82 *supra*, at 5.   [85] *Ibid.*

[86] S. Rep. No. 892, note 82 *supra*, at 5–6.

to permit the Supreme Court to keep abreast of its swollen docket and to give that tribunal more time to consider cases raising genuine constitutional issues.[87] Yet behind the efficiency facade lay the historic issue of federal-state court relations and collaterally the accessibility to harassed property owners of appellate federal forums. As Sidney Ulmer has noted, the framers of the Judiciary Act of 1789 built in a federal bias.[88] State court decisions upholding the constitutionality of state statutes as against federal constitutional challenge were made appealable as of right to the Supreme Court. But decisions upholding rights alleged under the federal Constitution, laws, and treaties were appealable only via certiorari. The 1925 Judges' Bill terminated Supreme Court review by right of decisions from federal courts of appeals, including decisions involving constitutional challenges to state statutes.[89] To charges that the measure rendered the intermediate federal appellate courts superior in status and power to the highest courts of the states, Taft replied:[90]

> . . . the bill is not intended to detract in any way from the dignity of the State courts of last resort or to exalt the dignity of the circuit courts of appeals. Neither will it so operate. There is no putting of one above the other.

At the heart of the Chief Justice's thinking, however, lay recognition that federal constitutional protections were safer in the hands of judges of United States courts than in those of state courts. Courts of Appeals, when confronted with state statutes alleged to conflict with the Constitution would, he asserted, "be more likely to preserve the Federal view of the issue than the State court, at least to an extent to justify making a review of its decision by our court conditional upon our approval."[91] But decisions of state courts were quite a different matter given the presence of elected judges, recall provisions, and ripples of progressivism at the state level.

---

[87] MASON, note 74 *supra*, at 111. See *Hearings on H.R. 10479 on Jurisdiction of Circuit Courts of Appeals, etc. before the House Committee on the Judiciary*, 67th Cong., 2d Sess., pt. 1 (1922).

[88] Ulmer, *Revising the Jurisdiction of the Supreme Court: Mere Administrative Reform or Substantive Policy Change?* 58 MINN. L. REV. 121, 134 (1973).

[89] 43 STAT. 936 (1925).

[90] Taft to Royal S. Copeland, 31 Dec. 1924, quoted in 66 CONG., REC. 2921 (1925).

[91] Taft to Copeland, 16 Jan. 1925, *id.* at 2922.

Thus the 1925 Judges' Bill fit comfortably into Taft's reform mosaic. It, like his other efforts, was designed to elude or erode state judicial power and procedures by enhancing that of the federal system.

IV. Reform Strategies: Hughes

Charles Evans Hughes maintained a much lower reform profile than did his predecessor. He never developed as complete a theory of judicial reform as did Taft. Nor did he even endorse all of Taft's reforms. He had entertained constitutional doubts about the 1925 Judges' Bill.[92] On Attorney-General Homer S. Cummings's initiative he continued to enact Taft's civil procedure reform.[93] In so doing Hughes acted more as shepherd than as midwife. But on the one judicial reform which he alone sponsored, he followed strategies diametrically opposed to those pursued by Taft. Where his predecessor had pressed for nationalism and administrative centralization, Hughes labored to implement principles of federalism and administrative decentralization.

The Administrative Office Act of 1939 provided an apt vehicle for Hughes's reform views. Enactment came in the wake of the court-packing crisis, a crisis that thrust Hughes into a political-reform leadership role. The President's Court Plan provided an immediate stimulus for the Chief Justice's somewhat delayed reformist response. Section 1 of the plan had struck at the work of the Supreme Court, but sections 2 and 3 related to the administration of the inferior federal courts wherein there admittedly existed problems of delay and judicial misbehavior.[94] Section 2 revived Taft's old nationalistic dream of judges-at-large, by enabling the Chief Justice to assign any district or circuit judge thereafter appointed to any other district or circuit in the absence of objection from the presiding judge of the assigned judge's home circuit. Section 3 created a Court proctor appointed by the Supreme Court and acting under its direction. This official would gather information on the business of district and circuit courts:[95]

> investigate the need of assigning district and circuit judges to other courts and to make recommendations thereon to the Chief Justice; . . . recommend with the approval of the Chief

---

[92] Mason, note 74 supra, at 111.

[93] 2 Pusey, note 50 supra, at 683–84.

[94] S. 1392, 75th Cong., 1st Sess. (1937).

[95] Ibid.

Justice, to any court of the United States, methods for expediting cases pending on its docket; and . . . perform such
other duties consistent with his office as the court shall direct.

Hughes found the structural changes proposed in sections 2
and 3 unacceptable. He assailed the vesting of greatly enlarged
intercircuit assignment powers in the Chief Justice as compelling
him to "practically determine who should try cases for the Government in all the circuits or districts of the country."[96] The proctor idea held some attraction. After defeat of the Court-Packing
Bill, it lingered on, promoted by Attorney General Cummings,
American Bar Association President Arthur T. Vanderbilt, and
Ninth Circuit Judge William Denman, who had originally pressed
it on Cummings.[97] S. 3212 introduced in the Seventy-fifth Congress
by Senator Henry F. Ashurst, chairman of the Judiciary Committee, conformed to the recommendations of Attorney General
Cummings in that it placed foremost responsibility for the work
of the director on the Chief Justice and the Judicial Conference.[98]
At hearings on the bill, Arthur Vanderbilt attacked this bifurcation
of responsibility. He urged that the measure be "recast" in such
a way that the supervision of the Chief Justice is understood to be
continuous . . . so that the Chief Justice has the sole responsibility."[99]

Hughes gave a cold reception to all efforts to create an executive-centered administrative system for the federal courts. Such a
Taft-type system failed to accord with his Court Plan strategy and
with his long-held administrative and political theories. Centering
primary responsibility for federal judicial administration on the
Chief Justice would, Hughes believed, pose dangers for the Chief
and his Court. Scandals or other problems in faraway courts might
reflect badly on the Chief Justice "as the responsible officer who
apparently had been neglectful in a matter which did not seem important perhaps at the time but later developed importance."[100] In

---

[96] Quoted in Chandler, *Some Major Advances in the Federal Judicial System: 1922–47*,
31 F.R.D. 307, 343–44 (1963).

[97] See FISH, note 2 *supra*, at 613.

[98] S. 3212, 75th Cong., 3d Sess. (1937).

[99] *Hearings on S. 3212 on Administrative Office of the United States Courts before the
Senate Committee on the Judiciary*, 75th Cong., 3d Sess. 52 (1938).

[100] *Extract*, note 53 *supra*, at 5–6.

light of Roosevelt's admittedly valid attack on inferior court performance,[101] the Chief Justice regarded a hierarchical system as
affording opportunities for "making the Chief Justice and the Court
itself a center of attack."[102] If the attorney general's bill ran counter to Hughes's strategy for dealing with past and future politically
inspired attacks on the Supreme Court, it was also out of harmony
with his theories of administration. As he told the 1938 Judicial
Conference, the fatal feature of the then pending proposal was its
"undue centralization."[103]

The Chief Justice entertained no objection to centralizing housekeeping or staff functions, especially as severance of the judiciary's
budget from that of the Department of Justice was included. But,
if he deferred to the doctrine of separation of powers, he adamantly
opposed centralization of executive or control powers within the
judicial system. At the 1938 Conference where he assumed reluctant leadership of the reform movement, Hughes unveiled his own
plan:[104]

> Instead of centering immediately and directly the whole re-
> sponsibility for efficiency upon the Chief Justice and the Su-
> preme Court, I think there ought to be a mechanism through
> which there would be a concentration of responsibility in
> the various Circuits. . . . immediate responsibility for the work
> of the courts in the Circuits, with power and authority to
> make the supervision all that is necessary to insure compe-
> tence in the work of all the judges of the various districts
> within the Circuit.

To this end, the Administrative Office Act provided for circuit
judicial councils composed of all judges of the several courts of
appeals.

Even the council composition reflected the chief's deep-seated
fear of centralized power. The Conference discussed making the
senior circuit judges solely responsible for exercising the council's
extensive powers, but Hughes favored multimember councils, because he "thought it . . . very unwise to impose upon the Senior
Circuit Judge all of the corrective power over District Judges."[105]

---

[101] *Id.* at 10.   [103] *Id.* at 14.

[102] *Id.* at 6.   [104] *Id.* at 14–15.

[105] *Id.* at 15–16. See Judge Groner to Members of the Conference of Senior Circuit
Judges, 21 Dec. 1938. D. Lawrence Groner Papers, Box 4 (University of Virginia,
Charlottesville, Va.).

Diffusion of power rather than its concentration appealed to him, perhaps because the latter promoted control while the former fostered voluntarism, independence, and individual freedom.

Hughes's council plan thoroughly accorded with his belief in local autonomy and responsibility. In his 1932 address to the Fourth Circuit Judicial Conference, he had declared: "We are apt to look too far away for the accomplishment of reforms. Improvement is generally a personal and local matter."[106] The plan also coincided with his judicial philosophy. As Chief Justice, Hughes joined by newly appointed Justice Owen J. Roberts dramatically altered the judicial reception extended to exercises of state authority. Taft had favored state actions only about 25 percent of the time. But Hughes and Roberts voted to uphold state authority 52 and 48 percent of the time respectively.[107] Both thus took a middle road on federalism questions. But more significantly, the Hughes-Roberts bloc was capable of providing a pro-state Court majority when combined with the once outnumbered Holmes-Brandeis-Stone and later Stone-Cardozo-Brandeis blocs.[108]

Hughes's acknowledged concern for the states and interest in pragmatically balancing central and local governmental powers became evident in the outline of the 1939 act. If the new Administrative Office provided "the centralized and executive administration necessary to give coherence and efficiency," the circuit council concept gave the decentralization which Hughes thought "necessary to buttress the sense of local responsibility" and would facilitate "speedy correction of local defects in administration and consultation as to local problems."[109] Such a plan he argued offered "de-centralization and a distribution of authority which . . . will greatly promote efficiency and will put the responsibility

---

[106] Hughes, note 41 *supra*, at 447.

[107] SPRAGUE, note 65 *supra*, at 96–97.

[108] *Id*. at 96–106. See 2 PUSEY, note 50 *supra*, at cc. 66–68. According to SMALL, ed., THE CONSTITUTION OF THE UNITED STATES OF AMERICA: ANALYSIS AND INTERPRETATION 1453–90 (1964), Taft sat on 114 cases or 12.67 per year in which the Supreme Court voided state legislative acts. Hughes, whose tenure on the Court exceeded Taft's by two years, voted in 82 cases or 7.46 per year overturning state acts. But 14 of these cases involved state legislation determined to have infringed on non-property First, Fifth, and Fourteenth Amendment rights. Only a maximum of 7 and a more realistic minimum of 3 cases decided by the Taft Court involved unconstitutional state violations of fundamental personal rather than property rights.

[109] *Address of Honorable Charles Evan; Hughes, Chief Justice of the Supreme Court of the United States*, 17 A.L.I., PROCEEDINGS 30 (1940).

immediately and directly where it belongs with respect to the administration of justice in the respective Circuits."[110]

Moreover, the council system cemented the federalism analogy to the administrative system of the United States Courts. "[A]s we have the States as *foci* of administration with regard to local problems pertaining to the States," the former governor told the assembled senior circuit judges in 1938, "We have in the various Circuits of the country *foci* of federal action from the judicial standpoint for supervision of the work of the federal courts."[111] For Hughes, the optimum means of assuring an independent federal judiciary and insulating it from future hostile popular tides lay with the decentralization of administrative, but not judicial, power. The core of the latter remained unimpaired in the Supreme Court of the United States.

V. CONCLUSION

Major reforms in the administration and procedures of the United States Courts had their inception and consummation during the two decades of the Taft and Hughes Chief Justiceships. As conservative reformers both jurists played prominent roles. Taft, however, was by far the more visible. Both perceived the American polity as pluralistic in nature but that the rule of law required a special place be given courts, especially those of the United States. Consequently both Taft and Hughes vigorously defended federal judicial institutions: Taft, against popular democracy centered primarily in the states, and Hughes from the same force transmitted through Congress and subsequently the presidency.

If the sources of political dangers differed, so did the responses. For Taft the answer lay with a federal judiciary of strengthened powers, administration, and status. The means to this end required a reform program emphasizing centralization and nationalism. The ultimate end for Taft involved ensuring existence of a federal judiciary ready, willing, and able to repel local and regional majorities antagonistic to private property rights. For Hughes property constituted a less absolute concept than it did for Taft. Moreover by the 1930s the world political climate had been transformed. Individual freedom broadly construed was threatened not by local tyrannies, but by modern centralized political and military power.

---

[110] *Extract*, note 53 *supra*, at 21.   [111] *Id*. at 14.

Under these circumstances the ultimate value for Hughes was not property rights alone but preservation of balanced government in order to assure maintenance of independent courts and the rule of law. To that end his halting and pragmatic reform effort reflected a felt need for balance in federal-state relations as well as among branches of the national government. The former concept was applied to the federal judiciary's administrative system while that systemic reform itself constituted a means of strengthening the independence and status of United States courts vis-à-vis the coordinate branches.

Economy, efficiency, speedy justice, and inexpensive litigation are the traditional stock in trade of conservative judicial reformers. Yet they hardly account for the enactment of major changes in the federal judicial system during the 1920s and 1930s. Rather they were but rhetoric behind which operated politically astute Chief Justices who sought realization or protection of important political values. By altering administrative structures and judicial procedures they sought to maintain an equilibrium that appeared threatened by other elements in the political system. Judicial reform thus meant more than the rhetoric indicated. It entailed different use of federal judicial manpower, a changed rule-making locus, altered jurisdiction of the Supreme Court, and a reformed administrative system. Each of these reforms had at least the potential for rendering the substantive or policy actions of the federal judiciary less responsive to popular impulses. Alternatively, such reforms were overtly designed to expand the judiciary's capacity to meet recognized increased quantitative demands made upon them. Thus in the end, judicial reform may be synonymous with "good government." But it may determine in a vital fashion the ultimate allocation of values and resources in society. It may, in short, be a decisive aspect of politics.

HOWARD B. ABRAMS and

ROBERT H. ABRAMS

GOLDSTEIN v. CALIFORNIA:

SOUND, FURY, AND SIGNIFICANCE

Some cases in the Supreme Court involve controversies of enormous immediate importance with little potential for effecting doctrinal constitutional change. Other cases seem of minimal moment, but call into question basic doctrinal issues whose resolution might have broad and serious effects. *Goldstein v. California*[1] falls into the second category. The obvious and dramatic limitation that *Goldstein* places on the scope of the Copyright Act[2] may have obscured its more subtle revisions of constitutional doctrine in other areas. For *Goldstein* not only defines the spheres of federal and state competence for copyright legislation; it also reinterprets precedents on preemption and supremacy principles that forebode substantial revision of these basic areas.

I. THE GOLDSTEIN DECISION

In *Goldstein v. California* the Supreme Court upheld the validity of a state criminal statute[3] outlawing unauthorized duplication of sound recordings[4] originally manufactured prior to 15

Howard B. Abrams is a member of the Illinois Bar; Robert H. Abrams is Associate Professor of Law, Western New England College of Law.

[1] 412 U.S. 546 (1973).   [2] 17 U.S.C. §§ 1 *et seq.*

[3] CAL. PENAL CODE § 653h(a) (1) (1970).

[4] The phrase "sound recordings" is used in the article to include phonograph records, prerecorded tapes, and other technological forms of sound reproduction.

February 1972, the effective date of the 1971 Sound Recording Amendment[5] to the Copyright Act.[6] The facts of the *Goldstein* case provide a typical example of the prohibited activity. Petitioners would buy a single copy of a popular phonograph record or prerecorded tape. Without authorization by either the performing artists or the owner of the rights in the original recorded performance, petitioners would duplicate the recording on blank tapes which would then be incorporated into cartridges. The cartridges were labeled with the title of the original recording and the names of the performing artists and then distributed to retail outlets for sale to the public. No payments were made by petitioners to the performing artists, producers, or other persons involved in the creative process, to the owner of the original sound recordings, or to defray any of the initial recording costs. Petitioners were convicted in the California courts and sought relief in the Supreme Court.

Chief Justice Burger, writing for the five-man majority,[7] recognized three issues:[8]

> First, they [petitioners] contend that the statute establishes a state copyright of unlimited duration, and thus conflicts with Art. I, § 8, cl. 8, of the Constitution. Second, petitioners claim that the state statute interferes with the implementation of federal policies inherent in the federal copyright statutes. . . . Finally, petitioners argue that 17 U.S.C. § 2, which allows States to protect unpublished writings, does not authorize the challenged state provision; since the records which petitioners copied had previously been released to the public.

In upholding the California statute against petitioners' preemption challenge, Chief Justice Burger framed the discussion by reference to Hamilton's famous statement in *Federalist* No. 32, that the several states surrendered their sovereignty to the Union in only three instances:[9]

> [W]here the Constitution in express terms granted an exclusive authority to the Union; where it granted in one instance

---

[5] 17 U.S. C. §§ 1(e),(f), 5(n), 19, 20, 26, 101(e).

[6] Hereinafter cited as 1909 Copyright Act.

[7] Chief Justice Burger was joined by Justices Powell, Rehnquist, Stewart, and White. Mr. Justice Douglas dissented and was joined by Justices Blackmun and Brennan. 412 U.S. at 572. Mr. Justice Marshall dissented and was joined by Justices Blackmun and Brennan. *Id.* at 576.

[8] 412 U.S. at 551.   [9] *Id.* 553.

an authority to the Union, and in another prohibited the States from exercising the like authority; and where it granted an authority to the Union, to which a similar authority in the States would be absolutely and totally *contradictory* and *repugnant.*

The Chief Justice then noted that state copyright statutes presented a case in the difficult third category, requiring a determination of whether the exercise of copyright authority by the states would be contradictory and repugnant to the exercise of copyright authority by the federal government. The language recited in the opinion is the time-honored formulation of *Cooley v. Board of Wardens:* "Whatever subjects of this power are in their nature national, or admit only of one uniform system, or plan of regulation, may justly be said to be of such a nature as to require exclusive legislation by Congress."[10]

Is copyright of such a nature? Chief Justice Burger concluded that it was not. Relying heavily on his interpretation of the statement of James Madison in *Federalist* No. 43,[11] the Chief Justice took the position that this nation's diversity implies a need for a corresponding diversity of regulation. He concluded: "Although the Copyright Clause thus recognizes the potential benefits of a national system, it does not indicate that all writings are of national interest or that state legislation is, in all cases, unnecessary or precluded."[12] To buttress this conclusion, the majority argument attempted an inquiry into the positive need for preemption by asking whether a grant of state copyright protection "will prejudice the interests of other States."[13] This type of inquiry raises two questions. First, under a Commerce Clause type of analysis, does a local regulation burden people not within the enacting jurisdiction? Second, as more explicitly recognized in Chief Justice Burger's subsequent opinion in *Kewanee Oil Co. v. Bicron Corp.,*[14] how should the national interest be identified and evaluated? The opinion found no harm done to the interests of other states because their citizens remained free to purchase unauthorized copies of sound recordings. And Chief Justice Burger saw no difficulty with "the concurrent exercise of the power to grant copyrights by Con-

---

[10] 12 How. 299, 319 (1851).   [12] *Id.* at 556–57.

[11] Quoted 412 U.S. at 555–56.   [13] *Id.* at 558.

[14] 416 U.S. 470 (1974). See Goldstein, *Kewanee Oil Co. v. Bicron Corp.: Notes on a Closing Circle,* 1974 SUPREME COURT REVIEW 81.

gress and the States"[15] because Congress could forbid state regulation of items Congress wished to be free of such regulation. The
possibility that a perpetual state copyright would frustrate a constitutional policy that the limited time of a copyright monopoly must
ultimately yield to the public domain is dismissed as a restriction
which pertains to Congress but not to the states.[16]

Petitioners' second argument, the Supremacy Clause challenge,
was measured by the yardstick of *Hines v. Davidowitz*,[17] "whether,
under the circumstances of this particular case, [the state's] law
stands as an obstacle to the accomplishment and execution of the
full purposes and objectives of Congress." Here Chief Justice Burger began his argument with the demonstration that prior to the
1971 Sound Recording Amendment, the Copyright Act did not
permit copyright protection of the performances embodied in
sound recordings. He concluded that Congress left sound recordings "unattended"[18] in the 1909 Copyright Act, implicitly ruling
that the fact that sound recordings as such were not eligible for
copyright was not intended to preclude other forms of protection.
Sears Roebuck & Co. v. Stiffel Co.[19] and *Compco Corp. v. Day-
Brite Lighting, Inc.*[20] were distinguished on the ground that the
subject matter in those cases was eligible for patent protection
although the items in question did not meet the prerequisite patent
standards, while sound recordings as a class were ineligible even
to be considered for copyright protection because they were outside the ambit of the 1909 Copyright Act. At the end of this part
of the opinion, Chief Justice Burger relegated the last of the three
issues he originally defined to a footnote, stating that whatever
limits Section 2 of the Copyright Act[21] may have placed on state
regulation of published works had no relevance to "categories of
writings which Congress has not brought within the scope of the
federal statute."[22]

---

[15] 412 U.S. at 559.

[16] *Id.* at 560–61.

[17] 312 U.S. 52, 67 (1941).

[18] 412 U.S. at 570.

[19] 376 U.S. 225 (1964).

[20] 376 U.S. 234 (1964).

[21] 17 U.S.C. § 2, provides: "nothing in this title shall be construed to annul or limit
the right of the author or proprietor of an unpublished work, at common law or in equity,
to prevent the copying, publication, or use of such unpublished work without his consent,
and to obtain damages therefor."

[22] 412 U.S. at 570 n.28.

Strictly speaking, the *Goldstein* case presented no issue that directly involved interstate commercial transactions. Section 653h(a) (1) of the California Penal Code, on which the petitioners were convicted, deals only with the question of the manufacture of the prohibited articles. The right of an out-of-state duplicator to sell his products in California provided they had been legally manufactured in his home state is not an issue between the parties in *Goldstein*. Nevertheless, the Commerce Clause cannot be divorced from any analysis of the *Goldstein* opinion. Section 653(a)(2) of the California Penal Code[23] explicitly prohibits the sale of sound recordings made by unauthorized duplication. In the opinion Chief Justice Burger makes it abundantly clear that not only is the activity prohibited but its products are likewise taboo even if manufactured in another state where such reproductions are not banned by law.[24] The opinion is quite explicit that "individuals who wish to purchase a copy of a work protected in their own State will be able to buy unauthorized copies in other States where no protection exists."[25] They must be "willing to travel across state lines in order to purchase records or other writings protected in their own State."[26] The Commerce Clause pronouncements of *Goldstein* may technically be dicta, but they leave little room for doubt as to how the majority would rule on the question.

The question whether state copyright laws would inhibit freedom of speech and therefore be constitutionally repugnant to the First Amendment is not even considered in *Goldstein*. The issue was not raised by the petitioners, although it seems an obvious and relevant concern. In abbreviated form, the First Amendment challenge to state copyright laws would probably run along the following lines. Any copyright statute granting a monopoly on a particular expression is an inhibition of freedom of speech. The federal government is permitted to do this because of the need to balance and reconcile the Copyright Clause with the First Amendment. The First Amendment, applicable to the states by virtue of the Fourteenth Amendment without the ameliorating effect of the Copyright Clause, does not permit the states to regulate the dissemination of ideas and their expressions by state copyright laws.

---

[23] *Id.* at 548, n.1.   [25] *Id.* at 558.

[24] *Id.* at 558–59.   [26] *Ibid.*

II. GOLDSTEIN AND PREEMPTION PRECEDENT

The *Goldstein* majority expresses a specific reliance on preemption cases which span more than a century of judicial decision making. Doctrinally, many views of preemption were espoused, adopted, and rejected in that period. The historical development of preemption leads to an understanding of the modern cases sufficient to cast doubt on the soundness of the *Goldstein* reasoning.

A. THE EARLY CASES: GIBBONS, BLACK BIRD, AND COOLEY

Historically, preemption of state laws was first used as a ground of decision when state regulation of related activity adversely affected transportation interstate commerce. In *Gibbons v. Ogden*,[27] Chief Justice Marshall, concentrating on defining the sphere of federal competence, laid little firm basis for evaluating claims of preemption. To the extent that *Gibbons* provides any criteria for determining preemption, they may be found in the passage Chief Justice Burger quoted with approval in *Goldstein*:[28]

> The genius and character of the government seem to be, that its action is to be applied to all the external concerns of the nation, and to those internal concerns which affect the states generally; but not to those which are completely within a particular state, which do not affect other states, and with which it is not necessary to interfere, for the purpose of executing some of the general powers of the government.

Striking down New York's state-granted steamboat monopoly in *Gibbons*, Marshall's language seems more concerned with establishing federal Supremacy Clause rhetoric than in finding preemption. He emphasized the fact that Congress had acted in the field and defined the issue as whether New York law conflicted with the federal enactment. He chose the argument that the right "to regulate" implies a full power over the area regulated and found in the congressional decision to limit the scope of its licensing provisions an intent to exclude state action in the areas left unregulated. He stated this thesis in the following language:[29]

> [R]egulation is designed for the entire result, applying in those parts which remain as they were, as well as to those which are altered. It produces a uniform whole, which is as

---

[27] 9 Wheat. 1 (1824).   [28] *Id.* at 195.   [29] *Id.* at 16.

much disturbed and deranged by changing what the regulating power designs to leave untouched, as that on which it has operated.

Marshall's concern with supremacy considerations continued in *Willson v. Black Bird Creek Marsh Co.*[30] Although he upheld the right of the state to license a dam, Marshall explicitly restricted the decision to non-action by Congress. His opinion stated: "If Congress had passed any act which bore upon the case; any act in execution of the power to regulate commerce, the object of which was to control state legislation over those small navigable creeks . . . we should feel not much difficulty in saying that a state law coming in conflict with such act would be void."[31]

Despite the vast doctrinal significance of establishing federal preeminence, Marshall's opinions give little guidance in the resolution of preemption disputes.[32] There is little direction in *Gibbons* or *Black Bird* for a resolution for the issues of *Goldstein*. Marshall's arguments suggest, if anything, that the California statute must fall. *Gibbons* did not offer a pervasive federal legislative scheme as intricate as the Copyright Act. Marshall's blanket invalidation of state legislation in the interstices of a federal regulatory scheme has at least as much validity in the context of *Goldstein* as in the context of *Gibbons*. Indeed, an application of the criteria set forth in the passage of *Gibbons* quoted in *Goldstein* seems to demand invalidation of the California statute on numerous levels. Copyright is one of "the external concerns of the nation"[33] as well as one of "those internal concerns which affects the states generally."[34] Correspondingly, state copyright regulation affects subject matter which is not "completely within a particular state,"[35] which does "affect other states,"[36] and whose application makes it "necessary to interfere"[37] with the execution of one "of the general powers of the government."[38] The *Goldstein* decision would seem to violate all of these criteria.

Application of the *Black Bird* dicta would also call for invalidation of the California statute. It seems clear from the Copyright

---

[30] 2 Pet. 245 (1829).   [31] *Id.* at 252.

[32] See FRANKFURTER, THE COMMERCE CLAUSE c. 1 (1937).

[33] 9 Wheat. at 195.   [35] *Ibid.*   [37] *Ibid.*

[34] *Ibid.*   [36] *Ibid.*   [38] *Ibid.*

Act itself and its accompanying legislative history[39] that Congress created a scheme of regulation in the Copyright Act which provided a niche for sound recordings in its scope. This apparent simplicity of decision, however, belies the difficult decision whether a state law in fact conflicts with a federal law.

For almost thirty years following *Gibbons*, the preemption-supremacy area remained a morass of diverging judicial attitudes towards state regulation. The decision in *Cooley v. Board of Wardens*[40] in 1851 is usually considered the beginning of a clearly articulated preemption doctrine and is the rock upon which Chief Justice Burger built his opinion in *Goldstein*. In *Cooley*, enforcement of a local statute imposing a fine for failure to engage a local pilot in the Philadelphia harbor was sanctioned. The congressional statute involved, enacted twelve years earlier, expressly delegated to the states the major share of pilotage regulation. Against the background of broad supremacy implications suggested by *Gibbons* and *Black Bird*, Justice Curtis in *Cooley* had first to limit the scope of inferences possible from the naked grant of power in the Commerce Clause and second to apply whatever test he devised to the facts confronting the Court. According to Chief Justice Burger in *Goldstein*, the test chosen to resolve the preemption issue was whether "Whatever subjects of this power are in their nature national, or admit only of one uniform system, or plan of regulation, may justly be said to be of such nature as to require exclusive legislation by Congress."[41] It is essential to note that the formulation of the issue based on this single quotation overstates the *Cooley* holding. The *Cooley* opinion carefully balanced the extremes, subjects requiring national uniformity and subjects requiring local diversity, describing the various aspects of the regulation of commerce as: "some imperatively demanding a single uniform rule . . . in every port; and some, like the subject now in question, as imperatively demanding that diversity, which alone can meet the local necessities of navigation."[42]

The facts of *Cooley* disclose a subject matter, pilotage, which has aspects of both national and local interest. As a result, the precedential value of the *Cooley* holding lies in the explicit congressional declaration of the local nature of the subject matter. Moreover,

---

[39] See text *infra*, at notes 106–23.

[40] 12 How. 299 (1851).

[41] 412 U.S. 553–54.

[42] 12 How. at 319.

Cooley gives little substantive guidance to determining whether a given subject falls into either of the two enumerated categories.[43] It is incorrect to read *Cooley*, as the Chief Justice did, as authority for the proposition that there is preemption only if there is a showing that the subject demands national exclusivity. Instead *Cooley* suggests that absent a congressional declaration to the contrary, an overriding national interest in the subject matter is a sufficient condition for preemption, and implicitly suggests that this is not a necessary condition for preemption.

In *Goldstein*, Chief Justice Burger conceded the scope of a national copyright system, but also found merit in a claim of local interest. He concluded, therefore, that there had been no preemption and turned to the Supremacy Clause issue. In contrast, under *Cooley* the identification of dual interests, both local and national, did not resolve the issue of preemption. *Cooley*, however, did not announce any standards by which to decide the issue other than the existence of congressional declaration of intent.

When then is the relationship between *Cooley* and *Goldstein?* *Cooley* relied in significant measure on the finding that pilotage in the Philadelphia harbor was so unique that the use of local pilots was required for the safety of vessels using the harbor. One cannot easily draw an analogy to *Goldstein* as there are no clear parallels. The California statute punishes behavior which may physically take place largely outside the jurisdiction and affects the economic well-being of only a small segment of the local population. This is hardly the same safety concern that arises when navigating in strange waters in a major port. There is nothing about record production which is inherently local; recording studios, phonograph record pressing plants, tape duplicating plants, and the like operate almost anywhere. To say industry concentration in California is unique and therefore within the *Cooley* doctrine is to say that every state which finds itself host to a concentration in an industry may regulate in all available interstices of congressional acts absent a positive showing of the need for uniformity.

Thus *Cooley* does not support *Goldstein*'s conclusion that the California statute is not preempted. Indeed, the absence of a congressional declaration endorsing local regulation and the failure of any reasonable analogy between the facts of the cases suggest the opposite.

---

[43] See FRANKFURTER, note 32 *supra*, at c. 2.

B. THE EVOLUTIONARY CASES

The Supreme Court grappled with the preemption area in several ways in the century following *Cooley* eventually claiming in *Southern Pacific Co. v. Arizona*,[44] to have reaffirmed as its preemption standard, the local-national subject matter dichotomy, announced in *Cooley*. To make this simplifying leap, as the majority in *Goldstein* did, obscures the complex issues that attend the definition of the respective powers of state and federal government.

Cooley's impact was widely felt in the expansionist era following the Civil War. Railroads and other primary carriers of both interstate and intrastate shipments of goods were the subject of a great deal of state regulation and subsequent litigation. In *Wabash, St. L. & P. Ry. v. Illinois*[45] there arose an issue typical of this genre of cases "how far such regulations, made by the States and under State authority, are valid or void, as they may affect the transportation of goods through more than one State, in one voyage." There a state statute forbade carriage pricing that discriminated against short hauls or inconvenient points of shipment or delivery. State courts found the railroad to be in violation of the statute when it charged more for shipment of goods from Gilman, Illinois, to New York City than it charged for a like shipment from Peoria, which was eighty-six miles farther from New York City. The Supreme Court held the Illinois statute placed an unconstitutional burden on interstate commerce drawing a clear distinction between the case at bar and a purely intrastate shipment. Although the majority opinion of Justice Miller did not cite *Cooley*, the opinion nevertheless distinguished *Cooley*, holding that railroad regulation is treated as being in:[46]

> that class of regulations of commerce which, like pilotage, bridging navigable rivers, and many others, could be acted upon by the States in the absence of any legislation by Congress on the same subject.
>
> By the slightest attention to the matter it will be readily seen that . . . the local rules which shall govern the conduct of the pilots of each of the varying harbors of the coasts of

---

[44] 325 U.S. 761 (1945).

[45] Wabash, St.L. & P. Ry. v. Illinois, 118 U.S. 557, 564 (1886).

[46] *Id.* at 568.

the United States, depend upon principles far more limited
in their application and importance than those which should
regulate the transportation of persons and property across the
half or whole of the continent.

In terms of emerging preemption doctrine, *Wabash* is significant
as it comes one year prior to the congressional entry into the field
with the Intrastate Commerce Act of 1887.[47] Therefore, it is fair
to treat *Wabash* as a pure preemption case.[48] Moreover, the explicit reference to the national-local determination and the narrow
reading of *Cooley* help to clarify what the Supreme Court saw as
the basis for that division. The explicit recognition of the validity
of purely intrastate regulation inescapably leads to the conclusion
that the *Wabash* application of the *Cooley* preemption test includes
as a crucial factor the existence of an identifiable extraterritorial
effect of the regulation.[49] In essence, a burden on interstate commerce could not be upheld. Were one to apply the extraterritorial
burden test suggested by *Wabash* to *Goldstein*, the result would be
preemptive invalidation of the California statute. The burdens of
the California statute frequently fall on those acting legally in localities outside the jurisdiction.

The clarity and simplicity suggested by the *Wabash* opinion
soon vanished when *Smith v. Alabama*[50] was decided in 1888. Alabama had passed a law in the wake of the Interstate Commerce Act
of 1887 requiring locomotive engineers operating trains within
Alabama to obtain state licenses. Smith, operating a train for the
Mobile and Ohio Railroad without a state license, was taken into
custody by the sheriff of Mobile County, Alabama. A writ of
habeas corpus was sought on the ground that the Alabama licensing scheme was constitutionally invalid and it was established that
the bulk of Smith's runs beginning in Alabama ended in another
state. Justice Matthews, speaking for the majority,[51] started with

---

[47] 24 Stat. 379 (1887).

[48] There is little scholarly explication of the difference between preemption and
supremacy as a ground for the invalidation of state enactments. Nevertheless, the two
are almost invariably treated as separate concepts, as is done by Chief Justice Burger
in *Goldstein.*

[49] Extraterritorial effect and its due process implications do not leave this view of
Wabash without subsequent effect. *Cf.* Edwards v. California, 314 U.S. 160 (1941).

[50] 124 U.S. 465 (1888).

[51] Justice Bradley dissented without opinion. Justice Lamar took his seat during the
interim between argument and decision and did not participate.

the premise that it is uniquely a matter of state law to define the standards of conduct of carriers upon which liability for injuries might be predicated: "A carrier exercising his calling within a particular state, although engaged in the business of interstate commerce, is answerable according to the laws of the State for acts of nonfeasance or misfeasance committed within its limits."[52] The logical extension followed rhetorically: "Why may [a state] not define and declare what particular things shall be done and observed by such a carrier in order to insure the safety of the persons and things he carries?"[53]

Thus, *Smith* established that the Commerce power standing alone did not preempt state regulation of railroad safety. The more subtle and difficult question of accommodating the preemption and supremacy problems which arise when the Congress has acted were also explored. Justice Matthews said that if Congress were to "prescribe the qualifications of locomotive engineers"[54] the case would be similar to *Sinnot v. Davenport*,[55] where a state law calling for registration of interstate steamboats was struck down. The *Sinnot* Court had said that for a state's exercise of a reserved power to be subject to Supremacy Clause invalidation "the repugnance or conflict should be direct and positive,"[56] and concluded that such a repugnance existed given the extensive federal scheme regulating the coasting trade.

Justice Matthews could have reconciled *Sinnot* and *Smith* on narrow grounds by pointing out that the Interstate Commerce Act of 1887 made no attempt at governance of safety standards, thus leaving state laws intact. He declined this opportunity and instead concluded on a more general plane that the Alabama act placed only an indirect burden on interstate commerce: "[S]o far as it affects transactions of commerce among the States, it does so only indirectly, incidentally, and remotely [and] it is not in conflict with any express enactment of Congress on the subject, nor contrary to any intention of Congress to be presumed from its silence."[57]

By failing to limit the decision in *Smith* to a narrow Supremacy Clause inquiry as was done in *Sinnot*, doctrinal problems arose in

---

[52] 124 U.S. at 476.

[53] *Id*. at 477.

[54] *Id*. at 479.

[55] 22 How. 227 (1859).

[56] *Id*. at 243.

[57] 124 U.S. at 482.

the preemption field. *Smith* and its progeny[58] may be viewed as creating a direct-indirect test for preemption. If the burden on interstate commerce is "direct," the regulation must fall; the opposite conclusion obtains if the burden is indirect, incidental, or remote. The *Wabash* concern for extraterritorial effect receded into the background, at most a factor in burden weighing.

The *Blow-Post Cases*[59] continued the direct-indirect approach. These two cases involved a Georgia statute requiring all trains to blow their whistle and check speed when approaching grade crossings. The disputes arose when the railroads defended personal injury actions based upon negligent noncompliance with the blow-post statute by claiming the statute was a direct burden on interstate commerce and therefore preempted by the federal law. In the earlier of the cases, owing to a defect in the railroad's pleadings, no evidence of the actual effect of the statute on interstate commerce was allowed. The Supreme Court held that, "In the absence of facts . . . showing the unreasonable character of the statute"[60] the railroad had failed adequately to raise the issue of Commerce Clause preemption. Warned by the first case, the railroad in the second case alleged and proved that obedience to the Georgia law would greatly delay interstate service. The Supreme Court concluded that "the statute is a direct burden upon interstate commerce, and, being such, is unlawful."[61]

It is interesting to return to *Goldstein* with the direct-indirect test in mind. Record piracy statutes to some degree burden interstate commerce. *Goldstein* recognized these commercial aspects of record piracy, yet failed to attempt a Commerce Clause preemption study. Had the "direct-indirect" line of cases been decided narrowly like *Sinnot* as seemed possible before *Smith v. Alabama*, more credence could be given the superficial factual inquiry of *Goldstein*. Instead, the *Blow-Post Cases* indicate that even the "direct-indirect" preemption inquiry includes an examination of the statute's operation, and the degree to which it burdens commerce. *Goldstein*'s failure in this area is even more glaring when one recalls the criticism of Mr. Justice Stone which eventually led

---

[58] *E.g.*, Seaboard Air Line Ry. v. Blackwell, 244 U.S. 310 (1917); Southern Ry. v. King, 217 U.S. 524 (1910); DiSanto v. Pennsylvania, 273 U.S. 34 (1927).

[59] Southern Ry. v. King, 217 U.S. 524 (1910); Seaboard Air Line Ry. v. Blackwell, 244 U.S. 310 (1917).

[60] 217 U.S. at 537.   [61] 244 U.S. at 316.

to the rejection of the "direct-indirect" approach: "In this case the traditional test of the limit of state action by inquiring whether the interference with commerce is direct or indirect seems to me too mechanical, too uncertain in its application, and too remote from actualities, to be of value."[62] Thus *Goldstein* fails to satisfy even the most mechanistic of the evolutionary preemption standards by the limited scope of its factual inquiry and by its blithe double standard regarding economic interests; those of the protected industries of the enacting states are considered, those of the duplicating entrepreneur and the consumer are not.

C. THE MODERN CASES

1. *Barnwell and Southern Pacific*. Justice Stone authored the majority opinions in *South Carolina State Highway Dep't v. Barnwell Bros.*[63] and *Southern Pacific Co. v. Arizona*.[64] These two cases renounced the "direct-indirect" test and adopted instead a renewed allegiance to *Cooley* in a more modern setting. *Barnwell*, which established the new approach, construed the test narrowly, resulting in a finding of nonpreemption. Seven years later, *Southern Pacific* in large measure reiterated the new test but liberalized its application, setting the tone for future adjudication.

Barnwell involved a South Carolina statute regulating the width and weight of trucks using the state highways. Congress had passed the Motor Carrier Act of 1935,[65] which required the Interstate Commerce Commission "to regulate common carriers by motor vehicle [and] establish reasonable requirements with respect to . . . safety of operation and equipment." Elaborate findings made below by a three-judge district court were explicitly noted by the Supreme Court:[66]

> [T]hat a gross weight limitation of that amount, especially as applied to semi-trailer motor trucks, is unreasonable as a means of preserving the highways; . . . and that the width limitation of 90 inches is unreasonable when applied to standard concrete highways of the state, in view of the fact that all other states permit a width of 96 inches, which is the standard width of trucks engaged in interstate commerce.

---

[62] DiSanto v. Pennsylvania, 273 U.S. 34, 44 (1927).

[63] 303 U.S. 177 (1938).   [65] 49 STAT. 543, 546 (1935).

[64] 325 U.S. 761 (1945).   [66] 303 U.S. at 183–84.

Nowhere in the opinion did Stone suggest that there was not some notable burden on interstate commerce. Instead of focusing on the burdens imposed by the South Carolina legislation or whether the burden was direct or indirect, the opinion concerned itself with defining the spheres of power of Congress and the state legislature. Although not explicitly stated, Stone's opinion seems premised on the non-action of Congress in the field, despite the aforementioned language of the Motor Carriers Act.

Two points need be made here. First, § 225 of the Motor Carrier Act could have been used to buttress the argument for implied congressional inaction, for that section authorized the Interstate Commerce Commission to study the need for federal regulation of vehicle size, etc. Second, and more fundamental, it is clear that Justice Stone divorced all supremacy clause considerations from his opinion. He wrote:[67]

> Congress, in the exercise of its plenary power to regulate interstate commerce, may determine whether the burdens imposed on it by state regulation, otherwise permissible, are too great, and may, by legislation designed to secure uniformity or in other respects to protect the national interest in commerce, curtail to some extent the state's regulatory power . . . inquiry whether the state legislature in adopting regulations such as the present has acted within its province, and whether the means of regulation chosen are reasonably adapted to the end sought.

Clearly a break with the prior cases is made. The problem of burden weighing is relegated to Congress, and, in the absence of congressional action (and the attendant supremacy inquiries which arise) the Court has only two functions: (1) to determine whether state authority existed at all (preemption), and (2) to insure that the enactment comports with due process standards in terms of being reasonably related to the end sought. It is the first inquiry, the preemption issue, which is of particular concern here.

Initially, Stone contended that there was some Commerce Clause[68] preemption without any congressional action, particularly

---

[67] 303 U.S. at 189–90.

[68] *Id.* at 184 n.2. The whole passage bears quotation: "State regulations affecting interstate commerce, whose purpose or effect is to gain for those within the state an advantage at the expense of those without . . . have been thought to impinge upon the constitutional prohibition even though Congress has not acted. . . . Underlying the stated

in those cases where the effect of a state regulation is to create an advantage for intrastate commerce at the expense of interstate commerce. He added, however, that, "it has been recognized that there are matters of local concern . . . which, because of their local character and their number and diversity, may never be fully dealt with by Congress."[69] The opinion then carefully examined whether highway regulation is local subject matter, reciting precedents at great length.

The importance to Justice Stone of placing significant stress on the "local nature of the subject matter" may be seen by comparing his decision in *Barnwell* with his opinion in *Southern Pacific*. In the latter, writing as Chief Justice, he concluded that the Arizona statute limiting train lengths was preempted by the interstate commerce power. The factual similarity to *Barnwell* is striking. Evidence below was equivocal as to the safety gains flowing from the regulation. There was clear indication in both cases that the bulk of interstate traffic did not conform with the state statute and that compliance would equally affect those in interstate commerce as well as those in intrastate commerce. In neither case had Congress or the Interstate Commerce Commission attempted a comprehensive regulation of the specific subject, though the nascent power to do so was conceded to exist. Although the results varied between the cases, the local-national subject matter inquiry, considered at length in both opinions, was dispositive of the preemption issue. To that extent the *Barnwell-Southern Pacific* line of cases is completely consistent with *Cooley*; similarly, to that extent the *Barnwell-Southern Pacific* line of cases casts serious doubt on the adequacy of the sketchy local subject matter reasoning in *Goldstein*.

2. *The economic barrier cases.* There is a suggestion in the *Barnwell* opinion that the protection of intrastate interests cannot be achieved at the expense of interstate commerce. Nowhere is this more clearly stated than in *H. P. Hood & Sons, Inc. v. DuMond.*[70] In *Hood*, an interstate commercial dairy company was denied a license to operate a shipping depot in New York because it "would

---

rule has been the thought, often expressed in judicial opinion, that when the regulation is of such a character that its burden falls principally upon those without the state, legislative action is not likely to be subjected to those political restraints which are normally exerted on legislation where it affects adversely some interests within the state."

[69] *Id.* at 185.   [70] 336 U.S. 525 (1949).

tend to a destructive competition in a market already adequately served"[71] in violation of a New York statute. Justice Jackson's majority opinion,[72] while granting that the public health aspects of milk regulation generally sustained state action in the area, emphatically concluded:[73]

> Our system, fostered by the Commerce Clause, is that every farmer and every craftsman shall be encouraged to produce by the certainty that he will have free access to every market in the Nation, that no home embargoes will withhold his exports, and no foreign state will by customs duties or regulations exclude them. Likewise, every consumer may look to the free competition from every producing area in the Nation to protect him from exploitation by any.

The broad ruling in *Hood* is an apt summation of the judicial reception given those state regulations found to deny access to local marketers interstate buyers or sellers. Similarly, in *Dean Milk Co. v. Madison*,[74] Justice Clark, writing for the majority, struck down a local ordinance requiring the local production of milk which could be sold in the city of Madison, Wisconsin. In holding the Madison ordinance unconstitutional under the Commerce Clause, he stated:[75]

> In thus erecting an economic barrier protecting a major local industry against competition from without the State, Madison plainly discriminates against interstate commerce. This it cannot do, even in the exercise of its unquestioned power to protect the health and safety of its people.

Indeed, the cases are legion that local economic protectionism is invalid under the Commerce Clause.

Although the Court was not called upon to decide this issue in Goldstein,[76] Chief Justice Burger's sweeping dicta made it clear this precise type of economic discrimination, which is embodied

---

[71] *Id.* at 529.

[72] Justice Black dissented, joined by Justice Murphy; Justice Frankfurter dissented, joined by Justice Rutledge, 336 U.S. at 564. It is interesting that the dissents are almost diametrically in conflict on a doctrinal level. Black would adhere to the narrow *Barnwell*-like deference of burden-weighing to Congress, while Frankfurter is almost insistent that the Court must scrutinize the degree to which a regulation impinges on interstate prerogatives.

[73] 336 U.S. at 539.   [75] *Id.* at 354.

[74] 340 U.S. 349 (1951).   [76] See text *supra*, at notes 23–26.

in § 653h(a)(2) of the California statute, was given the blessing
of the Court when the subject matter is sound recordings. Without
any inquiry into the facts, the majority opinion claimed, as if by
fiat, "We do not see here the type of prejudicial conflicts which
would arise, for example, if each State exercised a sovereign power
to impose imports and tariffs; nor can we discern a need for uniformity such as that which may apply to the regulation of interstate
shipments."[77] *Goldstein* gave no scrutiny to the interstate economic
consequences of the insular protection granted the California record
industry. The opinion ignored the out-of-state manufacturer who
is excluded from marketing his products in the most populous state
of the union and gave scant attention to the California consumers
who lose the advantages of a competitive market place. This shal-
low treatment of the Commerce Clause issues may be explained
away as mere dicta, but the implications of *Goldstein*'s pronouncements indicate that state-legislated economic barriers designed to
protect local industry will be more kindly received by the Supreme
Court in the future than they have in the past. Chief Justice Burger's explicit endorsement of the purposes of the statute, the protection of "the continued production of new recordings, a large
industry in California,"[78] suggests the possibility of future shifts in
Supreme Court attitudes on Commerce Clause issues.

3. *Other modern cases.* A third aspect of modern preemption
doctrine has been developed apart from the *Southern Pacific* safety
regulation line of cases and the *Dean Milk* economic barrier line of
cases. The issue posed in this third line of cases is whether congressional action has foreclosed the possibility of concurrent state regulation. Should the issue be resolved in the negative, the Court
must then inquire whether the state regulation conflicts with the
federal scheme.

The major focus of the preemption tests in these cases is the
existence of a dominant national interest, as exemplified in *Hines
v. Davidowitz*[79] and *Pennsylvania v. Nelson*.[80] This inquiry is an
obvious tangent emanating from the pronouncements of *Cooley v.
Board of Wardens*. Like *Cooley*, both *Hines* and *Nelson* dealt with
subjects where the challenged state statute touched upon a field
where there was extant federal legislation. Unlike *Cooley*, and to

---

[77] 412 U.S. at 559.

[78] *Id*. at 571.

[79] 312 U.S. 52 (1941).

[80] 350 U.S. 497 (1956).

some extent unlike *Barnwell*, in *Hines* and *Nelson* there was no explicit congressional recognition that the prospective subject matters, alien registration and sedition, were uniquely local. In distinguishing the *Cooley* type of concerns, the *Hines* Court was careful to examine the intent of the federal scheme passed in furtherance of the constitutional grant to Congress, to create a "Uniform Rule of Naturalization."[81] *Nelson*, on the other hand, emphasized that the problem (as opposed to the solution) of governmental subversion was a problem of national scope and that the federal legislation was "so pervasive as to make reasonable the inference that Congress left no room for the States to supplement it."[82]

Use of the analytic framework surrounding *Hines* and to a lesser extent *Nelson* has continued to the present. This intent-oriented inquiry has usually been coupled with a keener appreciation of the distinction between preemption and supremacy issues. In both *Huron Portland Cement Co. v. Detroit*,[83] and *Askew v. American Waterways Operators, Inc.*,[84] a stated congressional acknowledgment of the need for concurrent local legislation obtained a nonpreemption result. In the absence of such declarations, other decisions inquire into congressional intent, although they tend to read such intent broadly. For example in *Campbell v. Hussey*[85] a nonconflicting but additional state-required marking of tobacco was held preempted by the federally enacted Tobacco Inspection Act. To reach the result Mr. Justice Douglas found highly significant the fact that federal inspection standards were denominated *"the official standards of the United States."*[86]

The *Hines-Nelson* views of preemption are somewhat merged in *City of Burbank v. Lockheed Air Terminal, Inc.*[87] In striking down a local ordinance which regulated times of jet aircraft operation, Justice Douglas noted and examined the scope and purpose of the plethora of federal regulations applicable to the subject. He also spoke about the local and national aspects of the problem of aircraft noise and the threat to national planning posed by multiple similar enactments, thus weaving together almost all the threads of preemption doctrine spawned by *Cooley*.

---

[81] 312 U.S. at 72.

[82] 350 U.S. at 502.

[83] 362 U.S. 440 (1960).

[84] 411 U.S. 325 (1973).

[85] 368 U.S. 297 (1961).

[86] *Id.* at 299.

[87] 411 U.S. 624 (1973).

Thus, after the *Goldstein* Court determined that the Copyright Clause did not preempt state copyright legislation a priori, *Hines* and the other cases just mentioned indicate the next logical step would be to inquire whether the Copyright Act of 1909 excluded state copyright legislation protecting sound recordings. Chief Justice Burger's opinion decides this issue as part of its Supremacy Clause inquiry.

D. THE NATIONAL-LOCAL SUBJECT MATTER INQUIRY IN GOLDSTEIN

After deriving the preemption criteria for *Goldstein* from *Cooley v. Board of Wardens*, Chief Justice Burger conducted an inquiry into the nature of copyright to determine if state copyright legislation was preempted by the Copyright Clause. The inquiry begins with the Copyright Clause which grants Congress the power "To promote the Progress of Science and useful Arts, by securing for limited Times to Authors and Inventors the exclusive Right to their respective Writings and Discoveries."[88] The *Goldstein* opinion then found that: "The objective of the Copyright Clause was clearly to facilitate the granting of rights national in scope."[89]

For further guidance as to the purpose of the Copyright Clause, Chief Justice Burger turned again to James Madison's statement in *Federalist* No. 43:[90]

> The utility of this power will scarcely be questioned. The copyright of authors has been solemnly adjudged, in Great Britain, to be a right of common law. The right to useful inventions seems with equal reason to belong to the inventors. The public good fully coincides in both cases with the claims of individuals. The States cannot separately make effectual provision for either of the cases, and most of them have anticipated the decision of this point, by laws passed at the instance of Congress.

Madison's concluding comment, that "States cannot separately make effectual provision" for copyrights and patents, is interpreted by the Chief Justice as simply a comment on the territorial limitations of state protection and the burden of multiple registrations placed on an author who desires protection in two or more states. He ignores the equally plausible corollary that any system of state

---

[88] 412 U.S. at 555.   [89] *Ibid.*   [90] *Id.* at 555–56.

by state protection would create undesirable confusion resulting from the vagaries of many overlapping statutes.

Leading into the central text of his ensuing argument, the Chief Justice concluded from his discussion that a national copyright system "allows Congress to provide a reward greater in scope than any particular State may grant to promote progress in those fields which Congress determines are worthy of national action."[91] He then immediately stated his conclusion: "Although the Copyright Clause thus recognizes the potential benefits of a national system, it does not indicate that all writings are of national interest or that state legislation is, in all cases, unnecessary or precluded."[92] To support this conclusion, he made two arguments. First, he cited six examples of patents granted by the states in the eighteenth century.[93] Second, he argued that because of the diversity of modern United States, "it is unlikely that all citizens in all parts of the country place the same importance on works relating to all subjects."[94] On this reasoning he reached his ultimate conclusion on this issue: "Since the subject matter to which the Copyright Clause is addressed may thus be of purely local importance and not worthy of national attention or protection, we cannot discern such an unyielding national interest as to require an inference that state power has been relinquished to *exclusive* federal control."[95]

This brief portion of the *Goldstein* opinion contains the crucial determination that copyright is not only a matter of potential national concern, but can also be a matter of "purely local importance." A closer examination of this reasoning casts serious doubt on its validity. The two arguments that the Chief Justice employed do not support his conclusions. The six examples of state-granted eighteenth-century patents that he cited all predate the adoption of the Constitution and are thus totally irrelevant to any discussion of constitutional preemption. The other spoke of "the diversity of people's backgrounds, origins, and interests" and of "the variety of business and industry."[96] From this he derived the conclusion that "it is unlikely that all citizens in all parts of the country place the same importance on works relating to all subjects."[97] This second diversity is a diversity of aesthetic and intellectual priori-

---

91 *Id.* at 556.   94 *Id.* at 557–58.   96 *Id.* at 557.
92 *Id.* at 556–57.   95 *Id.* at 558.   97 *Id.* at 557–58.
93 *Id.* at 557 n.13.

ties. There is absolutely nothing inherently local about such diversity. The aesthetic tastes and concerns of a resident of one state may be in complete harmony with those of a stranger living thousands of miles away, but antithetical to those of his next-door neighbor. The intellectual and aesthetic diversity which *Goldstein* relied on exists not only nationally but locally. There is no geographic element inherent in such diversity as with the local harbor of *Cooley* or the state roads in *Barnwell*. Thus, the existence of the diversity which Chief Justice Burger postulated does not support his conclusion that the subject matter of copyright is not national in character.

Perhaps an even more important element of *Goldstein*'s holding on this issue is the progression from "fields which Congress determines are worthy of national action," to "writings . . . of national interest," to "subject matter . . . of purely local importance."[98] These semantic changes are more than mere substitutions of phraseology. These changes shift the definitions of the nature of the subject matter of copyright, thereby enabling the *Goldstein* opinion to reach its conclusion.

The first phrase, "fields which Congress determines are worthy of national action,"[99] appears in the discussion of Madison's commentary on the Copyright Clause and is used to indicate those classes of subject matter which Congress might grant copyright protection. The determination of which writings are "worthy of national action" is an undoubted congressional prerogative, and no exception can be taken to *Goldstein*'s usage of that language.

The usage of the second phrase should be considered in its full context: "Although the Copyright Clause thus recognizes the potential benefits of a national system, it does not indicate that all writings are of national interest or that state legislation is, in all cases, unnecessary or precluded."[100] Insofar as this reaffirms that Congress may choose to protect some writings but not others, it creates no difficulties. The fuller context suggests, however, that the majority opinion is creating a dichotomy between writings of national interest and writings of local interest. Upon examination, this particular concept proves to be so amorphous as to be chimerical. Obviously no two works will have identical appeal throughout the nation, and the same can be said for different categories of po-

---

[98] *Ibid.*   [99] *Id.* at 556.   [100] *Id.* at 556–57.

tentially copyrightable works, thus reflecting a diversity of intellectual and aesthetic concerns. But this alone is not sufficient to localize the concern with a particular work or category of works. *Goldstein* gives no examples of works of local interest. A search for such examples yields the conclusion that specific works or writings may have local appeal but their categories do not seem to be able to be so aligned. For example songs such as state songs, school fight songs or "alma maters" or songs celebrating a particular location may have an intense local appeal. The category of songs cannot be so localized. The broader the category of subject matter, the more any purely local interest disappears. An illustrative progression might be from a particular "western" novel set in Texas, to western novels to novels to fiction to prose to literature to writing. Thus *Goldstein*'s division of the subject matter of copyright into national and local categories disappears as the definitions of the categories expand. The national-local distinction has little if any reality when applied to classifications of any scope beyond specific works.

The final phrase, "subject matter . . . of purely local importance"[101] concluded *Goldstein*'s inquiry into the national or local nature of the subject matter of copyright. The implications of the previous discussion are made concrete. The geographic element that the prior verbal formulation suggests is explicitly proclaimed. As in the preceding passage, no examples are given and no authority is cited. The change in language makes *Goldstein*'s argument more emphatic but adds no substance. In effect, *Goldstein* proclaims that copyright may be purely local subject matter by fiat without any support or foundation in fact.

III. GOLDSTEIN: THE SUPREMACY AND COPYRIGHT ISSUES

After determining that the Copyright Clause of the Constitution did not preempt state copyright legislation a priori, the Goldstein opinion next had to deal with the question whether the 1909 Copyright Act prevented such state legislation with respect to sound recordings. Chief Justice Burger began his analysis by examining the definitions of the words "Writings" and "Authors" as they appear in the Copyright Clause. He adopted the definition of an "author" from *Burrow-Giles Lithographic Co. v. Sarony*[102]

---

[101] *Id.* at 558.   [102] 111 U.S. 53, 58 (1884).

as being the "originator" or "he to whom anything owes its origin." The word "writings" likewise was broadly defined "to include any physical rendering of the fruits of creative intellectual or aesthetic labor."[103] From this he cautiously concluded: "Thus, recordings of artistic performances may be within the reach of Clause 8."[104] The opinion then stated the tautology that "[w]hether any specific category of 'Writings' is to be brought within the purview of the federal statutory scheme is left to the discretion of the Congress."[105] In short, congressional intent is determinative.

A. CONGRESSIONAL INTENT AND THE 1909 COPYRIGHT ACT

Chief Justice Burger's next step in the *Goldstein* opinion was to demonstrate that the 1909 Copyright Act did not permit copyright protection of the performances embodied in sound recordings. But he ignored the crucial issue whether this omission of protection was an intentional element of the federal regulatory scheme. Historically there is a strong case that the unique treatment given to sound recordings was deliberate. In *White-Smith Music Publishing Co. v. Apollo Co.*,[106] which arose prior to the enactment of the 1909 Copyright Act, the Supreme Court held that the unauthorized manufacture and sale of perforated music rolls (player piano rolls) did not infringe the copyright of the underlying musical composition. Relying on the dicta in *Burrow-Giles Lithographic Co. v. Sarony*[107] limiting copyright to "all forms of . . . visible expression," *Apollo* held that a perforated roll was not a "copy" within the meaning of the Copyright Act because it was not "a written or printed record . . . in intelligible notation."[108] *Apollo* thus established definitions of "copy" and "writing" which excluded mechanical sound reproducing devices, including sound recordings, from the scope of the then existing Copyright Act.

When Congress made a wholesale revision of the copyright laws in 1909, one of the concerns that Congress felt was a need to define the scope of the coverage of the pending legislation. Section 4 of the Copyright Act provides: "The works for which copyright may be secured under this title shall include all the writings of an

[103] 412 U.S. at 561.

[104] *Id.* at 56.

[105] *Ibid.*

[106] 209 U.S. 1 (1908).

[107] 111 U.S. at 58.

[108] 209 U.S. at 17.

author."[109] After listing specific classes of works for which copyright may be secured, § 5 of the Copyright Act concludes with the provision that "the above specifications shall not be held to limit the subject matter of copyright as defined in section 4 of this title."[110] The congressional adoption of the constitutional terminology of " writings" and "authors" was a deliberate effort to enlarge the scope of the statute to be coextensive with the scope of the Copyright Clause.[111] In the report on the predecessor bill[112] of the 1909 act, the Senate committee complained that the listing of separate categories in the then existing statute had the unwanted effect of "requiring frequent additions to cover new forms or new processes." Speaking of the bill that was ultimately adopted, the House Committee stated that the word "writings" was deliberately taken from the Constitution with the expectation that it would be given "the construction which the courts have given it."[113]

Turning to the question of mechanical reproduction of musical compositions, Congress incorporated a provision designed both to reverse the result of the *Apollo* decision and to alleviate fears of a music monopoly. This provision, contained in § 1(4) of the 1909 Copyright Act,[114] was a curious compromise designed to accommodate two distinct concerns which might otherwise conflict. It granted the copyright proprietor of a musical composition the exclusive right to make the first reproductions embodying the composition on "parts of instruments serving to reproduce mechanically the musical work," but, after doing so, "any other person may make similar use of the copyrighted work on payment to the copyright proprietor of a royalty of two cents on each such part manufactured." This denied the copyright proprietor the exclusive right to be first, which would presumably give him a headstart in the marketplace, plus the statutorily prescribed two cent royalty. These benefits are less than unlimited copyright protection as a deliberate antimonopoly measure.

Against this background, the courts prior to *Goldstein* have consistently held that the phrase "writings of an author" as it

---

[109] 17 U.S.C. § 4.   [110] 17 U.S.C. § 5.

[111] H.R. Rep. No. 222, 60th Cong., 2d Sess. 10 (1909).

[112] S. Rep. No. 6187, 59th Cong., 2d Sess. 4 (1907).

[113] H.R. Rep. No. 222, note 111 *supra*, at 10.

[114] 35 Stat. 1075 (1909).

appears in § 4 of the Copyright Act does not include the performances embodied in sound recordings even though such performances may be "Writings" of "Authors" for purposes of the Copyright Clause of the Constitution. The courts reached this conclusion in several cases, the most notable of which is *Capitol Records, Inc. v. Mercury Records Corp.*[115] Prior to World War II, Capitol had obtained an exclusive license to manufacture phonograph records in the United States duplicated from master recordings owned by Telefunken, a German company. After the war, Mercury obtained a license to manufacture phonograph records of the same recorded performances from a Czechoslovakian company. The Czechoslovakian company had originally obtained its rights in the recordings from Telefunken prior to World War II as had Capitol, but the German rights were forfeited in Czechoslovakia following the war. Speaking for the majority, Judge Dimock[116] held that state law should be applied because sound recordings could not obtain copyright protection under the federal copyright laws. To buttress this conclusion, Judge Dimock quoted the same passage of the House Committee Report on the 1909 act that Chief Justice Burger quoted in *Goldstein:* "It is not the intention of the committee to extend the right of copyright to the mechanical reproductions themselves, but only to give the composer or copyright proprietor the control, in accordance with the provisions of the bill, of the manufacture and use of such devices."[117]

Judge Dimock read this passage in conjunction with the following passage of the same House Committee Report as justifying the removal of recorded performances from the intended coverage of § 4 of the Copyright Act:[118]

> Section 4 is declaratory of existing law. It was suggested that the word "works" should be substituted for the word "writings," in view of the board construction given by the courts to the word "writings," but it was thought better to use the word "writings" which is the word used in the Constitution. It is not intended by the use of this word to change in any way the construction which the courts have given it.

---

[115] 221 F.2d 657 (2d Cir. 1955). See also RCA Mfg. Co. v. Whiteman, 114 F.2d 86 (2d Cir. 1940); Aeolian Co. v. Royal Music Roll Co., 196 Fed. 926 (W.D. N.Y. 1912); but see Fonotipia Ltd. v. Bradley, 171 Fed. 951 (E.D. N.Y. 1909).

[116] He was joined by Judge Medina; Judge Learned Hand dissented.

[117] 221 F.2d at 661.   [118] *Ibid.*

Reasoning that the 1909 act did not change the denial of copyright protection to phonograph records that resulted from *Apollo*, the *Capitol* opinion concluded that phonograph records were not subject matter entitled to copyright under the statute. Judge Learned Hand, dissenting from the majority conclusion that state law should be applied to grant Capitol an injunction against Mercury, concurred in the majority's conclusion that a phonograph record was a constitutional writing but not a statutory one.[119]

In *Goldstein*, Chief Justice Burger reaffirmed the conclusion of *Capitol* and other authorities that §§ 4 and 5 of the Copyright Act do not permit an independent copyright for sound recordings. Unfortunately, he did not consider the issue whether this omission was a deliberate intent to exclude sound recording from protection. Every available indication is that Congress created a hybrid status for sound recordings only after conscious deliberation of the impact of unlimited copyright of sound recordings on a potential monopoly situation. The result, a statutory royalty in lieu of an unlimited copyright for the statutory term was created by design and not by oversight. From this it follows that the *Goldstein* conclusion is erroneous. By sanctioning state legislation in this area, *Goldstein* permits the states to frustrate the regulatory design of Congress. By any reading of the various preemption and supremacy formulas that may be chosen, the result is unjustified. Considering the natural sympathy one feels for the recording artist and those deriving their rights through the artist, the results of a contrary decision in *Goldstein* would have been harsh and distasteful. Nonetheless, the appropriate remedy is not the endorsement of state circumvention of congressional intent.

There is another important dimension to this particular issue which remained unarticulated in *Goldstein*. The argument for the *Goldstein* result most forcefully stated is that the 1909 Act provided a limited protection to the author of the musical composition but provided none for the performer who is the "author" of the performance which is embodied in a sound recording; Congress failed to recognize this second authorship by oversight and not by intent; therefore, *Goldstein* is correct in concluding not only that Congress did not legislate in this area but that Congress did not consider this issue in formulating its legislation. Since this gap in

---

[119] *Id.* at 664.

the coverage of the 1909 act was not created as a deliberate element of the regulatory scheme adopted by Congress, it would justify *Goldstein*'s holding that Congress left this area "unattended" and, if one accepts the balance of the *Goldstein* opinion, open to state legislation.

This analysis, however, is incomplete. A performer may be the "author" of a performance, but the very concept of performance requires the existence of subject matter to be performed. The performance of a subsisting work logically fits into the provisions of § 7 of the Copyright Act: "Compilations or abridgments, adaptations, arrangements, dramatizations, translations, or other versions of . . . copyrighted works when produced with the consent of the proprietor of the copyright in such works . . . shall be regarded as new works subject to copyright."[120] Thus performances of an underlying work would fit into that category commonly referred to as "derivative works,"[121] and the right to claim copyright therein would belong to the author of the underlying work, unless he agreed otherwise. For example, for a radio station to broadcast a musical composition or for a performer to perform a musical composition in a place of entertainment requires the consent of the copyright proprietor. The fact that Congress in § 1(e) of the 1909 act[122] granted the copyright proprietor of the underlying musical composition much less than unlimited monopoly rights in sound recordings of the composition, does not imply that the rights of the performer were overlooked, as these rights are inherently derivative. It can be argued that the rights of an author of a performance which *Goldstein* suggests Congress overlooked, were rights which in fact the author of the performance did not have in the first place.

Neither of these approaches is wholly satisfactory. It does not follow that the congressional limitation on the rights of the composer to control sound recordings of his composition thereby automatically creates independent rights in the performer whose rendition of the composition is embodied in the sound recording. The compulsory licensing provisions of § 1(e) of the 1909 act grant others the right to make "similar use" of the underlying compo-

---

[120] 17 U.S.C. § 7.

[121] This phraseology is adopted from NIMMER ON COPYRIGHT, §§ 39–45 (1974 ed.).

[122] 35 STAT. 1075 (1909).

sition but do not grant the similar users an independent property right in the resulting sound recording. This result could be achieved on an implied license theory, *i.e.*, the compulsory license granted by the statute carries with it an implied license to own the rights in the recorded performance. This approach is not unreasonable and would seem to accord with the *Goldstein* holding on this issue. This does not, however, accord with the practice of the music industry. The owner of a master sound recording may manufacture, distribute, and sell copies of the sound recording but he can make no further use of the recording without the consent of the owner of the underlying composition. The sound recording cannot be performed on radio or television, synchronized with a motion picture, used in a commercial advertisement, or played in a discotheque without the consent of the owner of the composition.[123] It should also be noted that the performer cannot publicly perform the composition for profit without the owner's consent, notwithstanding the fact that he has recorded the composition under the compulsory license provisions of § 1(e) of the Copyright Act.

From this the more logical conclusion would seem to be that the rights in the performance are in fact derivative or both joint and derivative. The problem this analysis poses for the *Goldstein* decision is that the rights of the owner of the composition in sound recordings are limited by statute to the two-cent compulsory license, and it is difficult to see how the owners of derivative rights or of joint rights in a derivative work could have greater rights than the owner of the underlying composition originally had in the composition. Since these rights are defined and, in the case of sound recordings, expressly limited by statute, a state law providing greater rights than the federal statute would run afoul of the Supremacy Clause.

B. SEARS AND COMPCO

The next major step in the *Goldstein* opinion was to distinguish the cases of *Sears, Roebuck & Co. v. Stiffel Co.*[124] and *Compco*

---

[123] Associated Music Publishers, Inc. v. Debs Memorial Radio Fund, Inc., 141 F.2d 852 (2d Cir. 1944); Jerome v. Twentieth Century Fox Film Corp., 67 F. Supp. 736 (S.D. N.Y. 1946), *aff'd* 165 F.2d 784 (2d Cir. 1948); Herbert v. The Shanley Co., 242 U.S. 591 (1917).

[124] 376 U.S. 225 (1964).

Corp. v. DayBrite Lighting, Inc.[125] in which the Supreme Court had ruled that manufactured articles that did not qualify for patent protection could not be protected from copying by state common law theories of unfair competition, holding that such laws were preempted. There, the Court had explicitly stated, "when an article is unprotected by a patent or a copyright, state law may not forbid others to copy that article. To forbid copying would interfere with the federal policy, found in Art. 1, § 8, cl. 8, of the Constitution and the implementing federal statutes, of allowing free access to copy whatever the federal patent and copyright laws leave in the public domain."[126] On the basis of the sweeping language of *Sears* and *Compco* and their holdings that state laws of unfair competition were preempted by the federal patent and copyright powers, the result in *Goldstein* seems at first glance to be anomalous.

Chief Justice Burger distinguished *Sears* and *Compco* in the following rather ambiguous passage which sets out the entirety of his discussion of the issue:[127]

> In regard to mechanical configurations, Congress had balanced the need to encourage innovation and originality of invention against the need to insure competition in the sale of identical or substantially identical products. The standards established for granting federal patent protection to machines thus indicated not only which articles in this particular category Congress wished to protect, but which configurations it wished to remain free. The application of state law in these cases to prevent the copying of articles which did not meet the requirements for federal protection disturbed the careful balance Congress had drawn and thereby necessarily gave way under the Supremacy Clause of the Constitution. No comparable conflict between state law and federal law arises in the case of recordings of musical performances. In regard to this category of "Writings," Congress has drawn no balance; rather, it has left the area unattended, and no reason exists why the State should not be free to act.

This passage suggests the most likely basis for the differential treatment the inventions in *Sears* and *Compco* and the sound recordings in *Goldstein*. In *Sears* and *Compco*, the items in question

---

[125] 376 U.S. 234 (1964).

[126] *Id.* at 237.

[127] 412 U.S. at 569–70.

were clearly proper subject matter for patent protection but failed to meet the requisite standards of novelty, utility and non-obviousness, the prerequisites for patent protection.[128] By contrast, sound recordings, the subject matter in *Goldstein,* could not have been subject to copyright whether or not the particular works in question satisfied the threshold copyright standards of originality and creativity. The distinction is one based on the eligibility for federal statutory protection of the class to which the specific item under consideration belongs. On this basis *Goldstein* does not overrule or alter the holdings of *Sears* and *Compco,* but limits their applicability to subject matter which is covered by the federal copyright and patent laws.

While limiting the scope of *Sears* and *Compco* to statutory rather than constitutional writings does not create an unavoidable conflict with these decisions, *Goldstein*'s premise that sound recordings are not covered by the 1909 Copyright Act is still open to serious question. The deficiency of *Goldstein*'s treatment of *Sears* and *Compco* is the discernible intent of Congress to accord a unique treatment of sound recordings. Congress drew a perhaps unwise but very precise balance between the rights of the author of a musical composition and the public policy of preventing monopolies. The legislative history of the 1909 act belies the Court's blithe assumption that "Congress has drawn no balance; rather, it has left the area unattended."[129]

C. THE PUBLICATION ISSUE

Chief Justice Burger brushed aside with a footnote[130] the last of the three issues he originally defined, rejecting petitioners' claim that the sound recordings in question has been "published," thereby forfeiting all protections except those authorized by the Copyright Act. Petitioners' contention rested on § 2 of the Copyright Act which provides: "Nothing in this title shall be construed to annul or limit the right of the author or proprietor of an unpublished work, at common law or in equity, to prevent the copying, publication, or use of such unpublished work without his consent, and to obtain damages therefor."[131] They argued that § 2 defined the boundaries of permissible state copyright protection, whether by

---

[128] 35 U.S.C. §§ 101–03.

[129] 412 U.S. at 570.

[130] *Id.* at 570 n.28.

[131] 17 U.S.C. § 2.

statute or case law. Arguing further that the sound recordings in question had been published, petitioners concluded from their syllogism that the sound recordings in question had been removed from the ambit of congressionally authorized state protection. Consistently with the rest of his opinion, Chief Justice Burger took the position that sound recordings belonged to those "categories of writings which Congress has not brought within the scope of the federal statute," concluding the term "publication" has no application.[132]

Certainly, the Chief Justice's treatment of this issue follows logically from his prior conclusions. If one accepts the premise that the limit of state copyright regulation is statutory rather than constitutional "writings," then the definition of "publication" for works outside the scope of the Copyright Act must be a question of state law, and any disagreement with this conclusion must rest on the issue of congressional intent underlying § 1 (e) of the 1909 act already discussed.

Some of the ramifications of Chief Justice Burger's position on this issue deserve mention. *Goldstein* implies that the distribution and sale of sound recordings is not a publication of the underlying musical composition for purposes of § 2 of the Copyright Act. Also, that the series of state court civil cases[133] which have enjoined unauthorized duplication of sound recordings now rests on a solid constitutional foundation. Finally, while seeming to be congruent with the case of *Wheaton v. Peters*,[134] which also looked to state common law for a definition of "publication," *Goldstein* could be the key that opens the door to the erosion of the *Wheaton* doctrine that publication is divestive of common law rights.[135]

D. GOLDSTEIN AS AMPLIFIED BY KEWANEE

The Chief Justice's opinion for the majority in *Kewanee* posed the issue "whether state trade secret protection is preempted by

---

[132] 412 U.S. at 570 n.28.

[133] Capitol Records, Inc. v. Spies, 130 Ill. App.2d 429 (1970); Capitol Records, Inc. v. Erickson, 2 Cal. App.3d 526 (1969); Liberty U/ A, Inc. v. Eastern Tape Corp., 11 N.C. App. 20 (1974); Capitol Records, Inc. v. Greatest Records, Inc., 43 (N.Y.) Misc. 2d 878 (1964).

[134] 8 Pet. 591 (1834).

[135] *Id.* at 664.

operation of the federal patent law."[136] The pattern of analysis parallels that of *Goldstein*. Preemption is considered first, and, as in *Goldstein*, the standard is that of *Hines v. Davidowitz*, whether the challenged state law "stands as an obstacle to the accomplishment and execution of the full purposes and objectives of Congress."[137] *Kewanee*, however, considered the public policy objectives of the patent laws, which it identified as the quid pro quo of monopoly for disclosure, balancing the encouragement of invention with the interest in disseminating knowledge both for its own sake and to stimulate further discovery.[138] The policies of the trade secret laws were identified as the "maintenance of standards of commercial ethics and the encouragement of invention."[139] An extensive inquiry into the overlapping spheres of patent and trade secret law followed, and the conclusion was "that the extension of trade secret protection to clearly patentable [but unpatented] inventions does not conflict with the patent policy of disclosure."[140] While there is ample room for disagreement with the conclusion that no conflict exists, what is of greatest significance is the broad scope of the inquiry into the public policy served by the patent laws and the expansion of the *Goldstein* decision.

Whether or not one is persuaded by Chief Justice Burger's arguments, the fact is he engages in a lengthy and serious inquiry into the economic gains resulting from business secrecy and finds that while the trade secret and patent laws overlap, they do not conflict. Admitting the risk that an inventor with a clearly patentable invention might eschew the seventeen years of patent protection in reliance on the perpetual protection of trade secret laws and thereby frustrate the federal patent policy of disclosure and its beneficial effects on the progress of science and technology, he argued the superior protection of the patent laws will obviate this potential problem. Although confronted with a contradictory example in the case before him, Chief Justice Burger postulated that the "possibility that an inventor who believes his invention meets the standards of patentability will sit back, rely on trade secret law, and after one year of use forfeit any right to patent protection . . . is remote indeed."[141] He continued: "Nor does society face

---

[136] 416 U.S. at 472.

[137] *Id*. at 479.

[138] *Id*. at 480–81.

[139] *Id*. at 481.

[140] *Id*. at 491.

[141] *Id*. at 490.

much risk that scientific or technological progress will be impeded from the rare inventor with a patentable invention who chooses trade secret protection over patent protection."[142] It is striking, however, that the *Kewanee* opinion never mentioned the ultimate dedication of the invention to the public domain as one of the federal policies of the Patent Act but talked solely of disclosure.[143]

Kewanee represents a significant expansion of the holding in *Goldstein* and an abrupt shift in emphasis in Supremacy Clause decision making. Conflicts between state and federal laws and frustration of the purposes of federal acts are constitutionally permissible provided the Court can classify the occurrence of these incidents of conflict and frustration as "remote" and "rare." It would seem that all that is now required of state laws which may overlap federal laws is a reasonable congruence of purpose and a lack of frequently occurring points of conflict.

Goldstein is far more cursory than *Kewanee* in its attempts to identify the underlying public policy interests that are embodied in the relevant constitutional and statutory provisions. The *Goldstein* opinion appropriately begins its inquiry with the Copyright Clause, which grants Congress the power "To promote the Progress of Science and useful Arts, by securing for limited Times to Authors and Inventors the exclusive Right to their respective Writings and Discoveries." The Chief Justice defined the purpose of the Copyright Clause and the method by which Congress may achieve this purpose: "In other words, to encourage people to devote themselves to intellectual and artistic creation, Congress may guarantee to authors and inventors a reward in the form of control over the sale or commercial use of copies of their works."[144] Having identified the goal of the Copyright Clause as the encouragement of "intellectual and artistic creation,"[145] he made no further inquiry into the national public policies embodied in the Copyright Clause or the Copyright Act.

At issue in *Goldstein* was the question whether the challenged state statute, by creating a copyright of unlimited duration, violated that portion of the Copyright Clause which provides that copyrights may be granted only "for limited Times." The manner in which Chief Justice Burger dealt with this issue was super-

---

[142] *Ibid.*

[143] *Id.* at 480–81.

[144] 412 U.S. at 555.

[145] *Ibid.*

ficial. Citing no precedent or other authority, he concluded that the "limited Times" requirement is a limitation on the power of Congress and had no application to the states.[146] This point cannot be laid to rest so easily. The copyright monopoly provides economic incentive encouraging aesthetic and intellectual creations which presumably benefit society. The limited time requirement of the Copyright Clause is given a precise limit in the Copyright Act of twenty-eight years plus a renewal period of an additional twenty-eight years.[147] Both the Constitution and the statute entail an ultimate dedication of all copyrighted works to the public domain where all citizens will have the right to free and unlimited use of the work in question. Two consequences flow from the expiration of a copyright. First, on an economic level, the public is relieved of the burden of monopoly price structures for any work entering the public domain. Second, the public domain is enriched. Thus the bargain which rewards the artist for his creative efforts with an economic monopoly also requires that the product of these efforts will ultimately enter the public domain. The consequences of the "limited Times" mandate of the Copyright Clause illustrate the policy that can be attributed to this requirement. Carefully avoiding any use of the word "policy" or any statement of what the dangers are that may be perceived, the Chief Justice disposed of the issue peremptorily:[148]

> Moreover, it is not clear that the dangers to which this limitation was addressed apply with equal force to both the Federal Government and the States. When Congress grants an exclusive right or monopoly, its effects are pervasive; no citizen or State may escape its reach. As we have noted, however, the exclusive right granted by a State is confined to its borders. Consequently, even when the right is unlimited in duration, any tendency to inhibit further progress in science or the arts is narrowly circumscribed.

In *Goldstein* Chief Justice Burger found that the challenged statute's inhibition of "further progress in science or the arts is narrowly circumscribed."[149] Yet he did not deny and may even be said to admit that some circumscription of the constitutional requirement of limited copyright duration does occur. In *Kewanee*,

---

[146] *Id.* at 560–61.

[147] 17 U.S.C. § 24.

[148] 412 U.S. at 560–61.

[149] *Id.* at 561.

he admitted that the policy of disclosure inherent in the patent laws may be frustrated by state trade secret laws, but stated that these are tolerable as they are "remote" or "rare." *Goldstein* explicitly treated the required expiration of a copyright as being only a limitation on Congress, thus avoiding consideration of the policy question posed by a perpetual state copyright. *Kewanee* identified a national interest in disclosure[150] but the ultimate dedication to the public domain was never really considered. In light of the pervasiveness of this theme in the literature of the law of patents and copyrights, the almost studied oversight of this issue by the *Goldstein* and *Kewanee* decisions is difficult to rationalize.

IV. SOME CONCLUSIONS AND IMPLICATIONS OF GOLDSTEIN

A. THE PREEMPTION ISSUE

The *Goldstein* decision reaffirms the rhetoric of the national-local subject matter test of *Cooley v. Board of Wardens*, thereby confirming the resurgence of this doctrine which began with *South Carolina State Highway Dep't v. Barnwell Bros.* and *Southern Pacific Co. v. Arizona*. While the precedents remained controlling, there can be no doubt that the direction of the preemption inquiry has been subtly but significantly altered. *Cooley* demands an inquiry into whether the subject matter of the regulation in question demands either national unformity or diversity. In *Goldstein*, the ultimate inquiry is whether the Court can or "cannot discern such an unyielding national interest as to require an inference that state power . . . has been relinquished to *exclusive* federal control."[151] This passage indicates that while the language of the test remains the same, the standards are in fact different.

B. THE SUPREMACY ISSUE

Beyond the immediate realm of patents and copyrights, *Goldstein* and *Kewanee* clearly lower the barriers of preemption and supremacy which might invalidate state legislation. Although the standard for testing state and federal conflicts is that adopted from *Hines v. Davidowitz*, a certain level of impingement on federal policy enunciated in a federal statute, not to mention a clause in the Constitution, is permitted the states, a result that would have

---

[150] 416 U.S. at 480–81.   [151] 412 U.S. at 558.

been intolerable in *Hines*. The reach of the Supremacy Clause has been limited.

C. COPYRIGHTS AND PATENTS

The implications of *Goldstein* and *Kewanee* for the future of the copyright and patent areas are troublesome. Clearly the Supreme Court has read both statutes as having a lesser scope than the constitutional clause. Thus not only sound recordings but other interstices in the federal Copyright and Patent Acts have been left open for state protection. Now that the states have a green light, it is only a question of time until such subject matter as dress designs, new breeds of animals, etc., are granted the blessings of perpetual state monopoly protection.

Perhaps the most troublesome of all of the problems left in the wake of *Goldstein* and *Kewanee* is Chief Justice Burger's definition of the public interest involved in the federal constitutional and statutory provisions. To the Chief Justice, the public policies embodied in the statutes are the encouragement of intellectual and aesthetic creation for copyright, and the encouragement of invention for patents. The statutory monopoly is the reward. The inventor's exchange is disclosure and the author's presumably publication. The "limited Times" provision of the Constitution is dismissed as simply a limit imposed on Congress, not on the states. There is no recognition of a public policy requiring ultimate dedication to the public domain in return for the time of the monopoly.

The *Goldstein* decision is something of an anticlimax for the recording industry. The 1971 Sound Recording Amendment,[152] which became effective on 15 February 1972, over a year prior to the *Goldstein* decision, provides federal sanctions, both civil and criminal, against the unauthorized duplication of sound recordings. Thus the importance to the recording industry of the *Goldstein* decision appears of minor consequence, particularly in light of the fleeting nature of phonograph record popularity. Nevertheless, the record industry has not abated the campaign for the enactment of further state criminal legislation outlawing unauthorized duplication of sound recordings.[153] Thus, the question whether the enforcement of a state statute of the type considered in *Goldstein*

---

[152] 17 U.S.C. §§ 1(f), 5(n), 19, 20, 26, 101(e).

[153] It would seem that more than half the states have recently enacted some legislation.

is preempted by the present Copyright Act may continue to be an issue for decision.

Moreover, the effect of the *Goldstein* opinion on the pending Copyright Revision Bill[154] is intriguing. Unlike § 4 of the present Copyright Act, § 102(a) of the Revision Bill abandons the constitutional language of "Writings" and "Authors" and instead speaks of "works of Authorship." The key passage provides:

> Copyright protection subsists, in accordance with this title, in original works of authorship fixed in any tangible medium of expression, now known or later developed, from which they can be perceived, reproduced, or otherwise communicated, either directly or with the aid of a machine or device. Works of authorship include the following categories:
> (1) literary works;
> (2) musical works, including any accompanying words;
> (3) dramatic works, including any accompanying music;
> (4) pantomimes and choreographic works;
> (5) pictorial, graphic, and sculptural works;
> (6) motion pictures and other audiovisual works;
> (7) sound recordings.

The Revision Bill does not define "works," "authors," and "works of Authorship." The phrase "works of Authorship" implies that something different is meant from the constitutional "Writings of Authors." While § 103 of the Revision Bill defines "fixed" sufficiently broadly to avoid the requirement of visible notation adopted by *White-Smith Music Publishing Co. v. Apollo Co.*[155] and *Burrow-Giles Lithographic Co. v. Sarony*,[156] it would seem that further limitation on the scope of the proposed statute is intended beyond the requirements that the works must be "original" and "fixed in any tangible medium of expression." At first glance, the listed categories of subject matter would seem to be the obvious boundary for the coverage of the Revision Bill. The word "include" used in § 102(a), however, is defined as "illustrative and not limitative." The problem of defining the boundaries of the subject matter eligible for federal copyright protection will remain a clouded issue under the Revision Bill, although the particular question of sound recordings raised in *Goldstein* is settled.

---

[154] S. 22, 94th Cong., 1st Sess. (1975). The identical companion bill is H.R. 2223, 94th Cong., 1st Sess.

[155] 209 U.S. 1 (1908).   [156] 111 U.S. 53 (1884).

The Copyright Revision Bill poses additional questions of the application of the *Goldstein* decision. Section 301(a) of the proposed bill specifically provides: "[A]ll rights in the nature of copyright in works that come within the subject matter of copyright as specified by sections 102 and 103 . . . whether published or unpublished, are governed exclusively by this title . . . . [N]o person is entitled to copyright, literary property rights, or any other equivalent legal or equitable right in any such work under the common law or statutes of any State." This would seem to resolve one of the lingering problems of *Goldstein* and *Kewanee* whether concurrent state copyright legislation is to be tolerated. Section 301(b)(1) of the Revision Bill, however, sanctions state protection of "unpublished material that does not come within the subject matter of copyright as specified by sections 102 and 103, including works of authorship not fixed in any tangible medium of expression." This leaves a curious gap for published material "that does not come within the subject matter of copyright as specified by sections 102 and 103." One possible argument is that if Congress had intended to sanction state protection of published works outside the scope of §§ 102 and 103, it would have done so explicitly as it did for unpublished works. Alternatively on the basis of *Goldstein*, it would seem that such material is proper subject matter for state regulation because Congress has excluded it from copyright protection under the Revision Bill. Since the Revision Bill is silent on the power of the states to regulate published subject matter outside the scope of §§ 102 and 103, and makes no explicit provision that such subject matter shall be free of regulation, it would be easy to reach the conclusion, following *Goldstein*: "In regard to this category of 'Writings,' Congress has drawn no balance; rather, it has left the area unattended, and no reason exists why the State should not be free to act."[157] In light of *Goldstein*, the latter result must be deemed more probable.

As to subject matter within the scope of §§ 102 and 103, § 301(b)(1) preserves the authority of the states to protect such subject matter prior to its being "fixed in any tangible medium of expression." In essence, this preserves state protection of essentially inchoate works as does § 2 of the present Copyright Act.[158] It substitutes a test of "fixation" which presents a more concrete

---

[157] 412 U.S. at 570.   [158] 17 U.S.C. § 2.

technical and factual issue for the present test of "publication" which has proved an amorphous and vexing concept for the courts to decide.[159] This passage of the Revision Bill also makes it clear that the phrase "fixed in any tangible medium of expression" is not part of the definition of "works of Authorship" but only defines the form a work of authorship must be in to secure federal copyright protection. Section 301(b)(1) of the Revision Bill provides further indication that the phrase "works of Authorship" is not as extensive in scope as the word "writings" in the Constitution, but does not give any guidance for clear measurement of the difference.

A restriction on federal preemption is found in § 301(b)(3) of the Revision Bill, which preserves the right of the states to grant protection "not equivalent to any of the exclusive rights within the general scope of copyright as specified in section 106, including breaches of contract, breaches of trust, invasion of privacy, defamation, and deceptive trade practices such as passing off and false representation." Since the Revision Bill defines the words "such as" "illustrative and not limitative," this could be interpreted to permit state court protection under the copying-misappropriation distinction that evolved from *International News Service v. Associated Press*.[160] But there is some indication in the legislative history of the Revision Bill that state protection against misappropriation was deemed equivalent to state copyright protection and therefore ought to be precluded under § 301(a).[161]

Finally, it need be said that the quality of the opinions in *Goldstein* and *Kewanee* leaves much to be desired. The precedents cited are familiar and respected, but little if any consideration was given to their content or the context within which they arose. They seem to be little more than a gloss upon analysis of the opinions. The result is that the Court's conclusions seem to be erroneous. A reading of the preemption precedents strongly suggests that the Copyright Clause and the Commerce Clause require the invalidation of the challenged statute. The failure to discern a national

---

[159] NIMMER, note 121 *supra*, at §§ 46–59.

[160] 248 U.S. 215 (1918).

[161] See H.R. Rep. No. 83, 90th Cong., 1st Sess. 100 (1967). [Since this was written, the Senate subcommittee has revised the bill substantially, authorizing state control whenever the subject is not specifically controlled by the terms of the bill. See S. Rep. No. 94-473, 94th Cong., 1st Sess. (1975).]

policy in the "limited Times" requirement of the Copyright Clause leads to the conclusion that the issue was deliberately fudged, and the reading of the legislative history of the 1909 Copyright Act by the Court surely cannot be justified.

Even more disturbing, perhaps, is the casual and one-sided nature of the opinion's empirical analysis of the social and economic policies and effects of its decisions. Almost devoid of any supporting authorities, *Goldstein*'s analysis of the effects of the challenged statute gave no scrutiny to the interstate economic consequences of the insular protection granted the California record industry and the subjection of the California consumer to a monopoly market. *Goldstein*'s identification of local industry as sufficient local subject matter to justify state regulation insulating the market from outside competition is surprising, however gratuitous *Goldstein*'s pronouncements may be. Hard cases may make, but do not justify, bad law.

It is ironic that the *Goldstein* opinion highlights its concluding section by citing Brandeis's famous dissent in *International News Service v. Associated Press:* "The general rule of law is, that the noblest of human productions—knowledge, truths ascertained, conceptions, and ideas—become, after voluntary communications to others, free as the air to common use."[162] Although one's sympathies lie with the recording artists and the authorized record producers, it must also be recalled that, while to "appropriate and use for profit, knowledge and ideas produced by other men, without making compensation or even acknowledgement, may be inconsistent with a finer sense of propriety . . . the law has heretofore sanctioned the practice."[163]

---

[162] 248 U.S. at 250.   [163] *Id* at 257.

JAMES BEARDSLEY

CONSTITUTIONAL REVIEW

IN FRANCE

From the fall of the *ancien régime* until 4 October 1958, the French resisted every effort to subject legislation to effective constitutional restraint. The judges of both the judicial and the administrative courts refused to examine any plea founded on the unconstitutionality of an act of Parliament or, indeed, of any other manifestation of *la loi*. Several attempts to establish nonjudicial organs of constitutional review foundered in institutional weakness and in the political impossibility of effectively restraining imperial or parliamentary legislators.

The Constitution of 4 October 1958[1] profoundly altered the distribution of lawmaking power in the French Republic and made some measure of effective constitutional review indispensable. By confining the legislative authority of the Parliament to certain fundamental matters and empowering the Government to make law by decree in all areas not expressly saved to Parliament, the 1958 Constitution split the lawmaking authority of the state. Encroachment by either lawmaker on the domain of the other was to be restrained by two institutions. The Conseil d'Etat, was to exercise its long-settled powers of judicial review of administrative acts. The newly created Conseil constitutionnel was empowered to determine the limits of parliamentary authority.

James Beardsley is Associate Professor of Law, The University of Chicago.

[1] [1958] Journal Officiel, édition Lois et Décrets, 9151 [hereinafter "J.O."]; [1958] Bulletin Législatif Dalloz 661 [hereinafter "B.L.D."].

A large part of what had been undivided and unlimited legislative power of parliaments, transmuted into autonomous regulatory authority in the Fifth Republic, had in this way become subject to substantive constitutional review in administrative litigation before the Conseil d'Etat. This, the highest administrative court, required the Government to comply not only with those constitutional provisions which define its regulatory competence, but equally with substantive norms said to be rooted in the Preamble to the Constitution.[2]

The Conseil constitutionnel was more circumspect. Not a tribunal to which the ordinary citizen might repair, the Conseil conceived of its role in constitutional review as that of a guardian of the frontier between parliamentary and governmental rule-making competences. For nearly thirteen years it performed this function without suggesting that its authority to test the constitutionality of acts of Parliament might include the application of substantive constitutional limitations restricting parliamentary authority within its zone of subject matter competence. Then, in 1971, when Parliament adopted a statute amending the law relating to nonprofit associations, the Conseil struck it down on the ground that it violated constitutionally protected freedom of association.[3]

Since the 1971 decision, there has occurred a series of events, some legal, some political, which strongly suggest that France, which has consistently and dogmatically resisted "government by judges" since the Revolution put an end to the legislative pretensions of the *anciens parlements*,[4] has indeed given to "the principle of constitutional supremacy the sanction which it has so long lacked."[5] To be sure, the judges of the administrative and judicial

---

[2] *E.g.*, Syndicat Général des Ingénieurs-Conseils, [1959] Recueil Sirey 202 [hereinafter "S."], [1959] Recueil Dalloz 541 [hereinafter "D."] (Cons. d'Et., 26 June 1959); Société Eky, [1960] D. 264 (Cons. d'Et., 12 Feb. 1960).

[3] Decision of 16 July 1971, [1971] J.O. 7114, [1971] Semaine Juridique (hereinafter "J.C.P."). II. 16832, [1971] Actualité Juridique, édition Droit Administratif 537 (Note Rivero) [hereinafter "A.J.D.A."]. The decision is analyzed at length in Beardsley, *The Constitutional Council and Constitutional Liberties in France*, 20 AM. J. COMP. L. 431 (1972). A comparison of the methods and reasoning of the Conseil in the 1971 decision with those of the United States Supreme Court is to be found in Haimbaugh, *Was It France's Marbury v. Madison?* 35 OHIO ST. L.J. 910 (1974).

[4] Throughout this paper, the word *parlement* will be used exclusively to refer to the royal courts of the *ancien régime*, while *Parliament* will be reserved to identify the national legislature under the several republican regimes.

[5] *Exposé des Motifs*, PROJET DE LOI CONSTITUTIONNELLE, ASSEMBLÉE NATIONALE Doc. No. 1181, Prem. sess. ord. 1974–75.

tribunals still adhere to the old dogma, but the new regime, and the recent decisions of the Conseil constitutionnel are subjecting the tradition of judicial deference to Parliament to considerable, unaccustomed strain.

In a country whose citizens are reputed to change the constitution more readily than they change their minds, it is only with great reservation that one dare assert that fundamental and durable constitutional change is occurring without upheaval through the interplay of old and new institutions. The assertion is especially hazardous when based on the developments of only four—or even seventeen—years. But the evidence is there, is cumulating, and is persuasive.

I. The Hostile Tradition

The *ancien régime* knew a kind of constitutional review in the *remontrances* which the *parlements* addressed to the King asserting the right and the duty of those courts to refuse to register royal decrees which they held to violate the fundamental law of the realm.[6] The exercise by the royal judges of the right of remonstrance and, graver still, their claim to share in lawmaking power through the issuance of general regulatory orders not connected with actual litigation (*arrêts de règlement*) were prerogatives not to be tolerated in a new constitutional system preoccupied with the separation of powers[7] and with the supremacy of *la loi*.[8] Judicial review—the enforcement of constitutional norms by the ordinary courts in the course of civil, criminal, or administrative litigation—was not to be permitted. Nonjudicial constitutional review

---

[6] See, *e.g.*, Ford, Robe and Sword 80–104 (1953); Esmein, Cours Élémentaire d'Histoire du Droit Français 518–43 (5th ed., 1903); Shennan, The Parlement of Paris 285–324 (1968). The right of remonstrance did not, however, embody a power to finally avoid legislation. The King, appearing in person in a proceeding known as the *lit de justice*, might, and often did, compel the recalcitrant judges to register the decree.

[7] "Any society in which . . . there is no separation of powers has no constitution." Decl. of Rts. of Man and Citizen of 26 Aug. 1789, Art. 16. Separation of powers theory can be, of course, handily applied either to attack or to defend constitutional review according to the version of the theory to which one subscribes and the nature of the arrangements for review which are under consideration. *Cf.* Vile, Constitutionalism and the Separation of Powers 157–58 (1967).

[8] *La loi* will sometimes be used in this paper as a broader category than "statute," its typical rendering in English, to encompass the variety of acts—imperial decrees, parliamentary legislation, certain ordinances—to which French public law attaches the quality of *la loi*.

—review by an organ independent of the judiciary and closely linked to the political process—was yet conceivable, but difficult, if not impossible, to organize effectively. These two persistent themes—hostility to judicial review and a certain receptiveness to the notion of "political" review—marked French constitutional thought for nearly two centuries. The unusual characteristics of the system of constitutional review emerging in the Fifth Republic are in large measure the outgrowth of an effort to design a constitutional system whose integrity is absolutely dependent upon the supremacy and enforcement of certain constitutional rules, but within the limits imposed by these notions.

A. JUDICIAL REVIEW: REVOLUTIONARY LEGISLATION AND JUDICIAL
   DEFERENCE

1. *Substantive review by the judicial tribunals.* Having set in motion the process that would lead to the abolition of the *parlements*,[9] the Constituent Assembly addressed itself in 1790 to judicial reform.[10] Among its concerns was the adoption of measures calculated to preclude frustration of the legislative will by a reformed judiciary. The celebrated Law of 16–24 August 1790 required the judges to apply to the legislature, whenever it might prove necessary, to interpret a statute, and prohibited them from "taking any part, directly or indirectly in the exercise of the legislative power" and from "obstructing or suspending the execution of the decrees of the Corps-législatif."[11] The Constitutions of 1791 and 1795 contained similar provisions.[12] As early as 1797 the Court of Cassation, invoking the Constitution of 22 August 1795, had occasion to deny the competence of the courts to consider the constitutionality of an act of the legislature.[13] In a number of nineteenth-century cases, the Court's refusal to judge the consti-

[9] CARRÉ, LA FIN DES PARLEMENTS 135–46 (1912).

[10] See GODECHOT, LES INSTITUTIONS DE LA FRANCE SOUS LA RÉVOLUTION ET L'EMPIRE 143–55 (2d ed., 1968), for a short account of the debates.

[11] Law of 16–24 Aug. 1790, Title II, Arts. 2, 3, 10, and 12, 1 DUVERGIER, COLLECTION COMPLÈTE DES LOIS 361, 363 (1824) (hereinafter "DUVERGIER").

[12] Const. of 3 Sept. 1791, chap. V, art. 3, 3 DUVERGIER 275; Const. of 22 Aug. 1795 (5 Fructidor An III), art. 203, 8 DUVERGIER 277, 289. Both texts are reproduced in DUGUIT, MONNIER & BONNARD, LES CONSTITUTIONS ET LES PRINCIPALES LOIS POLITIQUES DE LA FRANCE DEPUIS 1789, 1, 73 (7th ed., 1952) [hereinafter "BONNARD"].

[13] Decision of Criminal Chamber, 18 Fructidor An V (3 Sept. 1797), 30 DALLOZ, RÉPERTOIRE DE LÉGISLATION, DE DOCTRINE ET DE JURISPRUDENCE 196, n.1 (1853).

tutionality of legislation was founded not on the revolutionary prohibitions on judicial intervention in the legislative process, but on those provisions of the Constitution of 1799 which had for the first time instituted nonjudicial constitutional review through the attribution of powers of review to the Sénat conservateur.[14] Reasoning *a contrario* from the existence of a specialized organ of review, the Court held that review by ordinary tribunals was constitutionally precluded.

With the demise of the Constitution of 1799, and with it the Sénat conservateur (to reappear in the Constitution of 1852), the Court returned to the theory of separation of powers underlying the revolutionary legislation in what has become the leading decision on the incompetence of the judicial tribunals to examine the constitutionality of legislation. In the *affaire Paulin*, decided in 1833 under the regime established by the Charte of 1830,[15] the Court of Cassation declared: "[A] statute . . . adopted and promulgated in the manner constitutionally prescribed by the Charte, establishes the law for the courts, and cannot be attacked before them on the ground of unconstitutionality."[16] There is no reference to the revolutionary legislation and no hint of a theory of incompetence in the Court's decision, but the arguments of the *avocat-général*[17] suggest adherence by the Court to the theory that any judicial refusal to give effect to an authentic act of the legislature would constitute an impermissible intervention by the judges in the legislative power.

But *Paulin* did not immediately settle matters. Several later decisions undercut the Court's pronouncement in *Paulin* and were to provide some support to the proponents of judicial review in the doctrinal debates of the later nineteenth and early twentieth centuries.[18] Most important were two judgments rendered in 1851 in

---

[14] See, *e.g.*, Leveque, [1791-An XII] S. 627 (Cass. crim., 1 Floréal An X [20 Apr. 1802]); Lecabec, [1819–21] S. 79 (Cass. crim., 27 May 1819); Contributions Indirectes v. Potelle, [1819–21] S. 181 (Cass. crim., 3 Feb. 1820). On the *Sénat Conservateur* see text *infra* at notes 96–101.

[15] BONNARD 194.   [16] [1833] S. I.357.   [17] *Id.* at 360.

[18] Gauthier, [1851] D. I. 145 (Cass. crim., 15 March 1851); Gent [1851] S. I. 707 (Cass. crim., 17 Nov. 1851); Doyen et Lemaire, [1838] S. I. 314 (Cass. crim., 12 April 1838); Alliot, [1863] S. I. 350 (Cass. req., 15 April 1863). *Doyen* sustained legislation adopted prior to the *Charte* of 1830 against a claim of inconsistency with the *Charte* and consequent implicit abrogation. The Court, had it sustained the claim, would have merely been affirming the implicit abrogation of a prior statute by a later inconsistent one— a result to which the constitutional character of the *Charte* was purely incidental. In

which the Court of Cassation explicitly examined the substantive constitutionality of a statute purporting to subject civilians to courts-martial during a state of siege.[19] The Constitution of 4 November 1848 prohibited the creation of extraordinary tribunals, but it also authorized the National Assembly to determine by statute the conditions and effects of the declaration of a state of siege.[20] The latter authority, declared the Court, was sufficient to sustain the statute as a constitutional exercise of legislative power. Although the 1851 decisions certainly amounted to exercises in constitutional review (albeit less intrusive than a decision striking down a statute), the Court returned to the *Paulin* position in subsequent cases.[21]

2. *The position of the administrative courts.* The administrative courts did not squarely confront the issue until 1901.[22] In a decision of that year,[23] the Conseil d'Etat adhered to the rule adopted by the Court of Cassation in *Paulin*. The position of the Conseil d'Etat was more ambiguous, however, due to its development and application of nonstatutory principles which, in some applications, look remarkably like constitutional concepts.

Perhaps the best early example of this kind of decision is that which was handed down in the *Winkell* affair of 1909.[24] Winkell was a civil servant who had participated in a strike and was, for that reason, dismissed by his employer, the postal administration. In dismissing Winkell, the administration failed to comply with

---

Alliot the petitioner alleged that a penal statute was retroactive in effect and violative of Art. 2 of the Civil Code to which petitioner sought to attribute constitutional character. The court held that the statute in question was not retroactive and went on to observe that Art. 2 of the Civil Code was not in any event a constitutional rule.

[19] Law of 9 Aug. 1849, Art. 8, 49 DUVERGIER 268 at 274.

[20] Const. of 4 Nov. 1948, Arts. 4 and 106, BONNARD at 212, 214, 224.

[21] *E.g.*, Toutain v. Caisse artisanale vieillesse de Basse-Normandie, [1956] Bulletin des Arrêts de la Cour de Cassation II.464 (Cass. civ., 20 Dec. 1956) [hereinafter "Bull. civ."]; Schiavon, [1974] D. 273 (Cass. crim., 26 Feb. 1974), discussed in text *infra*, at notes 223–34.

[22] In an earlier decision, Dame Massois, [1853] Recueil des arrêts du Conseil d'Etat 1012 (Cons. d'Et., 2 Dec. 1853) [hereinafter "C.E."], petitioner alleged that the statute in question had not been adopted in conformity with the procedural requirements of the *Charte* of 1814. The language used to reject this claim asserts that the statute in question was "voted . . . promulgated and published according to the constitutional forms" and thus makes a constitutional determination but only on the procedural questions relating to the creation of the statute. See text *infra*, at notes 229–34.

[23] Delarue, [1902] D. III.87 (Cons. d'Et., 23 May 1901).

[24] [1909] S. III.145 (Cons. d'Et, 7 Aug. 1909).

the provisions of a 1905 statute requiring the government to inform a civil servant of the contents of his file before taking disciplinary action.[25] The Conseil d'Etat upheld the dismissal on the ground that a strike by civil servants was illicit even if not prohibited by statute because "in accepting the employment conferred upon him, the civil servant subjects himself to all of the obligations deriving from the needs of the public service and waives all rights incompatible with the essential continuity of the national life . . . ."[26] The strike violated this principle of "the continuity of the public service" and the strikers were held to have suffered in consequence a kind of outlawry, "placing themselves by a collective act beyond the application of laws and regulations adopted for the purpose of guaranteeing the exercise of the rights which they derive individually from the contract of public service."[27]

Maurice Hauriou argued that the decision could only be explained satisfactorily as a refusal to apply the 1905 statute for constitutional reasons—the "continuity of the public service" being a constitutional principle, not because it was to be found in the written document, but because it embodied a "condition necessary to the existence of the state."[28] Hauriou's arguments—advanced in notes to *Winkell* and other decisions as well as in his other writings[29]—provoked considerable doctrinal resistance[30] and failed to persuade the Conseil d'Etat that it had embarked upon, and should continue, the exercise of judicial review of the constitutionality of acts of Parliament. Despite the remarkable effects which the application of such principles might have in cases like *Winkell*, the powers of the administrative judge in relation to parliamentary legislation were no different from those of his colleagues in the judicial tribunals. As the Conseil d'Etat put it in the *Arrighi*

---

[25] Law of 22 Apr. 1905, Art. 65, [1905] J.O. 2573 at 2577, 105 DUVERGIER 269 at 285.

[26] [1909] S. III.145 at 151.

[27] *Ibid.*

[28] *Ibid.*, HAURIOU, PRÉCIS DE DROIT CONSTITUTIONNEL 145–47 n.9 (2d ed. 1929).

[29] Notes under Tichit, [1913] S. III.137 (Cons. d'Et., 1 March 1912), and Heyriès, [1922] S. III.49 (Cons. d'Et., 28 June 1918); HAURIOU, note 28 *supra*, at 284–87. The position adopted in *Winkell* in respect of the civil servant's right to strike was reversed in 1950 in *Dehaene*, [1950] C.E. 426 (Cons. d'Et., 7 July 1950).

[30] See, *e.g.*, Jèze, *Le contrôle juridictionnel des lois*, [1924] REVUE DU DROIT PUBLIC ET DE LA SCIENCE POLITIQUE EN FRANCE ET À L'ETRANGER 399 [hereinafter "REV. DR. PUB."], and 1 CARRÉ DE MALBERG, CONTRIBUTION À LA THÉORIE GÉNÉRALE DE L'ETAT 393–94, n.8 (1920).

decision of 1936:[31] ". . . in the present state of French public law, this ground of appeal [unconstitutionality of the statute underlying an administrative act] may not be raised before the Conseil d'Etat."

3. *The "general principles of law."* The principle of continuity of the public service invoked in *Winkell* is an important example of the then emerging phenomenon of "general principles of law" which was to form an important basis of the administrative case law and an aspect of that law which has been of enormous importance for the development of constitutional review in France. Although typically reticent about their nature and origin, the Conseil d'Etat progressively developed a catalog of principles applicable in the review of administrative action and rule-making and in the interpretation of legislation which included such notions as equality before the law,[32] freedom of conscience,[33] principles embodying what might be called procedural due process,[34] the non-retroactivity of administrative acts,[35] and the right to bring the *recours pour excès de pouvoir* in respect of administrative decisions.[36]

Under the regime of the Third Republic (1875–1940), it was extremely difficult to identify any legal source for these general principles other than the praetorian powers of the judges. The constitutional laws of 1875 contained no declaration of rights or any other statement of similar principles. No statute explicitly consecrated such principles as rules of law to be applied by the administrative courts. Serious attempts at theoretical explanation of the general principles were not forthcoming until after World War II.[37] Writing in 1951, M. Letourneur, a member of the Conseil

---

[31] [1938] D. III.1 (Const. d'Et., 6 Nov. 1936).

[32] *E.g.*, Roubeau, [1913] C.E. 521 (Cons. d'Et., 9 May 1913).

[33] *E.g.*, Chaveneau, [1949] C.E. 161, [1949] S. III.49 (Cons. d'Et., 1 Apr. 1949).

[34] *See* JEANNEAU, LES PRINCIPES GÉNÉRAUX DE DROIT DANS LA JURISPRUDENCE ADMINISTRATIVE 76–91 (1954), and the decisions there cited.

[35] *E.g.*, Soc. l'Aurore, [1948] C.E. 289, [1948] S. III.69 (Cons. d'Et., 25 June 1948).

[36] *E.g.*, Rey, de Labordes et Lauth, [1950] C.E. 110 (Cons. d'Et., 17 Feb. 1950). An especially important (because of its political repercussions) later decision on this point is Canal, Robin et Godet, [1962] C.E. 552 (Cons. d'Et., 19 Oct. 1962).

[37] See Rivero, *Le juge administratif français: un juge qui gouverne?*, [1951] D. 21, and see generally JEANNEAU, LES PRINCIPES GÉNÉRAUX DU DROIT (1954); Jeanneau, *La nature des principes généraux du droit en droit français*, in ETUDES DE DROIT CONTEMPORAIN, VIᵉ CONGRÈS INTERNATIONAL DE DROIT COMPARÉ—RAPPORT FRANÇAIS, 203 (1962); Letourneur, *Les "principes généraux du droit" dans la urisprudence du Conseil d'Etat*, in [1951] ETUDES ET DOCUMENTS 19–31.

d'Etat, argued that the general principles were nothing more than interpretations of the will of the legislator, presumed to guide legislative activity even in the absence of an explicit manifestation of that will in statutory form.[38] Other writers pointed out that, even if, as M. Letourneur insisted, the principles are only applied in the "absence of an express manifestation of legislative will to the contrary,"[39] the influence of the general principles in the administrative courts' interpretation of statutes raised considerable doubt about whether those principles could properly be regarded as anything other than judge-made law *tout simple*.[40]

The advent of the Fourth Republic and with it a constitution which incorporated the 1789 Declaration of Rights in its Preamble brought a new element into the theory of the general principles. The Conseil d'Etat came to refer in its decisions to the "general principles of law . . . deriving, notably, from the Preamble to the Constitution."[41] It was never quite clear whether the Conseil regarded the Preamble as declarative of the general principles (deriving their force from some other source as the logic of continuity from the Third to Fourth Republics might seem to require) or whether the Preamble simply created a new foundation for at least some of these previously difficult to explain concepts. To the extent that the Conseil was applying a general principle, such as that of the continuity of the public service, which could not, by any stretch of the imagination, be derived from the Preamble, some other source was still to be supposed.

None of this was of great practical importance so long as the supremacy of Parliament remained unchallenged and the judges adhered to the rule that an act of Parliament was immune from attack either as a violation of the general principles or as an unconstitutional act.[42] But if some of the powers of the administration were to be founded directly on the Constitution and Parliament was thus deprived of its supremacy, the source of the "general

[38] Letourneur, note 37 *supra*, at 28–30.

[39] *Id*. at 30. The formula quoted appears in *d'Aillères*, [1947] C.E. 50 (Cons. d'Et., 7 Feb. 1947).

[40] See JEANNEAU, note 37 *supra*, at 169–71.

[41] *E.g.*, Syndicat Général des Ingénieurs-Conseils, [1959] C.E. 394 (Cons. d'Et., 26 June 1959).

[42] The inconclusiveness of Fourth Republic doctrinal debates on the source and legal value of the general principles is well demonstrated in JEANNEAU, note 37 *supra*, esp. at 249–55.

principles" and the question of their constitutional force would become extremely important, for it would determine their applicability to the autonomous acts of the administrative authorities.[43]

Entirely apart from the importance of the "general principles" as a precursor and perhaps essential support to judicial review of the constitutionality of administrative acts in the Fifth Republic, it is also important to recognize that this preexisting body of law had already consecrated the principles which have so far been applied by the Conseil constitutionnel in its substantive constitutional decisions.[44] The Conseil had only to add the label "constitutional." Moreover, the attribution of legal force to the Preamble by the Conseil constitutionnel was certainly made a good deal easier by the Conseil d'Etat's earlier veiled recognition of the Preamble's constitutional force.

B. THE DOCTRINAL DEBATE UNDER THE THIRD AND FOURTH REPUBLICS, 1875–1948

Even as the post-revolutionary legislators and constitution-makers sought to confine the judiciary within limits which would save it from the errors of the *parlements*, the Abbé Sieyès, arguing for "nonjudicial" constitutional review, was insisting that "a constitution is either an obligatory body of law or it is nothing."[45] But the notion that this body of law, like any other, ought to be applied by judges found no great champions until the Third Republic had begun to send down the roots which were to hold that improvised regime in place through a number of storms until the fall of France in 1940.[46] Between the 1880s and the 1920s a num-

---

[43] See VEDEL, DROIT ADMINISTRATIF 278–87 (1973); *compare* 1 DE LAUBADÈRE, TRAITÉ ELÉMENTAIRE DE DROIT ADMINISTRATIF 248 (6th ed., 1973).

[44] See decisions of Conseil constitutionnel discussed in the text *infra*, at notes 152–92. *Cf.* Association amicale des Annamites de Paris et Sieur Nguyen-Duc-Frang, [1956] C.E. 317 (Cons. d'Et., 11 July 1956) (liberty of association, but note that the principle is identified in this decision as a "fundamental principle recognized by Republican statute" as to which see Beardsley, note 3 *supra*, at 448–52); Guieyesses, [1944] REV. DR. PUB. 166 (Cons. d'Et., 4 Feb. 1944) (equality before the law in tax matters); and Azoulay, [1948] C.E. 474 (Cons. d'Et., 17 Dec. 1948) (restrictions on liberty of citizen can only be imposed by statute).

[45] Quoted in BASTID, SIEYÈS ET SA PENSÉE 608 (2d ed., 1970).

[46] Certain members of the physiocratic school did, however, make a place for judicial review in the constitutional systems which they proposed. See EINAUDI, THE PHYSIOCRATIC DOCTRINE OF JUDICIAL CONTROL (Harv. Pol. Studies, 1938), and Chavegrin, *Les doctrines politiques des physiocrates* in MÉLANGES CARRÉ DE MALBERG at 71 (1933).

ber of eminent names in French legal scholarship rallied to the cause of judicial review: Thaller,[47] Jalabert,[48] Duguit,[49] Hauriou.[50]

The focus was on the "exception of unconstitutionality"—the right of a party to litigation to assert that a statute invoked against him was in conflict with the constitution and not therefore to be applied in his case—rather than upon the institution of a direct action for avoidance of unconstitutional legislation analogous to the *recours pour excès de pouvoir* which might be instituted against an administrative act.[51] The American experience was central to the debate and the reasoning of the proponents of judicial review was straight out of *Federalist* No. 78[52] and Marshall's judgment in *Marbury v. Madison*[53] (to which reference was frequently made):[54]

> The court, in effect, finds itself confronted with two contradictory texts: the constitution and the act of Parliament; it must assure the application of the law in force. Which is it? It is obviously the constitution, for there is no doubt that an ordinary statute cannot abrogate the constitution. The defective statute is already null; it is nonexistent.

As an abstract proposition and as a principle of judicial decision in a republic possessed of a proper and intelligible hierarchy of

---

[47] 31 Bull. de la Société de Législation Comparée 249–52 (1901–02).

[48] *Id.* at 252–54.

[49] 3 Duguit, Traité de Droit Constitutionnel 673 (2d ed., 1923); "In the first edition of this work . . . I had with some hesitation refused to recognize the power of the French courts to examine the constitutionality of statutes . . . . I was mistaken . . ."

[50] Hauriou, note 29 *supra*, at 279–93. A remarkable indication of the level of interest in judicial review and doctrinal support for it is to be found in a series of articles published by the newspaper *Le Temps* in 1925. A member of the Senate, M. Ratier, had refused to testify under oath before a parliamentary commission of inquiry concerning his campaign financing and was prosecuted under a 1914 statute authorizing the taking of such testimony by parliamentary commissions. His lawyer, Paul Reynaud, argued that the 1914 statute embodied an unconstitutional violation of the principle of separation of powers (only judicial tribunals, he argued, could properly take testimony under oath). *Le Temps*'s reporter interviewed Profs. Barthélemy, Duguit, Mestre, Rolland, and Hauriou and reported their views and approval of Reynaud's position in a series of articles appearing 14, 15, 19 and 29 Nov. and 15 and 27 Dec. 1925. The judges were not persuaded. See Billiet v. Min. Publ., [1926] Dalloz Hebdomadaire 378 (Cass. crim., 11 June 1926).

[51] On the recours pour excès de pouvoir, see de Laubadère, note 43 *supra*, at 505–51.

[52] *Federalist* No. 78 (Hamilton).	[53] 1 Cranch 137 (1803).

[54] *Notions sur le contrôle des délibérations des assemblées délibérantes*, 53 Revue Générale d'Administration 401, at 410–11 (1895). While Jèze was prepared to extend qualified support to judicial review in 1895, he was to be counted among the opposition by 1924. See note 31 *supra*.

legal norms, the argument was irresistible. Moreover, it offered the publicists of the day an unparalleled opportunity to influence profoundly the constitutional evolution of the Third Republic without invoking the political process. No constitutional amendment was required. It was only necessary to persuade the judges to exercise the powers already in their hands. So confident were the promoters of judicial review that Leon Duguit was able to declare, in a series of lectures given at the law faculty in Cairo in 1926, that the current running in favor of judicial review was "stronger than the courts and the resistance of certain traditional doctrinal writers."[55]

Why then did this movement fail to attain its objective? The answer certainly lies mainly in the training and traditions of the French judiciary, in the success with which the post-revolutionary regimes had molded a new model magistracy utterly disinclined to contest the legislative will.[56] But it is also true that the proponents of judicial review—perhaps because of the profound natural law bias which their work reflects—failed to deal effectively with objections founded on a more positivistic view of the Constitution of 1875 and of the relevant statutes, and that they found no adequate response to a more realistic account of the American experience.

The Law of 16–24 August 1790 remained on the books and had to be confronted. If it meant what it appeared to mean (and had always been taken to mean), judges were forbidden to refuse effect to statutes "sent to them."[57] Had the courts—at least the highest courts—acquired constitutional status coordinate with the legislature, it might have been argued that the 1790 legislation was ineffective to compel application of an unconstitutional statute, but, like the lower federal courts in the United States, the courts of the Third Republic were entirely the creatures of statute and could claim no powers other than those conferred by a statutory scheme which included the 1790 law.

The *Marbury* rationale might have been taken to exclude unconstitutional statutes from the operation of the 1790 statute on

[55] DUGUIT, LEÇONS DE DROIT PUBLIC GÉNÉRAL 292–93 (1926).

[56] Barthélemy and Duez favored judicial review in principle but considered it, regrettably, unsuited for France, because French judges did not enjoy the prestige necessary to make judicial review acceptable to Parliament and public. See BARTHÉLEMY & DUEZ, TRAITÉ ÉLÉMENTAIRE DE DROIT CONSTITUTIONNEL 219–22 (1926).

[57] Law of 16–24 August 1790, Title II, art. 11, 1 DUVERGIER at 363.

the ground that they were not statutes at all.[58] But the general purpose of the revolutionary legislator—to preclude refusal of application on any ground including those of "fundamental law" advanced by the *parlements*—severely undercut that argument.[59] So
a narrower ground was chosen. It was argued that the 1790 legislation was directed at the specific forms of misbehavior attributed
to the *parlements*—the arrogation to themselves of general legislative powers through the refusal to register royal edicts and the
issuance of general regulatory decrees—and that, its advocates maintained, was not what judicial review was about. A refusal to apply
a statute as a rule of decision in a particular case on constitutional
grounds was altogether different from a refusal a priori to recognize the validity of legislation; it was of this latter excess that the
parlements had been guilty. No member of the reformed French
judiciary would dream of arrogating such powers to himself.[60]
Cessat ratione legis, cessat lex. It wasn't a bad argument, but it was
totally dependent on the *Marbury* perception of what in fact
judges do in testing the constitutionality of a statute. That perception involves both a political judgment and judgment about the
nature and precision of the constitutional norms which the judges
are to apply. There were grave difficulties on both counts.[61]

The constitutional laws of 1875 were notably barren of substantive restrictions on parliamentary authority. To be sure, the
provisions relating to parliamentary immunity might have given
rise to questions of substantive constitutionality, had Parliament
sought by legislation to make its members civilly liable for statements made in parliamentary debate.[62] A court might, and to a
limited extent the French courts did, test legislation against the
procedural rules prescribed by the Constitution, but this was essentially a matter of verifying the existence of the statute.[63]

---

[58] *Cf.* Duguit, note 49 *supra*, at 668–69.

[59] See Duez, *Le contrôle juridictionnel de la constitutionnalité des lois en France*, in
Mélanges Hauriou 211 at 230–32 (1929).

[60] See Hauriou, note 28 *supra*, at 281–82.

[61] See Larnaude, *Etude sur les garanties judiciaires qui existent, dans certains pays au profit
des particuliers contre les actes du pouvoir législatif*, 31 Bull. de la Société de Législation
Comparée 175 (1902–03); and the commentaries of Saleilles and Lèvy-Alvarès, *id.* at
240 and 246.

[62] Constitutional Law of 16 July 1875, Arts. 13 and 14, Bonnard 294, 296.

[63] See passage from *Paulin*, quoted *supra*, at note 16, and *Dame Massois*, note 22 *supra*.
The scope of the inquiry into the existence of the law undertaken by the courts is examined in Druesene, *La jurisprudence constitutionnelle des tribunaux judiciaires sous la*

The great interest of judicial review, however, was in its use as a method of protecting individual rights. For that purpose it was essential to locate a body of substantive limitations which—if not part of the 1875 texts—had some claim to a status in positive law superior to that of ordinary legislation. Implicit constitutional principle was invoked by those professors who, in connection with the *Ratier* affair of 1925, had argued that the power to take testimony under oath was uniquely judicial in character and could not be constitutionally granted by Parliament to one of its own commissions. But the most serious doctrinal effort was devoted to the attempt to demonstrate that the 1789 Declaration of Rights was binding on Parliament and enforceable by the courts.

Duguit argued that the Declaration of Rights had been separately adopted by the Constituent Assembly of 1791 to *precede* the Constitution of that year and had thus survived subsequent revisions and replacements of the constitutional text itself.[64] Others seized upon the incorporation of a version of the 1789 Declaration in the Constitution of 1848,[65] and upon Article 1 of the Constitution of 1852 which "recognized, confirmed and guaranteed the great principles of 1789 which are the basis of French public law,"[66] to support their contention that the Declaration of Rights had acquired settled constitutional authority which was not to be denied merely because the draftsmen of 1875 had failed *per incuriam* to incorporate or affirm the Declaration in the constitutional texts of that year.[67]

The most elaborate conception was that of Hauriou, who sought to distinguish between the "political constitution" which established and regulated the organs of the state and the "social constitution" which embodied its pact with the citizen.[68] So long as the judges refused to examine the constitutionality of acts of the Parliament,

---

V⁰ République, [1974] Rev. Dr. Pub. 169 at 173–89. The difficulty of distinguishing between this kind of judicial review and substantive review was underscored by Eisenmann in his note to Arrighi, note 31 *supra*. No reference to this aspect of the matter would be complete without citing the famous South African decision of Harris v. Min. of Interior, 1952 (2) S.A.L.R. 428 (A.D.). See generally MARSHALL, PARLIAMENTARY SOVEREIGNTY AND THE COMMONWEALTH (1962).

[64] DUGUIT, note 49 *supra*, at 558–69.

[65] Const. of 4 Nov. 1848, Chap. 1, BONNARD 212, 214–15.

[66] BONNARD 249, 250.

[67] See, *e.g.*, DE LAPRADELLE, COURS DE DROIT CONSTITUTIONNELLE 529–31 (1912).

[68] HAURIOU, note 28 *supra*, at 624–37.

the "social constitution" was without effective sanction and it was this deficiency which made the institution of judicial review an urgent and imperative matter.[69]

Neither Duguit's attempt to make positive law of the Declaration by separating it from the succession of constitutional texts, nor the effort to achieve this result by resort to what amounted—even in Hauriou's theory—to an argument from constitutional custom, stood up well to positivist attack. Either the Declaration was part of the 1791 Constitution, in which case it disappeared with that instrument and only reentered the positive law—with such force as might then be attributed to it—when readopted in later constitutional texts, or it was not part of the Constitution, in which case its value was only that of a hortatory declaration of principle, or, at best, an ordinary statute subject to revision and hence not binding upon later legislatures.[70] Custom alone could not put the principles of the Declaration beyond the reach of the legislator.[71] It was, of course, possible to admit that these principles might have acquired positive force against the administration through their recognition as "general principles of law" by the administrative courts, without recognizing them as binding upon the Parliament.[72]

It was in the attempt to grapple with the problem of constitutional supremacy that the judicial review school encountered the greatest theoretical difficulty. Constitutional supremacy is the cornerstone of the *Marbury* argument. It was largely taken for granted by the proponents of judicial review until Raymond Carré de Malberg undertook to demonstrate, not only that the 1875 regime was one of unrestrained parliamentary supremacy, but that the cherished, if slippery, notion of separation of powers was, in the system of 1875, nothing more than a description of the technique of organization of the organs of the state imposed and maintained by a sovereign Parliament.[73] Carré de Malberg argued

---

[69] *Id.* at 612.

[70] See 2 CARRÉ DE MALBERG, note 30 *supra*, at 579–82; 1 ESMEIN, ELÉMENTS DE DROIT CONSTITUTIONNEL FRANÇAIS ET COMPARÉ 555–62 (7th ed., 1921).

[71] 2 CARRÉ DE MALBERG, note 30 *supra*, at 582, n. 10. See also Laferrière, *La coutume constitutionnelle*, [1944] REV. DR. PUB. 20.

[72] 1 CARRÉ DE MALBERG, note 30 *supra*, at 682, n.11; and see Jèze, *Valeur juridique des déclarations des droits*, [1913] REV. DR. PUB. 685.

[73] 1 CARRÉ DE MALBERG, note 30 *supra*, at 225–27; and especially CARRÉ DE MALBERG, LA LOI EXPRESSION DE LA VOLONTÉ GÉNÉRALE 103–39 (1930).

from the identity (as he perceived it) of the legislative and the constituent powers under the 1875 Constitution. The principal constitutional law of 1875 provided that the legislative authority would be exercised by the Chamber of Deputies and the Senate acting separately while for purposes of amending the 1875 constitutional statutes, the two chambers would unite and act jointly as the National Assembly.[74] The identity of the persons whose consent was essential to the making of an ordinary law with those whose consent is required for a constitutional amendment led Carré de Malberg to the conclusion that the regime was in fact one of parliamentary supremacy in which Parliament could do as it pleased, and, consequently, that an unconstitutional statute was logically impossible.[75]

While Carré de Malberg was attacking the case for a judicial power of constitutional review under the 1875 Constitution, Edouard Lambert was laying before his countrymen an analysis of the American paradigm of judicial review which made the social conservatism of judges a centerpiece in the debate and threat of "government by judges" a menace (and a catch-phrase) to which every proponent of constitutional review in any form had thereafter to respond. Lambert's study, *Le gouvernement des juges et la lutte contre la législation sociale aux Etats-Unis* (Government by Judges and the Struggle against Social Legislation in the United States), published in 1921, was devoted to the role of the United States Supreme Court in relation to social and economic legislation between 1883 and 1920. Quitting the realm of constitutional theory for that of judicial behavior, Lambert proffered these cautionary conclusions:[76]

> On the day when the French judiciary shall have acquired the power to review the constitutionality of legislation, it will find in our Declaration of Rights all of the essential elements of the multipurpose instrument which I have described under the name *due process of law* and which has enabled the American judiciary to bend the legislatures beneath its supremacy. The same surreptitious and patient play of constitutional decisions which permitted the American case law between 1883 and 1900 to ensnare legislation in a network of

---

[74] Constitutional Law of 25 Feb. 1875, Arts. 1, 3 and 8, BONNARD 290–92.

[75] Compare Harris v. Min. Int., note 63 *supra*.

[76] LAMBERT, LE GOUVERNEMENT DES JUGES ET LA LUTTE CONTRE LA LÉGISLATION SOCIALE AUX ETATS-UNIS 227–37 (1921).

constitutional limitations which daily becomes more dense, would probably permit ours to succeed in binding the French legislature just as quickly and quite as tightly.

.   .   .   .

It is possible with vigilance—our French legislators have displayed such vigilance from the Revolution until recent times—to prevent the introduction of judicial review into our constitutional system. But, once it enters the system, there is no way to confine it to a limited role or to eliminate it in peaceful and constitutional fashion . . . . In giving to the courts of justice the right to speak in the name of the Constitution, it [judicial review] supplies them with the means of watching over the resistance of each link in the chain of judicial supremacy[77] and, should one give way, of replacing it with a new and stronger one.

.   .   .   .

Is it not evident that in investing the courts of justice with the power to direct the social policy, and, above all, the economic policy of the country—which constitutes the very purpose of judicial review once it moves beyond the settlement of federal disputes [i.e., the allocation of lawmaking authority among the elements of a federal system] the judges inevitably become involved in the quarrels and passions of electoral politics? And will not the faith of litigants in the impartiality of the courts in the daily administration of justice be greatly diminished when the parties, in order to carry out their programs, must work to obtain a majority on the supreme court?

Lambert wrote before the United States Supreme Court's abandonment of the uses of "substantive due process" which he had described,[78] and he didn't live to know of the decision in *Brown v. Board of Education* and the evolving doctrine of "substantive equal protection."[79] He might today be obliged to frame his language but not his arguments differently.[80] The importance of his book

---

[77] Lambert considered that the nature and extent of judicial review in the United States was such as to give the Supreme Court effective control over the very process of amending the Constitution. *Id.* at 109–30.

[78] West Coast Hotel Co. v. Parrish, 300 U.S. 379 (1937).

[79] 347 U.S. 483 (1954).

[80] For a modern view, see Mathiot, *Les offensives du Congrès des Etats-unis contre la jurisprudence constitutionnelle de la cour suprème*, 1 MÉLANGES WALINE 47 (1974); and Pinto, *La fin de gouvernement des juges*, [1950] REV. DR. PUB. 833.

was not, however, in the quality or prescience of his description of the American experience through the years of which he wrote, nor in the intrinsic validity of the conclusions which he drew from it for his countrymen. What mattered was that Lambert had left theoretical argument aside, and produced concrete and persuasive evidence that the judges of a modern democratic state were perfectly capable of behaving precisely as had the old *parlements* and that the American system of judicial review was not the model of constitutional virtue to which a France concerned with social change ought to adhere.

The doctrinal debate under the Third Republic was concerned less with what the constitution ought to say than with what judges ought to do in the existing constitutional framework, but there was no shortage, during the same period, of proposals to institute judicial review by constitutional amendment.[81] Parliament was quite as unwilling to create a system of judicially enforced substantive constitutional limitations as the judges were to impose one and no action was taken on these proposals. Thus it was only after the collapse in 1940 of France's most durable republican regime that the opportunity arose for a fresh attack on parliamentary supremacy.[82]

It was in the public discussions of the nature of the postwar constitution and the debates of the Constituent Assemblies of 1946 that the question was most seriously confronted. Postwar constitutions restored judicial review in Germany[83] and established it in Italy,[84] but in the French Constituent Assemblies of 1946 a hopeless struggle by the parties of the right to institute judicial review was doomed to failure in face of Christian Democrat (M.R.P.),

---

[81] *E.g.*, PROPOSITION ROCHE of 28 Jan. 1903, [1903] Journal Officiel—Documents de la Chambre de Députés (hereinafter cited as "J.O. Doc. Ch.") 97; PROPOSITION BENOIST of 28 Jan. 1903, *id.* at 99; PROPOSITION BONNET of 10 Jan. 1924, [1924] J.O. Doc. Ch. 6 at 13; PROPOSITION BONNET of 27 Feb. 1925, J.O. Doc. Ch. 336 at 344; PROPOSITION ENGERAND of 17 Mar. 1925, J.O. Doc. Ch. 442.

[82] One of the more remarkable and ironic initiatives of Marshall Pétain was his proposal in 1943 of a constitution for the Vichy regime which would have established a supreme court with powers of constitutional review. *Projet de Constitution du Gouvernement de Révolution Nationale*, Arts. 33 and 34, BONNARD 386, at 392. Concerning this document, see LAFERRIÈRE, MANUEL DE DROIT CONSTITUTIONNEL 339–40, n.1 (2d ed., 1947).

[83] Basic Law of 23 May 1949, Arts. 93–94 and 100. See Dietze, *Judicial Review in Europe*, 55 MICH. L. REV. 539, 545–48 (1957) on judicial review in the Weimar Republic.

[84] Const. of 22 Dec. 1947, Arts. 134–37, and Art. VII of Transitional Provisions.

Socialist, and Communist opposition.[85] The conservative position of the parties favoring judicial review and Lambert's analysis of the American experience stood as convincing evidence that judicial review could only obstruct the achievement of the social and political goals of the parties of the left. The Preamble to the 1946 Constitution[86] reaffirmed the 1789 Declaration of Rights and the Republican commitment to "fundamental principles recognized by the laws of [Third] Republic," while proclaiming a new and not entirely consistent charter of less individualistic, social democratic principles. Their enforcement as positive law, however, was not to be put within the province of the courts and was expressly excluded from the competence of that feeble and ineffective organ of political review, the Constitutional Committee, whose creation was the constituents' sole concession to the demand for constitutional review.

Despite the rejection of judicial review by the Constituent Assemblies, some Fourth Republic writers found in the new Constitution a basis for the reassertion of the doctrinal arguments of the prewar decades.[87] The Preamble, it was argued, furnished a number of concrete, substantive principles binding Parliament, against which legislation might be properly tested in the courts by way of the exception of unconstitutionality. It was no longer necessary to rely on abstract theories to attribute constitutional force to the 1789 Declaration or, for that matter, to the new principles of 1946. They stood at the head of the written text. There was room to debate whether the "solemn reaffirmation" of the Preamble did anything more than consecrate a hortatory statement of philosophical principle, but some commentators were prepared to recognize positive constitutional force to at least those principles which were formulated in the manner of legal norms.[88] It could, of course, be argued that the very creation of the Constitutional Committee (like the establishment of the Sénat conservateur) determined the

---

[85] The debates of the 1946 Constituent Assemblies—the positions of the participants and the basis of the resulting compromise—have been thoroughly studied in LEMASURIER, LA CONSTITUTION DE 1946 ET LE CONTRÔLE JURIDICTIONNEL DE LÉGISLATEUR (1954). This account is based mainly on that work.

[86] [1946] J.O. 9166; BONNARD 554–55.

[87] See, e.g., Geny, De l'inconstitutionnalité des lois . . . dans le droit nouveau de la Quatrième République Française, [1947] J.C.P. I.613.

[88] Cf. id., with BURDEAU, MANUEL DE DROIT CONSTITUTIONNEL 71–93 (5th ed., 1947).

scope and limit of constitutional review, precluding action by the courts.[89] But, on the other hand, the committee's competence did not extend to the Preamble, and the very nature of its role was mysterious enough to lend some support to the contention that the creation of such an institution could not support an argument *a contrario* precluding judicial review.[90]

No definitive resolution of the problem was possible except at the hands of the courts themselves and they, as even commentators favorable in principle to judicial review were prepared to recognize, would not take the initiative.[91] The only judicial concession of note to the position of the proponents of judicial review was in the Conseil d'Etat's equivocal recognition of a positive legal force to the Preamble for purposes of reviewing administrative acts, a concession which was to be of greater significance after 1958.

C. NONJUDICIAL REVIEW

Verification of constitutionality by an organ independent of the judiciary and closely related to the legislature or, still better, to the constituent power, has long exercised a certain attraction on Gallic minds divided between distrust of judges and a desire to assure constitutional limitations of political power. It is the only form of constitutional review of statutes which any French regime has known since the fall of the *parlements*. In the 1790s proposals for the institution of nonjudicial review followed hard on the heels of the legislative and constitutional measures prohibiting judicial interference in the making, or reticence in the application, of legislation. It was proposed in 1792 that a special bench of "censors" be established in the legislature to be charged with overseeing the constitutionality of legislative and executive action.[92] The proposal was said to have been modeled on a similar provision of the Pennsylvania constitution.[93] A year later Robespierre urged the creation of a "national grand jury" to vindicate the rights of citizens oppressed by the legislature.[94] But the only proposal of the period

[89] See VEDEL, MANUEL ELÉMENTAIRE DE DROIT CONSTITUTIONNEL 555 (1949).

[90] See Geny, note 87 *supra*.

[91] *E.g.*, LAFERRIÈRE, note 82 *supra*, at 335–38; Toutain v. Caisse artisanale de Basse-Normandie, *supra* note 21.

[92] Duez, note 59 *supra*, at 233, n.1.

[93] On the Pennsylvania provisions, see GOEBEL, ANTECEDENTS AND BEGINNINGS, 1 HISTORY OF THE SUPREME COURT OF THE UNITED STATES 102–03 (1971).

[94] Duez, note 59 *supra*, at 233, n.1.

to find its way into a constitution was that of the Abbé Sieyès in 1795.[95]

The "jurie constitutionnaire" proposed by Sieyès would have been chosen by the electors who elect the legislature itself. Its sole mission would have been to hear complaints (from anyone) that legislation adopted by the legislature was unconstitutional. Its powers were to include both the right to avoid legislation held to be unconstitutional and to impose a fine on the unsuccessful complainant. Sieyès's system was rejected by the draftsmen of the Constitution of 1795 but was partially implemented in the Sénat conservateur of the Constitution of 1799.[96]

The members of the Sénat conservateur were recruited by co-option from a list of candidates submitted by the Corps législatif, the Tribunat and the First Consul. Upon leaving office, the First Consul became a member of the Sénat. Article 21 of the 1799 Constitution provided that the Sénat "shall maintain or annul any act [acte] referred to it as unconstitutional by the Tribunat or the Government." Article 37 imposed on the First Consul the duty to promulgate the decrees of the Corps-législatif within ten days of their issuance by that body unless they had in the meantime been referred to the Sénat for a determination of their constitutionality. Once promulgated a decree was immune to constitutional challenge before the Sénat. The Sénat conservateur never exercised its powers of constitutional review and disappeared from the constitution in 1815.

The Sénat was revived in somewhat different form by Louis Napoleon, who modeled the imperial constitution of 1852 on that of 1799.[97]

The Sénat of the Second Empire differed in several respects from its ancestor of 1799. The Constitution announced that the Sénat was the guardian of the constitution and that no statute might be promulgated without first being submitted to the Sénat, whose duty was to "oppose" the promulgation of unconstitutional legislation.[98] Article 29 provided that the Sénat "shall maintain or

---

[95] BASTID, note 45 *supra*, at 433–35.

[96] Const. of 22 Frimaire An VIII (13 Dec. 1779) BONNARD 109.

[97] Const. of 14 Jan. 1852, BONNARD 249, and see Proclamation of the same date, BONNARD 245.

[98] *Id.*, Const. of 14 Jan. 1852, Art. 26; BONNARD 247, 252.

annul every act [*acte*] referred to it as unconstitutional by the Government . . . or by citizen petition," apparently permitting legislation to be challenged by private citizens either before or after promulgation. (It has been suggested, however, that this provision did not apply to legislation, the duty of the Sénat to approve such legislation before promulgation being the sole sanction of its constitutionality.)[99] Its membership consisted of the cardinals, marshals, and admirals of the Republic as well as such other persons as the President of the Republic might wish to appoint.[100] The Sénat, like its First Empire ancestor, was never to annul any act as unconstitutional.

The failure of the Sénats led Duguit and Hauriou to condemn the system of nonjudicial constitutional review.[101] A political organ with effective powers of constitutional review and the requisite independence would have been too powerful, displacing the Government itself. To be effective, Hauriou argued, constitutional review must be both inoffensive to the political system and the work of an independent body.[102] For that it is necessary to turn to the courts and to confine constitutional review to litigated cases outside the political arena. In making the failure of the Sénats an argument for judicial review, Duguit and Hauriou exposed one of the persistent dilemmas confronted by proponents of either system. Judicial review, Lambert pointed out, politicizes the courts, injects them into the legislative process, threatens the integrity of the judicial system, and violates the principle of separation of powers.[103] Nonjudicial review responds to these concerns, but doesn't work because it is conceived as a political device and fails to achieve the necessary authority and independence. As we shall see, the 1974 debates on the amendment of the constitutional provisions regulating the reference of legislation to the Conseil constitutionnel reflect continuing concern with precisely this difficulty.

The Sénats of 1799 and 1852 were respectively the fruit of the constitutional labors of a small group of "repentant revolutionaries" in 1799 and of the entourage of Louis Napoleon in 1852. Whatever their imperial and autocratic inspiration, they might at least have

---

[99] 1 ESMEIN, note 70 *supra*, at 598.

[100] Const. of 14 Jan. 1852, Art. 20.

[101] 3 DUGUIT, note 49 *supra*, at 665–66; HAURIOU, note 28 *supra*, at 268.

[102] HAURIOU, note 28 *supra*, at 268.

[103] LAMBERT, note 76 *supra*.

laid claim to something resembling a coherent—if plainly undemo-
cratic—constitutional theory.[104] The new system of constitutional
review produced in 1946 in the political turmoil of liberated France
reflected only an incoherent compromise between reform-minded
insistence on parliamentary supremacy and the far weaker demands
of those who sought to impose effective constitutional limitations
on legislative authority.[105] The task of Fourth Republic's Constitutional Committee, to be performed only upon the joint demand
of the President of the Republic and the President of the Conseil
de la République, was to determine whether a statute adopted by
Parliament "implied revision of the Constitution."[106] Before deciding that issue, but presumably only where the committee perceived a problem of constitutionality, it was to attempt to mediate
between the Assembly and the Conseil de la République[107] (an
upper house of otherwise closely limited powers whose consent was
required for an amendment of the Constitution adopted by means
other than referendum).[108]

In the twelve-year history of the Fourth Republic there was
but one decision by the Constitutional Committee[109] which did not
fail to elicit charges of usurpation and improper interference in the

---

[104] See GODECHOT, note 10 *supra*, at 549–77; and the Proclamation of Louis Napoleon
of 14 Jan. 1852, BONNARD 245.

[105] See generally LEMASURIER, note 85 *supra*.

[106] Const. of 27 Oct. 1946, Art. 91, BONNARD 554.

[107] *Id.*, Art. 92.

[108] See *id*. Arts. 20 and 90.

[109] In June 1948 the committee was called upon, at the urgent request of the Government, to deal with legislation adopted by the National Assembly providing financial assistance to a state-owned company which manufactured aircraft engines and which was
then in desperate financial straits. The Conseil de la République refused to be hurried
and insisted upon delaying its own action long enough to permit a deliberate examination
of the bill. The Conseil's assent was not required for enactment. A bill could be adopted
and promulgated over the objections of the Conseil. This is what the National Assembly
sought to accomplish by treating the Conseil's failure to act within the period fixed by
the Assembly's by-laws as tantamount to a refusal of the measure justifying the Assembly
in proceeding to the unilateral adoption of the bill. The bill adopted by the Assembly was
referred to the Constitutional Committee. In its decision the committee observed that
the fixing of an unreasonably short period for examination of legislation by the Conseil
de la République would tend to frustrate the purposes of Art. 20 of the Constitution,
which provided for the examination by the Conseil, and therefore asked (1) that the
two chambers collaborate with each other to put their rules into conformity with the
purposes of Art. 20, and (2) that the President of the Republic exercise his power to
require a reconsideration of the legislation in question by both chambers so that Art. 20
might be respected. Decision of 18 June 1948, [1948] J.O. 5970. The background of
decision is treated in LEMASURIER, note 85 *supra*, at 221–31.

legislature's process.[110] The most important constitutional development under the Fourth Republic—the reinstitution of the practice of delegating legislative authority to the Government which the 1946 Constitution had sought to suppress—escaped altogether from the process of constitutional review established by that constitution.[111] In sum, as Eisenmann and Hamon have pointed out, the constitutional life of the Fourth Republic was carried on precisely as if the Constitutional Committee did not exist.[112] The utter futility of the constitutional review arrangements of 1946 appears to have stood as a warning, seriously taken by the draftsmen of 1958, that a powerless and essentially inaccessible organ of review, while free of any taint of "government by judges," cannot be relied upon to regulate and enforce complex constitutional relationships.[113] Accessibility and real power, however limited, are indispensable.

II. The Advent of Constitutional Review: The Constitution of 4 October 1958

Charles de Gaulle's distaste for "legalism" was probably matched only by his aversion to party government. The ultimate legalism of a rigid constitution did not escape his contempt:[114]

> Three things count in constitutional matters. First, the higher interest of the country—that which the Romans called *salus patriae*. That comes before all else and of that I alone am judge. Second, far behind, are the political circumstances, arrangements, tactics. They must be taken into account. Other-

---

[110] See the remarks of the Communist Deputy, M. Dreyfus-Schmidt, before the National Assembly on 22 June 1948, quoted in LEMASURIER, note 85 *supra*, at 232–33.

[111] "The National Assembly alone votes *la loi*. It cannot delegate this right [*droit*]." Const. of 27 Oct. 1946, Art. 13. The Law of 17 Aug. 1948, [1948] J.O. 8082, [1948] B.L.D. 734, delegated broad authority to the Government in a number of areas. The constitutionality of such delegations was considered by the Conseil d'Etat in an advisory opinion of 6 Feb. 1953, [1953] J.C.P. III.17697, which dealt in inconclusive fashion with the extent to which regulatory power might be delegated to the Government by Parliament without amending Art. 13 of the Constitution. See DE LAUBADÈRE, note 43 *supra*, at 68–69, and the works there cited.

[112] Eisenmann & Hamon, *La Jurisdiction Constitutionnelle en Droit Français*, in MAX-PLANCK-INSTITUT FÜR AUSLÄNDISCHES ÖFFENTLICHES RECHT UND VÖLKERRECHT, VERFASSUNGSGERICHTSBARKEIT IN DER GEGENWART (*Constitutional Review in the World Today*) 231, at 243 (1962).

[113] See LA DOCUMENTATION FRANÇAISE, TRAVAUX PRÉPARATOIRES DE LA CONSTITUTION DU 4 OCTOBRE 1958—AVIS ET DÉBATS DU COMITÉ CONSULTATIF CONSTITUTIONNEL 76 [hereinafter "TRAVAUX PRÉPARATOIRES"] (1960).

[114] Quoted in TOURNOUX, LA TRAGÉDIE DU GÉNÉRAL at 437 (1967).

wise the undertaking will come to nothing. Third, much further behind, there is legalism [*juridisme*]. . . . I have accomplished nothing in my life except by putting the welfare of
the country first and by refusing to be entrapped in legalisms.

Both in his words[115] and in his actions[116] the General frequently
displayed a fine disregard for constitutional limitations. There is,
therefore, more than a little irony in the emergence of real constitutional limitations on the powers of the state and, indeed, of a
new constitutionalism, out of the Gaullist Constitution of 4 October 1958. Yet this was an important consequence of the means
chosen to deliver France from the perceived evil of a parliamentary
government in the hands of perpetually unstable majorities. Limiting the powers of Parliament in a still fundamentally democratic
regime required the creation of an effective constitutional sanction
for violation of those limitations. The establishment of that sanction
gave France its first operative mechanism of constitutional review.

A. THE ALLOCATION AND CONTROL OF LAWMAKING AUTHORITY IN
   THE 1958 CONSTITUTION

From the identity of legislative and constituent authority under
the Constitution of 1875, Carré de Malberg argued that an unconstitutional law was logically impossible in the system of the
Third Republic. In his view there were no restrictions upon the
subject matter which the Parliament, sole legislative authority in
a unitary state, was competent to regulate, and nothing in the positive law imposed substantive limitations on the use which Parliament might make of that competence. The 1946 Constitution imposed restrictions on amendment sufficient to distinguish legislative
from constituent power and, arguably, subjected parliamentary authority both to procedural restraints (the prohibition on delegation
of legislative authority) and to substantive limitation (if the Preamble bound the legislature). But judicial deference to Parliament

---

[115] "Do you really believe that I am bound by the Constitution?" de Gaulle once
asked Professor Teitgen. *Id.* at 438.

[116] The classic example is the constitutional amendment of 1962 providing for the
election of the President of the Republic by universal suffrage. See Constitutional Law,
No. 62-1292 of 6 Nov. 1962, [1962] J.O., 10762, [1962] B.L.D. 725, adopted by referendum on 28 Oct. 1962, without prior approval by Parliament as required by Art. 89 of
the Constitution. Compare Art. 11 of the Const. invoked by de Gaulle in his decree submitting the proposal to referendum. Decree no. 62-1127 of 2 Oct. 1962, [1962] J.O.
9555, [1962] B.L.D. 625.

and the weakness of the Constitutional Committee left those restrictions without sanction. Moreover, and more importantly in light of later experience, there was no other constitutional organ with strong countervailing constitutional interests to defend against trespass by Parliament. The 1958 Constitution radically altered the conditions affecting constitutional review by profoundly changing the relationship between Government and Parliament.

The basic system was laid out in Articles 34 and 37. Article 37 reserves matters other than those which are to be regulated by statute (*la loi*) to the Government to be dealt with by decree. Article 34 provides:

> Statutes are voted by Parliament.
>
> Statutes fix the rules concerning:
>
> —civil rights and the fundamental guarantees accorded to the citizens for the exercise of public liberties; the requirements which the National Defense imposes on the persons and goods of the citizens;
>
> —nationality, the status and capacity of persons; matrimonial regimes, successions and donations;
>
> —the determination of crimes and delicts—as well as the punishments applicable thereto; criminal procedure; amnesties, the creation of new classes of courts and the status of magistrates;
>
> —the bases, rates and methods of collection of taxes of every kind; the regime for the issuance of money.
>
> Statutes also fix the rules concerning:
>
> —the electoral system for the parliamentary and local assemblies;
>
> —the creation of categories of public establishment;
>
> —the fundamental guarantees accorded to civil servants and members of the military;
>
> —the nationalization of enterprises and the transfer of the property of enterprises from the public to the private sector;
>
> —education;
>
> —the regime of property, real rights and civil and commercial obligations;
>
> —labor law, law relating to labor unions and the social security system.
>
> Finance statutes determine the resources and obligations [*charges*] of the state in accordance with the conditions and subject to the restrictions prescribed by an organic law.
>
> Program statutes [*lois de programme*] determine the objectives of the social and economic action of the State.

The provisions of this article may be defined and completed
by organic law.

Certain other matters, including the ratification of some types of
treaties[117] and the declaration of war,[118] required parliamentary
action. Even as to the matters reserved to Parliament by Article 34,
the decree-law practice of the Third and Fourth Republics was
institutionalized by authorizing Parliament to delegate to the Government for a limited time the power to deal with Article 34
matters by the issuance of "ordinances."[119]

The text of Article 34 reveals serious interpretive problems, not
only in the definition of subject matter, but in the distinction
between "rules" and "fundamental principles," and between these
two concepts and the normative activity not constituting the creation of "rules" or "fundamental principles" which the use of these
terms might allow the Government in respect of Article 34 matters.
If the system was to work, authoritative interpretation was indispensable. Moreover, on the reasonable assumption that the Government and the Parliament would overstep the boundary from time
to time, authority to interpret would have to be accompanied by
authority to invalidate the ultra vires act. At least for these purposes a mechanism of constitutional review was essential. The competing claims of Parliament and Government would give the task
and the institution which carried it out a seriousness of purpose and
centrality of function which insured that it would not be con-
signed to the limbo inhabited by the Sénats conservateurs and the
Constitutional Committee.

The draftsmen opted for a divided, headless system of review.
The Conseil d'Etat, whose existence and authority had been in the
past, and would be under the 1958 Constitution, entirely dependent
upon statute,[120] was to be relied upon to police Government infringement of parliamentary prerogatives.[121] Because the Article
34/37 complex gives rise to an autonomous normative power on

---

[117] Art. 53, [1958] B.L.O. 667.

[118] Art. 35, [1958] B.L.O. 645.

[119] Art. 38, [1958] B.L.D. 665, fn.22 and see note 111 *supra*. See also DE LAUBADÈRE,
note 43 *supra*, at 79–82.

[120] Ordinance no. 45-1700 of 31 July 1945, as amended, [1945] D. 197; Decree no.
63-766 of 30 July 1963, [1963] B.L.D. 423, 519.

[121] See TRAVAUX PRÉPARATOIRES 77.

the part of the Government—a power deriving directly from the Constitution and not dependent upon parliamentary delegation—a sizable and important segment of the total lawmaking authority of the state, once united in the Parliament and immune to judicial review, passed under the control of the administrative judges.[122] But this result was achieved not by subjecting *la loi* to judicial review but by withdrawing a large, residual category of normative activity from the domain of *la loi*.

Despite the obvious dangers of divergent interpretation, the imposition of effective restraints on Parliament was thought to call for a solution at least arguably responsive to the concern to avoid "government by judges."[123] The task was assigned to a new institution, the Conseil constitutionnel.[124] The Conseil is entirely without the framework of the judicial and administrative courts. There are no appeals from these tribunals to the Conseil, and no provision is made for the reference of constitutional questions by these courts to the Conseil constitutionnel.[125] Access to the Conseil in constitutional matters is not open to private citizens.[126] Its only point of contact with the courts is in the effect to be given its decisions. Article 62 provides that the decisions of the Conseil are binding upon all governmental organs and judicial and administrative authorities.[127]

The Conseil consists of nine appointed members plus all living former Presidents of the Republic. Appointments to the Conseil are made by the President of the Republic, the President of the National Assembly, and the President of the Senate. Members serve for nine years. Their terms are staggered, the appointing authorities

---

[122] See Syndicat Général des Ingénieurs-Conseils, [1959] S. 202, [1959] D. 541, (Cons. d'Et., 26 June 1959); and Société Eky, [1960] D. 263 (Cons. d'Et., 12 Feb. 1960). It might, of course, have been argued that any exercise of constitutionally conferred normative power partakes of the essential quality of *la loi* and is immune to judicial review. As the two cases cited demonstrate, the Conseil d'Etat experienced no hesitation on this score.

[123] See Debré's remarks quoted in text at note 136 *infra*.

[124] Const. of 4 Oct. 1958, Arts. 56–63, [1958] J.O. 9151.

[125] For a fleeting moment early in the drafting process, the possibility of allowing reference of questions involving the constitutionality of statutes to the Conseil constitutionnel by the Court of Cassation and the Conseil d'Etat was considered, and then promptly abandoned. See Art. G, under "Comité constitutionnel," in the draft submitted to the Ministerial Constitutional Committee about 30 June 1958. Text reproduced in J.-L. DEBRÉ, LA CONSTITUTION DE LA Vᵉ RÉPUBLIQUE at 88 (1975).

[126] See Art. 61, text *infra*, at note 207.

[127] But see text *infra*, at notes 226–33.

each nominating one new member every three years. Except in the case of appointments made to fill vacancies created by the death or resignation of a sitting member, appointments are not renewable.[128] Although a number of distinguished professors of public law, members of the Conseil d'Etat and legal practitioners have been appointed to the Conseil, there are no constitutionally imposed requirements of age or professional training, and persons without legal training have frequently been named to the Conseil.[129]

In addition to its functions of constitutional review, the Conseil has certain duties in connection with the holding of elections (a large part of its business has been the hearing of election disputes)[130] and certain advisory functions in connection with the exercise of emergency powers by the President of the Republic under Article 16 of the Constitution.[131] The Conseil's crucial and central tasks, however, are those which are assigned to it by Articles 37 (¶ 2), 41, and 61 of the 1958 Constitution. Articles 37 (¶ 2) and 41 are unequivocally addressed to the interpretation and enforcement of the limitations of competence imposed by Article 34 and Article 37 together. Article 61 is plainly aimed at the competence question as well but literally goes much further in authorizing the Conseil to examine the "conformity to the constitution" of legislation submitted to it.

The second paragraph of Article 37 establishes the process

---

[128] The appointment, terms and replacement of members of the Conseil are governed by Art. 56 of the 1958 Constitution.

[129] Since February 1974 (when three members of the Conseil were replaced upon expiration of their terms), the membership of the Conseil has included four non-lawyers (Roger Frey, Henri Rey, Jean Sainteny, René Brouillet), two professors of public law (François Goguel and Paul Coste-Floret) one of whom (Coste-Floret) is also a former member of the Court of Cassation (Dubois), another former member of the Conseil d'Etat (Pierre Chatenet), and one private practitioner (Gaston Monnerville). Monnerville is a former president of the Senate. All of the members have had active political careers. See Le Monde, 18–19 July 1971 and 24–25, and 26 Feb. 1974. See also Beardsley, note 3 supra, at 448, n.76, and Favoreu, Le Conseil constitutionnel régulateur de l'activité normative des pouvoirs publics, [1967] Rev. Dr. Pub. 5 at 73–88.

[130] Const., Art. 58. One of the 670 published decisions (including proclamations of election results) rendered by the Conseil from 4 Dec. 1958 through 15 Jan. 1975, 522 related to its duties in connection with elections. Favoreu & Philip, Chronique constitutionnelle et parlementaire française, [1975] Rev. Dr. Pub. 165 at 206–07 (hereinafter "Favoreu & Philip").

[131] From 4 Dec. 1958, through 15 Jan. 1975, the Conseil rendered one published advisory opinion relating to the exercise of emergency powers (Opinions of 23 April 1961, [1961] Recueil des décisions du Conseil constitutionnel 69 [hereinafter "C.C."] and 16 unpublished opinions concerning the application of emergency powers. Favoreu & Philip 208.

which has come to be known as "delegalization."[132] Texts in "legislative form"—those which have been adopted by Parliament, or by the Government pursuant to a parliamentary delegation under Article 38 or the interim powers conferred by Article 92—may be abrogated or amended by the Government if the Conseil constitutionnel first determines that their subject matter does not properly fall within the area of legislative competence reserved to Parliament by Article 34. In principle, the Conseil's decision under Article 37 (¶ 2) bears uniquely upon the interpretation of Article 34 and has nothing to do with substantive restraints on exercise of lawmaking power by the organ to which it is constitutionally allocated.[133] Once the Conseil has, by a decision under Article 37, excluded a certain subject matter from the parliamentary domain, the manner in which the Government exercises that authority is no longer subject to review by the Conseil constitutionnel, but passes under the surveillance of the Conseil d'Etat.

Article 41 provides a mechanism for resolving disputes over the scope of parliamentary authority under Article 34 arising between the Government and the Parliament in the course of the legislative process. Either the Government or the President of the Assembly which has the matter in question before it may ask the Conseil constitutionnel for a determination of its legislative or regulatory character. Again, the Conseil is concerned uniquely with the allocation of legislative authority under Articles 34 and 37.

Article 61, however, requires the Conseil to make a determination of "conformity to the Constitution" in respect of all organic laws,[134] the by-laws of the parliamentary assemblies, and authorizes the President of the Republic, the Prime Minister, or the President of either house of Parliament to refer ordinary legislation to the Conseil after adoption by Parliament and before promulgation for the same purpose. The right to refer legislation to the Conseil under Article 61 was extended to any sixty members of either house

---

[132] See Favoreu, *La délégalisation des textes de forme législative par le Conseil constitutionnel*, 2 MÉLANGES WALINE 429 (1974).

[133] But see Decision of 28 Nov. 1973, [1974] D. 269, discussed in the text *infra*, at note 156.

[134] "Organic laws" are statutes supplementing, completing, or defining various constitutional provisions dealing with the organization and operation of the institutions created by the Constitution. The Constitution expressly provides for the elaboration of many of its provisions by organic law. See, *e.g.*, the text of Art. 34, text *supra* at note 117. The conditions for the adoption of organic laws are fixed by Art. 46.

of Parliament by constitutional amendment in 1974. That Article 61 was intended to make of the Conseil an instrument of substantive review was much doubted before 1971 and, whatever the intent, it was considered unlikely that the Conseil would take up that task even if the opportunity to do so were presented to it.[135]

B. THE PROBLEM OF SUBSTANTIVE REVIEW UNDER ARTICLE 61

In submitting the draft constitution to the Conseil d'Etat in August 1958, Michel Debré, the first Minister of Justice of the new regime and one of the document's principal draftsmen, declared that "[t]he creation of a Conseil constitutionnel manifests the will to subordinate statutes [*la loi*], that is to say the decisions of Parliament, to the higher rules established by the Constitution."[136] Did he mean substantive rules such as those which might be extracted from the Preamble or from certain other provisions of the Constitution which are protective of certain civil and political rights? Or was he speaking exclusively of the constitutional rules restraining the Parliament's subject matter competence in favor of the Government, and those which were designed to assure the Government a strong hand in the direction of Parliament's legislative program? Despite the plain mandate of Article 61 to "determine conformity to the Constitution," Debré's remarks earlier in the same month before the Consultative Committee on the Constitution suggest that the constitutional rules which Debré had in mind were those fixing the competence of Parliament and regulating its procedures. Responding to a proposal to broaden the right to refer legislation to the Conseil, Debré argued that "it is possible to do more or less in the direction of what is called . . . the government of judges. But, at a certain point, recourse to the Conseil is incompatible with a parliamentary regime, for neither the . . . [Parliament] nor public opinion will accept the constant participation of judges in political life."[137] Later, responding to the suggestion that the Preamble (including the Declaration of Rights of 1789) be

---

[135] See, *e.g.*, BATAILLER, LE CONSEIL D'ETAT JUGE CONSTITUTIONNEL 38–39 (1966); Philip, *Note* to Constitutional Council Decision of 20 Jan. 1961, [1961] S. 164; DRAN, LE CONTRÔLE JURIDICTIONNEL ET LA GARANTIE DES LIBERTÉS PUBLIQUES 527–32 (1968).

[136] Debré, *La nouvelle constitution*, 9 REVUE FRANÇAISE DE SCIENCE POLITIQUE 1, 16 (1959). Following the quoted passage, Debré added: "It is not in the spirit of a parliamentary regime, nor in the French tradition, to give to the judiciary, that is to say, to individuals, the right to examine the value of a statute."

[137] TRAVAUX PRÉPARATOIRES 76.

expressly identified as part of the constitutional text applicable by the Conseil, Debré's close collaborator and the Government's representative before the committee, M. Janot, denied the constitutional force of the Preamble and argued that its inclusion in the body of the Constitution would risk "the creation of contradictions between the development of [Article 34] and the Declaration of 1789 in relation to the matters reserved to Parliament by the former: one can gloss without limit the constitutional tradition of 1789."[138] The fragmentary nature of the *travaux préparatoires* which have so far been published makes argument from the legislative history an uncertain business,[139] but the available documents certainly suggest great concern with the rationalization of the parliamentary regime, but little for the imposition of substantive restraints on legislative work of Parliament within its proper zone of competence.

The language of Article 61, authorizing the Conseil to examine "conformity to the constitution," is not decisive, for a broad mandate to the Conseil of this kind is essential even to the policing of the new relationship between Parliament and Government. Articles 37 and 41 are plainly and narrowly addressed to the maintenance of the boundary between parliamentary and governmental competence fixed by Article 34. But they do not exhaust the problem of protecting Government prerogatives against a Parliament determined to reassert its former supremacy. Parliamentary action may alter the equilibrium between its authority and that of the Government without violating the restrictions of Article 34 in a manner subject to correction through the application of Articles 37 and 41. For example, the question of governmental responsibility before Parliament (the vote of confidence or censure) is closely regulated by Articles 49 and 50 of the Constitution. Par-

---

[138] *Id.* at 101.

[139] The TRAVAUX PRÉPARATOIRES, officially published by *La Documentation Française*, include only the debates of the Constitutional Consultative Committee and even these are reproduced in analytical rather than integral form. See Waline, *Note Pratique sur la publication des travaux préparatoires de la Constitution*, [1960] REV. DR. PUB. 83. Prior drafts, and the opinion of the Conseil d'Etat remained unpublished until recently when some important additional materials were published in J.-L. DEBRÉ, LES IDÉES CONSTITUTIONNELLES DU GÉNÉRAL DE GAULLE (1974), J.-L. DEBRÉ, note 125 *supra;* and MOLLET, QUINZE ANS APRÈS: LA CONSTITUTION DE 1958 (1973). The relevance of the TRAVAUX PRÉPARATOIRES to the interpretation of a constitution adopted by referendum prior to the publication of any of the TRAVAUX PRÉPARATOIRES has been questioned by l'Huillier in his note to Société Eky, *supra* note 122.

liamentary by-laws facilitating the adoption of resolutions relating to the conduct of the Government may tend, politically if not in legal effect, to bypass the restrictions contained in those provisions. Some of the by-laws first adopted by the two houses of the new Parliament were held unconstitutional by the Conseil on this ground among others.[140] An organic law such as that authorized by Article 34 itself may, by the process of "definition and completion" of constitutional provisions, impinge on governmental prerogative. Ordinary statutes may violate provisions such as those of Article 40 reserving the initiative to the Government in respect of financing measures having the effect of "diminishing public resources or creating or increasing a public obligation [*charge*].[141] These are all matters which fall within Parliament's subject matter, legislative competence under Article 34, but which nonetheless raise constitutional questions because they may affect the distribution of power between Government and Parliament. Article 61 requires or permits their reference to the Conseil constitutionnel. It is thus possible to view Article 61 not as an invitation to the Conseil to engage in substantive constitutional review but rather as a catch-all enabling the Conseil to deal with any parliamentary decision which affects the constitutional distribution of normative power between Government and Parliament even when that decision falls within Parliament's subject matter competence under Article 34.

The restriction (in the original text) of the right to refer ordinary legislation to the Conseil to the President of the Republic, the Prime Minister, and the Presidents of either house of Parliament similarly reinforces this restrained view of the purpose of Article 61. While the suggestion of M. Triboulet of the Constitutional Consultative Committee that this restriction demonstrated the uselessness of the entire proceeding—"the system won't attack itself"[142] —has proved excessive, the limitation of the right of reference does suggest an intention to enable the appropriate representatives of Parliament and Government to act to protect the interests of their respective institutional constituencies. On the assumption implicit in M. Triboulet's remark that authorities empowered to refer

---

[140] See Decision No. 59-2 of 17, 18 and 19 June 1959, [1958–59] C.C. 58.

[141] See, *e.g.*, the Conseil's Decision of 20 Jan. 1961, [1961] C.C. 29, [1962] D. 177.

[142] TRAVAUX PRÉPARATOIRES at 76.

legislation to the Conseil would share the same political position (never true of the presidency of the Senate),[143] it is difficult to imagine reference to the Conseil for the purpose of enforcing substantive constitutional limitations.

The difficulty over the constitutional force of the Preamble also bears on the question, for if it is not part of the "constitution" to which Parliament's actions must conform, the Constitution of the Fifth Republic contains little in the way of substantive limitations on the exercise of governmental and parliamentary authority. It is not so barren in that respect as were the constitutions of the Third and Fourth Republics. Equality before the law, freedom from discrimination, freedom of association (at least for political purposes), a prohibition of arbitrary detention, and, arguably, certain protections for the freedom of the political and electoral processes, all find expression in the body of the 1958 constitutional instrument.[144] There couldn't have been much doubt about the Conseil's competence to give effect to those provisions under Article 61. But the basic charter of French liberties was still to be found in the Declaration of Rights of 1789 which was incorporated by reference in a Preamble which went no further than to affirm the nation's "solemn attachment" to that Declaration and to certain other principles. If the Preamble was not binding upon Parliament, and the draftsmen had indicated that it was not,[145] the new mechanism of constitutional review was not only deficient in the eyes of those who demanded constitutional protection of civil and political rights, but it was also plainly not intended as a serious instrument for the protection of those rights.

During the first thirteen years of its existence the Conseil did little to contradict this analysis.[146] While moving confidently and

---

[143] Concerning Alain Poher, the President of the Senate, and his predecessor, Gaston Monnerville, see Beardsley, *supra* note 3 at 439, n.38. Neither is a member of the ruling Gaullist political formation. The two decisions rendered by the Conseil on the substantive constitutionality of ordinary legislation, prior to the amendment of Art. 61 in 1974 to permit reference of legislation to the Conseil by members of Parliament, were both the result of the reference of the statutes in question to the Conseil by the President of the Senate.

[144] Arts. 2, 3, 4 and 66.

[145] TRAVAUX PRÉPARATOIRES 101.

[146] In 1966, Francine Batailler was prepared to conclude that "Constitutional practice had . . . caused the power of the Conseil constitutionnel to censure a statute on the basis of any part of the constitutional text, including the Preamble, to fall into desuetude." Note 135 *supra*, at 38–39.

with notable independence to resolve questions of competence and to bend Parliament to the restraints imposed upon its powers and proceedings by the new order, the Conseil acted with extreme deference and restraint when faced with substantive, or highly politicized, issues. When confronted with the 1962 amendment to the Constitution providing for the direct election of the President, adopted by referendum without compliance with the provisions of Article 89 governing the amendment process, the Conseil took the position that the amending law was a "direct expression of national sovereignty" which the Conseil was incompetent to review.[147] Faced with an organic law relating to the magistracy which appeared to pose questions of "equality before the law" and religious discrimination (in favor of a minority: judges adhering to the Muslim faith), the Conseil took no position on substantive constitutionality, noting that the legislation merely modified another organic law which had been adopted and promulgated, and whose conformity to the Constitution therefore "could no longer be contested."[148] Thus until 1971 there were sound, if not overpowering, reasons to see in the Conseil constitutionnel a new organ rather like the Sénat conservateur of 1799 but endowed with real authority reflecting not a change in French attitudes toward substantive constitutional review but rather the necessities of a new, complex, and closely articulated redistribution of lawmaking authority.

C. THE 1958 CONSTITUTION AND JUDICIAL REVIEW

The creation of the Conseil constitutionnel was certainly the major innovation of the 1958 Constitution in the domain of constitutional review. It was not, however, the only important development. I have already noted the subjection to judicial review of a substantial part of the normative powers of the state as they had existed (without limitation) under prior regimes by the transfer of those powers to the Government, where their exercise fell under the constitutional surveillance of the Conseil d'Etat. On the theoretical plane, at least, the 1958 Constitution also has some bearing on the constitutional review of parliamentary action by the judicial and administrative tribunals.

As had been true under the Constitutions of 1799, 1852, and

---

[147] Decision of 6 Nov. 1962, [1962] C.C. 27, [1962] D. 467.

[148] Decision of 15 Jan. 1960, [1960] C.C. 21, [1960] D. 293.

1946, the existence of a special nonjudicial organ charged with specific duties of constitutional review can be, and has been, taken to provide constitutional support for the unwillingness of the judicial and administrative courts to examine the constitutionality of statutes. Either because the provision of a mechanism of constitutional review in the Constitution directly implies the absence of powers of review elsewhere, or because legislation which has come into force without successful constitutional challenge is deemed to benefit from a conclusive presumption of constitutionality, the creation of the special organ of review has been thought to preclude judicial review. This argument seems to have prevailed among the publicists.[149] A notable exception is Maurice Duverger, who maintains that there is no obstacle under the 1958 Constitution to the examination of the constitutionality of legislation by the courts. He responds to the foregoing argument by insisting, in effect, that the Conseil constitutionnel must be viewed as a part of the lawmaking process which has no bearing on the rights of individuals before the tribunals.[150]

Other fundamental legal objections to judicial review voiced in the earlier doctrinal debate are largely overcome by the disappearance of parliamentary supremacy and the emergence of some substantive constitutional restrictions on parliamentary authority in the 1958 text. The political objections to judicial review continue to be heard, but there has been a remarkable evolution of attitudes in recent years.

---

[149] See, *e.g.*, Robert, *Propos sur le sauvetage d'une liberté*, [1971] REV. DR. PUB. 1171 at 1197–1200; VEDEL, note 43 *supra*, at 272.

[150] See Duverger's response in Le Monde, 7 Sept. 1971, to correspondence (appearing in the same issue) criticizing an earlier article by Duverger (*La Loi et les Juges*, Le Monde, 7 Aug. 1971) for failing to recognize the exclusive character of the Conseil constitutionnel's powers of constitutional review. Duverger also invokes the Constitutional Law of 3 June 1958 which, as one of the last acts of the Parliament of the Fourth Republic, fixed the conditions under which the new Constitution was to be drafted and adopted, and included certain stiuplations concerning the content of the new Constitution. Constitutional Law of 3 June 1958, [1958] J.O. 5326, [1958] B.L.D. 431. Among these provisions appears the following paragraph:

4. The judicial authority shall remain independent in order to be able to insure respect for essential liberties such as those which are defined by the preamble of the Constitution of 1946 and by the Declaration of the Rights of Man to which it refers.

Duverger argues that this provision, not having been abrogated by the new Constitution, remains in force and imposes upon the courts the duty to entertain the exception of unconstitutionality. DUVERGER, DROIT CONSTITUTIONNEL ET INSTITUTIONS POLITIQUES 653–54 (8th ed., 1965). But see Const. of Oct. 1958, Art. 66, [1958] B.L.D. 668.

III. The Role of the Conseil constitutionnel in Substantive
Review since 1971

After almost thirteen relatively uneventful years passed
mainly in deciding election disputes and picking out the boundary
between the normative competences of the Government and the
Parliament, the Conseil constitutionnel, acting on reference by the
President of the Senate, held unconstitutional certain provisions of
a proposed amendment to a 1901 statute on nonprofit associations.
In its decision of 16 July 1971,[151] the Conseil determined that the
imposition of prior restraints on the formation of nonprofit associations under the 1901 statute violated the liberty of association
which had been erected into constitutional principle by the incorporation of the Preamble to the 1946 Constitution in the Preamble
to the 1958 Constitution. No question of the distribution of lawmaking power was involved. The Conseil was invoking substantive
constitutional restrictions marking outer limits on the state's normative powers whatever might be the organ competent to exercise
them.

Since the 1971 decision, there have been several additional rulings by the Conseil on issues of substantive constitutionality, an
apparent shift of political opinion in favor of constitutional review,
a constitutional amendment extending the right to refer legislation
to the Conseil and some clear indications of the problems which
this new constitutionalism must confront.

A. THE DECISIONS OF THE CONSEIL CONSTITUTIONNEL ON SUBSTAN-
TIVE CONSTITUTIONAL ISSUES[152]

1. *16 July 1971.*[153] The President of the Senate referred to the
Conseil a statute which imposed a waiting period in connection
with the registration of nonprofit associations while the documents
submitted for registration were examined by the public prosecutor.

---

[151] Note 3 *supra.*

[152] Since this section was written, the Conseil has issued two further decisions, both
dated 23 July 1975, and rendered in respect of statutes referred to the Conseil by opposition groups in Parliament. [1975] J.C.P. III.43130, 43131. One of these decisions invalidated a statute authorizing the presiding judge of the *tribunal correctionnel* to determine whether a case would be tried before a single judge or a three-judge panel (the
latter being obligatory under prior law). The Conseil held that this provision violated
the principle of equality before the law affirmed by the 1789 Declaration of Rights in
that it would permit "citizens finding themselves in similar situations and prosecuted
for the same offenses to be judged by courts of different composition" at the sole discretion of the judge. Such distinctions would have to be established by legislation and

The Conseil constitutionnel held that the imposition of this prior restraint on the formation of registered nonprofit associations violated a constitutional guaranty of freedom of association. I have analyzed this decision at length in an earlier article.[154] For present purposes it will suffice simply to recall certain important points. First, the decision was an independent and politically courageous one, for its effect was to gut a statute proposed and urgently supported by the Government as an essential measure of internal security. Second, the Conseil based its decision on a constitutional guaranty of freedom of association which might have been attributed to Article 4 of the Constitution,[155] but which the Conseil based on the "fundamental principles recognized by Republican statutes," a notion contained in the Preamble to the 1946 Constitution which is in turn incorporated by reference in the 1958 Preamble. Reliance on the "fundamental principles" language—the least precise of possible constitutional sources—was, in itself, a remarkable initiative. The existence of the constitutional right and its content was asserted, and with it the constitutional force of the Preamble, without argument or explanation in the Conseil's decision, beyond the laconic observation that freedom of association is included among the "fundamental principles." Third, the Conseil's competence to rule on substantive constitutionality apparently presented no problems; the decision contains no reflections on the mission of the Conseil constitutionnel.

After the 1971 decision, no further occasion to rule on substantive limitations was presented until late in 1973.

2. *28 November 1973*.[156] This decision was not an Article 61 decision, and does not involve a determination of "conformity to the constitution." It is, however, an extremely important decision which belongs in spirit, and as a measure of the Conseil's new activism, to the short line of decisions which have established the

---

could not constitutionally be left to judicial discretion. The other decision upheld the institution of a new business tax replacing the old *patente* (a kind of business license tax). The constitutional issue concerned the proper application of Art. 40, *supra*, text at note 143, in the legislative process leading to the adoption of the challenged legislation. See Le Monde, 2 July and 25 July 1975, and see Schwartzenberg, *Le destin du juge unique*, Le Monde, 26 July 1975.

[153] Note 3 *supra*.   [154] Beardsley, note 3 *supra*.

[155] "Parties and political groups . . . may be formed and carry on their activities freely." Const., Art. 4. See also Dupeyroux, *La loi de 1901 et le destin du Conseil constitutionnel*, Le Monde, 16 July 1971.

[156] [1973] C.C. 45; [1974] D. 269.

Conseil's role as a guardian of individual constitutional rights against legislative infringement.

Acting under the provisions of Article 37 (¶ 2) the Prime Minister asked the Conseil constitutionnel to rule that certain provisions of a statute relating to the concentration of agricultural holdings were of regulatory character and therefore subject to amendment or abrogation by decree. The Conseil ruled as requested, but as to Article 188-9, 1° of the Rural Code[157] which imposed penal sanctions for failure to file required declarations or obtain necessary authorizations, the Conseil observed:

> Considering that above-mentioned provisions impose a penalty of 500 to 2,000F for failure to obtain prior authorization or to file a prior declaration in the case of concentration of agricultural holdings. . . . *Considering that the provisions of the Preamble, of paragraphs 3 and 5 of art. 34 and of art 66 of the Constitution, taken together, indicate that the determination of contraventions and of the punishments which are applicable to them is a regulatory matter when such penalties do not involve deprivation of liberty;* Considering that it appears from the provisions of arts. 1 and 466 of the penal code that fines which do not exceed a maximum of 2,000F are police penalties applicable to contraventions; that, consequently, the above-mentioned provisions of the Rural Code which provide only for a fine not exceeding 2,000F, are within the competence of the regulatory power [of the government].

This decision brought the Conseil constitutionnel into conflict with the Conseil d'Etat and has had significant repercussions before the judicial tribunals.[158] It also brought both the substantive constitutional limitations contained in the Preamble and the terms of Article 66 (forbidding arbitrary detention) to bear on the interpretation of the competence granted Parliament by Article 34.

The problem before the Conseil involved the allocation to Parliament by Article 34 of the exclusive power to make "rules concerning:—the determination of crimes and delicts—as well as the punishments applicable thereto." "Crime" (*crime*) and "delict" (*délit*) are technical terms of French criminal law, defined by the Penal Code, which group offenses on the basis of the punishments

---

[157] Law no. 62-933 of 8 Aug. 1962, Art. 8, [1962] J.O. 7962 and 8186; [1962] B.L.D. 535.

[158] See text *infra*, at notes 222–34.

applicable to them.[159] At the time of the 28 November 1973 decision the Penal Code classified as delicts those offenses punishable by a fine in excess of 2,000F or imprisonment for more than two months. Crimes were those offenses for which considerably more rigorous punishments were imposed. Beneath the delict threshold there is a third category of offense known as the *contravention de police*. At the time of the adoption of the Constitution in October 1958, the delict threshold had been even lower: 360F or ten days' imprisonment.[160] These limits were increased to the 1973 levels by an ordinance adopted under Article 92 of the Constitution in December 1958.[161]

In the drafting of the 1958 Constitution, the words "crime and delict" had been substituted for the more inclusive term "infractions" which had appeared in an earlier draft.[162] On the basis of that substitution, the Conseil d'Etat had concluded in 1960 that the draftsmen intended to include only the determination of crimes and delicts (in the Penal Code sense) in Article 34 and to leave the Government free to prescribe "contraventions" and their punishments.[163] The Conseil constitutionnel had taken the same position in several earlier decisions.[164] All of these decisions were open to question—not for their interpretation of the purpose of the modification in Article 34—but because they failed to grapple with the problems flowing from legislative definition (by the 1958 Ordinance) of the operative terms. If "crime and delict" possesses a constitutional meaning capable of limiting Parliament and conferring lawmaking power on the Government through Article 37, one would expect it to be the meaning attached to those terms by the legislation in effect when the Constitution came into force, and not that which resulted from subsequent legislative modification. The legislative definition of those terms did not rise to the level either of an organic law explicitly and properly defining the terms

---

[159] Code Pénal (hereinafter C. Pén.), Arts. 1, 7–9 and 464–66, and see generally 1 MERLE & VITU, TRAITÉ DE DROIT CRIMINEL 389–99 (2d ed., 1973).

[160] C. Pén., Arts. 464–66, prior to amendment by Ord. No. 58-1297 of 23 Dec. 1958, [1958] J.O. 11758, [1958] B.L.D. 164; and Law No. 56-1327 of 29 Dec. 1956, Art. 7, [1956] J.O. 12638, [1957] B.L.D. 15, 18.

[161] Ord. No. 58-1297 of 23 Dec. 1958, note 160 *supra*.

[162] Earlier versions are set out in TRAVAUX PRÉPARATOIRES at 211.

[163] Société Eky, note 122 *supra*.

[164] Decisions of 19 Feb. 1963, [1963] C.C. 27; 17 March 1964, [1964] C.C. 37 [1965] D. 681; 2 July 1965, [1965] C.C. 79.

of Article 34 nor to a delegation of legislative authority under Article 38.[165] But both Conseils had assumed that the subsequent legislative definitions of "crime," "delict" and "contravention" sufficed to shift lawmaking power from Parliament to Government under Articles 34 and 37, while simultaneously treating the Government's power as an autonomous one deriving directly from the Constitution.

The Conseil constitutionnel's 1973 decision still relies on statutory definitions of the domain reserved to Parliament to confirm that the Government can establish contraventions subject to a fine not in excess of 2,000F, but rejects those definitions in relation to imprisonment, insisting that "deprivation of liberty" can only be constitutionally prescribed by specific legislation, citing the Preamble, Article 66 and Article 34 (¶¶ 3 and 5). There is no basis in Article 34 for distinguishing between fines and imprisonment, although there is ample basis to dispute the existence of any autonomous regulatory power to define offenses if the system, as the decisions of both Conseils imply, extends to Parliament broad powers of definition whose exercise necessarily defines the upper limit of the "contravention."[166]

But difficulties with the rationale of the decision are not of crucial importance for present purposes. What matters is that the Conseil went out of its way to issue what amounted to an advisory opinion on how far the Government might go in the exercise of its regulatory authority and did so on the basis of the same broadly libertarian approach to the Constitution as had inspired the 1971 decision. The Conseil's observations on the scope of the Government's authority in penal matters were strictly obiter. Perhaps they were more disturbing for that reason.[167]

---

[165] The 1958 Ordinance had the hierarchical value of a simple statute adopted by Parliament. See Const., Art. 92. It did not purport to delegate parliamentary authority and probably could not have done so without complying with special requirements of Art. 38. Delegated authority would not in any event be the equivalent of autonomous Art. 37 power. Conceivably (though this is far from certain) a definition established by organic law (see Art. 46 and the last para. of Art. 34) might have sufficed to establish or confirm Art. 37 authority in the matter but the Ordinance did not purport to establish an organic law defining the terms of Art. 34.

[166] See, e.g., Georgel, *Aspects du Préambule de la Constitution du 4 octobre 1958*, [1960] Rev. Dr. Pub. 85 at 90–91.

[167] M. Krieg, Rapporteur of the National Assembly's Law Commission for the examination of the proposed amendment to Art. 61 in 1974, was to cite this decision as being perhaps indicative of a more "aggressive" attitude toward the exercise of its powers on the part of the Conseil. Assemblée Nationale Document No. 1190 at p. 11. (Première Session Ordinaire 1974–75) (hereinafter "Rapport Krieg").

3. *27 December 1973.*[168] An increasingly important weapon in the arsenal of the Direction générale des impôts is Article 180 of the General Tax Code which provides:[169]

> Every taxpayer whose personal, open or notorious expenditures, increased by the amount of his revenues in kind, exceed his total undeclared exempt income or whose declared income . . . [net of certain exempt or deductible items] is less than the total of such expenses and revenues shall be administratively assessed.[170] The basis of imposition for such a taxpayer, in the absence of certain information permitting the attribution of a larger income, shall be fixed at an amount equal to the sum of such expenses and revenues in kind . . . [reduced by the amount of certain exonerated items]. . . . And such taxpayer shall have no right to challenge such assessment by showing that he has used capital funds, or realized capital gains [not normally taxable in France], or that he receives, periodically or not, gifts from third persons or that some of his revenues would normally be the object of forfeitary evaluation.[171]

In effect the taxpayer may be taxed on his consumption—expenditures plus revenues in kind—rather than on his income. Once the tax administration is able to show that the taxpayer's "open or notorious personal expenditures" and his revenues in kind exceed his declared income and exempt revenue, he is subject to administrative assessment under Article 180, and can attack the assessment only by showing that the administration has erred in applying the relatively simple prescriptions of Article 180.

This is strong medicine for the understatement of income, and, given the very limited rights of defense, the Conseil d'Etat has tended to interpret Article 180 rigorously against the government mainly through narrow, literal construction of the requirement that the expenses considered be "personal" and "open" (*ostensible*)

---

[168] [1973] C.C. 25, [1974] J.C.P. II.17691.

[169] Code général des impôts, Art. 180 (ed. Dalloz, 1973).

[170] The expression in French is *taxé d'office* or *taxation d'office*. This is sometimes translated "unilateral determination of income." See NORR & KERLAN, TAXATION IN FRANCE 915–18 (World Tax Series, 1966). For convenience, I have used the less cumbersome but also less precise "administrative assessment."

[171] A meaningful English rendering of the French *forfait* or *forfaitaire* in the tax sense has eluded this writer as it apparently eluded the authors of *Taxation in France*, note 170 *supra*. See *id.*, at 344–62, for a general description of the *forfait* technique of taxation on the basis of estimated rather than analytically determined and declared income.

or "notorious" (*notoire*).[172] The Government, sensitive to criticism of the use and potential abuse of Article 180, has been at pains over the years to assure Parliament that it was and would be applied only with all of the judgment and discretion that might be thought desirable.[173] Nonetheless, during the parliamentary debates on the Finance Law for 1974 (a grand annual exercise dealing mainly with the budget, appropriations, and tax law revision), the Government found itself confronted with a proposal to amend Article 180 by substituting for the notion of open or notorious personal expenditures a set of relatively concrete standards for the determination of taxable income in cases in which the taxpayer's declared revenues were less than his expenditures.[174]

The Government countered with an amendment of its own which would merely have added the following paragraph to the existing Article 180:[175]

> The taxpayer to whom the provisions of the present article are applied may obtain the discharge of the assessment against him hereunder if he establishes before the tax court [*juge d'impôt*] that the circumstances do not permit one to presume the existence of hidden or illegal resources or of an attempt to avoid the normal payment of tax, and if his taxable income does not exceed 50 per cent of the upper limit of the amounts included in the highest income tax bracket.

The amended text proposed by the Government was approved, and the Finance Law for 1974, including the amendment to Article 180 was adopted by Parliament on 18 December 1973.[176]

---

[172] For an analysis of Art. 180 in the light of current decisions of the Conseil d'Etat, see Tixier, *La portée de l'article 180 du code général des impôts*, [1974] D. 751, and Gaudemet, *L'aménagement de la taxation d'office face aux exigences de l'égalité devant la loi et de la procédure budgétaire*, [1974] A.J.D.A. 236.

[173] See, *e.g.*, Réponse Ministérielle, [1971] Journal Officiel, édition Débats Parlementaires-Assemblée Nationale 4246 [hereinafter cited as "J.O., Déb. parl., A.N."], and Réponse Ministérielle, [1971] J.O., Déb. parl., A.N. 2455. Government sensitivity to criticism in respect of Art. 180 and its effort to meet that criticism without limiting the utility of the statute is also reflected in the *Instruction* laying down internal administrative ground rules for the application of Art. 180 which was published in the *Bulletin officiel de la Direction générale des impôts*, No. 19 of 29 Jan. 1974.

[174] PROJET DE LOI DE FINANCES POUR 1974, Art. 42 *bis* C (nouveau), ASSEMBLÉE NATIONALE DOC. NO. 827 at 18 (Première Session Ordinaire, 1973–74).

[175] [1973] Journal Officiel, édition Débats Parlementaires-Sénat 3062–63 [hereinafter cited as "J.O., Déb. parl. Sén."].

[176] [1973 J.O., Déb. parl. A.N. 7145; [1973] J.O., Déb. parl. Sén. 3066. The Finance Law for 1974 less the offending article, was promulgated as Law No. 73-1150 of 27 Dec. 1973. [1974] J.O. 13899, [1974] B.L.D. 22.

The amendment to Article 180 was referred to the Conseil constitutionnel on 20 December 1973 by Alain Poher, President of the Senate.[177] The possibility of referring the amendment—which had become Article 62 of the Finance Law for 1974—to the Conseil had been mooted in the Senate debates and Senator Dailly had noted that it would be necessary to be very prudent in that regard, referring only the offending last phrase to the Conseil, for otherwise the attempt to limit the discretion of the Fisc under Article 180 would fail altogether.[178] M. Poher's letter to M. Palewski, then the President of the Conseil constitutionnel, following Dailly's advice, asked only that Conseil consider the conformity to the Constitution "and its Preamble" of the last phrase of the amending article, i.e., that which limited the benefit of the right to contest the assessment to lower-bracket taxpayers. The President of the Senate contended in his letter to M. Palewski that "discrimination based on the real or supposed wealth of a certain category of citizens" violates the principle of "equality before the law."[179]

The Conseil's decision, rendered on 27 December 1973, rejected the amendment to Article 180 as unconstitutional in its entirety.[180] In the result, the original Article 180 and the extravagant powers of tax collection which it embodies were left intact and unamended to the satisfaction of the Government, while the President of the Senate was also upheld—in principle at least—in his view of the unconstitutionality of the reservation to lower-

---

[177] Communication from the Secretariat-General of the Presidency of the Senate, dated 28 May 1974 (in the author's files). Curiously the President of the Senate was unwilling to release the full text of his letter to the Conseil, this being "a text reserved strictly to internal use." Letter to the author from the Service de documentation of Le Monde, dated 30 May 1974.

[178] [1973] J.O., Déb. parl. Sén. 3063, records the following exchange: M. André Armendaud: "The question is very simple: it is a matter of knowing whether the article under consideration as proposed by the Government ought to be referred to the Conseil constitutionnel . . . . M. Dailly: We certainly agree. M. Armendaud is probably right, but the Conseil constitutionnel, if the matter were referred to it, by the President of the Senate, for example, has only the power to avoid the provision which doesn't conform to the Constitution. It is therefore necessary to be circumspect and only refer to it as the restricted passage relating to taxable income for one must not risk the elimination of the entire amendment."

[179] Note 177 supra.

[180] Note 168 supra. Only the last phrase with which Messrs. Dailly and Poher had been concerned was held unconstitutional, but the Conseil threw out the entire amendment on the ground that the remaining language was not severable from the offending phrase. See Ord. No. 58-1067 of 7 Nov. 1958, art. 22 (the Organic Law on the Conseil constitutionnel), [1958] J.O. 10129, [1958] B.L.D. 761, 762.

bracket taxpayers only of the right to contest an Article 180 assessment.

The Conseil again founded its decision on the Preamble, holding that the provisions in question would "discriminate against citizens in respect of the possibility of attacking an administrative tax assessment affecting them; that the said disposition thus infringes the principle of equality before the law contained in the Declaration of Rights of 1789 and solemnly reaffirmed by the Preamble of the Constitution."[181] For good measure the Council also invoked the provisions of the organic law on Finance Acts which prohibits amendments to the Government's Finance Bill whose effect would be other than a reduction of expense or an increase in revenues.[182] Despite this seemingly adequate independent ground, the decision was cast in terms which left no doubt that the substantive constitutional restriction was dispositive.

4. *15 January 1975*.[183] The decision of 15 January 1975 was the second decision taken upon reference by a parliamentary minority under the 1974 amendment to Article 61.[184] Eighty-one deputies joined in referring to the Conseil the statute which was to become the Law of 17 January 1975 relative to the interruption of pregnancy.[185] Adopted on 20 December 1974, over substantial Gaullist opposition, the statute recited the law's "guaranty" of respect for every human being "from the beginning of life" and affirmed that this principle might be infringed only in "cases of necessity" and under the conditions prescribed by the new statute[186] and the Code of Public Health was amended to provide that:[187]

> A pregnant woman whose condition places her in a situation
> of distress may request that a doctor interrupt the pregnancy.
> This interruption may only be effected prior to the end of the
> tenth week of pregnancy.

---

[181] Note 168 *supra*. On the troublesome problem of the principle of equality before the law in tax matters, see generally Devolvé, Le Principe d'Egalité devant les Charges Publiques (1969).

[182] Ord. No. 59-2 of 2 Jan. 1959, Art. 42, [1959] J.O. 756, [1959] B.L.D. 297; and see Const., Art. 40, [1958] B.L.D. 665.

[183] [1975] J.C.P. II.18030, [1975] Rev. Dr. Pub. 203.

[184] The first was the Decision of 30 Dec. 1974, [1975] J.C.P. II.18037 (involving a question of regulatory and legislative competence rather than a substantive issue). On the 1974 amendment see text *infra*, at notes 194–207.

[185] Le Monde, 24 Dec. 1974, p. 8; Law No. 75-17 of Jan. 17, 1975, [1975] J.O. 739; [1975] B.L.D. 48.

[186] *Id*., Art. 1.

[187] *Id*., Art. 4, adding Art. L.162-1 to the Code of Public Health.

The statute contains a number of additional provisions assuring the right of doctors and private hospitals to refuse to perform abortions, imposing certain counseling requirements before and after the performance of the operation and otherwise regulating the medical and administrative application of the statute.[188] There is, however, no elaboration of the basic criteria of the availability of an abortion: "distress" and "necessity." That aspect of the matter is left entirely in the hands of doctor and patient.

Jean Foyer, one of the most vocal parliamentary opponents of the abortion bill, offered a statement of the views of the deputies who had referred the law to the Conseil in *Le Monde* of 24–25 December 1974.[189] Two principal substantive arguments were advanced, one founded on the Preamble of the 1958 Constitution, and the other based on the European Convention on Human Rights, ratified by France in 1973.[190] Invoking the 1958 Preamble, M. Foyer focused on the incorporated provisions of the 1946 Preamble, which opens with an expression of profound concern for the protection of the "inalienable and sacred rights of every human being" and, to this end, provides that "the nation guarantees to all, particularly to the child, [and] to the mother . . . the protection of their health." He argued from the legislative history of this language that it is a mere contraction of a proposal made in the Constituent Assembly of 1946 which would have explicitly protected the child's well-being "from conception and implied the prohibition of abortion." His argument from the Preamble concludes with the assertion that the Constitution is founded on "the fundamental principle of humanist civilization that no one has the right to dispose of another's life"; that to deny the application of that principle to the foetus is to deny biological fact—a difficulty which, M. Foyer conceded, "has not stopped either the Supreme Court of the United States or the French legislature." With respect to the European

---

[188] See generally *id.*, Arts. 4–16.

[189] It is interesting to note that in 1971 M. Foyer had insisted that it was inappropriate for professors of public law to make use of the "authority of *la doctrine*" to examine in the press the merits of the constitutional issues before the Conseil while those issues were *sub judice*. Le Monde, 17 July 1971, p. 5. His articles in the same newspaper on the abortion legislation suggest that he, too, may now recognize that no other method of "briefing" these issues for the benefit of the Conseil exists under present procedures, and that such argument must be of great value to the Conseil however unofficial its submission.

[190] See Decree No. 74-360 of 3 May 1974, [1974] J.O. 4750; [1974] D. III.181. On the European Convention, see Note, 80 HARV. L. REV. 1798 (1967).

Convention, Foyer argued from the provisions of Article 2 which proclaims that "The right to life of every person is protected by the law." That the right to life thus protected includes the life of the foetus is demonstrated, argued Foyer, by the nearly universal prohibition of abortion among signatory states at the time of the drafting and signature of the Convention.

The argument from the European Convention raised threshold questions of the constitutional status of treaty provisions and the competence of the Conseil to apply them to invalidate an act of Parliament. Article 55 of the Constitution provides:

> Treaties or agreements regularly ratified or approved have, from the date of their publication, an authority superior to that of statutes, subject, however, for each treaty or agreement to its application by the other party.

Article 54 provides for reference of treaties to the Conseil constitutionnel by any of the four officials originally entitled to refer legislation to the Conseil under Article 61. A declaration by the Conseil under Article 54 that a provision of a treaty or agreement is contrary to the Constitution blocks ratification until such time as the Constitution shall have been appropriately amended. The "superiority" language of Article 55 does not clearly confer constitutional force upon the ratified treaty, and Article 54 suggests rather strongly that a treaty does not have such force since it may itself be subject to constitutional challenge. If the ratified treaty does not have constitutional force, if it is not somehow assimilated into the Constitution, the competence of the Conseil to avoid a statute on the basis of treaty under Article 61 is highly doubtful since that Article authorizes the Conseil to judge only conformity to the "Constitution." On the other hand, it might be thought evident that a statute which is inconsistent with a ratified treaty is necessarily unconstitutional simply because it violates the constitutional provision according "superiority" to treaties over statutes.

The Conseil sustained the constitutionality of the abortion law, holding itself incompetent to rule on the conformity of a statute to a treaty and ruling that the statute did not violate the "principle of liberty posed by art. 2 of the Declaration of the Rights of Man and of the Citizen," nor any of "fundamental principles recognized by the laws of the Republic," nor the principle of the 1946 Preamble pursuant to which "the nation guarantees to the infant the protection of his health." The Conseil relied heavily on the statutory language purporting to limit the availability of abortion to "situations of distress" in which therapeutic motives are presumed operative. The statute, the Conseil concluded, does not violate "the principle of the respect of every human being from the beginning of his life, recited in Article 1 [of the statute], except in cases of necessity and in accordance with the conditions and restrictions which it defines; and thus does not infringe the principle of liberty set out in Article 2 of the Declaration of Rights" nor any other principle having constitutional force contained in the Preamble. As in the prior decisions of July 1971 and December 1973, the Conseil adhered to the laconic style typical of the decisions of the Conseil d'Etat and of the Court of Cassation, and merely recited the constitutional sources without explaining or elaborating the principle it drew from them.

The Conseil's handling of the treaty point, by contrast, was a good example of the kind of analytical reasoning from which it has assiduously abstained in relation to substantive restrictions derived from the Preamble. The provisions of Article 55, the Conseil pointed out, accord to treaties an authority superior to statutes but do not prescribe or imply that respect for this rule is to be assured under Article 61. Moreover, the authority of the texts submitted to the Conseil under Article 61 is unconditional, while the greater force accorded to a treaty is subject to the condition of reciprocity and may thus vary over time and in relation to different parties to the treaty. A treaty, the Conseil implies, thus does not necessarily override a contrary law in all the latter's applications and it would be improper to apply the blunt instrument of an Article 61 declaration of nonconformity to the Constitution to preclude promulgation of a statute which is only inconsistent with overriding treaty obligations as to some of France's treaty partners.

The decision suggests new sensitivity to suggestions that the Conseil's decisions under Article 61 go beyond the limits of a verification of conformity to the Constitution—verging on interference in the legislative authority[191]—for it is at pains to recite at the beginning of the decision that "article 61 of the Constitution does not confer on the Conseil constitutionnel a general power of evaluation and decision identical to that of Parliament, but only confers

---

[191] See, *e.g.*, Rapport Krieg, at 9-12.

competence to determine the conformity to the Constitution of statutes referred to the Conseil for examination."[192]

B. THE POLITICAL RESPONSE

In some measure the response to the Conseil's decision of 16 July 1971 was entirely predictable. It would please the proponents of constitutional review. It would trouble those for whom the Parliament and political process remain the essential and only democratic means of defining and protecting public liberties, and who could only see in the Conseil's decision a manifestation of that "government by judges" against which the history of *ancien régime* and Lambert's analysis of the American experience had set the minds and constitutional traditions of the French.[193] It would, as an ad hoc matter, satisfy those who had seen in the legislation in question an attempt to reinforce the already substantial apparatus available to the Government for the suppression of radical dissent.[194]

The unequivocal and broadly principled character of the decision would make it difficult for the Conseil thereafter to withdraw into its earlier reticence on substantive constitutional issues. The possibility remained, however, given the limited opportunities for the initiation of review and the control of that process by elected officials, that an adverse political reaction to the decision would deter the further development of substantive review by the Conseil, or even induce moves to restrict its competence. Neither of these things occurred, and, as subsequent decisions suggest, the political response was generally favorable, marking the 1971 decision as a decisive turning point in French attitudes toward substantive constitutional review.

The parties of the left participating in the Constituent Assemblies of 1946 were resolutely opposed to the introduction of judicial review and were unwilling to go beyond the creation of that futile instrument of nonjudicial constitutional review which became the Constitutional Committee. In 1972, the Common Program jointly adopted by the Socialist party and the Communist party

---

[192] Note 183 *supra.*

[193] *E.g.*, Jean Foyer, quoted in Le Monde, 18–19 July 1971, p. 5; and see the correspondence concerning the decision published in Le Monde, 1–2 Aug. 1971.

[194] *E.g.*, Badinter, *Le droit d'association*, in Le Monde, 30 June 1971 at p. 8.

announced a complete reversal of that position. According to the Common Program:[195]

> A Supreme Court will assure respect for the constitutional rules, the regularity of national elections and the guaranty of public, individual and collective liberties.
>
> Exceptions of unconstitutionality raised by litigants against legislative or regulatory provisions which they consider contrary to the liberties guaranteed by articles 7 to 11 of the Declaration of the Rights of Man and of the Citizen and by the Preamble to the Constitution shall be referred to the Supreme Court by the judicial and administrative tribunals. Its decisions shall not be subject to any appeal.
>
> It will be composed of nine members appointed for non-renewable nine-year terms: three elected by the National Assembly . . . [proportionally—two by the majority and one by the minority], three by the Senate under the same conditions, one by the President of the Republic and two by the High Council on the Judiciary.

Shortly after the May 1974 elections in which he narrowly defeated François Mitterand, candidate of the Socialist Communist Alliance,[196] President Giscard d'Estaing proposed the amendment of Article 61 of the Constitution to permit reference of legislation to the Conseil constitutionnel by parliamentary minorities and, more extravagant still, to permit the Conseil to initiate review on its own motion when newly adopted legislation appeared to the Conseil to be violative of constitutionally protected rights.[197] At a press conference on 25 July 1974, shortly after the proposed amendment had been approved by the Council of Ministers, the President was asked how far in this direction the Government proposed to go. His response:[198]

> Is it necessary to go further? We'll see. It must be understood first of all that we have absolutely no intention of copying the

---

[195] PROGRAMME COMMUN DE GOUVERNEMENT DU PARTI COMMUNISTE FRANÇAIS ET DU PARTI SOCIALISTE (27 June 1972) 145–46 (Editions Sociales, 1972).

[196] In the run-off election of May 19, Giscard d'Estaing received 50.81 percent of the votes cast against 49.19 percent for Mitterand. Conseil constitutionnel, Proclamation of Results, 24 May 1974, as reported in Le Monde Sélection Hebdomadaire, 23–29 May 1974, p. 2.

[197] Le Monde Sélection Hebdomadaire 11–17 July 1974, p. 7; the text of the proposal adopted by the Council of Ministers on 10 July 1974 is contained in PROJET DE LOI CONSTITUTIONNELLE, note 5 supra.

[198] Le Monde, 27 July 1974, p. 2.

Constitution of the United States of America. We do not live in a copied constitutional system; our institutions are different. . . . [In going beyond the present proposal] it is necessary to be careful that we not create in France what I shall call a "Republic of judges." The Parliament has certain attributions. It represents the popular sovereignty. It is essential not to withdraw its authority systematically by transfer of too much constitutional power to a tribunal. We are therefore using the experimental method in this first extension of the powers of the *Conseil constitutionnel.* We will see later—together with all who follow political events—whether it is necessary to go further.

Mme de Staël might have underscored the concern with originality.[199] More significant, however, is the evocation of the classic themes—government by judges, parliament as the embodiment of popular sovereignty—at the very moment at which there is proposed the creation of a "roving constitutional commission" whose power to avoid legislation, being subject to neither the existence of a "case or controversy" nor any other independent interest or initiative, would, during the period between adoption and promulgation, substantially exceed the powers of judicial review of the Supreme Court of the United States.

To become part of the Constitution the proposed amendments to Article 61 had first to be adopted in identical terms by the National Assembly and by the Senate, and then by three-fifths of the members voting at a joint session (Congrès).[200] The proposal to allow the Conseil constitutionnel to undertake review on its own initiative of legislation "which might infringe public liberties" did not survive the first step. The report of the Assembly committee charged with the examination of the Government's proposal was adverse to this autosaisine (as it came to be called) and it was rejected by an Assembly majority uniting a wide range of Gaullist and left-wing opinion.[201] Four principal, interrelated reasons were advanced by the opponents of the measure. First, it was thought inappropriate to give any extraparliamentary, nonelected body the

---

[199] Concerning the Constitution of 1791, she wrote, "A mad, almost literary, vanity inspires in the French the need to innovate." Quoted, LEMASURIER, note 85 *supra*, at 16.

[200] Const., Art. 89. The President of the Republic may decide to submit the proposal, after approval by both houses, to referendum rather than convening the Congrès.

[201] Rapport Krieg, [1974] J.O., Déb. parl. A.N. 4955.

equivalent of a power of veto over Parliament which could be systematically applied to all legislation.[202] Second, it was argued that the political character of recruitment to the Conseil does not assure that it will act with judicial independence and objectivity. The composition and recruitment of the Conseil was a matter of concern to almost every participant in the debates.[203] Third, members strongly approving the principle of constitutional review objected that autosaisine would inevitably politicize the Conseil by requiring it to exercise an initiative which would be seen—however judicious might be the Conseil's behavior—as essentially political and would consequently discredit the very process of constitutional review whose acceptability depended upon an image of the Conseil's independence. Fourth, there was much concern that the very notion of "public liberties" and the documents which are its principal written manifestations are so imprecise and contradictory as to leave the Conseil's power without effective measure or limit —a difficulty which already existed but which would redouble in importance with the substantial increase in the output of substantive decisions by the Conseil expected to result from the adoption of the amendments.

Each of these arguments, except the first, was also applicable in some degree to proposed extension of the right of reference to parliamentary minorities, but the conviction that constitutional review in some form is desirable, that the existing system had shown that it could work, and that the extension of the right of reference was a sensible method of making that system more effective without new departures from traditional principles sufficed to assure passage of this branch of the proposed amendment. On the left, and especially in the far left, the arguments against the amendment were linked to more tendentious claims that the proposal was an insignificant half-measure in which the Government was deliberately avoiding confronting the major issues of constitutional reform, and that, as it stood, it was not worth Parliament's time to consider it.

---

[202] See Rapport Krieg, the debates are reported in [1974] J.O., Déb. parl. A.N. 4859–70, 4948–58, 5158–61; [1974] J.O. Déb. parl. Sén. 1311–42, 1374–75; [1974] Journal Officiel, édition Débats Parlementaires-Congrès du Parlement 1–10 [hereinafter cited as "J.O., Déb. parl., Cong. du parl."]. See also Rapport Dailly, SÉNAT Doc. No. 33 (Première Session Ordinaire, 1974–75).

[203] See Schwarzenberg, Les neuf juges et la constitution, Le Monde, 3 Jan. 1974, p. 1, for a critique of the organization and methods of recruitment to the Council in light of its expanding role in the French constitutional system.

Other speakers were quick to point out that the left-wing formation would be the first and most important beneficiary of the proposed amendment.[204]

The most notable thing about the debates was the almost complete absence of opposition to the principle of effective constitutional review. The late Jacques Duclos, elder statesman of the
Communist party, strongly opposed the amendment but invoked
the solutions of the Common Program in so doing.[205] Socialists
Franceschi and Chandernagor opposed, but Franceschi insisted that
the right solution had been in Chandernagor's own earlier proposal
for the establishment of a Supreme Court.[206] Even expressions of
concern over the possible future role of the Conseil as an obstacle
to the social legislation of a left-wing majority were linked to criticism of the recruitment and composition of the Conseil rather than
to a principled rejection of the notion of external review. On the
other hand, there were a number of speeches by supporters of the
extended right of parliamentary reference which cautioned against
the creation of government by judges, against any review after
promulgation. The traditional position on judicial review was represented strongly enough to lead one to doubt the likelihood of
any move to establish a constitutional court by further amendment.
The amendment giving sixty members of either house the right to
refer ordinary legislation to the Conseil was adopted by the Congrès on 21 October 1974.[207] The first reference to the Conseil (by
a group comprised mainly of Socialist deputies) occurred two
months later, on 20 December 1974.

Substantive constitutional review is largely a matter of the enforcement of constitutionally protected civil and political rights
by some sort of judicial or nonjudicial organ. A further measure
of the political climate for the growth of constitutional review
may be found in recent efforts to reinforce or better define the
body of rights which are to be assured to Frenchmen by consti-

---

[204] The only serious dispute over the proposal to extend the right of reference to the
Conseil arose between the Assembly and Senate and had to do with the proportion of the
membership (or number of members) of each house which must join in the reference
to the Conseil. This was finally resolved by substituting a fixed number (60) of members
of either house for the proportion (one fifth) proposed by the Government.

[205] [1974] J.O., Déb. Parl. Sén. 1322.

[206] [1974] J.O., Déb. Parl. A.N., 4966 (Franceschi); [1974] J.O. Déb. Parl., Cong. du
Parl. 4–6 (Chandernagor).

[207] [1974] J.O., Déb. parl., Cong. du parl. 10; [1974] J.O. 11035.

tutional and other means. Reference to French ratification of the European Declaration of Human Rights has already been made.[208] Not long after the adoption of the amendment to Article 61, the Government created a special commission to prepare and propose for adoption by appropriate means a "Code of Fundamental Individual Liberties."[209] There is no suggestion in the decree, however, that such a code would be inserted in the Constitution. The only concrete legislative action which the commission is invited to consider is the modification of existing statutes and regulations to better assure the protection of such liberties. The most recent initiative comes from the Communist party which, in May 1975, published a draft charter of individual and collective, social, economic, and political rights and at the same time affirmed the position of the Common Program (in rather more restrained terms) by calling for a Supreme Court which will "contribute" to the respect of constitutional rules and individual and collective freedoms.[210]

It isn't necessary to know much about the underlying motives for these developments to conclude that they reflect, if not a genuine change of mind in the parties and political leadership, at least a perception of public opinion which is favorable to constitutional review. If opinion hasn't changed, then either political perception of it, or political responsiveness to it, has, and in either case it seems fair to say that the experience of constitutional review has contributed largely to the opening of new vistas for its development.

---

[208] See also Madiot, *Du Conseil constitutionnel à la convention européenne: vers un renforcement des libertés publiques*, [1975] D. Chron. 1.

[209] Decree No. 74-937 of 8 Nov. 1974, [1974] J.C.P. III.42206.

[210] L'Humanité, 17 May 1975, p. 3. A kind of political essay contest in the reformulation of fundamental rights would appear to be under way between the Government and the principal opposition parties. See remarks of J.-P. Cot, [1974] J.O. Déb. parl. A.N. 4957.

On 10 Dec. 1975, the Gaullist Union des démocrates pour la République issued a document entitled: "Réflexions sur la liberté" which observes: "One might imagine the existence in our country of a true Supreme Court, a guardian of freedom in the last resort. The Conseil constitutionnel might assume this role. The development of [its] case law and the reform of 1974 enlarging its competence have opened the way for such an evolution." Quoted in Le Monde, 12 Dec. 1975. In addition, recent declarations of M. Chirac, the Prime Minister, as well as the formation, on Gaullist initiative, of a special parliamentary commission (independent of the Government commission appointed in 1974, see note 209 *supra*) suggest that the proposal to establish some sort of "bill of rights" has and retains considerable political momentum. See Le Monde, 20 Dec. 1975, p. 10.

C. REVIEW BY THE CONSEIL CONSTITUTIONNEL SINCE THE 1974 CON-
   STITUTIONAL AMENDMENT

Article 61, after the 1974 Amendment, reads in relevant part
as follows:[211]

> Organic laws before their promulgation, and the by-laws of
> the parliamentary assemblies, before they come into force,
> must be submitted to the Conseil constitutionnel which pro-
> nounces on their conformity to the Constitution. For the same
> purpose, statutes may be referred to the Conseil constitution-
> nel, before their promulgation, by the President of the Re-
> public, the Prime Minister, the president of the National As-
> sembly, the President of the Senate or sixty deputies or sixty
> senators.

The new provision for reference by members of Parliament were
first invoked soon after the amendment became effective and even
before the necessary modifications to the organic law on the Conseil constitutionnel came into force.[212] Certain provisions of the
1975 Finance Act were referred to the Conseil by a group of Socialist deputies and the Abortion Law was referred to the Conseil
by a group of deputies who belonged mainly to the Gaullist and
center political formations.[213] At the end of the 1974–75 legislative
session on 30 June 1975, two additional statutes were referred to
the Conseil by parliamentary groups.

Prior to the 1974 amendment there had been only nine instances
in which ordinary legislation had been referred to the Conseil under Article 61.[214] The impact of the amendment of the Conseil's
very small "case-law" under Article 61 has thus already been pro-
portionally significant.

Important as an indicator of future development is the simple
fact that members of Parliament need no longer persuade the President of the Senate to refer legislation to the Conseil. The presidency of the Senate, occupied continuously by anti-Gaullists since

---

[211] Note 207 *supra*.

[212] Ord. No. 58-1067 of 7 Nov. 1958, [1958] J.O. 10129, [1958] B.L.D. 761; as
amended by Ord. No. 59-223 of 4 Feb. 1959, [1959] J.O. 1683, [1959] B.L.D. 521; and
Organic Law No. 74-1101 of 26 Dec. 1974, [1974] J.O. 13068, [1975] B.L.D. 11. On
the most recent amendment see Franck, *Le nouveau régime des saisines du conseil constitutionnel*, [1975] J.C.P. I.2678.

[213] Le Monde, 24 Dec. 1974, p. 8.

[214] See Favoreu & Philip, at 207; and see annexes to Rapport Dailly, note 202 *supra*.

the beginning of the Fifth Republic, has heretofore been the only position from which there was any realistic possibility that Article 61 review might be initiated for any purpose other than that of protecting Government prerogatives under allocative or procedural provisions like those of Articles 34/37 and 41.

To the extent that formal political alignments are indicative of probable recourse to Article 61 review by parliamentary groups, the composition of Parliament is also of interest. As of March 1973 (when the last general elections of members of the Assembly were held), the 490 Deputies were divided among six major and a number of minor political formations.[215] Of these the largest was the *Union des démocrates pour la République* (Gaullist) which held 178 seats. The Socialists and the Communists held, respectively, 89 and 73 seats, and either was thus in a position to initiate review under the amended Article 61. And a fraction of the U.D.R. might do the same in case of disagreement with its own leadership or the Independent Republicans (53 seats) of Giscard d'Estaing. This is in fact what happened in connection with the abortion legislation. In the Senate no single group held the necessary 60 seats after the last senatorial elections (September 1974) although the Socialists (52 seats), the Independent Republicans (57 seats), and the Union centriste des démocrates de progrès (54 seats) were all close enough to have an excellent chance of attracting the collaboration of the additional members necessary to initiate review.

Increased frequency of reference to the Conseil will obviously mean increased opportunity for the development by the Conseil of a coherent body of constitutional doctrine, and, perhaps, lead to increased acceptance of the review function. As the Conseil renders more decisions on substantive matters, it will certainly lead to increased pressure to rationalize other aspects of the application of the Constitution as positive law.

It is important to note that the 1974 Amendment has not changed the temporal conditions of review. Legislation may only be referred to the Conseil after definitive adoption by Parliament and before promulgation by the President of the Republic.[216] It does not alter the Conseil's procedures in constitutional review. There is no pub-

---

[215] All of the figures in this   aragraph are drawn from 1 EUROPE YEAR BOOK 1975, 674–75.

[216] Const., Art. 61.

lic hearing or adversary proceeding. The only argument received directly by the Conseil is that which may be contained in the letter of reference, and in the observations which the other officials named in Article 61 may offer in writing when informed of the initial reference. This right of reply—which finds its only textual basis in the Conseil's duty to inform the other Article 61 officials under the Organic Law relating to the Conseil[217]—will now presumably extend to all members of both houses. The position is unclear because the members may submit their letters of reference individually without forming a coherent group of sixty or adopting a common position.[218] The Conseil appoints a *rapporteur* to examine the matter and acts *in camera* on his report.[219]

Finally, the amendment does nothing to elucidate the appropriate sources of the substantive rules to be applied by the Conseil unless the adoption of the amendment is to be taken as implicitly approving (as it surely does politically if not legally) the application of the Preamble and sources incorporated in the Preamble in the manner of the 16 July 1971 and 27 December 1973 decisions.

IV. THE CONSEIL CONSTITUTIONNEL, THE COURTS, AND THE CONSTITUTION

From the constitutional lawyer's point of view, one of the more serious defects of the institutional mechanism for the adjudication of substantive constitutional issues in the Fifth Republic is its inability to deal with divergent interpretations of the basic law. Despite the unwillingness of the judicial and administrative tribunals to pass upon the constitutionality of acts of Parliament, both must inevitably take account of the Constitution in dealing with their respective adjudicative tasks. The Conseil d'Etat is equally bound to look to the Constitution in the exercise of its advisory functions.[220] There have been a number of manifestations of concern over the maintenance of a unified interpretation of the Constitution as between the Conseil constitutionnel and the Conseil

---

[217] Ord. No. 58-1067 of 7 Nov. 1958, Art. 18, note 212 *supra*.

[218] The duty to inform the members of each house of Parliament of the reference of a statute to the Conseil falls on the President of each house (who must be notified by the Conseil) under the Organic Law of 26 Dec. 1974.

[219] Ord. No. 58-1067, Art. 19.

[220] On the advisory functions of the Conseil d'Etat, see RENDEL, THE ADMINISTRATIVE FUNCTIONS OF THE FRENCH CONSEIL D'ETAT 113–47, 194–232 (1970).

d'Etat.[221] There are multiple possibilities for conflict, not only in the process of defining the boundary between the legislative and regulatory domains identified by Articles 34 and 37, but also in substantive matters. As for the judicial tribunals, the strength of their commitment to the traditional refusal to review will be sorely tested in any case in which they are called upon to give effect to a statute which—not having been subject to review by the Conseil constitutionnel—plainly violates in principle or in detail a constitutional rule consecrated by a decision of the Conseil constitutionnel. Events subsequent to the Conseil's decisions of 27 November 1973 and 15 January 1975 illustrate the difficulty and raise the question whether France is to have one constitution or three—depending upon which and how many of its three highest jurisdictions are called upon to deal with a given issue.

A. DISCORD OVER THE DECISION OF 27 NOVEMBER 1973

The decision of the Conseil constitutionnel of 27 November 1973 created a dilemma which the system has only been able to resolve by denying the authority of the Conseil's pronouncement in that decision on the scope of the Government's rule-making powers in penal matters. The principle announced by the Conseil —that imprisonment may be imposed only in virtue of a statute adopted by Parliament—calls into question the validity of existing regulations which had been adopted by decree and which punish "contraventions," such as violations of the Highway Code, with short terms of imprisonment. There was an immediate reaction in the lower courts. At least two lower courts refused to enforce such regulations in the weeks following the Conseil's decision on the ground of unconstitutionality.[222] The problem arose in two other cases before the Court of Cassation in February 1974.[223] In the meantime, the Government had submitted a draft decree modifying the Highway Code to the administrative sections of the Conseil d'Etat for an advisory opinion. The opinion rendered by the Con-

---

[221] See FRANCK, LES FONCTIONS JURIDICTIONNELLES DU CONSEIL CONSTITUTIONNEL 169–80 (1974).

[222] Min. Publ. v. Dame Lepas et Schmitt [1974] D. Sommaires 33 (Trib. gd. inst., Orleans, Jan. 14, 1974); see also the judgment of the Tribunal de Police of Pithiviers cited in the conclusions of Procureur-général Touffait in Schiavon, infra note 223.

[223] Schiavon, [1974] Bulletin des arrêts de la Cour de Cassation en matière criminelle 204 [hereinafter cited as "Bull. Crim."], [1974] D. 273, (concl. Touffait) (Cass. Crim., 26 Feb. 1974); Chaix, [1974] Bull. Crim. 201 (Cass. Crim., 26 Feb. 1974).

seil squarely confronted the Conseil constitutionnel's position and rejected it.[224] Technically, these developments put the question of the authority of the decisions of the Conseil constitutionnel and the extent to which that authority attaches to an utterance like the troublesome "petite phrase"[225] of the November 1973 decision. More broadly, they challenge the integrity of the curiously compartmentalized system for the legal resolution of constitutional questions which has grown out of the 1958 constitutional arrangements. The response to the technical question has formed the basis for dealing with the problem in the Conseil d'Etat and the Court of Cassation and must receive attention here.

The authority of the decisions of the Conseil constitutionnel is determined by Article 62 of the 1958 Constitution which provides:

> The decisions of the Conseil constitutionnel are not subject to any appeal. They are binding on the public authorities [*pouvoirs publics*] and on all administrative and judicial adjudicative authorities.

This provision, which would appear to give wide and final authority to the decisions of the Conseil constitutionnel and to oblige every organ of the state, including the courts, to conform its own decisions to those of the Conseil, in fact exercises only the weakest sort of unifying influence upon the decisions of the Conseil d'Etat and Court of Cassation. Article 62 is without sanction. The Conseil constitutionnel has no means of reversing or modifying judgments which are inconsistent with its own decisions. Moreover, the rule of Article 62 has been assimilated to the rule of the civil law which attributes *la force de la chose jugée* (to be called *"res judicata"* hereinafter for convenience without suggesting more than gross analogy between the French and Common Law concepts) to final civil judgments.[226] Normally, in civil matters, the *res judicata* effect attaches only to the *dispositif* of the judgment (*i.e.*, that part of the judgment which fixes the rights of the parties) and not the reasoning which supports the decision.[227] The Conseil constitutionnel has

---

[224] Opinion of 17 Jan. 1974, [1974] D. 280.

[225] The frequent references in the literature to the Conseil's dicta as "la petite phrase" are attributable to Vedel, *Encore une petite phrase* . . . , Le Monde, 5 Dec. 1973.

[226] See, *e.g.*, FRANCK, note 221 *supra*, at 134. On the civil law rule, see VINCENT, PROCÉDURE CIVILE 86–99 (16th ed., 1973).

[227] See VINCENT, note 226 *supra*, at 644–46.

claimed a somewhat broader *res judicata* effect for its decisions in asserting that the force conferred by Article 62 extends both to the *dispositif* and to the reasons which are its "essential support."[228] The Conseil's decision of 28 November 1973 put the question of the effect of Article 62 before the Conseil d'État and the Court of Cassation, and it was on the basis of restrictive interpretation of that article that both bodies denied legal effect to the *petite phrase*.

In the *Schiavon* decision of 26 February 1974 the Court of Cassation had to grapple with the claim that Schiavon's conviction for involuntary homicide was bad in law because it was founded on certain provisions of the Highway Code which had been established by decree and were sanctioned by imprisonment, a sanction which the Conseil constitutionnel had held could not constitutionally be prescribed by decree. The problem was examined at length by Procureur-general Touffait in his argument before the Court. The Conseil constitutionnel, like other adjudicative organs, Touffait maintained, is subject to the "fundamental principles of adjudicative procedure" which prohibit such bodies from deciding any issue other than that which is placed before them by the parties. It decides that issue. It does not establish general principles. In an important passage in his argument Touffait evokes the classic prohibitions on the rendition of *arrêts de règlement:*[229]

> ... [I]t is obvious that the Conseil constitutionnel cannot issue general regulatory orders [*arrêts de règlement*], an act which would be contrary to the principle of French public law set out in art. 5 of the Civil Code: "Judges are forbidden to pronounce by way of general disposition on the causes submitted to them." It cannot therefore announce rules which are binding in all analogous cases, for *it would thus overstep its role of review of laws and regulations in conformity with the Constitution in order to fulfill a legislative role and would seriously disturb the balance of powers established by the Constitution* with all of the consequences difficult to measure which such an interference by one power with another may produce. (Emphasis in original.)

The argument, it will immediately be recognized, goes far beyond the issue of judicial review and raises that of judicial prece-

---

[228] Decision of 15 Jan. 1962, [1962] C.C. 31, [1963] D. 303 (Note Hamon).

[229] Note 223 *supra*, at 274.

dent. The same texts which have been taken to preclude constitutional review by the judicial and administrative tribunals are
also fundamental to the problem of judicial precedent in French
law.[230] An examination of that problem is beyond the scope of this
paper, but it is essential to recognize that French law has rejected
the notion that judges are bound in any formal sense to apply the
announced reasoning of a prior decision in deciding later, like cases.
Qualifications on this principle in doctrine and practice are legion,
and there is—insofar as the style of French judgments permits assessment of parity of fact, principle, and reasoning in different cases—
much evidence that French judges seek to treat like cases alike, and
that lower courts tend to follow the decisions of higher courts.[231]
But the constraints that produce this functional facsimile of common law precedent operate most surely only within a unified judicial hierarchy. While it is to be expected that the Conseil constitutionnel will also seek to adhere over time to the principles and
reasoning announced in its decisions, its isolation from the hierar-
chies of the judicial and administrative courts gives the denial of
a more general law declaring force to the Conseil's decision, a far
greater negative impact on the unity of the system.

Now it might be thought that the maintenance of the unity of
the system was precisely the purpose of Article 62, even if the
absence of appellate control over the courts cast doubt on its effectiveness for that purpose. The Conseil constitutionnel seemed to be
claiming something of the sort when it asserted that the force
attributed to its decisions by Article 62 attached not only to the
dispositif but also to the *motifs* which are its essential support. But
Touffait, accepting the Conseil's formulation of the principle, insisted that—given the general rule against deciding issues other than
those raised by the petitions of the parties—the only part of the
28 November decision to which Article 62 force attached was the
dispositif (*i.e.*, the declaration that the dispositions in question were
of regulatory character) and the single "necessary" *motif* (*i.e.*,
that the prescription of contraventions subject to fines not exceeding 2,000F was within the regulatory domain).[232] The Prime

---

[230] See 1 MARTY & REYNAUD, TRAITÉ DE DROIT CIVIL (INTRODUCTION GÉNÉRALE À
L'ETUDE DE DROIT) 216–20 (1972).

[231] See, *e.g.*, DAWSON, ORACLES OF THE LAW 400–31 (1968), on the case law of the
judicial courts.

[232] Note 223 *supra*, at 274.

Minister had, after all, only put the question, the only one he could put under Article 37, whether a particular provision sanctioned by a fine not exceeding 2,000F was subject to amendment by decree. The Conseil's *petite phrase* envisaging a different result if the article in question had been sanctioned by imprisonment was thus purely hypothetical and irrelevant to the decision. This argument was difficult to fault from a technical point of view, and it relieved the Court of any obligation (under Article 62) to conform its decision to the reasoning of the Conseil.

The absence of an obligation to apply the principle announced by the Conseil constitutionnel did not settle the matter for the Court of Cassation, since there was no doubt about that Court's power to test the "legality" or constitutionality of a regulation or about the propriety of Schiavon's challenge to the regulation, quite apart from any question of the effect to be attributed to the Conseil's decision.[233] The competence of the judicial courts in this regard in criminal proceedings constitutes one of the most important exceptions to the principle of the exclusive jurisdiction of the administrative courts in respect of any challenge to the validity of acts of the administration.[234] The Court of Cassation thus had to deal with Schiavon's claim. If it were to deal with the substantive constitutional issue, it would remain difficult to avoid confronting the position of the Conseil constitutionnel.

The Court resolved the problem by falling back on the *Paulin* position: judicial tribunals are incompetent to test the constitutionality of a statute. The regulation challenged by Schiavon imposed penalties which fell within the limits described by the Penal Code definition of the "contravention" and its punishments. Because those definitions have statutory force, the court could not examine their constitutional validity. The statutory definitions in turn shielded the regulations from constitutional challenge. The difficulty, of course, is that the Government's regulatory powers in respect of "contraventions" had been thought to be autonomous powers deriving directly from Articles 34 and 37 of the Constitution (also cited by the Court of Cassation in its decision.) Nonetheless, a decision dealing with the constitutionality of the regulations as an exercise of autonomous regulatory power would necessarily have called into question the valadity of the statutory defi-

---

[233] See 1 MERLE & VITU, note 159 *supra*, at 251–58.

[234] See DE LAUBADÈRE, note 43 *supra*, at 462–64.

nitions. By focusing on the statutory character of the definitions, the Court was thus able to invoke its traditional position in respect of the constitutionality of legislation, and avoid tackling a difficult constitutional question.

Just over one month earlier, the Conseil d'Etat had rendered its advisory opinion to the Government on new draft Highway Code provisions which imposed sanctions impliedly involving a deprivation of liberty. The Conseil addressed itself to the November 1973 decision of the Conseil constitutionnel and rejected the notion that a punishment involving a deprivation of liberty could only be imposed by statute. The Conseil d'Etat relied on its own prior decisions and on a 1963 decision of the Conseil constitutionnel and made no effort to resolve the problem of the autonomous or delegated character of Government authority in the matter. The opinion delicately avoided any reaffirmation of constitutional autonomy for the Government in this area.

In the result, the state of the law on the prescription by decree of punishments involving deprivation of liberty is roughly as follows: The country's highest adjudicative body charged explicitly with the interpretation of the Constitution, the Conseil constitutionnel, has declared that such punishments can only be constitutionally prescribed by statute. The prescription of such punishments by decree is, however, not a matter which is subject to review by the Conseil constitutionnel. The Conseil d'Etat, charged both with advising the Government in the drafting of decrees and with the adjudication of claims that decrees adopted by the Government are in excess of its constitutional powers, has taken the position that the prescription of such punishments for "contraventions" is within the power of the Government. The Court of Cassation has declared that it will not inquire into the constitutionality of such decrees because they are shielded by a statutory definition of "contravention" which includes offenses punishable by a brief term of imprisonment. That definition was, of course, considered by the Conseil constitutionnel. There is no possibility of resolving this difficulty by recourse to a higher tribunal having jurisdiction over all three. The Frenchman who, knowing of the decision of the Conseil constitutionnel, goes to jail for violation of a regulation adopted by the Government in the exercise of its autonomous decree power under Article 37 would seem to have the right (nonconstitutional) to be more than a little perplexed.

B. THE TREATY PROBLEM

A different kind of discontinuity in the system is revealed in the handling of treaties under the 1958 Constitution and in the courts. Article 55 of the Constitution accords ratified treaties superiority over statutes. The provisions of Article 54 of the Constitution, tracking those of Article 61, permit reference of treaties to the Conseil constitutionnel by the President of the Republic, the Prime Minister, or the President of either house of Parliament for a determination of their constitutionality. The Conseil ruled on 15 January 1975 that it is not competent under Article 61 to void a statute on the ground that it conflicts with a treaty in force.

In 1968, the Conseil d'Etat sustained a statute in face of a contrary treaty provision.[235] The Conseil did not explain its conclusion that the existence of later, statutory provisions to the contrary prevented the application by the Conseil of a European Community regulation binding France under the Treaty of Rome notwithstanding the language of Article 55 of the Constitution. But the argument of Mme Questiaux, the Commissaire du gouvernement in this case, indicates the probable basis of the Conseil's reasoning:[236]

> [The *Conseil*] may not, we believe, examine the conformity of the Ordinance to the Treaty. To be sure, in accordance with art. 55 of the Constitution every treaty regularly ratified has an authority upon promulgation superior to that of statutes. The Constitution thus affirms the preeminence of the international law over internal law and numerous voices (almost all of the doctrinal writers) have been heard to insist that this provision, which makes of our Constitution one of the most receptive to an international legal order, must not remain a dead letter.
>
> But the administrative judge cannot do that which is asked of him without modifying, by his will alone, his place among our institutions.
>
> He can neither censure nor refuse to apply a statute. This consideration has always led him to refuse to examine grounds of appeal based on the unconstitutionality of a statute . . . and an abundant case law has declared inoperative grounds of appeal based on the assertion that a statute is contrary to the Constitution . . . or that a decision taken for the application of a statute and consistent with the statute violates the Con-

---

[235] Syndicat Général des Fabricants de Semoules de France, [1968] C.E. 149, [1968] A.J.D.A. 235 (Cons. d'Et., 1 Mar. 1968).

[236] [1968] A.J.D.A. 235, at 238.

stitution. And that which is true of the review of statutes in relation to the rules, superior in principle, of the Constitution, is equally true in relation to every text which, like an international treaty, is expressly given a value superior to that of statutes. It has, of course, been argued that the traditional abstention of the judge before the acts of the legislator is less justifiable since the Constitution no longer recognizes the supremacy of Parliament. But the Constitution has dealt precisely with the review of the constitionality of statutes, adopting a limited concept of review and confiding that power to the Conseil constitutionnel; moreover, while modifying the equilibrium between the legislative power and the regulatory power, it has not redefined the powers of the judge; the mission of the latter remains the subordinate one of applying the statute.

The Commissaire du gouvernement, and presumably the Conseil d'Etat itself, thus assimilated the treaty to the Constitution itself for purposes of the review of legislation, and, on familiar grounds, held that the judge, himself a subordinate official holding his powers by statute, may not refuse application of a statute on the basis of Article 55 of the Constitution and the provisions of a treaty in force. That assimilation, which might have formed the basis for review by the Conseil constitutionnel under Article 61, was rejected in the decision of 15 January 1975.

The Court of Cassation, on the other hand, has recently affirmed the position of the lower judicial courts in refusing effect to a statute adopted subsequently to, and inconsistent with, the provisions of a treaty in force.[237] The Court's decision in *Administration des Douanes v. la Société "Cafés Jacques Vabre"* declares:[238]

> . . . [T]he Treaty of 25 March 1957 [the Treaty of Rome] which, in virtue of article 55 of the Constitution, has an authority superior to that of statutes, institutes a particular juridical order integrated with that of the other member States; because of this specificity, the juridical order which it has created is directly applicable to the nationals [*ressortissants*] of these States and binds their Courts; it is therefore proper and within its authority for the Court of Appeal to have de-

---

[237] [1975] D. 497 (Cass. ch. mixte., 24 May 1975) (Concl. Touffait). The earlier decisions of the *tribunaux* and Courts of Appeal are collected in Touffait's *conclusions*, and in his recent article, *Du conflit du traité avec la loi postérieure*, 1 MÉLANGES ANCEL 379, at 385 (1975).

[238] [1975] D. 497, at 506 (1975).

cided that article 95 of the Treaty must be applied in this case
to the exclusion of article 265 of the Customs Code even
though the latter was adopted subsequently.

The Procureur-général was again M. Touffait who invoked the
decision of the Conseil constitutionnel of 15 January 1975 to in-
fer that competence to refuse application of a statute inconsistent
with a treaty must lie with the judicial tribunals since the Conseil
constitutionnel had denied its own competence in such matters.[239]
He further argued that the judges of the Court of Cassation were
not in this way engaging in constitutional review because the
Conseil constitutionnel's decision established that the conformity of
a statute to a treaty was not a constitutional question which could
be raised in proceedings under Article 61.[240] The remarkable aspect
of Touffait's argument is, of course, his major premise that there
must be a sanction somewhere for the constitutional principle established by Article 55. Seven years earlier, Mme Questiaux had
had no difficulty whatever with the contrary proposition before the
Conseil d'Etat. The problem of the incompetence of judges to test
statutes against the Constitution, with which she had been concerned, is met by Touffait with an argument which amounts to this:
A duly ratified treaty occupies a subconstitutional position in the
normative hierarchy permitting the judge to subordinate statute
to treaty without entering the forbidden domain of constitutional
review.[241] It is the treaty itself, and not the Constitution, which
overrides the statute. This, the minor premise of Touffait's argument, rests uneasily alongside his own and the Court's recognition
that it is "in virtue of article 55" that treaties override statutes.[242]

Even if it were conceded that Article 55 merely arranges treaties
and statutes in an hierarchical order whose application by the judge
does not involve the testing of statutes against the Constitution,
there remains the problem of the competence of the courts in dealing with the validity of statutes. It is the inviolability of the statute
and not its hierarchical position which has principally sustained

---

[239] *Id.* at 502.   [240] *Ibid.*   [241] *Id.* at 502.

[242] *Id.* at 502–03, 506. Touffait reinforces this argument with an invitation to the
Court to invoke a monistic conception of the national and international order which
might give extra-constitutional sanction to the superiority of treaties over statutes. *Id.*
at 503. But if the Court's decision reflects the use of that conception for purposes of describing the legal order resulting from the Treaty of Rome, it nonetheless leaves no
doubt that the Court's duty to give effect to that legal order flows from Art. 55.

the refusal to review, especially after the final demise of parliamentary supremacy under the 1958 Constitution. The judicial system is the creature of statute and is bound by statute to give effect without question to acts of Parliament. The courts are incompetent to give effect to any conflicting higher norm whether it be a constitutional rule or a treaty provision. This is surely the thrust of Mme Questiaux's argument from the "place of judges among our institutions."

It is certainly possible to have recourse to that explanation of judicial deference which is based on the notion that the very attribution of powers of review to the Conseil constitutionnel by Article 61 generally precludes the exercise of such powers by the courts. The Conseil's determination that it does not have the power to test statutes against treaties might then be seen as carving out an exception to this application of the maxim *expressio unius* in that field alone. The importance which Touffait accorded the Conseil's 15 January decision in his argument suggests this analysis. But Touffait invoked the decision for a different purpose. He maintained that it established that the conformity of a statute to a treaty was not a constitutional question, implying that the result might be different if it were.

Reconciliation of the refusal to test the constitutionality of statutes with the willingness of the courts to subordinate them to treaties thus depends on the assignment of a unique magic to the words of Article 55, a magic not shared by the rest of the Constitution when confronted before the courts with an inconsistent statute. There is no evident basis for attributing such special qualities to Article 55, no apparent reason for concluding that its command is intended for judicial execution while constitutional provisions like those invoked by *Schiavon* are not. If the Court's position can be explained historically and functionally in terms of a constitutional structure designed to reinforce the executive (which makes treaties) and restrain Parliament,[243] a legal rationale remains to be supplied. In its absence, we may only observe that the decision in *Société "Cafés Jacques Vabre"* has in fact preserved an existing breach in the wall of judicial deference and refused to yield terrain already gained to constitutional review.

---

[243] The bearing of this "decline of *la loi*" on the matter is considered by Touffait, note 237, *supra*, at 391–95.

V. Conclusion

The fragmentary, headless system of constitutional review which has grown willy-nilly out of the Constitution of 1958 reflects in 1975 all of the curious, conflicting tendencies which mark the history of the search for an appropriate sanction for the constitutional limits imposed—or sought to be imposed—on the French legislature. Resistance to judicial review—whether founded on a certain appreciation of the behavior of the royal courts of the *ancien régime,* or more theoretical conceptions of the separation of powers and the notion of the statute as the expression of the general will, or upon a Lambertian view of the evils of "government by judges"—has reinforced early legislative restraints on judicial review and consecrated a tradition of judical deference which continues to dominate the judicial and administrative courts of the Fifth Republic and to inform parliamentary attitudes toward constitutional review. The doctrinal writers have argued for greater judicial assertiveness on the basis of the *Marbury* rationale, and members of Parliament have proposed the deliberate institution of judicial review by way of constitutional reform, but the promulgated statute remains immune to constitutional inquiry (except in face of a conflicting treaty).

The institution in 1958 of yet another nonjudicial mechanism for constitutional review had to be defended against both the argument that it would lead to "government by judges" and the fear that it would not be able effectively to sanction constitutional rules. Tradition forbade the creation of a single Supreme Court fully empowered to refuse enforcement to unconstitutional legislation, and the Gaullist draftsmen of the 1958 instrument were not, in any event, much inclined to saddle themselves with enforceable, substantive constitutional restraints. The Preamble was to have no positive legal force. The instrument of review which they created was to play a very limited role—essentially that of protecting governmental prerogatives against a Parliament whose supremacy over government as well as judges had become settled doctrine in the two previous regimes.

The expansion of the domain of judicial review by the shifting of autonomous lawmaking authority to the Government was promptly confirmed when the Conseil d'Etat held that the exercise by the Government of its autonomous regulatory powers was subject to review testing conformity to the Constitution (including the Preamble) precisely as any exercise of rule-making power under previous regimes might be tested against the authorizing legislation or the "general principles of law." No question of the constitutionality of legislation arose, however, because the Conseil insisted that it could not consider a claim of unconstitutionality or of violation of the "general principles of law" if the exercise by the Government of its rule-making power was within the scope of authorizing legislation. Substantive constitutional review had progressed this far and no farther until 1971.

With its decision of 16 July 1971, the Conseil constitutionnel opened a new phase in the evolution of constitutional review. Like the Conseil d'Etat, the Conseil constitutionnel decided that the Preamble was an enforceable part of the Constitution which fell within the Conseil's jurisdiction under Article 61. Parliament was held subject to substantive constitutional limitations for the first time. The 1971 decision moved the Conseil to a central position in the matter of substantive review. The four years which have elapsed since that decision have largely confirmed the new orientation adopted by the Conseil in 1971. In considering the role and impact of the Conseil constitutionnel, it is important to be clear about what it is and what it is not in the matter of constitutional review. It is a body which may be called upon by designated officials or groups of officials (including, since 1974, any sixty members of Parliament) to determine the constitutionality of newly adopted parliamentary legislation prior to the promulgation of that legislation by the President of the Republic. It is not a body from which any other group or individual may seek relief for any alleged violation of constitutional rights. Nor does it exercise any advisory or appellate role in relation to other tribunals.

Despite these limitations, the Conseil has plainly made the point in the last several years that the Constitution imposes substantive restraints on Parliament which it, the Conseil, is prepared to enforce. That principle is not one which is readily limited: it must be plain to the most obtuse opponent of constitutional review that rules drawn from the Preamble must be the same for both Parliament and Government, and that a statute which has escaped review is no less unconstitutional for having acquired a certain immunity to challenge. There is only one constitution and it has become the supreme law of the land. Acceptance of that principle and of the role of the Conseil constitutionnel as the most authoritative interpreter of the Constitution, imposes severe strains on courts which seek to cling to the tradition of judicial deference, giving effect to statutes and regulations which cannot be constitutional if the decisions of the Conseil constitutionnel are to be definitive. These strains are apparent in the argument of M. Touffait in the *Schiavon* affair before the Court of Cassation. It is a rather special kind of *cri de coeur* by an able and devoted servant of the French legal system.

One response to those strains might be a retrenchment by the Conseil, a movement back toward its pre-1971 role. The generally favorable political reaction to the Conseil's substantive decisions would, however, seem to encourage quite the opposite behavior on its part. The reaction also makes unlikely a second possible response to the inconsistency of the present situation—that of a major reorientation of the system through a constitutional amendment to restrict the powers of the Conseil. Extension, not restriction, is the order of the day, and in the present climate it is easier to imagine the creation of a Supreme Court than the elimination of the function of constitutional review.

A third response, of which the Court of Cassation's recent treaty decision might be the harbinger, is the gradual and cautious abandonment by the judicial and administrative courts of their refusal to examine constitutionality—at least in those cases in which applicable principle has been laid down by the Conseil constitutionnel in an Article 61 decision. A response of this kind would only require a somewhat less restrictive reading of Article 62 of the Constitution which makes the decisions of the Conseil binding upon all judicial and administrative authorities. It is, in my view, not an unthinkable outcome and it would have the substantial advantage of recognizing the hierarchical superiority of the Conseil constitutionnel in the decision of constitutional questions, thus eliminating future conflicts of the kind which arose in connection with the Conseil's November 1973 decision, in all cases in which the Conseil has had a substantive constitutional issue properly before it under Article 61.

As the remarks of the President of the Republic concerning the future development of constitutional review clearly demonstrate, the traditional hostility to judicial review still claims its tribute, and it would be excessive to suggest that the creation of a Supreme

Court along American lines or the generalization of constitutional review in the judicial and administrative courts is likely in any predictable future. Indeed the French may well wish to avoid the development of a system of constitutional review which promises the constitutionalization and litigation of political, social, and economic issues of every size and stripe. The present system is not badly adapted to satisfy such a wish, but it is difficult to imagine the preservation of the *status quo* in face of repeated conflicts on constitutional questions between the Conseil constitutionnel and the Conseil d'Etat and the repeated application by the judicial tribunals of statutes and regulations whose constitutionality has been directly or indirectly denied by the Conseil constitutionnel.

However these problems are resolved, it seems safe to say that substantive constitutional review, debated and resisted in France for nearly two centuries, has come to stay, an assertion that could not confidently be made before the Conseil constitutionnel handed down its landmark decision of 16 July 1971.

MARK TUSHNET

THE NEWER PROPERTY:

SUGGESTION FOR THE REVIVAL

OF SUBSTANTIVE DUE PROCESS

The Supreme Court's judgments in recent years have not been marked by major doctrinal innovation. One such attempt, the resuscitation of a prohibition on irrebuttable presumptions, was so patently defective[1] that it seems to have had a lifetime of only one year.[2] Another innovation, however, seems to have settled into the Burger Court's standard approach to the analysis of claims that statutory procedures for the termination of property interests fail to satisfy the requirements imposed by the Due Process Clauses. Until *Board of Regents v. Roth*,[3] the analysis of such claims was

Mark Tushnet is Associate Professor of Law, University of Wisconsin at Madison.

AUTHOR'S NOTE: Gordon Baldwin, Fredricka Paff, and William Whitford made helpful comments on an earlier version of this paper. The research assistance of Lawrence Hansen was especially valuable.

[1] See Cleveland Bd. of Education v. LaFleur, 414 U.S. 632, 651–52 (1974) (Powell, J., concurring in the result); Note, 87 HARV. L. REV. 1534 (1974).

[2] I date its revival from Vlandis v. Kline, 412 U.S. 441 (1973), and its demise in Cleveland Bd. of Education v. LaFleur, 414 U.S. 632 (1974), although one can perceive some postmortem spasms in the Chief Justice's opinion for the Court in Jimenez v. Weinberger, 417 U.S. 628, 636–37 (1974); see *id.*, at 639 (Rehnquist, J., dissenting). Other commentators include Bell v. Burson, 402 U.S. 535 (1971), and Stanley v. Illinois, 405 U.S. 645 (1972), in the doctrine's new lifetime, see, *e.g.*, Note, note 1 *supra*, but I think that such an interpretation misreads those cases. See Tushnet, ". . . *And Only Wealth Will Buy You Justice"—Some Notes on the Supreme Court. 1972 Term*, 1974 WISC. L. REV. 177, 194–96.

[3] 408 U.S. 564 (1972).

unitary, in the sense that the Court addressed only the question of the fitness of the procedure for determining disputed issues of fact and law.[4] *Roth*, without citation of authority,[5] introduced a two-stage analysis. First, the Court must identify whether a property interest has been created by state law.[6] Second, it must assess the suitability of the procedures adopted to terminate that interest. The Court has adhered to this form of analysis, and commentators have accepted it as obvious and noncontroversial.[7]

I argue here that the two-stage analysis is wrong and unproductive. The inconsistencies in the positions adopted by various Justices in different cases are an indicator of these flaws.[8] Mr. Justice Stewart wrote the opinion for the Court in *Roth* and joined Mr. Justice Rehnquist's plurality opinion in *Arnett v. Kennedy*,[9] which argued that the procedural protections provided by statute defined the property interest protected by the Due Process Clause. But he vigorously dissented in *Mitchell v. W. T. Grant Co.*,[10] where the majority refused to accord procedural protections more stringent than those imposed by state law. Mr. Justice Powell rejected Mr. Justice Rehnquist's approach in *Arnett*.[11] But his own stand in *Goss v. Lopez*[12] was not different in substance from the Rehnquist line in *Arnett*:[13]

---

[4] See, *e.g.*, Goldberg v. Kelly, 397 U.S. 254 (1970); O'Neil, *Of Justice Delayed and Justice Denied: The Welfare Prior Hearing Cases*, 1970 SUPREME COURT REVIEW 161.

[5] 408 U.S. at 577–78.

[6] More accurately, by some source of law outside the federal Constitution. The source may be state law, statutory or judge-made, or federal statutory law. *Cf.* Perry v. Sindermann, 408 U.S. 593 (1972); Arnett v. Kennedy, 416 U.S. 134 (1974).

[7] See, *e.g.*, Note, 54 B.U.L. REV. 186 (1974); Note, 86 HARV. L. REV. 880 (1973); Griffis & Wilson, *Constitutional Rights and Remedies in the Non-renewal of a Public School Teacher's Employment Contract*, 25 BAYLOR L. REV. 549 (1973); Shulman, *Employment of Nontenured Faculty*, 51 DEN. L.J. 215 (1974). A few commentators have noted the extent to which the two-stage analysis undermines constitutional protections. *E.g.*, Note, 5 CONN. L. REV. 685, 695 (1973); Smith & Gebala, *Job Security for Public Employees*, 31 WASH. & LEE L. REV. 545, 559 (1974); Gellhorn & Hornby, *Constitutional Limitations on Admissions Procedures and Standards*, 60 VA L. REV. 975, 982–83 (1974). Only Note, 1974 DUKE L.J. 89, however, discusses at length the problems addressed in this article. Comment, 59 MINN. L. REV. 421 (1975), touches on some of the issues.

[8] I think it significant that Mr. Justice Stewart wrote *Vlandis v. Kline* and *Board of Regents v. Roth*, the two sources of doctrinal innovation and confusion.

[9] 416 U.S. 134 (1974).

[10] 416 U.S. 600 (1974).   [11] 416 U.S. at 166–67.

[12] 419 U.S. 565, 584 (1975) (Powell, J., dissenting).

[13] See also North Georgia Finishing, Inc. v. Di-Chem., Inc., 419 U.S. 601 (1975).

. . . the very legislation which "defines" the "dimension" of the student's entitlement, while providing a right to education generally, does not establish this right free of discipline in accordance with [state] law. Rather, the right is encompassed in the entire package of statutory provisions governing education in Ohio.

Even Mr. Justice White, who at least seems to have a settled position,[14] wrote in *Mitchell* that "the definition of property rights is a matter of state law,"[15] a proposition that can logically lead only to agreement with Mr. Justice Rehnquist, although Mr. Justice White in *Arnett* explicitly rejected such agreement.[16] Justices who adhere to the two-stage analysis and wind themselves into such inconsistencies with such ease, thereby fairly raise questions about the validity of the analysis.[17]

I. Mitchell v. W. T. Grant: The Prevailing Approach

Mitchell v. W. T. Grant upheld the constitutionality of Louisiana's summary repossession procedure, called sequestration, in consumer credit cases. Mitchell had purchased various major appliances from W. T. Grant, a national retailer with a record of consumer abuse[18] and corporate mismanagement.[19] Grant instituted a sequestration proceeding by alleging that Mitchell's payments to reduce an unpaid balance of $574 were overdue. In Louisiana, sequestration is a device by which a creditor with a lien on specific property may summarily recover possession of the property. The only issues when a debtor seeks to dissolve a sequestration are

---

[14] 416 U.S. at 607.   [15] *Id*. at 604.

[16] 416 U.S. at 177–78. Mr. Justice White's analysis relies on an unconcealed "substance–procedure" distinction but, even aside from the difficulties in determining what is substance and what is procedure, his analysis is framed in a way that makes the sheer arbitrariness of the distinction apparent. See text *infra*, at notes 49 and 50.

[17] Other evidence of the contortions that the two-stage analysis seems to encourage can be found in Judge Hufstedler's strained opinion in Geneva Towers Tenants Org. v. Federated Mortgage Investors, 504 F.2d 483, 493–98 (9th Cir. 1974), and in Note, 88 Harv. L. Rev. 41, 86 n.26 (1974) (distinguishing between liberty and "traditional" property, where unitary analysis is appropriate, and "new" property, where two-stage analysis is required).

[18] See, *e.g.*, the scheme described in Welmaker v. W.T. Grant Co., 365 F. Supp. 531 (N.D. Ga. 1972); N.Y. Times, 8 Dec. 1972, p. 65, col. 1; F.T.C. News Summary, 21 Feb. 1975, p. 2 (reporting consent judgment of $150,000 for violations of Truth in Lending Act).

[19] See, *e.g.*, Business Week, 19 Oct. 1974, at 46; 24 Feb. 1975, at 74–76.

the existence of the lien, the debtor's default, and the debtor's possession of the property. Defenses such as fraud or misrepresentation can be raised only in a subsequent trial on the merits, and although the motion to dissolve may be heard quickly, the trial on the merits is not advanced by such a motion.[20] Mitchell moved to dissolve the sequestration. He did not contest the fact that he had defaulted. But he contended that the procedures that led to the seizure of the appliances violated the Due Process Clause of the Fourteenth Amendment. His claims were rejected by the state courts, and the Supreme Court affirmed.

Mr. Justice White's opinion for the Court considered the crucial question to be whether the Louisiana procedures struck a constitutionally acceptable balance between the debtor's interest in retaining possession of the goods when he had not in fact defaulted in his payments and the creditor's interest in having some property out of which a judgment could be satisfied in the event that his dispute with his debtor were resolved in his favor. I would approach this question differently by considering what the primary objections to summary sequestration or repossession might be.

The objections fall into two categories.[21] First, we are told that summary procedures seriously affect low-income consumers, who are unfamiliar with legal processes generally and so do not attempt to vindicate their rights after repossession. In addition, low-income consumers are often victimized by deceptive sales practices, such as misrepresentation or breach of warranty. Thus, the story goes, many debtors actually have valid defenses to creditors' claims that the debtors have unjustifiably defaulted in their payments.[22] Sum-

---

[20] See Johnson, *Attachment and Sequestration: Provisional Remedies under the Louisiana Code of Civil Procedure*, 38 TUL. L. REV. 1, 26 (1963).

[21] By focusing on purely procedural questions here, I do not intend to minimize other objections, such as that summary procedures authorize unreasonable intrusions on privacy, a Fourth Amendment concern, or that they make it harder for the debtor to challenge the creditor's claim on the merits, what I consider an Equal Protection Clause concern. Neither of these objections was faced in *Mitchell*, and I postpone their treatment to Section III, *infra*.

[22] This is the story told by two attorneys for the plaintiff in Fuentes v. Shevin, 407 U.S. 67 (1972). See Abbott & Peters, *Fuentes v. Shevin: A Narrative of Federal Test Litigation in the Legal Services Program*, 57 IOWA L. REV. 955, 957–58 (1972). The story, while exaggerated, is generally supported by CAPLOVITZ, CONSUMERS IN TROUBLE: A STUDY OF DEBTORS IN DEFAULT (1974) (hereinafter cited as CAPLOVITZ), a study based on a survey of purchasers in New York, Philadelphia, Chicago, and Detroit against whom creditors had instituted legal action claiming default in installment payments. *Id*. at 37–41. Caplovitz found that in 19 percent of the cases, the debtors may have had defenses prem-

mary procedures, however, make it impossible for the debtor to assert his defenses before his use of the goods he has purchased is terminated, a situation that seems grossly unfair. The answer to this in *Mitchell* is easy. The apparent unfairness is created, not by the fact that the creditor can proceed *ex parte*, but by the fact that the issues in sequestration proceedings are sharply limited. Even if the sequestration hearing were adversary rather than *ex parte*, the debtor could not assert defenses. Mr. Justice White, resting on highly questionable precedents,[23] said in *Mitchell* that "issues can be limited in actions for possession."[24] Once that is accepted, the objection based on the unfairness of an *ex parte* procedure that forecloses defenses dissolves.[25]

The second category of objections is based on common experience. We all have run into stubborn computers that insist on billing us for goods or services that we never purchased or have already paid for. It seems unfair to allow the creditor to take possession of goods as a result of his own errors. Thus, we would like some guarantee, prior to repossession, that no mistakes have been made. In *Mitchell*, Mr. Justice White relied on a statutory requirement that the creditor provide rather detailed information about how the debt and default arose,[26] and on the creditor's self-interest.[27] Because actions for repossession are generally instituted

---

ised on sellor wrongdoing. *Id.* at 91–123. See also Note, 10 COLUM. J. LAW & Soc. PROB. 370, 375–76 (1974) (11 percent of consumers reported receiving nonconforming or defective goods). For an example in the cases, see Guzman v. Western State Bank, 516 F.2d 125 (8th Cir. 1975).

[23] He relied on Grant Timber & Mfg. Co. v. Gray, 236 U.S. 133 (1915), involving a possessory action for real property, one of Justice Holmes's cryptic two-page opinions which did, however, stress the historic uniqueness of procedures in possessory actions for land. What is more, the defendant in *Grant Timber* was the party in possession, and the Court held that the state "may protect an established possession against disturbance by anything except process of law." *Id.* at 135. Bianchi v. Morales, 262 U.S. 170 (1923), also cited by Mr. Justice White, was only one page long and treated the issue as the same as that in *Grant Timber*. Lindsay v. Normet, 405 U.S. 56 (1972), Mr. Justice White's only other authority, is another real property case and relied solely on *Grant Timber* and *Bianchi*.

[24] 416 U.S. at 607.

[25] *Di-Chem*, unlike *Mitchell*, does not emphasize the scope of the issues available when challenging a garnishment. *Cf.* 419 U.S. at 608. Although in a strict sense this does not undercut my analysis, since the Court held the procedure in *Di-Chem* unconstitutional even without considering the scope of the issues, it does suggest that the relevant portions of *Mitchell* were perhaps disingenuous, even though the Court's emphasis in *Mitchell* on the fact that the issues were susceptible of documentary proof is hard to understand independent of the limitation of issues.

[26] 416 U.S. at 617–18.   [27] *Id.* at 610.

after a series of dunning letters have been sent,[28] creditors will rarely misidentify their debtors entirely. To Mr. Justice White, the number of errors to be expected under certain procedures is relevant to a determination of constitutionality,[29] and self-interest and particularization would indeed seem to be adequate to control errors of identity.

They are inadequate, however, with respect to errors about payments. One study disclosed that debtors attributed their plight to misunderstandings about payments, including bookkeeping mistakes by the creditor, in over 8 percent of all suits by creditors.[30] I am not sure of the significance of that figure. (In *Arnett v. Kennedy*, Mr. Justice White characterized a much higher reversal rate as "a fair degree of frequency,"[31] and in *Fusari v. Steinberg*, Mr. Justice Powell's opinion for the Court characterized a rate of 19.4 percent as significant.[32]) But I am sure that specificity in the pleadings and the creditor's self-interest do not help to reduce the number of cases in which bookkeeping errors lead to repossession. No matter how specific the pleadings must be, in an *ex parte* proceeding the creditor can do no more than transfer the information on his books into the pleadings. Self-interest might be a more substantial constraint, if we were dealing with the whole range of consumer transactions. Retailers sometimes count on further business from initial purchasers or referrals by satisfied customers. And such retailers might well be cautious in "interrupting the transaction," as Mr. Justice White put it,[33] not so much because this transaction is so substantial but rather because future sales attributable to each purchaser loom large in his calculations. Unfortunately, debtors who get into credit trouble often are not representative of all consumers. For one thing, they are poorer,[34] and thus may be unable to take their business to other retailers. It may be that only companies like W. T. Grant would be willing to extend credit to them.

---

[28] See CAPLOVITZ, at 180; Note, note 22 *supra*, at 377–79.

[29] See Arnett v. Kennedy, 416 U.S. at 191, 194, 201 (White, J., concurring and dissenting). See also Wolff v. McDonnell, 418 U.S. 539, 567 (1974); Fusari v. Steinberg, 420 U.S. 955, 960–61 (1975); Goss v. Lopez, 419 U.S. 565, 580 (1975).

[30] CAPLOVITZ, at 125–26. I must emphasize that, at this point in the study, Caplovitz was concerned with all suits, not simply repossessions.

[31] 416 U.S. at 190–91, citing Handler, *Justice for the Welfare Recipient: Fair Hearings in AFDC—The Wisconsin Experience*, 43 SOC. SERV. REV. 12, 22 (1969).

[32] 420 U.S. at 960.   [34] CAPLOVITZ, at 14–15.

[33] 416 U.S. at 610.

To the extent that poor people have limited access to transportation, they may also have few alternatives but the friendly neighborhood consumer defrauder. Both of these factors suggest that the retailers run little risk of prejudicing future sales by being careless about their bookkeeping.[35] But the most dramatic evidence is that nearly one-third of all purchases leading to default and litigation are made from direct sellers—those who rely on door-to-door salesmen, not stores at fixed locations—whereas only 3 percent of all retail purchases are made in this way.[36] And many direct sellers, totally apart from their reputation for shoddy practices,[37] clearly do not rely on repeat business or word-of-mouth referrals.

The analysis in *Mitchell* balanced competing interests and, to my vision, struck the wrong balance. But my concern here is with method and not results.

II. SOME DIFFICULTIES WITH THE TWO-STAGE ANALYSIS

Initially, identifying the first stage of the two-stage analysis seems something that the very words of the Due Process Clause require. One wants to say, "Of course we must first decide whether a property interest is involved, and state law defines property rights." More specifically, state law confers on individuals the right to do something—use tangible goods, hold a public job, or whatever—provided that they satisfy certain conditions. If these conditions are not satisfied, the state may terminate the right. But the Due Process Clause defines the limitations on the process by which the state determines whether its conditions have been satisfied. The federal Constitution has nothing to say about either the type of right conferred—a state is free to prohibit conditional sales or to have no tenure for civil servants—or the conditions that must be satisfied.[38]

---

[35] One small bit of evidence that supports this interpretation is reported in 2 CAPLO-VITZ, DEBTORS IN DEFAULT: THE EVENTS FOLLOWING UPON THE DEFAULT 10–10 (1971) (an earlier version of CAPLOVITZ) (original creditors, such as retailers who hold their own paper, harass debtors as much as holders-in-due-course; concern for preserving goodwill seems to have little effect).

[36] CAPLOVITZ at 33.

[37] See, *e.g.*, Note, 78 YALE L.J. 618, 628 n.39 (1969); Sher, *The "Cooling-Off" Period in Door-to-Door Sales*, 15 U.C.L.A. L. REV. 717, 721–25 (1968).

[38] Except, of course, that the conditions may not violate specific limitations, apart from the Due Process Clause, of the Constitution.

Cases like *Goldberg v. Kelly*[39] certainly can be fit into this framework. *Roth*'s failure to cite authority for the proposition that property rights are defined by state law may reflect only that the proposition is self-evident.[40] The lack of authority may signal, instead, that a radical doctrinal innovation was occurring. I think that the better interpretation.

It is useful here to consider two other constitutional provisions that might be said to protect state-created rights. The first is the taking clause of the Fifth Amendment, as applied to the states through the Fourteenth Amendment.[41] In *Pennsylvania Coal Co. v. Mahon*,[42] the state had prohibited the coal company from mining in a manner that caused houses to subside. The company claimed that this was a taking of its property right to mine as it chose, for which compensation was required, but the state courts rejected this claim. One may interpret that decision as saying, in effect, that the State of Pennsylvania simply did not recognize the alleged property right.[43] If property rights really are defined by state law, that should end the constitutional dispute. The United States Supreme Court, however, reversed, and established that, notwithstanding a state's definition of property rights, the federal Constitution imposed its own definition. A similar analysis can be made of every taking case. If the two-stage analysis is correct, taking cases would present no problems. But they do.[44]

Another relevant constitutional provision is the Contracts Clause. In *Indiana ex rel. Anderson v. Brand*,[45] the Court addressed a problem similar to the one just discussed. Indiana had a teacher

---

[39] 397 U.S. 254 (1970).

[40] The two-stage analysis might be viewed as a resuscitation of the old dichotomy between rights and privileges. If so, Mr. Justice Stewart is in an awkward position, for in *Roth* he explicitly rejected the dichotomy as a viable tool of constitutional analysis. 408 U.S. at 571.

[41] Conceptually, the problem is the same with respect to taking by the federal government. See, *e.g.*, United States v. Causby, 328 U.S. 256 (1946); United States v. Willow River Power Co., 324 U.S. 499 (1945). One might, however, squeeze such cases into the two-stage analysis by interpreting the question they present as one of federal common law definition of property, not one of federal constitutional law. See United States v. Causby, 328 U.S. at 266. This possibility blurs the analysis, so I focus on state taking.

[42] 260 U.S. 393 (1922).

[43] See, *e.g.*, Demorest v. City Bank Farmers Trust Co., 321 U.S. 36 (1944).

[44] See, *e.g.*, Sax, *Takings, Private Property and Public Rights*, 81 YALE L.J. 149 (1971).

[45] 303 U.S. 95 (1938).

tenure act, the provisions of which were incorporated in contracts with each teacher. Anderson had achieved tenure according to the act. The legislature then repealed the tenure act, and Anderson was threatened with discharge, which could not have occurred if the tenure act remained in effect. Anderson claimed that her discharge would violate the Contracts Clause. The state courts characterized her rights as statutory, not contractual, and therefore rejected the claim. The Supreme Court reversed, saying that the existence of a contractual right was not exclusively a question of state law. This can only mean that the Contracts Clause, of its own force, imposes some limits on a state's definition of what constitutes a contract. Here, too, property rights are not fully defined by state law.[46]

Three points should be made about these cases. First, both constitutional provisions provide wide scope for permissible state regulation through the exercise of the police power. Our sense that state law defines property rights may derive from the very breadth of the police power. In most cases, the state law definition of property rights is justified as an exercise of the police power.[47] That is, in most cases, approaching the problem through state law would lead to the same result that approaching it through a federal constitutional definition of property or contract rights would. The federal constitutional definition gives states great latitude but, as *Mahon* and *Anderson* show, it does impose some limitations.[48]

Second, there are hints in *Mahon* and especially in *Anderson* that the problems arose because of loose language in the legislation and in judicial opinions. For example, the Court in *Anderson* empha-

---

[46] See also D'Oench, Duhme & Co., v. F.D.I.C., 315 U.S. 447, 470 (1942) (Jackson, J., concurring).

[47] Two cases decided just before *Anderson* are reconcilable with it on this ground. Both Phelps v. Board of Education, 300 U.S. 319 (1937), and Dodge v. Board of Education, 302 U.S. 74 (1937), involved limitations on teacher tenure justified as attempts to deal with the effects of the Depression. See also text *infra*, at note 99. These cases are discussed in Hale, *The Supreme Court and the Commerce Clause*, 57 Harv. L. Rev. 621, 666–70, 852, 861 (1944).

[48] Hart & Wechsler, The Federal Courts and the Federal System 501–02 (2d ed. 1973) treats *Anderson* and related cases primarily as posing questions about the standard of review to be applied when the Supreme Court reviews a state court decision that some right is or is not contractual. Perhaps the language in these cases that supports such an approach should be treated as an artifact of their procedural posture. *Cf.* Mishkin, *The Federal "Question" in the District Courts*, 53 Colum. L. Rev. 157, 170 (1953). Cases arising in the federal district courts under 42 U.S.C. § 1983 certainly highlight the possibility of an alternative analysis.

sized that the tenure act "was couched in terms of contract" and that such terms also appeared in prior interpretations of the act by the Indiana Supreme Court.[49] To make this determinative, though, would transform the Contracts Clause from a limitation on the substance of legislation into a device for sharpening draftsmanship and a trap for the unwary. Sometimes constitutional provisions can usefully be interpreted as contraints on draftsmen,[50] but I doubt that the Justices who wrote *Fletcher v. Peck*[51] and *Dartmouth College v. Woodward*[52] thought that that was what they were doing.[53] Finally, the Court in *Anderson* said that it must determine whether a contract right existed, applying federal standards, "in order that the constitutional mandate may not become a dead letter."[54]

The effect of the two-stage analysis, though, is precisely to deprive the Due Process Clause of the protective features that the Court had insisted upon in the *Mahon* and *Anderson* cases, as Mr. Justice Rehnquist's opinion in *Arnett v. Kennedy* makes this abundantly clear. Kennedy was a non-probationary employee in the Civil Service. He was discharged after a supervisor upheld charges that he had falsely stated that the supervisor attempted to bribe a third person. Under the Lloyd-La Follette Act, Kennedy was entitled to receive advance notice of the proposed discharge, the material on which the action would be based, and an opportunity to appear before the supervisor in order to answer the charges. After discharge, Kennedy was entitled to a full trial-type hearing. A three-judge district court held that the procedures utilized in the *Kennedy* case failed to comply with the Due Process Clause.

Mr. Justice Rehnquist's opinion, after sketching the history of the Civil Service, noted that the very sentence that limited the grounds for discharge to "such cause as will promote the efficiency of [the] service" also specified the procedures by which the deter-

[49] 303 U.S. at 105–07; see also 260 U.S. at 413.

[50] See, *e.g.*, Morey v. Doud, 354 U.S. 457 (1957).

[51] 6 Cranch 87 (1810).   [52] 4 Wheat. 518 (1819).

[53] On the relevance of prior state court characterizations, see Kauper, *What Is a "Contract" under the Contracts Clause of the Federal Constitution?*, 31 MICH. L. REV. 187, 191–92 (1932); Hale, note 47 *supra*, at 852–61. As these articles indicate, the problems arising under the Contracts Clause are vastly more difficult than I have made them out to be here. My presentation is premised, not on a belief that my view solves the problems, but on a belief that it yields some productive attitudes toward their solutions.

[54] 303 U.S. at 100.

mination of cause was to be made. Drawing on *Roth*, Mr. Justice Rehnquist argued that Kennedy's expectancy of continued employment was limited by the procedural provision of the statute that created the expectancy.[55] This approach, as the concurring and dissenting Justices agreed, deprives the Court of all leverage on the due process problem.[56] If the property right is defined by the procedures, then whatever procedures the legislature provides must be constitutionally adequate, so long as state law alone defined the property right.

There is something disquieting about an approach that leads to such a conclusion. Even Mr. Justice Rehnquist hinted at some limitations. He said that the Lloyd-La Follette Act could not be "parsed as discretely" as Kennedy desired, and that it represented a legislative compromise, granting new rights at the same time that it limited those rights in particular procedural ways.[57] Surely, though, he could not have found it significant that Kennedy was attacking the original legislation, for that would preclude Congress from amending the statute to provide greater procedural protections albeit short of full trial-type hearings. Yet once the anchor to the original legislation is cast aside, the suggestion that the act must be viewed as a unitary legislative compromise loses its value as a limitation on the analysis, for every amendment might similarly be viewed as a new but still unitary compromise.[58]

For all that he objected to Mr. Justice Rehnquist's analysis in *Arnett*, Mr. Justice White fell into the same trap in *Mitchell*, because the problem derives, I submit, from the belief that nonconstitutional law defines property rights. The opinion in *Mitchell* conceals that problem somewhat, but Mr. Justice White's characterization of the purchaser's right provides a starting point. Mr. Justice White said that "Mitchell's right to possession and his title were subject to defeasance in the event of default."[59] Why not say, in addition, that they were also subject to defeasance in the event that W. T. Grant complied with the state sequestration law? That

---

[55] 416 U.S. at 151–52. Cf. Goss v. Lopez, 419 U.S. at 587 (Powell, J., dissenting).

[56] 416 U.S. at 166–68 (Powell, J., concurring in the result); 177–78 (White, J., dissenting); 211 (Marshall, J., dissenting).

[57] *Id*. at 152, 154.

[58] See also Comment, 59 MINN. L. REV. 421, 427–28 (1975) (suggesting that intensity of legislative focus on procedures is determinative).

[59] 416 U.S. at 604.

is, state law established a vendor's lien that "encumbered" Mitchell's title, and another encumbrance was the state law establishing the possibility of sequestration. Nothing in Mr. Justice White's opinion suggests why the description of Mitchell's interest stops short of incorporating the state's sequestration procedure. Perhaps it must be so in order to avoid rendering the Due Process Clause meaningless, but the very arbitrariness of the limitation suggests that there is something wrong with saying that state law defines property rights.[60]

Another signal of difficulty is the sharp distinction drawn by Mr. Justice White between liberty cases and property cases. He explicitly stated in *Arnett* that his "views as to the requirements of due process where property interests are at stake does [*sic*] not deal with the entirely separate matter and requirements of due process when a person is deprived of liberty."[61] This disclaimer would be unnecessary if all that Mr. Justice White meant was that the balance between state and individual interests might be struck differently in a liberty case. That is implicit in his quotation from *Cafeteria & Restaurant Workers Local 473 v. McElroy*:[62] "[C]onsideration of what procedures due process may require under any given set of circumstances must begin with a determination of the precise nature of the government function involved as well as of the private interest that has been affected by governmental action." Thus, the distinction between liberty cases and property cases must mean that the methodology of the latter is inappropriate for the former.[63] And, indeed, in liberty cases the Court has

---

[60] Mr. Justice White in *Mitchell*, like Mr. Justice Rehnquist in *Arnett*, hinted at limitations on his analysis. Like Mr. Justice Rehnquist's, Mr. Justice White's limitations disappear when closely examined. Mr. Justice White emphasized the seller's joint interest in particular items of property. Arguably, sequestration differs from garnishment, because in garnishment all the debtor's property is subject to taking. See, *e.g.*, North Georgia Finishing Co. v. Di-Chem, Inc., 95 S. Ct. 719 (1975). Unfortunately, it is easy enough to formulate a creditor's interest in any nonexempt property of his debtor— the creditor has a contingent interest in that property because the property is subject to seizure pursuant to a garnishment order. Thus, the proposition that sequestration is special because it involves property in which the creditor and debtor have joint rights cannot serve as a limitation on Mr. Justice White's analysis.

[61] 416 U.S. at 178 n.6.

[62] 367 U.S. 886, 895 (1961), cited at 416 U.S. at 188 (opinion of White, J.), 168 (opinion of Powell, J.).

[63] In Wolff v. McDonnell, 418 U.S. 539 (1974), Mr. Justice White, writing for the Court, stated that the "analysis as to liberty parallels the accepted due process analysis as to property," citing, among other cases, *Roth* and *Arnett*. *Id*. at 557–58. This summarized the argument that, because a statutorily guaranteed right to good-time credit

not looked to state law to define the "grievous loss"[64] that triggers the due process inquiry. Here the best available example is *Goss v. Lopez*. The majority first set out the two-stage model and cited the relevant property cases, including *Arnett*. It then turned to the liberty interest in reputation. In contrast to the earlier discussion, which was dotted with citations to the Ohio statutes, the majority at this point cited no Ohio statutes or cases conferring a legal interest in one's good name.[65] Although the point is not made as explicitly as one would like, the implication certainly seems to be that, whereas property rights are created by state law, liberty interests have an independent federal source.

These difficulties with the two-stage analysis do not show that it is logically incoherent. One could consistently apply the two-stage analysis with no difficulty. The Justices who espouse it, however, seem unwilling to follow through on its implications, and that suggests that they are utilizing an inadequate tool for proper constitutional analysis.

III. ALTERNATIVES: OTHER CONSTITUTIONAL PROVISIONS AND SUBSTANTIVE DUE PROCESS

When a majority of the Supreme Court employs competing, unsatisfactory methods of due process analysis, it becomes appropriate to search for other methods. I think that the most fruitful involves recognizing that substantive constitutional guarantees derive from the Due Process Clause as well as other provisions of the Constitution. Failure to provide certain procedural protections would then be seen as impairing those rights. The other constitutional requirements may be traditional ones like those of the Fourth Amendment, or they may be novel ones that should be treated as substantive due process cases.

---

was eliminated when prisoners were disciplined, a protected liberty is taken. As Mr. Justice Marshall noted, however, the Court stated that the same analysis was proper when "a major change in the conditions of confinement [transfer to solitary confinement] is at issue." *Id.*, at 581 n.1 (Marshall, J., dissenting in part), citing *id.*, at 571–72 n.19. While in Nebraska there was arguably a statutory right to confinement in the general prison population, the Court's footnote emphasized only that a "major change in the conditions" was there involved, and suggested that the case of deprivation of statutorily guaranteed privileges might be different. See also Milleman, *The Prisoner's Right to Stay Where He Is*, 3 CAP. U.L.REV. 223 (1974).

[64] Morrissey v. Brewer, 408 U.S. 471, 481 (1972), citing Goldberg v. Kelly, 397 U.S. 254, 263 (1970).

[65] 419 U.S. at 572–76.

Repossession procedures generally authorize state officials to enter a debtor's house and seize the goods in the debtor's possession. Ordinarily, the Fourth Amendment limits state officials in their attempts to enter and seize property. Not surprisingly, then, the debtors in *Fuentes v. Shevin* attacked the Florida replevin statutes as violations of the Fourth Amendment.[66] As the Court noted, however, its disposition of the due process claim made it unnecessary to address the Fourth Amendment claim.[67] Suppose that the Court had taken the other path; what would the Fourth Amendment require in these circumstances?

Clearly, to satisfy the Fourth Amendment, the state could authorize an entry and seizure only upon issuance of process by a neutral and detached magistrate who had been provided with adequate information upon which he could make an independent determination that probable cause existed. And, in fact, that is just what the Court has demanded. In *Mitchell*, for example, the Court relied on the fact that the writ of sequestration could be issued only by a judge, and carefully refrained from indicating how the case would have been resolved had it arisen elsewhere in Louisiana, where the clerks of the court could issue the writ.[68] Similarly, the Court there stressed the judge's duty under Louisiana law to make an independent determination of the existence of the debt and default.[69] The Court's insistence that detailed information be provided to the judge also supports the interpretation of *Mitchell* as a Fourth Amendment case.[70]

The Court in *Fuentes* relied on, and in *Mitchell* distinguished,

---

[66] 407 U.S. 67, 71 n.2.

[67] *Id*. at 96 n.32.

[68] 416 U.S. at 606 n.5. The emphasis on judicial oversight recurred in North Georgia Finishing Co. v. Di-Chem, Inc., 419 U.S. at 607, a garnishment case with muted Fourth Amendment overtones, although the Court relied heavily on *Fuentes* and *Mitchell*. But see *id*. at 611 n.3 (Powell, J., concurring in the judgment); Shadwick v. City of Tampa, 407 U.S. 345 (1972).

[69] 416 U.S. at 620 n.14. This interpretation of Louisiana law was disputed by the dissenters, *id*. at 632–33 n.4, but even if the Court misconstrued the requirements of state law, its misconception was important in how it viewed the case. *Cf*. Guzman v. Western State Bank, 516 F.2d 125, 130–31 (8th Cir. 1975).

[70] 416 U.S. at 616. See also North Georgia Finishing Co. v. Di-Chem, Inc., 419 U.S.-at 607, and note 58 *supra*.

In Gerstein v. Pugh, 420 U.S. 103 (1975), the Court held that the Fourth Amendment permitted the use of *ex parte* procedures to determine probable cause to continue the detention of a defendant proceeded against by information. The analysis in *Gerstein* could be taken over quite directly into the replevin and sequestration cases.

Sniadach v. Family Finance Corp.,[71] a garnishment case that can, with a little effort, be interpreted as a case relying on something more than simple procedural due process. Garnishment ties up the debtor's wages or, as in *North Georgia Finishing Co.*, the equivalent liquid assets of a corporation. As the Court in *Sniadach* noted, this places enormous pressure on the debtor to settle the dispute quickly and presumably on less favorable terms than he would without such pressure.[72]

I believe that these considerations call into play what I call the "equal footing" principle, which, although nowhere clearly stated, seems to lie at the base of many arguments made about procedural devices. The "equal footing" principle is that, although procedural rules should be structured to compel out-of-court settlements of disputes, they should not be structured so as to make a settlement in favor of one party or the other more likely. The rules should treat the parties as having equal footing in settlement negotiations, which should proceed, as far as the rules can influence the matter, on the basis of the merits of the parties' claims, although of course the parties' assets and interests may affect how they approach settlement negotiations. One example of the "equal footing" principle in action is the objection to the federal class action rules as constituting "legalized blackmail," an objection that means, as I understand it, that the rules place pressure on corporations to buy off meritless claims simply to avoid expensive litigation.[73] Of course, one example does not establish the vitality of the principle in general, nor its details, but it is enough to suggest that we could analyze some procedural due process cases, particularly *Sniadach*, in terms different from the standard ones.

---

[71] 395 U.S. 337 (1969).   [72] *Id.* at 341–42.

[73] See, *e.g.*, Handler, *The Shift from Substantive to Procedural Innovations in Antitrust Suits*, 71 COLUM. L. REV. 1, 9 (1971), cited with approval in Eisen v. Carlisle & Jacquelin, 479 F.2d 1005, 1019 (2d Cir., 1973), aff'd, 417 U.S. 156 (1974). See also American Timber & Trading Co. v. First National Bank, 511 F.2d 980, 985 (9th Cir. 1973) (Chambers, J., concurring); Kline v. Coldwell, Banker & Co., 508 F.2d 226, 234–35, 237–38 (9th Cir., 1974). This interpretation is supported by the emphasis in this literature on the fact that the plaintiffs do not face large attorneys' fees if they lose, the assumption being that the attorneys are working on a contingent fee basis. If the actual mechanism of the violation of the "equal footing" principle were worked out in more detail, the picture would be more complicated. Just as in the garnishment case the leverage on the garnishee is not exerted directly by the creditor but rather by the garnishee's employer through the threat of dismissal, so the leverage in the class action case may be exerted primarily by the effect a pending class action has on the defendant's position in the equity markets.

Roth and *Arnett*, however, do not implicate constitutional guarantees other than the Due Process Clause and so cannot be analyzed as *Fuentes* and *Mitchell* can. Perhaps this means only that Mr. Justice Stewart and Mr. Justice Rehnquist were correct in finding that whatever procedures the state chose to use were constitutionally acceptable. But there are two difficulties with bifurcating the cases into one group implicating only the Due Process Clause and another implicating other guarantees. First, the analysis of neither group would call for any special contribution from the Due Process Clause. In the former category, the Due Process Clause is automatically satisfied, and in the latter the procedural deficiencies could be treated as violations of the other constitutional guarantees. The failure to provide a prompt hearing in obscenity cases, for example, could be treated as a denial of First Amendment rights.[74] Second, a majority of the Supreme Court in *Arnett* rejected Mr. Justice Rehnquist's analysis.[75] The problem, then, is to devise a method of constitutional adjudication that would avoid these difficulties.[76]

Mr. Justice Marshall attempted to fit *Roth* and *Arnett* into the framework suggested here. In *Roth*, he argued that "every citizen who applies for a government job is entitled to it unless the government can establish some reason for denying the employment,"[77] and in *Arnett* he found, although much less explicitly, a constitutionally conferred property interest in continued employment in a tenured governmental position.[78] This resembles the analysis of *Fuentes* as a Fourth Amendment case, but there is an obvious, and major, difference. In *Fuentes*, we can refer to an explicit constitutional provision other than the Due Process Clause, but in Mr. Justice Marshall's analysis, the source of the constitutional right is, to say the least, unclear. The clue lies in Mr. Justice Marshall's citations, in *Roth*, of *Truax v. Raich*[79] and *Meyer v. Nebraska*.[80] These cases have taken on a new cast recently, *Truax* as an equal

---

[74] See Monaghan, *First Amendment "Due Process,"* 83 Harv. L. Rev. 518 (1970).

[75] See text *supra*, at note 47.

[76] That method, I must emphasize, is to be used only in those cases where no other constitutional guarantee is implicated. Thus, in order to defend *Fuentes*, I need not establish a constitutional right to consumer credit, since the Fourth Amendment is available.

[77] 408 U.S. at 588.

[78] 416 U.S. at 209, 226–27.

[79] 239 U.S. 33 (1915).

[80] 262 U.S. 390 (1923).

protection case about aliens[81] and *Meyer* as a case about family rights.[82] But when they were decided, they were clearly substantive due process cases. And that is the use to which Mr. Justice Marshall would put them. Mr. Justice Marshall's opinions in *Roth* and *Arnett* should be treated as attempts to revive substantive due process, although reviving substantive due process generally evokes shudders of horror.[83]

IV. SOME STANDARDS FOR DETERMINING SUBSTANTIVE DUE PROCESS RIGHTS

Unquestionably, substantive due process has a bad reputation. There seem to be three basic objections to substantive due process. (1) The cases following the doctrine were wrongly decided. (2) The doctrine has no roots in the constitutional text; the Constitution gives no guidance as to what rights should be treated as constitutionally protected. (3) The doctrine unjustifiably limits experimentation by rigidly confining the legislature in devising socially beneficial arrangements. All three objections are well taken, but it may still be possible to invoke the doctrine of substantive due process.[84]

Cases like *Lochner v. New York*[85] and *Coppage v. Kansas*[86] were wrongly decided in several ways. They denied the factual validity of at least arguably correct empirical assumptions.[87] They unjustifiably rejected goals that should have been recognized as permissible in a federal system.[88] And they identified, as due process rights, interests that should not be given special constitutional

---

[81] See, *e.g.*, Graham v. Richardson, 403 U.S. 365, 371 (1971); *In re* Griffiths, 413 U.S. 717, 720 (1973).

[82] See, *e.g.*, Griswold v. Connecticut, 381 U.S. 479 (1965); Boddie v. Connecticut, 401 U.S. 371, 376 (1971).

[83] See, *e.g.*, Ely, *The Wages of Crying Wolf: A Comment on Roe v. Wade*, 82 YALE L.J. 920 (1973); Epstin, *Substantive Due Process by Any Other Name: The Abortion Cases*, 1973 SUPREME COURT REVIEW 159.

[84] As the title of this article indicates, my analysis has links to Reich, *The New Property*, 73 YALE L.J. 733 (1964). The strength of Reich's work was its perception of an emerging principle that might unify the analysis of many apparently different cases. Its weakness was its failure, implicit in the enterprise, to differentiate among the various constitutional provisions that might protect the new property. In this article, I am concerned exclusively with cases in which no constitutional provision other than the Due Process Clause is available to that end.

[85] 198 U.S. 45 (1905).   [87] See, *e.g.*, 198 U.S. at 57–59, 62–64.

[86] 236 U.S. 1 (1915).   [88] See, *e.g.*, 236 U.S. at 16–18.

protection.[89] The first of these is no reason to reject the method of analysis; it is only a reason to urge the Court to do the job well rather than poorly. The other two proceed on the assumption that there are right and wrong ways to go about identifying goals and rights.

As a historical matter, *Lochner* and *Coppage* were regarded as wrongly decided because they failed to take account of the growing importance of the organized labor movement. Professor Bickel attempted to generalize this observation into a principle. The Court should do its best to anticipate the future.[90] I am afraid, however, that as a general principle, this is inadequate, because we have no warrant for believing that the Justices are better at that job than anyone else. Another criterion that will not work is that the Court should not substitute its value judgments for those of democratically elected legislatures. Such a rule would prohibit judicial review entirely.[91] But we have refined the criterion to make it work. The Supreme Court should not substitute its judgment for the legislature's unless the Constitution commands that it do so. It would be simple, but arbitrary, to consider this as a straightforward limitation on the Court's charter. The document to which it refers does not single out the Court as the special guarantor of the rights the document secures. There are functional reasons, however, for insisting that the Court confine itself to arguments that are rooted in the constitutional text.[92] Although the words of the document rarely compel conclusions,[93] they do force the Court to structure its arguments in particular ways. Structuring the argument is important because it allows evaluation of the Court's work, not simply by asserting that we would have, and that the Court should have, chosen otherwise, but in ways that rely on reason and fact. Rational discussion, after all, is—or should be— what opinion-writing is all about. A basis in the constitutional text keeps the Court from retreating into chambers and emerging with constitutional decisions full blown from the heads of the Justices.

---

[89] See, *e.g.*, Adair v. United States, 208 U.S. 161, 172 (1908).

[90] BICKEL, THE SUPREME COURT AND THE IDEA OF PROGRESS c. 4 (1970).

[91] For persuasive arguments that the standard "social-economic v. human" rights distinction is unacceptable, see McCloskey, *Economic Due Process and the Supreme Court: An Exhumation and Reburial*, 1962 SUPREME COURT REVIEW 34; Ely, note 83 *supra*, at 938–39.

[92] This argument derives from Ely, note 83 *supra*, at 942–44, 948.

[93] See, *e.g.*, Wesberry v. Sanders, 376 U.S. 1 (1964).

If, however, all we require is some sticking point around which the constitutional argument can focus, the words of the Constitution need not be the only candidate; almost any publicly disclosed standard will do. The Brandeisian objection to substantive due process should warn us to be careful in choosing that standard. In *New State Ice Co. v. Liebmann,* Brandeis wrote:[94]

> To stay experimentation in things social and economic is a grave responsibility. Denial of the right to experiment may be fraught with serious consequences to the Nation. It is one of the happy incidents of the federal system that a single courageous State may, if its citizens choose, serve as a laboratory; and try novel social and economic experiments without risk to the rest of the country.

Any standards for substantive due process must, therefore, guarantee adequate scope for state variation. It is worth remembering, though, that experiments sometimes yield results. For example, the experiment in providing some form of free public education ended long ago. It would be doctrinaire to insist on state autonomy when any benefits from experimentation have long since been established.

Against this background, I would specify some criteria for elaborating substantive due process rights, and elucidate them by explaining how they would be applied in a variety of cases. First, no substantive due process right should be established unless there is general agreement on the social importance of that right. Social importance, in turn, can be established by referring to the recognition given that right in nonconstitutional contexts, the relationship between the right and other constitutionally guaranteed rights, and the exercise of ordinary common sense by the Justices.[95] Second, a substantive due process right should be established only to the extent supported by the settled weight of responsible opinion. The Court should look to sources like the American Law Institute, the Commissioners for Uniform State Laws, and more specialized

---

[94] 285 U.S. 262, 311 (1932) (Brandeis, J., dissenting). See also Kewanee Oil Co. v. Bicron Corp., 416 U.S. 470, 493 (1974). For indications that the doctrine is not confined to the "social and economic" field, see Miranda v. Arizona, 384 U.S. 436, 467 (1966); United States v. Wade, 388 U.S. 218, 239 (1967); Miller v. California, 413 U.S. 15, 30–31 (1973).

[95] See Tushnet, note 2 *supra,* at 190. *Cf.* Faretta v. California, 95 S. Ct. 2526, 2530, 2532 (1975) (widespread statutory and state constitutional recognition of right of self-representation "form[s] a consensus not easily ignored").

commissions of inquiry such as the Administrative Conference.[96] The two criteria are not entirely distinct, but in general judgments of social importance will probably be more useful in defining a broad area in which a right should be recognized, while the views of informed experts will probably be more useful in defining the precise contours of the right. Application of these criteria would guarantee that substantive due process opinions be subject to rational discourse, that adequate scope be given for local variation when local variation is important, and nonetheless that constitutional rights not be subject entirely to majoritarian decisions.

One preliminary objection should be addressed. By relying on the settled weight of opinion, would not the Court improperly transfer the responsibility for constitutional decision to persons not appointed for life by the President and confirmed by the Senate? The Court still has the duty to make judgments about what the weight of opinion on a given matter is, and about whose opinions ought to count as "responsible."[97] There seems to be no qualitative difference between making such judgments and the Court's current task of making judgments about what procedures produce a fair balance between individual and governmental interests. Finally, I believe that it would be useful to acknowledge openly that the American legal system no longer consists solely of the three traditional branches of government, and that the proliferation of associated institutions such as the American Law Institute is a social fact that sensible adjudication ought to take into account.[98]

Let me begin with an easy question: Should a constitutionally protected right to education be found in the Due Process Clause? The question is easy because almost every state recognizes such a right even without a federal constitutional command, and the right's relationship to the constitutionally protected right to vote and right of free expression is clear.[99] Finding a right to education

---

[96] Cf. TAYLOR, TWO STUDIES IN CONSTITUTIONAL INTERPRETATION 3–4 (1969). See also Wolff v. McDonnell, 418 U.S. 539, 565 n.16 (1974).

[97] As to the latter, the Court might fairly conclude, for example, that the editorial process of law reviews ordinarily does not produce student work that reflects a mature and comprehensive judgment, and so could severely discount the weight of student notes and, probably, other law review articles as well.

[98] A full exploration of this suggestion would require consideration of the impact of proposals like mine on the efforts of interest groups to have their views represented in these associated institutions.

[99] See San Antonio Independent School District v. Rodriguez, 411 U.S. 1, 111–15 (Marshall, J., dissenting); WISE, RICH SCHOOLS, POOR SCHOOLS . . . (1968).

in the federal Constitution would scarcely limit state experimentation on the question. Indeed, one can read the opinion of the Court in *San Antonio Independent School District v. Rodriguez* as recognizing a state's obligation to provide a minimum education to its residents.[100] Beyond that minimum, questions arise. *Goss v. Lopez*[101] dealt with the procedures by which states could go about terminating a student's ability to procure any public education at all for a short time. Agreement approaching unanimity was clearly lacking in existing procedures, but the Court's result in *Goss* was supported by the substantial weight of responsible opinion, both that of the courts[102] and that of the commentators.[103] The Court's imposition of minimal due process standards in *Goss* would not therefore deny the nation the results of any experiments that could reasonably be regarded as likely to yield beneficial results.

The problem in *Rodriguez* was very different, and the Court's resolution of the problem is consistent with my criteria.[104] The Court recognized that serious dispute existed over what sort of school financing systems led to the best education for all; responsible opinion was sharply divided.[105] In addition, simply declaring Texas's financing scheme unconstitutional under the Equal Protection Clause would, if history is a guide, stifle state experimentation.[106] The Court recently tried to unblock a stagnating system of voter apportionment through the use of the Equal Protection Clause, but its efforts led inexorably to rigid rules whose impact could be limited only in the most arbitrary manner.[107] If courts find it difficult to handle more flexible rules within the confines of the Equal Protection Clause, then perhaps the Court was wise

---

[100] See, *e.g.*, 411 U.S., at 24; Clune, *Wealth Discrimination in School Finance*, 68 Nw. L. Rev. 651, 658–60 (1973).

[101] 419 U.S. 565 (1975).   [102] See cases cited *id*. at 577 n.8.

[103] See generally Buss, *Procedural Due Process for School Discipline: Probing the Constitutional Outline*, 119 U. Pa. L. Rev. 545 (1971); Wright, *The Constitution on the Campus*, 22 Vand. L. Rev. 1027 (1969).

[104] The precise issue in *Rodriguez* was, of course, an equal protection one. Given the Court's analysis, however, resolution of the equal protection claim turned on deciding whether education was a "fundamental" right, which in the Court's terms, meant deciding whether education was a right guaranteed by the Constitution. See 411 U.S. at 33–34. If it was, the Court would have to face the problems discussed in the text.

[105] See 411 U.S. at 41–43, 56–58.   [106] *Id*. at 43.

[107] See Tushnet, note 2 *supra*, at 179–80 n.6; Areen & Ross, *The Rodriguez Case: Judicial Oversight of School Finance*, 1973 Supreme Court Review 33, 38–41.

to refrain from federalizing school financing and to leave the job to state courts.[108]

Similar problems justify the Court's refusal in *Lindsey v. Normet*[109] to declare a federal constitutional right to housing. As the Court noted, common sense tells us that housing is quite important. But a right to housing has only sporadically been recognized in nonconstitutional situations.[110] Its link to other constitutional rights is tenuous at best. And the precise contours of even a minimal right to housing have not received the general agreement of informed observers.

Much the same could be said of Mr. Justice Marshall's suggestion of a prima facie right to governmental employment.[111] I am not here concerned, however, with the correctness of prior decisions. I would only show that we can specify criteria that allow us to structure arguments over substantive due process rights and preserve adequate scope for state experimentation.

The dissenting opinions in *Roth* and *Arnett* deserve close attention in this connection. *Roth* involved a probationary university teacher whose contract was not renewed at the end of its one-year term. The teacher alleged that the nonrenewal was unconstitutional because it was based on his exercise of his right to freedom of speech, and because his employer provided neither reasons for the nonrenewal nor an opportunity for a hearing. The district court granted partial summary judgment on the latter issue, and the Court of Appeals affirmed. Thus, as the case was presented to the Supreme Court, no First Amendment claims were involved.[112] Nonetheless, Mr. Justice Douglas's dissent properly emphasized the link between academic freedom and the First Amendment.[113] Even if academic freedom were not a constitutional guarantee,[114]

---

[108] See Areen & Ross, note 108 *supra*, at 55; *Future Directions for School Finance Reform*, 38 LAW & CONTEMP. PROB. 293–581 (1974).

[109] 405 U.S. 56 (1972).

[110] But *cf*. Housing Act of 1949, § 2, 63 STAT. 413.

[111] Board of Regents v. Roth, 408 U.S. 564, 588 (1972) (Marshall, J., dissenting).

[112] After remand and trial, Roth was awarded $5,246 in compensatory and $1,500 in punitive damages, the jury finding that he had indeed been discharged for constitutionally impermissible reasons. *Wis. State Journal*, 11 Nov. 1973, p. 4.

[113] 408 U.S. at 580–85 (Douglas, J., dissenting).

[114] *Cf*. Presidents Council, Dist. 25 v. Community School Board No. 25, 457 F.2d 289 (2d Cir. 1972); Ahern v. Board of Education, 456 F.2d, 399, 403–04 (8th Cir. 1972); Adams v. Campbell County School District, 511 F.2d 1242, 1247 (10th Cir. 1975). But *cf*. Webb v. Lake Mills Community School Dist., 344 F. Supp. 791 (N.D. Iowa 1972).

still it surely plays an important part in increasing the public's knowledge on matters of public importance, which is the point of the First Amendment. This should make us cautious in allowing administrators to dismiss teachers without explanation because, as Mr. Justice Marshall noted in *Roth*, when explanations are required, administrators are likely to be more careful to premise their action on grounds that do not impair academic freedom.[115]

Indeed, one might read *Indiana ex rel. Anderson v. Brand* as establishing that the Constitution requires the courts to be especially careful when dismissals of teachers are at issue. Indiana's teacher tenure act at first applied to all teachers in the state, but in 1933 it was repealed as to teachers in township schools, of whom Anderson was one. Teachers in cities and towns were unaffected by the 1933 act. Such a partial repeal ought to trigger our suspicions—if tenure for teachers is a good idea in cities and towns, why is it not a good idea in townships?[116] Perhaps the fiscal problems of townships in the Depression were more serious than those of cities. Perhaps less stringent protection of teachers was required in order to facilitate consolidation of rural schools. But each of these concerns could easily be alleviated by invoking the state's reserved police power, and the tenure statute evidenced no intention to preclude these reasons for dismissal. The record before the Court did not rule out the possibility that Anderson's dismissal would affect academic freedom and, in fact, the Court took offense at the suggestion that the Board, in dismissing Anderson, could permissibly be motivated by "political or personal" factors.[117]

The question of civil service tenure, too, has important constitutional overtones. As Chief Justice Hughes recognized in *Crowell v. Benson*,[118] the civil service bureaucracy has great potential for adversely affecting the constitutional rights of the citizen. He saw the problem as one of subordination of the bureaucracy to the varying wishes of the elected branches of the government and sought therefore to subject the bureaucracy to the scrutiny of the independent judiciary. *Crowell* is, after all, a decision about the scope of Article III. Pressures for conformity also arise from the

---

[115] 408 U.S. at 591–92 (Marshall, J., dissenting).

[116] This question sounds more in equal protection than in due process. My point, though, is that legitimate concerns about abuses and manipulation of state tenure systems should incline us to invoke whatever constitutional doctrines may be available to control such abuses.

[117] See 303 U.S. at 108–09.   [118] 285 U.S. 22, 56–67 (1932).

hierarchical nature of the bureaucracy.[119] Aside from judicial review, civil service tenure helps free lower level bureaucrats from political control.[120] Of course, tenure may also lead to unresponsiveness to citizen demands, just as academic tenure may lead to sloth and indifference, but the constitutional decision, validated by nearly one hundred years of experience, has been to risk unresponsiveness in order to protect against majoritarian overreaching.[121] The sheer number of governmental employees, when taken in conjunction with these constitutional overtones, supports the conclusion that civil service tenure ought to be recognized as constitutionally protected.

The next step requires identifying what the precise contours of that protection ought to be. In *Arnett*, Mr. Justice Marshall drew on a report to, and the recommendations of, the Administrative Conference of the United States, and on the experience of nine major federal agencies, as guides in this task. Mr. Justice Powell, following the regrettable practice established by his predecessors of confining the discussion of what ought to be the central issue to the footnotes,[122] countered by citing the government's "general practice to the contrary."[123] These sources might provide the framework for a rational discussion of the procedural requirements of due process. Mr. Justice Marshall might have discussed why the experience of his nine agencies should be considered more important than the experience of other agencies, and Mr. Justice Powell might have discussed why the Administrative Conference's recommendations should be disregarded. In sharp contrast to the structure of argument that these sources would create are the opinions of Mr. Justice White and Mr. Justice Powell in *Arnett*. Both enumerate the relevant interests, and then simply conclude that "on balance"[124] or "in any event"[125] certain procedures would

---

[119] See 416 U.S. at 205–06 (Douglas, J., dissenting).

[120] See, *e.g.*, Illinois State Employees Union, Council 34 v. Lewis, 473 F.2d 561 (7th Cir. 1972).

[121] For an analysis of civil service reform as an act of constitutional significance, because it changed the balance of power, see BETH, THE DEVELOPMENT OF THE AMERICAN CONSTITUTION, 1877–1917 at 24–26 (1971).

[122] See Tushnet, note 2 *supra*, at 191. See also Sampson v. Murray, 415 U.S. 61, 92 n.80 (1974), 101 (Marshall, J., dissenting).

[123] 416 U.S. at 168–69 n.4 (Powell, J., concurring in the result).

[124] *Id*. at 171 (Powell, J., concurring in the result).

[125] *Id*. at 195 (White, J., concurring in part).

satisfy the Due Process Clause. This has all the hallmarks of the methodological evil of the bad old days before the demise of substantive due process. For all that appears, the Justices simply retreated to their chambers and pondered over what would be best, and emerged with conclusions that cannot be criticized except by saying that the critic, were it up to him, would have arrived as a different balance.[126] I think it of some significance that the practitioners of this style nowhere in their opinions are able to engage each other in discussion.

Mitchell is an even better example of the impossibility of discussion under Mr. Justice White's approach, and the contrast with his opinion in *Arnett* is instructive in a new way. At the point in *Mitchell* that the Court assesses the competing interests, and again where it distinguishes *Fuentes*, not a single prior case is cited.[127] Mr. Justice White's opinion in *Arnett*, on the other hand, is surfeited with citations. This is significant because prior cases, no less than expert reports, can serve to structure legal arguments. Difficulties arise, however, when the Justices seek to require something less than a full trial-type hearing by relying on prior cases, since until recently the cases required either a full hearing or none at all. The first time the Court defines some intermediate position, it is necessarily driven to inarticulate balancing. The next time, though, the Court has its prior case as a reference point.

The process is illustrated in the citation of *Arnett* in *Wolff v. McDonnell*,[128] involving the procedural protections needed when prison officials seek to discipline prisoners. In *Arnett*, Mr. Justice White argued that cross-examination need not be provided prior to termination, where the issue is one of probable cause.[129] When he wrote the opinion of the Court in *Wolff*, Mr. Justice White repeated the argument. The existence of *Arnett* did provide some structure for the argument, but really not enough. First, and perhaps hypertechnically, *Arnett* and the cases there cited by Mr. Justice White all involved probable cause determinations. *Wolff* involved an administratively final adjudication. Second, the reason for relying on prior cases is that the experience gained as the prior

---

[126] See also Tushnet, *Judicial Revision of the Habeas Corpus Statutes: A Note on Schneckloth v. Bustamonte*, 1975 WIS. L. REV. 484, 501.

[127] 416 U.S. at 608–10, 615–16. There is a "cf." citation at 609.

[128] 418 U.S. 539, 588 (1974).

[129] 416 U.S. at 200–01 (White, J., concurring in result).

cases are applied in practice can enlighten the Court as to the costs and benefits of its decisions in the past, and so can provide relevant information for resolving current problems. Unfortunately, the time span between *Arnett* and *Wolff* was only two months.[130] Third, the Court in *Wolff* rejected the analogy to *Morrissey v. Brewer*,[131] though the setting there, parole revocation, is obviously closer than that in *Arnett* to the setting *Wolff*. Once again, the ground for rejecting the analogy was an ordinary assessment of what the Court perceived as the realities of prison life. One can fairly question, I think, the capability of men as isolated from day-to-day life as the Justices are to make that judgment.[132] The common-sense judgments of social importance that I have made a part—but only a part—of my criteria for determining whether a right is guaranteed by substantive due process are rather different, because those judgments are not about such details as concerned the Court in *Wolff*.

V. Conclusion

It may seem that I have not accomplished very much. To that, I enter a partial plea in confession and avoidance, and join issue only in part. Plainly, I cannot contend that I have provided a full discussion of any of the particular substantive due process rights that I have touched on. For example, even assuming that a constitutional right to civil service tenure for lower-level bureaucrats ought to be recognized, determining at what point in the hierarchy that right ought to disappear is hardly an easy task.[133] At each point in the preceding discussion, numerous complexities

---

[130] A similar objection can be made to the Court's practice of deciding one case, examining the cases it has held pending that decision, and granting review of one held case to clarify the decided case. The petition for certiorari in *Di-Chem*, 417 U.S. 907 (1974), for example, was granted two weeks after the decision in *Mitchell*, and on the same day that review was denied in two other cases similar to *Mitchell*, Carmack v. Buckner, 417 U.S. 901 (1974), and Spielman-Fond, Inc. v. Hanson's Inc., 417 U.S. 901 (1974).

[131] 408 U.S. 471 (1972).

[132] It may be significant that the Court noted that some form of cross-examination was allowed in a majority of the states. 418 U.S. at 567 n.18. A fair reading of this portion of the Court's opinion indicates that the Court was indeed making its own assessment of reality, although a few, quite muted, hints of Brandeisian concerns are dropped. See, *e.g.*, *id.* at 569 ("in a period where prison practices are diverse and somewhat experimental").

[133] The Court has suggested, though, that the task is not beyond its powers. Sugarman v. Dougall, 413 U.S. 634, 642–43 (1973).

relating to particular rights might be elaborated and explored. My aim, however, is both more modest and more grandiose. More modest, in that I have tried simply to open up these questions in a more satisfactory way than the prevailing views on the present Court do. More grandiose, in that I am concerned with establishing the viability of a method that could be used to analyze many particular rights.

Thus, I am not concerned with specifying results in any particular area. Neither am I troubled that the method I propose would not guarantee that the Court would conclude that some given right is protected by the Due Process Clause. A right to civil service tenure, a right to housing, a right to a public job—each of these may or may not be found socially important and recognized by the settled weight of responsible opinion. I certainly have not canvassed the views of those who must be consulted under my scheme. But again, that is not my concern here. I am skeptical of claims that we can provide general methods of constitutional analysis that guarantee results.[134] Since I doubt that we can eliminate the exercise of judgment on the part of judges, the best we can hope for, I think, are methods of structuring constitutional arguments.[135]

The framework for which I have argued is such a method. The criterion of social importance, for example, calls on the Court to see whether some right is recognized in nonconstitutional contexts, an ordinary exercise in legal research; whether it is closely related to other constitutional rights, an ordinary exercise in legal analysis;[136] and whether it is important in common sense terms.[137] All of these, as well as the second criterion that looks to the weight of responsible opinion, are subject to rational legal argument. The framework that I have proposed also lacks the defects of pre–New Deal decisions on substantive due process. While those cases limited beneficial experimentation, reliance on settled judgment in nonconstitutional decision-making permits experimentation where it is desirable. While those cases identified rights without constitutional roots and so could not be addressed in the ordinary

---

[134] *Cf.* Tribe, *From Environmental Foundations to Constitutional Structures: Learning from Nature's Future*, 84 YALE L.J. 545, 553–55 (1975).

[135] See Christie, *Objectivity in the Law*, 78 YALE L.J. 1311 (1969).

[136] See Tushnet, note 2 *supra*, at 190 n.78.

[137] *Cf.* Repouille v. United States, 165 F.2d 152 (2d Cir. 1947).

terms of legal argument, the criteria proposed here do set appropriate terms for discussion. In short, to the objection that I have not done very much, I answer that, while indeed I have not, what I have done is critical.

The Burger Court's performance in the recent cases discussed here has been technically inadequate and indeed, to the extent that the Court has been relying on essentially untutored, quasi-legislative judgments of what is proper in particular settings, evokes memories of what was deficient in the days of substantive due process. I have tried to suggest methods of adjudication that I believe avoid those deficiencies.

WILLIAM H. CLUNE III

THE SUPREME COURT'S TREATMENT OF WEALTH DISCRIMINATIONS UNDER THE FOURTEENTH AMENDMENT

Wealth discriminations present a special problem for the Supreme Court in its interpretation of the Fourteenth Amendment, a problem which derives from the pervasiveness and ethical ambiguity of wealth as a principle of organization in our society. Both critics and supporters of wealth stratification recognize the ethical power of claims against wealth discriminations. Supporters confine their recognition to extreme examples in selected areas without necessarily being able to define an extreme case or defend the selection of areas. Critics damn the whole system. Because they believe, however, that wealth is a basic principle of organization in our society, they concede the improbability of claims ever being successful except for some extreme examples. The instability of this boundary between acceptable and unacceptable, vulnerable and immune, becomes critical when it is the subject of a claim of right under the Fourteenth Amendment. For, once the basic ethical claim has been embodied in a judicial doctrine, the problem of finding a stopping place becomes difficult.

William H. Clune III is Associate Professor of Law, University of Wisconsin at Madison.

AUTHOR'S NOTE: The research for this paper was supported by funds granted to the Institute for Research on Poverty pursuant to the provisions of the Economic Opportunity Act of 1964. Special thanks are owed to my research assistant, Sebastian Geraci, and my colleague, Mark Tushnet.

Courts, especially the Supreme Court, cannot make fluid compromises as legislatures do.[1] Consistency and neutrality are more than the touchstones of the best analytic work of the Court;[2] to many, they are justice itself in the modern liberal state.[3] Thus, if a doctrine is open to claims of wealth discrimination, in the sense that the elements of the doctrine are isomorphic with the ethical sentiments, an acceptable stopping place will not be found until the ethical strength of the claims diminishes. Yet wealth discriminations do not concentrate in special sectors of the society; they are to be found in smooth gradients throughout. For this reason, an open or authentic doctrine, which is also neutral and principled, may be swept irresistibly into problems vastly beyond the competence of courts. Could the doctrine simply not be open to all? Callous indifference to the extreme cases would be difficult to sustain against the ethical background of our society. What about partial openness, a doctrine that recognizes the injustice of wealth discriminations in some oblique, non-expansive way? The answer to that question, and some suggestions about some other ways to solve the paradoxes of constitutional condemnation of wealth discrimination, are the subjects of this article.

It is maintained here that the beginnings of open doctrines about wealth discriminations established by the Warren Court have been halted or reversed by the Burger Court, principally through doctrines which are not open, or sensitive, to these discriminations. The process of desensitizing legal doctrines from ethics and politics

---

[1] Among the institutional and societal forces for consistency are the written published opinion, the rule of *stare decisis*, the ideals and beliefs of the legal profession, the concentration of resources of that profession in and around the work of the Court, especially around the Equal Protection Clause because of the magnetism of the idea of equality in the modern world.

[2] "The insistence on reason in the judicial process, on analytical coherence, and on principled judgment no matter how narrow its compass, is traditional." BICKEL, THE SUPREME COURT AND THE IDEA OF PROGRESS 8 (1970); BICKEL, THE LEAST DANGEROUS BRANCH 49–65 (1962); BLACK, THE PEOPLE AND THE COURT: JUDICIAL REVIEW IN A DEMOCRACY (1960); JAFFE, ENGLISH AND AMERICAN JUDGES AND LAWMAKERS 38–39 (1969); Wechsler, *Toward Natural Principles of Constitutional Law*, in PRINCIPLES, POLITICS, AND FUNDAMENTAL LAW 27–28 (1961). Even those who most severely criticize the Wechslerian and later Bickel formulation of neutrality and principle in constitutional law recognize that at some point conflicting cases must be reconciled and the obscurely perceived principle clearly stated. Wright, *Professor Bickel, the Scholarly Tradition, and the Supreme Court*, 84 HARV. L. REV. 769, 778–79 (1971); Rostow, *American Legal Realism and the Sense of the Profession*, 34 ROCKY MT. L. REV. 123, 138 (1962).

[3] Excellent expositions of this point may be found in UNGER, KNOWLEDGE AND POLITICS (1975) and LAW IN MODERN SOCIETY (1976), both soon to be published.

needs a name; I will refer to it in this article, following Professor Judith Shklar, as formalism. Legalism, as defined by Shklar, includes a tendency to regard law as separate from morals and politics. Formalism is a greater degree of legalism and strives for a more complete separation of law from reality by giving increased attention to definitions, that is, the orderliness and internal consistency of concepts.[4] Note the distinct meanings of formalism as used here. Formalism is not arbitrariness if arbitrariness means lack of logical consistency, because consistency is a primary goal of formalism. Indeed, if the Court responds to powerful pressures, internal consistency will be common to both open and closed doctrines. In open doctrines it might be called legalism, because consistency of rules is one thing that distinguishes law from ethics and politics; and consistency is the force of expansion within open doctrines that thrusts the law toward economic contradictions and creates the difficulty of finding a defensible stopping place. Either type of doctrine may also be logically inconsistent if the minimal demands of legalism are not met.

Formalistic doctrines tend to become arbitrary in application, however, because their emphasis is exclusively upon clarity and consistency. Because the internal logic of formalistic doctrines is not tailored to recognition of underlying ethical problems, the natural tendency of the formalistic model is to lead the Court away from ethically significant breaches of equal protection; that is, problems which are logically prior in the model may be socially insignificant. If the Court follows the internal logic, critics will wonder what possible set of priorities can explain the allocation of judicial relief. The lack of underlying ethical priorities will seem

---

[4] "[L]egalism . . . is the ethical attitude that holds moral conduct to be a matter of rule following . . . ." As a social outlook, it includes "the dislike of vague generalities, the preference for case-by-case treatment of all social issues, the structuring of all possible human relationships into the form of claims and counter-claims under established rules, and the belief that rules are 'there' . . . ." SHKLAR, LEGALISM 1, 10 (1964). Formalism treats "law as a conceptual pattern entirely distinct from all political, moral, and social values and institutions." "The idea of treating law as a self-contained system of norms that is 'there,' identifiable without any reference to the content, aim, and development of rules that compose it, is the very essence of formalism." *Id.* at 33–34. Formalism strives to be immune from politicians and moralists, in order to achieve dispassionate objectivity, *id.* at 35–36, and was conceived as an alternative to natural law, which openly equated law with morality. *Id.* at 36–37. Whereas natural law may exacerbate conflict, formalism, or positivism, seeks to avoid ideology and partiality in political discourse and life; but withdrawing from social conflicts does not solve them. Thus, "the price which this formalism has paid in terms of excessive abstractness and remoteness from law as a social phenomenon seems particularly exorbitant." *Id.* at 37–38.

arbitrary because the Constitution itself is believed to express the ethical priorities common to our people. On the other hand, to counter this tendency, and to recognize the great force of claims against extreme abuses, the Court may apply the formalistic doctrines mainly to the same kind of problems that would have received attention under non-formalistic doctrines. Then, the opposite kind of arbitrariness becomes apparent. Instead of asking why the Court is not following the Constitution, critics will ask why it is not following its own doctrine. The outlines of what would be the open doctrine become discernible in holdings and the rationales of dissenting Justices who adhere to the open doctrines will seem increasingly apt.

The particular tendency toward formalism (it is not formalism full blown) which has stymied the open doctrines of the Warren Court is a model of "due process" (in a non-technical sense embracing some equal protection decisions). The model was basically established by Justice Harlan in his dissent in *Griffin v. Illinois*.[5] Narrow in focus, it concentrates on the individual before the Court rather than on social classes or institutions or patterns of sociolegal conflict, on the explicit words and verbal categories of laws rather than their actual effect, on the dominance of the law in a situation rather than the interaction of law with other factors, on the technical neatness of the means-ends relationship rather than the end and actual effect of the law, and on the possible purpose of a law discerned from its logical properties rather than the actual purpose known from its social and political context. There is a master dichotomy here, a familiar one in constitutional law; it might be called law-sensitive vs. reality-sensitive, de facto/ de jure writ large.[6]

Showing the presence of this model, and criticizing it, are the major purposes of this article. Criticism would fall short, however, if it stopped at the flaws of the formalistic model. Those flaws

---

[5] Griffin v. Illinois, 351 U.S. 12, 29–39 (1956).

[6] This dichotomy, and the willingness of the Court to look beyond conceptual categories, has been central in at least two other major events of constitutional law: congressional authority under the Commerce Clause, and application of the Fourteenth Amendment to racial discrimination. *Compare* Plessy v. Ferguson, 163 U.S. 537, 551 (1896), *with* Brown v. Board of Education, 347 U.S. 483, 494 (1954).

In "state action" cases, too, the Court has been reality-sensitive. Burton v. Wilmington Parking Authority, 365 U.S. 715, 722 (1961); Reitman v. Mulkey, 387 U.S. 369, 378 (1967); see Black, *"State Action," Equal Protection, and California's Proposition 14*, 81 HARV. L. REV. 69, 90 (1967).

are inescapable if open doctrines cannot be designed which include a defensible stopping place short of the unenforceable judicial order to remake the face of society. I will argue here that suitable stopping places can be found. A proper constitutional doctrine of wealth discrimination, based upon the special role of the Court, would have an acceptably narrow focus and, within that focus, the task of actually proving wealth discrimination is difficult. In other words, the conceptual expansiveness of the authentic doctrines is less than is often represented, and, in addition, is properly checked by stern problems of proof. To exploit the possibilities of this counterpoise, however, the Court must be somewhat more creative with remedies than it has been, and must deal differently with social science as a body of knowledge. Perhaps it should be made explicit that conceptual restraint is not the same as formalism, which is only an extreme form of conceptual restraint. Open doctrines may possess conceptual limits; the difficulty will be to find principled limits.

I. The Public Fruits of Wealth: Two Legal Mechanisms

The Supreme Court has not been confronted with the legal mechanisms of creating wealth discriminations, which are vast and mysterious, but only with those necessary to enjoy wealth, which are fewer, simpler, and more visible. The need for legal mechanisms might be questioned in view of the apparent sufficiency of merely possessing private wealth. But if we judge from the type of cases reaching the courts, there is a need, on the one hand, to place certain activities in the public sphere because of economies of scale or equitable sharing of the cost of public goods,[7] together with, on the one hand, the obvious desirability (from the point of view of wealthier people) of causing public benefits to flow toward private wealth. Whether or not government activity is redistributive in net terms or in particular areas does not do away with this basic tension. Government could be very "socialistic" in the sense of greatly diminishing private wealth differences, yet there would always be competition for the marginal unit of unredistributed public benefits. An assumption here, perhaps a vital one, is that competition for government benefits runs strongly along lines of private wealth. If any assertion at such a level of generality can be

---

[7] See TULLOCH, PRIVATE WANTS, PUBLIC MEANS (1970).

accepted a priori, that one can.[8] Moreover, the very existence of the legal mechanisms reviewed by the Court is evidence of the competition.

One group of legal mechanisms of wealth enjoyment which has reached the Court functions to reinforce the geographical dispersion and concentration of wealth. Geographical isolation of wealth is apparently an essential precondition of enjoying wealth, or at the least, an extreme convenience. Social scientists tell us that "social distance" is the most prized of all goods and, as confirmation, that residential location of people can be most lucidly predicted and understood in terms of wealth and status.[9] The legal mechanisms undergirding geographical wealth concentration include legal authority for the local capture of tax resources, legal obstacles to residence of poor people in wealthy areas (such as majoritarian defeat of housing and exclusionary zoning),[10] and legal obstacles to participation of poor people in local government benefits, which also function as incentives against taking up residence. In summary, the legal mechanisms of geographical wealth concentration include not only those which allow wealthier people to live together apart from poorer people but also those which permit the wealth, once congregated, to stay where it is.

The second major mechanism of causing government benefits to flow toward wealth is the price for government service. Prices both complement and overlap with the mechanisms of geographical dispersion. The complementary function occurs in regulating

---

[8] See PLOTNICK & SKIDMORE, PROGRESS AGAINST POVERTY: A REVIEW OF THE 1964–1974 DECADE ch. 7 (1975); Heffernan, The Failure of Welfare Reform: A Political Farce in Two Acts (Institute for Research on Poverty, Discussion Paper 216–74, University of Wisconsin, Madison 1974); Clune, Wealth Discrimination in School Finance, 68 Nw. U.L. REV. 651, 667–68, and n.50 (1973).

[9] See Duncan & Duncan, Residential Distribution and Occupational Stratification, 60 AM.J. Soc. 493 (1955); SHEVKY & BELL, SOCIAL AREA ANALYSIS (1955); Hawley & Duncan, Social Area Analysis: A Critical Appraisal, 33 LAND ECON. 337 (1957).

[10] The Court denied standing to challenge exclusionary zoning in the Seldin case, discussed at the end of this article. See text infra, at notes 164–97. The constitutionality of exclusionary zoning has not been decided. Cases upholding zoning apart from any anti-poor basis are Village of Euclid v. Amber Realty Co., 272 U.S. 365 (1962), and the recent case of Village of Belle Terre v. Borass, 416 U.S. 1 (1974), reaffirming Euclid's test for determining zoning ordinance constitutionality, see generally, Sager, Tight Little Islands; Exclusionary Zoning, Equal Protection, and the Indigent, 21 STAN. L. REV. 767, 783 (1969).

State courts, however, recently have begun to treat zoning ordinances with a new rigor due to anti-poor bias. E.g., Southern Burlington City N.A.A.C.P. v. Town of Mount Laurel, 67 N.J. 151 (1975). See also note 179 infra.

the flow of services which are not cut off to the poor by geographical isolation, particularly those offered and financed on a statewide basis, such as access to and effectiveness in state courts. The overlap of prices and geographical isolators is definitional in that any mechanism which permits private wealth to generate more public service is likely to operate something like a price because it allows wealthy people to use their wealth to buy something. In this definitional sense, the geographical wealth-isolating mechanisms function either by raising the price of living in an area or by putting a price tag on local government. For example, the state declares, as to local government, that each locality must bear its cost: this is a price system.

Prices for government service are vivid examples of wealth discrimination, which makes judicial analysis of them especially interesting. They are neither more nor less than a vehicle for translation of private wealth into public services. It is true that prices, or fees, may help support the cost of the service, and offer a way to ration them according to the intensity of need. But there are ways of achieving these other functions while at the same time blocking the disproportionate flow of services toward wealthier users, *e.g.*, financing out a redistributive tax and rationing by use of waiting time. In theory, then, the price mechanism calls for a judicial evaluation of intentional wealth discrimination. The manner in which such an evaluation is avoided, particularly by formalistic doctrines, is one of the more interesting facets of the jurisprudence of wealth discrimination; and creating doctrines to strike down some, but not all, prices is an especially clear example of the difficulty of dealing with wealth discriminations in a principled way under more open doctrines.

II. THE PRICE OF FREEDOM—FROM GRIFFIN TO WILLIAMS

Griffin[11] and *Williams*[12] concerned appeals from criminal convictions in Illinois courts, decided by the Supreme Court thirteen years apart. The *Griffin* Court, which really introduced the modern era of doctrines concerning wealth discrimination, included Justices Clark, Harlan, Frankfurter, Burton, Minton, and Reed. The *Williams* Court had only Harlan, Douglas, and Black in com-

---

[11] 351 U.S. 12 (1956).

[12] 399 U.S. 235 (1970).

mon with the *Griffin* Court.[13] Now that Harlan, too, is gone, it is curious and interesting that the approach he took in dissent in *Griffin* seems have set a guide for the Burger Court.

In *Griffin*, the plaintiffs wanted the state to pay for stenographic transcripts of the trial because, under their uncontradicted affidavits, they could not afford to pay,[14] and under Illinois law, a transcript was either necessary for an appeal, or necessary for an effective appeal, or very helpful for an effective appeal, at least in most cases.[15] The contrast in *Griffin* between the majority opinion (which required the state to pay) and Harlan's dissent reveals almost all of the basic dynamics of the wealth cases—the moral persuasiveness of the claim of those without wealth, the problems of containing this claim once recognized, and the basic tools preferred both by those who favor and those who disfavor judicial evaluation of wealth discriminations.

Justices Black, for the majority, and Frankfurter, concurring, approached the question boldly as one of discrimination against the poor, offending both the Due Process Clause and the Equal Protection Clause. Both Justices made wealth discrimination analytically central. First, they emphasized, the nature of the right would not carry the case. The state could take away transcripts, or even appeals, entirely; it was the differential taking that offended. Second, not just any differential taking would raise judicial condemnation; the singling out of the poor was especially offensive. Clearly, some differential takings might pass judicial scrutiny, for example, those who defaulted under a system requiring self-help or those less in need in a system which examined need.[16] Furthermore, singling out the poor offended democratic values in a formal sense (equality for the poor being one of those values) and,

---

[13] Many cases decided after *Griffin* are not discussed in this section, including Douglas v. California, 372 U.S. 352 (1963). See generally GUNTHER, CASES AND MATERIALS ON CONSTITUTIONAL LAW 812–21 (9th ed. 1975).

[14] 351 U.S. at 13.   [15] *Id.* at 13–14.

[16] "[A]t all stages of the proceedings the Due Process and Equal Protection Clauses protect persons like petitioners from invidious discriminations." *Id.* at 18. Justice Frankfurter, concurring with Justice Black's remarks, said: "[N]or does the equal protection of the laws deny a State the right to make classifications in law when such classifications are rooted in reason . . . [but nothing] sanctions differentiations by a State that have no relation to a rational policy of criminal appeal or authorizes the imposition of conditions that offend the deepest presuppositions of our society. Surely it would not need argument to conclude that a State could not, within its wide scope of discretion in these matters, allow an appeal for persons convicted of crimes punishable by imprisonment of a year or more, only on payment of a fee of $500." *Id.* at 21–22.

practically, added to the burdens of those who are already short-changed by the legal apparatus.[17] Both Justices recognized implicit limitations on the ability of the Court to protect the poor. One limitation might be on the type of government service; perhaps the poor could validly be excluded from some services, not explicitly, of course, but by the price mechanism.[18] Where to draw the line was left for future cases, the Justices contenting themselves with references to distinctive characteristics of the facts before them —the importance of personal freedom, the centrality of fair criminal process to democratic institutions, and the intensity of the state action involved (the state was solely responsible both for the requirement that those convicted have a transcript in order to appeal and for the requirement that they pay for transcripts out of their own resources).[19]

Frankfurter saw another limitation. There might be cases, those concerned with the availability of equally skilled lawyers in criminal cases, as to which both the nature of the interest and the nature of the discrimination argued for judicial action but such action would not be feasible. There are "contingencies of life which are hardly within the power, let alone the duty, of a state to correct or cushion."[20] In summary, the majority stepped firmly and explicitly into the question of a constitutional remedy for discriminations against the poor, leaving future cases to the future.

The sociological and economic analysis, more than the result, roused Justice Harlan to a vigorous, prophetic dissent. Objection was made to the generality of the issue decided by the majority; Harlan would have preferred that the trial court determine such questions as whether Illinois appellate procedure did, in fact, require a transcript;[21] whether the particular plaintiffs needed a transcript for the particular errors they were alleging;[22] whether, and

---

[17] "In criminal trials a State can no more discriminate on account of poverty than on account of religion, race or color." *Id*. at 17. "There can be no equal justice where the kind of a trial a man gets depends on the amount of money he has. Destitute defendants must be afforded as adequate appellate review as defendants who have money enough to buy transcripts." *Id*. at 19.

[18] *Id*. at 20, 24.   [20] *Id*. at 23.

[19] *Id*. at 19, 24–25.   [21] *Id*. at 30.

[22] "The Illinois cases cited by the petitioners establish only that trial errors cannot be reviewed in the absence of a bill of exceptions, and not that a transcript is essential to the preparation of such a bill. To the contrary, an unbroken line of Illinois cases establishes that a bill of exceptions may consist simply of a narrative account of the trial proceedings prepared from any available sources—for example, from the notes or mem-

in what sense, they could not afford to pay.[23] Particularity of this kind is sometimes portrayed as a canon of all craftsmanlike legal analysis. Actually, it is a characteristic of the due process approach —was this particular individual provided the elements of a fundamentally fair procedure? But, even if particulars were ignored, and the more general question reached, Harlan thought the equal protection model was quite wrong. The plaintiffs really were asserting a due process claim to a fragment of state criminal procedure, thought Harlan, rather than complaining about the "classification" embodied in the price. They were asking to be treated differently rather than similarly, asking in fact, for a specific entitlement. Because they could not be entitled constitutionally to every resource needed or wanted for an appeal, Harlan argued that the particular necessity of this resource was the true issue, a traditional due process inquiry. Similarly, Harlan believed that treating the price as a classification of rich and poor was not what the majority really meant. If this classification was bad here, it ought to be bad anywhere; and the majority disavowed any intention of abolishing all fees for government service. Yet, if the nature of the particular entitlement was decisive, why advert to the wealth classification at all?[24]

Analytical frameworks do not, it is said, decide cases,[25] and, to be sure, the same facts do work their way into both approaches. The majority starts with a sensitivity toward exclusion of the poor and asks whether the importance of the interest, the intensity of the state action, and feasibility, require a remedy. Harlan would first examine the importance of the interest, verify that poverty caused the exclusion (other causes, like laziness, not deserving constitutional remedy), and conclude by weighing the state's legitimate interests. Nevertheless, the tools cut quite differently in *Griffin* and other kinds of cases. At bottom, equal protection makes one ask the

---

ory of the trial judge, counsel, the defendant, or bystanders—and that the trial judge must either certify such a bill as accurate or point out the corrections to be made." *Id*. at 30–31.

[23] The majority established the petitioner's poverty by noting that in an uncontradicted allegation "[t]hey alleged that they were 'poor persons with no means of paying the necessary fees . . . .' " *Id*. at 13. Justice Harlan, however, said that "[t]he record contains nothing more definite than the allegation that 'petitioners are poor persons with no means of paying the necessary fees . . . .' " *Id*. at 30.

[24] *Id*. at 35–36.

[25] Ely, *The Necklace*, 87 HARV. L. REV. 753 (1974).

wealth question; due process does not. Under the due process approach, new cases would emerge as increments to the federal constitutional definition of the essentials of ordered liberty.[26] No special significance would be given to poverty as the cause of the exclusion.[27] Under the equal protection approach, the distributive question is what brings the case up, and maldistributions of the right, other than according to wealth, would lack even prima facie constitutional significance. Equal protection also should frequently require social science or demographic evidence. In a due process case, we ask, Was this plaintiff excluded because of poverty? In an equal protection case, we should ask, in addition, How many poor people are injured and how much?[28] Thus, recognition of the wealth classification naturally draws attention to a wide variety of legal entitlements which are distributed by wealth; and, as to each, the Court must find something in the unimportance of the interest, the relative lack of involvement of the state or the sheer infeasibility of remedy, which precludes relief.

Fourteen years after *Griffin*, in *Williams v. Illinois* a majority of the Court again granted relief to an Illinois convict who could not afford to protect his right not to be in jail.[29] Williams had received the maximum sentence under Illinois law for petty theft—

---

[26] "[A] due process approach . . . considers each particular case on its own bottom to see whether the right alleged is one 'implicit in the concept of ordered liberty,' see *Palko* v. *Connecticut*, 302 U.S. 319, 325 (1937)." Williams v. Florida, 399 U.S. 78, 129 (1970).

[27] But see Goodpaster, *The Integration of Equal Protection, Due Process Standards, and the Indigent's Right of Free Access to the Courts*, 56 IOWA L. REV. 223, 239 (1970): "There is a "virtual identity of the new equal protection to due process." Hence, "Harlan's preference for the use of due process over equal protection in many of the recent equal protection decisions is a preference of form, rather than substance, simply *elegantia juris*, as is equally the majority's preference for the use of equal protection." *Id.* at 245.
Wealth is often mentioned in due process cases but is not the triggering mechanism requiring the invocation of due process protection. Gideon v. Wainwright, 372 U.S. 335 (1963); Boddie v. Connecticut, 401 U.S. 371 (1970); Fuentes v. Shevin, 407 U.S. 67 (1972); Goldberg v. Kelly, 397 U.S. 254 (1970); Mitchell v. W.T. Grant, 416 U.S. 600 (1974).

[28] Problems of quantitative analysis as to whether minority groups were injured as a class arose in San Antonio School Dist. v. Rodriguez, 411 U.S. 1 (1973); see generally, Clune, note 8 *supra*, at 659 n.10; Jefferson v. Hackney, 406 U.S. 535 (1972); see Bennett, *Liberty, Equality and Welfare Reform*, 68 Nw. U. L. REV. 74, 91–92 (1973); Hobson v. Hansen, 327 F. Supp. 844 (1971); see generally the three review articles in 7 J. HUM. RES. 275–325 (1972).

[29] 399 U.S. 235 (1969). See Paroutian v. United States, 471 F.2d 289, 290 (6th Cir. 1972); Hart v. Henderson, 449 F.2d 183, 185 (5th Cir. 1971); Wade v. Carsley, 433 F.2d 68, 69 (5th Cir. 1970); and United States v. Gaines, 449 F.2d 143 (2nd Cir. 1971).

one year in prison, a five-hundred-dollar fine and five-dollar court costs. Unable to pay the fine, he was sentenced to work it off in a prison at five dollars a day.[30] The Court, after reference to studies showing the enormous numbers of prisoners in jail for the same reason,[31] held that, under the Equal Protection Clause, Illinois could not imprison a man for failure to pay a fine, at least not until other, less onerous collection devices were attempted. Here was an age-old problem of equal justice for rich and poor—the ability of the wealthy to buy their way out while the nonwealthy spent time in our (often) nightmarish prisons. The majority did not fail to rest on equal protection grounds, and Harlan did not fail to take exception.[32] Curiously, however, Harlan concurred in the result, on due process grounds, and chided the majority for the careful limits placed on its holding, limits which Harlan accepted as consistent with the due process but not the equal protection approach.[33] Thus, Harlan agreed with all but the label. To see how Harlan approved

---

[30] 399 U.S. at 236.

[31] *Id.* at 240 n.13. The Court specifically cited two studies. (1) SIVERSTEIN, DEFENSE OF THE POOR IN CRIMINAL CASES IN AMERICAN STATE COURTS 123 (1965), reported that an estimated "5,000,000 persons a year are charged with misdemeanors in state courts." The report further estimated that "there are 1,250,000 indigent misdemeanor defendants a year." *Id.* at 125. Its estimate of how many defendants were jailed for failure to pay a fine, however, is flawed by an almost total lack of accurate data. The nationwide figure of 700,000 is based upon an extrapolation of the total number of persons jailed for misdemeanors in New Jersey. (2) RUBIN, THE LAW OF CRIMINAL CORRECTIONS (1965). The most recent data this study presented to the Court were nine years old but showed rather low rates of jailing for nonpayment.

Despite the inadequacy of the data cited by the Court, the plight of those too poor to pay fines is harsh. Rubin reported in a second edition of his work, published in 1973, that "[i]n Baltimore a ten month study in 1965 showed 80 percent of the 20,000 inmates were there for failure to pay fines. Of 27,000 persons fined in that period, 16,000 were unable to pay. In 1969, 43 percent of the persons serving post conviction jail terms in Arkansas were imprisoned in lieu of payment of fines. In New Jersey, 46 percent of the committed defendants were sentenced for nonpayment. Miami, Florida, also had a 46 percent ratio of nonpayment sentences to total commitments." *Id.* at 287 (2d ed. 1973). See also PRESIDENT'S COMM'N ON LAW ENFORCEMENT AND THE ADMINISTRATION OF JUSTICE, TASK FORCE REPORT: THE COURTS 18 (1967); REPORT OF THE PRESIDENT'S COMM'N ON CRIME IN THE DISTRICT OF COLUMBIA 394 (1966).

[32] 399 U.S. at 259–66. Some of the conclusions of the analysis of equal protection and due process presented throughout this section have been independently arrived at by others. See, *e.g.*, Note, *The Decline of the New Equal Protection: A Polemical Approach,* 58 U. VA. L. REV. 1489 (1972).

[33] "Today's holding, and those in the other so-called equal protection decisions, *e.g.*, *Douglas* v. *California, Anders* v. *California,* offer no pretense to actually providing equal treatment. . . .

"The reluctance of the Court to carry its equal protection approach to its most logical consequences accents what I deem to be the true considerations involved in this case, namely, whether the legislature has impermissibly affected an individual right or has done so in an arbitrary fashion." 399 U.S. at 261–62.

of a case extending *Griffin* is to see one essential way that the Burger Court has begun to constrain the earlier approach of the Court to wealth discrimination.

The significance of Williams as law is evidenced by the way the Court prospectively limited its holding. A broad, but logical, reading of the case, absent the Court's explicit rejection of it, would be that *Griffin* had been extended to the whole area of criminal sentencing. On this reading *Williams* could have opened the door to consideration of all reasons why poor people end up in worse jails for longer times than non-poor. At the extreme, scrutiny might have reached the statutory scheme of harsh sentences for crimes that poor people tend to commit, often because they are poor, and differential patterns of arrest, parole, and assignment to minimum security institutions.[34] Speculation about the ultimate sweep of the decision is hardly warranted, however, because the Court explicitly precluded so broad a reading. *Williams* can be read narrowly as being concerned only with the problem of poor people being in jail because they cannot pay a fine, that is, with the general tendency of the criminal justice system to let the non-poor pay a fine rather than go to prison. This would be the narrowest way to articulate the sense of justice offended by Williams's situation, and the one under which the ties to the *Griffin* precedent are kept very close; both cases are concerned with the state putting a price tag on freedom. Evidently aware of the logic of this interpretation, the Court took pains to warn off some of the common kinds of cases that might be forthcoming. The Court limited its holding to situations in which the prison sentence was

---

[34] "Indigent defendants receive unfavorable treatment at nearly all stages of criminal procedure and in all types of cases." Nagel, *Inequalities in the Administration of Criminal Justice*, 6 Mun. Ct. Rev. 27 (1966). The plight of the poor is so harsh that even "[racial] factors show less disparity than do the economic ones." *Id*. But see, Bullock, *Significance of the Racial Factor in Length of Prison Sentences*, 52 J. Crim., L.C. & P.S. 411 (1961). In Bullock's study, however, the economic factor was not separately or explicitly treated.

Arrests: see Katz, *Patterns of Arrest and the Dangers of Public Visibility*, 9 Crim. L. Bull. 311, 313, 317, 321 (1973); President's Comm'n on Law Enforcement and Administration of Justice Task Force Report: Crime and Its Impact—an Assessment 78 (1967). *Hearings:* Nagel, *supra*, at 1272, 1279; Berger, *Police Field Citations in New Haven*, 1972 Wisc. L. Rev. 382 and n.3, 383; Report of the Attorney General's Committee on Poverty and the Administration of Federal Criminal Justice 72–77 (1963); Kaplan, Criminal Justice 309–10 (1973). *Failure to have a grand jury indictment:* Nagel, *supra*, at 1280–81. *Conviction:* Rankin, *The Effect of Pretrial Detention*, 39 N.Y.U.L. Rev. 640, 641, 642 (1964); Berger, *supra*, at 383 n.4; Gerard, *A Preliminary Report on the Defense of Indigents in Missouri*, 1964 Wash. U.L. Q. 270, 315 (1964) [hereinafter cited as Gerard]. Landes, *An Economic Analysis of the Courts*, 14 J. Law & Econ. 61, 100 (1971) [hereinafter Landes]. *Probation:* Nagel, *supra*, at 1281 and 1282.

explicitly announced in the statutory scheme as a way of working off a fine.[35] There also may be, however, situations where the poor are sent directly to jail without the option of a fine under discretionary systems of sentencing, when the judge is able to discern, without specific inquiry, that the defendant would not be able to pay a fine if one were levied. Of particular concern was the common type of statute which allows prison or fine in the alternative or in combination, *e.g.*, a maximum sentence of ten thousand dollars or one year in jail.[36] Studies might show that under such statutes, poor people tend to go to jail while richer people go free on payment of fines.[37] The Court did not want to consider this kind of situation. But why?

The answer, I believe, is one of epistemology. Judicial investigation of such patterns would necessarily involve difficult questions. When the Court limits itself to de jure discrimination, as it did in *Williams*, I suspect that it does not want to ponder competing explanations of an empirical state of affairs. Often, this reluctance is expressed by a refusal to examine the "intent" of a statute or pattern of decisions by individual state officials.[38] There can be

[35] "Nothing in today's decision curtails the sentencing prerogative of a judge because . . . the sovereign's purpose in confining an indigent beyond the statutory maximum is to provide a coercive means of collecting or working out a fine . . . . [O]ur holding does not deal with a judgment of confinement for non-payment of a fine in the familiar pattern of alternative sentence of '$30 or 30 days'. We hold only that a State may not constitutionally imprison beyond the maximum duration fixed by a statute a defendant who is financially unable to pay a fine. . . . [N]o conclusion reached herein casts any doubt on the conventional '$30 or 30 days' if the legislature decides that should be the penalty for the crime." 399 U.S. at 264 (Harlan, J., concurring).

[36] See, *e.g.*, Mo. Stat. § 557.480; Cal. Penal Code § 19 (West 1970); and N.M. Stat. Ch. 40A-29-3(A).

[37] While I found no direct statistical data on this point, an inference can be drawn from the existing data. In his national study, Landes discovered that "[c]onvictions leading to prison sentences were lower in districts where estimates of the average wealth were higher, while convictions resulting in monetary fines were greater where average wealth was higher. One interpretation of this result is that the effect of wealth on the defendant's investment of resources into his case depended on whether penalties were jail sentences or fines." Landes, note 34 *supra*, at 101. Another interpretation is possible. Professor Gerard's study of the criminal process in Missouri discovered that "the indigent defendant not released on bail was about twice as likely to be sent to prison, [and] one-third as likely to be let off with a fine . . . as his counterpart." Gerard, note 34 *supra*, at 316. Thus a judge sentencing a convicted indigent is not as likely to levy a fine as he would if he were sentencing a wealthy convicted defendant.

[38] Jefferson v. Hackney, 406 U.S. 535, 541 (1972); San Antonio Independent School District v. Rodriguez, 411 U.S. 1, 26 (1972); see Ely, *Legislative and Administrative Motivation in Constitutional Law*, 79 YALE L.J. 1205 (1970); MacCallum, *Legislative Intent*, 75 YALE L.J. 754 (1966); Brest, *Palmer v. Thompson: An Approach to the Problem of Unconstitutional Legislative Motive*, 1971 SUPREME COURT REVIEW 95.

good reason for such reluctance. Lack of knowledge about precisely what is wrong may demand prickly cynicism by judges about
other branches of government (often in the form of presumptions)
and astringent remedies which cure an assumed harm by cutting
off the ability to act at all. In the judicial process, as well as outside it, ignorance plus power breeds distrust and oppression. Demonstrating how the problem of epistemology might lead to minor
judicial tyranny can, for purposes of discussion, be considered in
two parts, the problem of proof and the problem of substantive
equality.

A. THE PROBLEM OF PROOF

Let us assume an action against the state claiming that sentencing
under alternative fine-or-prison statutes tended to disfavor the poor.
Normally, it would be impossible for any one defendant to show
facts in his case that demonstrated that he was in jail because he
was poor. Of course, if the judge made a finding on this ground,
presumably *Williams* itself would control. In the vast majority of
cases, however, the defendant could only rely on statistical evidence of the pattern of imprisonment together with supporting
descriptive evidence about how sentencing usually operates under
the fine-or-prison statute (interviews with, and public statements
by, judges, expert testimony, etc.). Merely to enter this statistical
thicket could create difficulties that deter judicial action. The
Court might prefer the case-by-case approach simply to fend off
assembly and analysis of a mountain of data, or to save the criminal
justice systems of the states from system-wide audits by federal
courts. There are further problems. Once in the thicket, the Court
could not escape without making some hard judgments, hard both
in substance and methodology. To begin with, sentencing could
be compared only for similar crimes. Comparison across similar
crimes is certainly possible, but any time a control variable is
introduced into statistical analysis, statistical complexity is also admitted.[39]

---

[39] See note 28 *supra*. Perhaps the most awesome debate of all time over the importance
of variables is about the effect of schooling on test scores and social and economic mobility, a debate which looms over school finance lawsuits. To get a flavor of the vast
literature on this topic, see JENCKS, INEQUALITY: A REASSESSMENT OF THE EFFECT OF
FAMILY AND SCHOOLING IN AMERICA (1972), and the review of Chapters 6 and 7, Hauser
& Dickinson, *Inequality on Occupational Status and Income*, INSTITUTE FOR RESEARCH ON
POVERTY, Notes and Comments, October 1973.

Moreover, there is an important substantive question which must be answered on the basis of the comparison across crimes. Suppose we do find that for similar crimes, the poor receive heavier sentences and lighter fines than the non-poor. The Court in *Williams* makes the point that the length of sentences depends upon a multitude of facts in individual cases—how serious the intent, how many previous convictions, how severe the injury from the crime, and so on.[40] Could it be that the poor tend to rank higher in such factors? The Court might dismiss such a notion on abstract egalitarian suppositions about the equality of men. Surely, any comprehensive empirical investigation probably would be unpersuasive (although adding a few of the more obvious factors to the analysis, like previous criminal record and the amount stolen, might, if the anti-poor bias remained, strengthen the plaintiff's case). In other words, as always happens, empirical analysis can resolve only a finite number of possible explanations of an observed pattern. In the final analysis, the Court would have to assume that the state judges were not reckoning with the proper factors; and the state would have to strive to equalize the average sentences of poor and non-poor. Any system adopted by the state to guarantee equal sentences probably would represent an unparalleled centralization of the sentencing process. Perhaps the only feasible solution that would not violate the due process rights of individuals would be to impose uniform sentences on all defendants or, as Mr. Justice Blackmun suggested in the *Tate* case, do away with the fine-or-prison statute entirely.[41] Thus, the Court might be led to a position where the system permitting the anti-poor bias would have to be sacrificed in order to eliminate the bias. The good effects would go with the bad effects. Good effects, such as more benign sentencing in appropriate cases, presumably do exist. Equally important, the Court obviously prefers precise surgery to amputation of an entire facet of the criminal justice system of the states. What began as a problem of proof might lead, through inexorable assumptions and the legitimate need for sweeping remedies, to the conclusion that

---

[40] 399 U.S. at 243.

[41] "[T]he reversal of this Texas judgment may well encourage state and municipal legislatures to do away with the fine and to have the jail term as the only punishment for a broad range of traffic offenses. Eliminating the fine whenever it is prescribed as alternative punishment avoids the equal protection issues that indigency occasions." Tate v. Short, 401 U.S. 395, 401 (1970).

the Court vowed in *Williams* to avoid, that a state legislature may not constitutionally enact a certain type of criminal sentence.[42]

B. THE PROBLEM OF SUBSTANTIVE EQUALITY

Lurking beneath the problem of proof is a problem of substance which, if solved, could do away with the need for distrustful assumptions and draconian remedies, but demand, instead, judicial creativity akin to judicial legislation. Justice Harlan, in *Williams*, made the disarming point that if a man is absolutely without funds, prison is the only way to punish him under an alternative-type statute,[43] establishing at least one situation in which the state has no choice but to make poverty lead to the prison door, unless it is willing to leave unpunished and undeterred the crimes of poor people. Actually, for a small fine, the special problem of the utterly penniless man is not very serious in view of the Court's willingness to urge on the state such collection devices as the installment plan and such substitute transfer as the work farm.[44] But a realistic case is not hard to envisage, and Harlan discussed it, albeit obscurely.[45] The poorest man can come up with a hundred dollars out of his own earnings over twelve months, or in the economic value of part-time work for the state, but he can never, by any means, come up with ten thousand dollars. If the state may constitutionally impose a ten-thousand-dollar fine on a poor man, it may constitutionally send him to prison; for the ten thousand will never be collected; and all the poor men will go unpunished while all the rich men pay their fines. An escape from this Hobson's choice may be to impose a smaller fine on the poor man. If the problem be that he receive equal pain (and that his fellow potential poor criminals be threatened with equal pain), surely one thousand dollars, or even one hundred, hurts him as much as ten thousand does the rich man. Aware of this potential direction in the case, the perspicacious Harlan foresaw ominous consequences:[46]

---

[42] "The Constitution permits qualitative differences in meting out punishment and there is no requirement that two persons convicted of the same offense receive identical sentences . . . . 'The belief no longer prevails that every offense in a like legal category calls for an identical punishment without regard to the past life and habits of a particular offender.'" 399 U.S. at 243.

[43] *Id.* at 265–66.

[44] *Id.* at 244 n.21.

[45] *Id.* at 266.

[46] *Id.* at 261.

> If equal protection implications of the Court's opinion were
> to be fully realized, it would require that the consequence of
> punishment be comparable for all individuals: the State would
> be forced to embark on the impossible task of developing a
> system of individualized fines, so that the total disutility of the
> entire fine, or the marginal disutility of the last dollar taken,
> would be the same for all individuals.

Justice Harlan was nothing if not consistent. As in *Griffin*, he
viewed the problem in due process style as demanding investigation
of the situation of each and every individual defendant. Accordingly, the claim of the poor man for smaller fines cannot be distinguished from the claim of all men for a punishment exactly
fitting the criminal and the crime. Harlan was on firm ground
in not assigning this godlike task to human judges. But he was
wrong in thinking the task to be so great. First, in an equal protection framework, the problem is limited to the harm to poor
people. Once the differential harm to the protected class is remedied, there need be no further concern with differential burdens
which do not systematically affect protected classes.[47] Second, even
among poor people, the remedy need not be individually tailored.
The Court could require a schedule of fines fairly and thought-
fully designed to produce equal disutility on the average. One
possibility would be a fine of an equal percentage of earnings
(what are called "day fines" in the literature).[48] If the poor continued to be jailed more frequently under such a uniform schedule,
perhaps the schedule of fines could be made more progressive
with respect to wealth. On grounds of simplicity, however, the
Court might properly require no more than the simple, flat percentage system. Such a system would go most of the way toward
curing the wrong but would not represent a great interference
with the states' systems of criminal justice. Fines would not have
to be altogether abandoned nor would it be required that all prison
sentences for the same crime be equal. Trial judges possibly would
try to impose larger fines on the poor, feeling that the small fines

---

[47] That sentences vary enormously has been well documented. RUBIN, LAW OF CRIMI-
NAL CORRECTION 136–41, 266–69, 552–53 (2d ed. 1973).

[48] See, *e.g.*, Comment, 57 CAL. L. REV. 778, 812–21 (1969); Note, 101 U. PA. L. REV.
1013, 1024–26 (1953); Note, 64 MICH. L. REV. 938 (1966); see also, Fox, CONTEMPT
OF COURT 126–27 (1927); ABA, SENTENCING ALTERNATIVES AND PROCEDURES § 2.7,
Commentary 128 (Approved Draft 1968); NATIONAL COMM'N ON REFORM OF FEDERAL
CRIMINAL LAWS, STUDY DRAFT OF A NEW FEDERAL CRIMINAL CODE § 3302(4) (1970);
A.L.I., MODEL PENAL CODE § 302.1(1) (Proposed Official Draft 1962).

collected from persons of very small incomes would not be effective punishments. On the other hand they might not, especially with clear statutory instruction. Or the schedule of rates for a given crime could have a minimum of absolute dollars. In any event, the primary wrong, poor people in jail because of the outright impossibility of paying especially large fines, would be cured. The Court would not worry at all about individual poor (or non-poor) defendants who received larger than average fines (rates) or sentences, since it could now be assumed that poverty played no role in the outcome.

In summary, there could be both problems and solutions in future cases seeking to extend *Williams*. It is unfortunate that the Court seemed disposed not even to consider these problems in the proper case at the proper time, but that is not the most important criticism of the case. The real difficulty is the particular instrument of limitation chosen by the Court, the limitation to de jure discriminations. The limitation to de jure discriminations relieves the Court from inquiring why a state of facts exists; the state tells why in the statute. For this reason, de jure analysis is compatible with due process analysis; the law as applied to the facts of each case reveals on what basis the individual has been burdened. Thus, the broader significance of *Williams* may be that the limitations expressed there have taken the heart out of the equal protection analysis of *Griffin*, while seeming to extend the principle of that case. The one essential principle of *Griffin*, its departure from earlier cases, was the willingness to look beyond the law, which might appear equal, to the effect of the law. That is what bothered Harlan and caused him to dissent. Certainly there may be good reasons of judicial competence and restraint not to look beyond the law; but there also may be no reason. The danger in *Williams* is that the new majority on the Court has found a way never to consider empirical evidence about the fate of the poor, never to grant relief outside the area of de jure discriminations no matter how clear the facts.

It could be answered that such pessimism is not warranted by the facts. The Court has not in fact decided any cases extending the *Williams* principles.[49] Furthermore, *Griffin*, while not involving

---

[49] Except for the Court's decisions in *Tate* and *Schoonfield*, the Court has not returned to this area. The lower federal courts and the state courts have been very active on behalf of indigents. See note 37 *supra*, and cases collected in 31 A.L.R.3d 926 (Supp. 1974).

a de jure discrimination, did not involve an empirical investigation either. But pessimism returns when we consider that formalistic principles may afford a solution to the paradox of condemning wealth discriminations; the de jure principle releases the Court from the tug of reality because most of reality is not relevant to it. Rightly considered, *Griffin* should be a signal for a gradual careful investigation of the fate of poor people before our systems of criminal justice. The *Griffin* principle has a natural tendency to unearth wealth contradictions; the de jure principle has no such tendency. If the Court limits itself to de jure discrimination, it need only supervise the majestic consistency of the law, and the relative ease of that task may prove impossible to resist.

Concurring in *Griffin*, Justice Frankfurter quoted Anatole France's satirical observation that "the law, in its majestic equality, forbids the rich as well as the poor to sleep under bridges, to beg in the streets, and to steal bread."[50] *Griffin* was bold insofar as it purported to look beyond that majestic equality; *Williams* may have returned the scrutiny of the Court to its earlier focus.

III. The Price of Remedy—Boddie, Kras, and Ortwein

The series of cases dealing with fees for civil remedies which poorer people cannot afford (exclusionary access fees) has had shorter history, intense doctrinal evolution, and less favorable outcome for the poor than the criminal process cases. To hold unconstitutional a price on a government activity other than the criminal process was a step of potentially enormous significance.[51] Justice Harlan for the majority in *Boddie* minimized this potential for expansiveness with a due process approach that might have served well to discipline the unruly tendencies of many types of poverty cases.[52] But the Burger Court, with Mr. Justice White in an increasingly characteristic alliance, preferred no expansiveness. In *United States v. Kras*[53] and *Ortwein v. Schwab*,[54] *Boddie* was dis-

---

[50] 351 U.S. at 23.

[51] Note, 26 VAND. L. REV. 25 (1973).

[52] Boddie v. Connecticut, 401 U.S. 371 (1971). The restrictiveness of Justice Harlan's due process analysis has been pointed out by others. Note, 48 IND. L.J. 105, 108–09 n.13 (1972); Note, 20 KAN. L. REV. 554, 561 (1972). It has also been suggested that "[i]n their use of the due process standard, the majority apparently sought to provide the State legislature and courts with a definite set of guidelines for deciding future questions of access to civil courts." Note, 46 TUL. L. REV. 799, 803 (1972).

[53] 409 U.S. 534 (1972).   [54] 410 U.S. 656 (1972).

tinguished with such formalistic, hair-splitting precision that it was effectively limited to its own facts. What began as a restrained, somewhat formalistic expansion of the rights of the poor died still-born in an exercise of pure and empty logic.

Boddie was the mirror image, or film negative, of *Griffin* and, hence, a semblance of *Williams*. Aside from the civil-criminal distinction, the facts of *Boddie* and *Griffin* are similar. The complaint of the appellants in *Boddie* was that they could not afford court fees and the service of process (usually amounting to about sixty dollars), Griffin's that he could not afford stenographic transcripts. The inverted resemblance of the two cases occurs in that Harlan's due process argument is found in the majority in *Boddie*, whereas the equal protection approach is found in an opinion concurring in the result,[55] and in dissent in *Kras* and *Ortwein*.[56] A further symmetry, ironically intentional, is that Mr. Justice Douglas, concurring in the result in *Boddie*, criticized the majority's opinion as being too expansive and unprincipled.[57] Lest matters seem excessively balanced, Justice Black, the author of the Court's opinion in *Griffin*, wrote a vigorous dissent in *Boddie*, objecting to the extension of *Griffin* outside the criminal process.[58]

Harlan's effort to forge due process into a tool that bridges the civil and criminal process and also operates solely for the benefit of the poor is impressive. To reach civil cases, he identified the essence of due process as the right to notice and hearing in civil cases.[59] In order to limit the holding to the poor, or more precisely to those poor who are excluded by access fees, Harlan used two devices. First, he pointed out that other cases involving the right to be heard recognized special characteristics of groups as bearing on the need for constitutional protection. For examples, in *Mullane v. Central Hanover Trust Co.*,[60] notice by publication was held insufficient for known as opposed to unknown creditors, and in the *Covey* case, for an incompetent.[61] By this means, Harlan was able to recognize the fact that poor people have a unique claim without focusing on poverty as the nature of the uniqueness.

---

[55] 401 U.S. at 383–86. (Douglas, J., concurring in result.)

[56] 409 U.S. at 457–58; 410 U.S. at 661–64.

[57] 401 U.S. at 384–85.   [59] *Id.* at 337 and n.3.

[58] *Id.* at 389–94.   [60] 399 U.S. 306 (1950).

[61] Covey v. Town of Sommers, 351 U.S. 141 (1956).

Poor people simply have an acceptable excuse for not paying; poverty is important only insofar as it removes the ordinary interpretation put on nonpayment, that is, waiver or default. The second way that poverty is recognized without adverting to a wealth classification is by giving small weight to the state's interests in the price system. The Court has two principal tools with which to minimize state interests. Interests directly conflicting with granting the constitutional right can be shrunken with "mereness."[62] The Court will frequently say something like "mere cost and efficiency are not sufficient to justify the denial of important constitutional rights."[63] The other means are variants of the less onerous alternative: the interest can be achieved by a means which does not deny constitutional rights.[64]

In *Boddie*, both techniques were used. The Court discussed the state's interest in allocating scarce resources, a euphemism for not raising more taxes, and found simply no cause for denying access to the courts.[65] Two other state interests were raised by the defen-

---

[62] "We have therefore repeatedly held that laws which actually affect the exercise of these vital rights cannot be sustained merely because they were enacted for the purpose of dealing with some evil within the State's legislative competence, or even because the laws do in fact provide a helpful means of dealing with such an evil. Schneider v. State, 308 U.S. 147 (1939); Cantwell v. Connecticut, 310 U.S. 296 (1940)." U.M.W., District 12, v. Illinois State Bar Ass'n., 389 U.S. 217, 222 (1967). "Mereness" is just a conclusory label used to identify a valid interest which the Court thinks does not take precedence over a competing interest. See text *infra*, at notes 65–68; see also, Wisconsin v. Yoder, 406 U.S. 205, 213–15 (1972); Tinker v. Des Moines Independent Community School District, 393 U.S. 503, 506–07, 509 (1969); Chaplinsky v. New York, 315 U.S. 568, 571–72 (1942); Baird v. State Bar of Arizona, 401 U.S. 1, 6–8 (1971); Graham v. Richardson, 403 U.S. 365, 374–75, 376 (1971); Traux v. Raich, 239 U.S. 33, 42 (1915).

[63] In Stanley v. Illinois, 405 U.S. 645, 656 (1972), the Court stated that "the Constitution recognizes higher values than speed and efficiency." As regards the public purse, the state "must do more than show that denying welfare benefits to the new residents saves money. The saving of welfare costs cannot justify an otherwise invidious classification." Shapiro v. Thompson, 395 U.S. 618, 633 (1968). "The conservation of the taxpayers purse is simply not a sufficient state interest to sustain a durational residence requirement which, in effect, severely penalizes exercise of the right to freely migrate and settle in another State." Memorial Hospital v. Maricopa County, 415 U.S. 250, 263 (1974).

[64] Aptheker v. Secretary of State, 378 U.S. 500, 508 (1964). See Struve, *The Less-Restrictive-Alternative Principle and Economic Due Process*, 80 HARV. L. REV. 1463 (1967); Wermuth & Mishkin, *The Doctrine of the Reasonable Alternative*, 9 UTAH L. REV. (1964).

[65] "We are thus left to evaluate the State's asserted interest in its fee and cost requirements as a mechanism of resource allocation or cost recoupment. Such a justification was offered and rejected in Griffin v. Illinois, 351 U.S. 12 (1956). In *Griffin* it was the requirement of a transcript could be waived as a convenient but not necessary predicate to court access, here the State invariably imposes the costs as a measure of allocating its judicial resources. Surely, then, the rationale of *Griffin*, covers this case." 401 U.S. at 382.

dant: prevention of frivolous litigation and paying for notice to the defendant. As to the first, the Court urged means more directly aimed at frivolous litigation, noting that payment of a fee no more certifies genuine claims than nonpayment signified frivolous ones.[66] As to the second, a similar rebuttal was issued, notice to defendants could be had without the plaintiffs paying for it.[67] It might be pointed out that the Court's treatment of the asserted state interests is somewhat conclusory. Clearly, there is a limit to the cost the Court will or can impose on states. If providing a service free exceeds this limit, the interest in allocating scarce resources will be found to outweigh denial of rights. Likewise, paying a fee does have some effect in discouraging frivolous claims and, although most ends can be achieved by many different means, the means before the Court may be by far the most productive and inexpensive.[68] The real questions are whether the degree of cost and the number of claims discouraged outweigh the rights denied. When the Court judges the cost insufficiently high, or is willing to demand other means, it signals what balance has been struck without telling us how it was struck—"mereness" is a conclusion, not a reason. It may be, however, that the ultimate balancing and weighing of factors for which we pay judges is an inarticulable process. The most that can be expected from doctrine is a clear signal of that process.

Analytically, Harlan's due process approach to exclusionary fees is strained. Consider the reformulation of poverty as simply a waiver or default beyond the control of the potential plaintiff. This would suggest that other examples of nondeliberate waiver might be forgiven by the Court, for example, the inaction of the invincibly ignorant or incompetent (to take the facts of *Mullane* and *Covey*). But this direction is obviously barren. *Boddie* was about people who could not afford fees; its extensions would concern fees for other types of remedies, not other reasons why people

---

[66] "Not only is there no necessary connection between a litigant's assets and the seriousness of his motives in bringing suit, but it is here beyond present dispute that appellants bring these actions in good faith. Moreover, other alternatives exist to fees and cost requirements as a means for conserving the time of courts and protecting parties from frivolous litigation, such as penalties for false pleadings or affidavits, and action for malicious prosecution or abuse of process, to mention only a few." *Id.* at 381–82.

[67] *Id.* at 382.

[68] Ely, *The Constitutionality of Reverse Racial Discrimination*, 41 U. Chi. L. Rev. 723, 729 (1974); see also Ely, *Flag Desecration: A Case Study in the Roles of Categorization and Balancing in First Amendment Analysis*, 88 Harv. L. Rev. 1482, 1485 (1975).

do not take advantage of remedies.[69] The comparison of nonpayment of a fee to lack of notice is also inapt. The point of procedural due process cases is that the state may not finally change and determine legal rights without telling the owner of the rights about the proceeding and giving him a right to be heard. In *Boddie* situations, the state takes no action affecting the rights of any individual. It takes no action at all, but merely waits receptively for individuals to bring their claims forward. When the potential plaintiff does come forward and is refused a free trial of his claim, he is even less in a position of lack of notice. There is a sense in which he is denied a hearing by the demand for a fee which he cannot pay, but not the same sense as in the hearing cases, which dealt with people who never learned of the hearing.[70] If a fee for a hearing is a denial of due process as to those unable to pay the fee, the analogy would seem irresistibly complete. Any hearing as to which an outright exclusion would be unconstitutional must be made free for those unable to pay a fee. Again there is the problem in holding a de facto exclusion equivalent to a de jure one.

Harlan's escape from the logic is brilliant. As in *Williams*, he apparently saw the problem and tried to deal with it. Rather than focusing exclusively on the fee as a denial, he carved out a class of civil claims where the state can be thought of as affecting individual rights even though it takes no action, that is, one where the state has a monopoly on changing legal relationships.[71] *Boddie* involved the marriage relationship. The parties to a marriage must obtain a judicial decree before they are legally entitled to act con-

---

[69] Before *Kras*, the lower federal courts applied *Boddie* to bankruptcy fees, *In re* Naron, 334 F. Supp. 1150 (D. Or. 1971), and to prisoner prepayment of court appearance costs in their private suits, Brant v. Power, 339 F. Supp. 65 (W.D. Wis. 1972). Since *Kras*, *Boddie* has been cited for the proposition that procedural due process requirements are flexible. Crowe v. Eastern Bank of Cherokee Indians, Inc., 506 F.2d 1231, 1237 (4th Cir. 1974), and that the state may not establish any prerequisites for access to divorce courts, Stottlemeyer v. Stottlemeyer, 224 Pa. Sup. 123, 135–36 (1973).

[70] Goldberg v. Kelley, 397 U.S. 254 (1970); Wisconsin v. Constantineau, 400 U.S. 433 (1971).

[71] 401 U.S. at 376–77. Professor Michelman has pointed out: "It is unclear whether the 'monopolization' of relief deemed important in *Boddie* . . . was monopolization by the judiciary or monopolization by the government as a whole (where the only alternative to judicial relief is a governmental concession) . . . . That the *Ortwein* opinion does not cite appellant's opportunity to negotiate with the welfare officials as an alternative avenue to relief . . . may perhaps be taken as suggesting the latter interpretation." Michelman, *The Supreme Court and Litigation Access Fees: The Right to Protect One's Right—Part 1*, 1973 Duke L. Rev. 1153, 1157 n.15 (1973).

trary to the legal strictures of marriage; they may not execute a consensual agreement that can be later relied on as a defense of their actions. In this sense, then, the state stands perpetually active against a change in the relationship and denial of the hearing that could produce a change is, to that extent, similar to denial of a hearing that would create a change. Harlan's logic transforms nominal plaintiffs into substantive defendants, and invites a cautious exploration of the areas in which the state could be said to have a monopoly over legal relationships.

The monopoly doctrine has little to recommend it but its caution. As dissenters in *Boddie* observed,[72] the state has a monopoly on all final determinations of legal rights. What seems more relevant than the absence of any possible private settlement is the importance to individuals of the legal remedy. Again, the difficult de facto/de jure problem. The relevance of no private settlement is really that the claimant may be in desperate need of a legal remedy. This situation may be found in many areas where private settlements are available.

Though Harlan's conclusion in *Boddie* was cautiously drawn, it does not foreclose the possibility that the monopoly test might have been relaxed enough to include remedies as to which private settlement was merely difficult.[73] No flood of lawsuits or slippery slope need have been produced by such limited permissiveness, especially since Harlan attached another condition, that the substance of the claim be constitutionally protected, in other contexts, called a "fundamental interest."[74] The monopoly test and the importance test,

---

[72] "A State has an ultimate monopoly of all judicial process and attendant enforcement machinery. As a practical matter, if disputes cannot be successfully settled between the parties, the court system is usually 'the only forum effectively empowered to settle their disputes. Resort to the judicial process by these plaintiffs is no more voluntary in a realistic sense than that of the defendant called upon to defend his interests in court.'" 401 U.S. at 387 (Brennan, J., concurring in part).

[73] "[W]e wish to re-emphasize that we go no further than necessary to dispose of the case . . . . We do not decide that access for all individuals to the courts is a right that is, in all circumstances, guaranteed by the Due Process Clause of the Fourteenth Amendment so that its exercise may not be placed beyond the reach of any individual." *Id.* at 382.

[74] But see Mr. Justice Stewart dissenting, in United States v. Kras, 409 U.S. 434, 456 n.7 (1972).

Mr. Justice Harlan indicated marriage's fundamentality by calling it a "fundamental human relationship." Boddie v. Connecticut, 409 U.S. 371, 374 (1971). He noted that "this Court on more than one occasion has recognized, marriage involves interests of basic importance in our society." *Id.* at 376. Concurring in Griswold v. Connecticut, 381 U.S. 479, 499–502 (1964), and dissenting in Poe v. Ullman, 367 U.S. 497, 522–25

under a due process umbrella, might have served well as a more conservative way to approach the problem than a pure equal protection approach. Of course, due process still does not explain why fees as exclusion are singled out from the universe of exclusionary influences; but this is a minor point. The real point is that Harlan had fashioned a tool by which the access of the poor to important civil remedies could be explored on a case-by-case basis without a constant question being raised by the tools of analysis as to how the poor could be legitimately excluded from any remedy.

Given its first opportunity to expand *Boddie* slightly,[75] however, the four Justices appointed by President Nixon, plus Mr. Justice White, decided instead to take the monopoly test literally. If any private action could have the juridical significance of the civil remedy, fees could be demanded for the remedy. The context makes it clear that the approach is indeed this extreme. *United States v. Kras* involved a debtor who could not afford the fee in bankruptcy. It is true that debts, unlike marriage, can be adjusted privately. Private settlement of debts will be given juridical significance. Yet the remedy of bankruptcy is predicated upon such settlement being impossible (the debtor having nothing to bargain with)[76] or, at the least, undesirable, lest a debtor be required to mortgage his future. Thus, in practice, and under the explicit policy of the federal bankruptcy laws, the private remedy is either no remedy at all or worse than no remedy. There could not be an easier case to decide under the standard of a difficult, as opposed to nonexistent, private remedy. Are there any civil cases outside the area of family law where private settlement is not possible? Perhaps in order to forestall efforts to pursue the vanishing possibilities under the monopoly doctrine of *Boddie*, the *Kras* Court found a separate and independent ground for denying the claim. The pecuniary interest in being free from debt lacked the constitutional importance at-

---

(1961), Justice Harlan said that marriage is a fundamental interest because it is one of the basic values " 'implicit in the concept of ordered liberty.' " 381 U.S. at 500. See generally, Kauper, *Penumbras, Peripheries, Emanations, Things Fundamental and Things Forgotten: The Griswold Case*, 64 MICH. L. REV. 235, 236 (1965).

The classic criticism of Justice Harlan's due process analysis is that "it leaves judges without any fixed textual standard in determining which rights are fundamental." Redlich, *Are There "Certain Rights . . . Retained by the People?"* 37 N.Y.U.L. REV. 787, 799 (1962). See text *supra*, at note 58.

[75] United States v. Kras, 409 U.S. 434 (1972); see Note, 48 IND. L. REV. 452, 460 (1973); Note, 40 B'KLYN L. REV. 168 (1973).

[76] 409 U.S. at 455.

tached to marriage.[77] It is true that Harlan's limitation of *Boddie* to fundamental interests was problematic from the outset. But foreclosing importance to the individual as a relevant criterion, just as *Dandridge*[78] and *Rodriguez*[79] did in the equal protection area, was unquestionably one of the most restrictive possible interpretations.[80]

To the dissenters in *Kras*, it was clear that the majority had overruled *Boddie sub silentio* by limiting the *Boddie* principle to its own facts.[81] In the later case, *Ortwein*,[82] two Justices limited their protestation of the demise of *Boddie* to the perfunctory comment that although *Boddie* seemed to compel relief, the majority remained firm in their view.[83] Was there anything in the cautious *Boddie* holding that deserved such confinement, especially when *Boddie* represented a kind of belated triumph for the due process approach to poverty recommended by Harlan in *Griffin?* It is hard to see how. *Kras* can be read only as a wholesale retreat by the Court from the problem of exclusionary fees for civil remedies. The barrier of judicial formalism against poverty analysis is stronger when no case of a certain kind can succeed than when some can succeed. If we regard *Boddie* as a cautious alternative to the pure equal protection analysis of exclusionary fees, it seems that the majority did not regard the general problem as sufficiently important to be worthy of even a cautious compromise.

IV. A COST OF MOVEMENT—DURATIONAL RESIDENCY REQUIREMENTS

The durational residency cases are concerned with the requirement that before a person may become eligible for a beneficial government program, like welfare, college education, or medical care, he must have resided in a place for a certain period of time, often one year. These cases are a nice complement to *Rodriguez*[84] because the advantage to wealthier citizens of capturing tax re-

---

[77] *Id.* at 445, 446.

[78] Dandridge v. Williams, 397 U.S. 471, 484–86 (1970).

[79] San Antonio Independent School District v. Rodriguez, 411 U.S. 1, 30–34 (1973).

[80] Jefferson v. Hackney, 406 U.S. 535, 546 (1972); Richardson v. Belcher, 404 U.S. 78, 81 (1971); Lindsey v. Normet, 405 U.S. 56 (1972).

[81] 409 U.S. at 453–57, 458.

[82] Ortwein v. Schwab, 410 U.S. 656.

[83] *Id.* at 661, 664 (Brennan and Stewart, JJ., dissenting).

[84] See Part VII *infra.*

sources is lessened to the extent that poorer persons can simply move in. Indeed, if poor persons could move anywhere freely, there might be little or no geographical dispersion of average family wealth. Another way to say approximately the same thing is that we can equalize tax resources either by moving resources to people, as was tried in *Rodriguez*, or people to resources, as is done when a poorer person moves to a wealthier place. Durational residency requirements are a cost of movement, a cost which excludes people who dare not move unless they can rely on essential public services as soon as they arrive. Durational requirements are probably not the main obstacle to movement. Zoning laws which impose expensive conditions on living in a wealthy residential area are probably primarily responsible.[85] These have not been reviewed by the Supreme Court except that a case to be discussed later,[86] denying standing to challenge such laws, was decided last Term. Another obstacle, similar to zoning, is the exclusion of low income housing by law, the constitutionality of which has been considered by the Court in *James v. Valtierra*,[87] also to be discussed later herein.

Three cases dealing with durational residency requirements will be considered here. *Shapiro v. Thompson*,[88] *Vlandis v. Kline*,[89] and *Memorial Hospital v. Maricopa County*[90] deal respectively with welfare, college education, and health care. Again, the pattern is that an exploratory holding by the Warren Court, using an equal protection approach founded upon a sensitivity to the real plight of the poor before the legal order, has been replaced by the Burger Court with a due process approach which is highly unpredictable and, in this area, not even especially tailored to the plight of the poor. As with *Griffin* and *Williams*, the argument here is that there has been a clear retreat in doctrine even though in all cases the plaintiffs win. (John Marshall's technique was said to be seizing power while seeming to turn it down;[91] the Burger Court's may be abandoning doctrines by seeming to extend them).

---

[85] See note 10 *supra;* see also, Note, 84 HARV. L. REV. 1645 (1971); Babcock & Bosselman, *Suburban Zoning and the Apartment Boom*, 111 U. PA. L. REV. 1040, 1068–72 (1963); Branfman, Cohen & Trubek, *Measuring the Invisible Wall: Land Use Controls and the Residential Patterns of the Poor*, 82 YALE L.J. 483 (1973).

[86] See Part VII *infra*.   [89] 412 U.S. 441 (1972).

[87] 402 U.S. 137 (1971).   [90] 415 U.S. 250 (1974).

[88] 394 U.S. 618 (1968).

[91] In Marbury v. Madison, 1 Cranch 137 (1803), the Court was in "the delightful position . . . of rejecting and assuming power in a single breath." McCLOSKEY, THE AMERICAN SUPREME COURT 42 (1960).

Shapiro certainly dealt with a problem of poor people. Legislative history of the provisions of the several states imposing durational residency requirements left no doubt that the explicit purpose was to limit the influx of poor people seeking higher benefits.[92] (Connecticut would waive the one-year requirement if the migrant came with a job or three months' funds, indicating it was not prejudiced against poor people as long as they become poor in Connecticut.)[93] The majority in *Shapiro* found essentially two faults with the requirements. The first was that not all those excluded were shown to have moved for the purpose of obtaining higher benefits.[94] To the extent a law does not even achieve the purpose intended by the legislature, the Court owes it little deference. Sloppy laws which infringe on constitutional rights without achieving majority aims have the least chance of being upheld. But the Court was not saying that had the legislature passed a more refined law, which excluded only those who migrated solely for the purpose of obtaining higher welfare benefits, the law would have been upheld. On the contrary, the second fault was that the purpose of excluding such people is an unconstitutional one,[95] so that even if a hearing were held to determine each person's intent, a durational residency requirement could not be sustained. The emphasis here was not so much that poor people were excluded as opposed to non-poor as that the right of the poor to travel was as great. *Shapiro* stands more for the constitutionally protected right of travel than it does for the constitutional invalidity of selectively harming the poor. Yet the result really could not be reached without both elements. The dissenters point out that the travel interest in the case is weak. For one thing, the burden on travel, in the sense of number of persons actually deterred, was slight.[96] Probably, the

---

[92] 394 U.S. at 627–33.

[93] A person who is " 'living in an established place of abode and the plan is to remain' . . . does not have to wait a year for assistance if he entered the State with a bona fide job offer or with sufficient funds to support himself without welfare for three months." *Id.* at 636 n.16.

[94] "In actual operation . . . the three statutes enact what in effect are nonrebuttable presumptions that every applicant for assistance in his first year of residence came to the jurisdiction solely to obtain higher benefits. Nothing whatever in any of these records supplied any basis in fact for such a presumption." *Id.* at 631.

[95] "[A] State may no more try to fence out those indigents who seek higher welfare benefits than it may try to fence out indigents generally." *Ibid.* "[N]either deterrence of indigents from migrating to the State nor limitation of welfare benefits to those regarded as contributing to the State is a constitutionally permissible state objective." *Id.* at 633.

[96] *Id.* at 650, 671–72.

one-year requirement did not impose a nearly large enough cost to deter migration for higher benefits, that is, taken as a whole, high benefits plus the one year wait, still amounted to a strong net stimulus to interstate travel.[97] On the one hand, the special constitutional status of the right to travel was certainly necessary to the result. Mr. Justice Brennan expresses the dual nature of the grounds when he said that the state could no more reduce its welfare expenditures by excluding the poor than reduce its school expenditures by this means.[98]

Of course, the state must be free to reduce expenditures, and any time the state reduces welfare expenditures it excludes only indigents. Must every welfare cut be declared unconstitutional because it falls discriminatorily upon the poor? Hardly. It is the combination of travel and poverty that rises to constitutional importance. In one sense, the combination is even more important than the sum of its parts. For the poor, the right to travel and resettle is particularly vital as a means of escaping poverty. Even in *Shapiro*, the state was concerned with persons who were trying to escape poverty by obtaining higher welfare benefits. The converse of this view is the one with which I begin. The ability of wealthier persons in one place to keep out poorer persons from another place is one of the most powerful mechanisms for maintaining a system of wealth stratification.

Vlandis v. Kline[99] did not technically involve a durational residency requirement, but rather a statutory definition of college students as non-residents. Unmarried college students with a legal address outside Connecticut anytime during the year preceding registration could not thereafter become a resident for purposes of paying resident tuition as long as they remained students, notwithstanding any other indicia of residence, *e.g.*, driver's license, voter registration, home ownership, marriage to a Connecticut resident with a job in Connecticut.[100] Married students could escape nonresident status by residing in Connecticut at the time of applica-

---

[97] *Ibid.*   [99] 412 U.S. 441 (1972).

[98] *Id.* at 633.

[100] In *Vlandis*, one appellee married a lifelong Connecticut resident and moved to a permanent residence in Storrs, Connecticut, from California. She had a Connecticut driver's license, her car was registered in Connecticut, and she was registered to vote in Connecticut. The other appellee was unmarried. She too had moved her residence to Connecticut, had a Connecticut driver's license, had her car registered in Connecticut, and was a registered Connecticut voter. *Id.* at 443–44.

tion.[101] Of course, these definitions are the functional equivalents of a durational residency requirement inasmuch as they impose a waiting period before a migrant is entitled to the benefits of a government program, but unmarried students could never become qualified so long as they remained students.

The line-up of the Justices around the result, which struck down the Connecticut statute as violative of the Due Process Clause, indicates some of the problems in the case. Mr. Justice Douglas joined in dissent with Mr. Justice Rehnquist; Mr. Justice Marshall wrote a concurring opinion which was joined by Mr. Justice Brennan. Again, the heart of the controversy was the use of the Due Process Clause. The *Shapiro* equal protection problem in the case was whether the state could require college students to wait four or more years to become residents. Connecticut had somewhat masked this issue by purporting to allow all bona fide residents the lower tuition. Nevertheless, it was obvious that the only fact that blocked students from becoming residents was that they came to the state primarily to take part in the government program, the same fact which required the welfare applicants in *Shapiro* to wait a year.

The equal protection issue on these facts is rather straightforward: Can the discrimination between the two classes be justified? Mr. Justice Marshall joined the majority in basing the decision on the irrebuttable presumption doctrine, but strongly hinted that even a one-year waiting period, not concealed by a presumption of non-residency, should be void on equal protection grounds. For him, the travel interest in *Shapiro* had sufficient vitality to support relief where a poverty aspect was at least not readily apparent.[102] The Douglas joinder in the Rehnquist opinion which approved the

---

[101] "With respect to married students, § 126(a)(3) of the Act provides that such a student, if living with his spouse, shall be classified as 'out of state' if his 'legal address at the time of his application for admission to such a unit was outside of Connecticut.'" *Id.* at 442–43.

[102] Mr. Justice Marshall saw *Vlandis* as involving "only the validity of the conclusive presumption of non-residency erected by the State, and as such, concerns nothing more than the procedures by which the State determines whether or not a person is a resident for tuition purposes." *Id.* at 455. He saw, however, that the Court's opinion suggested the larger issue whether a state "may impose a one-year residence requirement as a requisite to qualifying for in-state tuition benefits." *Ibid.* Citing *Dunn* and *Shapiro*, Mr. Justice Marshall expressed serious doubt as to a state's ability to set such requirements "in light of well-established principles, under the Equal Protection Clause of the Fourteenth Amendment, which limits the States' ability to set residence requirements for the receipt of rights and benefits bestowed on bona fide state residents." *Ibid.*

Connecticut statute as a reasonable way to determine residence under the circumstances shows that Mr. Justice Douglas regarded
wealth discrimination as an essential element of *Shapiro* and one
lacking in *Vlandis*.[103]

The equal protection analysis, then, amounts to a weighing of
the interests actually in conflict—the constitutional status of the
burdened activity (higher education), the identity of the group
harmed (poor or non-poor), and the interests of the state in maintaining the burden (making non-residents pay more, determining
who are residents by some feasible method). In contrast, the due
process analysis of the majority rests on a rather minor technical
aspect of the statute, the fact that not all of the students classified
as non-residents could validly be presumed to be in Connecticut
solely for the purpose of attending college. To the majority, this
"irrebuttable presumption" was the fatal flaw. To be sure, the flaw
is real for some students whose attendance at a Connecticut college
is only a part of a firmly held purpose to reside in the state. The
same type of flaw in *Shapiro*, however, was merely noted in passing
because it was not the important constitutional infirmity of the
statute.

Why should such flaws have constitutional significance? As Justices Rehnquist and Douglas pointed out, it is no answer to say
that the statute is sloppy.[104] The Supreme Court of the United
States is not charged with the housecleaning of state statutes. There
are really only two satisfactory answers, both of which lead back
to equal protection analysis. First, there may be a satisfactory way
for the state to determine, on an individual basis, what a student's
real intentions are. Much would still depend on what evidence the
state would be allowed to consider against the student (*e.g.*, living
in a dormitory vs. owning a house). Even so, the real question is
why should the Constitution be used to compel the state to be so
careful? Many commentators on *Vlandis* and similar cases have
pointed out that almost every law involves an "irrebuttable pre-

---

[103] Justices Douglas and Rehnquist claimed that it is not the student plaintiffs who
are discriminated against or even most severely affected by the Connecticut statute.
Rather, Connecticut parents are really those most interested in the Court's decision.
Id. at 468–69. They are the ones whose tax dollars have paid and will continue to pay
for the state university.

[104] "[T]he fact that a generally valid rule may have rough edges around its perimeter
does not make it unconstitutional under the Due Process Clause of the Fourteenth
Amendment." *Id.* at 465–66.

sumption."[105] A 55-mph speed limit irrebuttably assumes that every driver is unsafe at a greater speed; a "no picnicking" sign assumes that every picnicker is messy or noisy. Such statutes take no account of *grand prix* drivers and woodsmen eating organic food. The job of refining general laws to fit individuals is both limitless and pathless, if there is nothing special about the people hurt or the interest protected, especially where the state has good grounds for not refining the law. The alternative assumption is that the state could not constitutionally use any external evidence to classify a student as a non-resident other than that used for non-students; with regard to the disputed element of intention to abide in the state, the state would have to take the student's word just as it takes the word of non-students. Here, the need for an equal protection analysis is even clearer because, as in *Shapiro*, the Court would be holding that the state could not constitutionally discriminate against persons coming solely to take part in a government program.

Some have praised the Court for its approach in demanding that the mechanisms of a statute fit its purpose.[106] The advantages are that individuals who were not intended to be burdened can be protected; constitutional rights can be protected without contravening any interest of the state; the result is costless liberty, an ideal solution for a judicial conservative. But the disadvantages are also great. Why should the Supreme Court devote its own scarce resources to the task of general legislative housecleaning; why not let well-represented groups take care of themselves in the legislative process? What standards can possibly guide the Court under a housecleaning mandate? Of course, it is possible to combine an equal protection approach with a means-ends approach. To the extent that special protection is justified on substantive equal protection grounds, a tighter relationship of mechanism to purpose will be required.[107] There is no particular reason not to adopt this blend of conservatism and activism. *Shapiro* itself rested both on

---

[105] Tushnet, ". . . *And Only Wealth Will Buy You Justice*"—*Some Notes on the Supreme Court, 1972 Term*, 1974 Wis. L. Rev. 177, 183 (1974); Note 72 Mich. L. Rev. 800, 834–36 (1974).

[106] See Gunther, note 2 *supra*, at 43–46.

[107] In Professor Gunther's means-focused approach, "when classifications such as race or interests such as speech are involved, tighter reins on the legislatures would remain appropriate." *Id.* at 24. Professor Gunther's model would establish constraints on legislative choices in other areas as well.

a legislative burdening of those not intended to be covered and the constitutionality of burdening those who were intended to be covered. The greater danger in *Vlandis* is that the Court will abandon all links with the new equal protection. The attractions of so doing are those of judicial formalism. Not being tied to such recurrent social problems as those of poor people, the Court is spared much of the constant pressure to widen its protections. Moreover, the tool, being without principles, is easy to limit. If the test is the outrageousness of the classification, how much consensus can be garnered for the proposition that one law upheld by the Court is really much more outrageous than another struck down? The Court is able to intervene with a display of ingenuity and craftsmanship in an occasional case of blundering injustice, yet is not bothered by the constant challenge of deciding whether the judicial process is capable of taking another step toward solving some endemic problem of justice.

Memorial Hospital v. Maricopa County[108] illustrates a new frontier in *Shapiro*-type cases as they relate to poor people, as pointed out in Mr. Justice Douglas's concurring opinion. An Arizona statute required a year's residence in a county as a condition to a patient's receiving non-emergency care at the county's expense. The county refused either to reimburse Memorial Hospital for its treatment of a resident indigent or to provide care itself through the county hospital. Mr. Justice Marshall's opinion for the Court struck down the statute on the basis of *Shapiro*. The only difference between *Shapiro* and *Maricopa* was that between welfare and non-emergency health care, a point disposed of by the majority on the ground that non-emergency care was as much a necessity as a welfare check.[109] The cavalier brusqueness of *Shapiro* greeted the state's argument that it needed to limit the cost of its program: "a State may not protect the public fisc by drawing an invidious distinction between classes of its citizens, . . . so appellees must do more than show that denying free medical [*sic*] to new residents saves money."[110] Mr. Justice Rehnquist, in dissent, made the point that, given a fixed amount of resources for medical care, if more people become eligible for care, the income defi-

---

[108] 415 U.S. 250 (1974).

[109] *Id*. at 259.   [110] *Id*. at 263.

nition of indigency may go up.[111] Another possibility is that the level of benefits would go down. Why is it more important to protect potential patients who have not lived in an area for one year than patients who fall just above an income condition or patients who cannot be admitted because of overcrowding? The answer, in *Shapiro* terms, is the additional weight of the interest in travel. It is constitutionally better simply to spend less across the board than to exclude poor interstate travelers.

Here, Mr. Justice Douglas parted company with the majority. Like Rehnquist, he found the disincentive to interstate travel posed by the failure to provide free non-emergency care too attenuated to be given constitutional recognition. The ground he did regard as adequate was discrimination against the poor, but not the poor traveling interstate. For Mr. Justice Douglas, *Rodriguez* implied the constitutionality of a state providing its best medical services where there are the fewest poor people.[112] To provide, further, that the poor may not move to the better places unless they wait a year to qualify for health services was too much. Mobility of the poor from county to county is significantly discouraged by the Arizona statute. This aspect of the Douglas opinion is interesting because it suggests, as a fallback position in the wake of *Rodriguez*, that a state may have a constitutional choice between providing services to poor people or not limiting their mobility toward places where there are services.

There is a further and more remarkable part of the Douglas opinion. The opinion begins with a sentence that refers the reader to an appendix: "The legal and economic aspects of medical care are enormous; and I doubt if decisions under the Equal Protection Clause of the Fourteenth Amendment are equal to the task."[113] The appendix itself,[114] called "Gourmand and Food—A Fable," is a farcical, classical libertarian tract on the effects of government intervention. The "Fable" begins with government certification of all cooks, which raises the price of eating in a restaurant, proceeds through prepaid insurance and government cash grants to allow all citizens unlimited meals in restaurants of choice, and

---

[111] "Given a finite amount of resources, Arizona after today's decision may well conclude that its indigency threshold should be elevated since its counties must provide for out-of-state migrants as well as for residents of longer standing." *Id.* at 279.

[112] *Id.* at 271.   [113] *Id.* at 270.   [114] *Id.* at 274–76.

ends with licensed dishwashers, national compulsory restaurant insurance, elaborate equipment, and, finally, when everyone in the country is discovered one day to be either preparing or eating or providing food, economic collapse. Readers of Supreme Court opinions have a hard enough time understanding what is going on without being subjected to the multiple meanings of fables and parables, yet the meaning of this one seems clear enough. Mr. Justice Douglas seemed to be saying that, given the nature of our health services industry, he would hesitate at declaring a place at a first-class hospital a fundamental right even if good medical care as such were to be considered a fundamental right. Making more people eligible for the expensive health care may be only subsidizing a lot of waste and hastening the day of an apocalypse. Of course, his objection is dangerous. It is essentially the same one that leads to defense of low educational spending on the ground that more dollars produce nothing for the children; the factual assumption is rather sweeping and gratuitous. Nevertheless, by concurring in the result, Mr. Justice Douglas limited the danger. He apparently would be willing to see states experiment with various methods and levels of health care, for various subgroups of the population, as long as protected minorities do not systematically carry the downside risk. In the area of health care, he would apparently accept the presumption of the need for fancy treatment, as a constitutional matter, only on behalf of those who least frequently obtain it. In marked contrast to the wide-ranging speculation, the Douglas opinion was the posture of the Chief Justice and Mr. Justice Blackmun. They concurred on the result without opinion. Perhaps talk in the majority opinion about the necessities of life disturbed them because it smacked of extending fundamental interests into the social and economic areas fenced off by *Dandridge* and *Rodriguez*. There is another possibility. One of the advantages of formalism, discouragement of future litigation, is perhaps most perfectly served by the absence of any opinion at all. Silence is perfect formalism.

The three travel cases provide excellent contrasts between formalistic and authentic models of decision-making as well as particularly clear proof of how difficult the factual questions may be under an authentic doctrine. Are excluded college students predominantly poor? Is modern medicine a waste? In Marshall's *Mari-*

copa opinion, we catch a glimpse of the problems of isolating the *Shapiro* travel interest from poverty as a suspect classification, the theme next to be explored.

V. Post-Script, 1974 Term

In the 1974 Term, the Court decided two cases that develop the themes treated in this section. In *Sosna v. Iowa*,[115] a one-year residency requirement for divorces was upheld. Mr. Justice Rehnquist for the majority (including Mr. Justice Douglas) distinguished *Shapiro* (and *Dunn v. Blumstein*)[116] on the ground that the interest of the state in regulating family life is stronger than in the fiscal and administrative interests asserted in the earlier cases.[117] *Vlandis* was distinguished because it involved a statutory presumption rather than a reasonable waiting period,[118] a formalistic distinction not to be taken seriously by legislators and thus granting *Vlandis* only technical vitality. The dissent of Justices Marshall and Brennan placed exclusive emphasis on the fundamentality of the travel interest in the earlier cases.[119] The conspicuous absence of Mr. Justice Douglas from the usual triumvirate of dissenters in individual rights cases was surely for the same reason which led him to dissent in *Vlandis* and to concur, with reservations, in *Maricopa*, the absence or ambiguity of the poverty interest. Thus, Mr. Justice Douglas now occupies the exact opposite of the position formerly held by Justice Harlan. Rather than routinely denying wealth as a preferred ground in equal protection cases, however, Mr. Justice Douglas now insists upon it in cases where the fundamentality of the protected interest is not particularly compelling.

The other case, *Weinberger v. Salfi*,[120] involved a different kind

---

[115] 419 U.S. 393 (1975).

[116] *Id.* at 405–07. While *Shapiro* involved the right to travel, *Dunn* was a class action brought against a Tennessee law "which barred persons from registering to vote unless, at the time of the next election, they would have resided in the State for a year and in a particular county for three months." *Id.* at 400. The Court struck down the Tennessee law as a violation of the Equal Protection Clause on the grounds that a suspect classification, recent interstate travel, was being used to infringe upon a fundamental right, the franchise for less than compelling state interests. Dunn v. Blumstein, 405 U.S. 330, (1972), noted in 86 Harv. L. Rev. 104 (1973); 1973 Wis. L. Rev. 914.

[117] 419 U.S. at 407.

[118] *Id.* at 409.

[119] *Id.* at 418–27.

[120] 95 S. Ct. 2457 (1975).

of waiting period, a nine-month "duration of relationship" test for social security benefits. The terms "widow" and "child" were defined in the statute to exclude surviving wives and children who had their respective relationships to the wage earner less than nine months prior to his death. Mr. Justice Rehnquist wrote the Court's opinion for a majority of six.[121] He had been a consistent, powerful critic of the doctrine of irrebuttable presumptions.[122] His analysis left little doubt that the basic technique of requiring individualized hearings to effect statutory purpose, while still available to the Court as a remedy, will henceforth be invoked only when certain widely accepted constitutional limits are exceeded. In other words, the doctrine that an "irrebuttable presumption" offends the Constitution is apparently dead.

Mr. Justice Rehnquist's opinion is an authoritative exegesis of recent cases involving the irrebuttable presumption and similar doctrines. The statutory provision of the Social Security Act was faced squarely in terms of its likely purpose, the discouragement of marriages entered primarily to obtain social security benefits. It was frankly conceded that the nine-month provision was a "prophylactic rule," a term used in the opinion to denote a rough classification which filters out many applicants who do not fit the purpose of the statute, and fails to filter out many who do.[123] Such rules are legitimate, Mr. Justice Rehnquist tells us, if they satisfy the following standards (here I interpret somewhat from his treatment of prior cases in addition to relying upon explicit statements): (1) There is an abuse which Congress might legitimately desire to avoid. (2) The prophylactic device rationally can be thought to protect against occurrence of the abuse (without necessarily preventing most abuses or even a substantial amount of them). (3) The expense and other difficulties of individual determinations justify imposition of a rule.[124] (In connection with this requirement, the likely effectiveness of hearings is obviously relevant. Mr.

---

[121] Mr. Justice Douglas wrote a separate dissent in which he does not address the question of poverty but claims the statutory provision "invades the right to a jury trial." *Id.* at 2476.

[122] Mr. Justice Rehnquist has consistently attacked the doctrine that an irrebuttable presumption is per se unconstitutional. See U.S. Dept. of Agriculture v. Murry, 413 U.S. 508, 522–27 (1972); Vlandis v. Kline, 412 U.S. 441, 463–69 (1973); Cleveland Board of Education v. LaFleur, 414 U.S. 632, 657–60; Sosna v. Iowa, 419 U.S. 393, 409 (1975); see also, U.S. Dept. of Agriculture v. Moreno, 413 U.S. 528, 545–47 (1972).

[123] 95 S. Ct. at 2473.   [124] *Id.* at 2469–73.

Justice Rehnquist argues that, on the facts of the *Salfi* case, hearings would likely not be any improvement over the duration of relationship test.[125] The superiority of hearings over the statutory presumption is also the only, and somewhat weak, explanation offered of *Vlandis*.)[126] (4) Constitutionally protected interests are not burdened, as in *Stanley* and *LaFleur*.[127] (5) The rule was not motivated by a "bare Congressional desire to hurt politically unpopular groups" (explaining *Murry* and *Moreno*).[128] Thus, the "irrebuttable presumption," as an independent source of constitutional invalidity, is dead, and the remedy of requiring individual hearings to determine the applicability of legislative purpose to individuals, is now tied to substantive constitutional standards.[129]

VI. WEALTH AS A SUSPECT CLASSIFICATION

The threshold issue I would now address is whether poverty shall even be recognized as a suspect classification.[130] Presently, the Court is divided. The Nixon Justices deny the existence of the doctrine. Holdings of the Warren Court in which wealth discrimination played a significant role are interpreted by these Justices as resting exclusively on the fundamentality of the interest burdened,

---

[125] *Id.* at 2475–76 and n.15.

[126] Mr. Justice Rehnquist said that the *Vlandis* Court held that where a state purports "to be concerned with residency, it might not at the same time deny to one seeking to meet its test of residency the opportunity to show factors clearly bearing on that issue." *Id.* at 2470. He goes on, however, to say that a hearing is not required in the present case because "the benefits here are available upon compliance with an objective criterion, one which the legislature considered to bear a sufficiently close nexus with underlying policy objectives to be used as the test for eligibility." *Ibid.*

[127] *Id.* at 2470.

[128] *Id.* In Weinberger v. Wiesenfeld, 420 U.S. 636 (1975), the Social Security Act provision, 42 U.S.C. § 402(g), providing widows but not widowers with survivors' benefits while caring for minor children was struck down by the Court as a violation of the equal protection guarantees of the Fifth Amendment on the grounds that the provision employed an entirely irrational gender-based distinction which denigrated the efforts of women whose earnings significantly contribute to their families' support.

[129] Barring a showing of invidious discrimination, petitioners can "present evidence that they meet the specified requirements [of the federal or State eligibility test]; failing in this effort, their only constitutional claim is that the test they cannot meet is not so rationally related to a legitimate legislative objective that it can be used to deprive them of benefits available to those who do satisfy that test." 95 S. Ct. at 2470.

[130] See, *e.g.*, Nowak, note 18 *supra*, at 1109–22; Coons, Clune & Sugarman, *A Workable Constitutional Test for State Financial Structures*, 57 CALIF. L. REV. 305, 348, 358–71, 386 (1969); Note, 82 HARV. L. REV. 1068, 1124 (1968); Note, 81 HARV. L. REV. 435 (1967); Michelman, *Protecting the Poor through the Fourteenth Amendment*, 83 HARV. L. REV. 1355 (1969).

specifically voting and the criminal process.[131] Brennan, Douglas, and Marshall recognize wealth discriminations as affecting the intensity of judicial scrutiny.[132] Whenever the other Justices join with these three, the preferred ground is, verbally, a traditional means-end approach[133] or the kind of due process approach employed in *Vlandis*.[134] Presumably, part of the reason why only three Justices support the doctrine goes to the question, once recognized, How can the doctrine be limited, when all aspects of our society and government are permeated by wealth effects? There is also, however, a genuine issue as to the theory of suspect classifications, which I will focus on first. One view of the basis of suspect classifications, which I call the individualistic view, regards the evil identified by the phrase "suspect classification" as treatment of an individual as though he is exclusively a member of a group, that is, not as a unique individual.[135] The other, which might be

---

[131] In *Rodriguez*, Justices Powell, Stewart, Blackmun, Rehnquist, and Chief Justice Burger cited Harper v. Virginia Bd. of Elections, 383 U.S. 663 (1966), to show that strict judicial scrutiny is triggered by the presence of a fundamental interest and not mere wealth discrimination. 411 U.S. at 29.

In Ross v. Moffit, 417 U.S. 600 (1974), Justices Rehnquist, Stewart, White, Blackmun, Powell, and Chief Justice Burger formed a majority which held that an indigent who had already had one appeal and court appointed counsel did not have a right to have counsel appointed for a subsequent discretionary appeal to the state's highest court. Mr. Justice Rehnquist, writing for the Court, cited *Griffin v. Illinois* and *Douglas v. California* for the proposition that the Fourteenth Amendment requires only that an indigent have an adequate opportunity to present his claims, and said that both clauses are necessary to explain the result. Justices Brennan, Douglas, and Marshall dissented. They wrote that *Douglas*, which rested heavily on *Griffin*, "was grounded on concepts of fairness and equality: not notions of adequacy.... [T]he 'same concepts of fairness and equality, which require counsel in a first appeal of right, require counsel in other and subsequent discretionary appeals.'" 417 U.S. at 621. The underlying perception is "that 'there can be no equal justice where the kind of appeal a man enjoys depends on the amount of money he has.'" *Id.* at 619.

[132] "This Court has frequently recognized that discrimination on the basis of wealth may create a classification of a suspect character and thereby call for exacting judicial scrutiny." 411 U.S. at 117 (Marshall, J., dissenting). To determine if such scrutiny will actually be applied, "we have generally gauged the invidiousness of wealth classifications with an awareness of the importance of the interests being affected and the relevance of personal wealth to those interests." *Id.* at 122.

Justices Brennan and Douglas, in dissent, have written that "wealth . . . like race, is a suspect classification." Britt v. North Carolina, 404 U.S. 226, 241 (1971).

[133] U.S. Department of Agriculture v. Moreno, 413 U.S. 528 (1973).

[134] U.S. Department of Agriculture v. Murry, 413 U.S. 508 (1973).

[135] "[W]hat differentiates sex from such nonsuspect statutes as intelligence or physical disability, and aligns it with the recognized suspect criteria, is that the sex characteristic frequently bears no relation to ability to perform or contribute to society. As a result, statutory distinctions between the sexes often have the effect of invidiously relegating the entire class of females to inferior legal status without regard to the actual

called the class conflict or counter-majoritarian view, emphasizes the disability of whole groups in the political process and the concomitant special need for judicial protection of certain groups.[136] By and large, the individualistic view is predominant on the Court. It explains why the expansion of suspect classes has run more to women,[137] illegitimate children,[138] and aliens[139] than to the poor. On a scale of anti-individualism, poverty is not the worst offender. Poverty is relative (compare the largely dichotomous categories of race, sex, alienage, illegitimacy), less visible and stigmatizing, and, for the individual, less permanent—upward and downward economic mobility are common. On a scale of class disabilities, however, poverty would rank very high. It is an endemic aspect of every part of our social and economic life; its relativity is one of the most startlingly stable social phenomena (the strata of personal income have remained in uncannily stable ratios to each other for decades);[140] it seems totally immune to political attack

---

capabilities of its individual members." Frontiero v. Richardson, 411 U.S. 677, 686–87 (1973). See also DeFunis v. Odegaard, 416 U.S. 312, 332–33 (1974) (Douglas, J., dissenting).

[136] Clune, note 8 *supra*, at 659 n.10.

[137] Frontiero v. Richardson, 411 U.S. 677 (1973); Reed v. Reed, 404 U.S. 71 (1971). A majority of the Court has not declared sex a suspect classification in explicit terms. For a summary of the Court's sex discrimination decisions in the 1974 Term, see Ginsburg, *Gender in the Supreme Court: The 1973 and 1974 Terms*, 1975 SUPREME COURT REVIEW 1.

[138] Weber v. Aetna Casualty & Surety Co., 406 U.S. 164 (1972). Mr. Justice Powell employed a strict scrutiny approach in *Weber* because he believed the state's actions touched on "sensitive and fundamental personal rights." *Id.* at 172. However, Mr. Justice Marshall writes that "[a] clear insight into the basis of the Court's action is provided by its conclusion: "[I]mposing disabilities on the illegitimate child is contrary to the basic concept of our system that legal burdens should bear some relationship to individual responsibility or wrongdoing. Obviously, no child is responsible for his birth and penalizing the illegitimate child is an ineffectual—as well as an unjust—way of deterring the parent. Courts are powerless to prevent the social opprobrium suffered by these hapless children, but the Equal Protection Clause does enable us to strike down discriminatory laws relating to status of birth. . . .'"
"Status of birth, like color of one's skin, is something which the individual cannot control, and should generally be irrelevant in legislative considerations. Yet illegitimacy has long been stigmatized by our society. Hence, discrimination on the basis of birth—particularly when it affects innocent children warrants special judicial consideration." San Antonio Ind. School District v. Rodriguez, 411 U.S. 1, 108–09 (1973) (Marshall, J., dissenting).

[139] Graham v. Richardson, 403 U.S. 365 (1971).

[140] Lampman, *What Does It Do for the Poor?—A New Test for National Policy*, 34 THE PUBLIC INTEREST 66, 72 (1974): Shares of "Total Money Income" Received by Fifth

or even war;[141] the disabilities and abilities associated with wealth are pervasive and among the most highly important on our scale of values. Thus, the suspectness of poverty depends pretty much on what is the proper theoretical basis for the doctrine of suspect classifications. What is the proper basis?

The individualistic perspective seems both misleading and incomplete. Consider the matter of an individual's ability to escape from the status, *e.g.*, the commonplace of escaping poverty by upward mobility versus the difficulty of a black passing as a white. Whether or not some individuals escape is insignificant compared to those who do not. If the non-escapees are vulnerable and weak economically, socially, and politically, their situation is identical to another class whose individual members are less able to escape. Imagine a society like some of the Pygmalion experiments,[142] where people are randomly assigned in rotation to the status of being "black" and thus suffer the same disabilities as blacks in our society. If we were to rank the protected minorities to determine the intensity of judicial protection, a topic addressed by Justice Marshall in his *Rodriguez* dissent,[143] should the ability of individuals to es-

---

of Families, Ranked by Income:

Families	1950	1970
Lowest fifth	4.5	5.5
Second fifth	12.0	12.0
Third fifth	17.4	17.4
Fourth fifth	23.5	23.5
Highest fifth	42.6	41.6

For the same comparison of 1947, '49, '59, '64, and '67, see LAMPMAN, ENDS AND MEANS OF REDUCING INCOME POVERTY 47 (1971).

[141] "It is remarkable that [the distribution of money income] shows little change over decades . . . , in spite of staggering changes in the size and role of the family (with the decline of the three-generation extended family); the pattern of participation in the labor force (with men starting to work later and retiring earlier and more women working away from home); the decline of farming and self-employment and the rise of service industries, government employment, and professional and technical occupations; a rise in the median income of black, relative to white families; the increase in taxes and government spending; the growth of fringe benefits; and the conversion of ordinary income into capital gains. The explanation must be that some of these changes offset others in such a way as to sustain a constancy in the shares of the several fifths, but we have no good explanation as to why the offsetting changes should balance out so neatly." Lampman, note 140 *supra*, at 71–72.

Regarding the theoretical significance of a pattern of constancy amid continuous dislodging forces, see the discussion of "equifinality" in STINCHCOMBE, CONSTRUCTING SOCIAL THEORIES (1968).

[142] ROSENTHAL & JACOBSON, PYGMALION IN THE CLASSROOM (1968).

[143] The care with which the Court scrutinizes discrimination against a minority will vary with the relative political power of the group, with the relevance of the discriminated characteristic to any constitutionally acceptable legislative purpose, and with the constitutional significance of the interests affected. 411 U.S. at 104–05, 109.

cape the social category be determinative, or the intensity of domination by the majority?

There is also the question of what kinds of laws should be stricken. The term "hostile legislation" has been used.[144] Certainly, the fact that a few black people happen to be injured by a law is not enough to defeat the law if most black people are intentionally aided by it. From *Plessy*[145] onward, the inquiry has been toward both intent and effect[146] because the Civil War Amendments were directed at a systematic pattern of intentional domination and stigmatization.[147] Thus, we cannot even recognize what legal behavior violates the equal protection of the laws without engaging in a type of class analysis which takes into account both the overall impact on the protected minority, an empirical question which is often intensely problematic, and the orientation of the whole social and legal process to the minority on the particular issue, what is called the question of intent. That question, too, is often so empirically baffling that a restraint-minded judge needs no doctrine but only factual skepticism to resist a claim of discriminatory intent. It might be said that the Civil War Amendments changed the focus of "individual rights" (as they are called in textbooks) from government versus the individual to majority versus minority.

The second question to be addressed is how to limit the doctrine once it is recognized as having even greater strength than Mr. Justice Marshall suggests. Because of its importance, this problem will be attended in both the next section and in the conclusion. Here I note only the broad outlines of the problem and some solutions. If wealth effects were sufficient in themselves to invalidate a government program, programs would fall in such numbers that the conformity of the result with constitutional intent might well be doubted.[148] The Court has already provided an essentially satisfactory solution to this problem summarized by the Marshall dissent

---

[144] Fairman, Reconstruction and Reunion, 1864–88 1228 (1971).

[145] Plessy v. Ferguson, 163 U.S. 537 (1896).

[146] Palmer v. Thompson, 403 U.S. 217 (1871); Jefferson v. Hackney, 406 U.S. 535 (1972). See note 38 *supra*.

[147] Fairman, note 144 *supra*, at 1213–14, 1228, 1237.

[148] "The economic status of an individual is, by definition, ubiquitous and persistent in its significance. . . . To undertake a constitutional challenge to all . . . indirect wealth classifications would be to commence a fool's errand." Carrington, *On Egalitarian Overzeal: A Polemic against the Property Tax Cases*, 1972 Ill. L.F. 232, 247 (1972).

in *Rodriguez.*[149] Wealth effects would be fatal only when coupled with fundamental interests. Such interests may be those with special connections to constitutional rights (arguably education) and those with subsistence value to the recipients.[150] I would urge another category, interests which have a special relevance to escaping poverty, *e.g.*, both travel and education. Anytime the legal system is employed to reinforce the existence of the disability which gives rise to special judicial protection that protection ought to be at its most intense. Notice that the theory of suspect classifications has an effect on the ranking of interests as well as the ranking of the minorities. If importance to the individual is the key, probably subsistence rights, like housing and welfare, are most important. If, however, a flaw in the majoritarian process is the guideline, then of first importance is the use of the legal system to maintain wealth stratification; of second importance are general disabilities in the representative process, like high primary fees and perhaps education as it relates to political efficacy; while of last importance are subsistence rights. Subsistence rights do not do anything with the basic pattern of poverty; and the Court cannot do much about them anyway, since improvement ultimately implicates all the basic mechanisms of redistributing income.[151] In sharp contrast, striking down principal legal mechanisms of maintaining wealth stratification could have a large impact. Consider two discussed in this article: the ability of urban communities to price out poor neighbors by means of zoning and the ability of rich localities to keep local tax resources for local services.

Discussion of flaws in the representative process leads us to the third topic, instances where state action should be struck down re-

---

[149] "[A]s the nexus between the specific constitutional guarantee and the nonconstitutional interest draws closer, the nonconstitutional interest becomes more fundamental and the degree of judicial scrutiny applied when the interest is infringed on a discriminatory basis must be adjusted accordingly." 411 U.S. at 102–03.

[150] "In *Shapiro*, the Court found denial of the basic 'necessities of life' to be a penalty. . . . [G]overnmental privileges or benefits necessary to basic sustenance have often been viewed as being of greater constitutional significance than less essential forms of governmental entitlements." Memorial Hospital v. Maricopa County, 415 U.S. 250, 259 (1974).

[151] An effective guarantee of subsistence would involve the Court in the entire spectrum of welfare programs, because the government can take away from one program what it gives with another, or demand the remedy of a transfer payment of a size sufficient to meet all subsistence needs. The idea of a Court-ordered national negative income tax is unthinkable. The Court must direct its energies toward more limited objectives.

gardless of the interest affected. If legal maintenance of wealth stratification is antithetical to the spirit of the Fourteenth Amendment, then any state action with this as its primary purpose and effect ought to be invalid. That is one reason why *James v. Valtierra*[152] is such a disturbing case. At issue in *James* was Article XXXIV of the California state constitution which required a majority vote in a referendum as a precondition for construction of governmentally subsidized housing for low income persons. The Article was adopted to negate a previous ruling of the California Supreme Court which removed the decision to build public housing from the routine constitutional power of referendum over legislative acts. The purpose of the Article, to vest the majority with power over the minority, was as clear as the constitutional issue.

The Court had previously held, in *Hunter v. Erikson*,[153] that open housing laws could not be singled out for advance approval by referendum. Nothing could more offend the spirit of the Fourteenth Amendment than isolating the volatile racial issue from the rest of the legislative process. If the coercive power of the majority is the danger, then it cannot be constitutional to require a plebiscite on issues as to which the constituency is known to be divided along majority/minority lines. Obviously, *James* was the same kind of case except it involved wealth divisions (with race in the background). The Court faced the issue squarely. Justice Black, joined by Justices Burger, Harlan, Stewart, and White, held simply that in *Hunter* the offensiveness of racial discriminations was the key. The dissenters, Justices Marshall, Brennan, and Blackmun, cited *Douglas v. California*[154] for the proposition that the state may not discriminate between rich and poor. No wonder the case was received as a blow to the possibilities of poverty as a suspect classification. It involved what have been urged here as the two most invidious forms of legal wealth discrimination: (1) a burden on an interest essential to the escape from poverty—residence in a wealthier place; (2) an intentional disabling of the poor in the legislative process.

The conservatism of the majority of the Court on the doctrine of wealth as a suspect classification, considering all three points made here, is not formalistic but frankly negative. It is the formal-

---

[152] 402 U.S. 137 (1971).

[153] 393 U.S. 385 (1969).   [154] 402 U.S. at 144.

ism of the friends of the doctrine that is surprising and interesting. On that ground, for example, Mr. Justice Marshall's otherwise superb dissent in *Rodriguez* may be soundly criticized. Indeed, that part of his opinion that expresses the mobility view is really of a piece with the effort of the judicial conservatives over fourteen years to focus scrutiny on the individual rather than the class. Marshall proposed that wealth is a weak suspect classification because of its low visibility, relativity, and non-permanency for the individual. Examined closely, these attributes boil down to an affirmation of the traditional American ethic that inequality may be tolerated as long as there is economic and social mobility.[155] No matter how permanent the pattern of equality or how serious its ramifications in the legal order, it may be tolerated if a significant turnover of individuals exists. As argued above, this view represents a confusion of values. If a pattern of discrimination exists in the political process, the only reference to individuals ought to be that those seeking relief are members of the injured class. The "mobility view" has the unacceptable consequence that grievous injuries produced by a serious flaw in the constitutional process can be regarded as of small importance. Of course, once the importance of the classification is denied, the other points follow, that neither acts of government which burden a fundamental interest nor acts with the sole purpose of reinforcing the bias irrespective of the nature of the interest are of any importance either.

Because the doctrine of wealth as a suspect classification is the most open way to recognize the ethical significance of wealth discriminations, it touches on pure paradox. The extreme importance and pervasiveness of wealth in our society argue for making wealth one of the most suspect of classifications. But the same facts certainly protect the vast majority of wealth discriminations from judicial remedy. Under these circumstances, the importance of principled limits is great. Some limits have been described and suggested in this section; the next section, on *Rodriguez*, and the conclusion, search for more.

---

[155] The idea that opportunity for the individual is the essential test of the justice of a system of economic and social stratification was expressed in COONS, CLUNE & SUGARMAN, PRIVATE WEALTH AND PUBLIC EDUCATION (1970). The central point of JENCKS, note 39 *supra*, is that there is no known means of providing such opportunity, particularly not through schooling, so that the distribution of wealth must be changed by direct means.

VII. The Price of Local Services—Rodriguez

San Antonio School District v. Rodriguez[156] is known as a school finance case. Certainly, had the plaintiffs prevailed, it would have been unlikely in the extreme that the principle of the case would have been expanded to all other services provided by local government. Nevertheless, it is as interesting to view the case as a poverty case as an education case. The legal policy which allows tax resources to be kept inside local boundaries is surely one of the most important ways by which the legal structure reinforces wealth stratification. It is interesting how the municipal boundary, as a kind of physical embodiment of legal formalism, is the bulwark against real factual problems seeking some solution. In the area of wealth classifications, this boundary was the focus of the travel cases, of *James v. Valtierra*, and of *Rodriguez*. In the racial area, it has apparently made unattainable the logical conclusion of the long development of school desegregation litigation begun with *Brown*.[157]

The unwillingness of the Court to recognize wealth as a suspect classification in *James* is probably based on the kind of problems raised by the *Rodriguez* case which in turn are those of *Williams*, *Boddie*, and *Vlandis* except on a larger scale. But the Court could not so easily brush aside claims of wealth discrimination in *Rodriguez* because the combination of education and wealth discrimination obviously presented a much more powerful case, at least to crucial swing members of the Court, than the *James* combination of wealth and housing.[158] As a matter of factual proof, the Court

---

[156] 411 U.S. 1 (1973).

[157] Brown v. Board of Education, 347 U.S. 483 (1954).

The proper constitutional weight to be given to local boundaries and local autonomy was the central question in Milliken v. Bradley, 418 U.S. 717 (1974). Chief Justice Burger gives these interests high value. *Id*. at 741–42. The dissenters took the position that, in Michigan, these interests were unusually lightly regarded by the state. *Id*. at 758–59, 768–69 n.4, 770, 783. Whether the boundaries can ever be crossed may depend on the timing of litigation and the corresponding personnel on the Court. Chief Justice Burger's majority opinion seemed to require that school officials caused the school or residential segregation, a seemingly impossible task. Mr. Justice Stewart, in a concurring opinion, seemed to accept the segregative impact of the actions of any local official. *Id*. at 755–57 and n.2. See Buchanan v. Evans, 96 S. Ct. 381 (1975) (Delaware statute drawing school district boundary).

The municipal boundary is also the organizational factor in exclusionary zoning, discussed in the next section in connection with Warth v. Seldin, 95 S. Ct. 2197 (1975).

[158] Mr. Justice White rested his dissenting opinion on the rational basis test, but the extent of justification he required of the state, indicated that some priority was given to the underlying interests. Mr. Justice Powell's majority opinion indicated that he could imagine a combination of education and wealth exclusion that would rise to constitutional significance. 411 U.S. at 25, n.60.

was correct in its position that discrimination on the basis of family wealth had not been made out.[159] As in *Williams*, however, the Court ventured beyond the facts before it to announce stringent, discouraging standards, some formalistic, others simply negative, to govern the application of the doctrine of wealth classification should it ever be recognized in the educational context.

I will deal with the significance of these limits here. The limits are: (1) The plaintiffs must be provided less than an adequate minimum of the service; that is, there is no constitutional right to the higher levels of services; and the inability to pay must be complete, that is, the plaintiffs must be completely without funds.[160] (2) Those unable to pay, and thus suffering the deprivation, must all be poor people; those able to pay, and especially those benefited, must be entirely non-poor people; that is, there can be no diversity of those affected with respect to income class.[161] The clear case in which both requirements are satisfied would exist if the public schools were financed by tuition; and some poor families, utterly unable to pay, were unable to provide their children with any education at all.[162]

Limiting relief to this analytically clear case serves the same function as the de jure approach in *Williams*, the monopoly rationale of *Boddie*, and the due process approach of *Vlandis*. It insulates against consideration of more important and common factual occurrences of the problem to which it pretends to respond in the less important case. And, as before, there is no sound basis for the refusal to go beyond the conceptually clear case. It is, in fact, the obvious force of the contrary position that creates the need for a clear stopping place. Similarly, although once the de jure position is abandoned the logical force of expansion is strong, problems of proof and implementation would thwart the rapid expansion that is feared.

A. LEVEL OF SERVICE AND ABILITY

I consider first the idea that the plaintiff must be completely unable to pay for the privilege in question. Although Mr. Justice Powell asserted total lack of funds to be a characteristic of plain-

---

[159] See Clune, note 8 *supra*.

[160] 411 U.S. at 20, 21, 25.

[161] *Id*. at 26.   [162] *Id*. at 25, n.60.

tiffs in the criminal process case,[163] in fact, inability to pay was merely an uncontested pleading in those cases.[164] Thus, the difficult question of exactly how poor is poor was never really answered. To simplify discussion, let us consider that the potential purchasers (whether an individual or a tax entity) may be possessed of three different amounts of wealth with respect to the amount required to purchase the privilege in question (a transcript, a given level of educational services, etc.): (1) Liquid and liquifiable assets are literally insufficient to pay; the net worth of the person could not buy the service. (2) Such assets are literally sufficient, but purchasers almost invariably, or usually, choose to purchase other things, that is, usually would sacrifice the privilege rather than pay. (3) Such assets are abundant enough that purchasers almost always or usually, choose to pay for the privilege if they must, but also are willing to claim they cannot afford it, that is, they will either pay for it or take it free if it is offered.

The controversy presumably concerns how far out of category (1), but short of (3), shall adjustments for wealth effects be made. The polar cases are easy; indeed they are virtually self-defining. To demand that a penniless man pay ten thousand dollars is not only heartless but ridiculous. Similarly, a rule that no one need pay who would rather not is merely impossible. If the state does not collect fees coercively it will collect taxes coercively instead, or else not offer the service. But when is it fair also to demand a little more sacrifice from poorer people for the exercise of a right? There does not appear to be one precise, easy solution to this general problem. But a number of guidelines can be formulated which collectively are far superior to the notion that, regardless of what the service is, the plaintiff must be completely unable to pay.[165]

The question boils down to how much wealth to redistribute through a fee system; there are two extremes. The minimum redistribution consistent with an idea of right would be that neces-

---

[163] See Wright v. Council of Emporia, 407 U.S. 451, 477 (1972) (Burger, C. J., dissenting).

[164] *Griffin*, 351 U.S. at 13; *Douglas*, 372 U.S. at 354; *Williams*, 399 U.S. at 237.

[165] If the state provides the service to all on an equal basis, free of charge, that is tax paid, the poor man might or might not be forced through the tax system to sacrifice more than the rich man, but the poor man's claim of unfairness could not be tied to the wrongful distribution of the particular service.

sary to permit the poorest man enough to pay for the privilege without going into bankruptcy. This minimum redistribution presumably would leave strong wealth effects in that richer people could afford the service increasingly easily, but the service would at least be practically available to all poor people who really needed it, the index of real need being willingness to undergo serious financial sacrifice. The maximum redistribution is where we try to make everyone equally wealthy, as in the power equalization plan for education. Instead of charging one hundred dollars for a service, we might charge 1 percent of income. If 1 percent of the incomes of very many people exceeds the cost of providing the service privately, we have two choices: (1) exclude the private service, as in many aspects of the criminal process, or (2) put a ceiling on the fee at the private cost, keeping the percentage low enough so that everyone can easily pay (if not 1 percent, then 0.5 percent, etc.) and recapture the cost of the program through general taxes.

What should determine whether the minimum wealth redistribution or the maximum would apply? There would seem to be a variety of relevant factors: (1) the importance of the exercise of the privilege to the workings of the constitutional process versus private importance to the individual, *e.g.*, education and voting versus, say damages for a tort; (2) the educative effect of the exercise, that is, the extent to which preferences in favor of the process are formed by exercising it, *e.g.*, officeholding, voting, and education; (3) the extent to which many who might decline to pay do not on that account suffer the loss of a direct benefit, *e.g.*, education; (4) the extent to which the state forces individuals to consume some of the service, but reserves superior service to the few, *e.g.*, the criminal process and education; (5) the emergency and subsistence character of the need, *e.g.*, medical care, food, and housing versus education.

The question of what degree of sacrifice to require is closely related to the other question, what level of service to guarantee. Indeed, it is impossible to know how much wealth is being redistributed without knowing both kinds of facts; and the constitutional question should be what combination of level of service and degree of sacrifice is appropriate. The particular combination suggested in *Rodriguez* has nothing to recommend it, on logical grounds, except greatest hostility to claims of the poor. In fact, no combination can be recommended on logical grounds. The question can only be discussed in terms of a particular service. As an illustration, consider the four combinations yielded by division of both service and sacrifice (see table).

SERVICE AND SACRIFICE

	SERVICE	
	Equal	Minimum
SACRIFICE	(1)	(2)
Equal	Equal service available at all levels for same tax rate (e.g., power equalizing)	Minimum service at equal tax rate (e.g., foundation plans in education)
	(3)	(4)
Maximum	Equal service available at all levels of service but at a maximum sacrifice for the poor	Minimum service available to poor at a maximum sacrifice

The four models imply different value judgments about services. The minimum amount of redistribution is found in (4) (minimum service at a maximum sacrifice). In order to apply this model, we should have in mind guaranteeing a minimum of the service to the poor in circumstances of great need, but excluding them altogether from any of the higher (more expensive) levels. Perhaps nonessential services which could readily be privately provided belong in this category—tree trimming, new sidewalks, travel, lectures at the public library, golf courses, swimming pools, nature trails, municipal museums. Between (2) and (3), it is hard to say which represents greater redistribution. Consider (3) first, the guarantee of an equal level of service at all levels but at a "maximum" sacrifice for the poor. For example, the poor might be guaranteed the minimum level for 30 percent of income and the maximum for 50 percent. As can be seen, this could be more accurately considered as offering the maximum service at a truly maximum sacrifice and the minimum service at a sacrifice that is substantial, but not maximum. The poor could not be offered all levels at the same sacrifice or they would always choose the highest levels (if we actually want to force consumption of any level, we should simply offer it free, *i.e.*, tax paid). In order to choose this model, we should have in mind a service the highest quantities of which are sometimes required on an emergency basis. Perhaps medical care, given the high cost of certain treatments, belongs in (3). Foundation plans in education are described in (2), including the one challenged in *Rodriguez*. Every purchaser equally can afford some minimum ir-respective of wealth, in the sense that the same tax rate is required of all, but there is no redistribution at all above the minimum level. This model should apply to services as to which we desire to make the minimum not only possible but likely, irrespective of wealth differences. We do not wish wealth differences to have any influence at the minimum, but we can accept the increasing influence of wealth differences as spending levels increase, including the impossibility of the poor affording the highest levels. The type of service apt for such treatment would be one with a crucially important minimum level, but with less and less importance at higher levels. Here could belong many services: housing, nutrition, a decent public library, adequate voting facilities. In the table (1) represents an attempt to make all purchasers equally wealthy with respect to every level of the service, that is, to remove all effects of wealth. It describes both power equalization in education and the system of day fines discussed previously in connection with the *Williams* case and is appropriate for services as to which wealth effects are considered unacceptable at any level.

Several qualifying remarks can profitably be inserted at this point. First, any fee system, of which all four models are examples, stands in opposition to all non-fee systems; and many non-fee sys-tems exist for distribution of government services. Fees presume that some value is accorded the operation of choice or preference. The four models differ precisely in the extent to which, and the levels of service at which, they try to eliminate wealth from the operation of preferences. But it is also possible to eliminate choice, as in a rationing system (*e.g.*, equal amounts for all) or to choose a different type of sacrifice as the index of choice (*e.g.*, waiting time, queues, rather than financial sacrifice). Second, the four models are neither comprehensive nor very sophisticated as a de-scription of possible fee schedules. The models actually exist on a continuum which could be expressed in graphic or algebraic terms. Certain logical parts of the continuum are not even present, *e.g.*, the possibility of negative fees (payments to users), or sacrifice negatively related to wealth (*e.g.*, to influence the poor to consume more of the service, or, conceivably, an equal amount). Such modifications are readily constructed, however. The purpose here is only to demonstrate that the level of service and amount of sacrifice are interrelated in ways that express implicit policy judgments about the significance of the service. In light of the number of different possibilities shown to exist, it is possible to see the significance of Mr. Justice Powell's assertion that the plaintiffs must be completely unable to afford a minimum level of service. Even if it exceeds formalistic lip service, this standard of correcting wealth discrimination is very low; it is, in fact, model (4). A more balanced perspective should allocate services to the various models.

It is appropriate, at this point, to correct the impression that I am arguing that the Court should establish a comprehensive system of taxes in varying progressivity for practically all services of government. There is nothing about the models discussed to prevent the Court from entering one area, or part, at a time. And the order of the Court could be verbal and summary rather than mathematical and detailed. For example, the Court might take a case involving non-emergency health service (like *Maricopa*) and specify, in a general way, what levels of service must be available for what degree of financial sacrifice. The purpose here was merely to show that defensible conceptual tools exist beyond the notion that the plaintiff must be completely unable to pay. Once again an analogy to *Williams* suggests itself. Just as there, Justice Harlan seemed to be concerned about reviewing the constitutionality of the size of fines, because the inquiry would lead to a Court-imposed schedule of fines, here the concern about going beyond complete inability to pay is because the inquiry will lead to court-imposed tax rates or fee schedules. The answer in both cases is the same: a rough-hewn judicial schedule fashioned on a case-by-case basis is infinitely superior to no relief at all.

B. SECOND LIMITATION: NO DIVERSITY OF IMPACT

The above discussion of service and sacrifice applies whether the purchaser is an individual or a taxing collectivity. The second stringent dictum that the Court imposed on the application of wealth as a suspect classification could only apply to a taxing body.

Indeed, the extreme importance of the second limitation is that it withdraws patterns of local taxation from constitutional scrutiny. When a price is imposed on individuals, exclusion is proportional to the wealth of individuals. When it is imposed on taxing collectivities, however, the exclusion of individuals is imperfect. Poor taxing bodies contain wealthy people and vice versa. The Court indicated that where the impact of wealth discrimination is diverse in this way, a suspect classification might never be found; in effect, the doctrine might be limited to fees on individuals. The reasons for the limitation are not clear. It may be that the Court was simply requiring proof of the actual impact by income class, an impact that can be readily assumed when a fee is levied on individuals. That would be a reasonable requirement, and it was not satisfied in *Rodriguez*. If, however, the Court meant to exclude consideration of the impact of collective wealth irrespective of its relationship to personal wealth, strong objection must be made.

Assume a case where the impact of variation in collective wealth is strongly correlated with personal wealth. As earlier stated, this would boil down to the fact that the distribution of industrial and commercial property does not compensate for the geographical distribution of personal income. Assume further that the politics surrounding the lack of redistribution of collective wealth could be shown to be largely absorbed in the politics of the income classes. On these facts, why should diversity of impact be important? The degree to which some poor and non-poor unaccustomedly find themselves together on one side of the fence ought not to be enough to upset the type of invidious political dynamic that the Fourteenth Amendment is designed to counteract. This is a vitally important point because, compared to general local taxation, fees pay for few and unimportant services.

The idea that diversity of impact is inconsistent with wealth discrimination is really a species of the individualistic view of wealth as a suspect classification. It suggests that, unless the legal system examines the wealth of each individual, and burdens the poorer ones, there is no discrimination. Refusal to look at impact on classes of people, to do what the Justices sometimes disparagingly call "sociological analysis,"[166] is a very direct way to deny

---

[166] See Wright v. Council of Emporia, 407 U.S. 451, 477 (1972) (Burger, C.J., dissenting).

any relief for injuries which befall classes rather than individuals. Unfortunately, the most powerful wealth effects of the legal system probably affect classes, as the problems of *Rodriguez*, and the *Seldin* case, discussed below, demonstrate. Perfect discrimination in each service is surely not required to reinforce the system of wealth stratification. For the Court to declare that only fees can harm poor people would be, as in *Williams*, to blink the potentially more significant problems out of existence.

VIII. EXCLUSIONARY ZONING IN THE 1974 TERM

The Court's resistance to claims of wealth discrimination generally, and, particularly, to attacks on legally fostered geographical wealth stratification, was well illustrated by *Warth v. Seldin*,[167] decided late in the 1974 Term. A number of individuals and organizations sought to challenge the exclusionary zoning ordinance of Penfield, New York, a suburb of Rochester, on grounds that its purpose and effect, on the face of the statute and as administered, were to exclude persons of low and moderate incomes in violation of the Constitution and civil rights statutes.[168] Affirming the Second Circuit, a majority of five Justices (the four appointed by President Nixon, joined by Mr. Justice Stewart), held that none of the plaintiffs had standing to challenge the ordinance.[169]

In many ways, the case is a fulfillment of all that has been said in this article. Substantively, it is an important case for three reasons: (1) Exclusionary zoning is arguably the cornerstone of the anti-poor locational laws, another variety of which was challenged in the travel cases. (2) The plaintiffs in *Seldin* alleged intentionally anti-poor administration and amendment of the ordinance, thereby presenting a direct analogy to *James v. Valtierra*. (3) Tax capture for local services and freedom of residence are

---

[167] 95 S. Ct. 2197 (1975).

[168] Petitioners alleged violations of their First, Ninth, and Fourteenth Amendment rights and their rights under 42 U.S.C. §§ 1981, 1982, and 1983. *Id*. at 2202.

[169] "[T]he District Court held that the original plaintiffs, Home Builders, and Housing Council lacked standing to prosecute the action, that the original complaint failed to state a claim upon which relief could be granted, that the suit should not proceed as a class action, and that, in the exercise of discretion, Home Builders should not be permitted to intervene. The court accordingly denied the motion to add Housing Council as a party-plaintiff, denied Home Builders' motion to intervene, and dismissed the complaint. The Court of Appeals affirmed, reaching only the standing question." *Id*. at 2204. The Supreme Court also addressed only the standing issue.

intertwined, as pointed out in the previous discussions of the *Maricopa* and *Rodriguez* cases. Analytically, the majority opinion, again written by Mr. Justice Powell, who seems to be the specialist of the majority of five in the constitutionality of the mechanisms of state and local government,[170] closely followed the models of formalism already discussed in this article.

There are at least four separate senses in which the opinion can be seen as formalistic, each of which will be considered separately in subsequent paragraphs. (1) Procedure versus substance: Reliance on the standing doctrine to dispose of the case inevitably led to finicky parsing and nit-picking of the pleadings; yet, standing probably will be recognized in another case; and the probable result on the merits was made quite clear from the discussion of standing. (2) Individualism versus class perspective: The doctrine of standing was defined in such a way that the poor person, as a poor person, could never have standing. Actual harm to particular individuals was made the criterion. (3) Arbitrariness versus principle: The doctrine of standing is renowned for its conspicuous absence of principles.[171] But in *Seldin*, the Court surpassed itself in particularistic analysis, employing what might be called the technique of the "fatal flaw." Each type of standing asserted by various plaintiffs was greeted with such metaphysical nit-picking, hole-punching, and point-shaving, as to suggest the hand of a Philadelphia lawyer. (4) Trap standards: As in *Rodriguez*, some of the analysis in *Seldin* consists of enunciation of legal standards which are represented as capable of proof but at a deeper level determine that the claim is legally impossible.

1. The majority's choice of the standing doctrine to dispose of the case represented a procedural flourish without any discernible purpose and was criticized as such by the dissenters.[172] In dictum, the Court indicated it would find standing if individual plaintiffs were the intended residents of a particular proposed housing project and organizational plaintiffs were those economically interested in

---

[170] Justices Powell, Burger, Stewart, Blackmun, and Rehnquist joined together as a majority not only in *Seldin* but also in *Rodriguez* and in *Milliken*. In Keyes v. School District No. 1, Denver, Colo., 413 U.S. 189 (1972), Justices Stewart, Powell, Burger, and Blackmun were part of the majority or concurred in the result.

[171] Scharpf, *Judicial Review and the Political Question: A Functional Analysis*, 75 YALE L.J. 517, 533–35 (1966).

[172] 95 S. Ct. at 2215, 2216.

the construction of a currently proposed project.[173] The five cases cited approvingly by the majority in connection with this dictum all involved plaintiff organizations which had title, or its equivalent, to land on which a housing project would be built but for the blocking action of some legal authority (rezoning, denial of a building permit, etc.).[174] Such limits on standing to challenge exclusionary zoning, whatever their wisdom, should be rather easy to satisfy. An organization need only to purchase some land, or obtain an option, seek approval for a project, and, probably, exhaust state remedies in being denied approval.[175] If this is true, the issues will surely come up again.

Whether or not anything is gained by waiting for the kind of plaintiff preferred by the Court, there are certainly some losses. The individual plaintiffs in *Seldin* alleged they had looked for housing they could afford in Penfield but couldn't find any because of the ordinance.[176] Some of the organizations alleged they would construct housing, and one said that it actually had tried to do so at one time.[177] Requiring them to go forward and develop plans for a particular project is burdensome and futile, because their efforts would be wasted at the local level (the ordinance being clear); and their federal claim (on wealth grounds, anyway) almost certainly would be rejected by the Supreme Court.[178] Furthermore, the Court creates an undesirable situation when it uses a procedural device, like standing, to block litigation of the merits in federal courts, when, at the same time, state courts are quite willing to dispense with the procedural problems and reach the merits of the federal constitutional questions. The Supreme Court can deny certiorari from the state court, letting stand for that state a decision

---

[173] *Id.* at 2209, 2210, 2214.

[174] United Farmworkers of Florida v. City of Delray Beach, 493 F.2d 799 (5th Cir. 1974); Park View Heights Corporation v. City of Black Jack, 467 F.2d 1208 (8th Cir. 1972); Crow v. Brown, 457 F.2d 788 (5th Cir. 1972); Kennedy Park Home Association, Inc. v. City of Lackawanna, 436 F.2d 108 (2d Cir. 1970); Dailey v. City of Lawton, 425 F.2d 1037 (10th Cir. 1970). In addition to the distinction referred to in the text, all of these cases involved racial discrimination.

[175] 95 S. Ct. at 2214 n.23.

[176] *Id.* at 2204.   [177] *Id.* at 2204, 2214.

[178] The best evidence of this may be in a footnote. "[Z]oning laws and their provisions . . . are peculiarly within the province of state and local legislative authorities. . . . [C]itizens dissatisfied with provisions of such laws need not overlook the availability of the normal democratic process." *Id.* at 2210 n.18. Relegation to the majoritarian process seems a direct way to deny plaintiffs' status as a protected minority.

on the merits (and tolerating the anomaly of conflicting results in different states).[179] Or it can take the case, with the anomalous result that a claim clearly satisfying the substantive jurisdictional requirements of lower federal courts can only be tried in state courts;[180] or it can federalize the law of standing to prevent litigation in state courts, an action properly not available under the modern nonconstitutional interpretation of the standing doctrine.[181] Thus, for many reasons, the choice of a procedural basis to dispose of the litigation creates nothing but pointless difficulties.[182]

2. The second formalistic aspect of the Court's analysis hearkens back to the strain of individualism versus class analysis which characterizes so much of the Court's response to wealth discriminations, including the way in which the doctrine of wealth as a suspect classification is defined and applied. As explained in the preceding paragraph, the Court established a strict standard of causality as its test of standing, finding against the plaintiffs because there was "no actionable causal relationship between Penfield's zoning ordinance and plaintiffs' asserted injury."[183] The notion is quite explicit that unless a claimant has a place reserved in a particular project he is not injured. In effect, the Court equates the position of the poor person without a reserved place to the "concerned citizen," whose only relationship to an unconstitutional

---

[179] In Doremus v. Board of Education, 342 U.S. 429 (1952), the Court dismissed an appeal from a state court on the ground that taxpayers lacked federal standing. Professor Freund believed that the Court in *Doremus* did "not go far enough" because, while it showed a commendable willingness not to follow the state's definition of standing, it allowed the ruling below to stand, instead of vacating that ruling, thereby making possible lack of uniformity among states in decisions on a federal question. CAHN, SUPREME COURT AND SUPREME LAW 35 (1954).

[180] In the exclusionary zoning area, the Pennsylvania line of cases seems to be based on both state and federal grounds. Nat'l Land & Investment Co. v. Kohn, 419 Pa. 504, 522 n.20 (1965). The *Mount Laurel* case (New Jersey) is discussed in note 10 *supra*.

[181] Flast v. Cohen, 392 U.S. 83, 91–101 (1968).

[182] Mr. Justice Douglas, in his dissent, seems to imply that the majority turned the case down in order to reduce its workload, which Douglas again claimed was light, even while he was in the hospital. A conventional defense of the Court's action touched on by the other dissenters, 95 S. Ct. at 2216, might be that the issue in the case was extremely important, with enormous problems of judicial role and enforcement, great legal and factual complexities, yet had not received sufficient analysis in courts and scholarly literature. The propriety of avoiding constitutional issues on such grounds, especially in cases involving civil rights, is debated in Bickel, *The Passive Virtues*, 75 HARV. L. REV. 40 (1961), and Gunther, *The Subtle Vices of the "Passive Virtues"—A Comment on Principle and Expediency in Judicial Review*, 64 COLUM. L. REV. 1 (1964).

[183] 95 S. Ct. at 2209.

action is the very fact that he objects to it.[184] It is true that the mere fact of being poor does not guarantee that a particular individual is excluded by a zoning ordinance. Living in Penfield might be the last thing the individual wants. More important, however, many more people are excluded by zoning ordinances than can acquire reserved places in proposed housing projects. Most individuals in the injured class have a kind of "statistical injury," a lessening of opportunities to live in other places, which is built up from the effects of the whole structure of residential wealth stratification, but which cannot be tied to particular proposed housing projects, mainly because the ordinances themselves chill proposals. The class is thus unique both in being larger than individuals excluded from proposed housing projects and smaller than the class of all concerned citizens.

The Court's emphasis on the excluded individual is more than merely unnecessary; it is undesirable in terms of the policies which the standing doctrine is designed to further. The kind of plaintiff preferred by the Court is actually worse than the ones before it in *Seldin.* Through the standing doctrine, the Court identifies the plaintiff whose personal stake in the lawsuit adequately represents the claim of injury being made.[185] In the zoning area, the essence of

---

[184] In *Richardson,* Mr. Justice Powell said that "[r]elaxation of standing requirements is directly related to the expansion of judicial power. It seems to me inescapable that allowing unrestricted taxpayer or citizen standing would significantly alter the allocation of power at the national level, with a shift away from a democratic form of government. I also believe that repeated and essentially head-on confrontations between the life-tenured branch and the representative branches of government will not, in the long run, be beneficial either." 481 U.S. at 188. He goes on to say that "we risk a progressive impairment of the effectiveness of the federal courts if their limited resources are diverted increasingly from their historic role to the resolution of public interest suits brought by litigants who cannot distinguish themselves from all taxpayers or all citizens." *Id.* at 192.

But see Davis, *The Liberalized Law of Standing,* 37 U. CHI. L. REV. 450, 471 (1970); Jaffe, *Standing to Secure Judicial Review: Private Actions,* 75 HARV. L. REV. 255, 305 (1961).

[185] "The fundamental aspect of standing is that it focuses on the party seeking to get his complaint before a federal court and not on the issues he wishes to have adjudicated. The 'gist of the question of standing' is whether the party seeking relief has 'alleged such a personal stake in the outcome of the controversy as to assure that concrete adverseness which sharpens the presentation of issues upon which the court so largely depends for illumination of difficult constitutional questions.'" Flast v. Cohen, 392 U.S. at 99. "This personal stake is what the Court has consistently held enables a complainant authoritatively to present to a court a complete perspective upon the adverse consequences flowing from the specific set of facts undergirding his grievance." Schlesinger v. Reservists to Stop the War, 418 U.S. 208, 221 (1974). But see Davis, note 184 *supra,* at 470. Therefore, in a class action, "it is essential that a plaintiff must be a part of that class, that is, he must possess the same interest and suffer the same injury shared by all members of the class he represents." 418 U.S. at 216.

this claim is the statistical injury to the class, rather than exclusion from an individual housing project, because the real problem is that proposals for housing projects are unrealistic in light of the ordinances. There is a sense, then, in which the Court in *Seldin* turns the standing doctrine on its head. Instead of preferring plaintiffs whose personal stakes best represent the claim (poor people with a statistical injury), the Court disqualifies them for the reason they ought to be preferred. The exclusion complained of becomes the bar to complaining; the family without a chance of residence in the suburbs cannot, for that very reason, raise the merits of the exclusion in federal court. The more flawlessly and totally the exclusion operates, the more invulnerable it is to constitutional attack. It would be like denying standing to a black child excluded from a segregated school on the ground that he was not on the waiting list for the white school. The result may be, once again, permitting challenges to the less important examples of the basic problem. Not one of the lower court cases cited by the Supreme Court, for example, involved the type of exclusionary zoning challenged in *Seldin* under which planning for low income housing is futile.[186] And, although the Court's requirement of a proposed project may be technically surmountable almost anywhere, the effort will not be made in many places when the only reason for making it would be the opportunity for an almost certainly unsuccessful constitutional challenge.

3. The Court's narrow interpretation of who is excluded also led to a third formalistic technique: legalistic (*i.e.*, technical and unprincipled) criticism of the pleadings and anachronistic emphasis on fact pleading. Legalistic reasoning can be seen in the excessively ingenious parrying of every claim of standing, noticeable not so much as to any one claim as cumulatively and in the absence of supportive reasoning. Plaintiffs alleging personal exclusion were denied for the absence of causal connection between the ordinance and their exclusion. The claim of Rochester taxpayers alleging poorer services for higher taxes was dismissed as an "ingenious academic exercise in the conceivable."[187] The claim of injury from segregation (the "white ghetto" claim) was rejected, in the first place, as limited to a claim of racial segregation arising under the

---

[186] The zoning ordinances in each case cited by the Court either already permitted the proposed building or could have been reasonably changed to allow the construction.

[187] 95 S. Ct. at 2210.

1968 Civil Rights Act,[188] and, in the second place, as available exclusively to residents, rather than, as in *Seldin,* to an association with injured residents as members. Note that the Penfield residents suing individually would escape one objection leveled at the other plaintiffs in that they were subject to the ordinance; but, in the absence of congressional command, the Court will apparently refuse to recognize the type of injury they alleged as a basis for standing.[189] The claim of the Home Builders for damages was no good because the damages, if any, would vary according to the individual circumstances of the member, and, for prospective relief, because it was not alleged that any member had applied for a variance or building permit.[190] Yet, although it was alleged that one of the members of the Housing Council had applied for a variance in 1969, there was no allegation that the project "remained viable in 1972 when this complaint was filed,"[191] or that administrative remedies had been exhausted.[192]

An unwarranted emphasis on fact pleading can be seen in many of these legalistic requirements and in the importance attached to the failure of plaintiffs to allege factual minutiae. Harris alleged he is a Negro, but did not allege he ever looked for a home.[193] Reyes, Sinkler, and Broadnax described themselves as persons of low and moderate income; this definition is inadequate; and the record reveals the plaintiffs' income in fact varied.[194] Penfield Better Homes and O'Brien Homes alleged they would build low and moderate income housing, but there is no indication that any of the plaintiffs could afford one of the units, or that any of the proposed units would be adequate to meet any of the plaintiffs' housing needs.[195] The kind of fact pleading which seems to be required by the Court in order to fill in every syllogistic filament in plaintiffs' argument has been explicitly rejected in standing cases[196] and represents a discredited tradition of formalism in pro-

---

[188] *Id.* at 2212 and n.21.

[189] *Id.* at 2213.

[190] *Id.* at 2213–14.

[191] *Id.* at 2214.

[192] *Id.* at 2214 n.23.

[193] *Id.* at 2203 and n.3.

[194] "[T]he complaint nowhere defines the term 'low and moderate income' beyond the parenthetical phrase 'without the capital required to purchase real estate.' In addition to the inadequacy of this definition, the record discloses wide variations in the income, housing needs, and money available for housing among the various 'low and moderate income' plaintiffs." *Id.* at 2203 n.5.

[195] *Id.* at 2208–09 & n.15.

[196] United States v. SCRAP, 412 U.S. 669, 689–90 (1973).

cedure. There is substantial arbitrariness in it as well. Potential plaintiffs obviously have no way of knowing which of the vast number of factual links in their case they might be required to allege.

4. The fourth formalistic technique is trap definitions. Attention has already been given to the device of denying standing on the basis of the very state action alleged to be unconstitutional. The other noteworthy example is the definite suggestion by the Court that the individual plaintiffs might be too poor to claim they couldn't afford a house in Penfield. This device, as the precise opposite of the requirement in *Rodriguez* that plaintiffs be "completely unable to pay," deserves some attention. Specifically, the Court found the "record devoid of any indication" that possible projects "would have satisfied petitioners' needs at prices they could afford."[197] Making reference to the low wealth of the individual plaintiffs,[198] the Court said that their exclusion from Penfield apparently "is the consequence of the economics of the area housing market rather than of respondents' assertedly illegal acts."[199] To raise such complex factual issues on the pleadings is itself extraordinary. The plaintiffs clearly alleged there would be housing available but for the ordinance.[200] If one were to resolve the factual dispute from the pleadings on judicial notice, however, it seems obvious that, since housing can be built which the plaintiffs can afford, especially given federal subsidies, the legal possibility of building it in new areas will result in its being built. Of course, flaws in the political process may prevent low income housing from being built. But invidious patterns in the political process which make such projects politically unlikely can hardly serve as a justification for a judicial approval of that same process rendering them legally impossible through zoning laws.

There is an interesting puzzle suggested by the Court's point about excessive poverty. That is the disparity between the cost of some housing that would be built after the demise of the exclusionary zoning laws and the means of some poor people. Some of the beneficiaries of non-exclusionary zoning would not be poor. Zoning laws in the richest places probably protect housing that is beyond the means of 95 percent of the American people. The

---

197 95 S. Ct. at 2209.

198 *Id.* and n.16.

199 *Ibid.*

200 *Id.* at 2216.

Court says the excluded class is too poor to have standing. Should we not anticipate the opposite problem that the class is too rich to be considered a protected minority on the merits? If the 95 percent of the people of California who cannot afford to live in Beverly Hills do not like exclusionary zoning laws, they certainly have the political power to abolish such laws by state legislation or even constitutional amendment. Can we consider the poorest one-fifth of the population to be a protected minority when they are included within such a massively powerful political alliance?

The same problem arose in a different guise in *Rodriguez*, and I discussed it at some length in another article dealing exclusively with wealth discrimination in the school finance context.[201] It is useful to consider the parallels. First, in a system of wealth distribution and non-redistribution, it is impossible for 95 percent of the people to benefit from any mechanism. Subject to many qualifications, we could anticipate that complete freedom to reside anywhere would benefit the poorer half of the people and hurt the richer half; *i.e.*, relatively poorer people would tend to get somewhat more desirable housing, and relatively richer somewhat less desirable. Although representatives of 95 percent of the people might think they would benefit from opening Beverly Hills, some of the richer ones moving in actually might lose because they would now find poorer people than where they came from. In other places, communities which used to be for the 80th–85th percentile would be mixed, and so on. My article on school finance tried to show the empirical extent of this averaging process for school spending in Illinois.[202] Even assuming only about half the people would show a net benefit from the death of exclusionary zoning, we are still confronted with a difficult question—how can approximately half the electorate be considered a protected minority? There are at least two answers. The superior political potency of the wealthier half, bound together effectively by powerful incentive to prevent redistribution, and the relative lack of injury to most of the lower half. Most of the lower middle class who might benefit somewhat by destruction of the system of exclusionary zoning also must consider the felt undesirability of living near poor people, especially since the political process often

---

[201] See Clune, note 8 *supra*.

[202] *Id.* at 690–93.

seems to target low income housing near working-class people who are striving to leave poverty behind and lack the abundant resources sometimes necessary to cope with problems of change. In addition, it is the poor alone whose harm from the present system is sufficiently severe to warrant accepting the risks of change. Thus, a political remedy for the poor, whose housing needs are the only extreme ones in the wealth spectrum, is stifled because many people are somewhat benefited, by the present system, while most of those hurt are not hurt much and thus have little to gain from a change. For these reasons, an effective constitutional remedy for those with low incomes must be a remedy for those of moderate income as well and judicial provision of the remedy does not contradict the underlying theory of protected minorities.

IX. CONCLUSION

Three conclusions seem conspicuous from the foregoing analysis. One is that the Court is not committed to formalism but has found compromises between authenticity and formalism, such as Justice Harlan's due process approach in *Boddie* and the criminal process cases. While these doctrines are highly restrained conceptually, because they do not admit poverty as an explicit factor, they are responsive to the ethical problem of wealth discriminations. To respond to a problem but not to refer to it is a considerable achievement but a doctrinal flaw. Only a judge of the stature of Harlan, who wanted to provide some relief, but feared the wealth doctrine as illimitable, could carry it off. Justice Harlan, however, probably exhausted the possibilities of compromise. The due process analysis in each area depended upon considering the problem in individual terms before the court. The individualistic perspective fails as a way of analyzing the more "demographic," and socially important, problems like local tax capture, exclusionary zoning, and the general fate of the poor in the criminal process. Applied to such problems, it leads, as in *Rodriguez* and *Warth v. Seldin*, to the conclusion that there is no problem. In the final analysis to avoid the flaws of less-than-formalistic doctrines, to have a consistent doctrine for all problems, and to have some doctrine for the most important problems, there is no choice but the explicit recognition of wealth as a factor in the analysis.

Such explicit recognition of the wealth factor confronts two challenges, both implicit in the entertainment of the more demographic kind of case (where the situation of a whole class must be analyzed). One is the problem of proof. How shall the impact of existing laws and proposed remedies be analyzed? This is an enormous and largely ignored problem, an important dimension of which is a new relationship with social science. Courts have sometimes tried to settle problems of proof within the confines of the courtroom by a priori reasoning or by permitting competing studies to be introduced in evidence: *E.g.*, economies of scale exist in educational spending.[203] Does housing code enforcement help or hurt the poor?[204] Such techniques are highly unsatisfactory because conclusions about such complex matters cannot be trusted until they emerge clear and robust from the process of social science. Even if a judge were to require less than clear proof, so that the burden would not be insurmountable, reference to social science would help guard against obvious mistakes in theory and measurement. But good procedures for informing courts about the significance of social science conclusions are lacking.

The second challenge comes from the necessity of solving the redistributive equation, the determination of what level of service to guarantee and what to charge the poor for the guarantee. In the earlier cases, the problem was handled categorically, and perhaps unconsciously, by saying that if a person is poor, the service is free. Again, in the more demographic kind of case, the true nature of the underlying problem becomes obvious. In this article, discussion of service and sacrifice is focused on the closely related questions of fees and local taxes; but the need to set the level of service and sacrifice is endemic. Consider exclusionary zoning, where the question is how many units of low and moderate income housing should be made available at what price. Courts should be able to meet the challenge of the redistributive equation by announcing simple standards to guide the more quantitative labors of experts (*e.g.*, "all levels at an equal percentage of wealth," "a basic minimum within the reach of the poorest man").

Taking all three conclusions together, I understand why today's Court will not accept a doctrine that condemns wealth discriminations. It is true that I see the doctrines of the Warren Court as the

---

[203] See Hobson v. Hansen, 372 F. Supp. 844 (1971) and the review articles, in 7 J. OF HUMAN RESOURCES, 275–325 (1972).

[204] See Komesar, *Return to Slumville: A Critique of the Ackerman Analysis of Housing Code Enforcement and the Poor*, 82 YALE L. J. 1175 (1973).

only ones that are ultimately defensible and I see the doctrines of restraint fashioned by the Burger Court as largely indefensible. But, in the early cases, there was not much to choose between the doctrines. The point at which authentic doctrines begin to create the unique problems which formalistic doctrines seek to keep out of court was not reached by the Warren Court. It was a great deal easier to remove the conceptual restraints than to impose empirical ones. Nevertheless, the existence of factual complexity and difficulty of remedy ought to provide more than an adequate check against conceptual expansiveness and permit the Court to solve problems one at a time in priority of constitutional importance. Hence, no reason exists for complete, conceptual insensitivity to wealth discriminations other than a disregard for the constitutional importance of the problem itself. That does not seem defensible under any conception of the Fourteenth Amendment broader than its central focus on race.

HARVEY S. PERLMAN and
LAURENS H. RHINELANDER

WILLIAMS & WILKINS CO. v. UNITED STATES: PHOTOCOPYING, COPYRIGHT, AND THE JUDICIAL PROCESS

Once Caxton introduced the printing press into England in 1474, it became inevitable that the common law would be forced to consider the propriety of printing another's works without his consent. After the demise of the royal monopoly in the eighteenth century, the rhetoric of the legal arguments was pronounced in terms of "natural rights," "property," and "monopoly." Could the common law with its dedication to equity and its approval of individual initiative deny the "natural right" of a person to profit from his own intellectual effort or sanction another's unjust enrichment by the exploitation of that effort? Could the common law with its abhorrence of monopoly award such monopoly to authors and, if so, under what limitations? What incentives were necessary to create or publish written works? What interest did the public have in access to works thus created and to what extent could the creator restrict that access?

The nature of the historical development of copyright resulted in delayed judicial consideration of an author's rights to his manu-

Harvey S. Perlman and Laurens H. Rhinelander are Professors of Law, The University of Virginia.

The authors wish to acknowledge the helpful comments of their two colleagues, G. Edward White and Warren F. Schwartz, and of Edmund Kitch, who read and criticized parts of an earlier draft of this article, but who bear no responsibility for the authors' errors or omissions.

script. The royal grant of power to the Stationers' Company to govern the printing of books, with the undeniable purpose of censorship, may have forestalled direct litigation of an author's rights. The eventual liberalizing of the rights of English subjects to publish and enactment in 1709 of the Statute of Anne—the forerunner of modern copyright statutes—raised the issues in distinct ways. The first important judicial consideration of the rights of authors occurred in 1769 in the famous case *Millar v. Taylor;*[1] it required not only a judicial examination of the common law but a consideration of legislative enactments regulating the same interests.

Andrew Millar had purchased a perpetual copyright in a book of poems written by James Thomson entitled "The Seasons." Robert Taylor printed an edition in competition and was sued by Millar. The copyright term granted by the Statute of Anne had expired. The King's Bench examined, first, whether an author had a perpetual copyright at common law and second, if so, whether it was affected by the Statute of Anne. Three of the four judges discovered a common law right of authors in their works, unaffected by enactment of the copyright statute. Lord Mansfield joined the majority, noting that the case was the "first instance of a final difference of opinion in this Court, since I sat here. Every order, rule, judgment, and opinion, has hitherto been unanimous."[2]

The majority position largely ignored the difficulties of fitting literary productions into traditional common law concepts of property. As Judge Willes noted:[3]

> I have avoided a large field which exercised the ingenuity of the Bar. Metaphysical reasoning is too subtle; and arguments from the supposed modes of acquiring the property of acorns, or a vacant piece of ground in an imaginary state of nature, are too remote. Besides, the comparison does not hold between things which have a physical existence, and incorporeal rights. It is certainly not agreeable to natural justice, that a stranger should reap the beneficial pecuniary produce of another man's work.

Justice Yates in dissent presented the classic argument against recognition of common law rights in authors. Literary "property" becomes a "monopoly in intellectual ideas." The "natural rights"

---

[1] 4 Burr. 2303, 98 Eng. Rep. 201 (K.B. 1769).

[2] *Id.* at 2395, 98 Eng. Rep. at 250.

[3] *Id.* at 2334–35, 98 Eng. Rep. at 218.

of authors is seen as conflicting with the "natural and social rights" of mankind:[4]

> I wish as sincerely as any man, that learned men may have all the encouragements, and all the advantages that are consistent with the general right and good of mankind. But if the monopoly now claimed be contrary to the great laws of property and totally unknown to the ancient and common law of England; if the establishing of this claim will directly contradict the legislative authority, and introduce a species of property contrary to the end for which the whole system of property was established; if it will tend to embroil the peace of society, with frequent contentions;—(contentions most highly disfiguring the face of literature, and highly disgusting to a liberal mind;) if it will hinder or suppress the advancement of learning and knowledge; and lastly, if it should strip the subject of his natural right; if, these, or any of these mischiefs would follow; I can never concur in establishing such a claim.

A writ of error was filed but not prosecuted. After the death of Millar the copyrights were sold at auction and obtained by Becket and others who were eventually forced to sue Donaldson for his part in printing another unauthorized version of "The Seasons." This time the cause came before the House of Lords who called in various judges to answer a series of five questions involving authors' rights and the effect of the Statute of Anne.[5] While a majority of the judges believed the common law originally provided a property interest in an author's works, six of the twelve judges found that the common law was abrogated by enactment of the statute. Five judges, on the other hand, thought that the author's interest was not limited to that conferred by the statute. Lord Mansfield was the twelfth judge. Because he was a peer he did not participate. His opinion in *Millar*, however, strongly indicates that had he done so the judges would have been evenly divided. The House of Lords concurred with the six-judge majority.[6] Thereafter, the author's right in his creations was an exclusive creature of legislation.

The issues facing these early English judges arose from the tech-

---

[4] *Id.* at 2394, 98 Eng. Rep. at 250.

[5] Donaldsons v. Becket, 4 Burr. 2408, 98 Eng. Rep. 257 (K.B. 1774).

[6] Donaldson v. Beckett, 2 Bro. P.C. 129, 1 Eng. Rep. 837 (H.L. 1774).

nological development of the printing press. The previously unknown opportunity for dissemination of knowledge and learning
throughout the Empire was at hand. A classic confrontation between private right and public interest was perceived. Did authors
or publishers need the incentive of financial reward provided
through recognition of a property interest in published works or
did such an interest make dissemination of written works more
difficult and more expensive?[7] And perhaps as important, could
such a complex question be answered by the disorderly processes
of the common law or did it require detailed resolution through
legislation? American copyright law replayed the arguments and
the passions of the intellectual property debate sixty years later,
and in *Wheaton v. Peters*[8] the United States Supreme Court followed the judgment of the House of Lords.

It is not surprising that a new technological advance in printing
comparable to the printing press should stimulate anew the questions muted but not silenced in *Donaldson* and *Wheaton*. The
photocopy machine, or perhaps more importantly the cheap photocopy machine, supplied the necessary technological advance, and
Williams & Wilkins Co. v. United States[9] provided the forum. The
Supreme Court affirmed the judgment of the Court of Claims by
an equally divided vote with Mr. Justice Blackmun not participating. The Court of Claims,[10] by a 4-to-3 vote had reversed the
trial judge who had ruled in favor of the copyright holder against
an unauthorized copying.[11]

Law has the infinite capacity to alter the perspective of a problem without altering the problem itself. In the eighteenth century,
the debate involved common law property interests. In *Williams
& Wilkins*, the plaintiff had complied with the copyright statute.
In the latter case the applicable legal doctrine, seemingly adopted

---

[7] There is no doubt that the House of Lords faced this issue directly. Lord Camden,
who moved the question against the authors' position, noted: "It was not for gain that
Bacon, Newton, Milton, and Locke instructed the world; it would be unworthy such
men to traffic with a dirty bookseller for so much a sheet of letterpress. When the bookseller offered Milton five pounds for his 'Paradise Lost,' he did not reject it and commit
his poem to the flames, nor did he accept the miserable pittance as the reward of his
labour; he knew that the real price of his work was immortality, and that posterity
would pay it." Quoted in SCRUTTON, THE LAW OF COPYRIGHT 39 (2d ed. 1890).

[8] 8 Pet. 591 (1834).   [10] 487 F.2d 1345 (Ct. Cl. 1973).

[9] 420 U.S. 376 (1975).   [11] 172 U.S.P.Q. 670 (Ct. Cl. 1972).

by those on both sides of the argument, became "fair use." Is it a "fair use" of a copyrighted work to duplicate it for research or educational purposes? Having in 1774 solemnly paid deference to the legislative will by declaring an author's rights limited to those provided by statute, the courts were now asked to limit the statutory rights by a judicially conceived doctrine of "fair use." Thus this bicentennial intellectual property case shifted the perspective from examination of the limits legislation placed on the common law to what limits the courts should place on legislatively created rights.

As so often happens in the fortuities of litigation, fundamental questions become disguised in shifting legal doctrines and oftentime escape recognition. But in *Williams & Wilkins* the United States Supreme Court essentially faced the same questions that were central to the eighteenth-century intellectual property debate: What rule will best enhance the dissemination of knowledge and learning, and which instrument of government, the legislature or the courts, is best suited to fashion that rule? The purpose of this article is to face those central questions as they relate to the current controversy over reprography[12] and copyright and to examine them in the context confronting the Supreme Court in *Williams & Wilkins*. Issues which over a span of two centuries divided Lord Mansfield's bench for the first time and evenly divided both the judges consulted by the House of Lords and the Justices of the United States Supreme Court are ones fraught with complexity and not easily resolved.

Our efforts lead us to the conclusion that in the face of a congressional grant to copyright owners of the exclusive right to "print, reprint, publish, copy, and vend the copyrighted work,"[13] the courts should not construct a privilege authorizing the photocopying of scholarly articles, particularly on the pretext that such a privilege is necessary to stimulate scholarly activity. While our conclusion may lend little assistance to resolution of the reprography-copyright conflict, we are convinced that it focuses the re-

---

[12] "Reprography" has become the technical word for the art of facsimile reproduction and encompasses a variety of methods in addition to the traditional photocopy machine. Since the thrust of our article does not depend on the method employed to reproduce the copyrighted work, we use "reprography" and "photocopy" interchangeably. Being interested in trademark law as well we have studiously avoided using the term "xeroxing" in deference to the Xerox Corporation's attempt to preserve its mark.

[13] 17 U.S.C. § 1(a)(1970).

sponsibility for resolution where it properly belongs—on Congress —and, if adopted, may save the Court the embarrassment of an extended, fruitless experience with an issue it is ill-equipped to resolve.

I. WILLIAMS & WILKINS IN CONTEXT

The forces which eventually brought the issue of accommodating photocopying to copyright before the Supreme Court began shortly after Congress enacted the present copyright statute in 1909. Highlights of the history of the controversy as it raged, both in the private offices of publishers and libraries and in the halls of Congress, may help to put the case and the legal doctrines advanced therein in proper perspective.

In its consideration of *Williams & Wilkins* the Court of Claims was impressed by the contributions to both copyright revision and photoduplication of Herbert Putnam, the Librarian of Congress and a public advocate of the 1909 revision.[14] While Putnam contributed substantially to passage of the 1909 act, the rule he established for his library in the same year authorized "photocopying" of copyrighted articles, and an amendment to the rules in 1913 added "photoduplication of books, newspapers, etc.," as a service provided by the library. The clash between photography and copyright was perceived by the Court of Claims as existing contemporaneously with passage of the 1909 act. As the technology became more advanced, and duplication more extensive, however, the interests came more fully into conflict.

In 1935, a "gentlemen's agreement" was reached between researchers and book publishers which authorized libraries to make photographic reproductions of copyrighted books and periodicals for scholars in lieu of loan or manual transcription.[15] In 1941 the American Library Association promulgated the "Reproduction of Materials Code" which, adopting for the most part the provisions of the "gentlemen's agreement," also recognized the possible detri-

---

[14] 487 F.2d at 1351.

[15] The agreement was formally approved by the Joint Committee on Materials for Research of the American Council of Learned Societies and the Social Science Research Council and the National Association of Book Publishers and is published in full text at 2 J. DOCUMENTARY REPRODUCTION 31 (1939). See also Smith, *The Copying of Literary Property*, 46 LAW LIB. J. 197 (1953). The background to the "gentlemen's agreement" is related in Saunders, *Origins of the "Gentlemen's Agreement" of 1935*, in HATTERY & BUSH eds., REPROGRAPHY AND COPYRIGHT LAW 159 (1964).

ment to publishers: "Reproduction of in-print material, however, is more likely to bring financial harm to the owner of the copyright, and it is recommended that libraries be even more careful than in the case of out-of-print material."[16]

These early attempts at accommodation between publishers on the one hand and libraries and scholars on the other were conducted in tones moderated perhaps by the expense involved with existing duplicating techniques. Photoduplication was performed primarily by the Photostat method, a time-consuming and expensive per page reproduction system. It was not until 1950 that reprographic techniques which were inexpensive and provided instantaneous clear copies became commercially available.[17] These developments, which provided a copy for a dime or less per page, changed the tenor of the debate. The stage was set for a clash of interests the intensity of which was depicted in the recent statement of the Register of Copyrights: "I don't regard authors and publishers and teachers and librarians as natural enemies. It is extremely painful to see them at each other's throats."[18]

In the decade of the 1960s the debate focused on Congress.

A. THE LEGISLATURE FAILS TO ACT

For twenty years the idea of a general revision of the copyright law has been before Congress, beginning with appropriations in 1955 to the Copyright Office to make studies as the groundwork for revision. The battle lines were quickly drawn between publishers and authors[19] on the one hand, and librarians and educators on the other, over whether Congress should recognize the "right"

---

[16] 35 Am. Lib. Ass'n Bull. 84, 85 (1941).

[17] Hawkens, *Reprographic Technology: Present and Future*, in Hattery & Bush, note 15 *supra* at 39. For an additional review of the reprographic technology, see 15 U.C.L.A. L. Rev. 931, 941 (1968).

[18] 33 Cong. Q. 1177 (7 June 1975).

[19] Authors as a class have mixed reactions to the problems of reprography and copyright. Those who make their living directly from copyright royalties can be expected to side with the publishers against the copiers. The financial rewards of publishing for authors of most scholarly material, however, is more indirect, and these authors tend to perceive of their own needs of access to copyrighted materials as more important than the indirect disadvantage to their own publishers. In addition, these scholars may obtain direct financial rewards in terms of increased salary or more lucrative offers from other institutions as a direct result of wider dissemination of their works. Of course, if in fact the photographic duplication of scholarly materials does adversely affect the economic well-being of publishers generally, the end result of diminished publication capacity would inure to the detriment of those scholars who publish.

to make "single copies" for research or educational purposes without paying royalties to the copyright holder. The proposed revision bill also attracted controversy over the rights of cable television and jukebox owners, and the extent to which copyright should apply to computer input and output. Thus, while the House passed a version in 1967 and the Senate passed one in 1974, the efforts of those seeking statutory resolution of copyright problems created by the new technology have not been successful. The history of these legislative efforts has been reviewed elsewhere.[20] Of particular relevance here, however, is an examination of those efforts as they may have influenced both the Court of Claims and the Supreme Court in resolving *Williams & Wilkins*.

The 1955 appropriation resulted in publication by the Copyright Office of a number of studies on significant copyright issues,[21] and a report on copyright revision by the Register of Copyrights in 1961.[22] On 20 July 1964, in the Eighty-eighth Congress, at the Register's request, Senator McClellan and Congressman Celler introduced identical copyright revision bills[23] which were reintroduced with some changes in the Eighty-ninth Congress.[24] Hearings were held in the House by a Subcommittee during the spring and summer of 1965,[25] and a year later, on 12 October 1966, a bill was reported favorably to the full Judiciary Committee with many changes.[26] A substantially identical bill was introduced in the House

---

[20] Schulman, *Fair Use and the Revision of the Copyright Act*, 53 IOWA L. REV. 832 (1968).

[21] Thirty-four studies were written from 1955 to 1959 and published in 1960 and 1961 by the Subcommittee on Patents, Trademarks, and Copyrights of the Senate Committee on the Judiciary, 86th Cong., 1st & 2d Sess. (Comm. Print 1960). Two of these are relevant, No. 14, "Fair Use of Copyrighted Works," by Alan Latman, who subsequently represented Williams & Wilkins in both the Court of Claims and the Supreme Court, and No. 15, "Photoduplication of Copyrighted Materials by Libraries," by Borge Varmer.

[22] *Report of the Register of Copyright on the General Revision of the U.S. Copyright Laws for House Comm. on the Judiciary*, 97th Cong., 1st Sess. (Comm. Print 1961).

[23] S. 3008 and H.R. 11947, 88th Cong., 2d Sess. (1964).

[24] S. 1006 and H.R. 4347, 89th Cong., 1st Sess. (1965).

[25] H.R. REP. No. 83, 90th Cong., 1st Sess. (1967).

[26] Before making its report, the House Subcommittee held 59 executive sessions reviewing the points made at the hearings. *Id*. at 2. Meanwhile the Senate Subcommittee on Patents, Trademarks, and Copyrights had held hearings in August 1965, then again a year later, devoted to the troublesome question of the applicability of copyright to cable television, but took no action on the bill before adjournment of the Eighty-ninth Congress. S. REP. No. 93-983, 93d Cong., 2d. Sess., 101 (1974).

in the Ninetieth Congress as H.R. 2512.[27] This bill was reported favorably to the House by the full Judiciary Committee in March 1967[28] and was eventually passed in the House by an overwhelming margin.[29]

The question whether libraries should be entitled to photocopy copyrighted works for research purposes was the subject of one of the studies conducted by the Copyright Office.[30] The study, after consideration of the present ambiguity of copyright law and the contemporaneous resolution of the dilemma by foreign countries, suggested two basic strategies: First, Congress could resolve the problem directly by statutory provisions. Second, Congress could merely encourage "libraries, publishers, and other groups concerned to develop a working arrangement, in the nature of a code of practice, to govern photocopying by libraries." Reference was made to the "gentlemen's agreement" as illustrative of a possible solution to the problem. The Register, however, in his own report on copyright revision recommended the statutory approach, urging a provision that would authorize the "single photocopy of one article in any issue of a periodical, or of a reasonable part of any other publication . . . when the applicant states in writing that he needs and will use such material solely for his own research."[31]

The bill eventually introduced at the request of the Register did not make specific provisions for the photocopy machine. A preliminary draft had contained an express privilege for libraries to supply single copies of "no more than one article or other contribution to a copyrighted collection or periodical issue" without any investigation as to the planned use of the copy. In addition the libraries could supply one copy of an entire work if upon reasonable investigation it was discovered the work was not available from trade sources. These provisions were dropped prior to introduction at the request of both publishers and libraries, the former arguing it would open the door to wholesale copying, the latter

---

[27] H.R. 2512, 90th Cong., 1st Sess. (1967).

[28] H.R. REP. No. 83, note 25 *supra*.

[29] 113 CONG. REC. 9022 (1967).

[30] Varmer, note 21 *supra*.

[31] Report of the Register, note 22 *supra*, at 26.

contending it would curtail established services.[32] The only surviving provision which in any way affected the growing controversy was a restatement of the judicial doctrine of "fair use" under which certain minimal uses of copyrighted works had been
declared privileged.[33]

By the time the bill was reported to the full House in 1967,
however, the libraries had succeeded in obtaining express recognition of a limited photocopy privilege. The bill, H.R. 2512, contained two relevant sections. The first, entitled "Fair Use," had
been expanded to provide that "fair use of a copyrighted work,
including such use by reproduction in copies . . . , for purposes
such as . . . teaching, scholarship, or research is not an infringement." Added also was a provision which had appeared in the
1964 bill but had been dropped in 1965 which listed the factors
courts were to utilize in determining which uses were "fair." The
factors to be considered included: "(1) the purpose and character
of the use; (2) the nature of the copyrighted work; (3) the amount
and substantiality of the portion used in relation to the copyrighted
work as a whole; and (4) the effect of the use upon the potential
market for or value of the copyrighted work."[34]

Section 108 of H.R. 2512, entitled "Reproduction of works in
archival collections," dealt directly with library photocopying and
was of very limited scope, permitting a "nonprofit institution" having "archival custody over . . . unpublished works to reproduce
them for "preservation and security, or for deposit for research
use in any other such institution." Wholly lacking was any provision giving a broad exemption to educators or libraries, as had
been strongly urged at the hearings.[35] The committee did, however, include a provision permitting a court on finding infringe-

---

[32] *Supplemental Report of the Register of Copyright on the General Revision of the U.S.
Copyright Law for the House Comm. on the Judiciary,* 89th Cong., 1st Sess., pt. 6, at 26
(Comm. Print 1965). The supplemental report contains a comparative table of the provisions of the 1909 act and those recommended in a "preliminary draft," the 1964 bill,
and the 1965 bill. *Id.* at 192–93.

[33] The Register's bill introduced in 1964 provided that "fair use of a copyrighted
work to the extent reasonably necessary or incidental to a legitimate purpose such as
. . . teaching, scholarship, or research is not an infringement." H.R. 11947, 88th Cong.,
2d Sess. § 6 (1964). The bill reintroduced a year later had been whittled down to the
statement that "fair use of a copyrighted work is not an infringement." H.R. 4347,
89th Cong., 1st Sess. § 107 (1965).

[34] H.R. 2512, note 27 *supra*, at § 107.

[35] H.R. REP. note 25 *supra*, at 31 and 36.

ment by a teacher to exempt him from damages if he proved that he reasonably believed that his classroom use of a copyrighted work was a "fair use under Section 107."[36] The committee was strongly of the view that this was as far as the bill should go as it was thought unwise to do more for educators and libraries than to let them try to have their practices approved by the courts under "fair use."[37] Resolution of the central issue in the reprography-copyright controversy was avoided.

Revision efforts in the Senate proceeded slowly, but at each significant turn the libraries obtained an extension of their photocopying privilege. The Senate failed to act on the House passed version in 1967 preferring to hold its own hearings which began in 1969. While the provision dealing with "fair use" remained the same, § 108 of the proposed revision picked up baggage protecting the library from infringement. Thus in S. 644, introduced by Senator McClellan in 1971, libraries were free to make a single copy of an entire copyrighted work upon the request of a user of the collection, if the user established he could not obtain a copy at normal prices from known trade sources and the library had no reason to believe the copy would be used for other than "private study, scholarship, or research."[38] But revisionists did not obtain Senate approval of a revision bill until 1974.

S. 1361, as reported by the Senate Judiciary Committee and eventually passed by the Senate in 1974, offered substantially broader privileges with regard to some forms of photocopying. Separate provisions dealt with duplication of entire works and duplication of a "small part" of a work. Included in the section dealing with "small parts" was reproduction of "no more than one article or other contribution to a copyrighted collection or periodical issue."[39] To reproduce an entire work, the user still had to demonstrate that he could not obtain the work elsewhere at normal prices. This requirement was dropped with regard to "small parts" and single articles in periodicals. Photoduplication

---

[36] H.R. 2512 *supra* note 34, at § 505 (c) (2).

[37] H.R. REP. note 25 *supra*, at 130–31.

[38] S. 644, 92d Cong., 1st Sess. § 108 (1971).

[39] S. 1361, 93d Cong., 1st Sess. § 108 (1973). The bill passed the Senate by a 70-to-1 vote. 120 Cong. Rec. 16167 (9 Sept. 1974).

was privileged if the library had no notice that the copy would be used for other than scholarly purposes.[40]

The major ambiguity remaining in S. 1361 was that the privilege to photoduplicate extended only to the "isolated and unrelated reproduction . . . of a single copy . . . of the same material on separate occasions," but not to "systematic reproduction . . . of single or multiple copies." It was unclear whether systematic reproduction of the same article upon the isolated and unrelated requests of different users was included within the privilege. In any event, it appeared that in the Senate the libraries had gained the momentum. The House on the other hand and particularly the House Judiciary Committee were busy impeaching a President.

The legislative history of the general copyright revision bill should have provided some instructive lessons for the Court as it examined its options in *Williams & Wilkins*. It was clear that the issue the Court was being called upon to decide was not one that had escaped congressional attention. Indeed much of the legislative debate and delay can be attributed to the "new technology" issues of copyright reform. In fact the difficulty experienced by Congress in accommodating the competing interests and the intricacy of fashioning a legislative solution should have encouraged judicial caution. Like eighteenth- and nineteenth-century judges, Congress found the problem of a proper balance between authors and public intractable.

On 17 December 1974, the Supreme Court heard oral arguments in *Williams & Wilkins*. Two days later both the Senate and the House enacted Public Law 93-573 which established a National Commission on New Technological Uses of Copyrighted Works and directed it to study and compile data on, among other things, "the reproduction and use of copyrighted works of authorship . . . by various forms of machine reproduction."[41] In justifying the commission study the House Report noted:[42]

---

[40] The bill as passed by the Senate contained the following additional conditions: (1) no more than one article from each periodical could be copied per request; (2) the copying must be done without profit for the library; (3) the copy must become the property of the user; (4) the copy must contain a notice of copyright; and (5) the library must be open to the public. The privilege granted by the section while protecting the libraries did not extend similar protection to the researchers themselves. Their privilege, if any, depended on the application of "fair use." S. 1361, note 39 *supra*, at § 108.

[41] 88 STAT. 1873.

[42] H. R. REP. No. 93-1581, 93d Cong., 2d Sess. (1974).

Moreover even though section 108 of the revision bill deals with certain aspects of library photocopying and other aspects of the problem are now before the Supreme Court in the Williams & Wilkins case, neither enactment of the revision bill nor a definitive decision in the lawsuit can be expected to solve the copyright problems presented by library photocopying or reprography generally.

B. THE COURT FAILS TO ACT

On 25 February 1975, much to the disappointment of a great many interested authors, publishers, educators and librarians, the Supreme Court proved unable to find a majority in *Williams & Wilkins.* As a result, the majority ruling of the Court of Claims, finding no infringement, was "affirmed by an equally divided Court."

This suit, which the Court of Claims called "ground-breaking," was filed 27 February, 1968, by a publisher of copyrighted medical periodicals against the United States for damages from the alleged infringement of eight articles in four medical journals by photocopying in governmental libraries.[43] The libraries based their defense on the judicial doctrine of "fair use," what they called long-existing "custom" of making single copies for scholars for their personal use. This, argued the libraries, was merely an extension of the well-recognized privilege of scholars to copy material in longhand or to have their secretaries type it. On the other hand, publishers vigorously asserted that this practice violated their exclusive right to "print, reprint, publish, copy and vend" their works under Section 1 of the 1909 Copyright Act.[44] The controversy still unresolved by Congress had moved into the courts.

The National Institutes of Health (NIH), one of the alleged infringers, with its technical library of 150,000 volumes, subscribed to 3,000 medical and other scientific journals, including the four in suit. Since subscription copies did not satisfy the research worker's needs, "as an integral part of its operation," NIH operated a photocopy service exclusively for its staff members. In doing so, the library did not ask the reasons for requests and the photocopies remained the property of the researchers. Some limits

---

[43] The action was brought under 28 U.S.C. § 1498(b)(1970), which authorizes suit against the United States for copyright infringement but limits recovery to actual damages only.

[44] 17 U.S.C. § 1.

were imposed; for example, only a single copy of an article limited to 40 pages would be made without special permission, and not more than one article per journal issue. In 1970 four employees were assigned to operate the photocopying equipment on an $86,000 budget; 93,000 articles containing some 930,000 pages were copied.

The National Medical Library (NLM), the other alleged infringer, was essentially a "librarian's library" which supplied material in its collection to other libraries, usually at the request of one of its patrons. Most requests came from other libraries or government agencies, but about 12 percent came from private or commercial organizations, including drug companies. While these were usually called "inter-library loans," in the case of requests for journals rarely was the original sent; a photocopy was used instead. Again limits were imposed: only one article per request was duplicated and never an entire journal issue. Requests for the latest and most widely available articles were rarely filled, unless from a governmental library or someone who had been unsuccessful in obtaining them elsewhere.[45] In 1968 NLM filled 120,000 requests for single articles, totaling over 1,000,000 pages. As in the case of NIH, NLM made no attempt to find out the ultimate use of the photocopy. At least one photocopy of each of the eight articles at issue was made at the request of NIH researchers and an Army medical officer stationed in Japan, in all cases for their professional work and "used solely for those purposes." Seven articles were more than two years old and the other almost as old.

In the Court of Claims the controversy focused on the doctrine of "fair use." The majority noted that the doctrine had developed because of a tension between copyright owners' desires to reap financial benefit and the constitutional purpose "to promote the Progress of Science and the Useful Arts." While the majority in analyzing the applicability of "fair use" considered a variety of

---

[45] Since 1968 NLM's policy had been not to copy more than one article from a single issue, nor more than three from a journal volume. Journals less than five years old on a "widely available list," including all four in suit, were not copied except for the Government, or in exceptional cases, such as where the requester reported he could not find the journal elsewhere. Requests for more than fifty pages were rarely filled, and those for more than one copy were always rejected. As a general rule not more than twenty copies per month were made for an individual, or thirty per month for an institution.

different factors, the holding of the Court of Claims was based on
three core propositions:[46]

> First, plaintiff has not in our view shown, and there is inade-
> quate reason to believe, that it is being or will be harmed sub-
> stantially by these specific practices of NIH and NLM; sec-
> ond, we are convinced that medicine and medical research
> will be injured by holding these particular practices to be an
> infringement; and third, since the problem of accommodat-
> ing the interests of science with those of the publishers (and
> authors) calls fundamentally for legislative solution or guid-
> ance, which has not yet been given, we should not, during the
> period before congressional action is forthcoming, place such
> a risk of harm upon science and medicine.

These three propositions were expanded in the majority opinion
by more detailed consideration of eight factors which when "fused"
together convinced the court that the libraries' practices were
"fair."[47] Three judges dissented.[48] The central problem for the

---

[46] 487 F.2d at 1354.

[47] The "eight factors" briefly summarized are: (1) "the hallmark of the whole enterprise of duplication" was "scientific progress, untainted by any commercial gain"; (2)
both libraries imposed "reasonably strict limitations" on photocopying so that the total
is relatively small in proportion to the number of journals on hand, and "duplication
of articles . . . does not appear at all heavy"; (3) library photocopying had existed
since the 1909 act with little complaint until ten or fifteen years ago; (4) "medical
science would be seriously hurt if such library photocopying were stopped"; (5) the
publisher had not shown financial injury, but relied on "general business common sense"
to show loss; (6) "this is now preeminently a problem for Congress," and with "the
grave uncertainty" whether "copy" in the 1909 act covers the case, "on balance and
on this record" it seemed "less dangerous to the varying interests at stake" to find fair
use; (7) Congress had been considering a change for many years and the "influential"
views on "fair use" of the House Committee on the Judiciary in its 1967 report "indicates the correctness of our general approach"; (8) many other countries "with problems
and backgrounds comparable to our own" have legislation which "would cover" what
NLH and NLM did.

[48] Chief Judge Cowen, dissenting, characterized the situation as "wholesale machine
copying and distribution . . . on a scale so vast that it dwarfs the output of many small
publishing companies." He rejected "fair use" for four basic reasons: First, the limits
imposed by the libraries were "illusory" as they allowed duplication of "the same
article over and over again." Second, the photocopies were "copies of completed copyrighted works" and "were intended to be substitutes for . . . the original articles"
which is "the very essence of wholesale copying and, without more, defeats the defense
of 'fair use.' " Third, the scholar's fair use privilege to quote parts of copyrighted works
did not cover "the massive copying and distribution" by the libraries, and if a nonprofit
motive automatically excused the copying, it would render useless the statutory consent
to suit for copyright infringement since all government copying is nonprofit. Fourth,
he noted that while a copyright plaintiff need not prove actual damages, the record supported the trial judge's view that distribution of free copies would draw potential customers away from the publisher. Judge Cowen argued that a holding limited to reason-

Court of Claims and the one confronting the Supreme Court remained the definition of the function and purpose of the copyright law.

II. The Functions of Copyright

Copyright can be seen performing one of two often conflicting functions: (1) protection of the author's interests in the fruits of his creative efforts, or (2) promotion of the general welfare by regulating the allocation of scarce resources to intellectual production. The first alternative in the context of the history of copyright is largely motivated by noneconomic concerns. Emphasizing the producer's interest can involve notions of natural rights and property interests without regard to the implications of resource allocation. The second justification for copyright protection, which emphasizes the public interest, is predominantly governed by economic theory.

The discussion of the "natural rights" of an author may, at the outset, seem obsolete, particularly in an area so heavily burdened with economic implications.[49] Giving full play to a "natural rights" approach would dictate a perpetual copyright protecting the author from all unauthorized uses, a proposition unlikely to garner much support. The concept of "natural rights"—the apparent fairness of insuring that the benefits of a work will be secured to its creator and the perceived injustice of allowing unauthorized enrichment from the labors of others — has played and continues to play an important role in copyright cases. The acceptance in *Wheaton v. Peters* of the predominance of the legislative branch in defining the extent of the author's interest in his works did not end the matter. The controversy became one of statutory interpretation and the extent to which the courts could be persuaded to expand or restrict the language of the copyright statute. It is in this context

---

able royalty payments would not injure medical research and might encourage a satisfactory agreement among the parties. 487 F.2d at 1363 *et seq.*

Judge Nichols in a separate dissent declared he could not find a "fair use" where the user benefits extensively from copyrighted material and "adamantly refuses to make any contribution to defray the publisher's costs, or compensate for the author's effort and expertise." 487 F.2d at 1387.

[49] The possible theoretical justifications for a patent system are reviewed and analyzed in Machlup, *An Economic Review of the Patent System*, Study 15 for the Subcommittee on Patents, Trademarks, and Copyrights of the Senate Committee on the Judiciary, 85th Cong., 2d Sess. (Comm. Print 1958). For the most part copyright has not received such extensive treatment, and there are sufficient differences in the respective scopes of the patent and copyright monopolies to suggest caution in drawing the analogy.

that the original debate over the justification for protecting authors surfaced again in *Williams & Wilkins*.

A. COPYRIGHT AS PROPERTY

The eighteenth-century intellectual property debate was in a certain sense won by those who argued that the author had a natural right in his intellectual labors. In *Millar v. Taylor* a majority of the Kings Bench adopted this view, while eight of the twelve judges in *Donaldson v. Becket* agreed. The additional holding in *Donaldson*, however, followed in *Wheaton v. Peters* by the United States Supreme Court, that the common law interest was supplanted by statute, made further discussion on the foundation of copyright largely irrelevant. Interpretation of the copyright legislation became the critical inquiry, and in most instances pursuit of the more basic question of the function of copyright was thought unnecessary. The tension between the various interests involved and the unresolved nature of the function of copyright may account for a willingness on the part of the courts to adopt judicial doctrines that add to or at times directly contradict the language of the statute. Indeed, the complexity of the basic premise may explain why Congress has been content to allow the judiciary to resolve these issues.[50]

At common law the difficulty with perceiving a property interest in intellectual creations resulted from the common law's adherence to doctrines of possession. Ideas and other incorporeal intellectual achievements once published were not subject to exclusive possession. Indeed the analogy to the law governing animals *ferae naturae*, where the hunter "owned" the animal as long as it was possessed but upon escape (publication?) it returned to a natural state, was almost irresistible.[51] On the other hand, commentators

---

[50] See KAPLAN, AN UNHURRIED VIEW OF COPYRIGHT 40 (1967): "I do not mean to reproach the draftsmen for failing to face squarely the questions of validity and infringement which are in the end insoluble. Rather I make the point that the statute, like its predecessors, leaves the development of fundamentals to the judges. Indeed the courts have had to be consulted at nearly every point, for the text of the statute has a maddeningly casual prolixity and imprecision throughout."

[51] See Millar v. Taylor, 4 Burr. 2303, 2363, 98 Eng. Rep. 201, 233 (1769) (Yates, J., dissenting). See also Justice Brandeis's dissenting opinion in International News Service v. Associated Press, 248 U.S. 215, 250 (1918): "The general rule of law is, that the noblest of human productions—knowledge, truths ascertained, conceptions, and ideas—become, after voluntary communication to others, free as the air to common use. Upon these incorporeal productions the attribute of property is continued after such communication only in certain classes of cases where public policy has seemed to demand it."

and philosophers argued strongly for the principle that a person should retain the fruits of his efforts, either as a matter of traditional common law doctrine or as a matter of natural right.[52] The notes to *Blackstone's Commentaries*, for example, contain a strong argument in favor of "property" by creative act to support the rights of authors in their published works.[53] The copyright can be perceived as a device to implement this "moral" right of an author in his works, the right to reap the fruits of his creation, to protect the integrity of his creation as an extension of his personality, and to obtain a reward for his contribution to society.[54]

The "natural rights" explanation of copyright has been found wanting both on moral and economic grounds. Professor Breyer has suggested that authors might well obtain fruits from their labors without copyright, and thus the copyright determines not whether reward will be forthcoming but the rate of return.[55] He found it difficult to construct an argument on moral grounds for adding to the "fruits" by granting copyright protection. It has also been argued that the right of an author in the integrity of his work may be protected by other tort principles, and, if society must reward authors, there are more efficient mechanisms such as prizes and other direct subsidies.[56] Whatever merit these arguments have they are not universally accepted nor conclusively established. And the principle that rejects the propriety of appropriating that which was created by others, continues to influence both courts and politicians alike. The Supreme Court, for example, has indicated in a variety of ways that the law protects against unjust enrichment from the labors of others regardless of the resulting economic consequences.[57]

Viewing the copyright granted by Congress as a property right would suggest an outcome in *Williams & Wilkins* in favor of the

---

[52] The philosophical basis for a property interest in intellectual creations is reviewed in Breyer, *The Uneasy Case for Copyright: A Study of Copyright in Books, Photocopies, and Computer Programs*, 84 HARV. L. REV. 281 284–91 (1970).

[53] 2 BLACKSTONE, COMMENTARIES 406–07 n.13 (1865 ed.).

[54] Hurt & Schuchman, *The Economic Rationale of Copyright*, 56 AM. ECON. REV. 421 (1966).

[55] Breyer, note 52 *supra*.

[56] Hurt & Schuchman, note 54 *supra*.

[57] International News Service v. Associated Press, 248 U.S. 215 (1918). The *INS* case and the subsequent history of its misappropriation doctrine are discussed in Part IV, *infra*.

publishers. The core propositions of the Court of Claims required a balancing of the advance of medical research stimulated by photocopying against the detriment to the publishers. Structured in this way, the public interest is seen as paramount. If copyright were recognized as a property interest, however, the court, in order to find for the libraries, would be required to distinguish between forcing authors and publishers, but not other property owners, to subsidize research. Authors have argued that the products of their labor cannot or should not be treated differently from the products of the Xerox Corporation, and if medical researchers or libraries on their behalf must compensate Xerox for use of its machines, why should they not also compensate the authors for use of their articles?[58]

B. COPYRIGHT AS INCENTIVE

In contrast to emphasizing the private property aspect, copyright can be viewed exclusively as a means to provide economic incentives to authors and publishers in order to preserve the public interest in the publication of writings. With this emphasis the private interests of the authors and publishers would be subordinate to claims for access where it can be demonstrated that the public interest will be better served by allowing frce use of copyrighted works. This approach requires an economic analysis of copyright doctrines. It was the course pursued by the Court of Claims in *Williams & Wilkins*. The difficulties with utilizing economic theory to justify the creation of a judicial privilege to copy copyrighted works is that neither a theoretical nor an empirical basis exists upon which to evaluate the claims of either party.

Writings fall within a category of goods designated by econo-

---

[58] See, *e.g.*, Statement of Rex Stout on behalf of the Authors' League of America, in *Hearings on H.R. 4347 before Subcomm. #3 of the House Comm. on the Judiciary*, 89th Cong., 1st Sess., ser. 8, pt. 1, at 88 (1965): "No one else's property or services are appropriated without charge for education, to serve the public interest. . . . The copy machines, paper, and other equipment used to disseminate his [the author's] writings are all sold to schools by profit-making enterprises. No one has suggested that they, too, be appropriated without charge."
Acceptance of the "natural rights" theory does not of course mean that there can be no limits on the power of the "property" owner or that his interests cannot be restricted for socially beneficial purposes. The traditional common law approach to the use of another's property out of the necessity to protect some interest of the actor has been to require compensation. Vincent v. Lake Erie Transportation Co., 109 Minn. 456, 124 N.W. 221 (1910).

mists as "public goods" or "collective goods."[59] The essential characteristic of a public good is that once it is produced, use by one individual does not diminish the amount available for others. For many public goods it is also difficult or impossible to establish a market for the goods and at the same time exclude persons who desire to use the goods but who refuse to pay for them.[60] Absent some form of copyright protection, the publisher would not be able to prevent the distribution of his work beyond those who have contributed toward its costs of production. These characteristics of public goods increase substantially the costs of enforcing negotiated arrangements for the sale and distribution of the goods. The difficulties in accommodating the interests of the publishers and the libraries in *Williams & Wilkins* is illustrative.

Under a regime in which libraries or their users were legally obligated to pay royalties for duplication, the costs of collecting and enforcing that obligation would be substantial. Individual negotiations for permission to photocopy would be very costly in relationship to the amount of the royalty likely to be exacted. A number of proposals call for a "clearinghouse system" similar to ASCAP whereby private arrangements are effectuated in order centrally to license photocopying rights.[61] It may or may not be

[59] See ALCHIAN & ALLEN, UNIVERSITY ECONOMICS 147 (3d ed. 1972); Breyer, note 52 *supra*, at 288–89.

[60] There are some public goods for which exclusion of freeloaders is possible. Pay television has been suggested as an example. Demsetz, *The Private Production of Public Goods*, 13 J. LAW & ECON. 293 (1970).

[61] The "clearinghouse proposal" is advanced in detail in Sophar & Heilprin, *The Determination of Legal Facts and Economic Guideposts with Respect to the Dissemination of Scientific and Educational Information as It Is Affected by Copyright—A Status Report*, Final Report, Prepared by the Committee to Investigate Copyright Problems Affecting Communication in Science and Education, Inc., for the U. S. Dept. of H.E.W. Project No. 70793 (1967).
It would appear that generally a publisher would have sufficient economic incentives to adopt some form of licensing policy. It is also possible for Congress to adopt a compulsory license provision similar to that applicable to the recording of musical compositions. 17 U.S.C. §1(e).
The experience of the Williams & Wilkins Company in its attempt to exploit the duplication rights subsequent to the trial judge's finding of infringement, while obviously affected by the uncertainties of the pending appeal, demonstrates the complexity of the relationships in this area. After winning at the trial, the publisher circulated letters to libraries stating that after 1 January 1973 subscription prices for journals would be raised on the average of $3.65 a year which would include a right to photocopy freely, including back issues, but would not include a license for purposes of interlibrary loan programs for which a five-cent-per-page royalty would be exacted. The director of NLM refused to pay the additional fee pending the appeal, and allegedly threatened to boycott Williams & Wilkins publications and to exclude them from the *Index Medicus*. There-

economical to administer such a system and distribute the pro-ceeds.[62] And, the implications of private price-fixing essential to most clearinghouse systems must be included on the negative side of such arrangements. The antitrust experience with ASCAP amply demonstrates the problem.[63]

Under a regime in which photocopying is "free," the copyright owner could in theory increase the price of the book to include a substitute for the royalty. If the demand for the book is respon-sive to price, however, subscriptions will decrease with the rise in price. It would be difficult, absent copyright protection, for the pub-lisher to discriminate in price between those who would use their copy for photoduplication and those who would not.[64] As the pub-lisher increased his price and decreased the number of subscribers, he would at the same time increase the potential market for dupli-cated copies. The logical extreme in the context of the advances in reprographic techniques and the increased use of "interlibrary loan" programs (in periodicals made up mainly of photoduplicated copies), becomes a copyright owner faced with a single potential buyer.[65] And, the ability of others to photocopy the photocopy

upon, the publisher withdrew its license offer but announced a new institutional rate which represented an average increase of $3.65. A representative of the company told a Senate committee that this "did not give the library any photographic copying rights at all. . . . [W]e didn't give the libraries what we wanted to give them." *Hearings on S. 1361 before the Subcommittee on Patents, Trademarks, and Copyrights of the Senate Com-merce Committee,* 93d Cong., 1st Sess. at 153–64 (1973) (testimony of Mrs. Andrea Albrecht, Director of Marketing Research, Williams & Wilkins Co.).

[62] See Breyer, note 52 *supra,* at 332–33.

[63] See United States v. ASCAP, 341 F.2d 1003 (2d Cir. 1965).

[64] It has been argued that the Court of Claims in fact shifted the costs of duplication from users to subscribers, since the publisher in order to cover costs must keep subscrip-tion rates higher than would be the case if he could distribute his costs among both sub-scribers and duplicators. Goldstein, *The Private Consumption of Public Goods: A Comment on Williams & Wilkins Co. v. United States,* 21 BULL. COPYRIGHT SOC. 204 (1974).

[65] Conventional interlibrary loan programs often utilize a photocopy as a substitute for sending an original copy of a requested periodical. There has been a growing trend to utilize facsimile transmission in which copies of articles can be instantaneously trans-mitted through telephone lines. The Sophar and Heilprin study indicated that of 76 li-braries surveyed, 57 participated in conventional programs and 19 used facsimile trans-mission. Sophar & Heilprin, note 61 *supra,* at 49. It has also been reported that a Uni-versity of California experiment used microwave to transmit articles between campuses. "Facsimile transmission will some day make it possible for one library in a network to use a single copy of a journal or book to supply all libraries in the network." 15 U.C.L.A. L. REV. 931, 947 (1968). Harvard, Yale, and Columbia Universities in cooperation with the New York Public Library have recently announced plans to share purchases of some journals. N.Y. Times, 24 Mar. 1974, at 59, col. 1.

would put the original purchaser in the same position as the publisher in attempting to recoup his acquisition costs.

It is reasonably clear that the legal rule regarding the duplication of copyrighted works will have an adverse effect on one of the two opposing interests and will determine, in part, the amount of publication and research which will be performed.[66] If photocopying for research purposes is privileged, publishers will lose income. If the copyright monopoly extends to the activities of the libraries, the costs of research will increase. In order to justify a judicial exception to the copyright statute on the basis of economics, a court must be able to demonstrate that the amount of publication and research resulting from its rule advances the public welfare to a greater extent than that produced under the regime imposed by Congress. It has been suggested that two separate assumptions may support the welfare analysis of copyright:[67]

> First, without copyright protection, the private economic return from literary creation (to author and publishers) will necessarily be smaller than the economic benefit of this activity to society. As a result, it is argued the quantity of literary creation will be insufficient to maximize welfare. Second, literary production, like education, should be encouraged because it has greater intrinsic merit than its alternative product, perhaps because of its long run neighborhood effects.

The second assumption equates the public welfare with the maximization of publication and research; the first assumption argues for an efficient allocation of resources.

Both sides of the debate over reprography and copyright seemingly have adopted the second assumption. Publishers maintain that the total level of publication will decrease if reprographic users do not contribute to the cost of production whereas users of published material argue that they will not produce as much if the costs of research are increased by the tribute paid to the copyright owner. Resolution of the issue requires a comparison of the amount of intellectual goods produced under either of two potential regimes —one in which reprography is an infringement and one in which it is privileged.

---

[66] The high costs of carrying on private transactions will cause the legal rule to have a significant impact on the amount of the goods produced. Coase, *The Problem of Social Cost*, 3 J. LAW & ECON. 1 (1960).

[67] Hurt & Schuchman, note 54 *supra*, at 429.

One of the difficulties in pursuing this analysis is that hard evidence is lacking either in the record of the *Williams & Wilkins* litigation or the presentations to Congress to show: (*a*) the extent to which current photocopying practices of libraries have detracted from the amount of intellectual material published;[68] (*b*) the extent to which royalties to copyright owners would detract from the research efforts of scholars;[69] and (*c*) the quantitative relationships between the amount lost or gained by publishers and the amount lost or gained by users. If the Supreme Court had sought to fashion a rule which would maximize the production and dissemination of scholarly works, it would have to do so by instinct rather than reason. Furthermore, the selection of scholarly research and publi-

---

[68] The Court of Claims bemoaned the absence of any "careful, thorough, impartial study" of the economic effect of photocopying on publishers, characterizing what was available as "conclusory generalizations of injury." 487 F.2d at 1358 n.22.

The appeals panel chose to emphasize that the publisher's business had prospered at a rate faster than the gross national product, even though there were years when some of the journals in question did not show a profit. 487 F.2d at 1357. A review of the history of attempts to study the economic impact of photocopying is provided in Sophar & Heilprin, note 61 *supra*, at 2. Reported therein are the results of a study commissioned by the National Science Foundation and conducted by George Fry and Associates which concluded that "economic damage does not exist in substance. It does exist in special circumstances; but in relation to the total picture, we do not consider it a major problem." *Id.* at 7. The Fry report was emphasized by the Court of Claims. 487 F.2d at 1358. The Sophar and Heilprin study which sought to remedy the lack of economic data succeeded in documenting the amount of photocopying being performed, but did not demonstrate the impact it had on publisher profits.

Other economic factors such as a cutback in public funding have caused some hardships for the publishers of scientific journals, and it may be impossible to establish a direct causal relationship between declines in revenues and any one factor. It has been noted that "the publishers have never been able to make a persuasive case that copying is destroying the journals. The point appears to be, rather, that *licensed photocopying could save them.*" Weinberg, *The Photocopying Revolution and the Copyright Crisis*, 38 PUBLIC INTEREST 99, 106 (1975).

[69] Rejecting untested hypotheses as an appropriate base from which to prove economic loss on the part of publishers, the Court of Claims determined it unnecessary to "spend time and space demonstrating" that "medical science would be seriously hurt if such library photocopying were stopped" because the court had "no doubt in [its mind]" that it would be. The court also thought it "wholly unrealistic" to expect researchers to increase the number of their personal journal subscriptions. 487 F.2d at 1356–57. The analysis is unquestionably correct if photocopying were prohibited. The court did not, however, analyze the more likely possibility that photoduplication could continue upon payment of royalties to the copyright owner. While the hypothesis that royalty charges would cut down the amount of photocopying is correct, evidence is lacking as to the extent to which this would be true. Indeed one of the findings of the Court of Claims contained a survey conducted by the Director of NLM which disclosed that the amount of royalties which would have been due to Williams & Wilkins at 2 cents per page over a ninety-day sample was "surprisingly small," and the administrative expense in collecting it would have been "substantially greater than the royalty itself." Petitioner's Brief for Certiorari, at App. 95.

cation as a preferred activity to be expanded without regard to competing interests, while perhaps defensible, is the type of political decision more appropriately made by Congress.

If the general welfare is not served by a rule that maximizes research and publication without regard to competing demands for resources, the Court must confront the formidable task of determining the scope of copyright protection necessary to produce an amount of scholarly effort society believes to be optimal in relation to other goods and services. In most instances, the free marketplace can be relied upon to determine the relative value of various goods. But economists have only recently begun to examine how producers of public goods respond to various market conditions and little consensus has emerged.[70] In fact there is little agreement as to whether any form of copyright protection is necessary to insure a sufficient supply of written work.[71] In short, while it has often been asserted that copyright protection serves the general welfare, the assertion is more a political hypothesis than an empirical certainty. While a judicial response to an interstitial issue of copyright law might well be based on the Court's own hunch about the general welfare, there is little in the economic literature which would buttress creating a privilege to do what Congress has expressly forbidden.

The Court had two alternative approaches from which to choose in reviewing the Court of Claim's decision in *Williams & Wilkins*. If the property approach were adopted, the Court of Claims's ruling is subject to grave inadequacies. If the Court had attempted to apply economic analysis, it is unlikely that it could have done more than fashion a rule based on the most tentative assumptions regarding the behavior of libraries, scholars, publishers, and authors. Nor could it have developed a holding that would have wide applicability. A rule which efficiently allocates resources in the field of medicine where there are heavy subsidies may well be

---

[70] *Compare* Demsetz, *The Private Production of Public Goods*, note 60 *supra*, with Samuelson, *Contrast between Welfare Conditions for Joint Supply and for Public Goods*, 51 REV. ECON. & STAT. 26 (1969); see also, Oakland, *Public Goods, Perfect Competition and Underproduction*, 82 J. POL. ECON. 927 (1974).

[71] Hurt & Schuchman, note 54 *supra*. But see Tyerman, *The Economic Rationale for Copyright Protection for Published Books: A Reply to Professor Breyer*, 18 U.C.L.A. L. REV. 1100 (1971). See also Breyer, *Copyright: A Rejoinder*, 20 U.C.L.A. L. REV. 75 (1972); Plant, *The Economic Aspects of Copyright in Books*, 1 ECONOMICA 167 (n.s. 1934). For an extensive economic analysis of the patent system see Machlup, note 49 *supra*.

counterproductive in other fields, such as law, where other conditions exist.[72]

III. "Fair Use"

While *Williams & Wilkins* contained the fundamental question of the function of copyright law, the legal argument revolved around the legal doctrine of "fair use." The issue of "fair use" has been termed "the most troublesome in the whole law of copyright,"[73] and it is nearly universally agreed among both courts and commentators that the doctrine is an evanescent body of distinguishable cases which offers little guidance in resolving new conflicts.[74] Surprisingly enough, this critical feature of American copyright law has never received the direct attention or blessing of the United States Supreme Court. Prior to *Williams & Wilkins*, the Court had a direct opportunity to consider "fair use" in two instances. In one the Court sent the case back because of an inadequate record.[75] In the other, as in *Williams & Wilkins*, the lower court was affirmed by an equally divided Court.[76] A single doctrine that has forced the Court to divide equally twice can claim some measure of difficulty.

The copyright statute of 1909 does not specifically define infringement but rather emphasizes the exclusive nature of the rights granted to the copyright owner. These "exclusive" rights include the right to "copy" the work. The statute affords the owner a variety of remedies for infringement, including damages, recovery of profits, and injunctive relief.[77] In addition, Congress provided statutory damages "in lieu" of proof of actual loss caused by an infringement.[78] The statute does not provide for privileged use

---

[72] The Court of Claims recognized this particular difficulty in emphasizing the limits of its holding: ". . . our holding is restricted to the type and context of use by NIH and NLM, as shown by this record. That is all we have before us, and we do not pass on dissimilar systems or uses of copyrighted materials by other institutions or enterprises, or in other fields, or as applied to items other than journal articles, or with other significant variables." 487 F.2d at 1362.

[73] Dellar v. Samuel Goldwyn, Inc., 104 F.2d 661, 662 (2d Cir. 1930).

[74] 2 Nimmer, Copyright § 145 (1975); Latman, note 21 *supra*.

[75] Public Affairs Assoc., Inc. v. Rickover, 284 F.2d 262 (D.C. Cir. 1960), *vacated for insufficient record*, 369 U.S. 111 (1962).

[76] Benny v. Loew's, Inc., 239 F.2d 532 (9th Cir. 1956), *aff'd by an equally divided court, sub. nom.* Columbia Broadcasting System, Inc. v. Loew's, Inc., 356 U.S. 43 (1958).

[77] 17 U.S.C. § 101.   [78] *Ibid.*

nor does it expressly require that the copyright owner suffer or prove economic loss in order to protect his interest. Thus the teaching of the statute is that a copyright owner need only show that the defendant copied his work. The judicial gloss on the statute, however, teaches the opposite. Since Justice Story's famous dictum in *Folsom v. Marsh*,[79] courts have been validating by word and deed a variety of copying activities. If the use is "fair" it is privileged.

A. ORIGINS OF FAIR USE

Although the Statute of Anne did not contain a section outlining privileged uses, the English courts were quick to recognize that one of the dilemmas of any copyright system is to balance the proprietary rights of authors against the public interest in access to information. Chief Justice Mansfield in a famous dictum noted:[80]

> [W]e must take care to guard against two extremes equally prejudicial; the one, that men of ability, who have employed their time for the service of the community, may not be deprived of their just merits, and the reward of their ingenuity and labour; the other, that the world may not be deprived of improvements, nor the progress of the arts be retarded.

Mansfield faced the issue in a difficult copyright context. The plaintiff held copyrights in four navigational charts. The defendant utilized the charts to make one larger chart. Expert testimony established that the defendant employed the mercator principle while the plaintiff did not. This made plaintiff's charts inaccurate as ships moved away from the equator. Mansfield held that the jury must determine whether the defendant's work product was a "servile imitation" (infringement) or whether defendant corrected errors in plaintiff's original work (no infringement). In the latter event, the use of plaintiff's maps would be permissible, because the copyright "guards against the piracy of the words and sentiments; but it does not prohibit writing on the same subject."[81] In context, Mansfield's view either emphasized the value of the corrected

---

[79] 9 Fed. Cas. 342 (1841).

[80] Sayre v. Moore, 1 East 361, 102 Eng. Rep. 139, 140 (K.B. ˙ ᷄).

[81] *Ibid.*

chart or the limitation on any author to appropriate to his exclusive use the geographical features of the world.

As we have noted, in American jurisprudence, the doctrine of "fair use" is generally traced to Justice Story's decision, on circuit, in *Folsom v. Marsh*.[82] Folsom was publisher of a twelve-volume work by Jared Sparks on George Washington containing a vast amount of Washington's correspondence. Charles Upham subsequently published a two-volume work containing an originally written narrative of the life of Washington and reproductions of 319 letters originally published in the Sparks work. Sparks successfully claimed his copyright covered the letters.

In confronting the major issue whether the taking constituted an infringement, Justice Story, after declaring the issue to be "intricate and embarrassing" calling for "subtile," "refined," and "evanescent" distinctions, stated: "[W]e must often, in deciding questions of this sort, look to the nature and objects of the selections made, the quantity and value of the materials used, and the degree in which the use may prejudice the sale, or diminish the profits, or supersede the objects, of the original work."[83] From this language "fair use" developed.[84]

The difficulty with Story's opinion is that, while he provided the factors to be weighed in answering the question, he failed to articulate the purpose of his inquiry. In one instance, early in the opinion, he seemed to indicate that the problem was whether the taking by Upham was substantial. He subsequently noted: "[I]t is not only quantity, but value that is always looked to."[85] The tenor of the opinion suggests that Story was primarily concerned with whether the alleged infringement would serve as a substitute for the original work, in other words, whether the economic incentive provided by the copyright laws would be substantially defeated and the copyright owner directly injured by the infringing work.

Whatever the ambiguities, it is clear that Story did not attempt to balance the interests of the copyright owner against the spillover benefits obtainable by the reading public. There is little to

---

[82] Note 79 *supra*.   [83] *Id*. at 348.

[84] The early "fair use" cases are discussed in Cohen, *Fair Use in the Law of Copyright*, 6 COPYRIGHT L. SYM. 43 (1955). The current proposed general revision of the copyright law contains a statutory adoption of Story's analysis. See, *e.g.*, S. 1361, 93d Cong., 1st Sess., § 107 (1973).

[85] 9 Fed. Cas. at 348.

suggest that Story perceived, in adopting what subsequently became the language of fair use, a need to limit the copyright owner's monopoly in order to facilitate the creation of new works. In fact, Story found Upham's work an infringement "not without some regret, that it may interfere, in some measure, with the very meritorious labors of the defendants, in their great undertaking of a series of works adapted to school libraries."[86] In fact Story's opinion expressly recognized the copyright as a device to protect the property interest of the creator:[87]

> If so much is taken, that the value of the original is sensibly diminished, or the labors of the original author are substantially to an injurious extent appropriated by another, that is sufficient, in point of law, to constitute a piracy pro tanto. The entirety of the copyright is the property of the author; and it is no defence, that another person has appropriated a part, and not the whole, of any property.

The ambiguities created by the failure to explain exactly what purpose the factors of fair use were designed to serve is compounded in *Folsom* by Story's failure to indicate the source of the doctrine. He utilized the English cases as precedent, but his previous participation in *Wheaton v. Peters*, where the Court held that the author's interest in his published works was peculiarly statutory, would suggest that he should have tied his decision either to some statutory phrase or to some constitutional directive. The absence of any specific reference to source or policy allowed, indeed encouraged, courts to engraft on the copyright system a variety of privileges under the rubric of "fair use."

Justice Story did not in *Folsom* use the language "fair use," although his decision is thought to have spawned the approach generally taken by contemporary courts under that doctrine. In 1879, in *Baker v. Selden*,[88] the Supreme Court rendered a decision which may explain the holding if not the rhetoric in some "fair use" decisions. In *Baker*, the copyrighted work was a treatise by Charles Selden explaining a bookkeeping system and providing forms neces-

---

[86] *Id.* at 349. Story's concern about the potential markets for the copyrighted work appeared to be well founded. Chief Justice John Marshall, a partner with Sparks in the original venture, subsequently published an abridgment of the longer work especially for children. BAKER, JOHN MARSHALL: A LIFE IN THE LAW 647 (1974).

[87] 9 Fed. Cas. at 348.

[88] 101 U.S. 99 (1879).

sary to put the system into practice. Baker subsequently published account books utilizing the forms originated in the Selden work. The Court held that there was no infringement. While the explanation of a new system was protectible under the copyright law, the system itself could only be protected by a patent. Copyright protected the manner of expression not the underlying idea of the work. And while the forms might be considered part of the manner of expression, they were necessary to practice the art and were thus not protected by the copyright: [89]

> The very object of publishing a book on science or the useful arts is to communicate to the world the useful knowledge which it contains. But this object would be frustrated if the knowledge could not be used without incurring the guilt of piracy of the book. And where the art it teaches cannot be used without employing the methods and diagrams used to illustrate the book, or such as are similar to them, such methods and diagrams are to be considered as necessary incidents to the art, and given therewith to the public; not given for the purpose of publication in other work explanatory of the art, but for the purpose of practical application.

The Court did not precisely explain the source of its doctrine that copyright only protects the expression and not the idea although there was ample precedent in the common law.[90] In part, the Court was attempting to separate the patent and copyright systems, arguing that since unlike the copyright system the patent laws required pre-issuance evaluation by the patent office, exclusive rights in ideas and arts themselves should not be created unless such an evaluation had occurred. On the other hand, it also appears that the Court was interpreting the statutory provision which provided for copyright in "books." This, in turn, may reflect the constitutional directive of the Patent and Copyright Clause that Congress can grant exclusive rights only in "writings." In any event, the Court's approach in *Baker* examined and defined the subject matter protectible under the copyright law, establishing the metes

---

[89] *Id.* at 103. Two cases which illustrate the point that the expression can be appropriated if necessary to practice the underlying art are: Continental Casualty Co. v. Beardsley, 253 F.2d 702 (2d Cir. 1958) (insurance forms copyrightable but not infringed); Morrissey v. Procter & Gamble Co., 379 F.2d 675 (1st Cir. 1967) (rules for contests).

[90] See Holmes v. Hurst, 174 U.S. 82, 86 (1899) (citing Lord Mansfield for the proposition that "ideas are as little susceptible of private appropriation as air or sunlight."

and bounds of the property interest granted by the copyright statute.[91]

The *Baker* opinion does not utilize the terminology of "fair use" and can arguably be limited to apply only to works based on "facts" as opposed to works created primarily for aesthetic purposes.[92] On the other hand, some decisions based on "fair use" have in fact been holdings that the alleged infringer did not appropriate that part of the copyrighted work which was protected.[93] In these cases, "fair use" served as a short-hand expression for a finding of no infringement rather than a privileged infringement. The distinction is critical and reflective of the fundamental copyright dilemma.

Where "fair use" is used as a substitute for finding no infringement of protectible subject matter, it parallels the *Baker v. Selden* approach. And, *Baker* is fully consistent with an analysis that (1) regards copyrights as a recognition of the natural rights of an author to a property interest in his creative works; (2) defers to the judgment of Congress as to the appropriate scope of the copyright monopoly. The *Baker* case limited that interest, in the context of a constitutional provision directed to "authors" and "writings," to the manner of expression, leaving the patent system free to protect the "discoveries" (ideas) of "inventors." If "fair use" is, on the other hand, a privileged infringement, the courts must, without congressional assistance, assert some public interest sufficient to limit the statutory grant of copyright protection. In this context, "fair use" becomes the means by which courts could elevate the public's interest in dissemination of information above the author's interest. The ambiguity of the early precedents for the doctrine of "fair use" provides support for both sides in the photocopy-copyright debate.

B. "FAIR USE" AS BALANCING

The Court of Claims in *Williams & Wilkins* discovered support in the "fair use" cases for a judicial balancing of the needs of the

---

[91] For an excellent review of the *Baker* analysis, see Gorman, *Copyright Protection for the Collection and Representation of Facts*, 76 HARV. L. REV. 1569 (1963). Another view of the merits of the idea-expression distinction is presented in Libott, *Round the Prickly Pear: The Idea-Expression Fallacy in a Mass Communications World*, 16 COPYRIGHT L. SYM. 30 (1966).

[92] KAPLAN, note 50 *supra*, at 63.

[93] Latman, note 21 *supra*.

producer and the consumer of intellectual goods. The facts presented an attractive basis for such balancing since the potential
social gain from advances in medical science was substantial. It is
difficult to argue with the goal pursued by the court. The issue,
however, is whether "fair use" provides an appropriate vehicle
for that pursuit. While the basis for the "fair use" doctrine remains
unclear, there are a number of different factual situations around
which most of the cases are clustered. And a plausible explanation
of these cases weakens their application in favor of library photocopying.

1. *Review, criticism, and parody cases.* If "fair use" protects any
activity it is the practice of taking small portions of a copyrighted
work for review or critical purposes. While agreement with this
proposition is universal, in 1964 in his report on "fair use" to the
Copyright Office Alan Latman indicated no reported American
decision.[94] A case close to the point is *Consumers Union of United
States v. Hobart Mfg. Co.,*[95] in which a manufacturer whose dishwashers were rated second in *Consumer Reports* quoted part of the
report in a rebutting sales bulletin. In a suit for copyright infringement the court, without relying on "fair use," held that an author
cannot use the copyright law to insulate his works from criticism.
The critical review cases can be explained by application of the
Baker v. Selden analysis. *Baker* teaches that the facts or ideas of
a copyrighted report are not protected, and a subsequent copier
can utilize those facts in his work critical of the first. Moreover,
if the manner of expression is necessary in order to capture and
use the idea—which it is in many instances of critical reviews—then
Baker authorizes the taking of the expression as well. On the other
hand, a reviewer could not publish the entire work reviewed.

The parody cases dramatize the issue of review and criticism.
Parody is a form of criticism in which part of the underlying work
must be presented—appropriated if you will—in order to make the
parody effective. Parody as an art form surely enjoys society's
protection. On the other hand, the creator of the parody benefits
as a result of the owner's earlier efforts.

The courts have not had an easy time accommodating parody
and copyright. In *Benny v. Loew's Inc.*, the Ninth Circuit held
that Jack Benny's burlesque of the copyrighted play "Gaslight"

---

[94] *Id.* at 9.
[95] 189 F. Supp. 275 (S.D. N.Y. 1960).

was an infringement. The court found that Benny had taken a substantial part of the copyrighted work, including "detailed borrowing of much of the dialogue with some variation in wording." Rejecting the applicability of the doctrine of "fair use," the court noted that " 'wholesale copying and publication of copyrighted material can [never] be fair use.' "[96] The case was affirmed by the Supreme Court on an equally divided vote.

The Second Circuit faced the parody question in *Berlin v. E.C. Publications, Inc.*,[97] where *Mad* magazine published parody lyrics which were to be "Sung to the tune of" plaintiff's copyrighted music. The musical score itself was not published in the magazine. The Court held: "At the very least, where, as here, it is clear that the parody has neither the intent nor the effect of fulfilling the demand for the original, and where the parodist does not appropriate a greater amount of the original work than is necessary to 'recall or conjure up' the object of his satire, a finding of infringement would be improper."[98]

The court justified its conclusion by asserting that courts ought to subordinate the copyright owner's financial return "to the greater public interest in the development of art, science and industry," citing the constitutional directive to Congress in the Patent and Copyright Clause to "promote the Progress of Science and useful Arts."[99] Indeed the *Berlin* case has been utilized often to support the proposition that courts, in deciding infringement questions, must make the balancing decision between the public interest in information and the copyright owner's monopoly. The *Baker v. Selden* inquiry as to what it is that is protected in a copyrighted work, however, provides not only a suitable governing rule for accommodating parody and copyright but also a suitable explanation for the rule announced in the *Berlin* case.

While the distinction between idea and manner of expression is more easily seen in works describing a practical art, it can be equally applicable to works of fiction. As Judge Learned Hand recognized in his series of opinions pursuing various alleged infringements of dramatic works, the "dramatic work" contains vari-

---

[96] 239 F.2d at 536.

[97] 329 F.2d 541 (2d Cir. 1964).

[98] *Id.* at 545.

[99] *Id.* at 543–44.

ous ideas including theme, plot, setting, etc., which cannot be monopolized.[100]

In the parody context, as in instances where works are reviewed or criticized, the "idea" is the work itself. The writing of an author and his manner of expression is subject to his monopoly but the *fact* that he wrote it and the judgment of its quality is not. Thus a reviewer should be free to criticize, and *Baker* allows appropriation of expression where necessary for that purpose. Short quotations in a review or appropriation of parts of a work in a parody, to "conjure up" the original work, is fully consistent if not illustrative of the analysis of *Baker v. Selden*.

2. *News, history, and biography.* "Fair use" is often thought to have some special role to play when the copyrighted work involves news, history, or biography. The significant public interest in access to this type of information makes the apparent power of the copyright owner particularly suspect. In these cases, the *Baker v. Selden* analysis of the boundaries of the copyrightable subject matter supports both the societal and author's interest. And while the "news" cases may be inviting opportunities for courts to reaffirm their role in protecting the advancement of knowledge and insuring an informed electorate, such posturing is largely unnecessary, for *Baker* indicates that the copyright law does not inhibit the dissemination of news. The news itself—the happening or the event reported—is not subject to copyright protection; the expression used in reporting the event might be.[101] And, if the event can only be reported by others by adopting part or all of the manner of expression of the original report, then the appropriation is privileged.

An example of a court using too large a weapon for too small a prey is *Rosemont Enterprises, Inc. v. Random House, Inc.*[102] Howard Hughes purchased a copyright in three *Look* magazine articles which discussed various aspects of his life and attempted to obtain an injunction for copyright infringement against the publication of a biography of Hughes by Random House. The biography was admittedly based in part on the *Look* articles. The

---

[100] See Nichols v. Universal Pictures Corp., 45 F.2d 119 (2d Cir. 1930); Sheldon v. Metro-Goldwyn Pictures Corp., 81 F.2d 49 (2d Cir. 1936).

[101] International News Service v. Associated Press, 248 U.S. 215 (1918); Chicago Record-Herald Co. v. Tribune Ass'n, 275 Fed. 797 (7th Cir. 1921).

[102] 366 F.2d 303 (2d Cir. 1966).

Second Circuit, while not clearly indicating the extent to which the *Look* articles were appropriated, held the biography to be a "fair use."

The Court viewed "fair use" as facilitating a judicial accommodation of the copyright owner's rights with the public interest in wide dissemination of information. The author of the opinion for the three-judge panel found the fundamental justification for the doctrine of "fair use" in the promotion-of-science language in the Constitution. Two concurring judges suggested that "fair use" emanated from the First Amendment. Both opinions raised the issue to unnecessary dimensions. Under *Baker v. Selden* the copyright owned by Hughes could not be used to prevent utilization of the facts about his life contained in the *Look* article but could be used to prevent wholesale appropriation of the expression of the article itself.

In *Time Inc. v. Bernard Geis Associates*,[103] the "fair use" privilege was applied in a more difficult context. The question was whether the defendants could use charcoal sketches of frames of the copyrighted Zapruder film of the assassination of President Kennedy. The defendant used the sketches as part of a book developing a thesis on the assassination contrary to the Warren Commission Report. The defendant argued that the films were necessary to demonstrate or prove his thesis and therefore his use was "fair." The court first held the photograph was copyrightable, and that the photograph was not absolutely necessary to set forth the events in Dallas.[104] Thus, implicitly, *Baker v. Selden* was not applicable. The court then found that "fair use" justified the use by the defendant:[105]

> There is a public interest in having the fullest information available on the murder of President Kennedy. Thompson [the defendant] did serious work on the subject and has a theory entitled to public consideration. While doubtless the theory could be explained with sketches of the type used . . . the explanation actually made in the Book with copies is easier to

[103] 293 F. Supp. 130 (S.D. N.Y. 1968).

[104] The court rejected the application of the "doctrine" of Morrissey v. Procter & Gamble Co., 379 F.2d 675 (1st Cir. 1967), which provided that where the means of expressing an idea are limited, the copyright owner's expression can be freely used by others.

[105] 293 F. Supp. at 146.

understand. The Book is not bought because it contained the
Zapruder pictures; the Book is bought because of the theory
of Thompson and its explanation, supported by Zapruder
pictures.

There seems little, if any, injury to plaintiff, the copyright
owner. There is no competition between plaintiff and defendants.

While the case is not without its difficulties, it could be argued
that the graphic picture of the assassination contained within it
both the event that occurred and Zapruder's expression of that
event in film. The idea in the *Baker* sense is, in the context of the
defendant's use, the theory of the "second gun." That idea cannot
be developed without appropriating the expression. The *Baker*
analysis is capable of resolving the *Time* controversy without
raising the more difficult issues of constitutional dimension.

3. *Scholarly and educational uses.* As one of the factors found
to support the application of "fair use" to the photocopying in
Williams & Wilkins, the Court of Claims gave weight to the fact
that the researchers were promoting scientific progress without
regard to commercial gain:[106]

> On both sides—library and requester—scientific progress, un-
> tainted by any commercial gain from the reproduction, is the
> hallmark of the whole enterprise of duplication. There has
> been no attempt to misappropriate the work of earlier scien-
> tific writers for forbidden ends, but rather an effort to gain
> easier access to the material for study and research. This is
> important because it is settled that, in general, the law gives
> copying for scientific purposes a wide scope.

The court's reasoning was essentially twofold: First, that for some
reason scholarly, educational, or scientific progress deserves some
special protections. Second, that noncommercial motives will justify the appropriation of a copyrighted work. Whatever merit
there is in either proposition, neither appears to be supported in
the case law on "fair use" other than in dicta. Both, on the other
hand, raise serious questions of policy as to their intrinsic merit and
as to whether they are appropriate doctrines to be adopted by judicial decree.

Traditional copyright doctrine, while containing language sug-

---

[106] 487 F.2d at 1354.

gesting some broader leeway for copying for scholarly or educational purposes, can be explained primarily as a recognition of
the scope of copyrightable subject matter as defined in the *Baker*
case. Scholarship and education utilize published works revealing
facts and ideas. Even in the fine arts the existence of a particular
work is an idea or event which authorizes certain appropriations.
It would not be surprising for the courts to be confronted more
often with "fair use" assertions to justify taking for scholarly or
educational uses. The issue, however, remains the same—the definition of the boundaries of the copyrighted work.

The cases that have directly raised the propositions that scholarly
or educational uses deserve greater protection have generally rejected the assertion. In *Macmillan Co. v. King*,[107] one Harvard
professor made an outline of the textbook of another Harvard professor and utilized it for classroom purposes in addition to assigning
the textbook itself. The court found an infringement commenting
also that it did not "believe that the defendant's use of the outlines is any the less infringement of the copyright because he is
a teacher, because he uses them in teaching the contents of the
book, because he might lecture upon the contents of the book
without infringing, or because his pupils might have taken their
own notes of his lectures without infringing."[108]

In *Wihtol v. Crow*,[109] a high school music teacher made a new
arrangement of a copyrighted song and duplicated his version for
the high school choir. The work was performed once by the choir
at a school chapel service and once on Sunday at the local Method-
ist church. The court found an infringement although there was
no commercial motive, the use was educational or religious, and
the copying resulted in a new arrangement of the song.[110]

---

[107] 223 Fed. 862 (D. Mass. 1914).

[108] *Id.* at 867.

[109] 309 F.2d 777 (8th Cir. 1963).

[110] Of the cases cited by the Court of Claims in *Williams & Wilkins* for the proposition that "fair use" has a greater prominence in scientific works, none provide a direct
holding to that effect. In Greenbie v. Noble, 151 F. Supp. 45 (S.D. N.Y. 1957), the
infringement question involved a novel. In Thompson v. Gernsback, 94 F. Supp. 435
(S.D. N.Y. 1950), the court doubted that a magazine devoted to sexual enlightenment
was "scientific," but held there was a triable issue of fact on the defense of fair use in
any event. In Henry Holt & Co. v. Liggett & Myers Tobacco Co., 23 F. Supp. 302
(E.D. Pa. 1938), taking of three sentences from a scientific treatise on cigarettes for
use in connection with the advertising of cigarettes was declared an infringement. The
other two cases cited by the court, *Rosemont* and *Benny v. Loew's, Inc.*, have been discussed above and do not directly hold the proposition for which they are cited.

Nor does it appear that the nonprofit character of the defendant's use has insulated that use from liability. The teachers in *Macmillan* and *Wihtol* were not shown on the record to have been motivated by direct commercial gain. More important, the copyright statute evidences an intent by Congress to prevent not-for-profit uses in some instances. The exclusive right to "copy" is unlimited although the exclusive right to deliver a lecture is limited to delivery "in public for profit."[111] Performances of dramatic works in public are infringements without regard to profit motives;[112] but performances of musical compositions infringe only if done for profit.[113] Thus Congress has demonstrated its ability to distinguish between profit and nonprofit uses of copyrighted works and did not make profit motives essential when the infringing act was copying.[114]

Even so, characterization of the activities in *Williams & Wilkins* as devoid of commercial motives requires a simplistic definition of "commercial gain." It is perhaps true that the two government libraries did not profit from duplication in other than very indirect ways, but the researchers requesting copies were surely not governed by purely altruistic motives. Publication of their own research leads to advances in salary and position.[115] Patents or copyrights may result from such research. While the photocopying isolated from the context in which it occurs was not done for profit, the "taint" of profit infected the enterprise.

4. *Economic detriment.* One of the four factors listed by Justice Story in *Folsom* as useful in determining whether a given use is fair was whether the second work served as a substitute for the copyrighted work. There has been a strong trend suggesting that any use is fair—or at least presumptively fair—if the copyright owner

---

[111] 17 U.S.C. § 1(c).   [112] *Id.* at § 1(d).   [113] *Id.* at § 1(e).

[114] Chief Justice Burger in Goldstein v. California, 412 U.S. 546 (1973), in describing the copyright system stated that the copyright owner could "preclude others from copying his creation for *commercial* purposes without permission. In other words, to encourage people to devote themselves to intellectual and artistic creation, Congress may guarantee to authors and inventors a reward in the form of control over the *sale* or *commercial* use of copies of their works." (Emphasis added.) The references to commercial use were unnecessary to decide the case and in all likelihood were not intended to be restrictive.

[115] Where Congress has limited infringements to uses "for profit" the Supreme Court has recognized that indirect commercial gain is included. See Herbert v. Shanley Co., 242 U.S. 591 (1917), where a live performance of a musical composition in defendant's public dining room was a "for profit" performance, even though no separate charge was made for the entertainment.

suffers no direct economic loss as a result of the use by others of his work. Several commentators have suggested that economic loss is at the heart of the doctrine of "fair use."[116] Economic detriment to the copyright owner has been an important factor in several "fair use" cases.[117] The Court of Claims in *Williams & Wilkins* weighed heavily against the publisher the fact that no direct economic harm had been proven. Adoption of an economic loss test alone, however, is insufficient to assist the court in determining which uses are "fair." It is possible to hypothesize some loss from almost any use of another's work. If economic loss is a relevant factor, the court's definition of what type of loss is required for copyright infringement will be controlling and that definition will depend in large measure on the court's perception of the function of copyright.

It appears that the Court of Claims would require the copyright owner to show a loss of subscription sales directly attributable to the photocopying of articles contained in the copyrighted periodical. The court observed that (1) between 1958 and 1969 subscriptions to the journals in question increased; (2) annual taxable income increased until 1966 and then fell in the following three years; (3) the four journals were a small part of the publisher's business and each showed a profit in the three-year period; and (4) the publisher's business grew faster than the gross national product.[118] Williams & Wilkins, on the other hand, did not prove direct loss, relying on "general business common sense and things that you hear from subscribers, librarians and so forth."[119] The court found the evidence insufficient to prove economic loss.

Williams & Wilkins argued, however, that some researchers unable to obtain a duplicated copy of the periodical article would subscribe, and therefore the publisher lost potential sales. But the court rejected such "untested hypothesis, reminiscent of the abstract theorems beloved of the 'pure' classical economics of 70 or 80 years ago" as neither "obvious nor self-proving."[120] The court argued that a researcher might not subscribe but might instead wait for the library's copy or forgo reading the article entirely.

---

[116] See a review of the literature in Latman, note 21 *supra*, at 14.

[117] *E.g.*, Hill v. Whalen & Martell, Inc., 220 F. 359, 360 (S.D. N.Y. 1914) ("One test which, when applicable, would seem to be ordinarily decisive, is whether or not so much as has been reproduced will materially reduce the demand for the original.")

[118] 487 F.2d at 1357.   [119] *Ibid*.   [120] *Id*. at 1358.

While this may be true, it is hardly an answer to the contention, for even if the availability of free photocopies caused only one researcher not to subscribe, economic detriment is shown.

The copyright law has not generally required that a copy must directly compete with the copyrighted work. The different media cases are good examples. The courts have generally declared it an infringement to adapt a copyrighted work into another media. It has been held that making three-dimensional toys by copying two-dimensional copyrighted cartoon characters is an infringement. The Second Circuit commented that the copyright owner is entitled to "any lawful use of his property whereby he may get a profit out of it. . . . It is the commercial value of his property that he is protected for."[121] Only in a very general sense do toys compete with comic books; the infringer had interfered with the potential market of the copyright owner. Professor Nimmer has suggested the same analysis in declaring that making a motion picture of a copyrighted novel is not a fair use.[122] A logical extension of this rationale would prohibit any duplication of a copyrighted work.

Congress has also provided ample evidence that direct economic loss is not required. The Court of Claims rejected hypothesized proof of loss in the face of a statutory scheme which authorizes the copyright owner to recover statutory damages "in lieu" of proof of actual loss. These provisions suggest a remedy for cases like *Williams & Wilkins*, where evidence of direct economic injury is unavailable.[123]

In the last analysis reliance on economic loss as a determinant for infringement does not resolve the cases. The extent to which a given court is willing to pursue the concept of economic loss to include potential markets would be of critical importance. And in turn the scope given to the potential markets would depend on the court's emphasis—whether it was placed on the author's interest in reward or the public's interest in the creation of new works.

---

[121] King Features Syndicate v. Fleischer, 299 Fed. 533 (2d Cir. 1924).

[122] 2 NIMMER, note 74 *supra*, at § 145 646–47. Professor Nimmer undercuts his own argument by apparently certifying as correct the conclusion that publishing copyrighted song lyrics in a literary piece was fair use because the two works served separate functions. *Id.* at 647. See also Goldstein, *Copyright and the First Amendment*, 70 COLUM. L. REV. 983, 1030–31 (1970), justifying the award of profits in copyright infringement cases as based on providing a remedy for loss in potential markets.

[123] Although not completely free from doubt, it appears that "in lieu" damages may be awarded even in cases where no injury is shown. For a review of the cases see 2 NIMMER, note 74 *supra*, at § 154.11.

C. MORE BALANCING

Judge Wyatt in the "Zapruder film" decision was candid enough to confess that "fair use" "is entirely equitable and is so flexible as virtually to defy definition."[124] The precedent contains rhetoric sufficient to support almost any plausible contention. Yet the underlying issue masked in "fair use" language remains the critical accommodation of the interests of the author with the interests of society—the conflict between the property doctrine of misappropriation and the competitive principle which seeks to serve the consuming public.

The confusion and ambiguities in the precedents involving "fair use" result in large measure from the unwillingness of courts to face the issue directly. And the problem is compounded by the failure of early decisions to articulate the source of the doctrine or the purpose it was intended to serve. In *Rosemont Enterprises,* however, the three-judge panel did attempt to determine the justification for a judicial doctrine of "fair use," one judge arguing that it was necessary to implement the constitutional directive to "promote the Progress of Science and useful Arts" and two concurring judges finding "fair use" to be a First Amendment imperative. We have suggested that if "fair use" is a device to define the metes and bounds of the copyright owner's interest, it is likely to be derived from either the constitutional language authorizing the protection of the "writings" of "authors" or from the statutory language providing protection to "books" and other tangible methods of expression. On the other hand, if the promotion clause or the First Amendment serves as its basis, "fair use" would authorize the courts to adopt a more flexible balancing approach—to pursue, as did the Court of Claims, questions of resource allocation. While the Supreme Court has not dealt specifically with "fair use," it has had several occasions to interpret both the promotion language of the patent and copyright clause and the First Amendment in analogous contexts. In examining those precedents, we find little to support the course pursued by the Court of Claims.

1. *The copyright clause.* Article I, § 8, cl. 8 of the Constitution gives power to Congress: "To promote the Progress of Science and useful Arts, by securing for limited Times to Authors and Inventors the exclusive Right to their respective Writings and Discoveries." Some who argue that the photoreproduction of copy-

[124] 293 F. Supp. at 144.

righted works is a "fair use" assert that the doctrine implements the introductory clause of the provision, that it is a judicial device to insure that the grant bestowed by Congress is limited to the constitutionally mandated purpose. By this analysis any use is "fair" that serves to promote the dissemination of knowledge, and the courts are obligated to test each alleged infringement against that directive. The Court of Claims in *Williams & Wilkins* appears to have at least caressed, if it did not fully embrace, the argument.[125]

The promotion clause can be interpreted in one of three ways. It can be construed as merely a preamble to the constitutional grant of power, explaining its purpose without limiting its exercise.[126] Second, the phrase can be interpreted to provide a limitation on the subject matter upon which Congress can bestow a limited monopoly. Under this view not all "writings" of "authors" could be protected, only those that pertained to "Science" and the "useful Arts." A third view would construe the phrase as a limitation on the extent of the monopoly Congress may grant. The emphasis in this interpretation would be on "promote," and any congressional action under the clause would be unconstitutional unless it served the announced purpose. It is this third view that the advocates for liberal photocopying privileges advance. In balancing the interest of the copyright owner and the interest of the copier, it is argued, science is more effectively promoted by free photocopying of copyrighted works.

The history and background of the formulation and adoption of the patent and copyright clause is largely unrecorded. James Madison's notes of the constitutional convention indicate that on 18 August 1787 he proposed a number of congressional powers to be considered by a committee. Among Madison's proposals were three related to copyrights and patents:[127]

> To secure to literary authors their copyrights for a limited time
> To establish a University
> To encourage by premiums & provisions, the advancement of useful knowledge and discoveries

---

[125] 487 F.2d at 1352.

[126] 1 NIMMER, note 74 *supra*, at § 3.

[127] 2 FARRAND, RECORDS OF THE FEDERAL CONVENTION OF 1787 324–25 (rev. ed. 1966). The editor noted that Madison's original record indicates that he also proposed the language, "To secure to the inventors of useful machines and implements the benefits thereof for a limited time." *Id.* at 324 n.3.

On the same day, Charles Pinckney proposed the following powers: [128]

> To establish seminaries for the promotion of literature and the arts & sciences
> To grant patents for useful inventions
> To secure to Authors exclusive rights for a certain time
> To establish public institutions, rewards and immunities for the promotion of agriculture, commerce, trades and manufactures

On 5 September, David Brearley for the Committee on Detail reported a recommendation for a patent and copyright clause which was included in the Constitution unchanged.[129] There are no explanations of the meaning of the language.[130]

The context in which the Madison and Pinckney proposals must have been considered within the committee provides some basis for speculation about the intent of the drafters of the promotion clause. Neither of the proposers felt compelled to attach limiting language to the provisions for protecting authors and inventors other than suggestions for limiting the time of copyright. Viewed as a package of suggestions, the issue before the committee was, more likely than not, "what is the proper role of the federal government in promoting science and useful arts" rather than "how should we limit the power of Congress to grant copyrights and patents?"

The Supreme Court has not had an extended history of interpretation of the "promotion clause," but from the cases which do exist it seems clear that the Court has consistently viewed the language as either explanatory or as a limitation on the subject matter capable of protection and then only to supplement the definition of "writing." In early copyright cases, issues were often resolved without citation to source or legal doctrine, but some implications are discernible as to how the Court viewed its role in copyright litigation.

---

[128] *Id.* at 325.   [129] *Id.* at 505.

[130] Madison presented the defense of the provision in *The Federalist* No. 43 but added little to interpretation of the language used. He did recognize that England had declared the copyright of authors to be a right at common law and that inventors should be similarly treated. "The public good fully coincides in both cases with the claims of individuals." It would appear that Madison did not view the introductory language as limiting the claims of individuals by the public interest, since he did not perceive a conflict in the two.

The Supreme Court confronted the question of the copyright of judicial opinions in a series of early cases. If the Court had wished to adopt a principle of judicial intervention when copyright did not serve the constitutional purpose, the cases presented the perfect opportunity. It can hardly be contended that the copyright monopoly is necessary to provide incentives for judges to write opinions. And while it is possible that the monopoly was necessary to assist the reporters of those opinions in publishing them, it is a close case considering the public nature and need for dissemination.[131] The Court did not approach the issue in this way.

In 1834 in *Wheaton v. Peters*,[132] the Court faced the assertion by its former reporter, Wheaton, that its then current reporter, Peters, had published an "abridged" version of Wheaton's case reports. The remand to determine whether Wheaton had complied with the copyright law made it unnecessary to decide directly the extent of the interest Congress could grant. But Justice McLean gratuitously added a final paragraph reporting a unanimous court on the proposition that no reporter could have a copyright in the written opinions themselves and that "the judges thereof cannot confer on any reporter any such rights."[133] The issue arose again in *Callaghan v. Myers*[134] where the Court held the reporter had no interest in the judicial opinions because he was not the "author." In the same year, in *Banks v. Manchester*,[135] the Court found the judge held no interest in his opinions because it would be against "public policy." It was unclear whether that policy was due to the fact that the judge was paid by public funds and the work was within the scope of his employment or whether there was a more fundamental, unarticulated, reason emanating from the Constitution.

The 1879 Term provided two opportunities to interpret the

---

[131] The copyright statute now denies copyright protection to "any publication of the United States Government," even in areas where the publishing agency is required by law to be self-supporting. 17 U.S.C. § 8. See testimony of Rene Tegtmeyer, Assistant Commissioner of Patents on H.R. 2223, before the House Subcommittee on Courts, Civil Liberties, and the Administration of Justice, as reported in PATENT, TRADEMARK, & COPYRIGHT JOURNAL No. 228, at A-7 (15 May 1975), arguing that agencies which must make their publications self-supporting should be granted copyright protection.

[132] 8 Pet. 591 (1834).

[133] *Id.* at 668. On the other hand, Peters in a footnote remarked that he did not report the argument of counsel on the point because he had been informed that the Court "did not consider it when the case was disposed of." *Id.* at 618 n.a.

[134] 128 U.S. 617 (1888).   [135] 128 U.S. 244 (1888).

copyright and patent clause. In the *Trade-Mark Cases*,[136] Congress had enacted a federal trademark registration system. The Court found the statute beyond the authorized powers of Congress, first, because it attempted to regulate intrastate as well as interstate commerce and could thus not be defended under the Commerce Clause, and, second, because a trademark was not a "writing of an author" and accordingly could not be protected by Congress pursuant to the patent and copyright clause. The Court held that the copyright clause included writings that were based "in the creative powers of the mind. The writings which are to be protected are the fruits of intellectual labor, embodied in the form of books, prints, engravings and the like."[137] The argument that trademarks are not "writings" or could not be the result of "creative powers" seems unusual unless the word "writings" is construed in the context of the promotion of science and useful arts language. Of course, business and commerce could be within the "useful arts," but the Court in *Higgins v. Keuffel*,[138] made it plain that they were not. In *Higgins*, the plaintiff sought copyright protection for labels bearing the words "waterproof drawing ink." The Court denied protection. One of the express grounds was that the label had "no connection with the progress of science and the useful arts." The Court used the phrase to limit the kinds of writings eligible for monopoly protection.[139]

In the same Term as the *Trade-Mark Cases*, the Court decided *Baker v. Selden*,[140] announcing the proposition that copyright protected the manner of expressing an idea but not the idea itself. The source of this declaration of copyright law was not disclosed. Of interest, however, was the Court's reliance on *Clayton v. Stone & Hall*,[141] an opinion by Justice Thompson on circuit, that daily market prices could not be copyrighted because they did not "pro-

---

[136] 100 U.S. 82 (1879).

[137] *Id.* at 94.   [138] 140 U.S. 428 (1891).

[139] The view that industrial activity is not within the "useful arts" was subsequently abandoned. Justice Holmes, fearful of judicial censorship of the arts, upheld the copyright in a chromolithograph used for advertising a circus. Holmes, while recognizing the promotion language as limiting the subject matter of copyright, refused to interpret that language strictly. Bleistein v. Donaldson Lithographing Co., 188 U.S. 239 (1903).

[140] 101 U.S. 99 (1879). For a more complete discussion of *Baker* see text *supra*, at notes 88 *et seq.*

[141] 5 Fed. Cas. 999 (1829).

mote science." Again the Court performed the role of establishing the boundaries of the copyright owner's interest.

In more recent cases the Court has continued to utilize the preamble as a limitation on the subject matter over which Congress may extend protection. In *Graham v. John Deere Co.*,[142] the Court emphasized the "nonobviousness" test as the standard of invention for patent validity and noted that the promotion clause was:[143]

> both a grant of power and a limitation. . . . The Congress in the exercise of the patent power may not overreach the restraints imposed by the stated constitutional purpose. Nor may it enlarge the patent monopoly without regard to the innovation, advancement or social benefit gained thereby. Moreover, Congress may not authorize the issuance of patents whose effects are to remove existent knowledge from the public domain, or to restrict free access to materials already available. Innovation, advancement, and things which add to the sum of useful knowledge are inherent requisites in a patent system which by constitutional command must "promote the Progress of . . . Useful Arts."

The Court in *Deepsouth Packing Co. v. Laitram Corp.*[144] rejected the idea that the Court could review the extent of a patent monopoly to determine if it most effectively promoted the useful arts. In *Deepsouth*, the owner of a combination patent sued a defendant who made all the elements of the combination in the United States and then exported the elements for assembly abroad. The issue was whether this violated the patent owner's exclusive right to "make" the patented article within the United States. The patentee argued that only a very technical interpretation of "make" would validate the defendant's activity and that the Court ought to focus on the promotion language for an interpretation which would best promote science. That suggestion was rejected by Mr. Justice White:[145]

---

[142] 383 U.S. 1 (1966). See Kitch, *Graham v. John Deere Co.: New Standards for Patents?* 1966 SUPREME COURT REVIEW 293.

[143] *Id.* at 6. Mr. Justice Douglas dissenting from a denial of certiorari in Lee v. Runge, 404 U.S. 887 (1971), argued that the Constitution—in part the introductory clause—required a stricter standard of originality for copyrighted works than generally thought necessary. While some language in his dissent suggests a willingness on his part to use the introductory clause to test a variety of copyright doctrines, the issue before him involved the appropriate subject matter for copyright.

[144] 406 U.S. 518 (1972).   [145] *Id.* at 530.

We cannot accept this argument. The direction of Article I is that *Congress* shall have the power to promote the progress of science and the useful arts. When as here the Constitution is permissive, the sign of how far Congress has chosen to go can come only from Congress.

At the time the Supreme Court heard arguments in *Williams & Wilkins,* there was little authority for the proposition that the promotion clause could be used by courts to excuse activity which would otherwise be an infringement. The effect of the argument in *Williams & Wilkins,* nevertheless, left its mark on various Justices. Late in the 1974 Term the Court rendered an opinion in another copyright case, *Twentieth Century Music Corp. v. Aiken,*[146] in which Mr. Justice Stewart adopted language suggesting a broader role for the courts in interpreting the copyright law. In *Aiken* the question was whether a restaurant owner infringed a musical composer's exclusive right to perform the work publicly for profit by extending a radio broadcast of the composition throughout his restaurant. On the one hand the Court faced an earlier opinion by Justice Brandeis holding similar activity by a hotel to be infringing,[147] and, on the other, Mr. Justice Stewart had fashioned a rule in two CATV cases which suggested the opposite result.[148] All these cases involved interpretations of the exclusive right of the copyright owner to "perform." Mr. Justice Stewart held in the television cases that listeners listen and broadcasters perform and cable television falls on the listener's side of the line. In *Aiken,* Mr. Justice Stewart for a majority of six Justices found no infringement; Mr. Justice Blackmun disagreed but concurred and the Chief Justice with Mr. Justice Douglas dissented.

Mr. Justice Stewart, in the course of his opinion, employed language implying that the Court should interpret the copyright law in certain instances to conform to the constitutional purpose of promoting science:[149]

The limited scope of the copyright holder's statutory monopoly, like the limited copyright duration required by the Constitution, reflects a balance of competing claims upon the

---

[146] 422 U.S. 151 (1975).

[147] Buck v. Jewell-LaSalle Realty Co., 283 U.S. 191 (1931).

[148] Teleprompter Corp. v. Columbia Broadcasting System, Inc., 415 U.S. 394 (1974); Fortnightly Corp. v. United Artists Television, Inc., 392 U.S. 390 (1968).

[149] 422 U.S. at 156.

public interest: Creative work is to be encouraged and re-warded, but private motivation must ultimately serve the cause of promoting broad public availability of literature, music, and the other arts. The immediate effect of our copyright law is to secure a fair return for an "author's" creative labor. But the ultimate aim is, by this incentive, to stimulate artistic creativ-ity for the general public good. . . . When technological change has rendered its literal terms ambiguous, the Copyright Act must be construed in light of this basic purpose.

This language suggests that an economic analysis is appropriate, at least where the statute is ambiguous. That does not, of course, support the creation of a judicial doctrine which would directly contradict the language of the act. In *Williams & Wilkins*, the Solicitor General, on behalf of the government libraries, argued that the CATV cases should be read broadly and that the same ambiguities that existed in the word "perform" existed in the word "copy."[150] Even Mr. Justice Stewart, the architect of the approach in the CATV cases, could not accept the analogy.[151] And there is little in the CATV cases to imply that the Court analyzed the economic consequences to determine which rule would best ad-vance the dissemination of information.

In *Aiken*, Mr. Justice Stewart utilized, for the proposition set forth above, a quotation from *Fox Film Corp. v. Doyal*[152] which suggested the predominance of the public interest in copyright cases.[153] In *Fox*, Chief Justice Hughes remarked: "The sole interest of the United States and the primary object in conferring the mo-nopoly lie in the general benefits derived by the public from the labors of authors."[154] Another quotation often employed for the same purpose is Mr. Justice Douglas's comment in *United States v. Paramount Pictures Inc.*,[155] that the "copyright law, like the patent

---

[150] Transcript of oral argument at 29.

[151] Q. [Stewart]. "Except, Mr. Solicitor General, the only thing to be decided in those 2 cases was the meaning of the word 'perform' under the 1909 Act. I can under-stand that casual readers of the opinion, perhaps, particularly in view of the dissenting opinions, might have thought those cases had to do with something else. But all they were directed to was a meaning of the statutory word 'perform.' And now here we have the statutory word 'copy.' Certainly there isn't any ambiguity about that." *Ibid.*

[152] 286 U.S. 123 (1932).

[153] 422 U.S. at 156.

[154] 286 U.S. at 127.

[155] 334 U.S. 131, 158 (1948). See 487 F.2d at 1352.

statutes, makes reward to the owner a secondary consideration." Both quotations have a preeminence far beyond what the context in which they were fashioned would dictate. In *Fox*, the issue was whether a copyright was exempt from state taxation on the grounds that it was a federal instrument. The Court held it was not, and the language of Chief Justice Hughes was designed to support the proposition that the federal government did not have a sufficient interest in the copyright to make it a federal instrument. In *Paramount*, producers of copyrighted movies asserted the right to force theaters to license movies in blocks, thus tying marginal films to popular films, making the package profitable to produce. The producers argued that the Court should create an exemption from the antitrust laws because the practice in essence promoted science by giving a greater return to copyright owners. The issue was not whether to restrict a right granted by Congress but whether to extend the monopoly power of copyright owners. Mr. Justice Douglas's comment read in that context does little to serve the interest of those advocating the judicial adoption of a doctrine creating a privileged infringement. And the Court in a subsequent review of the language recognized that while the point was correct, the patent and copyright clause was based on the conviction that "encouragement of individual effort by personal gain is the best way to advance public welfare."[156]

In none of the cases is there real support for the proposition that the courts ought to create privileged activities in order to insure the attainment of the purpose established for patent and copyright. While Congress in enacting the 1909 act recognized its responsibilities in this regard, it also asserted its exclusive right to make the necessary determinations as to when science and useful arts were

---

[156] Mazer v. Stein, 347 U.S. 201, 219 (1954). There are additional remarks in some patent misuse cases which suggest a broader role for the courts derived from the promotion language of the Patent and Copyright Clause. In those cases, as in *Paramount*, the issue was whether the monopoly conferred by Congress has been abused. In United States v. Masonite Corp., 316 U.S. 265 (1942), where Mr. Justice Douglas again emphasized the "main object" of the patent system as promoting science, he was directly concerned with whether the patent provides authority to attach price fixing conditions to a license to use the patented product. The issue was not, as it was in *Williams & Wilkins*, whether the patent owner can enforce his statutory right at all. There is also a distinction between the scope of the monopoly conferred by the copyright and patent systems. In the latter the statute confers the exclusive rights to "make, use and sell." 28 U.S.C. § 271. The patent misuse cases generally involve the problem of "use" and the conditions that can be attached thereto. This is a different problem from that in *Williams & Wilkins* where the only condition the copyright owner sought to attach to a license to "copy" was the payment of royalties.

effectively promoted.[157] And the Supreme Court, when directly called upon to do so, has refused to second-guess the Congress on this issue.

2. *The First Amendment.* In the past few years there has been a developing interest, surfacing primarily in law review commentaries, in the extent to which the First Amendment may limit the rights of a copyright owner or the power of Congress to extend copyright protection.[158] The First Amendment is designed to insure a free flow of information necessary to carry on the public dialogue essential to create a marketplace in which to test the soundness of ideas. If access to information is restrained, the dialogue is impeded. To the extent the copyright monopoly adds to the cost of information, it may interfere with basic First Amendment goals. Thus there exists a colorable case of conflict between a governmentally bestowed monopoly in "writings" and a constitutionally protected system of free and full debate.

In *Rosemont Enterprises,* two of the three panel members believed that the doctrine of "fair use" was the protector of First Amendment values: "The spirit of the First Amendment applies to the copyright laws at least to the extent that the courts should not tolerate any attempted interference with the public's right to be informed regarding matters of general interest when anyone seeks to use the copyright statute which was designed to protect interests of quite a different nature."[159] And in *Williams & Wilkins,* the amicus brief of the National Education Association was devoted exclusively to the proposition that the First Amendment required privileged access by means of the photocopy machine to copyrighted works: "*Amicus* respectfully suggests that 'fair use' (or the right of reasonable access to copyrighted materials) has consti-

---

[157] H.R. Rep. No. 2222, 60th Cong., 2d Sess. (1909).

[158] Nimmer, *Does Copyright Abridge the First Amendment Guarantees of Free Speech and Press?*, 17 U.C.L.A. L. Rev. 1180 (1970); Goldstein, note 122 *supra;* Sobel, *Copyright and the First Amendment: A Gathering Storm?* 19 Copyright L. Sym. 43 (1971). At least two of the Supreme Court Justices have noted and rejected the conflict between the First Amendment and a suit for copyright infringement. See Mr. Justice White joined by Mr. Justice Stewart, concurring, in New York Times Co. v. United States, 403 U.S. 713, 731 n.1 (1971): "[N]o one denies that a newspaper can properly be enjoined from publishing the copyrighted works of another."

[159] 366 F.2d 303, 311 (2d Cir. 1966) (Lumbard and Hays, JJ., concurring). In Walt Disney Productions v. The Air Pirates, 345 F. Supp. 108 (N.D. Cal. 1972), the court rejected the First Amendment contention of an infringer who published copies of several Walt Disney cartoon characters in a magazine of cartoons and argued he was parodying the Disney characters within his First Amendment rights.

tutional protection under the First and Ninth Amendments in the Bill of Rights. This constitutional dimension protects the right of reasonable access to the cultural, educational, scientific, historical, technical and intellectual heritage of the Nation."[160]

Unlike instances where the courts have been forced to balance the First Amendment against other socially beneficial activities, the purported conflict with copyright involves a quantitative judgment between two systems seeking the same end. While the First Amendment facilitates the flow of information by preventing government intervention, the copyright system encourages the development of information and its dissemination by providing incentives for publication. The conflict, if any, is in method not purpose.

There are four possible assumptions about the interaction of copyright incentives and First Amendment prohibitions. (a) The copyright monopoly fails to create an incentive to produce and substantially increases the cost of access to published material. (b) The copyright monopoly provides incentives that attract works which would otherwise not be published, but the quantity or quality of works thus attracted does not exceed the costs in restraints on access that the monopoly power creates. (c) The value of the works attracted by the copyright monopoly exceeds the costs in limiting access to copyrighted works. (d) The copyright monopoly provides some incentives and does not add to the costs of access to information. The same analysis would be applicable in considering whether any particular feature of the copyright, i.e., right to exact royalties for photoduplication, would conflict with the First Amendment.

If the first assumption were correct, there would be little gain in preserving the copyright monopoly, and courts could reasonably conclude that First Amendment values should take precedence. Under the fourth assumption, there would be no conflict with the First Amendment and the copyright protection could be preserved. More difficult questions are raised under either of the other two assumptions. The evaluation of the quantity or quality of the work produced would by necessity be prone to subjective judgments and would raise the specter of censorship. For example, if copyright encouraged comic books but discouraged scholarship in the fine arts, a difficult issue of policy would present itself, one which Jus-

---

[160] P. 11. The brief was recycled as a law review article. See Rosenfield, *The Constitutional Dimension of "Fair Use" in Copyright Law*, 50 NOTRE DAME LAW. 790 (1975).

tice Holmes warned judges to avoid.[161] Even if these judgments could be reasonably made, it is not clear that the First Amendment should inevitably triumph over copyright. Even under the second assumption, information would continue to flow into the market-place.[162]

We are, and will likely remain, in the uncomfortable position of not having sufficient information to determine which of the assumptions is factually correct, although we can reject assumptions (a) and (d) as extremes. Financial rewards produced by copyright protection must create some incentives to produce writings even though the incentives may create misallocation of resources from an economic efficiency perspective. On the other hand, the copyright does increase the cost of information. The power of the copyright owner to restrain the public dialogue, however, is considerably diluted by application of the *Baker v. Selden* doctrine that only the manner of expression is protectible. Access to the ideas contained in copyrighted works is not restrained; nor are there restraints on the use of those ideas in the public debate sanctioned and encouraged by the First Amendment. Giving substantial weight to First Amendment values, it cannot be shown that Congress would be clearly wrong if it determined that the incentives created by the copyright would, in the long run, result in a better balance of useful and diverse information than providing First Amendment privileges to reprographic activities.

The difficulty of accepting a First Amendment justification for the doctrine of "fair use" is enhanced by the Supreme Court's

---

[161] "At the one extreme some works of genius would be sure to miss appreciation. Their very novelty would make them repulsive until the public had learned a new language in which their author spoke. . . . At the other end, copyright would be denied to pictures which appealed to a public less educated than the judge." Bleistein v. Donaldson Lithographing Co., 188 U.S. 239, 251–52 (1903).

[162] It is possible that the relative balance between copyright incentives and free access will affect the source of the information produced—as between authors dependent on direct monetary rewards for writing and those who are dependent instead on indirect gain through grants or salaries. A decision to opt for free access might shift editorial resources from private enterprise to subsidized publication. If the assumption that government provides the greatest opportunity for subsidized research and publication is correct, elimination of the copyright monopoly might increase governmental power over information in derogation of First Amendment purposes. Whether the atomization of "government" would be sufficient to produce a variety of viewpoints is unclear as is the proof for the underlying assumptions on which the hypothesis is based. It does seem clear, however, that the Supreme Court did face in *Williams & Wilkins* the possibility that its decision would shift some publishing resources from private to public control.

reluctance to implement a First Amendment right of access in analogous circumstances. This is true regardless of whether the Court in defining the copyright interest would ultimately choose to emphasize the interest of the author or the public interest in the efficient dissemination of information. In cases raising First Amendment access claims the Court generally has weighed the balance against access.[163]

The claim by advocates of free photocopying for a First Amendment privilege is undercut by the Supreme Court's decision in *Miami Herald Publishing Co. v. Tornillo*.[164] The Court there invalidated a "right to reply" statute which required a newspaper criticizing a candidate for public office to provide, free of cost, equal amounts of space for his reply. The Court held the First Amendment prohibited this governmental interference on what the press could or could not print. In doing so, Chief Justice Burger, for a unanimous Court, rejected a First Amendment right of access to the media. The implications for the success of similar claims in *Williams & Wilkins* appear obvious and direct.

All members of the Court agreed that the First Amendment was designed to facilitate a wide dissemination of information productive of a robust debate of public issues. The argument for com-

---

[163] The access cases discussed in the text are generally analogous to *Williams & Wilkins* in that they pose conflicts between First Amendment access to information and a publisher's First Amendment rights of control over his own publication. In a variety of other settings the Court has found the claimed First Amendment right of access to information subservient to other governmental interests. Zemel v. Rusk, 381 U.S. 1 (1965) (power to withhold permission for Americans to travel to specified foreign countries); Kleindienst v. Mandel, 408 U.S. 753 (1972) (power to deny temporary visa to alien); Pell v. Procunier, 417 U.S. 817 (1974), and Saxbe v. Washington Post Co., 417 U.S. 843 (1974) (power to exclude press from conducting interviews with prison inmates); Sheppard v. Maxwell, 384 U.S. 333 (1966) (power to deny press access to information prejudicial to an accused right to a fair trial). As Chief Justice Warren remarked in *Zemel*, *supra* at 16–17; "There are few restrictions on action which could not be clothed by ingenious argument in the garb of decreased data flow."

Nor does it appear that the cases placing First Amendment limitations on defamation and privacy actions are particularly relevant to the statutory copyright. The balance in those cases was between the reputational interest of the plaintiff and the First Amendment interest in free public debate. The cases culminating in Gertz v. Robert Welch, Inc., 418 U.S. 323 (1974), which involved personal defamation actions, sought to prohibit barriers to discussions of fact or opinion. The privacy cases again involved the publication of facts about the plaintiff. The most recent case, Cox Broadcasting Corp. v. Cohn, 420 U.S. 469 (1975), held invalid a statute prohibiting the publication of the name of a rape victim which had earlier appeared in the court records. These cases may have some relevance to common law copyright under which an author may prevent the publication of his writings. The statutory copyright, however, contemplates publication and allows subsequent use of factual information by others.

[164] 418 U.S. 241 (1974).

pelled access in *Miami Herald* resembled in some critical elements the position of those advocating a privilege to reproduce copyrighted materials. The defenders of the "right of reply" statutes emphasized the monopoly power of single newspaper markets protected by the high costs of entry. Researchers defending their use of the photocopy machine emphasize the monopoly power of the copyright owner and the potential increased costs of research if royalties for photocopying are exacted.

In *Miami Herald*, the Court invalidated the right-of-reply statute on two basic grounds. First, it was not clear that enforcement of the statute would increase the dissemination of information, since the knowledge that free space must be made available to candidates might discourage the newspaper from critically commenting on candidates altogether.[165] Second, the Court found that even if there were no increased costs in publication and no disincentives to debate, the statute would still be invalid because it intruded into "the function of editors."

In terms of First Amendment values, *Miami Herald* appears to present a more compelling case for access than that advocated by the photocopiers. The Court admitted in *Miami Herald* that the editorial function could prevent certain ideas from ever reaching the marketplace and that nothing required the press to be "fair." On the other hand, the copyright owner has no protection in his ideas separate and apart from the manner in which he expresses them. Upon obtaining a copyright he has by definition added to the public debate by publishing his work. Furthermore, the newspaper monopolist not only controls his own ideas but those of others. The Court recognized that in many markets the costs of entry other than through a right of access would be prohibitive. While copyright royalties may indeed increase the costs of research, it is doubtful that the scope of the barrier they represent is in any way comparable to the costs of competing with a large metropolitan newspaper monopoly.

The *Miami Herald* case refused to permit the government to require a private individual to utilize his property to subsidize the attainment of the values associated with the First Amendment. While the copyright interest can be viewed as a private property

---

[165] The Court found support of this assumption in Lange, *The Role of the Access Doctrine in the Regulation of the Mass Media: A Critical Review and Assessment*, 52 N.C. L. Rev. 1 (1973).

concept, it could be argued that it more closely resembles a governmental license limited in scope by the public interest. From this perspective, *Miami Herald* can be distinguished, and the copyright subjected more easily to the limits imposed by the need for the widest expression of information and ideas. The Court, however, has been unwilling to grant rights of access in other areas of governmental licensing equally limited by public interest obligations and encumbered with First Amendment emanations.

In *Red Lion Broadcasting Co. v. Federal Communications Commission*,[166] the Court upheld against First Amendment attack Federal Communication Commission regulations requiring that broadcast licensees provide equal time to one personally attacked. The "fairness doctrine," said the Court, advanced rather than conflicted with the fundamental purpose of the First Amendment—to "preserve an uninhibited marketplace of ideas in which truth will ultimately prevail, rather than to countenance monopolization of that market, whether it be by the Government itself or a private licensee."[167] But in *Columbia Broadcasting System, Inc. v. Democratic National Committee*,[168] the Court held that absent affirmative governmental regulations, a licensed broadcaster could refuse to accept paid editorial advertisements without violating the First Amendment.[169]

To the extent that the copyright is perceived as an economic device to advance the public interest in dissemination of intellectual products it is comparable to a broadcast license. Both are monopolies granted by the government to facilitate the distribution of information. Both bear the same public interest burden. By analogy, the result of *Red Lion* and *CBS* would be to authorize Congress to limit the interest of copyright owners but to deny the courts the authority to provide for access to copyrighted works under the First Amendment.

In some important respects, the copyright differs from the broadcast license sufficiently to make the First Amendment argument for access even less compelling. Given the limited number of tele-

---

[166] 395 U.S. 367 (1969).

[167] *Id.* at 390.   [168] 412 U.S. 94 (1973).

[169] The precise doctrinal support for the *CBS* decision is far from clear. Chief Justice Burger and Justices Stewart and Rehnquist argued that the denial of access by a licensed broadcaster was not "governmental action" such as to invoke First Amendment restraints. Whether they would have similar views about a copyright infringement suit is left to speculation.

vision frequencies available, the monopoly bestowed on the broad-caster provides the power to exclude the views of others; the copyright gives the owner no power over others' views and only a limited power to increase the cost of access to his own ideas.[170] He not only cannot prevent the expression of ideas foreign to his own, he cannot prevent the use of his own views by others. In the scale of First Amendment concerns for free expression, the power of the broadcaster looms considerably larger than that of the copyright owner.

In *Red Lion* the broadcaster utilized an argument similar to that of the publishers in *Williams & Wilkins*. Authorizing access, argued the broadcaster, would provide incentives for self-censorship and thereby stifle public discussion because of the additional costs a broadcaster would incur by taking editorial positions. In *Miami Herald*, the Court accepted the basic premise of the argument in refusing to announce a First Amendment access right to news-papers. In upholding the "fairness doctrine" in *Red Lion*, the Court again assumed that access would provide some disincentives to public discussion, but the Court noted that the FCC had the power to force broadcasting of public issues. Thus in both cases, the Court assumed that protecting the interest of the publisher (broadcaster) would serve to increase the flow of information. Only where the government had the authority to counteract disincentives created by access did the Court uphold such regulations. Neither the Con-gress nor the Court could compel authors to write or publishers to publish. The upholding of affirmative access regulations in *Red Lion* provides no assistance for those arguing for privileged photo-copying.

A First Amendment costume for the issue in *Williams & Wilkins* lends little support to those who seek the right freely to reproduce copyrighted works. If the copyright were viewed as a property right, a "fair use" privilege based on First Amendment principles would be inconsistent with *Miami Herald*. On the other hand, if the copyright were considered an economic device to encourage publication, the Court has demonstrated that it is not convinced

---

[170] Mr. Justice White observed in *Red Lion* that there is nothing that requires Con-gress in its regulation of frequencies to grant an exclusive right of use. The Constitution, on the other hand, authorized Congress to grant "Exclusive" rights for limited times to authors. Whether the constitutional language forbids non-exclusive rights under the copyright clause, a question with some fascinating implications for photocopying and the doctrine of "fair use," has not been litigated. See 1 NIMMER, note 74 *supra*, at § 7.

that access will provide substantially more debate, at least absent a congressional judgment to the contrary.

IV. RECENT ANALOGUES

In a separate line of decisions beginning with *International News Service v. Associated Press*,[171] the Supreme Court faced issues similar to those presented in *Williams & Wilkins*. INS had appropriated uncopyrighted news stories from published Associated Press newspapers and distributed them to INS subscribers. The issue as framed for Supreme Court consideration was whether the common law of unfair competition prohibited the "bodily taking of the words or substance of complainant's news until its commercial value as news had passed away."[172] The Court ruled that it did, fashioning a judicial remedy for the misappropriation of the results of another's labor. The opinion, heavily laden with the language of property rights,[173] emphasized the injustice of defendant's conduct in "endeavoring to reap where it has not sown," and also recognized the public interest in insuring a sufficient economic return to newsgatherers to enable them to continue to gather news.[174] Justice Brandeis in dissent noted that the public interest might better be served by having two sources of news rather than one, and argued strongly that the Court should defer to the legislature which might better define the limits of any property right in uncopyrighted or unpatented material.[175]

Williams & Wilkins involved the question whether the Court should authorize the appropriation of copyrighted materials. The unfair competition cases were concerned with the appropriation of works not protected by a copyright or patent and the extent

---

[171] 248 U.S. 215 (1918).   [172] *Id*. at 232.

[173] "The rule that a court of equity concerns itself only in the protection of property rights treats any civil right of a pecuniary nature as a property right . . . ; and the right to acquire property by honest labor or the conduct of a lawful business is as much entitled to protection as the right to guard property already acquired." *Id*. at 236.

[174] The Court believed that unless INS were prohibited from using the news in competition with AP, "it would render publication profitless, or so little profitable as in effect to cut off the service by rendering the cost prohibitive in comparison with the return." *Id*. at 241.

[175] In a passage as relevant to the photocopying-copyright dilemma as it was to the case before him, Justice Brandeis proposed that if a property interest in news were recognized, a legislature might reasonably decide to prohibit injunctive relief while authorizing damages, or to provide a fixed measure of damages or a compulsory licensing system. *Id*. at 266–67.

to which the courts could grant protection in addition to that provided by statute. In both instances, however, the Court could perceive the problem as one of protecting a property interest resulting from a creative act or of fashioning a rule which would best allocate innovative resources, and in both the Court was faced with the limitations of judicial action in the face of the copyright and patent statutes. The legal guise in which these issues appeared in the copyright case was "fair use." The unfair competition cases presented the issue as a question of federalism, how best to accommodate state law with the policies of the federal copyright and patent systems. In the unfair competition cases the contrast between the approach taken by the Warren Court in the 1960s and that followed by the Burger Court in the 1970s not only dramatizes the unsettled nature of the issues but provides a source from which to speculate on the votes of the various Justices in *Williams & Wilkins*.[176]

In 1938 Justice Brandeis suggested that the patent laws served to limit the scope of common law doctrines protecting intellectual material in the public domain.[177] But it was not until 1964 that the Warren Court brought the message home explicitly. A pair of cases, *Sears, Roebuck & Co. v. Stiffel Co.*[178] and *Compco Corp. v. Day-brite Lighting, Inc.*,[179] held that the copyright and patent laws preempted state unfair competition doctrines which prohibited the copying of designs or other intellectual productions not protected by a patent or copyright. The result of *Sears* and *Compco* was to establish a national policy of competition in intellectual values except where Congress had provided monopoly protection through the patent or copyright system.

Like *INS*, *Sears* and *Compco* presented a conflict between innovators and appropriators of intellectual goods. In contrast to *INS*,

---

[176] The unfair competition cases have been the subject of considerable commentary and no attempt will be made here to duplicate those efforts. Our purpose is merely to suggest that *Williams & Wilkins* need not be viewed as a case of first impression for the Court but rather a new context for recurring problems. See, *e.g.* Treece, *Patent Policy and Preemption: The Stiffel and Compco Cases*, 32 U. CHI. L. REV. 80 (1964); Goldstein, *The Competitive Mandate: From Sears to Lear*, 59 CALIF. L. REV. 873 (1971); Brown, *Publication and Preemption in Copyright Law: Elegiac Reflections on Goldstein v. California*, 22 U.C.L.A. L. REV. 1022 (1975); Stern, *A Reexamination of Preemption of State Trade Secret Law After Kewanee*, 42 G. WASH. L. REV. 927 (1974).

[177] Kellogg Co. v. National Biscuit Co., 305 U.S. 111 (1938).

[178] 376 U.S. 225 (1964).

[179] 376 U.S. 234 (1964).

Justice Black for the Court in the latter cases paid little attention to the interest of the creator. Absent from the opinions are the ethical concerns about reaping without sowing. Indeed, the opinions highlight only the public interest in competition as reflected in the negative implications of the patent and copyright laws.[180] *Sears* and *Compco* can be read as affirming the preeminence of Congress in protecting intellectual values, an approach inconsistent with a court-created privilege to photocopy the works of those granted "exclusive" rights by Congress. On the other hand, the language of the opinions suggests that the Warren Court might have looked with favor on free photocopying. Emphasized in *Sears* was the predominance of the public interest in competitive activity; seemingly ignored were the noneconomic concerns of rewarding creative activity and preventing unjust enrichment.

The rise of the Burger Court signaled the decline of *Sears* and *Compco*. In two decisions involving copyright and patent preemption of state law the Court eroded the underlying assumptions of *Sears* and *Compco* while reaffirming their viability as precedent. Both new opinions, authored by Chief Justice Burger, suggest a heightened concern for creative values and impatience with activities which result in unjust enrichment. And at the same time, the Court eroded what was seen in *Sears* as the exclusive power of Congress over "writings" and "discoveries". Read in the context of this recurring conflict, the shift in the unfair competition cases forewarned of the difficulties the Court would have in *Williams & Wilkins*.

In *Goldstein* v. *California*,[181] the Court considered the validity of a California statute making it a criminal offense to appropriate a tape recording of the performance of a musical composition. The Court ruled that the federal copyright system did not pre-

---

[180] In a separate minority opinion in Lear, Inc. v. Adkins, 395 U.S. 653, 677 (1969), Justices Black and Douglas and Chief Justice Warren demonstrated the intensity of their dislike for any "natural rights" resulting from creative acts. In suggesting that the patent system prevented the licensing of trade secrets, Justice Black wrote: "One who makes a discovery may, of course, keep it secret if he wishes, but private arrangements under which self-styled 'inventors' do not keep their discoveries secret, but rather disclose them, in return for contractual payments, run counter to the plan of our patent laws, which tightly regulate the kind of inventions that may be protected and the manner in which they may be protected. The national policy expressed in the patent laws, favoring free competition and narrowly limiting monopoly, cannot be frustrated by private agreements among individuals, with or without approval of the State."

[181] 412 U.S. 546 (1973). See Abrams & Abrams, *Goldstein v. California: Sound, Fury, and Significance, supra* at 147.

vent the states from granting copyright-like protection to "writings" not protected by the federal system where Congress had expressed no intention to preempt the field. *Sears* and *Compco* were reaffirmed but limited to "mechanical configurations." Justices Douglas, Brennan, Blackmun, and Marshall dissented on the basis of *Sears* and *Compco*, arguing that "free access to products on the market is the consumer interest."[182]

The activities of a tape "pirate" in *Goldstein* were in many respects similar to those of the photocopying scholar. The "pirate" purchased an original tape recording on the open market and duplicated and sold the copies at lower prices, since he avoided the royalties and recording costs incurred by the original recording company. Both tape pirates and scholars obtained access to the original by legal means; neither violated any contractual agreement. And while the commercial motives in *Goldstein* were more intense and direct, in each case the Court faced a simple act of copying.

While the factual context differs, there is much in the Chief Justice's opinion in *Goldstein* which bears on the later resolution of *Williams & Wilkins*. Justice Black in *Sears* had interpreted the copyright and patent system as a pervasive and interrelated scheme of monopoly and competition designed to promote intellectual labor. Gaps in the protection granted by statute reflected a studied determination by Congress that competition (privileged appropriation) would best serve the public interest. To Justice Black, Congress had resolved the intellectual property question across the board! Chief Justice Burger, on the other hand, rejected the idea that the failure of Congress to extend copyright protection to a category of "writings" represented a mandate for free appropriation and competition. If Congress wanted that, it must say so! Absent such a clear directive, the states were free to give the results of intellectual activity the "attributes of property." Ignored, or rejected, was the possibility that the "Science and useful Arts" clause required Congress to promote innovation by withholding monopoly power as well as by conferring it. In *Williams & Wilkins* it was argued on behalf of the libraries that the Constitution requires a privilege to photocopy for research purposes in order to "promote science." This argument was by analogy rejected in *Goldstein*.

---

[182] *Id.* at 574. Justice Marshall wrote a separate dissent which appears also to emphasize the consumer interest. *Id.* at 579.

The return to concepts of private property and the rejection of the implicit competitive mandate of *Sears* may signal among at least five members of the Court a more heightened sensitivity to claims for the enforcement of ethical standards against those who reap where others have sown. Those justices who failed to find a privilege to appropriate where federal copyright protection was withheld, should have had difficulty in finding a similar privilege in *Williams & Wilkins* where copyright protection was extended. In the last analysis, what divided the Court in *Goldstein*, and in all likelihood in *Williams & Wilkins*, was the relative importance to be given to the consumer interest in competition (appropriation) as against the private interest in intellectual production. But at least one of the majority justices in *Goldstein* must have shifted positions in *Williams & Wilkins*.[183]

In *Kewanee Oil Co. v. Bicron, Corp.*,[184] the most recent of the unfair competition cases, the Court held by a majority of 6 to 2 that the Ohio law of trade secrets as applied to prohibit employees from disclosing their employer's proprietary information was not preempted by the policies of the federal patent system. The majority opinion reemphasized the shift in the Burger Court toward protecting creators of innovative activity against claims that the public interest would be better served through appropriation and competition.

The Chief Justice asked whether trade-secret protection under state law "clashes with the objectives of the federal patent laws."[185] In approaching the issue from an economic viewpoint, Chief Justice Burger concentrated almost exclusively on the costs of self-help to trade-secret owners in protecting their information in the absence of state trade-secret protection. He found the costs substantial and a serious barrier to innovative activity. He did not consider or attempt to evaluate the potential gain in dissemination of innovative information that would result from free appropriation. As Justice Black had ignored the interest of the creator in *Sears*,

---

[183] Justice Blackmun, who did not vote in *Williams & Wilkins*, dissented in *Goldstein*. Thus at least one of the five Justices who voted to authorize protection for the record company in *Goldstein* voted to deny protection to the publisher in *Williams & Wilkins*.

[184] 416 U.S. 470 (1974). See Goldstein, *Kewanee Oil Co. v. Bicron: Notes on a Closing Circle*, 1974 SUPREME COURT REVIEW 81.

[185] *Id.* at 480.

the Chief Justice relegated the values of competition to a similar fate in *Kewanee*.

In addition to resolving the economic analysis in favor of protecting the originator, the Court reemphasized the "ethical" ramifications of appropriation regardless of the economic consequences: ". . . there is the inevitable cost to the basic decency of society when one firm steals from another. A most fundamental human right, that of privacy, is threatened when industrial espionage is condoned or is made profitable."[186] The majority did not balance these "costs" against the benefits to consumers in added competition. Nor did it accept a compromise accommodation offered in Mr. Justice Douglas's dissent of awarding damages for the breach of a contract not to disclose secrets but withholding injunctive relief against use.

In the absence of a Supreme Court decision directly involving "fair use," the unfair competition cases provide an inviting source for conjecture upon the votes of the Justices in *Williams & Wilkins*. Many of the same policy questions, both economic and non-economic, flow through the cases, as well as the tension between court and legislature in fashioning the rules governing intellectual activity. The extent to which the Burger Court is willing to authorize copyright-like protection by the states absent legislation remains far from clear. In *Goldstein* the Court validated state legislation. It has not yet dealt with a common law attempt to provide protection to ideas or innovations that have been published.[187] Such a case would be a reincarnation of *Wheaton v. Peters*. *Kewanee* involved the common law of trade secrets and was not concerned with material that had been published, the traditional dividing line between common law and preemptive copyright legislation. Thus apart from its language, *Kewanee* fitted comfortably with traditional analysis and offered little direct assistance to the Court in *Williams & Wilkins*.

Arguably the Burger Court has retained a preference for legislative solutions. If so, advocates of free photocopying can find little consolation. But when, as in *Williams & Wilkins*, the Court does

---

[186] 416 U.S. at 487.

[187] The Court recently refused to hear a case which had sustained a common law copyright in published writings on the basis of the *INS* decision. Mercury Record Prod., Inc. v. Economic Consultants, Inc., 64 Wis.2d 163, (1974), *cert. den.*, 420 U.S. 914 (1975).

venture into the intellectual property arena, the preemption cases appear to offer some tentative indications of the views of a majority of its members on issues of competition, monopoly, and standards of ethical behavior, all inevitably involved in the application of the doctrine of "fair use."

V. CONCLUSION

In *Williams & Wilkins* the Supreme Court was asked to adapt a copyright statute enacted in 1909 to the age of the photocopy machine, the facsimile transmitter, and the computer. While the governing congressional enactment granted authors the exclusive right to "copy" their works, it was argued that mechanical reproduction by libraries for researchers was "fair use" and therefore privileged. The basic issues underlying the case were more fundamental. What was required was a new balancing of the author's interest in capturing the fruits of his efforts and the needs of society to reap the benefits of technological progress. In such a balance, the decision-maker would be forced to reexamine and perhaps choose between popular notions of what constitutes ethical behavior and economic theories which seek to insure an efficient allocation of scarce resources.

We have not offered a definitive blueprint to facilitate the choice between these competing concerns. We have, rather, examined the implications of the choice, some early history in the development of copyright law, and the available precedent to determine if there is a basis for a reasoned judicial approach which would authorize the photocopying in *Williams & Wilkins*. Our efforts convince us that no such basis exists.

The promotion of science and the useful arts is a constitutionally authorized activity that still retains widespread public support. The problem initially is how such activity is to be promoted. A copyright system may be too cumbersome to meet this objective in the era of printing on demand, in which information is not reduced to tangible, readable form until requested by a user. Other forms of incentives such as grants or prizes may be necessary. Direct public subsidy of publication may be required. Indeed, the present landscape of information management currently contains a combination of all these devices. If private gain to an author through a copyright system is retained as one method of encouraging publication, the secondary issue will be "how much" gain is necessary. Both the "how" and the "how much" seem political questions appropriate for the legislative branch.

The judicial system has been bracing itself for some time for the inevitable clash between technological change and traditional legal principles. The lesson of a case like *Williams & Wilkins* may well be that while the society upon which law operates is in constant change, the issues for the legal system are static and the alternatives for resolution of conflicts limited. The new issues of law and technology may test the judicial process—not to develop new and creative strategies or doctrines but to examine more closely the fundamental principles underlying the solutions of the past. Indeed, in the more than two centuries between enactment of the Statute of Anne and the failure of the Supreme Court definitively to decide *Williams & Wilkins*, only the names and context have changed; the issues have remained constant.

ROBERT H. BORK

ALEXANDER M. BICKEL,

POLITICAL PHILOSOPHER

It is hardly surprising that with his book *The Morality of Consent* Alexander M. Bickel moved from constitutional scholarship into explicit political philosophy. That would seem a natural, indeed almost an inevitable, progression for scholars of the Constitution. The wonder is less that Bickel developed in that way than that so many academic scholars of the Constitution do not. There is, of course, political feeling implicit in much constitutional writing, but too often it is disguised as legal analysis; it colors and distorts constitutional judgment rather than informing it.

This book, published posthumously, was Bickel's first foray into the realm of political philosophy. He came equipped, as the book makes evident again and again, with the intellectual apparatus of a profound lawyer as well as the historical learning that earned him an appointment at Yale as Chancellor Kent Professor of Law and Legal History, and an ease with political science that could easily have qualified him for a chair in that department as well.

The Morality of Consent needs to be seen in perspective. It is not a definitive work; it is not the full statement of Alex Bickel's political thinking. It was intended as a ranging shot in the task Bickel had set for himself: the reconstitution of a conservative intellectual tradition in this country. He was not entirely satisfied with the label "conservative." Although he applies it to himself here, at various points in the book he modifies it by referring to his views

Robert H. Bork is Solicitor General of the United States.

as "Whig in the English eighteenth-century sense." And he also claims, rightly, that it is he, rather than those whose thought he opposes, who is entitled to the name of "liberal," by which he meant liberal in the classical, European sense. The effort to find an appropriate label is confusing. Some idea of what Bickel meant may be gleaned from the fact that he thought *The Federalist* an example of the best American conservative thought, as Edmund Burke was of the English variety. In this sense, Bickel's conservatism was a habit of mind and a quality of spirit that rejected the doctrinaire, the derivation of conclusions about a highly complex, somewhat irrational, flesh-and-blood world from large abstractions and grand principles. He displayed instead the qualities of thoughtfulness about experience, prudence, modesty of ambition for political solutions to problems, respect for established values and institutions. He quotes approvingly from Burke concerning abstract theories of individual rights: "distinctions of rights . . . these metaphysical distinctions; I hate the very sound of them."

The distinction between those who reason from experience and those who reason from abstract principle, and the serious dangers posed by the latter, is a major theme of this book. Indeed, it opens with the observation: "Two diverging traditions in the mainstream of Western political thought—one 'liberal,' the other 'conservative' —have competed, and still compete, for control of the democratic process and of the American constitutional system. . . ." The liberal tradition or model is "contractarian" and "rests on a vision of individual rights that have a clearly defined, independent existence predating society and are derived from nature and from a natural, if imagined, contract. . . . The Whig [or conservative] model, on the other hand, begins not with theoretical rights but with a real society, whose origins in the historical mists it acknowledges to be mysterious. The Whig model assesses human nature as it is seen to be."

These days the contractarian model is having all the best of it, particularly in the academic world. Bickel alludes to some examples of that tradition but does not take direct, specific issue with those writers here, as undoubtedly he would have been required to do had he lived to develop the intellectual foundations of his own position. This book is not an explicit attack upon the premises of contractarianism. It is an excellent example of the opposed mode of argument, and it does suggest why contractarianism is to be

feared: "It is moral, principled, legalistic, ultimately authoritarian."
In our time, it is also egalitarian, a fact that, Alex Bickel thought,
poses special danger for freedom and safety in society. Egalitarian-
ism requires not only an equal chance in social and political processes but equal results obtained from those processes. That in turn
requires that the state control institutions once thought of as
private, as areas for the play of individual and group initiatives,
in order to ensure that they produce equality of outcomes. Of
necessity, this effort expands the state enormously and drains the
strength of centers of private power so that the individual is without buffer institutions that deflect and moderate the direct power
of the state. The upshot will not be equality; it may, both Alex
Bickel and Edmund Burke warn, be tyranny.

There is too much richness of insight in this book for summary
in brief compass. The book does not accomplish the restoration of
a conservative intellectual tradition—Bickel knew that to be a work
of enormous magnitude—but it is a noteworthy first step. He
succeeds in setting much of the framework in place and in display-
ing the mode of thought appropriate to that tradition. It is hard
to believe the work will not prove seminal, that the tradition will
not be elaborated by others.

FREDERICK BERNAYS WIENER

AMERICAN LAW FOR THE COFFEE TABLE—AN IMPOSSIBLE DREAM

"Sir," said Dr. Samuel Johnson, "a woman's preaching is like a dog's walking on his hinder legs. It is not done well; but you are surprised to see it done at all."[1] So it is with an effort to compress the history of law in America, covering both private and public law over 350 years, into a single illustrated volume designed for the coffee table.

The author of such a volume,[2] Professor Bernard Schwartz, is Edwin D. Webb Professor of Law at New York University. He is a prolific writer who, about a dozen years ago, undertook a multi-volume series on the Constitution of the United States. The late Professor Alexander M. Bickel was of the opinion that the earlier task was an impossibility.[3] Another review of that work's first two volumes arrived at a similar conclusion, but only after considering at some length those volumes' flaws of techniques and after revealing a long series of specific and demonstrable errors of law that they contained.[4]

Two careful readings of Schwartz's latest venture lead inexora-

---

Col. Frederick Bernays Wiener is retired from the practice of law. He had concentrated, both during his days in the Solicitor General's office and thereafter, on Supreme Court litigation.

[1] 1 Boswell's Life of Johnson 463 (Powell's revision of Hill's ed. 1934).

[2] Bernard Schwartz, The American Heritage History of the Law in America. New York: American Heritage Pub. Co. 1974. $25.00. Pp. 383.

[3] Book Review, 63 Col. L. Rev. 1347 (1963).

[4] Book Review, 58 Nw. L. Rev. 711 (1963).

bly to the same conclusion: This also represents an aim incapable of attainment; this also suffers from numerous errors and omissions, legal and factual, both easily demonstrable. Far more seriously, however, this new book is badly flawed by fundamental fallacies in outlook and approach.

The projected scope of this new volume is indeed formidable; only a listing of its chapter headings will adequately portray the breathtaking expanse of what is sought to be covered: I, The English Heritage; II, The New Nation: Public Law 1789–1860; III, The Golden Age: Private Law and Institutions 1789–1860; IV, Years of Laissez Faire: Public Law 1860–1910; V, Excess of Freedom: Private Law and Institutions 1860–1910; VI, Welfare of the Community: Public Law 1910–1950; VII, Gone with the Frontier: Private Law and Institutions 1910–1950; VIII, Search for New Values: Public Law since 1950; IX, Era of Transition: Private Law and Institutions since 1950.

Could any single individual, no matter how learned or gifted, no matter how many years he devoted to the enterprise, complete such an obviously Herculean task in truly satisfactory fashion? The difficulties of course increase in inverse ratio to the space available, for compression necessitates omission, while generalizations stripped of their qualifications inevitably become inaccurate.

The Law in America contains many perceptive passages and much cogent analysis. But, alas, the flaws predominate; the intelligent lay reader will not be able to derive from its pages a satisfactory account of what law has meant in the nation's past, much less an adequate explanation of what changing legal doctrines are doing to the country's present and future. It seems appropriate to list, in ascending order of importance, the shortcomings of the book now under review.

Not even the pictures pass muster. There is a portrait of Charles Evans Hughes whose caption mentions his term (1930–1941) as Chief Justice of the United States,[5] but the picture shows him as a very much younger man, when he was Governor of New York, a full generation earlier. Roscoe Pound, purportedly portrayed "about 1909, when he was teaching law at Northwestern University,[6] appears in his Cambridge LL.D. gown, a degree not con-

---

⁵ P. 257.   ⁶ Pp. 228–29.

ferred until 1922.[7] And there is a portrait labeled "James Otis aroused the colonies in 1761 with his fiery attack on writs of assistance in Boston."[8] Alas, the picture does not portray James Otis, Jr. (1725–83), protagonist of that memorable encounter, of which John Adams later wrote, "Then and there, the child Independence, was born."[9] Rather, it shows the advocate's father, James Otis, Sr. (1702–78). For the features of the younger Otis, the reader must turn to *Wroth & Zobel*.[10] Thumbnail biographies of both Otises will be found in the same volume.[11]

The Law in America abounds in other annoying factual errors and omissions, some of the more significant of which are listed here in order of their appearance.

1. Chapter I starts with the illustration of a medieval English court in session, and we are told that "The King's Bench (left) was England's principal court of common law."[12] Not so; Lord Coke himself declared that the Court of Common Pleas, not the King's Bench, was "the lock and key of the common law."[13] Indeed, when King James I at the instigation of Francis Bacon, Coke's rival, moved Coke from the Chief Justiceship of the Common Pleas to that of the King's Bench in the view that he would do less harm there, that step from Coke's point of view was a wholly involuntary kick upstairs.[14]

2. John Adams' defense of Captain Preston in the Boston Massacre trial, in the face of strong public sentiment for the accused's conviction, is strongly stressed.[15] But there is no mention of the fact that Adams' task was greatly eased by the circumstance that the jury trying Preston had been substantially stacked in the defendant's favor by the Tory sheriff, who, after challenges had

---

[7] 4 WHO WAS WHO IN AMERICA, 1961–68 (1969).

[8] P. 35.

[9] 10 GIPSON, THE BRITISH EMPIRE BEFORE THE AMERICAN REVOLUTION 126 (1961).

[10] WROTH & ZOBEL, EDS., LEGAL PAPERS OF JOHN ADAMS, facing p. 133 (1965). Data concerning the portrait of James Otis, Sr., are available in 1 PROWN, JOHN SINGLETON COPLEY 28, 225, plate 54 (1966).

[11] WROTH & ZOBEL, note 10 *supra*, at civ–cv.

[12] P. 15.   [13] 4 INST. 99.

[14] PLUCKNETT, CONCISE HISTORY OF THE COMMON LAW 244 (5th ed. 1956); 5 HOLDSWORTH, HISTORY OF ENGLISH LAW 436–38 (1923).

[15] Pp. 32–33.

exhausted the original panel, drew the necessary tales from other Tories on the street.[16]

3. The black cook who was not permitted to testify against the nephew who poisoned Chancellor George Wythe of Virginia was not a man as stated,[17] but a woman, Lydia Broadnax.[18]

4. In his discussion of the *Dartmouth College* case,[19] Schwartz fails to state that one result of that decision was the universal inclusion thereafter, in all legislative acts of incorporation, of a clause specifically reserving the state's power to amend or repeal.

5. Similarly, in commenting on the fact that spite fences were held legal in America, there is no mention of the English common law doctrine of ancient lights, which created a prescriptive negative easement of access to light and air.[20]

6. In discussion whether President Franklin Roosevelt's Court Plan of 5 February 1937 was responsible for the change in decision on the constitutionality of minimum wage legislation,[21] from *Morehead v. Tipaldo,*[22] to *West Coast Hotel Co. v. Parrish,*[23] Professor Schwartz, while quoting the contemporary witticism, "A switch in time saved Nine," concludes that it did not. Yet he fails to mention, what is clearly the most significant documentary proof of that conclusion, the memorandum by Justice Roberts, who was with the majority in both cases, which explains why he followed *Adkins v. Children's Hospital*[24] in the first but voted to overrule it in the second.[25]

7. Schwartz's discussion of the "incorporation theory," advanced by Justice Black in *Adamson v. California,*[26] to the effect that the Fourteenth Amendment so far incorporated the first Eight so as to make all of them binding on the states,[27] never reveals that the legislative history is conclusive against the Black contention.[28]

---

[16] 3 LEGAL PAPERS OF JOHN ADAMS 17–19 (1965), note 10 *supra*.

[17] P. 37.

[18] BOYD & HEMPHILL, THE MURDER OF GEORGE WYTHE 11–17, 37 (1955).

[19] Dartmouth College v. Woodward, 4 Wheat. 518 (1819).

[20] 7 HOLDSWORTH, note 13 *supra*, at 339–41.

[21] Pp. 198–99.   [23] 300 U.S. 379 (29 March 1937).

[22] 298 U.S. 587 (1 June 1936).   [24] 261 U.S. 525 (1923).

[25] Frankfurter, *Mr. Justice Roberts*, 104 U. PA. L. REV. 311, 314–15 (1955).

[26] 332 U.S. 46 (1947).   [27] Pp. 212–16.

[28] Fairman, *Does the Fourteenth Amendment Incorporate the Bill of Rights? The Original Understanding*, 2 STAN. L. REV. 5 (1949).

8. Roscoe Pound was only a Commissioner of the Supreme Court of Nebraska;[29] never actually a Justice of that tribunal, as here asserted.[30]

9. Far more significantly, Schwartz's discussion of "How the Supreme Court Works"[31] never once tells the reader that most appeals, taken as of right under jurisdictional statutes still in force, are actually dismissed for asserted insubstantiality quite as capriciously as hundreds of petitions for certiorari are regularly denied. Thus it is now the law that while a private club will forfeit its liquor license for refusal to admit blacks, it risks no such consequence if it excludes Jews. The first is racial and therefore condemned, the second is religious and hence wholly rational. Otherwise stated, the Constitution condones the anti-Semite but condemns the anti-Hamite, and the resultant dichotomy does not present a substantial federal question.[32] It will not occasion surprise that in the author's paean to civil rights laws,[33] he nowhere notes the foregoing fantastic holding.

10. Finally, Professor Schwartz appears to have caught the Watergate bug. After faulting the White House staff for being too big, adding, "Yet none of its personnel was confirmed by the Senate,"[34] he goes on to complain of the vast powers exercised by the Office of Management and Budget. He then makes this remarkable assertion: *"Though the Constitution requires senatorial confirmation for all federal officers,* none of the OMB officials, from the director down, was ever voted on by the Senate."[35] The italics have been added, impelled by Art. II, § 2, of the Constitution, one clause of which plainly provides that "the Congress may by Law vest the Appointment of such inferior Officers, as they think proper, in the President alone, in the Courts of Law, or in the Heads of Departments."

Unhappily also, there are at least two passages that should have been but are not set off by quotation marks. Schwartz says of Justice Cardozo, "To read his opinions today is, in a sense, to string pearls."[36] Back in 1927, Professor Frankfurter (as he then was)

---

[29] 86 N.W. iii (1901).

[30] P. 230.   [31] P. 299.

[32] B.P.O.E. Lodge v. Ingraham, 297 A.2d 607 (Me. 1972), *app. dism.*, 411 U.S. 924 (1973).

[33] Pp. 300–01.   [35] *Ibid.*

[34] P. 280.   [36] P. 201.

had written, "To consider Mr. Justice Holmes' opinions is to string pearls."[37]

There is another passage, likewise, that evokes reminiscent nostalgia; Schwartz's version is on the left,[38] its source on the right.

Rarely articulated considerations were the secret root from which the law drew its life. These were, of course, considerations of what was advantageous for the community. The felt necessities of the time, the prevalent philosophical and political theories, intuitions of what best served the public interest, even the prejudices that the judges share with their fellow-men —all had at least as much to do with the American version of the common law as the analytical jurisprudence the judges professed to be applying.	The life of the law has not been logic: it has been experience. The felt necessities of the time, the prevalent moral and political theories, intuitions of public policy, avowed or unconscious, even the prejudices which judges share with their fellow-men, have had a good deal more to do than the syllogism in determining the rules by which men should be governed.

The right-hand passage, of course, is from the very first page of Justice Holmes's immortal classic, *The Common Law*, published in 1881.

Let us move to broader topics—and broader criticisms.

Professor Schwartz says of his book that "It is a personal, not to say, kaleidoscopic survey."[39] The basic difficulty with such an approach is that it sets forth particularized and essentially dogmatic preferences without stating counter-arguments adequately— or even at all. Here are a few examples.

The decision sustaining the Japanese evacuation in World War II, *Korematsu v. United States*,[40] is characterized by the author as "America's Gravest Miscarriage of Justice."[41] Discussion begins with quotations from two dissents. There is no mention of the fact that the majority opinion was written by Black, J., and that concurring were Stone, C.J., and Frankfurter, Douglas, and Rutledge, JJ., not a single one of whom was ever insensitive to the demands of or the deference due civil liberties.

---

[37] Frankfurter, *Mr. Justice Holmes*, 41 HARV. L. REV. 121, 146 (1927).

[38] P. 77.   [40] 323 U.S. 214 (1944).

[39] P. 8.   [41] P. 208.

Moreover, Schwartz's discussion of the evacuation speaks only of the Army's Civilian Exclusion Orders. He never advises the reader that the evacuation was ordered by President Roosevelt pursuant to an Act of Congress; nor that this legislation was unanimously supported by every West Coast congressional delegation; nor that it was strongly supported by California's Attorney General, Earl Warren. And—perhaps needless to add—there is no discussion of the major premise underlying the evacuation, the fear that persons of Japanese descent, raised under wholly Japanese influences and living outside the mainstream of American cultural values, were not likely automatically to sympathize, in a war between Japan and the United States, with the latter simply because of the essential accident of birth on American soil. Before that fear is dismissed out of hand as chimerical, critics of the *Korematsu* case would be well advised to ponder where the loyalty of second or third generation Americans, born and living in, say, Venezuela, would lie, if their country of birth were suddenly to find itself at war with the country of their blood and spiritual ties.

Of course it is to be expected that the occupant of a named chair at New York University Law School would feel kindly disposed towards one of its former Deans. But less parochial observers may perhaps be pardoned for doubting whether Arthur T. Vanderbilt deserved a full-page portrait in color plus a second full page proclaiming his greatness.[42] To mention contemporaneously expressed doubts of this evaluation would be invidious; it seems sufficient to question in all kindliness whether such hyperbole is really justified, much less so disproportionately bestowed.

An easier—and less touchy—task is the demonstration of the fundamental fallacy of all that underlies Professor Schwartz's highly personalized judgments: "The true American contribution to human progress has not been in technology, economics, or culture; it has been the development of the notion of law as a check upon power. . . . this book . . . seeks to present the pageant of American legal development and all that it has meant in the history of freedom. When one thinks on this majestic theme, his eyes dazzle."[43]

Carried to its logical extreme, law as a check upon power in the history of freedom would, necessarily and inevitably, result

---

[42] Pp. 352–53.   [43] Pp. 7–8.

in unrestricted anarchy. The essence of total freedom, after all, is the complete absence of all restraints whatever, with no one obliged to obey or take directions from anyone else. For demonstration of the infirmity in this concept, obviously basic to Schwartz's outlook, one need only turn to two Holmes opinions. True, both were dissents, but both of the cases in which they were uttered have since been overruled.

"Contract is not specially mentioned in the text [Due Process Clause of the Fifth Amendment] that we have to construe. It is merely an example of doing what you want to do, embodied in the word liberty. But pretty much all law consists in forbidding men to do some things that they want to do, and contract is no more exempt from law than other acts."[44] "We fear to grant power and are unwilling to recognize it when it exists."[45]

Like the Nine Old Men of the twenties and thirties, Professor Schwartz fears power and seems never so happy as when all are free to do whatever their individual hearts desire. This is not to say that he adheres to the anti-Holmes cult that for more than thirty years has defaced a number of law reviews. To the contrary, he admires the Justice tremendously, quotes him constantly throughout the book, and attaches to a photograph of the old gentleman in his latter years the caption, "The powerful dissents delivered by Oliver Wendell Holmes from 1902 to 1932 set the theme for twentieth-century law."[46] Yet he remains completely and indeed blissfully unaware how far the two dissents just quoted, and indeed the basic teachings of this preeminent American judge, undercut his own fundamental notion of law as a brake on power and as a recital of the history of freedom.

Another thoroughgoing Schwartz failing is his repeated and indeed consistent emphasis on the asserted dichotomy between human or personal rights, and property rights.[47] That supposed difference is, actually, the litmus paper test of the demagogue. The fact of the matter is that the Americans of the Revolutionary Era never recognized any such distinction; their motto, phrased in the con-

---

[44] Adkins v. Children's Hospital, 261 U.S. 525, 568 (1923), overruled by West Coast Hotel Co. v. Parrish, 300 U.S. 379 (1937).

[45] Tyson v. Banton, 273 U.S. 418, 445 (1927), overruled *sub silentio*, when Gold v. DiCarlo, 235 F. Supp. 817 (S.D. N.Y. 1964), was affirmed without argument, 380 U.S. 520 (1965).

[46] P. 227.   [47] *E.g.*, pp. 34, 213, 285, 335.

junctive, was "Liberty and Property." Their "protests against taxation frankly and openly, indeed passionately, affirm the sanctity of property. . . . For eighteenth-century Americans, property and liberty were one and inseparable, because property was the only foundation yet conceived for security of life and liberty; without security for his property, it was thought, no man could live or be free except at the mercy of another."[48]

More than that, the framers of both the Fifth and the Fourteenth Amendments equated without differentiation life, liberty, and property. And anyone who has been so brainwashed by the consistent denigration of the third of this trio would do well to contemplate the Central European expropriations before and during World War II: What human rights are left an individual who has been stripped of every shred of property he ever owned?

There are other vital areas of contemporary American law that are either inadequately or less one-sidedly treated by the author. Thus, for all his expressed concern over the present overcrowding of our courts,[49] Schwartz seems unaware that much of this is due to expanded concepts of standing. Once *Massachusetts v. Mellon*[50] was brushed aside as currently inapplicable by *Flast v. Cohen*,[51] every taxpayer has been free to litigate his dislikes in a federal forum, once those were expressed in constitutional terms. Nowadays, when nearly every branch of law has become constitutionalized, that qualification presented few obstacles to even reasonably resourceful counsel. More recent cases, which reaffirmed the traditional requirement of a showing of particularized injury[52] were decided after the Schwartz volume went to press.

But nowhere does Professor Schwartz indicate to his readers, learned or lay, that the very concept of standing has a constitutional basis, *viz.*, the limitation of the judicial power to "Cases" and "Controversies."[53] Instead, he expresses regret that the Supreme Court followed existing law in avoiding a ruling on the legality of hostilities in Viet Nam.[54] That issue is currently at rest—at least

---

[48] MORGAN, ed., THE AMERICAN REVOLUTION 175 (1965).

[49] Pp. 326–28, 350–51, 354–55.

[50] 262 U.S. 447 (1923).   [51] 392 U.S. 83 (1968).

[52] United States v. Richardson, 418 U.S. 166 (1974); Schlesinger v. Reservists to Stop the War, 418 U.S. 208 (1974).

[53] Art. III, § 2.   [54] Pp. 278–79.

until the constitutionality of the recent War Powers Resolution[55] reaches the litigating stage. But the matter of busing schoolchildren to achieve racial balance is still very much alive, as the continuing Boston imbroglio bears witness. That sorry practice originated in the South, where it represented the unedifying paradox of classifying by race in order to extirpate all vestiges of racial classification.[56] But Boston had had a unitary school system for generations, and of course the cry of "quality education," loudly proclaimed to justify busing, was tragic nonsense: The very substantial sums spent on busing meant that much less money for the core process of teaching.

Even the lay reader may well question how busing in Boston —which, despite continuous distortion by the media, had nothing whatever to do with desegregation—can be squared with the Schwartz concept of "law as a check upon power" and as an epoch in "the history of freedom." Of course it cannot be—and that doubtless explains why Schwartz is deafeningly silent about busing for racial balance, or quotas, or "goals," or "affirmative action."

Not surprisingly, his generalized comments on equality,[57] on racial equality, and on "The Rights Explosion,"[58] reflect no awareness of the Supreme Court's approval of state action designed to curb "the discrimination inherent in the quota system."[59]

Indeed, the most consistently disturbing omission in the volume under review is the author's utter failure to realize, in the face of his repeated and indeed pervasive laudatory comments concerning Justices Holmes and Brandeis—he prints two pictures of the first[60] and quotes him over forty times, Brandeis on some thirteen occasions—that their frequently expressed views utterly condemn much if not actually most of the constitutional developments of the last twenty years.

"But the word 'right' is one of the most deceptive of pitfalls; it is so easy to slip from a qualified meaning in the premise to an unqualified one in the conclusion. Most rights are qualified." Thus

---

[55] 87 Stat. 555 (1973).

[56] Swann v. Charlotte-Mecklenburg Bd. of Educ., 402 U.S. 1 (1971), following United States v. Jefferson Co. Bd. of Educ., 372 F.2d 836 (5th Cir. 1966), 380 F.2d 385 (5th Cir. 1967).

[57] Pp. 289–92, 358.   [58] Pp. 300–06.

[59] Hughes v. Superior Court, 339 U.S. 460, 467 (1950).

[60] Pp. 189, 227.

spoke Holmes in 1921.[61] And, a little later in the same year, "The
dangers of a delusive exactness in the application of the Fourteenth
Amendment have been adverted to before now."[62] [W]e must be
cautious about pressing the broad words of the Fourteenth Amendment to a drily logical extreme" was an earlier expression."[63] "We
are bound to be very cautious," he had written in 1906, "in coming
to the conclusion that the Fourteenth Amendment has upset what
thus has been established and accepted for a long time."[64] And,
once again in 1921:[65]

> There is nothing that I more deprecate than the use of the
> Fourteenth Amendment beyond the absolute compulsion of
> its words to prevent the making of social experiments that an
> important part of the community desires, in the insulated
> chambers afforded by the several States, even though the ex-
> periments may seem futile or even noxious to me and to those
> whose judgment I most respect.

Let us turn to Justice Brandeis, writing in 1924:[66]

> Put at its highest, our function is to determine, in the light of
> all facts which may enrich our knowledge and enlarge our
> understanding, whether the measure, enacted in the exercise
> of an unquestioned police power and of a character inherently
> unobjectionable, transcends the bounds of reason. That is,
> whether the provision as applied is so clearly arbitrary or
> capricious that legislators acting reasonably could not have
> believed it to be necessary or appropriate for the public
> welfare.

All this Schwartz recognizes, at least in part: "The legislative
judgment might well be debatable. But that was the whole point
about the Holmes approach. Under it, the courts left debatable
issues, as respects business, economic, and social affairs, to legislative decision."[67] And, so limited, that represented the later Supreme
Court approach as set forth in *Ferguson v. Skrupa*,[68] from which
Schwartz several times quotes.[69]

---

[61] American Bank & Trust Co. v. Federal Reserve Bank, 256 U.S. 350, 358 (1921).

[62] Truax v. Corrigan, 257 U.S. 312, 342 (1921).

[63] Noble State Bank v. Haskell, 219 U.S. 104, 110 (1911).

[64] Otis Co. v. Ludlow Co., 201 U.S. 140, 154 (1906).

[65] 257 U.S. at 344.

[66] Jay Burns Baking Co. v. Bryan, 264 U.S. 504, 534 (1924).

[67] P. 137.   [68] 372 U.S. 726 (1963).   [69] Pp. 195, 196, 202, 203.

But—neither Schwartz nor the Court over the last twenty years has faced up to the circumstance that the Holmes and Brandeis standards condemn virtually all that has been decided in equal protection cases subsequent to *McGowan v. Maryland*.[70] (It is worth noting in passing that Judge Learned Hand refused to distinguish between the Due Process and the Equal Protection Clauses in dealing with judicial review under each.[71] Indeed, the very test for passing constitutional muster has been advisedly altered, particularly in classification cases.)

Traditionally, a state had broad powers of classification, which were not exceeded even if some inequality resulted, just so long as the classification was not without any reasonable basis, wholly irrational, and hence purely arbitrary.[72] But, beginning in 1968, the Court applied a wholly different standard, *viz.*, that where the classification touches basic or fundamental constitutional rights, a more strict scrutiny will be applied, and there must be a showing of some compelling state interest to save the statute.[73] Thus the burden of proof in constitutional cases was shifted from the attackers to the defenders of the legislative enactment. Of course this turned the Supreme Court into a far more jealous censor of legislation than the Nine Old Men of the twenties and thirties ever undertook to be.

In Schwartz's words, "The preferred position theory . . . is based on the view that the Constitution gives a preferred status to personal, as opposed to property, rights. The result is a double standard in the exercise by the courts of their review function. The tenet of judicial self-restraint does not rigidly bind the judge in cases involving civil liberties and other personal rights."[74] True, the double standard has long been a cherished tenet among American libertarians, going back to Thomas Jefferson. That worthy denounced the Sedition Act of 1798 as unconstitutional, going on to make it the occasion of the Kentucky and Virginia Resolutions— and they were the spiritual ancestors of secession. But, once become President of the United States, Jefferson regularly directed United

---

[70] 366 U.S. 420 (1961).

[71] HAND, THE BILL OF RIGHTS 56 (1958).

[72] *E.g.*, Lindsey v. Natural Carbonic Gas Co., 220 U.S. 61, 78–79 (1911), last reaffirmed in *McGowan*, note 70 *supra*.

[73] Levy v. Louisiana, 391 U.S. 68 (1968); Shapiro v. Thompson, 394 U.S. 618 (1969); Weber v. Aetna Casualty & Surety Co., 406 U.S. 164 (1972).

[74] P. 286.

States Attorneys to prosecute for criminal libel Federalist editors who were articulately disenchanted by John Adams' successor in the White House.[75]

Schwartz's approval of and consequent attachment to the double standard accordingly has the authority of libertarian precedent. Unhappily for the reader, however, he does not adequately treat the most significant current consequences of rejecting the Holmes-Brandeis due process standards in any case involving equal protection.

Item, the police power as it had been known and exercised for decades has been effectively gutted, and lest this is deemed an exaggeration by those primarily familiar with the *United States Reports,* it is suggested that any doubters look at the *Federal Supplement* over the past ten years or so, and check to see how much legislation has been invalidated by three-judge courts by a process of interpretation characterized by a "delusive exactness" in the construction of the Equal Protection Clause, which has consistently been pressed "to a drily logical extreme." Indeed, it would not be far from the mark to assert that this particular Clause has been applied, not just mechanically—compare the mechanical jurisprudence criticized by Pound—but in the manner of that mathematician's tool, the slide-rule. Can anyone imagine for a minute that Holmes, who sustained compulsory vaccination[76] and who with Brandeis upheld the compulsory sterilization of imbeciles,[77] would even have dreamed of denying to the states the power to forbid abortions?[78]

Item, despite mention of complaints over the years about the technicalities of the criminal law, a matter illustrated by contemporary cartoons,[79] the author sees no connection between that perennial discontent and the "Criminal Law Revolution" that he briefly summarizes.[80] For it is that line of decision which, by ignoring the basic social interest in public safety, has made the streets of every large city unsafe at night—and of many similarly unsafe even in hours of daylight.

---

[75] Levy, Legacy of Suppression 299–306 (1960).

[76] Jacobson v. Massachusetts, 197 U.S. 11 (1905).

[77] Buck v. Bell, 274 U.S. 200 (1927).

[78] Roe v. Wade, 410 U.S. 113 (1973); Doe v. Bolton, 410 U.S. 179 (1973).

[79] Pp. 176, 255.   [80] P. 288.

There is no mention of the harm done communities by current bail practices, pursuant to which a robber or burglar once apprehended is released to rob or burgle once again—unless of course that process is to be deemed comprehended in Schwartz's comment, "We have come to recognize that property rights must be restricted to an extent never before permitted in American law,"[81] the words "property rights" no doubt being understood to refer to the passerby's insistence that her purse be not snatched, or to the householder's hope that his television set be not carried away in his absence.

Significantly, although the author mentions by name[82] *Miranda v. Arizona*,[83] he does not comment on the notable circumstance that this decision appears to have been expressly designed to anticipate by prior announcement, and then to nullify because of the constitutional terms in which it was couched, the rules for questioning criminal suspects that were then in process of being formulated by the scholarly American Law Institute.[84]

Interpretations of statutes and of decisional law can be rectified by Congress and by state legislatures. But the *Miranda* interpretation of the Constitution covers with a cloak of unalterable sanctity theological in nature the result reached by the interpreters, and binds everyone—until such time as a later Court recedes from that decision. It is almost needless to add that Professor Schwartz does not undertake to explain just how the terms of the *Miranda* warning can be extracted from the four constitutional words, "due process of law."

Item, there is no discussion of the "void for vagueness"—or "for overbreadth"—doctrine, which has resulted in such heavy casualties among statutes and ordinances. Here also, Justice Holmes showed what a court should not be doing:[85] "The bill of rights for the Philippines giving the accused the right to demand the nature and cause of the accusation against him does not fasten forever upon those islands the inability of the seventeenth century common law to understand or accept a pleading that did not exclude every misinterpretation capable of occurring to intelligence fired with a

---

[81] P. 316.

[82] P. 288.   [83] 384 U.S. 436 (13 June 1966).

[84] A.L.I. PROCEEDINGS 1966 77–143, 157–264 (17–19 May 1966).

[85] Paraiso v. United States, 207 U.S. 368, 372 (1907).

desire to pervert." Substitute "United States" for "the Philippines," "this country" for "those islands," and "statute or ordinance" for "pleading," and those remarks would qualify as a mordant critique of the vagueness/overbreadth doctrine. Possibly—though perhaps only hopefully—*Parker v. Levy*[86] presages a return to sanity in this area.

Item, the author does note that "The Supreme Court's failure meaningfully to define obscenity resulted in a virtual abdication of public power; proliferation of pornography was a direct consequence of the law's failure to draw workable lines."[87] Passing the point that "abdication" should more accurately and with far more justification have been rendered as "destruction," a more serious lapse lies in overlooking that the current "proliferation of pornography" stems not from *Roth v. United States*,[88] decided in 1957, but from the case, decided nine years later, that held not obscene the classic item of eighteenth-century filth, *Fanny Hill*.[89] Nor does Professor Schwartz ever note, much less explain, the Court's abandonment of its earlier declaration that the lewd and the obscene were beyond the scope of First Amendment protection.[90] Right there can be found the reason why our cities are now infested with block after block of commercialized obscenity. True, Ralph Ginzburg went to jail because of *EROS* and its sales literature,[91] but that short-lived periodical was actually straitlaced by comparison with what today is hawked for sale on every newsstand.

Item, while Schwartz notes that over a 47-year period, 1890–1937, 55 Acts of Congress and 228 state enactments were declared unconstitutional, an average of 6 per year,[92] he is silent about the far greater mortality in the 19 years between 1953 and 1972. The toll in the later period comes to 24 Acts of Congress and 264 state measures, or an average of 26 per year.[93] True, cases are not fungible, and so the numbers jurisprudence is a notoriously unreliable tool. But the comparative figures go to show how much

---

[86] 417 U.S. 733 (1974).

[87] P. 306.   [88] 354 U.S. 476 (1957).

[89] Memoirs v. Massachusetts, 383 U.S. 413 (1966).

[90] Chaplinsky v. New Hampshire, 315 U.S. 568, 571–72 (1942).

[91] Ginzburg v. United States, 383 U.S. 463 (1966).

[92] P. 196.

[93] THE CONSTITUTION OF THE UNITED STATES, SEN. DOC. 92–82, 1597–1785 (1973).

more stringent judicial censorship has become in the present phase of what the author insists is "the history of freedom."

Of course Professor Schwartz is lawyer enough to be aware that many of the most far-reaching decisions of the last twenty or so years blazed new ground, quite at variance with judicial views earlier expressed. Thus, he recognizes that the result of the first school desegregation case, *Brown v. Board of Education*,[94] was directly contrary to what anyone thought about the Fourteenth Amendment when it was adopted.[95] Indeed, that Amendment would not and could not have been adopted had its sponsors proclaimed that *Brown* would be its consequence. Nor, in his encomium on Judge Learned Hand[96] does Schwartz note that this distinguished jurist expressed strong doubts distinctly more than philosophical in nature as to both the correctness and the inevitability of that celebrated decision.[97]

Similarly, Schwartz is fully aware that what the Supreme Court held to be "state action" in the 1960s, when it was engaged in stretching that concept in order to strike down virtually every instance of privately enforced segregation coming into litigation prior to the passage of the Civil Rights Act of 1964, was wholly contrary to the views of the congressional majorities who wrote and adopted the Fourteenth Amendment.[98] Perhaps a more rational and more realistic view of what is and what is not "state action" prevails at the moment.[99] But where the line will be drawn say ten years hence must, realistically considered, depend on who is selected to fill the judicial vacancies certain to be created during that interval.

Again, Schwartz recognizes[100] that the debates on the Civil Rights Act of 1866 quite belied the result reached in *Jones v. Mayer Co.*,[101] which held that that act prevented, by virtue of the Thirteenth Amendment alone, a private person's discrimination, on racial grounds, in the sale of his own property. He likes the result, commenting that, in consequence of the Court's reading of the 1866 act

---

[94] 347 U.S. 483 (1954).

[95] P. 128.

[96] Pp. 262–63.

[97] HAND, note 71 *supra*, at 54–55.

[98] P. 126.

[99] Moose Lodge No. 107 v. Irvis, 407 U.S. 163 (1972); Jackson v. Metropolitan Edison Co., 419 U.S. 345 (1974).

[100] Pp. 125–26, 297.

[101] 392 U.S. 409 (1968).

in the *Mayer* case, "Purely private discrimination is no longer beyond the reach of public power."[102] Unhappily he fails to advise his readers that this particular legislation was enacted by a Congress that, far from intending any such result, actually sat in chambers both of which had segregated galleries![103] The Fairman volume noting this fact is included in Schwartz's bibliography;[104] what a pity that he did not study it more closely. So too, although Schwartz fails to note that, by actual count, well over thirty decisions of the Supreme Court have been expressly overruled since 1953,[105] he does recognize the constitutional revolution effected by the Warren Court, so-called.[106] (Whether that phrase should be regarded simply as convenient shorthand to cover the years 1953–1969, when Earl Warren was Chief Justice; whether Chief Justice Warren was indeed the Court's intellectual leader as well as its presiding officer; whether, in actual fact, he ever wrote by himself any of the many transforming opinions to which his name was attached—all these are matters impossible to consider here.)

Schwartz recognizes that in its decisions in social welfare cases—notably *King v. Smith*,[107] and *Goldberg v. Kelly*[108]—the Supreme Court, while Warren presided, acted as a third chamber of the legislature,[109] and he recognizes also that "Transforming innovation, in the law as elsewhere, can take place for only so long."[110] But, here again, he fails his readers in significant particulars. In saying that "When Warren resigned in 1969, it could be said that, in all of American history, only John Marshall's Court had played so large a role in reshaping the law to meet the needs of the day,"[111] he ignores the vital distinction between the Court in Marshall's time, which was writing on a blank slate, and the Court during Warren's Chief Justiceship, which turned the existing law of the Constitution upside down.

Again, and this is the most serious flaw in a badly flawed book, Schwartz never faces up to the fact that the complaints about the Court that led to F.D.R.'s Court Plan of 1937 are precisely the

---

[102] P. 297.

[103] Fairman, Reconstruction and Reunion 1864–1888 1259 (1971), citing Cong. Globe, 39th Cong., 1st Sess., p. 766 (9 Feb. 1866).

[104] P. 378.

[105] Note 93 *supra*, at 1794–97.

[106] P. 318.

[107] 392 U.S. 309 (1968).

[108] 397 U.S. 254 (1970).

[109] P. 311.

[110] P. 319.

[111] P. 285.

same as those that shake public confidence in the Court today. In 1937 it was the view of many segments of the public that the Court in dealing with the Due Process Clause was acting as a super-legislature, writing its predispositions and its predilections into the invalidation of legislation deemed unwise. That was why Franklin Roosevelt proclaimed in support of his proposal that "We must save the Constitution from the Court and the Court from itself."[112]

Today the preferred tool of judicial censorship is the Equal Protection Clause, now (as has been seen) involving a shifting of the burden of proof in constitutional cases. Then, even the most indefensible decisions[113] paid at least lip-service to the presumption of constitutionality. But today the insistence on "some compelling state interest" shifts the burden to the litigant relying on the statute to establish its validity, in the face of a tribunal that "More and more . . . came to display its solicitude for individual rights."[114] True, Schwartz does express a qualm. He says that "it is not mere caviling to point out that judicial disposition toward the libertarian result may be a two-edged sword. Properly employed, it can maintain the essential balance between liberty and authority. Carried to its extreme, however, judicial libertarianism can lead the judges to assume undue authority over the other branches."[115] This is fine —as far as it goes. But it lacks something of what Justice Jackson said a quarter of a century ago in *Terminiello v. Chicago:*[116]

> This Court has gone far toward accepting the doctrine . . . that all local attempts to maintain order are impairments of the liberty of the citizen. The choice is not between order and liberty. It is between liberty with order and anarchy without either. There is danger that, if the Court does not temper its doctrinaire logic with a little practical wisdom, it will convert the constitutional Bill of Rights into a suicide pact.

The quoted dissent was uttered in a case involving demonstrations, and the prediction then ventured has been amply fulfilled. One has only to survey the quality of life today—crime rampant and unpunished, pornography flaunted everywhere, demonstrations evoked by every discontent (*e.g.*, the slaughtering of calves before

---

[112] Pp. 137, 196–97, 320–21.

[113] *E.g.*, Adkins v. Children's Hospital, 261 U.S. 525, 544 (1923).

[114] P. 285.   [116] 337 U.S. 1, 37 (1949).

[115] P. 320.

TV cameras), schoolchildren driven back and forth like so many sacks of grain, discrimination in reverse practiced in colleges and spreading into every form of employment, idiocies such as the action successfully brought to recall policemen's badges so that they will read "police-person"—to judge not only the prescience of Jackson in 1949 but also to evaluate the extent to which virtually every facet of American existence has been altered and indeed turned around by the uncontrollable mandate of five out of nine persons holding office for life.

Tenure during good behavior was the response of the Glorious Revolution of 1689 to the judicial removals effected by the last two Stuarts whenever there was disagreement with decisions rendered. Most of our fifty states have long since abandoned this arrangement, in the view that otherwise judicial independence would too easily become judicial irresponsibility. The national experience of the last twenty years at least poses the question whether representative government can safely continue when it is subject to the whim of five substantially irremovable Supreme Court Justices. Of the hundred-odd persons who have served on that bench, only one has ever been impeached, only to be acquitted, and only one has been forced to resign, because of (at least) unethical greed. The dispassionate observer may well ask whether these last twenty years of Supreme Court adjudication have not in fact transformed that tribunal into the Council of Revision that the Framers advisedly rejected.[117]

"The law must be stable and yet it cannot stand still," Pound wrote in 1923.[118] Of course the law cannot stand still, any more than any other human contrivance can do so. But the very nature of the law implies at least a modicum of stability, and stability in constitutional interpretation is precisely what the country has not had, if not in the last twenty years or so, then certainly since Justice Frankfurter retired in 1962.

When Frankfurter, J., was succeeded by the Hon. Arthur J. Goldberg, who spent three years on the Supreme Court between being Secretary of Labor and then becoming United Nations Ambassador, the process of change, the epoch of instability, began to accelerate. The events of the 1962 Term, the initial period of ac-

---

[117] FARRAND, THE FRAMING OF THE CONSTITUTION 50, 70, 79, 156–57, 202 (1913).

[118] POUND, INTERPRETATIONS OF LEGAL HISTORY 1 (1923), quoted at p. 316.

celeration, were chronicled by a journalist in bemused fashion, wholly without any display of amazement, and quite devoid of the slightest indignation.[119] Indeed, the tenor of Clayton's observations recalled the distinterest of the Queens, New York, inhabitants, who, seeing a woman neighbor assaulted and then murdered before their very eyes, not only did nothing themselves to prevent it, but never even called the police.

Clayton's book, and particularly the Queens incident, come most vividly to mind during careful study of the present volume. For Bernard Schwartz records therein the rape of the Constitution that has been effected since 1954, and simply walks by on the other side. Nay more, he approves the double standard of constitutional interpretation pursuant to which successive violations have occurred. It is that feature of his present work which is most disturbing to this reader. Unhappily it is this precise approach that quite fails to upset in the slightest one whose lodestar is "the notion of law as a check upon power," and who sees in the last two decades' overrulings and innovations primarily "the pageant of American legal development and all that it has meant in the history of freedom."

---

[119] CLAYTON, THE MAKING OF JUSTICE (1964).